Elvin F. Donaldson, Ph.D., The Ohio State University, is Professor of Finance in the College of Commerce and Administration, The Ohio State University. Dr. Donaldson is the co-author (with John K. Pfahl) of *Corporate Finance—Policy and Management,* Second Edition (The Ronald Press Company, 1963) and is a contributing editor to the *Financial Handbook,* Fourth Edition (The Ronald Press Company, 1964).

John K. Pfahl, Ph.D., The Ohio State University, is Professor of Finance in the College of Commerce and Administration, The Ohio State University. Dr. Pfahl has had wide experience as an investment, financial, and real estate consultant. He is a contributing editor to the *Financial Handbook,* Fourth Edition (The Ronald Press Company, 1964).

PERSONAL FINANCE

ELVIN F. DONALDSON
JOHN K. PFAHL
The Ohio State University

FOURTH EDITION

THE RONALD PRESS COMPANY · NEW YORK

4MP

Library of Congress Catalog Card Number: 66–16842
PRINTED IN THE UNITED STATES OF AMERICA

To Our Wives

Preface

Money is, perhaps, more difficult to manage than it is to earn. A person may devote years to learning some trade or profession and a good many more years to the painful accumulation of savings sufficient to afford protection for a rainy day and security for old age. Yet too often such savings are quickly and heartbreakingly swept away by foolish "investments." If an individual is willing to devote years to preparing himself for a better-paying job, he should surely be willing to devote some study to the vitally interesting and important subject of the sensible use and management of his money.

This book was written to give practical help to the person who wants to do a better job of managing his personal finances. The cordial reception that university professors, businessmen, and laymen accorded the previous editions is evidence of the need for a book which is not highly technical and which presupposes, not the fortunate possession of a considerable sum of money, but only an intelligent interest in personal money matters. The Fourth Edition of *Personal Finance* fully covers the content of college courses on the subject, yet its constant emphasis on practical applications will help anyone to whom personal finance is a matter of daily responsibility.

A person's interest in money problems arises long before he has accumulated enough money to become a fledgling investor. Most young adults encounter pitfalls in buying on credit, or they find that borrowing money is a nettlesome thing. The budgeting of income and the care and proper use of savings and checking accounts are also matters the elements of which can certainly be learned in ways other than by hard experience. These matters are carefully covered in this book. In addition, comprehensive attention is given to the manifold aspects of insurance and the features of various forms of savings.

Real estate law and home ownership are discussed in a single chapter, which also includes coverage of the rapidly expanding field of mobile homes. Some people, as they acquire more money, turn to stocks and bonds as a means of investing surplus capital. That their interest in the stock market is too seldom based on real knowledge has been, at times, acutely evident. Thus the chapters devoted to securities will be especially valuable and helpful to many readers. The chapter on mutual funds includes the actual ten-year performance of a fixed initial investment. Similar results for accumulative savings plans and systematic withdrawal plans are also shown.

No book on personal finance would be complete without a discussion of income taxes. These taxes consume, and will continue to consume, a very considerable portion of personal earnings. Our discussion includes a number of tax-saving devices.

Social security and Medicare are treated from the personal viewpoint, with special attention given to those provisions devoted to hospital coverage, medical insurance, and similar benefits. The important problems of retirement planning have been expanded to take into account tax-favored plans for the self-employed, the systematic withdrawal plan for mutual funds, and variable annuity plans. The final chapter—Owning a Business—may appear to be a subject which would more appropriately be included in a book on business finance. But, starting or operating a small business is very much a personal affair, and this book would not be complete unless we included some of the essentials of this type of endeavor.

The authors are indebted to many people for helpful comments on the first three editions and for material included in this Fourth Edition. Particular credit is due the following: Mr. Albert A. Anastasia of Dow Jones & Company, Inc.; Mr. Robert L. Baker of The National Industrial Conference Board; Mr. Robert A. Beach of The Kiplinger Washington Editors, Inc.; Mr. Robert C. Beetham of Teachers' Insurance and Annuity Association of America; Mr. John C. Burrows of Moody's Investors Service, Inc.; Mr. John D. Craigie of the Insurance Information Institute; Mr. E. Donahue of Standard & Poor's Corporation; Mr. B. F. Dunn of Estate Recording Company; Mr. Louis Engel of Merrill Lynch, Pierce, Fenner & Smith, Inc.; Miss Ruth Ann Farb of the Federal Reserve Bank of Chicago; Mr. Harry Fuller of National Consumer Finance Association; Mr. Thomas A. Gagan of Vickers Associates, Inc.; Mr. P. A. Gratton of The American Telephone and Telegraph Company; Mr. Richard C. Harland of the Investment Company Institute; Mr. Henry R. Hecht of Merrill Lynch, Pierce, Fenner & Smith, Inc.; Miss Leone Ann Heuer of Household

Finance Corporation; Miss Billie F. Jackson of the Federal Home Loan Bank Board; Mr. Hugh A. Johnson of Hugh Johnson and Company; Mr. Robert Lindquist of the Harris Trust and Savings Bank; Mr. Kahlman Linker of Data Digests, Inc.; Miss Meg McCluskey of Arthur Wiesenberger & Company; Mr. Harlan B. Miller of the Institute of Life Insurance; Mr. R. Duane Saunders, Director, Office of Debt Analysis, United States Treasury Department; Miss Elinor L. Price of the National Association of Mutual Savings Banks, and Mr. G. Weiner of *Forbes* Magazine. Dr. and Mrs. David W. Cole were extremely helpful in reading the manuscript.

ELVIN F. DONALDSON
JOHN K. PFAHL

Columbus, Ohio
April, 1966

Contents

PERSONAL FINANCE

1

Personal Financial Planning

This book is written for and about you and the millions of other people who are interested in obtaining the greatest possible value from their available resources. Scientific management theory tells us that the best way to accomplish economic objectives is to plan, organize, and control, with the objectives clearly in mind. Planning is the first function and should be accomplished far enough in advance of the desired attainment of the goal to enable the planner to study the possible alternatives, and to give him sufficient time to organize his resources and control his accomplishments along the way. Planning, therefore, is the first consideration in a book on *personal finance.*

No one can plan in a vacuum. Also, a plan must be closely correlated to the objectives to be obtained. Finally, the planner's personal objectives must take into account existing and expected external conditions over which he has no control.

IMPORTANCE OF MONEY

To most people the word "finance" means money and money problems. Therefore, this book deals with the money matters of individuals and families. Personal money matters include income, spending, saving, investing, insuring, estate planning, and retirement benefits.

Money means different things to different people. Some people equate money with power, independence, success, or social status. Others think of money as a means to gratification of desires, protection, and emotional security. We live in a *money economy.* Therefore, we tend to think of many things which are not money in terms of money equivalents; that is, we measure many non-money items in terms of money values. Money becomes a common denominator for many of the important things in our life. Americans have been accused of being overmaterialistic and money-conscious. The accusers have often confused the use of the dollar as a common denominator of value with emphasis on the material things a dollar will buy. The only way we can realistically compare such non-material things as the value of an education, the cultural worth of a painting, the value of good health, or the preservation of life is by placing equivalent dollar values on these items. It means that we are willing to give up *X* number of dollars' worth of other things we could have in order to acquire or preserve the intangible value under discussion. This is not being materialistic.

Definition of Money

Money is a generally accepted medium of exchange. This means that others are willing to take your "money" in exchange for goods and services which they have available. What is "generally accepted" changes from time to time. Economists in the United States count United States Government and Federal Reserve System coin and currency, and demand accounts (checking accounts) in commercial banks, as our money supply. Coin, currency, and checks are generally accepted by others in exchange for goods and services in our present economy. Prior to 1933, gold was included among the money components in the United States. Gold is still generally accepted in international trade, and therefore is still part of international money.

Money generally includes more than just legal tender. *Legal tender* is that form of money which the government declares must be accepted in payment of debt. If a creditor refuses to accept legal tender he cannot enforce his claim against the debtor in court. Checks are not included in legal tender, but United States Government and Federal Reserve System coin and currency are legal tender.

In addition to being a medium of exchange, money serves other purposes; of equal importance in personal finance is the use of money as the standard or measure of value. Because of its use as a common denominator, money is particularly important in personal financial planning and enables the planner to weigh various alternative expenditures in making his purchasing and investment decisions.

Money can also be used as a store of value; it may be held to acquire goods and services in the future rather than used immediately as a medium of exchange. Individuals store value in money by holding on to coin and currency and by maintaining balances in checking accounts for extended periods of time.

The Value of the Dollar

The dollar is a common measure when people think of income and expense and the kind of enjoyment they would like to receive for their life's effort. We speak of a house being worth so many dollars, food costing so much in dollars, or spending so many dollars for education. In these examples, we are thinking of the item under consideration as being worth a given amount of dollars. Actually, the dollar itself has no value except as measured by the goods and services it will purchase. It is just as logical to say that a dollar is worth so many loaves of bread or so many hours of labor as to say that bread or labor is worth so many dollars. *The value of the dollar is measured by the goods and services the dollar will purchase.*

The value in terms of dollars of specific goods and services can fluctuate while the overall value of the dollar remains constant. Some items rise in price while others fall, due to changing supply and demand for these items on the part of the general public. For example, a unit of electricity was at one time equal to a loaf of bread in dollar value. Today, three units of electricity equal the same loaf of bread in dollar value. If the loaf of bread and unit of electricity both sold for $1.00 initially, bread may now have risen in price to $1.50 and the unit of electricity fallen in price to 50 cents. The overall value of the dollar could still be constant.

Inflation and Deflation

Unfortunately, the dollar does not maintain a stable value over a period of time in terms of the overall goods and services it will purchase. When it takes more dollars to purchase a given amount of goods and services than in the past, the dollar has fallen in value and goods and services have risen in value relative to the dollar. In this case, *inflation* has taken place. Inflation becomes a very pressing problem in personal financial planning. The falling value of the dollar has brought insecurity to millions of people who thought they had provided sufficient amounts for retirement, for their children's education, for death benefits, and for other needs.

Most people are interested in money primarily for what it will buy for them. Thus their basic interest is in maintaining their purchasing power rather than maintaining a certain dollar income. In times of inflation, more dollars are necessary to maintain a given amount of purchasing power. Just the reverse is true in times of *deflation.* In recent economic history, there have been relatively few times of significant deflation of the dollar in the United States. On the other hand, there

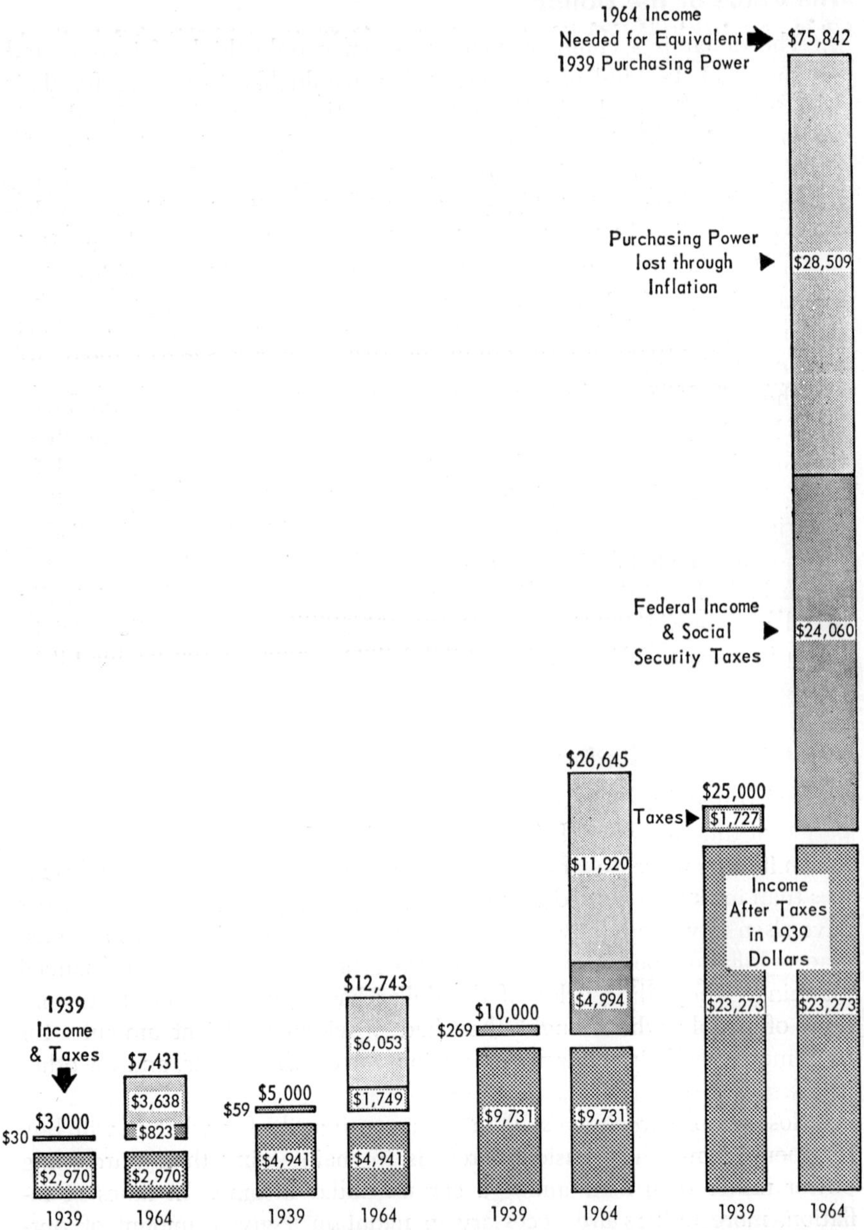

Fig. 1–1. Comparison of income and purchasing power for a married couple with two children in 1939 and 1964. (National Industrial Conference Board, Inc.)

have been long periods of inflation and a number of examples of very substantial inflation occurring in short periods of time.

Figure 1–1 indicates the erosion of the dollar from 1939 to 1964. Four different income levels for 1939 are shown. In 1964, family income of $12,743 per year was necessary to match the purchasing power of a $5,000 income in 1939. In 1939, a married couple with two children with a gross salary of $5,000 had $4,941 to spend after taxes. To maintain the equivalent purchasing power of this $4,941 in 1964, this family must have more than doubled its gross income from 1939 (to $12,743) because it must now pay the federal government $1,749 in federal income and social security taxes and forfeit $6,053 in purchasing power loss to inflation. Higher up on the income scale, the additional requirements become even greater. The $10,000-a-year family of 1939 requires $26,645 today to maintain the same purchasing power; $25,000 in 1939 is equivalent to $75,842 today.

It is apparent that inflation has substantially affected the purchasing power of the dollar in recent decades. It is certainly hoped by most people that the future will not bring as much inflation as has been experienced in the past twenty-five years. Nevertheless, the possibility of continued inflation is ever present and this must be considered in planning for the future. Of course, there is the possibility of deflation, which would have the reverse effect on dollar values. Some of the techniques which may be used to overcome the disadvantages of inflation and deflation are discussed in later chapters.

ECONOMIC CONDITIONS

While the actions of each of us have only a small influence on total economic conditions, no one who lives in a society can plan his economic future outside the environment of overall economic conditions within that society. Such major factors as wars, business depressions, or significant unemployment can completely change our personal economic plans. In general, we plan under the assumption that economic conditions will remain comparable to what they are today. In spite of past fluctuations (with the exceptions of major war periods), economic conditions have not changed so rapidly as to make personal financial planning meaningless. We in the United States have been particularly fortunate because even wars have not, to date, caused a complete upheaval of personal financial plans. While we have had our share of booms and depressions, we have generally experienced a more stable economy than most other countries. Furthermore, economic opportunities have been much greater in the United States than in many other countries. Most of us, in our personal financial planning, assume that this favorable economic environment will continue.

In the 1930's it was thought by many that the United States had become a mature nation and that business expansion would slow up. Our experiences since then have not substantiated this point of view. We are unquestionably in a dynamic economy which has grown rapidly in the past and which still has a great deal of future growth potential. Business capital expenditures have been rising steadily in the postwar period. New ideas are being developed and new businesses are coming into existence every day. National housing expenditures have expanded rapidly throughout the postwar period. In recent years consumer spending has risen steadily. While our economy exhibits problems of inflation and some permanent unemployment, the general outlook is still good. However, as the environmental economic conditions change, so must personal financial planning.

PERSONAL GOALS

The most fundamental institution in the American economy is the family unit. Each family, in planning its financial affairs, must answer two basic questions. First, what are the goals for the family unit? Second, how can these goals best be achieved? The answer to the second question can only follow the answer to the first. Most of this book will deal with answers to the second question, in the light of various objectives which different individuals and different family units may establish.

This chapter discusses the various common objectives of Americans. No formula is given and no recommended objective or group of objectives is determined for any particular individual. One of the great advantages of a free society is that each person and family may work toward different objectives. The various objectives that may be important to different individuals are discussed with no intention to imply relative importance or emphasis. Once you have determined your own objectives, the remainder of this book will help you in attaining them.

Happiness

Philosophers tell us that happiness is the goal of life for most people. While there is little disagreement that happiness is a common goal, the way to obtain a happy life is a complex problem confronting everyone. Considering the differences among human beings, it is understandable that the paths leading to this goal are many and varied. The artist finds happiness in pursuits different from those followed by the businessman.

Contrary to the idea held by many persons, psychologists tell us that people are happiest when they are regularly employed, even though they may not find their job particularly satisfying. Furthermore, leisure time, like money, appears to be more valuable the less one has of it. Many people spend their active years working and saving for their old age, with little thought of current enjoyment. This is a mistake. Only by building up varied interests during one's active life can one attain happiness and be interesting to other people during old age. Furthermore, death may overtake a person before he reaches the age at which he plans to start enjoying himself.

Money

For many people, money is to spend. This would seem logically to follow from the definition of money as a medium of exchange. Over a long period of time, all money is spent by someone. However, it has been noted that money can also be used as a store of value, for deferred spending or to meet other goals of the saver. The fewer the dollars one possesses, the greater the value of the dollar appears to be to that person. This value is based on what the dollar will purchase for this individual now or in the future. The enjoyment received from spending a specific dollar depends upon a variety of things. Psychologists say that the older one gets, the less enjoyment he receives from spending a dollar. Since most people accumulate more money as they grow older, and everyone grows older, it might be inferred from the above statements that one should spend all of his money as fast as he obtains it in order for him to enjoy himself the most. Such an interpretation is not intended. A balance must be determined between expenditures and savings.

The acquisition of money is not the goal of life, but it must be admitted that money is important in obtaining objectives. The person who devotes all of his time to working and accumulating a small fortune is usually, upon retirement, one of the unhappiest individuals on earth. If an individual has not learned to enjoy the things money will buy before he retires, he normally will not learn after he retires.

Health

While the conditions which create happiness vary substantially among individuals, there are certain common attributes. To most people, health is an important ingredient in happiness. You often hear the expression that health is wealth, or, in other words, good health is necessary for happiness. It is well known that money cannot buy health, even though it does make possible prompt and efficient medical and dental care. Fortunately or unfortunately, as the case may be, one's physical and mental condition at the time of birth has a lot to do with his health throughout life. But there is much that can be done to improve or to impair health. Medical science has made remarkable strides in recent years, and even greater medical accomplishments are anticipated in the future. Most people appreciate good health only when they have lost it. The value of money is realized in the happiness obtained through spending it, but without good health, money becomes worthless as a measure of happiness. It would thus be a shortsighted policy, to say the least, to ruin one's health for the sake of acquiring money.

Anticipation and Accomplishment

You have probably also heard the saying that anticipation is greater than realization. Many people have found out at one time or another that the pleasure derived from working toward a particular goal is often greater than that experienced when the objective is realized. It does not necessarily take money to strive for certain objectives. In fact, the absence of money may in itself be the reason why certain goals are attempted. The objective may be a better position, or more money, or it may be some goal which does not necessarily pay off in money, such as painting a picture, writing a book, or winning a race.

Learning

It is debatable whether education makes for greater happiness. Judging from personal observation, most of you could point out examples where apparently just the opposite occurred. However, it must be admitted that education does make it possible to enjoy more things than would otherwise be possible. Furthermore, the forms of enjoyment appear to be on a higher plane for the educated person. (Before they are misunderstood, the authors hasten to state that in their opinion, a high school diploma or a college degree does not necessarily evidence an education. Neither do they believe that long schooling is a necessary requisite of an educated person.)

Leisure

Many people receive a great deal of pleasure out of things they are not compelled to do. They hope to have interesting jobs but, in addition, they like to have sufficient leisure time to enjoy other types of activities. Having sufficient surplus funds to spend on leisure activities is important to many people. The pursuit of leisure activities need not present financial problems to the family, but the family income should be sufficient at least to meet other needs so that the head of the family does not have to devote all of his waking hours to earning a living. In addition, many of the generally accepted leisure activities today require some financial outlay.

Leisure activities should be given recognition in the family budget. Many people are able to continue working at some unpleasant job day after day only because of the enjoyment which they derive from their leisure-time activities. Leisure activities, therefore, become an important element in happiness.

Travel is becoming increasingly popular as a leisure activity of the average American family. Normally, the leisure time provided by a vacation period is the time devoted to travel, and many firms are giving increasing time to employees for vacations. A great deal of enjoyment can be obtained from sightseeing, visiting new places, getting away from normal surroundings, learning something of the history and culture of other places, and meeting people from other geographic areas. Travel, however, tends to be expensive and must be planned for over a considerable period of time. Families that are able to allow for travel in their income planning usually find that traveling contributes substantially to their enjoyment of life.

ECONOMIC GOALS

The problem of money is uppermost in the minds of many people from the time they assume adult responsibilities until they die. Furthermore, someone else must be concerned about individuals in a financial way before they are born, during their childhood, and after they are dead, since it costs a considerable amount of money to be born, a far larger amount to be reared, and a not inconsiderable sum to be respectably buried. Among adults, the greater part of the day is devoted to the pursuit of some form of work for the purpose of earning money. Much of the remaining time not consumed by sleeping is given to the spending of at least part of this money. The more fortunate find it necessary to allow a little time for the difficult task of investing part of their money. Truly, this quest for money is what causes the wheels of life to turn.

It is difficult therefore to separate economic objectives from social, cultural, religious, and other personal objectives. The kind of life desired by most individuals is a combination of these various objectives. Economic means are often important to the satisfaction of non-economic objectives. Some of the specific objectives which may be classified as economic, or which are met through economic means, are discussed below.

Security

Security means freedom from fear. Economic security implies freedom from fear of loss of the economic means to provide for needs. Almost everyone with family responsibilities has wondered at some time what would happen if he suddenly lost his income-earning potential. What will

ECONOMIC SECURITY — PROBLEMS AND PROTECTION

Economic Security Problem:	As members of family or other social unit:	As individuals:	As employees:	As citizens (under Social Security, public welfare and other government programs)
Unemployment	Earnings of other family members Assistance from friends and relatives Private welfare	Job skills Savings Life insurance cash values Property for sale or use as loan collateral	Annual salary, union contract or other wage guarantees Severance pay, deferred profit sharing, employee savings plans Supplementary unemployment benefits	Unemployment insurance compensation Public welfare
Old Age	Support by children Assistance from friends and relatives Private welfare	Part-time work Annuity or other guaranteed income Savings Life insurance cash values Property for sale or use as loan collateral	Pension Severance pay, deferred profit sharing, employee savings plans	Old Age, Survivors, and Disability Insurance (OASDI) Old Age Assistance Medical assistance for the needy aged
Death of Family Breadwinner	Earnings of other family members Assistance from friends and relatives Private welfare Fraternal society benefits	Life insurance Savings Property for sale or use as loan collateral	Group life insurance Group accidental death & dismemberment insurance Widow's pension Deferred profit sharing, employee savings plans	OASDI Workmen's compensation (if death was caused by job accident or illness) Public welfare
Illness	Assistance from friends and relatives Free treatment at hospitals if unable to pay Other private welfare	Individual health insurance Savings Life insurance cash values Property for sale or use as loan collateral	Group health insurance Employee savings plans Paid sick leave	Free medical care privileges for veterans and other special groups City, county and state hospitals (free care for the needy)
Disability	Earnings of other family members Assistance from friends and relatives Private welfare Fraternal society benefits	Loss-of-income insurance Savings Life insurance disability benefits & cash values Property for sale or use as loan collateral	Group loss-of-income insurance Paid sick leave or disability pay Pension Severance pay, deferred profit sharing, employee savings plans	OASDI (for permanent total disability only) Workmen's compensation (for job-connected disability) Temporary disability insurance (4 States) Public welfare

Fig. 1–2. Economic security—problems and protection. (Reproduced with permission, from *The Search for Economic Security*. New York: Institute of Life Insurance, 1965, p. 48.)

happen to my family when I die? How will my economic needs be met in my old age? These questions deal with the economic security of the individual and the family.

A feeling of economic security unquestionably contributes a sense of well-being and happiness. The means to meet this sense of economic security vary substantially from one individual or family to another. Some people pay little attention to personal security. They operate on the assumption that someone else will take care of them if they get into difficulty. Other people would be very unwilling to have to rely on others under any unexpected set of circumstances in the future.

If security were the only possible economic goal, personal and family financial planning would be very simple. However, other goals are also important to most people, and they face the problem of having to allocate their available resources to meet these different goals. Those people who cut back too severely on their standard of living and current enjoyment of life in order to obtain economic security may be as unhappy in their earlier years as are those who forget about security during the early years and later find themselves in substantial economic difficulty. Each individual or family must make its own decision on the relative importance of planning and providing for economic security. Figure 1–2 gives some types of security problems and some possible solutions.

Standard of Living

A standard of living is the level of consumption of material goods and services which is maintained by the individual or family. Most Americans would like to increase their standard of living; in fact, it is difficult to find people who are not striving, at least to some degree, for its improvement. Gains in a standard of living are normally attained through increased income, but they may also be realized by a reduction of savings for security or other economic objectives. Many people can look forward to rising standards of living throughout most of their lives. An outstanding economic aspect of the American system has been the steadily rising standard of living for nearly all elements of society. The material goods included today in the normal standard of living were unheard of a generation ago. The average American maintains a standard of living impossible for any but the very wealthy in many foreign countries. Electrical appliances and automobiles are commonplace, and modern housing is within the reach of most American families. It is one of the characteristics of the American society that regardless of their current standard of living, there are additional things that most people would like to purchase.

Some authors have complained about the materialistic emphasis of the American people and their constant striving for a higher standard of living. The standard of living, however, includes non-material things such as expenditures on travel, education, and leisure activities. In a free society, the choice of whether or not to reduce the emphasis on material goods is made by the individual. To many, increasing one's standard of living is a very important economic objective in life.

It must be remembered that increasing the standard of living is often achieved at the expense of other economic and personal objectives. While many may overemphasize current enjoyment of income, others probably would be much happier if they spent a little more of their income. Some people deprive themselves of many pleasures which can be enjoyed for the outlay of a small amount of money. If a pair of shoes hurts, why suffer when the expenditure of a few dollars can bring relief? One third of your life is spent in bed; the comfort and rest afforded by a good mattress and springs make their purchase well worthwhile.

Estate

Some people include providing an estate for their heirs as an important economic goal. (Providing an estate is differentiated here from providing security for a family in the event of an untimely death of the main income provider.) Many Americans have had little or no help from their families in launching their economic careers. They would like to see their children and grandchildren have an "easier" time in life than they themselves experienced, and are willing to sacrifice some of their own current enjoyment to save and invest for their heirs. This enables their children and grandchildren to start life and continue it on a higher economic plane. Other individuals consider that they have met their obligations to their descendants by merely providing an adequate education. Upon completion of his education, the child is placed on his own—and this, in the long run, may be best for the child. For some who are interested in providing an estate for their descendants, other economic goals must suffer in order that this may be done. Very few individuals attain sufficient wealth to meet all the economic goals they desire.

INCOME AND ASSETS

Personal income is the flow of economic values to individuals. We generally think of income on a weekly, monthly, or annual basis; but income continues to flow, and accumulated income to increase, throughout the working life of each individual. In fact, some income usually flows to an individual even during his non-working years through social security payments, insurance proceeds, or earnings on savings.

It is this income or flow of economic value which is used to acquire economic satisfactions. Thus, income becomes extremely important in personal financial planning. An individual is limited in reaching financial goals by the sum total of his potential income (including inheritance) during his lifetime.

Average family income in the United States has risen steadily in recent years. In 1929, one half of the nation's families had incomes under $3,000, and less than 10 per cent had incomes in excess of $10,000. By 1965, less than 20 per cent of the families had incomes under $3,000, and over 20 per cent had incomes over $10,000 per year. These figures are adjusted for the inflation which has taken place during this interval, and indicate, therefore, that real incomes of individuals and families have been rising. The average income in 1929 adjusted to 1962 dollars was $4,200 per family. The average income in 1962 was $6,400 per family, an increase in excess of 50 per cent.

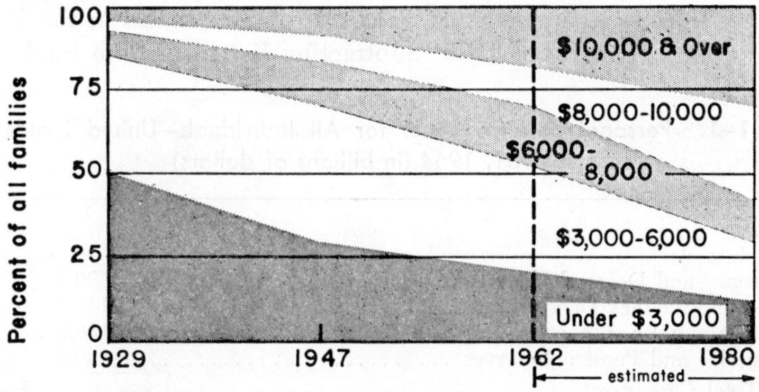

Fig. 1–3. Percentage of American families in various income classes. (Reproduced with permission, from data in Herman P. Miller, *Rich Man, Poor Man.* New York: Thomas Y. Crowell Co., 1964.)

Average incomes have risen more sharply in recent years. In terms of 1962 dollars, the average in 1952 was $5,200 (a gain of 24 per cent for the 23 years from 1929 to 1952). From 1952 to 1962, there was an increase in average family income in real dollars of $1,200, a growth of 23 per cent in only ten years. Figure 1–3 gives the percentages of all families in various income classes from 1929 to 1962 and projected estimates to 1980.

The figures quoted above are annual earnings. A typical college graduate in the 1960's can look forward to lifetime earnings of approximately half a million dollars, assuming no inflation. With inflation, his lifetime earnings will be much greater. In fact, even the non-college graduate with earning potential can look forward to a lifetime income of a quarter of a million dollars. Many college graduates of the 1960's will earn far in excess of a million dollars during the remainder of their lives. These are sizable figures and should cause us to stop and consider the wide variety of potentials we have for consuming or saving this income.

Assets

Most of the income we receive periodically is consumed within a relatively short time by the normal costs of living. However, many people do not consume their total income. The sum total of the savings or non-consumed income of an individual or family at any point in time is the *assets* of that family. These are items of wealth or economic value which the individual or family has accumulated for purposes of future consumption or security, or as part of an estate. If invested, assets produce future income. The assets an individual has at any given point in time, when added to his remaining lifetime expected earnings, give the total sum of economic value available to that individual for personal financial planning.

Table 1–1 lists the assets and liabilities of individuals in the United States at the beginning of 1965. Subtracting liabilities from total assets

Table 1–1. Personal Balance Sheet for All Individuals—United States, December 31, 1964 (in billions of dollars)

ASSETS		
Financial Assets		
Currency and Demand Deposits	$ 96.7	
Time and Savings Deposits	146.4	
Savings and Loan Accounts	108.9	
Insurance and Pension Reserves	290.6	
Total Cash Assets		$ 642.6
Savings Bonds	49.0	
Other U. S. Government Securities	29.4	
Local and Miscellaneous Government Securities	35.9	
Total Government Securities		114.3
Corporate Securities		615.4
Total Financial Assets		1,372.4
Fixed Assets		
Home Ownership	516.0	
Consumer Durables	249.5	
Total Fixed Assets		765.5
Total Assets		2,137.9
Less Liabilities		
Mortgage Debt	187.2	
Consumer Credit	76.8	
Total Liabilities		264.0
Net Worth		$1,873.9

SOURCE: National Consumer Finance Association, *Finance Facts*, 1965.

gives a net worth for all American individuals of $1,873.9 billion. Most of this is in *financial assets*—assets which are readily convertible into cash. *Fixed assets* include homes and durable goods such as automobiles and furniture and fixtures.

Total assets represent in excess of $1,000 for each man, woman, and child in the United States. These assets, however, are not equally spread; more than one fourth of American families have no liquid assets at all. Table 1–2 indicates the types of assets owned by families as a percentage

Table 1–2. Specific Types of Assets as a Percentage of Family Net Worth, by Income Levels—United States, 1962

		Assets as a Percentage of Net Worth			
Annual Income	Average Net Worth	Home and Auto	Equity in Business	Liquid and Investment Assets	Misc.
Under $3,000	$ 8,875	43.9%	16.0%	38.9%	3.4%
$ 3,000 to $ 4,999	10,914	36.2	17.4	42.7	7.1
$ 5,000 to $ 7,499	15,112	37.1	13.6	35.9	16.4
$ 7,500 to $ 9,999	21,243	39.4	12.1	35.3	16.5
$ 10,000 to $14,999	30,389	35.8	17.0	36.9	12.3
$ 15,000 to $24,999	74,329	22.9	12.2	53.7	11.9
$ 25,000 to $49,999	267,996	13.1	24.7	41.7	22.2
$ 50,000 to $99,999	789,582	6.2	31.9	49.1	13.4
$100,000 and over	1,554,152	5.8	18.6	68.1	8.3

SOURCE: *Federal Reserve Bulletin,* March, 1964.

of their net worth, classified by family income levels. It can be seen that fixed assets such as a home and an automobile are the major assets of low-income families. These become decreasingly important as the level of income rises. Liquid and investment assets (or financial assets as listed in Table 1–1) become increasingly important as the family's income rises. The amount of assets at a given point in time is particularly important in personal financial planning.

Sources of Personal Income

The major source of income to Americans is wages or salaries. Table 1–3 indicates that this source produces approximately 70 per cent of all personal income. However, income relative to employment is certainly not the only source of income. Other types of income can be almost equally important. The second most important source of income over the years has been proprietors' income. This includes profit from business ownership and from farm operation. The decreasing importance of this

Table 1–3. Sources of Personal Income, Percentage Distribution

Income Type	1929	1947–1957 Average	1963–1964
Wages and salaries	59.7%	66.7%	70.4%
Proprietors' income (includes farming)	17.5	16.0	10.6
Transfer payments (net) (social security, etc.)	1.6	5.3	5.2
Personal interest income	8.2	4.7	7.3
Dividends	6.9	3.7	4.0
Rental income	6.1	3.6	2.5
Total	100.0%	100.0%	100.0%

SOURCES: *National Income and Output,* Survey of Current Business Supplement (Washington, D. C.: Department of Commerce, Office of Business Economics, 1958), p. 46; and *Survey of Current Business,* June, 1965.

source of income at present is probably due to the decreasing percentage of farm income in the total income structure. Transfer payments–social security, workmen's compensation, unemployment compensation, insurance benefits, etc.–have been rapidly growing in importance in the past thirty years. These types of payments are particularly important to retired people and to families without a working head of household.

The effect of personal assets on personal income is illustrated by the importance of interest, dividends, and rental income. These three items combined accounted for 20 per cent of all personal income in 1929 but less than 14 per cent recently. The decline in importance of these three items indicates the increasingly diminishing position of personal assets as compared to employment in the personal financial income picture.

Value of a Job

How much is a $5,000-a-year job worth to you? Do you envy a person who is unable to work but has $100,000 in assets? Would you quit a job if you inherited $50,000 from some relative? How much is a job for the next 30 or 40 years worth?

The sum of $50,000 or $100,000 may sound like a great deal of money. But many people fail to recognize how much their job is worth to them in terms of future income. If a person were able to earn 5 per cent (and very few really safe investments would yield this amount) on his investments, the amazing principal sum of $100,000 would be required in order to receive an annual income of $5,000.

In other words, a $5,000-a-year job is worth $100,000 to you in terms of its future income and buying power. In this sense, the person who is earning $5,000 annually is currently worth about $100,000. If he is earning $10,000 every year, then he is currently worth $200,000. This method of figuring puts a high valuation on the earning power of a person; but after all, it would require a large amount of money to produce the same income. And is it not true that a person who has the ability to earn $10,000 a year is just as well off, from a current financial income viewpoint, as the $200,000 capitalist who is unable to work?

To find out the capitalized value of a certain salary, just capitalize it at the rate of 5 per cent. In other words, let the annual wage income equal 5 per cent, and then find out what 100 per cent equals. For example, assume that you earn $5,400 a year. If $5,400 equals 5 per cent, then 100 per cent equals $108,000 (100/5 × $5,400), the value of your earning power capitalized.

It might be argued that if you had $100,000, you could invest at least part of it at a rate higher than 5 per cent. To do so, however, might result in the loss of part of the principal amount, which would correspondingly reduce the annual income. Or it could be argued that an income higher than $5,000 a year could be obtained by using part of the principal each year, but this has the same shortcoming just described. It is generally true that people of wealth hesitate to use any of their principal because they are afraid that this may result in their not having enough to live on for the rest of their lives.

Another criticism that could be made of this method of capitalizing earning power is that there is no assurance a person will continue to be in the proper physical or mental condition to enable him to work until he dies. Even if he is in condition to work, he may not be able to secure employment; or if he does secure employment, he has no assurance that he will earn a fixed amount. In answer to this point, however, it should be realized that a person with a fixed amount of money is not certain of the rate of interest he will be able to earn on this money in the distant future, and furthermore, except for a limited number of investments, there is always the danger that part of the principal may be lost.

Another approach to the value of a job is to estimate future earnings. If you anticipate a starting salary of $400 per month, you will have an annual income of $4,800 per year. In ten years' time, that income could very easily grow to $7,500 per year or an annual average for the ten-year period of $6,500–$65,000 over the ten-year period. The average working lifetime is approximately forty years, and it would be anticipated by many people that during the remaining thirty working years income would rise still further. Even without inflation, increases to $10,000 per year could be anticipated. Thus, assuming an average income during the remaining thirty years of $8,500, the total income for the thirty-year period will be $255,000, or for the forty-year period, $320,000. That is almost a third of a million dollars in income received during forty working years. This substantial sum is due to the value of your job.

Life Cycle Pattern of Income

The typical college graduate spends approximately forty of his eighty years of total life expectancy in full-time employment. During these forty years, he must earn enough to support himself during his retirement, if he does not wish to become a drain on society. The typical American college graduate does not support himself for the first twenty-two years of his life—his parents do this for him. He in turn provides for his children during their first twenty-two years. But he also must save during his working years to provide sufficient income for his needs in the years of his retirement.

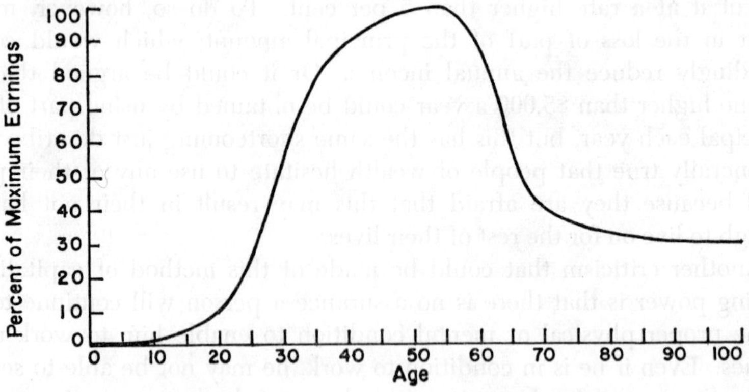

Fig. 1–4. Lifetime earnings cycle of average American male college graduate and head of household.

Figure 1–4 indicates the typical lifetime earnings cycle for a male college graduate. The earnings received after retirement at age 65 are income on investments, social security payments, and other types of receipts which are provided for during his working years. If an individual fully understands the earnings cycle indicated in Fig. 1–4, he will be better equipped to plan lifetime enjoyment of his total income received.

OCCUPATION

Since a person spends a large part of his life working, it is most desirable that his work be congenial. Some people actually enjoy their work; others, although they do not enjoy it, would be miserable if they were not working. Some absolutely hate their jobs. Since the type of work an individual does has much to do with his happiness, it is generally advisable for a person to choose work that he likes, even if the pay is less, rather than take some better-paying position that would be irksome to him. Although a person may like some particular type of work, he may find after he has worked at it for a while that he no longer obtains the same pleasure from it. This is natural; any position that requires one to be present for a certain number of hours five or six days a week will become tiresome after a while. When an attractive task becomes a job which must be done every day for livelihood, it loses much of its glamour. Another fellow's job may appear more interesting, but if you had to do it you might find it no more interesting to you than it is to him.

Very few people are able to find exactly the position they think they would like to have, but there is no harm in trying to get a job that one likes. An educated person usually has a better chance of obtaining the type of work he wants than does the less educated individual. In his quest for happiness through a congenial job, then, it is important for an individual to secure an adequate education.

Selecting an Occupation

Next to sleeping, gainful employment or occupation consumes more hours during an individual's lifetime than any other activity. Therefore, the selection of a vocation or occupation is an extremely important decision. Every young person has a potential choice from among a wide variety of lifetime occupations. As a person grows older and completes his education, he limits the number of potential occupations for which he is suited. Nonetheless, even in middle age, many people have an opportunity to change to another type of occupation or specific job. If a person decides at an early age what he wants to do vocationally, he has more time to develop in his occupation and is likely to make a greater contribution. Most college students and many college graduates do not really know what they want to do in their future life. The earlier they make this decision, the better off they will be; but they should not force themselves to an early decision that may turn out to be a wrong one. The costs of changing vocations can be much greater than the problems involved in waiting a little longer to make a selection.

Intelligent choice of vocation includes a determination of the objectives to be accomplished and the factors leading to this accomplishment. Each potential vocation must then be weighed in the light of these objectives and factors. In selection of a vocation, most people are immediately concerned with the factor of income. While income is important, there are a variety of different vocations or occupations which can produce sufficient income for most people.

Of equal or even greater importance in selecting a vocation are the sense of satisfaction one can obtain from working in his chosen field and the personal enjoyment he will obtain from his job. Working hours, working conditions, geographic location, work associates, and fringe benefits are other considerations in selecting a vocation.

Occupation and Income

The choice of an occupation greatly influences the amount of income one may anticipate. Unskilled, semiskilled, and clerical and service employees have much lower incomes than do professional people and business managers. People in the field of education, as a rule, earn more than unskilled factory workers but less than people in other professions. The clergy is often a very low paid profession, and medicine is a very highly paid profession. The occupations of low-income families tend to be substantially different from those in the high-income brackets. Potential income is thus an important factor in selecting one's occupation and, conversely, the choice of occupation is very important to the accomplishment of economic objectives.

Table 1–4 gives the lifetime earnings of various professional people and craftsmen. These lifetime earnings are from employment only and do not include earnings before entering the chosen profession or earnings after retirement, nor do they include income from sources other than the

Table 1–4. Lifetime Earnings by Occupation, Male—United States, 1962

Occupation	Lifetime Earnings (ages 18–64)	Occupation	Lifetime Earnings (ages 18–64)
Doctors	$717,000	Teachers	
Lawyers	621,000	College	$324,000
Managers and proprietors		High school	261,000
(with college degrees)	593,000	Elementary	232,000
Dentists	589,000	Accountants	313,000
Natural scientists		Electricians	251,000
Geologists	446,000	Airplane mechanics	248,000
Physicists	415,000	Plumbers	236,000
Biologists	310,000	Masons	209,000
Chemists	310,000	Plasterers	206,000
Social scientists		Automobile mechanics	187,000
Economists	413,000	Carpenters	185,000
Psychologists	335,000	Radio and television	
Statisticians	335,000	mechanics	183,000
Engineers		Clergymen	175,000
Aeronautical	395,000		
Electrical	372,000		
Mechanical	360,000		
Civil	335,000		

SOURCE: Herman P. Miller, *Rich Man, Poor Man* (New York: Thomas Y. Crowell Co., 1964).

job itself. The wide variation in lifetime earnings expectation is apparent from a study of this table.

Average annual income from occupation for various professions or vocations is given in Table 1–5. These data give the average annual

Table 1–5. How Earnings Change With Age

Occupation	Age and Income 25–34 Years	35–44 Years	45–54 Years	55–64 Years
Accountants, auditors	$ 5,993	$ 7,528	$ 7,793	$ 7,016
Artists, art teachers	5,841	7,131	7,317	6,612
Clergymen	3,864	4,547	4,301	3,973
College professors, instructors	5,488	8,208	8,936	9,129
Elementary school teachers	4,938	5,835	5,931	5,613
Secondary school teachers	5,130	6,492	6,961	6,883
Dentists	10,534	14,993	13,397	9,830
Designers, draftsmen	5,959	7,127	7,181	6,997
Editors, reporters	6,229	7,967	8,288	8,318
Aeronautical engineers	8,289	10,560	10,351	9,547
Civil engineers	6,968	8,291	8,477	8,566
Electrical engineers	8,048	9,369	9,396	9,374
Mechanical engineers	7,888	9,099	9,143	8,431
Lawyers, judges	7,220	12,006	13,844	12,057
Musicians, music teachers	4,854	6,017	6,027	4,859
Chemists	6,634	8,190	8,287	8,083
Physicians, surgeons	4,811	19,491	20,788	16,949
Economists	6,880	9,896	9,933	11,330
Electrical, electronic technicians	6,024	6,542	6,479	6,780
Store buyers, department heads	6,042	7,945	7,636	6,783
Public officials, administrators	5,604	6,835	6,998	6,545
Bank tellers	4,404	4,946	5,186	5,147
Clerical workers	4,898	5,436	5,369	5,132
Bookkeepers	4,647	5,170	5,145	4,701
Mail carriers	5,137	5,377	5,423	5,448
Postal clerks	5,196	5,433	5,528	5,579
Office machine operators	5,271	5,850	5,433	4,717
Salesmen, salesclerks	5,398	6,122	5,668	4,895
Insurance agents, brokers, underwriters	5,715	6,926	7,284	6,705

SOURCE: *Changing Times*, December, 1963, p. 16.

income by age bracket as well as by occupation. It is apparent that income changes not only with the choice of vocation, but with the age of the employed within his vocation. Between 50 and 55 years is the age generally considered to yield the peak earnings for most professional and semiprofessional people. Starting salaries and occupations are certainly not equivalent to average salaries and positions in these fields. In recent years the starting salaries of college graduates have risen very substantially, which has somewhat reduced the rate at which salaries increase during the early working years. However, starting salaries are not necessarily indicative of long-run income.

EDUCATION

Few people regret the time and money spent on an education. Aside from the potentially greater financial return in the future, a college education is usually worth, in intangible values, its cost in both time and money. Most people look back upon their college days as the happiest in their lives.

Considering the usual income benefits from a college education, the price paid for it is indeed low. The work of an educated person is usually more congenial, and in many instances, particularly in the professions, he enjoys a higher social esteem.

It must be remembered that education does not stop when one graduates from high school or college. Good formal education should create in the individual a desire to continue his learning process throughout the remainder of his life. A college graduate who believes that he knows it all will soon find his knowledge out of date, and he will be unable to benefit to the fullest extent from his formal education. Education after college takes many forms. Much of the continued learning process can be achieved with little expenditure of money; the major outlay is time. Continued study and learning should lead toward the more complete enjoyment of life.

Good education does not necessarily mean attending a college. Some people are not academically or temperamentally suited to college; nonetheless, they should obtain the best education available to meet their needs. Technical schools of a variety of types can be very important to the future economic and personal development of someone who does not attend college. Some people who plan to attend college never get there, or they attend but do not graduate. Only 10 per cent of the present labor force are college graduates; approximately 50 per cent of all boys and slightly over 45 per cent of all girls graduating from high school in 1960 planned to attend college. An additional 22 per cent of the boys and 17 per cent of the girls were undecided. One should seek the educational level for which he is suited and obtain as much as possible from the level of education he reaches.

Economic Value of Education

In addition to its other values, education pays off economically. The amount of a person's education influences his future income to the point where there is a strong correlation between earning power and the formal educational level achieved. This correlation applies for both men and women and for groupings of society based on color, nationality, and age. Unemployment, which leads to the lowest level of income, is most common for people with low formal educational achievements. Only a very small percentage of college graduates are unemployed, but a very large number of those who had no schooling or only elementary schooling are unemployed. Also, future prospects seem to indicate that unemployment may become relatively greater among those with low educational levels. The greatest need for future workers is in the professional and technical areas, which require a high level of education—and that need is increasing. Future need for farmers and farm workers, and for non-farm laborers, is expected to decline, and these are the areas of employment most suitable for those with less than high school education.

Certain kinds of occupations require a college degree and tend to be more highly paid than those available to non-college graduates. The change in earnings with level of educational achievement is indicated in Table 1–6. Among the many employment opportunities listed, only machinists earn more with four years of high school than others with four years of college. None of the listed occupations indicates higher earn-

Table 1–6. How Earnings Change With Education

	Years of School Completed and Income			
Occupation	8 Years Elementary School	1–3 Years High School	4 Years High School	4 Years College
Accountants, auditors	$6,498	$6,539	$6,530	$7,149
Designers, draftsmen	6,401	6,322	6,490	6,904
Electrical, electronic technicians	6,069	6,252	6,316	6,435
Medical, dental technicians	4,757	5,044	5,042	5,148
Store buyers, department heads	5,675	6,363	6,787	8,634
Public officials, administrators	5,068	5,765	6,288	7,684
Clerical workers	4,824	5,102	5,311	5,792
Bookkeepers	4,793	4,693	4,939	5,217
Office machine operators	4,778	5,166	5,457	6,157
Insurance agents, brokers	5,856	5,895	6,284	6,994
Real estate agents, brokers	5,070	5,552	6,499	7,942
Salesmen, salesclerks	4,509	5,128	5,664	7,388
Compositors, typesetters	6,047	6,118	6,187	6,304
Electricians	5,931	6,117	6,292	6,509
Foremen	6,300	6,635	6,964	8,367
Machinists	5,423	5,643	5,843	5,681
Mechanics, repairmen	4,752	5,101	5,383	5,707
Plumbers, pipe fitters	5,545	5,919	6,246	6,863
Toolmakers, diemakers, setters	6,407	6,617	6,749	7,092
Linemen & servicemen for telephone, telegraph, power companies	5,790	6,151	6,267	6,527

Source: *Changing Times*, December, 1963, p. 16.

Table 1–7. Number of American Families at Various Family Income Levels, and Education Level of Head of Household (Husband–Wife Families; Head Under 65)

Education Level of Head of Household	Under $3,000	$3,000 to $4,999	$5,000 to $6,999	$7,000 to $9,999	$10,000 to $14,999	$15,000 and Over	Median Income
Elementary							
Less than 8 years	1,971,788	1,661,134	1,290,381	832,418	334,200	85,426	4,399
8 years	953,041	1,365,739	1,457,874	1,122,978	488,696	133,829	5,617
High School							
1–3 years	854,827	1,618,100	2,130,153	1,730,604	745,330	214,958	6,219
4 years	708,407	1,666,369	2,646,414	2,354,245	1,076,942	358,887	6,725
College							
1–3 years	221,896	467,335	843,293	961,802	598,938	292,418	7,811
4 or more years	136,460	295,444	647,209	1,032,578	907,460	691,847	9,415
Total	4,846,419	7,074,121	9,015,324	8,034,625	4,151,566	1,777,365	6,332

SOURCE: "Sources and Structure of Family Income," *United States Census of Population, 1960* (Washington, D. C.: Department of Commerce, 1961).

ings for the elementary school graduate than for the person with four years of high school. In 1959, lifetime earnings of an average man with less than eight years of schooling were $143,000; the average man with five years of college or more had lifetime earnings of $455,000.[1]

Table 1–7 indicates the number of American families at various levels of income, and the education of the head of household. The median income is higher for each level of academic achievement than for the preceding one. It is apparent that a very high percentage of people with high incomes have completed four years or more of college. On the other hand, almost half of all families with income under $3,000 have a head of household who has had less than eight years of elementary schooling, and considerably more than half of these families have a head of household with no high school or college education.

Numerous studies have been made which prove that earnings of college graduates after they are out of school for several years exceed those of non-college graduates. Furthermore, the salaries of college graduates usually continue to increase over a longer span of years than for non-college graduates. A college graduate reaches his peak earning power in his fifties whereas the high school dropout tends to hit his peak earning power in his thirties. The salary lost while a student is in college is quickly made up. Even though the costs of college today are very high, the later financial reward more than justifies the investment. According to the National Consumer Finance Association average college graduates (with bachelors' degrees) in 1965 receive a starting salary of about $600 a month, which will go up $100 in two years; graduates with masters' degrees generally receive about $100 more per month. Technically trained Ph.D.'s command a beginning salary of at least $1,000 per month.[2]

Cost of Education

Education costs in two ways—lost income while in school, and the outlay necessary for education expenses. The lost income is relatively small compared to the future financial benefits, and the cost of education in today's society is rather low for the high school level. However, the cost of going to college can be very substantial.

Figure 1–5 indicates yearly costs of going to college at public and private institutions. The steady rise in college costs is much greater than the increase in most other prices during the same time period. As more and more people look toward advanced degrees, it must be recognized that this yearly cost will extend beyond four years. The typical four-year

[1] Herman P. Miller, *Rich Man, Poor Man* (New York: Thomas Y. Crowell Co., 1964), p. 148.

[2] National Consumer Finance Association, *Finance Facts* (March, 1965), p. 1.

graduate spends in excess of $10,000 during his college career. A master's degree may cost an extra $5,000 and various professional degrees much more. Tuition alone at some private schools is as high as $1,800 per year. It is expected that the annual cost of an education will continue to rise in coming years as rising living costs are reflected in higher tuitions.

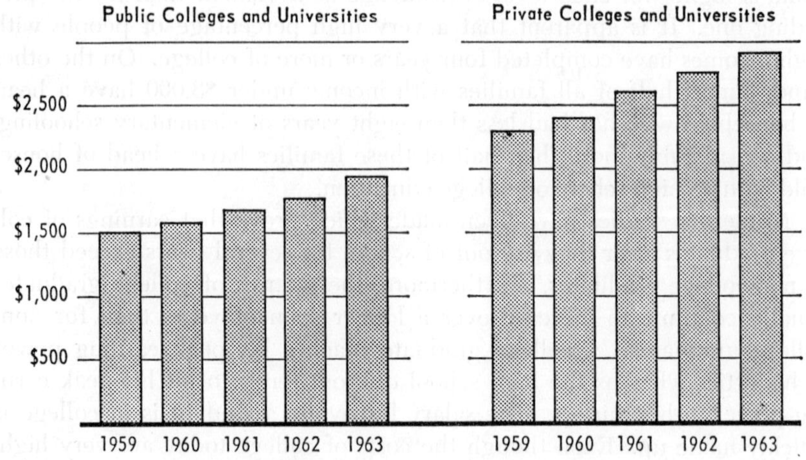

Fig. 1–5. Yearly cost of going to college—tuition, books, room, and board. (Department of Health, Education, and Welfare.)

Financing Education

The very substantial cost of education cannot normally be provided by the average family from its current income. Figure 1–6 gives the annual cost of college for a typical unmarried student, by sources of funds. His parents contribute almost two thirds of the total cost. His own earnings are second in importance, followed by scholarships and other sources. It is apparent that typical parents cannot expect to send two or three children to college, paying from one half to full support for them, without advance planning. While most people owe their parents for at least part of the cost of their own education, this obligation is commonly repaid by educating their own children.

Good students can help considerably in financing their own education. A wide variety of scholarships are available for top students, but, while scholarships are rising in number and dollar amount, the number of applicants is also increasing considerably. Students who are unable to obtain sufficient scholarship funds may be able to organize their time in such a way as to work part-time and contribute a portion or all of the total cost of college. However, with rapidly rising enrollments in colleges, the part-time opportunities have not kept up with the demand in many schools. Thus, unless the cost of education has been provided for in advance, many people are unable to meet the requirement financially or must borrow to do so.

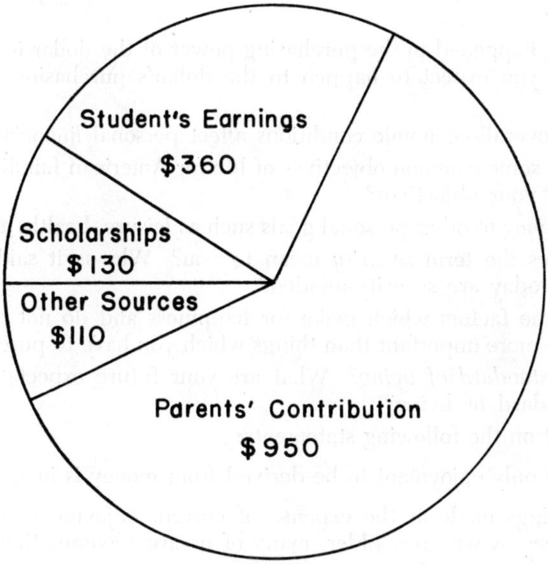

Total $1,550

Fig. 1–6. Sources of funds for annual college costs for average unmarried student. (Data from *Burroughs Clearing House*, 1963.)

In recent years a number of new borrowing plans have been developed, some with government assistance. Many schools have special loan funds, and some states have developed college loan plans which either lend directly to students or insure loans from banks and other financial institutions to pay for their college education. In 1964, federal savings and loan associations were authorized to make loans to college students for purposes of financing their education. In some cases, it is possible to borrow the total cost of going to college with no repayments due until after graduation. The importance of college education for those who have the ability to complete it is indicated by the increased emphasis placed by government and private organizations on financial aid for college students.

A college education is worth the cost even if the student must give up some time and social activities to work part-time, or if he or his family must borrow in order for him to complete college.

QUESTIONS

1. Define *finance*. What is the relationship between finance and money?
2. Differentiate money and legal tender.
3. What is meant by inflation? How does inflation affect personal financial planning?
4. What has happened to the purchasing power of the dollar in recent years? What do you expect to happen to the dollar's purchasing power in the future?
5. How do overall economic conditions affect personal financial planning?
6. What are some common objectives of life for American families? Which of these are your objectives?
7. Relate money to other personal goals such as leisure, health, and happiness.
8. What does the term *security* mean to you? Why is it said that college students today are security-minded?
9. Name some factors which make for happiness and do not cost anything. Are these more important than things which you have to purchase?
10. What is *standard of living?* What are your future expectations for your own standard of living?
11. Comment on the following statements:
    (a) The only enjoyment to be derived from money is in spending it.
    (b) Savings made at the expense of current enjoyment are unwise because, as we grow older, many of us are accumulating more money or other property.
    (c) Spend and grow rich.
    (d) Saving money is justified only if the future spending of it will bring more enjoyment than current spending.
12. Some people say they would rather get their education by traveling than going to college. Can an education be acquired in this way?
13. What are the problems of maintaining economic security?
14. How do personal assets relate to personal income?
15. What are the major sources of personal income for most Americans? What do you expect your future sources of income to be?
16. If prevailing interest rates are 5 per cent, what is the capitalized value of the earning power of a person who is earning a salary of $6,000 per year?
17. Since average life expectancy is approximately eighty years, how can you provide for financial support in your old age if you work for only forty years?
18. How would you go about selecting a lifetime occupation?
19. What is the monetary value of an education today? What other values accrue from education?
20. How much does a college education cost? How can a college education be financed?

CASE PROBLEMS

1. John Francis will be graduated from college in June with a Bachelor of Arts degree in civil engineering. As he has been a regular ROTC student during his four years of college, he is committed to a tour of duty in the army for three years. John is 21 years old and has no immediate marriage plans. He will graduate in the upper 10 per cent of his class, and several of his professors have suggested that he should go on for a graduate degree. He could obtain a small research assistantship, but the rest of his expenses would have to be met by his parents, with some financial sacrifice on their part. They are, however, willing to help. If he goes to graduate school, he will still face the time requirement in the army, but he can be deferred until he completes his graduate degree. Should he go to graduate school? List the advantages and disadvantages of so doing. State the basis on which you would make this decision if you were John.
2. John Brent has just inherited $100,000. Considering himself wealthy, John has quit his job and decided to live off his estate. George Smythe has a secure job paying $6,500 per year, but with little opportunity for further advancement. Both men are in their early thirties, are married, and have two children. Smythe is very envious of Brent's wealth. Which man is better off financially? Was Brent's decision to quit work wise? How could he get the greatest return on his investment without taking substantial risk? Which man would you rather be? Why?
3. Mary Wright has just graduated from high school where she was an average student. She took a college preparatory course. Mary's parents want her to go on to college to study liberal arts. She expects to get married in two years and may have to help support her husband until he gets his medical degree. She wants to go to work now rather than go to college. Are her parents right in encouraging her to go on to college? What advantages will the additional education have for her? If you were her fiancé, what would you advise her to do?
4. Bob and Mary Wilson were married at the beginning of Bob's junior year in college. Mary has had a teaching position for the past two years in an elementary school in the college town. This position has paid $4,500 per year. Bob has just graduated from college and has accepted a position as a management trainee in Indianapolis at an annual salary of $5,600 per year. They plan to take a vacation during the month of June to visit their families and Bob starts work on July 1. Should Mary apply for a teaching job in Indianapolis? They have no savings because it has taken all of Mary's earnings to support Bob in school. They would like to purchase a car, furniture, and a home. Which of these purchases should be made first? What kind of a savings program should they have? What are the advantages and disadvantages of Mary's continuing to work?
5. Robert Hammond is completing his college course in business administration. His father expects him to go to work in the family business which will some day be his. His father offers him a starting salary of $8,600 per year with periodic increases. He should become president of the company in eight years, when his father plans to retire. Hammond feels that he would

like to go on to graduate school and then to teach in college rather than go into the business world. Which action should he take? How important is the financial advantage of working for his father's firm? What advantages would the teaching position have? If you were Hammond's father and, against your wishes, your son decided to go on to graduate school rather than enter the family business, would you help him financially in obtaining the additional schooling?

6. Mike Perry is 35 years old, with a wife and three children. He owns his house outright and has $8,000 in savings accounts and other investments. He has a chance to go into a business of his own, but it would take all his savings as well as require a large mortgage on the house. He has always wanted to be in business for himself rather than working for others. Should Perry quit his secure job for a business of his own? What can he hope to gain by giving up his present position? Would it make any difference if he had no dependents?
7. Make a list of your personal objectives in life. Then attempt to list them in the order of their importance to you. Also list what you think were your parents' objectives in life at the time of their marriage. Have their objectives changed? Have they accomplished their objectives?

SELECTED READINGS

Bureau of the Census. "Income of Families and Persons in the United States." *Current Population Reports, Consumer Income.* Washington, D. C.: U. S. Department of Commerce. Latest edition.

Bureau of Labor Statistics. *Occupational Outlook Handbook.* Washington, D. C.: U. S. Department of Labor. Latest edition.

Calvert, Robert, Jr., and Steele, John E. *Planning Your Career.* New York: McGraw-Hill Book Co., 1963.

Career: The Annual Guide to Business Opportunities. New York: Careers, Inc. Published annually.

Carlson, Waldernar. *Economic Security in the United States.* New York: McGraw-Hill Book Co., 1962.

Department of Health, Education, and Welfare. *Financing an Undergraduate Education.* Washington, D. C.: U. S. Government Printing Office, 1964.

Endicott, Frank S. *Trends in Employment of College and University Graduates in Business and Industry.* Evanston, Ill.: Northwestern University, Annual Reports.

Finance Facts, 1964. Washington, D. C.: National Consumer Finance Association, 1964.

Goode, William J. *The Family.* Englewood Cliffs, N. J.: Prentice-Hall, Inc., 1964.

Hazlitt, Henry. *What You Should Know About Inflation.* New York: D. Van Nostrand Co., Inc., 1960.

Katona, George. *The Mass Consumption Economy.* New York: McGraw-Hill Book Co., 1964.

Katona, George, Lininger, Charles A., and Mueller, Eva. *1963 Survey of Consumer Finances.* (Survey Research Center.) Ann Arbor: University of Michigan Press, 1964.

Levy, William V. *How Much Is a College Degree Worth to You?* New York: Macfadden Publications, Inc., 1963.

Lowen, Walter. *You and Your Job.* New York: Thomas Y. Crowell Co., 1962.

Margolis, Sidney K. *How to Pay for your Child's College Education.* New York: Public Affairs Committee, 1963.

Miller, Herman P. *Rich Man, Poor Man.* New York: Thomas Y. Crowell Co., 1964.

Morgan, James N., David, Martin H., Cohen, Wilbur J., and Brazer, Harvey E. *Income and Welfare in the United States.* New York: McGraw-Hill Book Co., 1962.
Search for Economic Security, The. New York: Institute of Life Insurance, 1965.
Sinick, Daniel. *Your Personality and Your Job.* Chicago: Science Research Associates, 1960.
Survey of Consumer Finances. (Survey Research Center.) Ann Arbor: University of Michigan Press. Latest edition.
Vocational Guidance Manuals. New York: Grosset & Dunlap, Inc. Latest numbers.

2

Personal Budgeting

The establishment of personal and family long-range economic goals is the most important activity of personal financial planning. Personal economic goals, the base for financial planning, must be determined first. It is not the purpose of the authors to tell you which economic goals you should have, but rather to indicate ways of accomplishing whichever goals you select. Prudent family financial management is necessary for the fullest accomplishment of economic satisfactions in life.

All individuals and families have economic goals or objectives; the trouble is that many people have too many desires—all of which they wish to satisfy immediately. Proper financial management forces the consideration of economic goals in the order of their importance, and the selection of the more desirable objectives. Expected present and future resources are then allocated toward the accomplishment of the chosen goals in the order of their importance.

Everyone has a financial management program. Most personal programs, however, are poorly planned and accomplish little for the individuals involved. While most people recognize the importance of financial planning on the part of governmental agencies and business units, the majority of individuals fail to recognize the equal importance of *personal* financial planning.

Some people put their financial plans on paper, budget carefully, and keep an up-to-date record of expenditures. Others use a less formal program but are still familiar with the basic objectives of their personal financial plans and the ways in which they intend to accomplish them. Regardless of the formality of the financial program, the family with a wise financial plan for spending and saving has fewer financial problems and thereby enjoys greater peace of mind.

Sound personal financial management requires adequate data. You must know where your money comes from and where it goes. Equally important, you must know where you most *want* it to go. In addition, you need a knowledge of techniques of management that are applicable to your own personal circumstances. This chapter discusses the budget, the major technique used in personal financial management planning.

INCOME PLANNING

The average American family had a gross income of $7,510 in the year 1963. The 1963 total income represented a 3 per cent increase over 1962. Adjusting for price increases during the year 1963, the gain in *real* income during the year was 2 per cent. The average gain in real income per year from 1947 through 1963 was 1¼ per cent. Figure 2–1 indicates the aver-

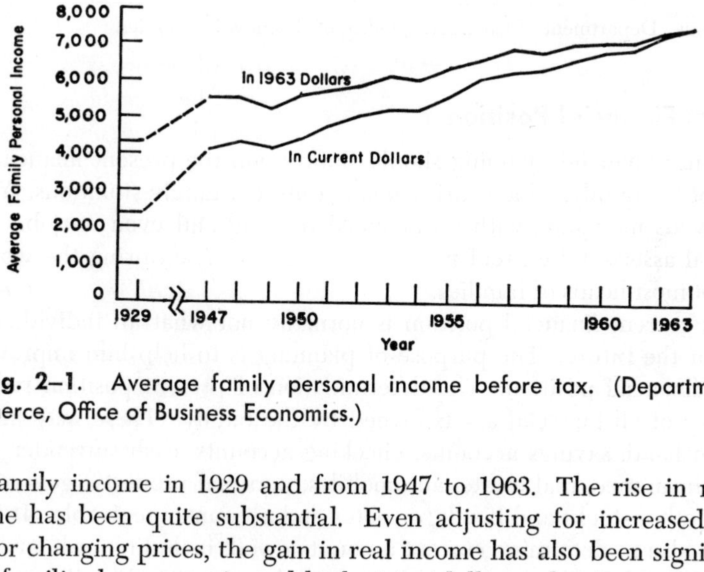

Fig. 2–1. Average family personal income before tax. (Department of Commerce, Office of Business Economics.)

age family income in 1929 and from 1947 to 1963. The rise in money income has been quite substantial. Even adjusting for increased taxes and for changing prices, the gain in real income has also been significant. Most families have experienced both rising dollar and rising real income in past years. Total family income tends to rise until the time of retirement. It is important that individuals and families attempt to estimate their present and future income, in order to do a better job of personal financial planning.

Table 2–1 gives the breakdown of American families into income categories in 1962. Note that, in spite of rising incomes in recent years, 12 per cent of the families still earn less than $2,000 per year. Many of these famiiles, of course, are retired or live on farms, where actual total income may exceed stated dollar income. While half of the American families still earned less than $6,000 in 1962, the number of families with incomes under this amount has been decreasing steadily since the 1930's. Almost 20 per cent of American families had incomes over $10,000 in 1962.

Table 2–1. Distribution of Consumer Units and Their Income—1962

Family Personal Income Before Income Taxes	Number of Families (millions)	Percentage Distribution
Under $2,000	6.9	12.0%
$ 2,000 to $ 3,999	10.6	18.3
$ 4,000 to $ 5,999	11.8	20.4
$ 6,000 to $ 7,499	8.2	14.1
$ 7,500 to $ 9,999	9.1	15.7
$10,000 to $14,999	7.1	12.3
$15,000 and over	4.2	7.2
Total	57.9	100.0%

SOURCE: Department of Commerce, Office of Business Economics.

Present Financial Position

Future financial planning should build upon the present financial position of the family, which varies among different family situations. Young newlyweds may start with no financial backing and even no job. Total financial assets and current income both tend to rise during the working years of most heads of families.

His current financial position is normally not what an individual desires for the future. The purpose of planning is to help him improve his future financial position. The determination of present position requires a survey of all financial assets owned by the family. These may include cash on hand, savings accounts, checking accounts, cash surrender value of life insurance, real estate, automobiles, personal property, government bonds, other stocks and bonds, or notes and accounts receivable. It is advisable also to determine current amounts owed, including ordinary bills, installment debts, mortgage balances, and notes payable. The net of current financial assets minus current amounts owed is available for future use, either to produce additional income or to be consumed.

Your present financial position also takes into consideration current income. Income from employment is normally the most important item, but dividends and interest on investments, rental incomes, and any other types of income you may have should also be considered. Your current income added to your financial assets gives the total financial value available to meet immediate financial objectives. Figure 2–2 is a form for use in determining present financial position.

how much are you worth today?
AND
what are your goals for the year?

OWNED	*Today*	*Goal in 1 Year*	*Actual in 1 Year*
CASH Savings Account Checking Acc't			
INSURANCE *(cash value)*			
REAL ESTATE *(market value)* Home Other			
OTHER PROPERTY Automobile *(listed value)*			
INVESTMENTS U.S. Bonds Other Bonds Stocks			
MORTGAGES			
NOTES *(receivable)*			
ACCOUNTS *(receivable)*			
TOTAL OWNED			

OWED	*Today*	*Goal in 1 Year*	*Actual in 1 Year*
CURRENT BILLS *(owed)*			
INSTALLMENT DEBTS			
MORTGAGES *(balance owed)*			
NOTES *(payable)*			
TOTAL OWED			

TOTAL OWNED MINUS TOTAL OWED IS YOUR NET WORTH ⟶

Fig. 2–2. Form for determining present financial position and planning goals. (Harris Trust and Savings Bank, Chicago.)

Increasing Income

Family income is merely a means to an end. Very few people are interested in income for income's sake. The real values in income received are the goods and services and the security and well-being which that income will purchase. These various values and uses of income were discussed in the preceding chapter.

One way to increase present and future satisfactions is to increase income, but many people are not in a position to increase their current income; they are presently earning to the limit of their capacities. Others, however, have opportunities for increasing their present or future income. Most younger people can look forward to rising incomes throughout much of their future lives. Many people work hard for job advancement—both in position and in salary. The income of most professional men tends to rise rapidly during the first ten or twenty years of work, and at a slower rate thereafter until retirement.

Salary increases contribute to future gains in income, but they do not generally help to solve the immediate income problem. Many family groups have found other ways to increase current income. Proper investment of savings can, for instance, lead to an increase in current income. It is becoming increasingly common in young families for the wife to contribute to the total family income by working part-time or full-time. Older children may take baby-sitting jobs, mow lawns, or do other odd jobs to provide part of their own spending money and thus, in effect, contribute to the total family income. Many employed men have found interesting and lucrative opportunities in addition to their normal full-time job to supplement the family's income. There are a large number of part-time insurance and real estate salesmen, for example, and many industrial workers supplement their income by television servicing and home maintenance work on weekends and in the evenings.

Working wives present a difficult problem in financial planning. If the wife is still of child-bearing age, the certainty of her continuing to work and to supplement family income is unknown. The desirability of a wife working must also be carefully considered. Studies have indicated that 40 per cent of the income earned by a working wife is taken to meet job cost expenses—thus only 60 per cent of what she makes aids the family budget. Other studies indicate that the higher the family income (up to $15,000) the more likely it is that the wife is working. Over 50 per cent of the wives of families whose incomes range from $7,000 to $15,000 are employed part-time or full-time. The average working wife contributes from one fourth to one half of the total family budget. Most working wives are saleswomen, office helpers, semiskilled factory workers, service workers, or teachers.

This discussion of working wives applies when they are the *secondary* breadwinners of the family. Obviously, where the woman is the only employed person in the family or the major contributor to the family budget, her job should be considered as primary and the other contributors to the family budget as providing the secondary income. This situation may arise where the husband is deceased, unemployed, disabled, retired, or going to college full-time.

Budgeting Receipts

Financial planning must necessarily start with expected income. Many people have income from only one source; others receive funds from a number of different sources. Figure 2–3 is an example of a form for

how much is your income now?

Estimate monthly income in pencil. If actual varies from estimate, make changes accordingly for your record.

HUSBAND

(Fill in Names of Months)

Source	*Estimated Annual Income*													*Actual Annual Income*
Salary or Wages														
Bonus														
Commissions														
Interest														
Dividends														
Annuities														
Rents														
Royalties														
Special Fees														
TOTAL														

WIFE

Salary or Wages														
Bonus														
Commissions														
Interest														
Dividends														
Annuities														
Rents														
Royalties														
Special Fees														
TOTAL														
GRAND TOTAL														

Fig. 2–3. Form for planning income. (Harris Trust and Savings Bank, Chicago.)

budgeting receipts. It suggests a separation of husband's income from wife's income. Nine different possible sources of income are listed and blank spaces are available to fill in any others. The user estimates his annual income from each of these sources and then breaks it down into months so that a monthly grand total of estimated income is given at the bottom of the chart. As actual income is received, the amount received is substituted for the amount estimated.

The amounts to be entered in the columns for estimated annual income and actual income received are the total amounts of income before any withholding. Amounts withheld for personal income tax, social security, hospitalization, retirement, and savings plans are truly expenses paid out of income. They should, therefore, be included in the income amount and later subtracted when studying the distribution of income to meet expenses.

Even if income is irregular, a budget is an important and practical device. With irregular income, the best approach might be to estimate the *least* amount that can be expected and plan on the basis of that amount. An overflow budget can be designed to include the expenditures that will be made if income exceeds minimum expectations. Planning is even more important for the person with uncertain income, so that he can be assured of not living beyond his means.

Note again that Fig. 2–3 breaks total expected income down into that provided by the husband and that provided by the wife. This is done for a specific purpose. If both incomes are used for living expenses, the family may be in serious financial difficulty when the wife stops working. It is very difficult for a family to adjust downward from two incomes to one. A safe plan for families in which both the husband and the wife work is to use the wife's income (over and above the expenses incident to her employment) for special purposes not related to day-to-day living expenses. Her income could be set aside, for example, toward the accumulation of a down payment for the purchase of a house. It could be used for special vacations, for the purchase of labor-saving equipment, or for new furnishings for the home. If the wife's income is used for a generally higher scale of living than the family would be able to enjoy on the husband's income alone, they may be headed for difficulty. It is generally impossible for a young married couple to anticipate the wife's working throughout her lifetime. Even though it may appear possible for her to continue to work, many families would consider it undesirable.

BUDGETING EXPENSES

Most people work hard for their income, but many of them waste part of it through poor buying and poorly planned expenditures. Often, lack of income is blamed for an unsatisfactory current financial position; however, those who complain about insufficient income could substantially increase their enjoyment of life by better planned spending. The solution to many personal financial problems is the proper control of expenditures.

Typically, a family that has financial difficulty spends more than it should on many "small items," which are often of a repetitive nature. In time, the summation of "small items" equals a large amount. Families rarely find themselves in financial difficulty due to the installment purchase of one item. It is when they purchase on installment a second, third, or fourth item before paying for the first one that they get into difficulty. Most families with financial problems spend more on housing, furnishings, clothes, food, or an automobile than is necessary. Instead of trying to keep up with the Joneses, it might be more satisfactory to just be the Smiths. The obligation to pay bills should come before satisfaction of the desire to live on the same economic level as the neighbors.

Importance of Expense Budgets

The family budget is an effective way of controlling expenses and providing for savings. The federal government and the various state and municipal governments find it absolutely necessary to maintain budgets, and most successful businesses have found that the budget is an important management tool. While it would seem logical that most individuals, therefore, should also budget, this is not the case. Most people do not keep a budget, but then most people are very poor personal financial managers. Keeping a budget is often "too much trouble." Most people do not want to be bothered by the detail. Figures worry people, and a budget is all figures. A budget compels them to look into the future, and for many people this is not easy to do. Why not face the issue? Almost everyone would profit by keeping a budget. The personal success of many individuals is due in large part to the fact that they were not afraid to face unpleasant things. Some people find that they are absolutely compelled to keep a budget in order to pay their current expenses or make payments on a loan. In fact, some lending agencies require that the borrower maintain a budget until the loan is paid off. This should be evidence enough that a budget usually makes possible larger savings.

Businesses and governmental units often have both expense and cash budgets. *Expense budgets* do not include investments but they do include expenses when they are incurred, whether they are paid for in cash at that time or not. *Cash budgets* cover planned cash outlays for expenses as well as cash outlays for investments, which are not considered expenses. For personal planning, the typical budget is a cash budget. "Savings" cannot technically be considered expenses but they are considered as a cash outlay in a personal expense budget. Principal payments on a mortgage and purchases of securities, a home, life insurance, and even an automobile are not technically expenses for the individual. However, they are cash outlays and must be planned for. The typical individual thinks in terms of cash income and outflow rather than the accounting concepts of income and expense.

Expense items are those which result in immediate consumption: food, recreation, travel, clothing, or utilities. The personal budget must also plan for cash outlays such as savings, investment, purchase of durable goods, or purchase of a home.

Reasons for Keeping a Budget

A major objective of budgeting is to help a person or a family live within a certain income. Let us concern ourselves with *your* budget. Every budget begins with an estimate of income. It is implicit in the budgeting process that you "make the budget balance." In so doing, you force yourself to provide only for expenses which your income can meet. With a fixed income and a carefully prepared budget rigidly adhered to, you need not fear spending beyond your means. A collateral advantage of budgeting is that it forces you to set priorities on your spending. In making your expenses stay within your income, you force yourself to place a relative importance upon each of the various alternatives for spending. By studying the worth to you of all potential expenditures at the same time, you are more likely to make reasonable selections on the basis of importance than if you make a decision whether to purchase an item when the specific circumstance arises. By determining your priorities in advance, you should end up actually doing the things that give you the most satisfaction. Without planned expenditures, you would be unlikely to accomplish this.

With a given amount of money and a given number of expense items, an apportionment to the various expense items must be made. The more income appropriated to one item, the less there is available for some other. In this way you are assured that there will be sufficient money available to pay for the essential expenses of living. This does not necessarily mean that a person must cut out entirely a certain expenditure—he may merely have to reduce the amount spent on that particular item. In some instances a budget will, by limiting the expenditure for certain items, enable an individual to enjoy the purchase of even more things than would have been possible if the budget had not been maintained.

Expense budgeting can also be very helpful in the systematic accumulation of savings. Most people save little or nothing. Others automatically save whatever is left from their income after they have spent all that they desire. Of those who are able to effect some form of saving, however, most do so only because of some systematic plan. This plan, in many instances, is forced upon them. In order to pay premiums on life insurance and annuities, or to meet payments on the mortgage on their home, they must budget their expenses. Life insurance and home ownership constitute the greatest savings of most persons. Without this forced saving, many people would save little or nothing. It is thus apparent that a budget can enable a person to save part of his income regularly. Since budgeting is a formal plan for spending, it leads to the greatest long-run satisfaction of financial desires and, as a corollary, makes a substantial contribution to freedom from worry.

The disadvantages of budgeting must also be mentioned. Most people who do not maintain budgets claim that keeping a budget is just too much trouble. The time consumed in record-keeping and the problems of establishing a budget system are considered by some to outweigh the advantages of a budget. Others claim that it is too difficult to estimate income and expense, and therefore budgeting is impractical. Neither of these arguments is sufficiently founded in fact to justify non-budgeting. Various types of systems are available from many published sources, but a budget system need not be time-consuming or complex. While it is often difficult to estimate income and expense, some estimate is obviously better than none. And, whether you keep a formal budget or not, you obviously, in your own mind, have some concept of what your future income will be when you are making your expenditure commitments.

It is strongly recommended that every family have some type of budget. For those whose income and expenditures have leveled off, the formal budgeting described below is perhaps not necessary. These people should, however, have reasonable estimates of their own income and spending desires for the funds available. Newlyweds, particularly, benefit from budgeting since it aids them in reaching some of their long-run financial objectives. Every time the family position changes, either by changing income or by size and circumstance of family, the budget plan should be reviewed and a new plan prepared.

Preparing the Budget

Before preparing a budget for expenditures, it is necessary to establish your financial objectives. The expenditures you should make are influenced by many things, including your age, the age of your family, your current financial position, the size of your family, your income, your future expectations, and your goals in life. No model spending pattern fits any one family or individual. There is no single formula which will tell you how you should spend your money. The best allocation of expenditures is the one which best meets *your* financial goals in the order of their importance to you.

When an individual begins to prepare a budget for the first time, he is confronted with the fact that he does not know how much to allow for most of the expense items. The amounts of a few items, such as rent, taxes, insurance, or utilities, can be ascertained from old receipts. Checkbook stubs also furnish considerable data. It will be necessary to make intelligent guesses concerning the expense items for which information is not available. These estimates can be revised later, after reviewing the experience of the first several months. Past expenditures are not a criterion of what should be spent, but they furnish a useful guide for setting up the original budget.

In addition to estimating future expenditures, an important part of budgeting is keeping a record of the actual expenditures for the various expense items. It is from such records that the budget can be set up more intelligently for the following months and years. A record of all cash expenditures should be classified and, for convenience, kept in the same book. The monthly totals can then be transferred from this book and the check stubs to the budget record. Figure 2–4 (pages 46 and 47) is an example of a daily expense record.

Before starting to assemble the expenditures for the past year (which will be used as somewhat of a guide for future budgeting), it is advisable to decide upon a grouping or classification for the various expense items. More effective control can be maintained over future expenditures if a large number of expense groups are used. Too large a number of groups, however, can make records somewhat cumbersome. Each person should decide for himself what expense classifications he needs. The ten classifications and their subdivisions listed on page 45 should be considered minimal.

After establishing the various classifications of expenses, it is necessary to estimate what regular annual expenses are included in each of these classifications. Many large expense items will come only once or twice a year. These major expenses should be anticipated and enough should be provided out of each month's income to meet these expenses when they fall due. The funds provided for these annual expenses can be set aside in separate envelopes or in separate bank accounts, or carried in an existing bank account. The latter is probably preferable, if the individual keeps in mind that these funds are not to be spent for other purposes. By setting aside amounts in the months in which the unusual expenses do not occur, the family will have the funds necessary to meet these payments. It is suggested that one twelfth of the annual expense for these items actually be prorated to each month under the appropriate heading so that the budget for that month does not show as surplus the amount necessary to meet these expenses.

Figure 2–5 gives an example of a planning and control chart to aid in budgeting annual outlays which are not paid at regular weekly or

EXPENSE CLASSIFICATIONS

Food
- All food items
- Meals taken out
- Beverages
- Tobacco

Housing
- Tenant
  - Rent
- Owner
  - Interest on mortgage
  - Real estate taxes
  - Assessments on property
  - Insurance on property
  - Maintenance on property
  - Property improvements

Household Operation
- Electricity
- Fuel
- Furniture repairs and insurance
- Garden supplies
- Gas
- Home decoration materials
- Home furnishings and equipment (including installments on past purchases)
- Laundry
- Refrigeration
- Telephone
- Water

Clothing
- Clothing
- Cleaning and pressing
- Alterations
- Storing

Automobile Expenses
- Automobile (including installments on past purchases)
- Garage
- Gasoline and oil
- Insurance
- Licenses
- Repairs
- Tires

Medical and Personal Care
- Barber and beauty shops
- Cosmetics and beauty supplies
- Drugs and medicines
- Health and accident insurance
- Hospital
- Medical supplies
- Professional medical services

Recreation and Entertainment
- Admissions
- Games
- Hobbies
- Musical instruments and supplies
- Photographic equipment
- Radio and TV expenses
- Reading materials
- Sporting goods
- Travel
- Vacation

Other Expenses
- Carfare
- Charity
- Christmas
- Church
- Club
- Education
- Gifts
- Taxes (other than real property and income taxes)
- Legal services
- Tips
- Miscellaneous

Income Taxes

Savings
- Annuity policies
- Life insurance
- Loan repayments
- Real estate
- Retirement plans
- Savings accounts
- Securities
- Social security
- Net increase in checking account

---

monthly intervals. The development of a monthly reserve to provide for these outlays is illustrated.

The budget maker should now determine other fixed expenses which are paid at regular monthly or weekly intervals: house payments, rent, installment payments, utilities bills. These fixed expenses are very easy to determine by checking past records. Day-to-day living costs such as food, family allowances, and household operation should then be determined. It should be recognized that many of these outlays can be varied to meet

WHERE DOES THE MONEY GO? **A Guide for Regular Saving —** **BUDGET AND**

Date	TOTAL INCOME	PAYROLL DEDUCTIONS	SPENDABLE INCOME	EXPENDITURES	MUST PAYMENTS * SAVINGS	FIXED EXPENSES	HOUSING	OPERATING HOUSEHOLD	FOOD	CLOTHING
Estimates for the Month $										
	Salary Commissions Interest Dividends Other	Income Tax Social Security Savings Bonds Other	or "Take-home Pay"	Daily or Weekly Totals	Savings Account Savings Bonds	Income Tax (Estimate & State) Life Insurance Other	Rent/or Taxes Interest Repairs/ Insurance, etc.	Gas, Heat Phone, Water Electricity Laundry Service Equipment	All Food Milk Meals Out	Wearing Apparel Cleaning Pressing For Entire Family
1										
2										
3										
4										
5										
6										
7										
8										
9										
10										
11										
12										
13										
14										
15										
16										
17										
18										
19										
20										
21										
22										
23										
24										
25										
26										
27										
28										
29										
30										
31										
TOTAL										
BALANCE—Subtract total for each column from Estimate for Month (see above)										

BALANCE OR RESERVE: The estimate made for certain items (for example: Clothing, Medical, Education) will not be spent each month. However, a definite sum should be allowed for these things, and the amount not spent can be added to the estimate for the next month — or, better yet, set aside as a Reserve Fund in your Savings Account. A record of the use to which this is put can be kept separately.

Fig. 2–4. Budget and expense record.

available income. Past records are also helpful in determining the amount required for day-to-day living costs.

The budget maker should not let the amount of his actual expenses in prior years serve as a requirement of what he *should* spend in the future. If he does this, his budget will not accomplish its purpose. Past experiences are used only to give a rough idea of amounts that will be

EXPENSE RECORD — and for **Wise Spending** For Month of ....19......

LIVING EXPENSES

PERSONAL		ADVANCEMENT					MEMORANDA
Carfare, Taxi, Papers Barber, Hairdresser, Other Personal Allowances Husband	Wife, Children	Medical Doctor Dentist Drugs	Education Books Magazines Recreation Vacation	Clubs Gifts Contributions Church	Car		
							1
							2
							3
							4
							5
							6
							7
							8
							9
							10
							11
							12
							13
							14
							15
							16
							17
							18
							19
							20
							21
							22
							23
							24
							25
							26
							27
							28
							29
							30
							31

★ **MUST PAYMENTS — Savings and Fixed Expenses —**

Each month set aside in a Savings Account a definite amount as a Cash Reserve and Emergency Fund.

Also, estimate Fixed Expenses for the year: Income Tax (Estimate of amount not withheld and State Tax) — Life Insurance — Payment and Taxes on home (if owned and not under Housing) — and any other fixed payments. Take 1/12 of the total and each month deposit this amount in a Special Savings Account so there will be money on hand to meet these payments as they come due.

(Union Dime Savings Bank, New York.)

spent in the future if spending habits are not changed. A study of past expenditures can lead to a determination of which expenditures should be reduced in the future to maximize satisfaction. If an individual's income is increased or decreased, or if the prices or amounts of his necessary expenses change, then his future budgets should be changed accordingly.

planning chart

LOOKING AHEAD TO REGULAR ANNUAL EXPENSES

	Amount	*Payment Schedule (Fill in Names of Months)*											
AUTOMOBILE Insurance License													
FEES School and other													
INSURANCE (*see page 31*)													
Annuities													
Fire and Theft													
Health and Accident													
Hospitalization													
Life													
Property													
MEMBERSHIP DUES													
MORTGAGE (If paid annually)													
PLEDGES Church Community Fund Other													
SUBSCRIPTIONS													
TAXES Property Income (*Estimate beyond amount withheld*)													
Social Security (*If not withheld*)													
TOTAL													
MONTHLY RESERVE (*1/12 of Total*)													

control chart—*Plan for Operation of Reserve Fund*

REGULAR ANNUAL EXPENSES

	Amount	*(Fill in Names of Months)*											
Amount of Reserve Carried Forward													
Added to Reserve													
Withdrawals for Expenses													
Balance of Reserve at End of Month													

Fig. 2–5. Form for planning expenses. (Harris Trust and Savings Bank, Chicago.)

The budget maker must decide his savings needs. Most families who do not provide for savings *first* find that they do not save. Also, if savings are not satisfied regularly, most people do not save. A form for planning savings is given in Fig. 2–6. (An approach to budgeting for savings is discussed later in this chapter.)

plan for savings

	Emergencies	*Opportunities*	*Security*	*Specific Wants*	*TOTAL*	
Goal to be Achieved						
Budgeted Monthly						
Savings Now on Hand						*Cumulative. Savings*
Month Amount Saved:						
Amount Saved:						
Amount Saved:						
Amount Saved:						
Amount Saved:						
Amount Saved:						
Amount Saved:						
Amount Saved:						
Amount Saved:						
Amount Saved:						
Amount Saved:						
Amount Saved:						
Total Savings at End of Year						←*Equals*↑

Fig. 2–6. Form for planning savings. (Harris Trust and Savings Bank, Chicago.)

Subtracting savings, the prorated portion of annual expenses, the fixed monthly expenses, and the day-to-day living costs from take-home pay should leave a balance available for future flexible expenses. Should the planned outlay exceed the expected income, you must go back and decide which anticipated expenses will have to be reduced. If the expected income exceeds total expenses, you are in a position to plan for the use of

Month	Food	Housing	Household Operation	Clothing	Automobile	Medical	Recreation	Other Expenses	Income Taxes	Savings	Debt Repayment	Total	Income
Budget for Year													
JAN. FEB. MAR. APR. MAY													
DEC.													
Total for Year													
Over													
Under													

Fig. 2–7. Summary budget and expense record.

surplus funds for such items as extra clothing purchases, purchases of equipment or furnishings, special vacation, or travel. These constitute luxuries, and should be planned for after the necessary items are met. You should list in order of importance all the things you would like to do but which are not necessary to maintain your normal standard of living. The income over and above fixed needs may be allocated to these items.

Budget Forms

Budget forms may be obtained from libraries, stationery stores, financial institutions, and various consumer organizations. Several different types of forms are available, from very simple to highly complex ones, and from one small page to several pages in length. While printed forms may be easier to use, they are not necessary for good budgeting practice. The average individual could prepare his own budget forms by merely filling in labeled columns on lined paper.

A series of budget forms has been given in Figs. 2–2 through 2–7. Present financial position and goals for the year are recorded on the form in Fig. 2–2. Figure 2–3 is a form for recording the income plan and the actual income received by month. Daily cash expenditures and the planned monthly budget are entered on the form illustrated in Fig. 2–4. Expenses paid by check may be entered on this form at the end of the month or on the day that a check is written. Cash expenditures should be recorded promptly so that they will not be forgotten. Total expenditures for the month are determined by adding up the various columns. The amount by which the classification of expenditure is over or under budget is recorded. Figure 2–6 is the plan for savings. The actual amount saved and the planned savings for each month can be recorded on the monthly expense record in Fig. 2–4.

Figure 2–5 is also a subsidiary form for Fig. 2–4. This is used to prorate expenses which are not paid at regular monthly or weekly intervals. Figure 2–7 is a summary budget record for both income and expense. At the end of each month, the totals from the monthly budget and expense record and from the monthly income record may be recorded on this summary. Yearly totals of budgeted income and expense are recorded, along with the yearly totals of actual income and expense.

It is generally advisable to keep a budget on a monthly basis, as indicated in the sample forms. This is particularly true when income is received on a monthly or semimonthly basis. Some people who receive their paychecks weekly may prefer to keep their budgets on a weekly basis, but this involves more work. The keeping of a budget should be done in the way that is easiest for the individual or family involved. If the budget plan adopted is too complex or too time-consuming, the family is likely to discontinue its budget process. It would be better to have a less detailed, more easily understood budget process which the family would continue for many years.

Using Your Budget

A budget is both a planning and a control tool. The importance of a budget in forcing a selection from among alternative expenditures has already been discussed. Planning what you would most like to do with the funds you expect to have available does not mean that you will accomplish your objectives. A budget is meaningless unless it is used to control expenditures. To do this, you must compare the actual expenditures with the planned expenditures, and if the actual exceed the planned, you must make some kind of an adjustment—either reduce that expenditure in the future or adjust other expenditures downward to make up for it.

It would generally be a good idea to study the actual expenditures each month, as indicated in Fig. 2–4. The actual expenditures relative to the amounts budgeted should be analyzed in the light of adjustments you will make in the future to bring the budget into balance. When an expenditure arises which has not been provided for in the budget, if you use your budget as a control device, you are forced to adjust other expenses downward. This causes you to make the best selection, among the alternative expenditures, in the light of what you most want to accomplish.

Fixed Income Problems

Those people whose future annual income will not increase in amount have a special budgeting problem. Most retired people are included in this category. Past expenditures are helpful in planning the future only if living requirements and prices do not change. Over long periods of time, we have experienced substantially rising prices in the United States. In 1936 a person who retired on $3,000 could live very well. If he continues to receive only $3,000 per year in 1966, his standard of living must be greatly reduced in order to make ends meet. Furthermore, as he grows older, he may have more medical expense and additional living expenses.

Inflation is particularly bad for people who must live on fixed incomes. While we hope that there will not be substantial inflation in the future, the past trend indicates that we are likely to have some. If this is the case, it may be wise for people who are planning on a fixed dollar income for a long period of years in the future to budget in such a way that they spend less of this income in the early years in order to accumulate some extra savings which could be applied to compensate for price increases in later years. (Investing part of one's savings in good common stock or real estate may offer a good hedge against inflation.)

AVERAGE CONSUMER EXPENDITURES

Over a lifetime, the average American family has an income of \$250,000. This is a quarter of a million dollars and sounds like a substantial amount of money. Where do we spend our quarter of a million? An analysis of overall American spending patterns indicates that this \$250,000 is spent as follows:

Housing	\$ 58,000
Food and drink	48,000
Taxes	36,000
Contributions, gifts, books, and dues	26,000
Transportation	24,000
Insurance	16,000
Clothing	12,000
Recreation	12,000
Personal expenses	12,000
Medical expenses	6,000
Total	\$250,000

Because of the lack of homogeneity in objectives, income, and conditions, budgets of other families have limited usage in making your own personal family budget. There is no such thing as the typical or the average family in the United States. Spending patterns of American families vary substantially among various geographic locations, rural and urban areas, families with different occupations and education levels of heads of household, and various stages in the life cycle of the family. Variations in distribution of expenditures by households based upon stage in the life cycle are indicated in Table 2–2. Keep the limitations of average or typical statistics in mind in studying the information given in Fig. 2–8.

Table 2–3 indicates total personal consumption expenditures nationwide by type of product in 1950 and in 1963. While expenditures for all products increased during this 13-year period, the increasing affluence of the American society can be seen by the more than proportionate increase in personal care, housing, medical care, personal business, and private education expenses. Many of these items would be considered luxury items. The more necessary food, clothing, household, and transportation expenses all decreased in relative importance.

Each of the major items included in normal family expenditures is discussed below.

Table 2–2. Share of Annual Household Expenditures by Stage in the Life Cycle

Expenditures	All Households	Household's Stage in the Life Cycle: No Children and Head Under 40	Younger Children	Older Children Only	No Children and Head over 40: Married Head	Single Head
All goods and services—total	100%	100%	100%	100%	100%	100%
Food, beverages and tobacco	29	26	30	30	29	28
Clothing and accessories	12	12	12	13	11	13
Medical and personal care	5	4	5	6	6	6
Home operation and improvement	19	19	20	15	18	23
Home furnishings and equipment	9	10	8	8	9	7
Recreation and recreation equipment	5	7	5	5	5	5
Automotive	14	17	14	15	14	10
Other goods and services	7	5	6	8	8	8

SOURCE: *Life Study of Consumer Expenditures.*

Where the money goes

	average for all city families	age of head of family: under 25	25-34	35-44	45-54	55-64
meals at home	19.3%	15.4%	18.0%	19.8%	19.2%	19.7%
meals out	5.1	6.0	5.2	4.9	5.1	5.6
tobacco, alcoholic beverages	3.6	3.3	3.7	3.5	3.8	3.5
shelter	13.8	15.6	15.2	12.8	12.5	13.4
fuel, light, refrigeration, water	4.5	2.9	3.9	4.3	4.4	5.0
household operations (laundry, cleaning, help, etc.)	5.9	5.8	6.3	5.8	5.5	5.8
home furnishings	5.2	6.4	6.0	5.7	5.0	4.6
clothing	10.2	9.2	9.8	11.1	11.3	9.8
personal care	2.9	2.7	2.8	2.8	2.9	2.8
medical care	6.4	5.8	5.9	5.8	5.9	7.2
recreation	4.0	4.4	4.4	4.4	4.2	3.3
education	1.1	1.2	.8	1.1	1.9	.9
car	13.0	17.6	14.1	13.3	13.0	11.9
other transportation	1.7	1.6	1.3	1.7	1.8	2.5

How spending differs from average

	under 25	25-34	35-44	45-54	55-64
ABOVE AVERAGE	meals out shelter home furnishings recreation education car	meals out tobacco, alcohol shelter household operations home furnishings recreation car	meals at home home furnishings clothing recreation car	tobacco, alcohol clothing recreation education other transport	meals at home meals out fuel, light, etc. medical care other transport
BELOW AVERAGE	meals at home tobacco, alcohol fuel, light, etc. household operations clothing personal care medical care other transport	meals at home fuel, light, etc. clothing personal care medical care education other transport	meals out tobacco, alcohol shelter fuel, light, etc. household operations personal care medical care	meals at home shelter fuel, light, etc. household operations home furnishings medical care	tobacco, alcohol shelter household operations home furnishings clothing personal care recreation education car

Some expense items are excluded, so total does not add up to 100%.
The average for all city families also includes older age groups not listed here.

Fig. 2–8. Expenditures for various adult age groups. [Reprinted by permission from *Changing Times,* the Kiplinger Magazine (March 1964 issue). Copyright 1964 by The Kiplinger Washington Editors, Inc., 1729 H. Street, N. W., Washington, D. C. 20006.]

Table 2–3. Personal Consumption Expenditures by Type of Product—1950 and 1963

	1950		1963	
	Millions of Dollars	Per Cent	Millions of Dollars	Per Cent
Food, beverages and tobacco	$ 59.7	30.6%	$ 95.2	25.3%
Household operation	29.0	14.9	52.4	13.9
Housing	21.2	10.9	48.9	13.2
Transportation and auto	24.7	12.6	47.2	12.5
Clothing, accessories, and jewelry	23.8	12.2	37.1	9.8
Medical care and death expenses	9.7	5.0	25.4	6.9
Personal, business, and financial	8.0	4.1	25.0	6.8
Recreation	11.3	5.8	22.7	6.2
Personal care	2.5	1.3	6.5	1.7
Private education and research	1.8	0.9	5.7	1.5
Religion and welfare activities	2.4	1.2	5.4	1.4
Foreign travel and remittances, net	1.1	0.6	3.5	0.9
Total	$195.0	100.0%	$375.0	100.0%

SOURCE: *Survey of Current Business*, 1964.

Savings

Savings is probably the most important single item in the family budget, but, unfortunately, many people consider it last and save only what is left over after all other outlays—which is usually nothing. Throughout the world there is the paradoxical situation that the people who need savings the most have the least and, conversely, those who perhaps need them least save the most. Part of this is beyond the control of the individual, but it is hoped that what is contained in this book may, in at least some instances, aid the individual in more effectively spending *and* saving his money. The maintenance of a budget will enable many persons to save who otherwise would be running into the red every year.

To save money most people find it necessary to adopt some plan of regular and systematic saving. Regardless of how small the income may be, a part of it, even though it may be insignificant in amount, should be saved. If unforeseen expenses arise, a genuine attempt should be made to cut down on other expenses rather than reduce savings. Admittedly, the latter is the easier way and will in most instances be followed. Saving through payroll deduction is one of the least painful ways of saving and it is highly recommended by the authors. This may take the form of deductions for the purchase of savings bonds, retirement plans, or insurance. A person cannot spend money that does not come into his hands. For spending purposes, the individual should consider his entire pay to be the net amount after the deductions have been made. It is surprising how small payroll deductions can result in appreciable savings over a long period of years.

An annual plan for savings has been shown in the form in Fig. 2–6. This form suggests that the savings be broken down into those amounts necessary for emergencies, special opportunities, security, and specific wants. Only the savings accumulated to meet specific wants should be used for those purposes. Specific wants would include the accumulation of a down payment toward the purchase of a house, the purchase of major durable goods, vacation uses, and similar expenditures. By planning for savings *first* in the budgeting process, and by sticking to that plan, you should be able to meet your long-run objectives.

Figure 2–9 indicates the regular monthly savings required to reach certain dollar goals in certain time periods, invested at various percentage returns. For example, if you will need $4,000 in 20 years to send a child to college, you should accumulate $11.05 per month if you have your savings invested at 4 per cent return. This amount must be saved regularly or the funds will not be available at the time they are needed. If a college fund is one of the goals for your savings, the amount necessary should be considered a fixed monthly outlay and be set aside regularly. The same approach should be taken for savings required for other future uses. The amounts you save through payroll deduction plans and through social security should be included in your plan for savings. Types of investments for saving, methods of saving, and the amount to be saved are discussed further in Chapter 6.

Food

As used here, food includes beverages and tobacco. The amount spent for food, beverages, and tobacco is the most important expenditure for most families, regardless of income level. In families with income less than $2,000 per year, 36 per cent of the annual household income is spent on this item. Although the *percentage* of the *total* income spent for food declines as the size of the income increases, the *actual* amount expended for this item increases.

Housing and Household Operation

Home operation and improvement is the second most important expenditure for most households. When home furnishings and equipment expenditures are added, housing and household operations consume 28 per cent of the average family's budget. In addition to the basic cost of shelter, housing and household operation expenses include utilities, tele-

Find your savings goal in this column	Here is the regular monthly saving needed to reach that goal if your money is invested at . . .							
	2½%	3%	3½%	4%	5%	6%	7%	8%
$500 in 5 years	$7.85	$7.80	$7.70	$7.60	$7.45	$7.25	$7.10	$6.95
10 "	3.70	3.60	3.50	3.40	3.25	3.10	2.95	2.80
15 "	2.35	2.20	2.15	2.05	1.90	1.75	1.60	1.50
20 "	1.60	1.55	1.45	1.40	1.25	1.10	1.00	.90
30 "	.95	.85	.80	.75	.60	.50	.40	.35
$1,000 in 5 years	$15.75	$15.55	$15.40	$15.25	$14.85	$14.55	$14.20	$13.90
10 "	7.40	7.25	7.05	6.90	6.50	6.20	5.90	5.60
15 "	4.65	4.45	4.25	4.10	3.80	3.50	3.25	2.95
20 "	3.25	3.10	2.90	2.75	2.45	2.20	1.95	1.75
30 "	1.90	1.75	1.60	1.45	1.25	1.00	.85	.70
$2,000 in 5 years	$31.50	$31.15	$30.80	$30.45	$29.75	$29.05	$28.40	$27.75
10 "	14.75	14.40	14.05	13.70	13.05	12.40	11.80	11.20
15 "	9.20	8.85	8.55	8.20	7.60	7.00	6.45	5.95
20 "	6.45	6.15	5.80	5.50	4.95	4.40	3.95	3.50
30 "	3.75	3.45	3.20	2.90	2.45	2.05	1.70	1.40
$3,000 in 5 years	$47.25	$46.70	$46.15	$45.65	$44.60	$43.60	$42.60	$41.65
10 "	22.15	21.60	21.10	20.55	19.55	18.60	17.65	16.80
15 "	13.85	13.30	12.80	12.30	11.40	10.50	9.70	8.90
20 "	9.70	9.20	8.75	8.30	7.40	6.65	5.90	5.25
30 "	5.70	5.20	4.80	4.40	3.70	3.05	2.55	2.10
$4,000 in 5 years	$63.00	$62.30	$61.55	$60.90	$59.50	$58.10	$56.80	$55.50
10 "	29.50	28.80	28.10	27.40	26.10	24.80	23.55	22.35
15 "	18.45	17.75	17.10	16.40	15.20	14.00	12.90	11.90
20 "	12.95	12.30	11.65	11.05	9.90	8.85	7.90	7.00
30 "	7.55	6.95	6.35	5.85	4.90	4.10	3.40	2.80
$5,000 in 5 years	$78.75	$77.85	$76.95	$76.10	$74.35	$72.65	$71.00	$69.40
10 "	36.90	36.00	35.25	34.25	32.60	31.00	29.45	27.95
15 "	23.05	22.20	21.35	20.55	19.00	17.50	16.15	14.85
20 "	16.20	15.35	14.55	13.80	12.35	11.05	9.85	8.75
30 "	9.40	8.65	7.95	7.30	6.15	5.10	4.25	3.50
$6,000 in 5 years	$94.50	$93.40	$92.35	$91.30	$89.20	$87.20	$85.20	$83.30
10 "	44.30	43.20	42.20	41.10	39.10	37.20	35.35	33.55
15 "	27.65	26.60	25.60	24.65	22.75	21.00	19.35	17.85
20 "	19.40	18.40	17.45	16.55	14.85	13.25	11.85	10.50
30 "	11.30	10.40	9.55	8.75	7.35	6.15	5.10	4.20

Fig. 2–9. Monthly savings needed to meet various savings goals. [Reprinted by permission from *Changing Times,* the Kiplinger Magazine (April 1959 issue). Copyright 1959 by The Kiplinger Washington Editors, Inc., 1729 H. Street, N. W., Washington, D. C. 20006.]

phone, home operation expenses, appliances, furniture, equipment, and related expenses.

For a family that does not own a home, housing means rent. A homeowner, on the other hand, will have to include all expenses incurred in owning a home: interest on the mortgage, taxes and assessments, insurance, and maintenance. It is to be noted that the amount of the monthly payment on a loan which applies to the reduction of the principal amount of the loan is not listed as an expense; it is properly considered as savings. Although depreciation is a factor which should be taken into consideration in connection with home ownership, it is not included as an expense in the cash budget, since no cash outlay must be made for this item.

Clothing

People with larger incomes spend more for clothing but the percentage of the income allotted for this item does not vary as much as for the other expense items. Most families spend from 11 to 14 per cent of their incomes for clothing. Single persons usually spend more for clothes than married people. Many persons spend too much on clothes, while others probably spend too little. Relatively high-priced clothes are not necessarily expensive. The wearing qualities of good clothes may in the long run make them no more expensive than lower-priced clothing.

Automobile Expense

Automobile expense includes both the purchase of the automobile and the periodic operating expenses—gas and oil, repairs, insurance, licenses, tires, and garage rent. Depreciation is a real cost of owning an automobile, but since no out-of-pocket outlay is necessary to cover it, the depreciation factor can be ignored in the personal cash budget. The purchase of an automobile is an expense in the budget, because a cash outlay is involved. Proper planning recognizes that cars do depreciate over time and that periodic replacement is necessary. This requires planning of available cash to provide for replacement when needed.

An automobile is a great convenience, but an expensive one. With cars as high-priced as they are, a considerable amount of money must be expended to buy a car even in the "low-price field." Also, unlike many other items, when you buy a car you are buying something which is going to cost you a considerable amount of money all the time that you have it. Automobiles depreciate rather rapidly, and although you do not include depreciation in the cash budget, it is a real cost and will show up in the form of increased maintenance costs and replacement cost when a new car is purchased.

Families that do not have the necessary cash to purchase a car outright will often use all the money they have to make a down payment on one. Then they have the remaining part of the purchase price to pay plus the interest on the unpaid balance. A bad situation is then made worse because they have to get cash in some way in order to operate the car. Although not an automobile expense, an automobile can take you to many places where you can spend money.

The cost of operating a car varies according to the type of automobile, its age, and the number of miles per year it is run. Repair charges also vary and tend to be higher in the larger cities. Automobile insurance is also more expensive in the large cities. The following would be typical of the average costs of operating a car in the low-price field in the United States:

Variable costs, average per mile	
Gasoline and oil	$ 0.0240
Repairs	0.0075
Tires and miscellaneous	0.0060
Total variable costs, per mile	$ 0.0375
Fixed cash costs, annual	
License	$ 20.00
Insurance	150.00
Total fixed cash costs, per year	$170.00
Other fixed costs	
Depreciation (during first three years), per year	$500.00

On the basis of 10,000 miles a year, the variable costs of 3¾ cents a mile would make the annual cost $375. Adding the fixed cash costs of $170 would make a total cash expense of $545 per year. This would be $45.42 per month. This monthly figure does not include monthly payments which are required for automobiles purchased on credit. It also does not include depreciation expense. Average annual depreciation on a new Chevrolet, Ford, or Plymouth would be $500 per year for the first three years. This increases annual automotive cost to $1,045 ($87.08 per month or 10.45 cents per mile). It becomes obvious that the family with less than $4,000 income per year would have great difficulty affording an automobile. Even an inexpensive used automobile with practically no depreciation involves substantial cost of operation. While many people today consider an automobile a necessity, the longer an individual can wait before he purchases a car the greater will be his financial gain.

Next to the purchase of a home, the purchase of a car is the most important single outlay for the average American family. Because of this, careful thought should be given to it, and the best possible purchase and arrangements should be made. The budgeting process includes the recognition of annual outlays in connection with owning a car as well as the initial purchase outlay. Advance planning can save substantially on annual outlays: the larger the down payment, the lower the installments. There is the basic question of whether one should buy a new or a used car. Certain types of new cars involve considerably less initial outlay than others. Long-run and short-run operation costs will vary with the type of car purchased. While used cars cost less initially, their operation expenses are generally higher. Even so, a good used car will normally average substantially lower annual cost, including purchase price, than a new car.

Some people have found it financially advantageous to rent an automobile rather than to own one. This is generally true if the car is driven for business as well as pleasure and if the annual mileage driven is much higher than average.

Proper selling of a car may also result in budget savings. It may not be advantageous automatically to trade a car in on a new one. In certain cases, it is more profitable to sell a car outright and to buy a new one without the trade-in.

Many American families have two cars. While the operating expenses per mile would tend to be the same for the second car as for the first, fixed expenses per mile are likely to be much higher for the second car because it is not driven as often. While a second car is a tremendous convenience for many families, its purchase must be considered in light of other expenditures which could be made before deciding whether the outlay required can be justified by the benefits gained.

Medical Expenses and Personal Care

Health is all-important. A person should always consult a doctor, a dentist, or an oculist when he believes that such services are needed. It may prove to be cheaper in the long run to have a complete medical examination every year or two. Little can be said in a book of this kind that would be of value to the individual in regard to his health, but the authors wish to stress the importance of this factor. People occupying responsible positions in the modern world are usually under considerable pressure, and it takes a good body and good nervous system to stand the strain. To possess the education and experience necessary to hold down a particular position which pays a high salary is of little practical value if the person does not have the health that is required to fill successfully the requirements of the job.

Full utilization should be made of free medical services offered by life insurance companies, schools, and many private companies. Health and accident insurance and group hospitalization plans should be looked into by the individual. These are discussed in Chapter 8.

Personal care includes such items as cosmetics, beauty aids, beauty implements, personal hygiene supplies, and barber and beauty shop expenses. These items are necessary for the maintenance of good personal appearance and are an important item in most household budgets. It is possible, however, through proper buying and usage, to reduce the expenses necessary for these items.

The amount spent on medical and personal care increases as the annual household income increases, but the percentage of total income spent on this item remains fairly constant. The typical family spends about 5 per cent of its annual before-tax income on medical expenses and personal care. It should be realized that persons in the lower-income groups probably receive more medical care than indicated, because the figures do not include the cost of free medical attention furnished by public and private agencies. Some people benefit substantially more than others from hospitalization insurance and medical payment programs.

Recreation and Other Expenses

The typical family in the United States spends between 5 and 6 per cent of its before-tax income for recreation. This applies to lower-income as well as higher-income families. The value of recreation and entertainment should not be overlooked. Relaxation and change are often necessary for an individual to do a good job in his daily work. Housewives need a change from the routine of cleaning house, cooking, and caring for children. In some instances, proper recreation may result in lower medical expenses. Many people have found that certain recreation activities may be engaged in without the expenditure of much money.

All expense items not included in any of the above groups can be placed under the heading of "other expenses." If it appears that too much money is being spent for these expenses, it would be advisable to separate some of the more important items and budget them separately. Again, the importance of education cannot be overemphasized. Money spent for this purpose is really an investment, but is not listed in the budget as a saving.

PROPER BUYING

One of the wonders of the American economic system is the wide variety of choices available to the consumer. The great number of alternatives, however, places upon the consumer the burden of selection. Inherent in good personal financial planning is obtaining full value for the money you spend. One of the best ways of stretching the budget dollar is to buy wisely. Good buying can result in an important reduction of expenditures for various types of items without substantially reducing total service received from the expenditures. Wise buying of food alone can save hundreds of dollars per year for the average family.

Good buying is based upon a prudent plan for buying. The buyer should know in advance what he wants to buy, rather than buy on impulse. A wealth of information on this subject is available to the average family buyer in advertisements, consumer service booklets, business-sponsored publications, and government bulletins. This information can help a buyer decide, independently from the influence of the seller, the kinds of things he wants to purchase. The customer should be alert to price. He should consider buying in quantity where the savings are sufficient to justify the quantity purchased. Buyers should be familiar with recognized standards of quality. Labels provide a great deal of information, in most instances, which can help the buyer make a wise purchase.

The buyer should choose the right time and place to shop. Sales and bargains are bargains only if they offer the possibility of getting something you want for less than it would ordinarily cost. Buying something you do not necessarily want because it is a bargain is hardly a way of aiding your budget. The method of payment used for purchases is so important that it is discussed separately in the next chapter.

A seller never offers "something for nothing." While this lure is hard to resist, rational buyers know that good buys do not exist under this heading. Be sure to watch package purchases—that is, the buying of one item to obtain another "free." If it is the "free" item that you want, then buy it separately without acquiring the other item, which you probably do not need. Know the advantages of the item you are purchasing. They would be based on the service it is to perform for you rather than what the seller may play up.

Be alert to price, but also recognize substantial variations in quality. A low price may lead to a poor purchase if quality is inferior. Just because an item has proved suitable for someone else does not mean that it will fit your needs. Once you have purchased an item, take care of it. Proper maintenance may defer replacement outlays for long periods of time. Furniture you can use for twenty years is just as good a buy as furniture at half the price, which lasts for only ten years. The way you take care of the furniture can make a substantial difference in how long it lasts. When a purchase lasts longer, so does your money. Also, after purchasing, be careful of waste, which is particularly common in such budgeted items as food, utilities, and clothing.

FAMILY BALANCE SHEET

In addition to budget and savings plans, it is advisable to know where you are at a given moment. It is recommended that the family periodically draw up a family balance sheet. This is a statement of the family's assets, debt, and net worth as of a specific time. New balance sheets can be prepared annually or at five-year intervals in the future so that the family can see how it is progressing. Many families do not really know how much they have in assets or what their total liabilities are. Such knowledge may cause certain families to change their planned financial actions. Balance sheets are useful in determining whether to buy on credit or to incur additional liabilities. They can be helpful in making decisions on life insurance, savings, and real estate. An example of a personal balance sheet is given in Fig. 2–10. Table 1–1 should also be

FINANCIAL STATEMENT 19......

ASSETS				LIABILITIES			
CHECKING ACCOUNT BALANCE				NOTES PAYABLE			
SAVINGS ACCOUNT BALANCE							
CERTIFICATE OF DEPOSIT							
CASH							
BONDS AND SECURITIES M'K'T VALUE							
STOCKS M'K'T VALUE							
NOTES RECEIVABLE NET				ACCOUNTS PAYABLE			
ACCOUNTS RECEIVABLE NET							
CASH VALUE LIFE INSURANCE							
TOTAL CURRENT ASSETS				TOTAL CURRENT LIABILITIES			
REAL ESTATE—HOME				MTGE. OR LIEN NOTES ON HOME			
OTHER REAL ESTATE				OTHER REAL ESTATE LIENS			
OTHER ASSETS				OTHER LIABILITIES			
				NET WORTH			
TOTAL				TOTAL			

Fig. 2–10. A personal balance sheet form. (Pfening and Snyder, Columbus, Ohio.)

referred to, for examination of the combined balance sheet of all American consumers.

THE FAMILY FINANCIAL PLAN

The total family financial plan includes long-term budgets, short-term budgets, the current balance sheet, planned future financial position, and a determination of overall goals. In this chapter, the authors have described part of the process of developing an overall financial plan. It should be emphasized that the financial plan is basically a family affair. It does no good to have a plan which is adhered to by only one member of the family. One of the most difficult problems in marriage is attaining agreement on economic goals by both husband and wife. Once they

AVERAGE FAMILY FINANCIAL PROTECTION IN 1900, 1929, 1935 AND TODAY

Type of Protection	1900	1929	1935	Today
Life insurance (average for all families)	$900	$3,000	$2,700	$13,000
Annuity or pension	None	None	None	Yes (maximum payment usually in $100-$150 per month range)
Health insurance	None	None	None	Hospitalization, surgical and medical expense benefits for self and family
Workmen's compensation for occupational injury	None	Yes	Yes	Yes
Unemployment benefits	None	None	Up to $15 a week	Up to $55 a week
Social Security payments for widow	None	None	None	Up to $254 monthly if there are dependent children
Retirement payments under Social Security Act for retired worker & wife	None	None	Up to $85 monthly	Up to $190.50 monthly ($254 if both husband and wife qualify for retirement payments)
Home equity (average for all homeowners)	N.A.*	$2,200**	$1,500**	$6,250**
Liquid assets (average for all families)	$150**	$ 940**	$ 710**	$2,200**
Balance of annual income above food, shelter, clothing and taxes (average for all families)	$150**	$ 600**	$ 300**	$2,200***

*Not available
**Estimated from Bureau of the Census figures
***Estimated from Bureau of Labor Statistics figures

Fig. 2–11. Average family financial protection. (Reproduced with permission, from *The Search for Economic Security*. New York: Institute of Life Insurance, 1965.)

have done this, they can plan together effectively and they are likely to accomplish their planned goals.

The improving financial status of the average family is indicated in Fig. 2–11. Significant increases in protection and assets are indicated. Family financial planning must consider all types of government and employee plans as well as activities of the individual family.

The changing nature of the financial plan and objectives should be recognized. Newlyweds have economic requirements that are considerably different from those of an established or growing family. A family that is contracting in size has still a different position. Retirement leads to different needs and incomes. Periodically review your plan—both short-term and long-term—to be sure it meets your expectation of future circumstances. A potentially useful checklist is:

1. Invest in yourself first, to assure future earning power.
2. Know where your money goes.
3. Make it go where you want it to go.
4. Try to buy on a cash basis except for very major purchases.
5. Accumulate some capital.
6. Make your accumulated capital earn money.
7. Base your plans on *net* income rather than gross before taxes and social security and other withholding.
8. Don't purchase luxuries before you have made provision for necessities, including protection for the family in the event of loss of income due to death, disability, or unemployment.

QUESTIONS

1. How is personal net worth determined? List the items which would be considered personal assets.
2. How does a "working wife" create special budget problems?
3. What sources of income are available to the average family? How can these sources be increased?
4. What is meant by budgeting receipts?
5. What is meant by overspending? What actions tend to lead to overspending?
6. Differentiate a cash budget from an expense budget.
7. What are the major reasons for keeping a budget?
8. Comment on the following statement: "The budget is only a tool; it is the budgeter who makes income and outgo balance."
9. How may the maintenance of a budget enable a person to buy more things?
10. How should a person make provision in his budget for meeting some relatively large expense, such as real estate taxes, which are paid only twice a year?

11. How much do you need to save each month in order to have $10,000 twenty years from now? Would your answer vary, based on how you planned to invest the money?
12. If, during a particular month or year, you spend more for an item than you allowed for this item in your budget, does it follow that your savings must be correspondingly less? Explain your answer.
13. How much does it cost to own and run a car? How do your car expenses compare with average figures?
14. How can you buy "something for nothing"?
15. What does proper buying have to do with budgeting?
16. What is meant by the statement that the federal government should balance its budget?
17. What is a family balance sheet? How should it be used?
18. Describe a complete family financial plan. What is meant by periodic review in connection with a family financial plan?
19. State why you do or do not maintain a budget.
20. Make an estimate of your income and expenses for the next thirty days and then keep a record of your actual income and expenses for that period in order to determine the accuracy of your estimate.

CASE PROBLEMS

1. Al Clarke has $275 in his checking account and $50 cash on hand. He also has $500 in a savings account. He owns a new Ford and the furnishings in his three-room apartment. He owes $1,000 on his car and has miscellaneous bills totaling $200. He has a $10,000 life insurance policy with a cash surrender value of $400. Make a personal balance sheet for Al.

   He is planning to marry shortly. His fiancée lives with her parents. She owns ten shares of General Motors stock which were given to her by her parents. In addition, her parents have promised her a wedding gift of $1,000. Prepare a balance sheet for Al and his wife after marriage and determine their net worth.
2. With an income of $5,400 per year, Jim and Doris Whit have had difficulty making ends meet. They live in a small rented house and have two children. They have twelve more payments to go on their furniture at the rate of $18 per month. While their appliances are old, they are fully paid for. Jim would like to buy a new car and use their old car as a down payment. Doris is worried about meeting the $46 per month payments on a new car for the next two years. Jim suggests that they cut spending somewhere else in order to make payments on the car. Do you think budgeting of income and expenses would help Jim and Doris? How should they go about setting up a budget? What information do they need to collect?
3. Jack Wright will graduate from college at the end of the term. He expects to get married immediately upon graduation and to take a furnished apartment for $115 per month. He has a job that will pay him $425 per month for the first year. While Jack did not budget his expenses in college, he estimates that he has been spending approximately $100 per month for room and board at the dormitory, $30 for cleaning and clothing, and $45 for other expenses. His parents have sent him $175 per month

and have paid his tuition directly. Since his income is increasing by $250 per month and he managed to get along without a budget before, does he need one now? Why was it easy for him to make ends meet without a budget while in college? Why might this be more difficult after graduation? Set up a tentative budget for Jack and his bride.

4. Cynthia Walsh has been encouraging her husband Ray to buy an automobile. Since their marriage six months ago, Cynthia and Ray have used public transportation for going to and from work and have taken cabs when they have gone out in the evening. Ray wants to wait six more months until he has a sufficient amount saved to buy a used car for cash. On the other hand, Cynthia wants to buy a new car now on the installment plan. She points out that the $150 per month that Ray plans to save to apply to a cash purchase can meet the payments on a new car installment plan. Which approach is best? Which approach is cheaper? Determine the financial advantage of following Ray's plan.
5. Herb Johnson has just finished a college preparatory course in high school. He plans to start college in the autumn at the state university 80 miles from his home. His parents will be unable to contribute anything toward his support or to help him financially in any way. He has been unable to obtain a scholarship. He has a summer job from which he will be able to save $900. His tuition and books will cost $850 per year. He has made arrangements for a part-time job while in school which will pay him $1.25 per hour. He expects to be able to work 20 hours per week. Assuming that he can get the same summer job each year and can continue with the part-time job at school, can Herb complete four years of college? What would you advise him to do? Set up a tentative budget for him for the coming year. Would he be better off to work a year or two to accumulate some savings before starting college? Is the effort of working his way through college worthwhile for Herb?
6. Carl and Bernice Cooke were married recently. Each is 21 years old and a college graduate. Cooke has a sales training position with a local company paying $5,400 per year. In six months, when his training is completed, his income will increase to $5,700, plus commissions. Commissions should build up over a period of time to a point equal to his salary but initially will amount to very little. His wife teaches grade school and earns $4,500 per year. She expects to teach for two to three years before becoming a full-time housewife. Should they be saving out of current income? If so, how much would you suggest? What should they do with their savings? Since they are so young, should they be thinking of retirement? Estimate their income for each year for the next ten years. How should the changing income in the next ten years influence their savings budget?
7. Make up a budget for yourself. Determine the percentage of your income you are saving. Is this enough to meet your future requirements? What is your future income potential?

SELECTED READINGS

Automobile Facts and Figures. Detroit: Automobile Manufacturers Association. Latest edition.

Blaunstein, B. J., and Gorman, Robert. *How to Have More Money to Spend.* New York: J. Messner, 1962.

Burkhart, Roy A., Hauver, Carl F., and Peterson, James A. *Money and Your Marriage.* Washington, D. C.: National Consumer Finance Association, 1963.
Family Budget Guide. Tacoma, Wash.: Pacific Federal Savings & Loan Association, 1963.
Family Financial Planner, The. Newark, N. J.: The Prudential Insurance Company of America, 1964.
Family Money Manager, The. New York: Institute of Life Insurance.
Finance Facts, 1964. Washington, D. C.: National Consumer Finance Association, 1964.
Fitzsimmons, Cleo. *Consumer Buying for Better Living.* New York: John Wiley & Sons, Inc., 1961.
How to Plan Your Spending. Hartford, Conn.: The Connecticut Mutual Life Insurance Co., 1960.
Katona, George. *The Powerful Consumer.* New York: McGraw-Hill Book Co., 1960.
Kreisman, Leonard T. *The Consumer in Society.* New York: Odyssey Press, 1964.
Life Study of Consumer Expenditures. Vol. I. New York: Time, Inc., 1957.
Margolis, Sidney K. *How to Stretch Your Money.* New York: Public Affairs Committee, 1960.
Money Management for the Young Adult. New York: Institute of Life Insurance, 1965.
Money Management—Your Automobile Dollar. Chicago: Household Finance Corp., 1963.
Money Management—Your Budget. Chicago: Household Finance Corp., 1962.
Personal Money Management. New York: American Bankers Association, 1962.
Ten Steps to Money Success. Chicago: Harris Trust and Savings Bank, 1963.

3

Buying on Credit

While there are widely varying opinions concerning the economic and social values of consumer credit, it must be recognized that consumer credit is an integral part of our economic system and that it is here to stay. While debt is almost as old as the human race, many people in the past have looked down upon buying consumer items on credit. They believed that credit utilization should be confined to business and government purposes. Today, it has been estimated, over 70 per cent of American families enjoy consumer credit in one form or another. Its use is no longer considered unethical or immoral.

Changing economic environment has been mainly responsible for the continued rise in consumer credit. Mass production demands mass distribution and mass distribution tends to require consumer credit. Growing populations and rising incomes lead to increased use of consumer credit. Borrowing is no longer restricted to times of distress—in many cases the consumer debt is undertaken to finance investments, which is the same as business use of credit. To a degree, continued use of consumer credit is a sign of prosperity and contributes to it.

Consumer credit is the credit used by individuals to facilitate the process of consumption. It is utilized in connection with the purchase of goods or services for personal and family consumption, with a promise of future payment. Business credit is normally used to purchase assets which will produce earnings sufficient in amount to repay the debt. Consumer debt, on the other hand, is generally repaid from the consumer's wage or salary income, and repayment is unrelated to the use of the goods or services purchased.

Types of Consumer Credit

Consumer credit (home financing is usually excluded) falls into two general classes: installment and non-installment. Table 3–1 shows that installment credit accounts for more than three fourths of the total, with automobile installment paper alone accounting for almost a third of total consumer credit. While non-installment credit has increased in recent years, the great rise in total consumer debt outstanding has been due principally to the rapid expansion of installment credit following World War II.

Figure 3–1 indicates the trend in consumer credit outstanding from 1929 to 1964, and Table 3–1 gives the percentage distribution for 1965.

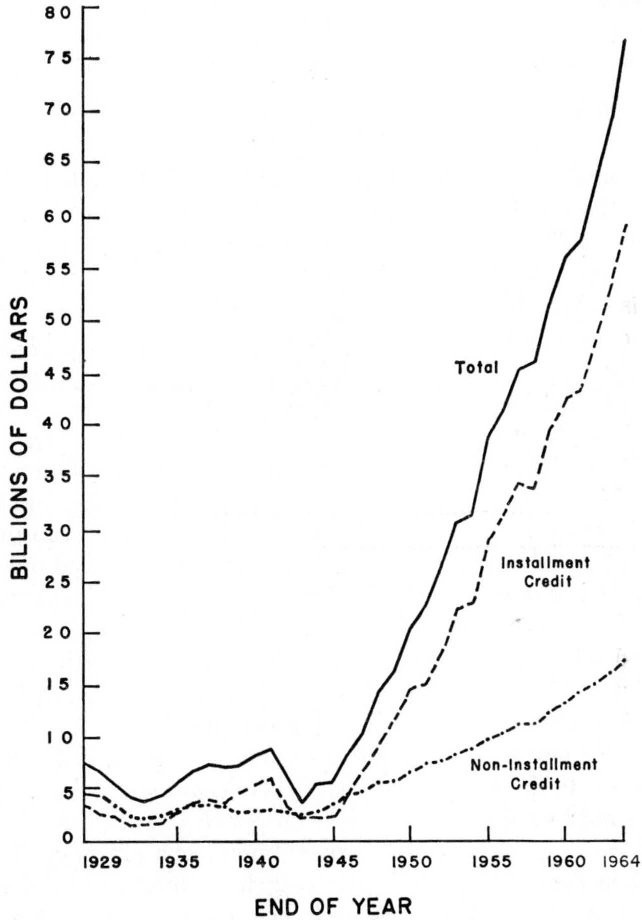

Fig. 3–1. Consumer credit outstanding. (Data from *Federal Reserve Bulletin.*)

Table 3–1. Estimated Consumer Credit, Short- and Intermediate-Term Consumer Credit Outstanding—January, 1965 (in millions of dollars)

Type of Credit	Amount		Percentage Distribution	
Installment credit				
Automobile paper	$24,574		32.2%	
Other consumer goods paper	15,204		20.0	
Repairs and modernizing loans	3,473		4.6	
Personal loans	16,091		21.1	
Total		$59,342		77.9%
Non-installment credit				
Single-payment loans	6,412		8.4	
Charge accounts	5,724		7.5	
Service credit	4,667		6.2	
Total		16,803		22.1
Total consumer credit		$76,145		100.0%

SOURCE: *Federal Reserve Bulletin.*

All of the classifications of consumer credit listed in Table 3–1 are directly related to the purchase of goods or services, with the exception of personal loans and single-payment loans. At least a portion of the latter items, however, is also directly related to buying on credit. The remainder is indirectly related, since it is used for the payment of old bills.

Total consumer credit outstanding at the beginning of 1965 was approximately 18 per cent of the total disposable personal income in that year. Figure 3–2 indicates the rapid rise in dollar amount of total consumer debt and relates total consumer debt to certain other consumer financial items. While total consumer debt increased over four times from 1950 to 1964, much of this rise is accounted for by inflation and by rising personal incomes and standard of living. As a result, total consumer debt as a percentage of disposable personal income has increased only slightly more than 70 per cent in the same time period. In 1950 all consumers had committed 38 days' worth of future income to repay completely consumer debt. By 1964, all consumers were in debt 64 days' worth of future income. Thus, while consumer income as a percentage of disposable income has not risen as rapidly as dollar consumer debt, it has still risen significantly. No one knows how far consumers can go in committing their future income to the repaying of past debts. Consumer debt, as discussed here, does not include mortgage debt on personal real estate.

While adding to their debt commitment, consumers have also increased their financial assets. Figure 3–2 shows total consumer debt as a percentage of financial assets (excluding corporate securities of consumers). This relationship has increased 50 per cent from 1950 to 1964.

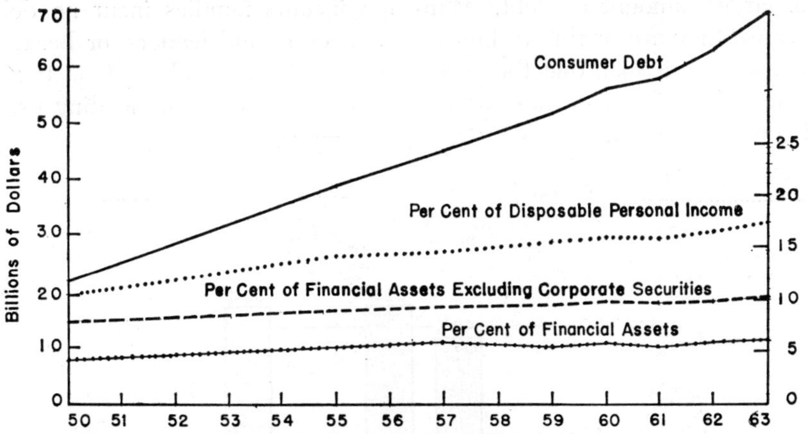

Fig. 3–2. Consumer debt in the United States. (Data from *Survey of Current Business,* and Securities Exchange Commission.)

Nonetheless, in 1964, it would have taken only 10 per cent of consumer financial assets, excluding corporate securities, to repay all consumer debt. If corporate securities are included in the measure of financial assets of consumers, it would take 6 per cent of the total to accomplish the same thing. Of course, these figures are for all consumers combined. Many consumers with a large amount of consumer debt have no financial assets and those consumers with the largest amounts of financial assets tend to have no consumer debt.

Table 3–2. Amount of Installment Debt by Spending Units—United States, 1962 (mortgage credit excluded)

Amount of Installment Debt	Percentage of Spending Units
None	54%
\$ 1–\$ 99	6
\$ 100–\$199	6
\$ 200–\$499	10
\$ 500–\$999	10
\$1,000 and over	14
Total	100%

SOURCE: Survey Research Center, University of Michigan.

Table 3–2 indicates the amount of personal installment debt by spending units (families and single individuals). At the time of this survey less than 50 per cent of all spending units were in debt. Figure 3–3 shows the percentages of spending units with personal debt by income groups. It can be seen that the lowest income groups are not the ones which have the largest amount of debt. Many low-income families incur no debt because they are unable to buy on credit or to find lenders, or because their income is such that they do not wish to incur an obligation. It can be seen from Fig. 3–3 that middle-income families are the leading users of consumer credit.

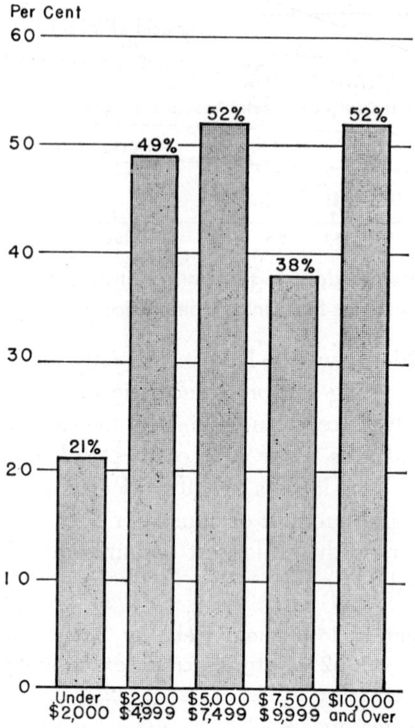

Fig. 3–3. Percentage of spending units with installment debt, by income groups. (Data from Survey Research Center, University of Michigan.)

Reasons for Buying on Credit

Not all consumer credit goes for purposes of buying. This chapter, however, is concerned only with buying on credit; borrowing money for other purposes is discussed in Chapter 4. An obvious reason for buying on credit is that it is the only way many persons can, at times, buy anything. A large percentage of wage earners live from hand to mouth. Their paycheck is usually spent by the time it is received. If anything is purchased before the next payday, it must often be on credit.

Many people utilize consumer credit, particularly the charge account, because of its convenience. If a person has a charge account, he can order goods over the telephone, or if he goes to the store, it is not necessary to use cash. Charging things is also cheaper and easier than writing checks.

Installment purchases commonly result in an increase in the standard of living of the individual or family. Many high-priced, durable consumers' goods such as automobiles, television sets, furniture, or washing machines could never be obtained by many people if they had to save enough to meet the entire purchase price in cash. The installment plan enables them not only to get the articles but also to enjoy their use while paying for them. Other reasons for or advantages of buying on credit will be mentioned later in the chapter.

Use and Abuse of Credit Buying

The advantages of buying on credit stated above express the viewpoint of the consumer. To the seller, selling on credit usually means larger sales and greater profits. Credit thus benefits both the buyer and the seller. It is realized, however, that the unwise use and overextension of credit works to the disadvantage of the consumer, the seller, and the nation.

Many people cannot resist the temptation of buying, especially when merchandise is elaborately advertised and displayed by retail stores. The credit departments of these establishments usually make it easy to purchase the merchandise either on the charge account or installment contract. Despite the ease with which goods may be purchased on credit, a person should never incur a debt unless he can see his way clear to pay off that debt.

No definite statement can be made as to how far a person or family should go in the incurring of debts. This varies according to the number in the family, the personalities of its members, its income and expenses, the age, health, and type of employment of the head of the family, and similar factors. For families in the lowest income groups it would be advisable not to spend more for current consumption goods than the amount which will be received at the end of the week. In other words, one week's income should be the maximum non-installment debt. As the family income increases, perhaps a current consumption debt equivalent to one and one-half or two times the weekly wages should be the maximum. When the debt is incurred for the purchase of durable consumers' goods which are acquired on the installment plan, higher debt limits are established. A person's debt limit is not only what he can borrow, but what he is going to be able to pay back. In setting your own credit limit, remember that you cannot borrow yourself out of debt.

Abuses have risen in connection with harsh collection methods, misrepresentation, and excessive interest rates, as well as in the form of over-

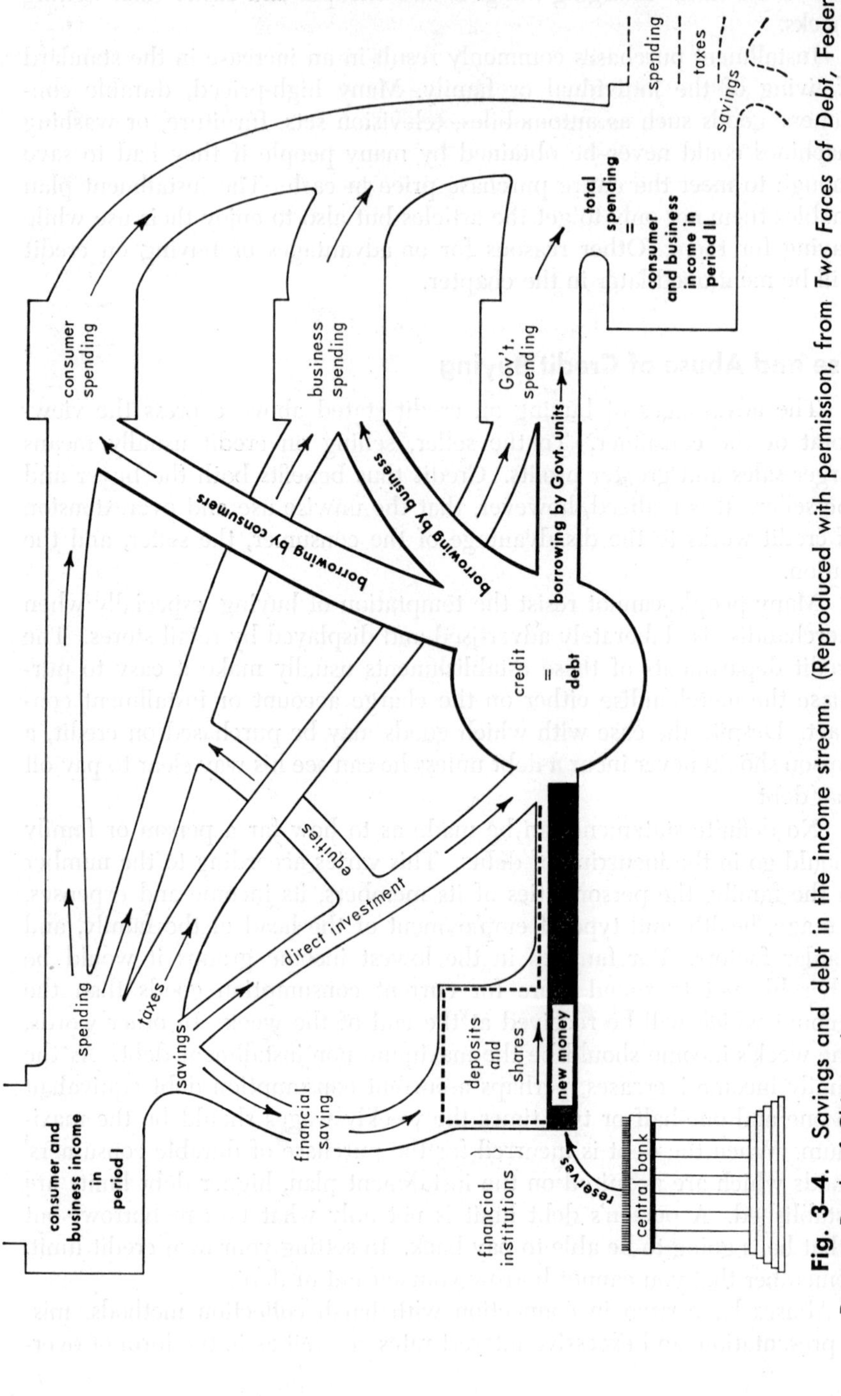

Fig. 3—4. Savings and debt in the income stream. (Reproduced with permission, from *Two Faces of Debt*, Federal Reserve Bank of Chicago.)

extensions of credit. The intelligent consumer can guard against these abuses, and much has been done in recent years through regulation, consumer education, and industry efforts to reduce their prevalence. The fact that consumer credit is often misused or that selling on credit is abused is no more a reason for eliminating it than would be the elimination of the automobile because of the improper or dangerous driving habits of some persons. The solution lies in the proper use of credit by both the buyer and the seller. Consumer credit is here to stay.

Consumer Credit in the Economy

Debt of all types, including consumer debt, is an important element in the national income stream. The flow diagram in Fig. 3–4 indicates the significance of consumer borrowing in the total savings and debt flow in the United States. Figure 3–5 shows that, while consumers are large borrowers, total consumer debt (including mortgage debt) owed by consumers represents only 15 per cent of the total debt *owed* in the

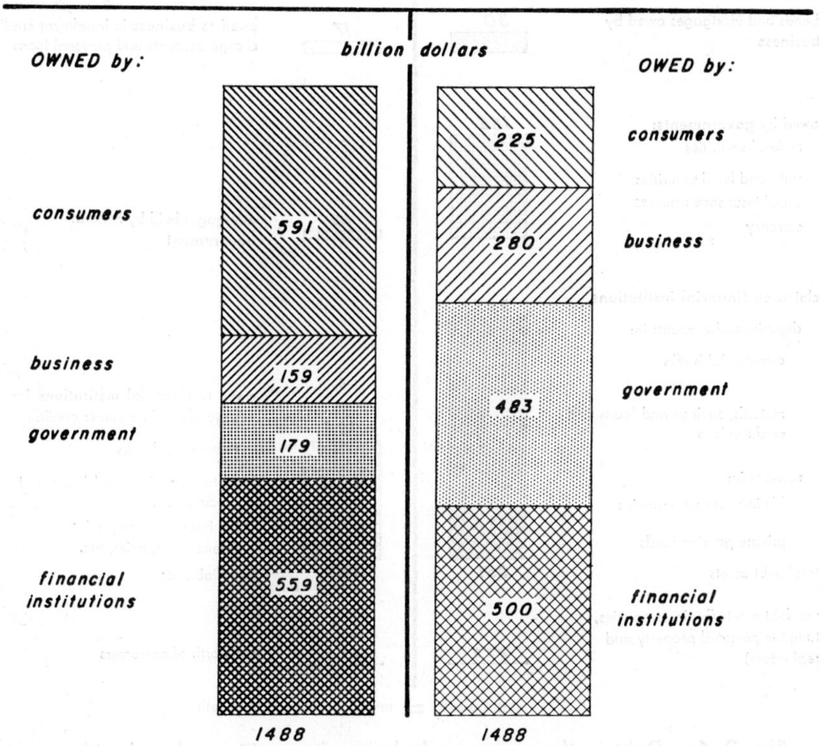

Fig. 3–5. Debt in the economy. (Reproduced with permission, from *Two Faces of Debt*, Federal Reserve Bank of Chicago.)

economy. Consumers *own* 40 per cent of the total debt in the economy. Consumers as a group are more important as lenders, or holders of debts of others, than any other segment of the economy, including financial institutions. The place of debt in the consumer balance sheet is illustrated in Fig. 3–6, which also indicates the claims consumers hold against others and the sources of debt currently outstanding in the consumer balance sheet.

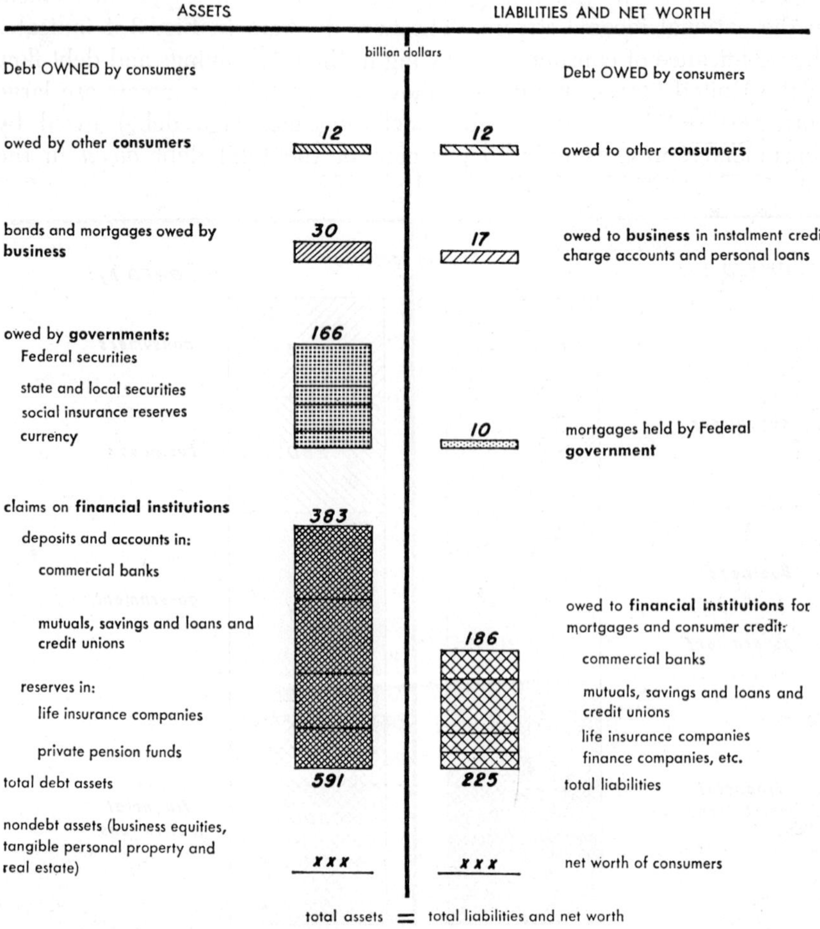

Fig. 3–6. Debt in the consumer balance sheet. (Reproduced with permission, from *Two Faces of Debt*, Federal Reserve Bank of Chicago.)

THE CHARGE ACCOUNT

While there are many different types of charge accounts, the most common ones involve the purchasing of goods or services with a promise to pay the seller the full amount at a specified future date. The buyer generally agrees to make payment a certain number of days after billing and does not specifically pledge the merchandise purchased as collateral for the amount owed. He merely gives his signature in receipt for the merchandise and later pays with cash.

While the use of charge accounts has continued to rise, charge account credit is no longer the most important segment of non-installment consumer credit. Table 3–1 indicates the importance of all non-installment consumer credit and the breakdown of the total amount into single-payment loans, charge accounts, and service credit. Single-payment loans are normally not related to the purchase of goods or services but are loans granted by financial institutions to consumers for various investment purposes. Service credit is credit granted to consumers in connection with the purchase of services rather than the purchase of commodities. In reality, service credit is really a type of charge account credit. Service credit and charge account credit outstanding combined represented over $10 billion at the beginning of 1965.

It is estimated that 70 per cent of American families hold credit cards or have charge accounts. Manufacturers grant credit to wholesalers, wholesalers in turn extend credit to retailers, and the latter give credit to consumers. Inability of the consumer to pay his bills causes trouble all along the channel of distribution. Charge account credit or service credit is granted not only by retail stores but also by doctors, garages, plumbers, and other professions and service industries.

The trend in recent years has been toward the wider adoption of charge accounts for the purchase of shopping goods. Department and specialty stores in particular have been doing an increasing charge account business. The rise of chain stores, discount houses, and grocery supermarkets has brought about a different trend in convenience purchases, but today some chain-store operations are turning to charge account credit. It appears that charge accounts and other types of consumer credit are becoming an increasingly important factor in many lines of retailing.

Advantages of Charge Accounts

It obviously costs a business something to sell on credit. Credit sales involve more bookkeeping, more billing, possible bad debt losses, collection costs, and interest charges on the money the concern has tied up in credit sales. All of these costs must be recovered in some way through business operations. In some cases, these costs may be paid directly by credit customers. In others, the total cost of the merchandise may be increased to recover these costs. Many retailers believe that they can sell on credit without raising prices because of the increased volume obtained. In other words, the efficiencies gained through larger volume pay the cost of the credit operation. However, the variation in price found in some sales lines between credit and non-credit stores indicates that, at least in certain cases, the consumer does pay the cost of credit. A recent study by the National Retail Merchants' Association indicates that total credit charges received from customers on all types of credit selling do not equal the costs of operating the credit department, including the cost of interest on the money tied up.

From the consumer's point of view, if the price paid for the goods purchased on charge account credit is no higher than it would have been had the consumer paid cash at this store or another store, it can be said that the consumer is paying no more for the use of charge account credit. In a great many cases, consumers will find that they can make purchases on regular charge accounts at no additional cost relative to cash prices paid for the same merchandise at any other store. If this is the case, the advantages of using charge accounts are obtained at no effective cost to the purchasers.

When merchandise is purchased through a charge account, the buyer obtains the use of the goods immediately, but does not have to pay for them until the following month. To a person who does not have the cash to pay for the merchandise but has immediate need of it, this is a distinct advantage.

Perhaps the greatest advantage of the charge account to the individual is its convenience. There is no need to anticipate a shopping expedition—the items to be purchased, their cost, etc.—and then draw the money from the bank. Writing checks for individual items, which is both time-consuming and costly, is also eliminated.

Another advantage of buying merchandise on credit is the greater willingness of the store to take back the goods if for some reason it becomes desirable to return them. Charge account customers also often have the advantage of receiving notice of special sales before the advertisements appear in the newspapers. A further advantage is that they receive a written statement of monthly purchases.

Disadvantages of Charge Accounts

The availability of a charge account often leads a customer to buy something that is not really needed, and the later payment for the merchandise may cause him substantial distress. Available cash places a limit on purchasers who buy for cash, but the only limit on charge account purchasers is the one placed by the retail outlet.

While many individual stores have installed charge accounts without having to increase prices, it seems logical to assume that, if all stores eliminated charge accounts and if sales remained the same, the cost of the charge account operation might be saved. This might result in an overall reduction in the price of merchandise.

The ease of buying with a charge account and the corresponding ease of returning the merchandise so purchased tend to cause customers to do less planning before making a charge account purchase. More merchandise may be returned because of the less careful buying that results.

Competition among merchants is important in retailing and often takes forms other than price competition. Competition between merchants with liberal credit policies may lead to unsound use of charge accounts by customers.

Opening an Account

Most people are familiar with the charge accounts maintained by many department stores and specialty stores. Securing a charge account is ordinarily a very simple procedure. The applicant usually applies in person at the credit office and is sometimes interviewed by the credit manager or by one of his assistants. A written application is filled out giving the name, age, and address of the applicant, husband's or wife's name, employer's name and address, position held, names of other stores in the city where the applicant has a charge account, and several references, including a banking connection. If the applicant is below legal age (which is 21 years in most states), the store will usually require that his parent or guardian guarantee his account.

The Credit Investigation

The credit office of a retail store will investigate most charge account applicants. This can be done by calling references or sending them a form to be completed and returned. It may also be done by contacting other stores, if any, at which the applicant has charge accounts. A common approach is to use a retail credit bureau if one is available. These bureaus collect a surprising amount of information on consumers in their locality from cooperating stores, public records, financial institutions, and other sources. The type of information available to a retail store from a retail credit bureau is indicated in Fig. 3–7.

From the information collected, the store's credit department determines whether or not to allow purchases by the applicant. If credit is

Factbilt REPORTS ARE BETTER

ASSOCIATED CREDIT BUREAUS OF AMERICA
INCORPORATED
AN ASSOCIATION OF CREDIT BUREAUS SINCE 1906

CONFIDENTIAL

STANDARD CONSUMER REPORT
ACBofA No. 1
compiled by member bureau

1 REPORT ON:
(Surname first) (Mr. or Mrs.) (Given Name) (Spouse's name)

2 RESIDENCE ADDRESS:
(Street Number) (City) (County) (State)

IDENTITY	3. Number of years covered: A. In file	A.
	B. In investigation	B.
	4. A. Age. (If near 21, confirm)	A.
	B. Racial extraction (White, Black, Red, Yellow, Brown)	B.
	5. A. Marital status	A.
	B. Number of dependents?	B.
HISTORY	6. A. Name of employer	A.
	B. Type of business	B.
	7. A. How long so employed	A.
	B. Position held	B.
	8. A. Does applicant have record of steady employment?	A.
	B. Any recent employment change? (If yes, explain in remarks)	B.
	9. Any suits, judgments or bankruptcies? (If yes, explain in remarks)	
Character	10. Is applicant well regarded as to character, habits and morals?	
	11. Is applicant favorably regarded by employer?	
	12. Any suspicion of illegal practice past or present?	
RESOURCES	13. A. Estimate monthly income from present employment	A.
	B. Estimate other income such as rentals, investments, etc.	B.
	C. Estimate income of others in household	C.
	14. Own home, rent or board?	

CREDIT RECORD: (If feasible include whether subject has satisfactory bank checking account.)

Trade Line	How Long Selling	Date of Last Sale	Highest Credit	Terms of Sale	Amount Owing	Amount Past Due	Manner of Payment

REMARKS: A. Give brief word picture of subject's history, explaining any unusual condition.
B. Amplify any incomplete or adverse information in answers above. Use other side also for full details.
C. Include estimate of net worth if possible.

Report for

Date **Prepared by**
Name of member reporting bureau City State

The confidential information given in this report is in answer to a request for same. This report is compiled simply as an aid in determining the propriety of extending credit, or the value or condition of an existing credit and is based upon information obtained from sources deemed reliable, the accuracy of which, however, is in no manner guaranteed. The inquirer, in accepting this report, agrees to hold same in STRICT CONFIDENCE for his own exclusive use, never to be communicated, and to be personally responsible for any damage arising from a violation of any of the above provisions.
(Printed in U.S.A.)

Fig. 3–7. A credit bureau report form.

allowed, a limit is normally placed on the total amount outstanding at any time.

People moving to new localities sometimes find that it takes a little time for them to establish their credit. In order to obtain credit readily, a person can, before moving, ask the retail credit bureau in the city in which he has been residing to forward his credit file to the credit bureau office in the city to which he is going. This can often be done even when a person is moving to a city in a foreign country.

The Three C's of Credit

In judging the credit risk of an individual, credit men give consideration to the three C's—character, capacity, and capital. The first of these qualities is perhaps the most important, particularly in connection with charge accounts. *Character* represents willingness to pay. A person of good character will usually see his way clear to pay a bill before he incurs the debt. If unforeseen circumstances arise to prevent immediate payment, an honest person will take care of the bill as soon as possible. On the other hand, there are many people of questionable character who, although they have a large income and a sizable amount of property, are notoriously slow payers.

Capacity or ability to pay is obviously important. A person who is in good health and who has a steady position or a profitable business is obviously a better credit risk than one who is unemployed. Where character and capacity are both present, a good credit risk exists. The amount of *capital* which a person or a business possesses denotes, in some degree, the financial ability to pay. If a person refuses to pay a debt, a lien may be secured against his property, and it may be sold to satisfy the debt. In investigating credit risk for charge accounts, however, more weight is given to character and capacity than to capital. These qualities may be somewhat related—a person's willingness to pay a bill may result from his capacity to pay it, as measured by his income or the property he possesses.

It is perhaps well to emphasize that a person should always keep his credit rating in good standing. Slowness in paying bills or a failure to pay a small account, even though it may have been in the past or at some distant place, can result in a poor credit rating and a later refusal of credit. Everyone should maintain a good credit rating, if for no other reason than to make it possible to obtain credit in an emergency.

Types of Charge Accounts

In recent years, many retailers have developed a variety of types of charge accounts. Many of them involve specific credit charges in addition to the price of the merchandise purchased. Most of them involve some combination of a regular charge account and an installment plan purchase. These combination plans have been developed to appeal to customers who cannot meet the total bill at the end of the normal charge account period.

30-Day Account. The most common type of charge account is the normal 30-day account: the buyer agrees to pay for all merchandise received during a monthly period upon receipt of his bill at the end of the month. There is normally no charge to the customer for the use of the 30-day account. In practice, the customer is given more than 30 days on items purchased early in the billing period and less than 30 days on items purchased at the end of the period. Department stores find that 30-day charge account purchases tend to be outstanding an average of 45 days. This indicates that not all customers pay their bill immediately upon its receipt. Further, there is a time delay between the date of billing and the receipt of the bill by the customer. Normally, all types of merchandise may be purchased on a 30-day charge account. Many stores use coin or card identification procedures for 30-day account holders.

Budget Charge Accounts. A variety of different combinations of normal charge accounts and installment accounts have been developed by retail stores to meet varying circumstances. These may be called budget charge accounts, deferred payment charge accounts, few-pennies-a-day plans, installment charge accounts, etc. In accounts of this type, customers are not required to pay the full bill during the next month. Instead, they pay only a portion of the bill each month for a period of three, six, or twelve months. This is, in effect, installment payment for goods purchased on a charge account. Some of these involve a constant monthly payment regardless of the amount purchased. In others, the monthly payment is determined by the principal amount outstanding. Accounts of this type usually involve an interest and/or credit fee. The most common credit charge used today is 1½ per cent per month, which is an annual rate of 18 per cent. These accounts are sometimes restricted to smaller unit items.

Option Charge Account. An option charge account is another variation of the combination of normal charge accounts and installment plan purchases. This account works just like a 30-day charge account as long as the customer pays his bill within a stated number of days after its receipt. Should a customer be unable to pay or for some reason not desire to pay his total bill, he is automatically converted to a deferred payment plan. He is charged interest on all amounts outstanding in the account for more than 30 days. The payment of these amounts may be spread out over a period of time—commonly three or four months. These accounts require that some percentage of the amount owed be a minimum payment each month. A minimum dollar payment such as $10 may also be required.

Revolving Credit Account. The budget charge plan and option charge account discussed above include a revolving credit arrangement. Revolving credit merely means that a customer may constantly bring his balance owed up to some maximum amount by new purchases, as long as he meets certain payment conditions. Some revolving plans may require equal monthly payments regardless of the amount of the principal while others require a percentage of principal to be paid each month. In the equal payment plans, for example, a customer may have a credit limit equal to twelve times his agreed-upon monthly payment. Thus, if he agrees to pay $20 per month, he may buy on credit any items he desires as long as the total balance owed does not exceed $240. All revolving credit plans include some interest charge, commonly at the rate of 1½ per cent per month. Revolving credit allows a consumer to make new purchases before he has paid in full for his previous purchases.

Charge Account Banking. *Charge account banking* is another type of charge account which is utilized in most sections of the country. In this plan, member retailers in the metropolitan area offer complete charge account service with an agreed-upon bank assuming all risk and cost. In effect, the retailer becomes the agent of the bank in each credit sale, and the bank in reality makes the loan directly to the retailers' customers. The customers may buy on credit in a number of retail stores and receive one bill at the end of each month. The retailer is normally charged 6 per cent of the total bill for each credit sale. In addition, in most cases the customer is also charged a fee for utilizing this service. However, some of the more recent plans involve no charge to the customer at all. The bank involved, rather than the individual retail store, checks the credit of the applicant. The bank pays the retail store immediately upon the sale of the merchandise and the customer in turn pays the bank at the end of the 30-day period. Some of the bank plans include budget accounts in which payments may be made over a period of months rather than in one month. For this type of service, an additional charge is made. Many banks offer charge account plans or revolving credit plans which are not tied in with specific purchases from stated retail outlets. These types of arrangements are discussed in the next chapter.

Script Book Accounts. In the *script book account,* customers are provided with coupons or script which can be exchanged for goods within the store which issues the coupons. In many cases script purchases must be paid before new script books will be issued. This effectively establishes a limit on the account. Sometimes the books are issued only after payment of cash by the customer equal to the amount of the script. A variation allows a customer to buy on account up to amounts of cash previously deposited with the store. When no script books are issued, this is called a *deposit account.* Accounts of this type are not really credit because there is no promise of future payment—payment is actually made in advance of purchase.

CREDIT CARDS

The credit card is just what its name suggests, a small card—usually made of plastic—which evidences the right of the holder to obtain goods or services on credit. Credit cards came into existence in the early 1920's as a device to encourage brand loyalty in the sale of gasoline, but it was not until the post-World War II period that their use expanded to other types of products and they became important as a credit device.

Credit cards are really just a variation of charge accounts; the major differences are in the way credit is granted and the fact that the card may be used at a number of different retail establishments. All that is necessary to obtain credit by using a credit card is to show the card and sign a sales slip. Since a number of different purchases are made from different retail outlets on the same card, there tends to be no maximum credit limit on the amount that may be purchased on any one card. Of course, the card may be withdrawn by the issuer if the buyer does not or cannot pay.

While normal charge accounts may commonly be used only at a single outlet, usually where the credit authorization was initially made, the credit cards have much broader acceptance. Even if a card is issued by a single company for use at its own outlets, such as gasoline credit cards, the company generally has a large number of outlets and the card may be used at any of them. Table 3–3 gives the credit card balances out-

Table 3–3. Credit Card Balances Outstanding—1957 and 1960–1964 (in millions of dollars)

Year	Total Charge Account Credit Outstanding	Credit Card Credit Outstanding	Credit Card Credit as a Percentage of Total Charge Account Credit
1957	$5,146	$317	6.1%
1960	5,329	436	8.2
1961	5,324	469	8.8
1962	5,684	505	8.9
1963	5,871	520	8.9
1964	6,300	635	10.0

SOURCE: *Survey of Current Business.*

standing in 1957 and 1960–1964. It can be seen that this type of credit is a growing portion of total charge account credit and now accounts for 10 per cent of the total.

National Credit Cards

A relatively new development in the charge account field is the national credit card sponsored by such organizations as Carte Blanche, American Express Company, and others. These national credit cards involve the use of the card at a variety of types of retail establishments across the country and in many foreign countries. These credit card companies charge the user a membership fee, which produces part of their income, but they also charge the retailer who makes the sale a certain percentage of the selling price for each purchase made with the credit card. National credit cards are particularly useful to people who travel a great deal and to people who desire receipts for travel and entertainment expenses. The only additional cost to the credit card holder is his initial or annual membership fee, which is relatively small.

Limited-Purpose Credit Cards

A great majority of the credit cards issued are usable at only one type or a limited number of types of retail establishments. For example, the universal air travel plan is a credit card jointly sponsored by the International Air Transport Association and the American Travel Agents' Association. This card requires a substantial deposit on the part of the holder. It may be used to charge the purchase of airplane tickets on most major airlines in the world. Because a substantial deposit is required, this credit card becomes an excellent credit reference or means of identification for a variety of purposes other than purchase of air travel tickets.

Many hotel systems have credit cards which are accepted at each of the hotels in the chain. The same is true of the major car rental systems. The American Telephone and Telegraph Company has a large number of credit cards outstanding for the charging of long-distance telephone calls while away from the phone to which the call is to be charged.

Petroleum companies are still among the major issuers of credit cards. If all of a person's petroleum purchases are made on a credit card, an excellent record is developed of automobile expenses and gasoline taxes for purposes of income tax determination and budgeting.

The great majority of special-purpose credit cards involve no membership fee or annual charge to the user. Since the price of the commodities purchased is the same whether the credit card is used or cash is paid, the holder of the credit card receives the advantages of convenience and later billing at no additional cost.

Regional Credit Cards

Several firms offer credit cards which are accepted only in certain geographic areas. The largest of these are BankAmericards issued by the Bank of America for use at a large number of establishments throughout the state of California. The cards are also good for personal loans up to $350 at any branch office of the Bank of America. The card holder may defer payments if he desires, but he must pay a minimum each month against his charges as well as interest on amounts due over 25 days.

Other regional credit card systems which include deferred payments and an interest charge are New York City's Unicard, and plans offered by the Marine Midland Trust Company in upstate New York, Atlanta's Citizens & Southern Bank, and the Bank of Hawaii.

THE INSTALLMENT PLAN

The *installment plan* is a type of credit purchase in which an agreed-upon amount is paid periodically until the total purchase price and carrying charges have been paid. Table 3–4 indicates the rapid growth in

Table 3–4. Consumer Installment Credit Outstanding (in millions of dollars)

Beginning of Year	Total	Automobile Paper		Other Consumer Goods Paper		Repairs and Modernizing Loans		Personal Loans	
		Amount	%	Amount	%	Amount	%	Amount	%
1930	$ 3,156	$ 1,318	41.8	$ 1,197	37.8	*		$ 643	20.4
1935	1,867	576	30.8	741	39.7	*		550	29.5
1940	4,503	1,497	33.3	1,620	36.0	$ 298	6.6	1,088	24.1
1945	2,176	397	18.2	791	36.3	119	5.5	869	40.0
1950	11,590	4,555	39.3	3,706	31.9	898	7.7	2,431	21.1
1955	23,568	9,809	41.7	6,751	28.6	1,616	6.8	5,392	22.9
1960	39,482	16,590	42.1	10,243	25.9	2,704	6.8	9,945	25.2
1965	59,397	24,521	41.3	15,303	25.8	3,502	5.9	16,071	27.0

* Included in personal loans.
SOURCE: *Federal Reserve Bulletin.*

consumer installment credit outstanding. About 20 per cent of all retail sales are made on the installment plan. Almost two thirds of all automobiles and half of all household appliances are sold in this way. Formerly, only people of very limited financial means purchased goods on the installment plan. A great increase in the use of this kind of credit took place in this country, however, beginning with World War I. Today, even some people who can afford to pay cash utilize the plan to avoid paying out a large amount of cash at one time. Table 3-5 indicates the usage of installment credit by various age groups.

Table 3–5. Users of Installment Credit

Age of Head of Household	Percentage with Installment Debt Outstanding in 1964
18–24	70%
25–34	64
35–44	59
45–54	53
55–64	35
Age 65 and over	20
Average for all cases	49

SOURCE: *Finance Facts Yearbook, 1965.*

The installment plan differs from the charge account in several respects. While the charge account is used for any kind of merchandise a store offers for sale, the installment plan is more commonly limited to higher-priced consumer goods. A regular charge account is supposed to be paid in full during the month following the sale; an installment account is paid off in monthly installments and may not be fully liquidated until several years after the purchase. On installment sales, interest is charged on the amount owed, whereas no interest is normally charged on a charge account. Charge accounts require no down payment; most installment plans do. A note or contract is normally signed in installment buying, but it is not normally required for charge account purchases.

It can be seen that several of the newer types of charge accounts discussed above involve many features of the installment plan. The primary differences are that under the installment charge account, a new contract is not written each time an additional purchase is made; any type of merchandise may be purchased, and title to the goods passes immediately to the purchaser.

The three C's discussed in connection with charge accounts are also of importance in installment accounts. Merchants are more liberal, however, in accepting risks under installment contracts than they are with charge accounts. For installment sales the merchant usually requires some down payment and, furthermore, retains title to the goods. Thus, in the event that payments are not made according to the contract, the seller may repossess the goods. Often payments are so arranged that after giving consideration to the depreciation, the goods are worth more than the unpaid balance. If this is done, only an accident or malfeasance on the part of the buyer would jeopardize the position of the seller.

The Installment Contract

It is good advice to say that one should always read the contents of any paper before signing it, and this certainly applies to the installment contract. The seller, or his lawyer, draws up or adopts particular forms used in connection with installment sales, so it would follow that in most instances the provisions in the contract are for his benefit—not the benefit of the buyer. Fine print should not discourage the buyer from reading the contract; in fact, the finer the print, the greater the need for reading it.

Legal documents used in connection with installment sales, along with the note, are usually chattel mortgages, conditional sales agreements, or bailment leases. In states which have adopted the Uniform Commercial Code (39 states by 1966), these contract forms are still used, but the security given is controlled by the Code and is, in most instances, identical in effect regardless of the contract form used. Each of these forms conveys to the creditor a *security interest* in the goods and this interest is governed by the common Code provisions.

Under the Uniform Commercial Code, a security interest must be created in writing unless possession of the collateral is taken by the creditor. An oral contract involving a security interest in personal property is ineffective. A security interest is of little value unless it can be enforced in bankruptcy or protected against the claims of the debtor's other creditors. The Code provides that a security interest in most kinds of personal property is protected when the creditor or his agent takes possession of the collateral. Thus, upon default by the debtor, the secured creditor would normally elect to take possession of the pledged property, which he may repossess by any peaceable means.

Under the Uniform Commercial Code, after repossession has been taken, the secured creditor may proceed to sell the collateral at public or private sale. The secured creditor has the right to buy in at a public sale or at a private sale if the collateral is regularly sold on a recognized market. Generally, a creditor who has retaken possession of the collateral may elect to keep it in full satisfaction of the debt instead of reselling it. In such a case, he must notify the debtor in writing of his intent and, if he does not receive objection from the debtor within 30 days, he may keep the collateral as his own. If objection is made, the goods must be sold.

Also, under the Code, there is one other specialized—though common—situation where the creditor *must* sell the goods. If the collateral consists of consumer goods (items purchased primarily for household or personal use, including automobiles), if the debtor has paid 60 per cent or more of the debt prior to default, and if the debtor after default has not signed a statement renouncing his rights in the goods, then the creditor is obligated to sell the goods within 90 days of taking possession. All three conditions must exist. At any time prior to sale or retention after notice, the debtor may redeem the property by tendering enough money to take care of the debt and expenses incurred up to that point. The money received at a sale is applied first to expenses, second to the secured obligation, and third to an inferior lien if there is one. Any resulting surplus must be returned to the debtor. The debtor would personally be liable for any deficiencies resulting from the sale of the goods.

In states where the Uniform Commercial Code has not been adopted, there are some differences between the chattel mortgage, the conditional sale, and the bailment lease. When one purchases goods and executes a *chattel mortgage* as security for the purchase price, title to the goods passes from the seller to the buyer as a consequence of the sale and back to the seller by virtue of the chattel mortgage. The seller thus holds legal title until final payment is made. The usual chattel mortgage entitles the seller (mortgagee) to repossess the goods in event of default. He can then sell them to some other party and apply the proceeds to the amount still owed. In most states, a copy of the chattel mortgage is filed by the seller with the proper county official. This makes it a matter of public record, and, generally speaking, no one can get a lien on the particular property equal to or superior to that of the seller.

When the conditional sales agreement is used, title to the goods remains with the seller until the final payment has been made. In practical effect, there is not much difference between the chattel mortgage and the conditional sales agreement.

In the bailment lease, title remains with the seller until the last payment has been made and then it is purchased for a nominal sum which is usually waived by the seller. In effect, the buyer merely hires the use of the goods until final title is purchased. If the buyer defaults, the seller simply takes back his goods and keeps the previous payments as rent rather than as partial principal payment.

Generally, the seller determines which form he will use depending upon the law of the state in which he operates. He will, of course, select the contract which offers the greatest protection to himself. The buyer generally has no choice.

Regardless of which form is used, in the event of the buyer's default on any payment, the seller usually has the right to declare all the remaining payments due. This right is brought about by the inclusion of an *acceleration clause* in the contract. If complete payment is not made, the seller then has the right to repossess the goods. Repossession and resale costs must be borne by the original buyer. If the goods sell for an amount insufficient to pay the deficiency, the original buyer is usually liable for the balance due.

The installment contract should be scrutinized for additional features. Waiver of certain legal rights possessed by the buyer may be included in the printed form. In many instances the seller will discount the installment notes with lenders who might take advantage of every opportunity to enforce the contract according to the strict letter of the law. In some instances the seller may repossess the goods with little or no notice—a procedure followed intentionally at times when it is known that the buyer is not in a position to get cash immediately. Some contracts make no provision for the recovery by the buyer of goods which have been repossessed.

The Note

At the time the buyer signs the chattel mortgage or conditional sales agreement, he also signs his personal note for the amount due under the contract. The note represents the promise to pay the debt; the mortgage or sales agreement is merely security for the note. Because of the note, the buyer is still liable for any balance due if there is a deficiency after default in the amount remaining unpaid on the note after the sale of the pledged goods. As the personal credit of the buyer is behind the note, the seller may get a judgment and attach some other property which the buyer possesses for the deficiency. The buyer should see to it that his note or notes are canceled after final payments have been made.

The two parties to the note are the maker and the payee. However, the payee may endorse the note to any new party he so desires. A *demand note* has no stated maturity date and may be presented for payment at any time. A *time note* has a specific maturity date. Some notes include a confession of judgment clause. In a note without this clause, if the holder sues the maker, it is necessary to go through the routine of legal action. To avoid delays in getting legal judgment, creditors in some states have the debtor sign notes which contain this clause. These are often called *cognovit notes.* If there is a default in the payment of the note, the holder's attorney will have another attorney sign a statement to the effect that the amount stated is owed, etc. This other attorney represents the debtor but the debtor need not be notified of this representation.

Interest on Installment Contracts

One of the most important parts of the installment contract is the provision relating to the interest or fees to be charged. If the seller charges no interest, the buyer can be certain that the selling price of the goods is made sufficiently high to include the added cost of selling on the installment plan. In a situation of this kind the buyer should ask the cash price of the goods. Invariably he will find that goods can be purchased for cash at a much lower price. The cash price, in fact, may be so much lower that he may realize the economy of postponing the purchase until he has sufficient cash saved.

The carrying charge which must be paid by the buyer on installment contracts covers more than mere interest. The cost of making the credit investigation of the buyer, collection costs, bookkeeping expense, the possible expenses in connection with repossession, reconditioning, and reselling of the goods, and bad debts are all part of the cost paid by the buyer. The seller usually has the goods insured against fire and theft, and sometimes against damage, and these expenses are also passed on to the buyer.

Some of the costs, such as investigation or bookkeeping, are usually as great for low-priced articles as for more expensive ones. Consequently, the total carrying charge for low-priced articles is usually a higher percentage of the sale price than in the case of higher-priced articles.

The carrying charges for the buyer on installment purchases are usually very high. The effective rate which he pays is often more or less concealed through the way in which the interest rate is stated. For example, the price tag on a particular article may show $60 to be the selling price. The seller indicates that it can be paid in six equal monthly installments with a carrying charge of only 6 per cent added. He then computes this carrying charge to be $3.60 (6 per cent of $60). Thus far the statement of a 6 per cent carrying charge is misleading in two respects. First, since the loan is for only six months and not one year, the charge of $3.60 for the use of $60 amounts to an interest charge of 12 per cent per year. (Interest is usually computed on an annual basis.) Second, since the full amount of $60 will be outstanding only one month and not six months, the rate being charged will obviously be much greater than 12 per cent. Furthermore, the seller may require a down payment equal to 10 per cent of the selling price of the article. So, after the cash payment of $6 is made, the amount of the debt is really only $54. This is to be paid off, then, at the rate of $9 a month. During the first month the debt amounts to $54, but during the sixth month it is only $9. Thus, the average debt outstanding during the six months is only $31.50 [($54 + $9) ÷ 2]. If $3.60 is paid for this loan for a period of six months, this would be equivalent to $7.20 a year, and interest charges of $7.20 for a loan of $31.50 for one year amount to 22.857 per cent. Thus, the real rate which the installment buyer pays is not 6 per cent, but almost 23 per cent.

The computation of the rate of interest in this example can perhaps be better understood by the tabulation of amounts that follows on page 94.

Amount owed during	
First month	\$ 54
Second month	45
Third month	36
Fourth month	27
Fifth month	18
Sixth month	9
Total	\$189

The amount owed on this installment purchase is thus equivalent to the sum of \$189 owed for one month. A charge of \$3.60 for a loan of \$189 for one month would be at the rate of 1.90476 per cent a month. Multiplying this by 12 to put it on an annual basis, we get 22.857 per cent for the annual rate.

The approximate effective rate of interest charged on common shorter-term installment contracts can be determined through the use of the following formula:

$$R = \frac{2Ni}{P\,(n+1)}$$

where

R = effective interest rate (expressed in decimal form)
N = number of payment periods in a year
i = actual interest charges (expressed in dollars)
P = net amount of loan or credit advanced
n = number of payments to be made

Substituting the above data for the symbols in the formula, we get:

$$R = \frac{2 \times 12 \times \$3.60}{\$54\,(6+1)}$$

$$= \frac{\$86.40}{\$378}$$

$= 0.22857$, or an effective rate of interest of slightly more than 22.85 per cent

Perhaps a word of explanation is needed in regard to the symbol N in the above formula. Although the payments extend over a period of six months only, since they are monthly payments this is at the rate of twelve payments a year.

In the above examples it is assumed that the interest charges of \$3.60 will be paid at the end of the six months' period. As a practical matter, however, the interest is usually added to the principal amount of the loan and the total is paid off in equal installments. Thus, the \$3.60 interest would be added to the loan of \$54, giving us a total of \$57.60. This latter amount would be paid off by six monthly installments of $9.60 each. This procedure would obviously make the actual interest rate slightly more than that computed in the above examples. The formula, however, for all practical purposes, gives a result which is reasonably close to the actual interest rate.

It was assumed in the above example that the "quoted" interest charge was based on the total purchase price. This is rarely done in practice, but was explained here merely to indicate the actual rate being charged in such instances. In most installment sales the quoted interest rate is applied to the balance due after the down payment has been deducted. Thus, in the example, the 6 per cent would be applied to the $54 instead of the purchase price of $60. This would make the interest charges $3.24 instead of $3.60, and the monthly payment would total $9.54. Using this figure in the formula would give us an effective rate of interest of 20.57 per cent.

The ease of buying a $60 article with a down payment of 10 per cent and $9.54 a month appeals to many individuals, and for this convenience they are willing to pay the charges of $3.24. The seller may point out to them that the carrying charges are less than 2 cents a day but the buyer should realize that he is paying carrying charges of more than 20 per cent. It is important to determine the real interest rate in order to compare it with the costs of using other techniques of financing the contemplated purchase. If the buyer must have the merchandise immediately and is willing to pay a carrying charge, he may find that it would be to his advantage to find some means of financing this purchase other than the 20 per cent charge being taken by the seller. Few people, however, take the trouble to figure out the rate of interest they are paying on installment purchases. It often means that they pay a much higher price for articles than necessary. In certain cases, where the dollar amount of the interest charge is small, the buyer may not care what effective interest rate is paid.

The above method of determining the effective interest rate is only an approximation. There is considerable disagreement on how effective interest rates should be determined under varying sets of installment charge circumstances. Different mathematically acceptable methods yield different effective interest rates in given circumstances. While the "true" rate is difficult to determine, the formula gives a general figure which is usable for most consumer purposes. The "truth in lending" bill which has been proposed in several sessions of Congress would require that finance charges be stated in effective rates for all installment finance purchases. Under certain circumstances, the effective rate may be as misleading to the buyer as the total dollar charge. Much of the controversy over determining effective rates has arisen because of the proposed requirement in this pending legislation.

The consumer's major use of an effective interest rate should be in comparison to other similar means of financing the same purchase so that the lowest cost source of funds may be determined. Note that a 6 per cent loan for one year, in which the total principal and interest are paid at the end of the period, requires more dollars of interest payment than a 12 per cent effective rate loan with monthly payments for nine months.

Clauses To Watch For in Installment Contracts

When buying on the installment plan, a person should deal only with a reliable firm. Some retailers have the buyer sign a contract in which all the charges—insurance, taxes, accessories, interest—are lumped together. If this is done, the buyer should be suspicious that he is paying for more than he is getting. This loading, if any, is called a *pack;* if the dealer discounts the notes with a finance company, the latter may split part of the excessive charges with the retailer.

When a person borrows money to buy a car, the agency lending the money wants to be sure that it will not lose anything on the transaction, so it will require the buyer to take out fire, theft, and collision insurance on the car. Naturally, the cost of this insurance is paid by the buyer. But he should make sure that he is paying no more for it than the rates which are set by the state authorities. These charges should be specifically itemized so that he knows what he is paying for. The automobile installment contract should contain the following in writing, not lumped together, but listed separately:

1. Price of the car exclusive of extras, taxes, etc.
2. All extras, itemized
3. Trade-in allowance
4. Down payment
5. Cost of insurance
6. Balance to be financed
7. Amount of monthly payments
8. Number of monthly payments
9. Statement of extra financing costs

The buyer should insist that all the above items be specifically listed. He should never sign any contract until all blank spaces have been filled in, and he should get his copy of the agreement at the time that he signs it.

Many installment buyers find out to their sorrow later that they signed a contract which contained a *wage assignment clause.* With such a provision the creditor can notify the buyer's employer that a portion of the buyer's wages are to be paid directly to the creditor. Some installment contracts include an *add-on clause,* an agreement which the individual should guard against. This type of contract covers a succession of installment purchases and allows the seller to retain title to all of the various items purchased until the last one is paid for in full. In this sense, the seller could repossess a large number of items in the event of default on some small item purchased recently.

The *balloon contract,* which has become more common in recent years, provides for a final installment payment much larger than each of the preceding installments. The contract may provide for payments of $25 a month for two years and a final payment of $400 or $500. The unsuspecting buyer is unaware that his final payment is larger and he is generally unprepared to meet it at the end of the time contract. Balloon notes are sometimes used to mislead buyers into thinking in terms of small monthly payments for the purchase of an item which they cannot really afford.

Advantages of Installment Buying

There is no doubt that installment buying has been at least partially responsible for the wide ownership of durable consumers' goods in this country. It is apparent that many consumers are unable to save sufficient funds in advance to purchase durable items for cash. The installment method allows them to save to buy the items while they are actually using them. In this sense an installment purchase is somewhat like saving to purchase a durable good in advance and then paying cash—the difference being that the article is purchased first and then the cash is saved. The advantages of buying on the installment plan can be summarized as follows:

1. The buyer gets the immediate use of the article by making only a small down payment.
2. It may be more convenient for the buyer to make a number of small payments than to make one large payment.
3. Some persons who otherwise would never save up enough in advance to buy the article are able in this way to enjoy its use.
4. If the installment payments did not have to be met, some individuals might waste their money on less durable goods.
5. The purchase of an item, such as a washing machine, can effect immediate savings (in this case, in the laundry bill).
6. The necessity of meeting installment payments may cause the individual to start limiting his expenses and budgeting his income, and thus begin thrift habits.
7. Installment buying may be the only way an individual has of buying something that is needed in his work, such as an automobile.
8. If something goes wrong with the article, the installment buyer can usually get better service than can the cash buyer.

Disadvantages of Installment Buying

The cost of purchasing consumers' goods on the installment plan has been discussed above. Obviously it is a costly way for consumers to acquire the goods they desire. In addition to the high carrying charges, installment sales are open to several other criticisms. By the time an individual has an article paid for, he may find that it has depreciated to the point where it is of little use. It is true, however, that he enjoyed the use of the article while paying for it.

Perhaps a more serious objection to installment buying is that in many instances people overbuy. The purchase of goods is made so easy for them that they buy more than their income permits. After having made some installment purchases in the immediate past, the current income of an individual may appear to be sufficient to make some additional ones. He may do so, only to realize later that too much of his current income is being absorbed in paying for past installment purchases to warrant those additional purchases.

Summarizing the many abuses which have crept into installment financing, the disadvantages to a purchaser of buying on the installment plan are as follows:

1. A higher price must be paid for the goods.
2. The carrying charges are usually very high.
3. The ease of such buying may cause overbuying and a resultant inability to meet one's obligations.
4. Inability to meet obligations may result in the loss of the money already paid and the goods as well. In some instances other property is also taken to satisfy the debt.
5. The future is mortgaged, despite the fact that the amount of future income is uncertain.
6. Pressure to meet installments may cause an individual to make unwise economies.

Installment Credit Life Insurance

As a protection to the seller and to the buyer's family, it may be desirable for the buyer to purchase life insurance in sufficient amount to cover the outstanding balance at any time on his installment purchases. This kind of insurance has come to be known as *credit life insurance*. It assures full payment of a loan in the event of the death of the buyer and leaves his survivors free of this indebtedness. Furthermore, it makes collection easier for the seller in the event of the death of the buyer. Many sellers insist that the buyer purchase life insurance. Where this is done, the buyer should be certain that he is paying only a reasonable price for the insurance.

Regulation of Installment Credit

In 1964, thirty-seven states had statutes relating to installment selling. About one half of these statutes covered only installment selling of motor vehicles; the remainder regulated all types of installment sales. In the thirteen states which do not have legislation on installment sales, the subject is dealt with, if at all, only indirectly in the Uniform Commercial Code or in the conditional sales or chattel mortgage laws of the state. These laws do not include a maximum legal rate of interest which may be charged. The trend is toward the enactment of installment legislation in most of the states which do not now have this legislation.

State statutes in existence generally provide for the licensing of firms doing a sales finance business. Most statutes require an itemization of costs and charges. They also set certain standards for contract form and execution, and they prohibit certain undesirable clauses. Some of the statutes prescribe the way in which insurance may be sold in connection with a sales finance contract. The laws also define repossession procedures and extension and refinancing.

Many state statutes set a legal limit on the maximum rate which may be charged in connection with the installment contract. Legislation in most states divides authorized finance charges into three or four classifications, depending upon the type of item purchased. The common types of classifications are: new motor vehicles, motor vehicles less than two years old, other used motor vehicles, and all consumer goods except motor vehicles. For new motor vehicles, New York allows a finance charge of $7 per $100 per year. This is an add-on charge and the effective rate for a one-year contract with monthly payments would be approximately 14 per cent. New York allows $10 for $100 per year for used motor vehicles less than two years old, and $14 per $100 per year for all other vehicles. California allows finance charges up to one per cent of the unpaid balance multiplied by the number of months to maturity, with a minimum charge of $25. Ohio allows a base charge of $8 per $100 per year on the original principal plus a service charge of 50 cents per month on the first $50 unit of the original principal for each month of the term of the contract, and an additional service charge of 25 cents per month for each of the next five $50 units or fraction thereof of the original principal for each month of the term of the contract. This allows a charge of $17 for a $100 purchase without down payment, to be paid for in twelve monthly installments.[1] This is an effective rate of 31 per cent per year.

[1] $8 charge plus $6 (50 cents per month for twelve months) for first $50, and $3 (25 cents per month for twelve months) for the next $50.

It should be noted that this is the maximum amount which may be charged and is not necessarily the actual charge included in all installment contracts.

SOURCES OF FUNDS FOR CREDIT BUYING

Of the $76 billion in consumer credit outstanding at the beginning of 1965, it has been estimated that approximately $50 billion or 66 per cent arose in connection with credit buying. About 20 per cent of this was charge account and service credit and about 80 per cent was in connection with installment payments for purchases. The major suppliers of funds for credit buying are the retailers themselves, commercial banks, sales finance companies, and other financial institutions.

Retailers

It is estimated that retailers financed approximately $18 billion or 36 per cent of the $50 billion in consumer credit for purchases outstanding at the beginning of 1965. This includes almost all of the charge accounts and service credit, and some portion of the automobile paper and other consumer goods paper in installment finance. Some of this amount financed by retailers may have been indirectly financed by financial institutions through discounting the paper at banks or sales finance companies. Accounts and notes receivable are a major asset of many retailers and are financed along with other asset requirements of the retailer.

Commercial Banks

Table 3–6 indicates that commercial banks are the most important of the financial institutions that extend installment sales credit. Over half of all automobile paper held by financial institutions is financed by com-

Table 3–6. Amount and Percentage Distribution of Installment Sales Credit Outstanding—January 31, 1965 (in millions of dollars)

Institution	Automobile Paper		Other Consumer Goods Paper		Total	
	Amount	%	Amount	%	Amount	%
Commercial banks	$12,828	53.1	$3,455	41.2	$16,283	50.0
Sales finance companies	8,648	35.8	3,943	46.9	12,591	38.7
Other financial institutions	2,689	11.1	996	11.9	3,685	11.3
Total	$24,165	100.0	$8,394	100.0	$32,559	100.0

SOURCE: Federal Reserve Board.

mercial banks, as are almost half of all consumer installment sales. (Commercial banks as a consumer lending institution are discussed in the next chapter.)

Sales Finance Companies

Unlike the commercial bank, which offers a variety of financial services, the *sales finance company* is a specialized institution which engages primarily in buying time sales contracts arising out of installment sales to customers from automobile dealers and other retailers. Sales finance companies pioneered in this type of financing, and commercial banks did not enter the field until the 1930's. Table 3–6 indicates that sales finance companies held approximately 39 per cent of financial institution installment sales credit outstanding at the beginning of 1965. (Sales finance companies should not be confused with consumer finance companies operating under the Small Loan Acts, which are discussed in the following chapter.)

Sales finance companies help those retailers and dealers who do not have sufficient capital to finance the installment sales of automobiles and other durable consumers' goods. Some sales finance companies will lend the dealer money on the collateral of a customer's endorsed notes, without the knowledge of the customer. In most cases, however, the finance company deals directly with the consumer rather than with the dealer. Sometimes when the dealer is involved, the transaction is on a *recourse* basis. This means that if the consumer defaults in his payments and repossession is necessary, any loss will have to be taken by the dealer. When a company operates on a *non-recourse* basis, any loss will be borne by the finance company. In addition to the note, the finance company has the security of a chattel mortgage or conditional sales contract.

There are many sales finance companies in operation in the United States, but five dominate the field: General Motors Acceptance Corporation, the C. I. T. Financial Corporation, Commercial Credit Company, Associates Investment Company, and Pacific Finance Corporation. While the last four listed are independents, General Motors Acceptance Corporation is known as a *captive* finance company. This means that it is owned by the manufacturer or retailer whose goods are financed. Many other large manufacturers have captive finance companies, including Ford Motor Company, General Electric Company, and Radio Corporation of America.

The consumer does not have to deal with the finance company or bank recommended by the dealer. In many cases, it pays for the consumer to shop for his financing rather than automatically accept the recommendation of a dealer. Many dealers receive rebates from financial institutions for sending customers to them. Even when there is a captive finance company, the consumer may arrange his own financing with another company if he so desires.

Other Financial Institutions

A number of other financial institutions operate directly or indirectly in the field of installment sales finance. While none of these is as important as the commercial banks and sales finance companies, each is still worth the consideration of the individual consumer. Credit unions (which are discussed in the next chapter) are growing rapidly in installment sales finance. Savings and loan associations, discussed in Chapter 6, often indirectly finance installment sales through refinancing of homes or through home improvement loans. Some insurance companies are interested in financing automobile paper. This is particularly true of the direct writing insurance companies, but independent insurance agents often finance automobile paper through related bank plans.

CASH DISCOUNTS

Many wholesalers and manufacturers and some retailers and service institutions will subtract a portion of the list price of an article or service if cash is given at the time of sale or shortly thereafter. This is called a *cash discount.*

A common cash discount is 2 per cent if the bill is paid within 10 days of the date of sale. Thus, if the bill net of discount is due in 30 days from the date of sale, this term would be expressed as "2/10, net 30." Under these terms, for a $100 purchase, the buyer, if he pays the bill within 10 days' time, will have 2 per cent deducted from the bill, leaving a net of $98 as the cost of the article. If the bill is not paid within 10 days, the full list price of $100 should be paid by the 30th day.

If this 2 per cent discount is converted to an annual rate of interest, it can be seen that appreciable savings result. As stated in the above example, if the purchaser pays by the end of the 10-day period, the article will cost him only $98, but if he waits an additional 20 days, he must pay $100. To keep the use of the $100 for this 20-day period thus costs the buyer $2. A year contains eighteen 20-day periods (that is, figuring 360 days to the year as bankers do in computing interest). So, paying $2 for the use of $100 for 20 days is the same as paying $36 (18 × $2) a year for the use of $100. Thus the 2 per cent cash discount amounts to a saving of 36 per cent (expressing it on an annual basis).

The above computation illustrates the savings effected by taking the discount, and is easy to understand, but it is not quite accurate. In the illustration, the $2 savings was expressed as a percentage of the $100.

Actually the $2 savings is effected by giving up the use of $98 for the 20-day period. Dividing $36 by $98, we get 36.73 per cent as the real savings obtained by taking the discount. Thus, if a person does not have the necessary cash on hand to take advantage of such a discount he would be justified in paying up to 36.73 per cent (annual basis) interest for borrowed money to pay the bill.

QUESTIONS

1. Define *consumer credit.* Why do people buy on credit?
2. Would we be better off if consumer credit were abolished? Why or why not?
3. What relationship is there between use of consumer credit and age and income of the borrower?
4. It is sometimes argued that the prices charged for merchandise in a store that grants credit are higher than those charged in an establishment which does not give credit. What argument can be used in reply to this assertion? What evidence is there to refute the assertion?
5. How important is charge account credit?
6. Which of the three C's of credit is most important in the field of consumer credit?
7. Explain *revolving credit.*
8. Differentiate national credit cards and limited-purpose credit cards.
9. How does the regular thirty-day charge account differ from the budget charge account?
10. What is charge account banking?
11. How does the installment plan of purchase differ from the charge account? Is it used for a different type of merchandise?
12. How are title, security, and repossession handled under the Uniform Commercial Code?
13. Distinguish among the bailment lease, the conditional sale, and the chattel mortgage plan of selling goods on credit.
14. In buying on the installment plan, a person may be required to sign a chattel mortgage and a note. Distinguish between these two instruments. Why should he have to sign both instruments?
15. Why may the quoted rate of an installment purchase differ from the effective rate?
16. What is a "pack" in installment buying? What may be included in the "pack"?
17. What is a balloon note? Why is it used?
18. Why is retail installment credit regulated in some states? Is it in your state?
19. (a) What is a sales finance company?
    (b) What kinds of products are ordinarily financed by these companies?
    (c) What rate of interest is usually charged by sales finance companies to finance the purchase of an automobile?
    (d) What are the largest sales finance companies?

20. What is a cash discount? How is the effective rate of interest in a cash discount determined?

CASE PROBLEMS

1. James Rawlings is purchasing a color television set from a large department store. He may pay cash, charge it on his thirty-day charge account, or put it on a budget account which requires monthly payments of $50 and has a service charge of one per cent of the unpaid balance each month. The set costs $495. How should James purchase the television set? What factors should influence his decision? Would you recommend that he consider financing through institutions other than the department store?
2. Ken Diehl is very proud of the fact that he has never had a charge account and that he has paid cash for all his purchases. He has a good income, and he and his family purchase many luxuries. His wife is anxious to open an ordinary charge account at the local department store, but Diehl insists they continue their old policy of cash for everything. Do you think his policy is wise? Why? If you were his wife, what arguments would you put forth for opening the account? What arguments could Diehl use to convince his wife they should not have an account?
3. Bill Baird has a large home in the most fashionable part of town. He is the vice-president of a small manufacturing company, and has a substantial income. He owns two large new cars and seems to live very well. The local credit bureau states that he is a slow-pay account and that he has been as far behind as six months in some payments. If you were a local credit manager, would you grant Baird credit? Why? Is he a better risk than a person with smaller income? As long as he pays eventually, does it matter that he is sometimes late? Is his credit good?
4. Ray Walsh and his wife are contemplating the purchase of an automatic dryer. His wife wants to buy it now on the installment plan. He prefers to wait three months until they have the money to pay cash for the machine. As their old machine has broken down, they will have to use the Laundromat until the new machine is installed. Which approach is best? Which approach is cheaper? What factors would have to be considered in determining the financial advantages of Walsh's plan? Could they buy the dryer and merely charge it to their charge account?
5. A new clothes dryer is advertised in the newspaper for $399. Terms of purchase are quoted which call for a $49 down payment and monthly payments of $25 for sixteen months. A similar dryer at a similar price is quoted elsewhere in the paper with terms of purchase calling for thirty-six monthly payments of $16.50 with no down payment. What is the effective interest rate in each plan? What is the dollar interest charge in each plan? Which plan would you prefer? What other alternatives would you consider?
6. Alfred Taylor wants to trade in his three-year-old car on a new model. His next-door neighbor works for a local Plymouth agency and tells Alfred that he will sell him a new Plymouth with his old car as a down payment and $50 per month for three years. Is this a good deal? What should Alfred do to determine the financial advisability of making this purchase versus some other? What additional information would Alfred need to determine the percentage carrying charge for this financing?

7. Janet Dodge has been shopping for a new sewing machine. She has determined a specific model of a national brand which she wants. Two stores in town have this model and she has the following quotations: Store A asks $149.50 with $25.00 off for her old machine in trade-in. It will give her a cash discount of 2 per cent of the cash difference if she pays upon delivery or will finance the machine for her for twelve months at $12.00 a month with her old machine as trade-in. Store B quotes a cash price of only $124.00. It will allow no trade-in and will not finance the sale. As Janet has no money to pay down, she has found out that she can borrow the $124.00 from a local bank for 12 months at a charge of 5 per cent on the original balance. What is the effective rate charged for credit at Store A? At the bank? Which is the better deal?

SELECTED READINGS

Beckman, Theodore N. *Credits and Collections in Theory and Practice,* Seventh Edition. New York: McGraw-Hill Book Co., 1963.

Black, Hillel. *Buy Now, Pay Later.* New York: William Morrow & Co., 1961.

Caplovitz, David. *The Poor Pay More.* New York: The Free Press of Glencoe, 1963.

Credit Management Yearbook. New York: National Retail Merchants Association. Latest edition.

Credit Manual of Commercial Laws. New York: National Association of Credit Men. Latest edition.

Hawyer, Carl F. *Family Money and Credit Management.* Washington, D. C.: National Consumer Finance Association, 1962.

Johnson, Robert W. *Methods of Stating Consumer Finance Charges.* New York: Columbia University Press, 1961.

Juster, Francis T. *Consumer Sensitivity to Finance Rates.* New York: National Bureau of Economic Research, 1964.

McAlister, Edgar R. *Retail Instalment Credit: Growth and Legislation.* Columbus: Bureau of Business Research, Ohio State University, 1964.

Margolis, Sidney K. *A Guide to Consumer Credit.* New York: Public Affairs Committee, 1963.

Mors, Wallace P. *Small Loan Laws,* Revised Edition. Cleveland: Bureau of Business Research, Western Reserve University, 1961.

National Consumer Finance Association. *The Consumer Finance Industry.* Englewood Cliffs, N. J.: Prentice-Hall, Inc., 1962.

Neifeld, Morris R. *Neifeld's Manual on Consumer Credit.* Easton, Pa.: Mack Publishing Co., 1961.

Phelps, Clyde W. *Retail Credit Fundamentals,* Fourth Edition. St. Louis: International Consumer Credit Association, 1963.

Shultz, William J., and Reinhardt, Hedwig. *Credit and Collection Management,* Third Edition. Englewood Cliffs, N. J.: Prentice-Hall, Inc., 1962.

Smith, Paul F. *Consumer Credit Costs 1949–1959.* Princeton, N. J.: Princeton University Press, 1964.

Two Faces of Debt, The. Chicago: The Federal Reserve Bank of Chicago, 1963.

4

Borrowing Money

Consumer credit in the United States was discussed in the preceding chapter. A part of this credit is for purposes of buying goods; the remainder is directly related to the borrowing of money. Buying goods on credit is really a form of borrowing money. Instead of paying cash, the buyer may borrow money from the seller in order to make payments for the goods purchased. While he often gives a lien on the goods purchased, he really promises to pay the dollars in cash at some later date. Consumer *cash* credit differs from *sales* credit in that the consumer obtains cash funds, rather than merchandise, in exchange for a promise of future cash payment.

The amount outstanding in cash installment loans has grown steadily throughout the post-World War II period. Personal installment loans in excess of $16 billion were outstanding at the beginning of 1965. In addition, over $6 billion more was outstanding in single-payment loans to consumers. Thus, at the beginning of 1965, consumers were in debt for more than $22 billion in connection with the actual borrowing of cash. While this seems like a large amount, consumer money loans outstanding amounted to only 5 per cent of disposable personal income, and the total volume of consumer money loans made during the year far exceeded the amount outstanding at the end of the year.

Reasons for Borrowing Money

Consumer money loans are usually made for the purpose of paying some relatively large extraordinary expense. Many such loans are granted for emergency help in meeting medical or hospital bills. Emergencies of this type not only increase expenses, but often reduce the income of the individual at the same time. Emergencies may occur and money may be needed to meet normal living expenses during periods of time in which the consumer does not have income due to illness, accident, strikes, unemployment, or other unusual conditions. Money may also be borrowed to take advantage of unusual bargains or special business opportunities. Or, money may be borrowed for items that will reduce operating costs, such as the purchase of storm windows to save on fuel bills. Borrowing money may also increase earning capacity when the funds are used for special training or education courses. Money is often borrowed to pay for large special-purchase items such as furniture or an automobile. An increasing use of borrowed money is to educate children.

Another use of borrowed money is to *consolidate* a number of outstanding debts. This should be done only where it involves a reduction in the interest rate or the amount of the dollar costs. Even then, careful analysis should be made before debt consolidation is undertaken. Some individuals get themselves involved financially with a number of different creditors. Many money-lending institutions advertise that they are willing to lend consumers sufficient amounts to pay all existing creditors. The new loan may be of such maturity that it can be paid off over a period of some months, thus allowing the borrower to meet all of his current obligations and to lump all of his monthly payments into one monthly payment. However, under this type of borrowing, those future monthly payments will have to be paid over many more months. The actual cost in dollars of such a transaction is undoubtedly higher due to the added cost of lending for the longer period of time.

A constant dilemma occurs for some individuals because some of their expenses have to be met daily but their wages are not paid until the end of a week, or two weeks, or a month. This predicament is further aggravated by the fact that the employer may hold back one or two weeks' pay. When payday comes, all the money is used to pay for expenses incurred in the past and to pay off loans. When the next pay period begins, they have no ready money and have to start borrowing all over again. Such individuals should cut their expenses so that after a few months they will not owe all their pay by the time they receive it.

Table 4–1 gives a percentage distribution of the number of consumer finance company loans made in selected years, classified according to purpose of the loan. The use of borrowed money to consolidate overdue bills is clearly indicated. The declining importance of borrowing for medical, dental, hospital, and funeral expenses may be due to the increasing use of various types of medical and hospital insurance. The purposes stated in Table 4–1 are for borrowing from consumer finance companies only, and are therefore not necessarily indicative of reasons for borrowing from all types of financial institutions.

Table 4–1. Percentage Distribution of the Number of Loans Extended By Purpose—Selected Years, 1948–1963

Purpose	1948	1950	1954	1958	1960	1963
To consolidate overdue bills	27.8%	30.2%	33.7%	39.5%	40.0%	39.0%
Travel, vacation, education expenses	7.8	7.4	8.4	9.3	10.0	10.0
Medical, dental, hospital, and funeral	17.6	17.5	11.1	7.9	*	*
Automobile purchase or repair	2.9	4.5	4.7	5.5	7.0	14.0
Clothing, food, rent, fuel, moving	11.7	10.5	9.7	7.2	*	*
Assistance to relatives	3.9	3.8	3.6	3.5	*	*
Home furnishings and appliances	3.3	5.1	5.2	4.7	8.0	3.0
Taxes, payments on real estate loans, insurance	6.5	6.1	7.7	7.6	*	*
Household repairs	8.3	7.3	6.8	5.1	4.0	3.0
All other purposes	10.2	7.5	9.3	9.7	31.0	31.0
Total **	100.0%	100.0%	100.0%	100.0%	100.0%	100.0%

* Included in all other purposes.
** Parts may not add to totals due to rounding.
SOURCE: National Consumer Finance Association.

Cosigning for Others

Creditors will sometimes require that the debtor obtain the signature of another person as a comaker or accommodation endorser when a loan is granted. This person is called an *accommodation party* or a *cosigner*. The effect of cosigning or endorsing someone else's note is the same as if you had borrowed the money directly yourself and in turn loaned it to the other person.

Many students have been able to finish their college courses because others have cosigned a note with them, and many people have secured personal loans because of the cosignature of a friend. Nevertheless, the wisdom of signing other people's notes is doubtful. The accommodation party often finds that he is compelled to pay the note at the very time when he is least able to stand it. At the time the loan was granted, the accommodation party may have been in good financial condition—otherwise he probably would not have been acceptable to the creditor. But usually the accommodation party does not set aside a reserve to meet the note in case the debtor cannot pay.

It might actually be better for the accommodation party to lend the money himself. He presumably had it at the time of signing and the failure of the debtor to pay the note at maturity may not be nearly so embarrassing to him as having to pay the note himself at that time. Furthermore, he may have been collecting some interest on the loan in the meantime. As an accommodation party, he gets no return. It should be kept in mind that, if the borrower's credit was good enough to get the loan, the borrower would not have had to obtain the signature of an accommodation party.

The authors may, perhaps, seem overly critical of the practice of signing other people's notes, but they have been considering it primarily from the viewpoint of the accommodation party. You will never lose money by refusing to sign someone else's note, and you usually gain nothing by doing it.

Sources of Borrowed Money

Money lenders and borrowers have existed since biblical times. One of the earliest forms of government regulation was in connection with money lending. History has indicated that if legal provision is not made for this type of lending, it will spring up outside the law. If the rate of interest permitted by law is not high enough to enable legal agencies to stay in business, the business will be diverted to illegal lenders. Judging from past experience, it is apparent that there is a place for legitimate consumer money lending institutions in our economy.

The average consumer has a large number of possible sources for borrowing money. These include the legal lending institutions, such as commercial banks, consumer finance companies, credit unions, industrial banks, and remedial loan societies. Those individuals who have policies or accounts may borrow from life insurance companies, savings and loan associations, and mutual savings banks. Others may borrow from pawnbrokers or from friends and relatives. In some cases, consumers will be taken advantage of by loan sharks. Table 4–2 gives the personal installment loans outstanding by type of lender in 1965. All of these possible lenders are discussed later in this chapter.

Each potential borrower should take the time to determine which possible lender is the most advantageous for his specific purpose. When shopping for a loan, borrowers should always deal with a reliable institution or lender. Factors which vary between lenders are the rate of interest paid, the dollar amount of interest paid, the dollar amount of money borrowed, when payments are due, size of payments, and type of security required.

Table 4–2. Personal Installment Loans Outstanding, by Type of Lender—United States, January 31, 1965 (in millions of dollars)

Type of Lender	Amount	Distribution
Consumer finance companies	$ 5,078	31.6%
Commercial banks	5,408	33.6
Sales finance companies	2,030	12.6
All other	3,575	22.2
Total	$16,091	100.0%

SOURCE: *Federal Reserve Bulletin.*

In judging among different classes of lenders, the total dollar cost and rate of interest required for the loan are often the most important factors. Even though total cost is often difficult to determine, the potential borrower should make the effort to determine the cost which would be charged by the various possible sources of loans. Cost can be compared on both a dollar base and by effective rate of interest. It is important that the borrower be certain that the terms of the loan are such that his income will enable him to make the payments involved so that default will not occur. The following factors should be considered in selecting a source of borrowed funds:

1. The dollar cost of the loan and the effective rate
2. The amount of the loan the lender will grant
3. The time allowed for repayment
4. The pledge of collateral required
5. The collection practices of the lender
6. The reliability of the lender
7. The size and timing of the payments

Each potential borrower should determine which lenders would be interested in lending to him and then select from among them the one which best meets his requirements at the lowest cost and on the most advantageous terms.

CONSUMER LOAN DEPARTMENTS OF COMMERCIAL BANKS

The First National City Bank of New York established a personal (consumer) loan department in 1928. This was the first such department in a large bank and it formally recognized a type of lending which was to become very important to all commercial banks. Today, commercial banks are the source of more than one third of all consumer installment credit. In their personal loan departments, commercial banks perform both a sales finance and a direct money lending function.

Prior to the domination of consumer installment credit by commercial banks, consumer finance companies and sales finance companies were the most important institutions in the field. The movement into the consumer loan field by banks represented a substantial departure from prior banking philosophy. While banks had granted loans to businesses for many years without the implication of borrowing being necessarily an indication of weakness, they applied different standards to personal affairs and operated under the philosophy that a resort to borrowing by an individual was indicative of unwise personal financial management. As the assets behind consumer loans are ordinarily of less value than business assets and are generally not productive of income, it was felt that the typical consumer loan offered poor security. Therefore, in general, such loans were considered too speculative for commercial banks. However, the shortage of good business loans in the 1930's, the higher return available on consumer loans, and the very low loss experience of other institutions in the field convinced commercial banks that consumer lending was a desirable activity for them.

The expense connected with granting consumer loans is greatly in excess of that incurred in handling commercial loans. Because of the greater risk involved, a more careful credit investigation of the borrower is necessary. Also, bookkeeping and collection costs are higher for installment payments. The average consumer loan of commercial banks is under $600, a much smaller amount than the usual business loan. Investigation costs tend to be as great for a small loan as for a large one. These higher expenses require a higher interest rate for personal loans relative to business loans. For commercial banks to enter the consumer loan field, the legal interest rates which they can charge must be sufficient to cover costs and return a reasonable profit to the bank.

Legislation

In many states, banks granting consumer loans still do so under the general banking laws, which do not specifically authorize the installment payment plan. Since 1935, a number of states have passed special statutes covering this type of commercial bank loan. Some of them set a maximum amount for the loan; in several instances it is $1,000. Some states specify a maximum maturity, and some require that the bank obtain permission from the proper state authorities before opening a consumer loan department. The maximum interest rate is stated in a few of the statutes; several such statutes provide for charges in addition to interest, while others permit only fines, court costs, and insurance premiums in addition to the discounted interest. Where there is no special law governing these loans in a particular state, the banks charge up to the maximum rate permitted for ordinary loans, but usually discount the note and add on some other charges for investigation, insurance, and similar expenses. Some states have special statutes which permit commercial banks, through the use of hypothecated accounts (a special account pledged as security for the loan), to charge an effective rate in excess of the maximum rate specified by the law. Under this method, the principal amount of the loan stays the same and the borrower makes his installment payments into a non-interest-bearing savings account. At the time of maturity, the savings account is used to pay off the personal loan.

The legal and maximum interest rates permitted on ordinary loans in the various states are given in Table 4–3. The *legal* rate of interest is the amount that can be collected by the creditor when no rate is specified in the contract. The *maximum* rate is the highest contract rate that can be charged on ordinary loans. In forty of the fifty states, the legal rate is 6 per cent. In nine of the remaining ten, it is either 5 per cent or 7 per

Table 4–3. Legal and Maximum Rates (Annual) of Interest

State	Legal Rate	Maximum Rate	State	Legal Rate	Maximum Rate
Alabama	6%	8%	Missouri	6%	8%
Alaska	6	8	Montana	6	10
Arizona	6	8*	Nebraska	6	9
Arkansas	6	10	Nevada	7	12
California	7	10	New Hampshire	6	Unlimited
Colorado	6	12	New Jersey	6	6
Connecticut	6	12	New Mexico	6	10**
Delaware	6	6	New York	6	6
District of Columbia	6	8	North Carolina	6	6
			North Dakota	4	7
Florida	6	10*	Ohio	6	8
Georgia	7	8	Oklahoma	6	10
Hawaii	6	12	Oregon	6	10*
Idaho	6	8	Pennsylvania	6	6
Illinois	5	7	Rhode Island	6	30
Indiana	6	8	South Carolina	6	7
Iowa	5	7	South Dakota	6	8
Kansas	6	10	Tennessee	6	6
Kentucky	6	6	Texas	6	10
Louisiana	5	8	Utah	6	10
Maine	6	Unlimited	Vermont	6	6
Maryland	6	6	Virginia	6	6
Massachusetts	6	Unlimited	Washington	6	12
Michigan	5	7	West Virginia	6	6
Minnesota	6	8	Wisconsin	5	12
Mississippi	6	8	Wyoming	7	10

* Higher for corporations.
** When a loan is unsecured, the rate may be 12 per cent.
SOURCE: *Credit Manual of Commercial Laws,* 1964.

cent, and in one state, North Dakota, it is 4 per cent. In all but 11 states, the maximum rate exceeds the legal rate. In these 11 states, the maximum rate is 6 per cent. The maximum rate exceeds 12 per cent in only four states; the median maximum rate is 8 per cent. Maximum rates of 6, 7, or 8 per cent are normally too low to cover the costs of consumer loans. As a result, in states with these maximums, commercial banks must operate in such a way that the effective rate can be higher than the maximum rates specified by law.

Borrowing Charges

One way to obtain a higher effective rate of interest than the maximum rate allowed is to *discount* the loan. Discounting the loan means taking the interest out in advance. Thus, a $100 loan for one year at 6 per cent would be discounted by subtracting $6 from $100, leaving a net amount borrowed of $94. The effective rate of a $6 cost for a $94 loan is 6.2 per cent. In some cases, commercial banks are permitted to charge maximum rates on the full amount of the loan even though the loan is to be paid off in installments. In these cases, the effective rate becomes much higher than the maximum rate given. A common charge (effective rate) for a consumer installment loan of a commercial bank is from 7 to 18 per cent per year. Although the effective rate to the borrower on the amount of money used may be in excess of the maximum rate prescribed by law, the stated rate is not in excess of the legal maximum.

If the maximum rate of interest permitted in a particular state is 6 per cent per year, the most that a person who wants to borrow $100 for one year can be charged for interest is $6. However, a charge to cover the cost of investigating the borrower's credit risk may be added. The commercial bank generally considers the cost of making the loan a separate item from interest. If the charge is 2 per cent, $2 would be added to $6 to give a total charge of $8. On a discount basis, this $8 is deducted from the $100 and the borrower is given the balance of $92. Thus, the borrower is paying $8 per year for the use of $92 which is at the rate of 8½ per cent rather than 6 per cent. But the real rate is even more than 8½ per cent if the loan is repaid in equal monthly installments. Since the face value of the note is $100 and not $92, twelve monthly installments of $8.33 will be paid by the borrower for the use of $92. As indicated in the preceding chapter, the borrower has the $92 for only one month and the average amount borrowed during the year is $46. This leads to a real interest charge of about 16 per cent. The formula for computing interest charged on installment purchases, which was presented in the preceding chapter, can be used to determine the effective rate of interest charged in this case.

Applying the formula,

$$R = \frac{2Ni}{P\,(n+1)} = \frac{2 \times 12 \times \$8}{\$92 \times (12+1)} = \frac{\$192}{\$1{,}196} = 0.16, \text{ or 16 per cent per annum}$$

In states where 8 and 10 per cent per annum are permitted, the effective rate could obviously be much higher than the example given above. Commercial banks do not necessarily charge the maximum allowable rate.

Nature of Loans

Most loans made through consumer lending departments of commercial banks involve installment payments on a monthly basis. These payments may be made into a special savings account or, in states which allow higher charges for personal loans, the payments may be made directly against the loan. In any case, the loan operates in the same manner as other types of installment credit.

There is usually no limit on the amount of the loan which may be made through the consumer loan department of the commercial bank. The security required is usually one or two cosigners on the note, although this is not necessary for persons of high credit rating. In some cases chattel mortgages may be taken against personal assets. Some commercial banks charge an investigation fee and require the purchase of credit life insurance in connection with consumer loans granted. Commercial banks tend to make larger personal loans than do other consumer money-lending institutions. Because their charges are generally less than those of other institutions, they cannot afford to make the small loan or the high-risk loan. As a result, the consumer loan departments of most commercial banks are patronized by the higher-income, better-financed consumer borrowers.

Most commercial banks actively promote their consumer loan departments, and a variety of plans have been developed to encourage their use. Some banks offer a combination savings and borrowing program. Others perform personal financial counseling for their customers.

In recent years many banks have developed revolving credit plans or charge account banking plans. The revolving credit concept represents a sharp departure from prior philosophy for commercial banks. While these plans vary in title and technique, the general approach is that the customer may write checks as he desires up to a stated credit limit, and he has no responsibility to inform the bank of his use of the funds. As the checks clear the bank, the amounts written are added to the principal of the loan outstanding to the individual. As the customer pays his credit obligation, he increases his available credit up to his credit limit at the same time. He is generally required to pay either a given dollar amount per month or a given percentage of the outstanding balance. Maximum credit limits range from $100 to $5,000. In effect, the borrower under a revolving credit plan has almost permanent use of a given amount of money. Of course, the bank charges interest on the account at its usual consumer loan rate.

CONSUMER FINANCE COMPANIES

Consumer finance companies are specialized institutions making small cash installment loans to consumers. While commercial banks are the most important consumer credit institutions, consumer finance companies dominate the field of small cash loans. These companies are also called small-loan companies and personal finance companies. Consumer finance companies have grown rapidly in recent years. In 1939, less than half a billion dollars was outstanding in consumer loans granted by consumer finance companies. By the beginning of 1965, the amount outstanding had risen to over $5 billion. The consumer finance field embraces a large number of small companies maintaining one-man offices, as well as such nationally known concerns as Beneficial Finance Company and Household Finance Corporation, which have more than 900 offices each. About one out of every seven families in the United States borrows money from a consumer finance company. More than $6 billion was granted in loans by these companies in 1964.

Legislation

The state maximum legal rates of interest are adequate for commercial loans made by banks to business organizations or to the government, but are not high enough to cover the costs of lending small amounts to consumers on an installment basis. Although the lawmakers thought that these maximum rates would give protection to the borrower, experience indicates that when legitimate financial institutions cannot profitably make consumer loans at maximum legal rates, loans are made by illegal lenders who charge exorbitant rates ranging up to 1,200 per cent per year.

The Russell Sage Foundation, after an extensive investigation, made a report in 1910 that showed the need for enactment of legislation which would permit the organization of consumer lending agencies with legalized rates of interest high enough to permit them to stay in business. Massachusetts was the first state to enact a small-loan law.

The Russell Sage Foundation, together with the National Federation of Remedial Loan Associations, drew up a Uniform Small Loan Act in 1916. With certain modifications, this law has now been adopted by 44 states. Three states and the District of Columbia have types of small-loan laws which are largely or wholly ineffective, due, in part, to the fact that the maximum rates of interest permitted are not high enough to enable

Table 4–4. Maximum Rates for Small Loan Companies

Alabama	3% per month on first $200; 2% on remainder to $300
Alaska*	4% per month on first $300; 2½% on next $300; 2% on remainder to $1,000
Arizona	3% per month on first $300; 2% on next $300; 1% on remainder to $1,000
California	2½% per month on first $200; 2% on next $300 (flat 2% if security insured); ⅚% on remainder to $5,000
Canada	2% per month on first $300; 1% on next $700; ½% on remainder to $1,500
Colorado	3% per month on first $300; 1½% on next $200; 1% on remainder to $1,500
Connecticut	$17 per $100 per year to $300; $9 per $100 per year for remainder to $1,000
Delaware*	6% per year discount; plus 2% service fee and 5% fine
Florida	3% per month on first $300; 2% on remainder to $600; 10% per year after 12 months
Georgia	8% per year to $2,500; fee of 8% on first $600 and 4% on excess
Hawaii	3½% per month on first $100; 2½% on remainder to $300
Idaho	3% per month on first $300; 2% on next $200; 1% on remainder to $1,000
Illinois	3% per month on first $150; 2% on next $150; 1% on remainder to $800
Indiana	3% per month on first $150; 2% on next $150; 1½% on remainder to $1,000
Iowa	3% per month on first $150; 2% on next $150; 1½% on remainder to $500
Kansas	3% per month on first $300; 10% per annum on remainder to $2,100
Kentucky	3% per month on first $150; 2% on next $450; 1% on remainder to $800
Louisiana	3½% per month on first $150; 2½% on remainder to $300; 8% per annum 12 months after maturity
Maine	3% per month on first $150; 2½% on next $150; 1½% on remainder to $2,500
Maryland	3% per month to $300
Massachusetts	2½% per month on first $200; 2% on next $400; 1¾% on next $400; ¾% on remainder to $3,000
Michigan	2½% per month on first $300; 1¼% on remainder to $1,000
Minnesota	2¾% per month on first $300; 1½% on remainder to $600
Missouri	2.218% per month on first $500; 8% per year on remainder
Montana*	$20 add on per $100 per year to $300; $16 on next $200; $12 on remainder to $1,000
Nebraska	2½% per month on first $300; 2% on next $200; 1½% on next $500; 1% on remainder to $3,000
Nevada*	$9 per $100 per year plus a graduated service charge
New Hampshire	$16 per $100 per year to $600; $12 on remainder to $1,500

Table 4–4 (Continued).

New Jersey	2½% per month on first $300; ½% on remainder to $500
New Mexico	3% per month on first $150; 2½% on next $150; 1% on remainder to $1,000
New York	2½% per month on first $100; 2% on next $200; ¾% on remainder to $800
North Carolina	$20 per $100 per year to $100; $18 on next $100; $15 on next $100; and $6 on remainder to $600
North Dakota	2½% per month on first $250; 2% on next $250; 1¾% on next $250; 1½% on remainder to $1,000
Ohio	$16 per $100 per year to $500; $9 on next $500; $7 on remainder to $2,000
Oklahoma*	10% per annum plus service charge, plus 5% initial charge, plus monthly charge
Oregon	3% per month on first $300; 2% on next $200; 1% on remainder to $1,500
Pennsylvania	3% per month on first $150; 2% on next $150; 1% on remainder to $600; 6% per annum after 24 months
Rhode Island	3% per month to $300
South Dakota*	3% per month on first $300; ¾% per month on remainder to $2,500
Texas	$19 per $100 per year to $100; $16 on next $100; $13 on next $100; $11 on next $200; $9 on next $500; $7 on remainder to $1,500
Utah	3% per month on first $300; 1% on remainder to $600
Vermont	2½% per month on first $125; 2¼% on next $175; 1% on remainder to $600
Virginia	2½% per month on first $300; 1½% on remainder to $600; 6% per annum after 23 months
Washington	3% per month on first $300; 1½% on next $200; 1% on remainder to $1,000
West Virginia	3% per month on first $200; 2% on next $400; 1½% on remainder to $800
Wisconsin	2½% per month on first $100; 2% on next $100; and 1% on remainder to $300
Wyoming*	3½% per month on first $150; 2½% on next $150; 1% on remainder to $1,000

* Laws are dissimilar to Uniform Small Loan Laws.

NOTE: Arkansas, District of Columbia, Mississippi, South Carolina, and Tennessee have ineffective or no small-loan laws.

a legitimate firm to stay in business. These states are Mississippi, South Carolina, and Tennessee. In one state, Arkansas, there is no small-loan law.

The Uniform Small Loan Act calls for a limit on the amount which may be loaned to each borrower by the regulated companies. Most of the laws originally specified a limit of $300 per loan and some states still have this limit, but the majority of states have increased the maximum loan to amounts ranging from $500 to $5,000. Loans of $1,000 or more are now permitted in 28 states. In some states, consumer finance companies may grant loans in excess of the amounts stated, but ordinary usury laws are applicable to the larger amounts. The *monthly* loan charge that may be made by consumer finance companies in states with workable laws ranges from 2 per cent in Massachusetts to 4 per cent in Alaska. A number of states apply a lower rate to that portion of the loan above a certain minimum amount. For example, a rate of 3 per cent per month may be charged on the first $150 of the loan, 2 per cent on the next $150, and 1 per cent on the balance up to the maximum amount allowed. Maximum charges permitted by regulated consumer finance companies in the various states are shown in Table 4–4.

Although the details vary somewhat among the states, the following are the main provisions of the Uniform Small Loan Act:

1. On loans of $300 or less the maximum rate of interest permitted varies among the states from 2 to 4 per cent a month. In some states this maximum is permitted on only the first $100 or $150 of the loan, with a lower rate for the balance.
2. The interest is computed on the unpaid balance of the loan.
3. Interest cannot be deducted in advance.
4. Security for the loan may be an endorsed promissory note, a chattel mortgage, or negotiable collateral such as securities.
5. With the exception of recording fees, and fees on loans of a small amount in several states, no charges of any nature other than interest may be made.
6. Companies formed under the law must be licensed, bonded, and subject to state supervision and examination.
7. A minimum capital—in some states $25,000—must be provided.
8. Penalties are provided for violation of the law.

Nature of Operation

While maximum legal lending limits range from $300 to $5,000, the average consumer finance company loan granted in the United States is approximately $500. More than half of the loans are for $250 or less. Industrial and office workers are the principal customers of these companies. Table 4–5 indicates that most borrowers are in the lower and middle income brackets.

While most loans are secured by chattel mortgages on automobiles or household goods, or involve cosigners, the principal security behind any loan is the promise to pay embodied in the borrower's note (Fig. 4–1).

Since the original amount of the loan usually exceeds the forced-sale value of the property mortgaged, it is only after a part of the loan has been paid that the lender would be likely to look to the chattel for satis-

Table 4–5. Percentage Distribution of the Monthly Income of Borrowers from Consumer Finance Companies—Selected Years, 1939–1963

Monthly Income of Borrowers	Number of Loans Extended						
	1939	1948	1950	1954	1958	1960	1963
$0.00–100.00	16.3%	1.4%	0.9%	0.4%	0.3%	0.3%	0.3%
$100.01–200.00	62.5	31.5	18.9	7.4	4.6	3.7	3.0
$200.01–300.00	21.1*	46.9	46.0	30.7	17.6	13.1	10.4
$300.01–400.00	. . .	13.0	20.6	32.1	30.6	23.8	19.9
$400.01–500.00	. . .	4.7	8.7	16.1	22.7	25.0	25.0
$500.01–750.00	. . .	2.4**	4.9**	12.0	21.4	26.6	30.1
$750.01–1,000.00	. . .	. . . .	. . . .	1.3***	2.3	6.0	9.1
$1,000.01 and over	. . .	. . . .	. . . .	. . . .	0.5	1.5	2.2
Total †	100.0%	100.0%	100.0%	100.0%	100.0%	100.0%	100.0%

* *Over $200.00.*
** *Over $500.00.*
*** *Over $750.00.*
† Parts may not add to totals due to rounding.
SOURCE: National Consumer Finance Association.

faction. Consumer finance companies will use all available methods of collection before resorting to the sale of the mortgaged property. If the borrower runs into unexpected trouble, the company will usually try to get him to pay something on the loan, and will spread the payments over a sufficient period of time to enable him to pay it off entirely.

The number of months over which the loan may be repaid depends upon the ability of the borrower to pay and is a matter of contract between him and the company. The amount of the payment is usually the same for each of the months during which the loan is being repaid and includes interest on the unpaid balance. Most states provide for a maximum of 36 months of payments. Figure 4–2 shows the monthly payments that would be made on a loan of the amount indicated for the period stated, according to an advertisement for a consumer finance company in Ohio. Most consumer finance companies offer credit life insurance to the borrower. This insurance pays the balance of the loan in the event of the death of the borrower. Some companies require the customer to purchase credit life insurance; others make it optional. These policies are normally sold to the borrower at the company's cost.

Consumer finance companies do a sizable repeat business. The same family may borrow from a consumer finance company five or six times during a ten-year period. Because of a continuing relationship with their customers, some consumer finance companies have developed debt counseling services whereby they attempt to aid their customers in all types of personal financial planning.

NOTE

CAPITAL FINANCE CORPORATION

PAYEE

, OHIO

ACCOUNT NUMBER	NAME AND ADDRESS	PHONE:	DATE WILL PAY
YOUR INSURANCE EXPIRES			

PRINCIPAL AND CHARGES PAYABLE IN ____ CONSECUTIVE MONTHLY INSTALLMENTS BEGINNING ____ 19__	PAYMENTS (EXCEPT FINAL)* $ EACH	FREQUENCY 3

CHARGES	CODE	DATE OF NOTE	SIZE CODE	AMOUNT OF LOAN (PRINCIPAL)	FINAL PAYMENT DUE
3-				$	

* The last payment shall include any unpaid principal balance and charges accrued on the date due. All unpaid principal in default shall bear charges stated below, until loan is fully paid.

The undersigned jointly and severally promise to pay to the order of the above named payee at its above address, the aforestated Amount of Loan on the terms and conditions herein set out, with agreed charges on the Amount of Loan of 3% per month on any of unpaid principal balance of $150 or less; 2% per month on any of unpaid principal balance over $150 but not over $300; 8% per annum payable monthly on any remainder of unpaid principal balance of loan. These charges are computed on the number of days actually elapsed, a month being any period of 30 consecutive days and day being 1/30 of a month.

Payment may be made in advance in any amount at any time but from any payment made, the proceeds shall be applied first to all charges in full to the date of payment, at the agreed rate. Failure to pay any installment when due shall cause the entire unpaid principal balance with accrued charges to become immediately due and payable at the option of the holder, without notice.

All parties to this note, whether maker, co-maker, endorser, guarantor, surety, or other party, hereby jointly and severally waive presentment, notice of dishonor and protest and diligence in bringing suit against any such party, and agree that discharge or release of any such party shall not discharge any other party, and that any time of payment may be extended, or the holder's right to enforce this note postponed, at any time without notice and without discharging any such party, and further, jointly and severally authorize irrevocably any attorney at law to appear in any court of record of Ohio or elsewhere at any time after any installment herein becomes due and unpaid, and waive the issuing and service of process and confess judgment against them, or any of them, in favor of the holder hereof for the total amount, including charges, unpaid on this note, together with costs of suit, and thereupon to release all errors and waive all right of appeal.

Witness our hands and seals:

Witnessed:

____________________ (SEAL)

____________________ (SEAL)

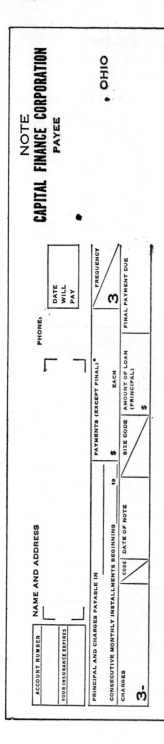

Fig. 4–1. A consumer finance company note.

	Monthly Payment Plans			
Cash You Get	36 payments	25 payments	18 payments	12 payments
$100		$ 5.33	$ 6.88	$ 9.66
300		16.00	20.66	29.00
500		26.66	34.44	48.33
1000		50.41	65.97	93.75
1500	$55.00	73.33	96.66	138.33
2000	71.80	96.25	127.36	182.91

Payments above include principal and charges if paid according to schedule.

Fig. 4–2. A typical advertisement for a consumer finance company.

Borrowing Charges

The maximum interest rates specified in Table 4–4 apply to the unpaid balance of the loan. Since the loans are reduced by monthly installments, the amount of the interest decreases as time goes on. Most consumer finance companies, however, arrange the total monthly payments so that they will be equal in amount. This means that the first month's payment on, for example, a ten-month loan will not be sufficient to retire one tenth of the principal of the loan. In those states which have lower rates on the higher balances of the loans, the first payments made against principal are charged against the higher balances. Thus, in a state which allows 3 per cent per month on the first $300 but one per cent on the remaining amount, a loan of $500 would involve interest of $11 (3 per cent of $300 and one per cent of $200) for the first month. If the first monthly payment reduces the principal to $400, interest charges for the second month would be $10 (3 per cent of $300 and one per cent of $100). When the loan is paid down to $300 or less, the interest charge would be 3 per cent of the unpaid balance.

Consumer finance companies do not generally quote percentage interest charges. Instead, they quote definite monthly payments which must be made to pay off a loan of a given amount over a definite period of time. With this information a person can compute the effective rate which he is being charged for the loan. If, for example, a $100 loan may be paid off in three equal monthly installments of $35.38, the borrower would be paying a total of three times $35.38, or $106.14, to the company. The difference between this and $100.00 is $6.14, the amount of the interest charges. Using the formula presented previously, we get the following:

$$R = \frac{2 \times 12 \times \$6.14}{\$100\ (3 + 1)} = \frac{\$147.36}{\$400} = 0.36$$

or a charge of 36 per cent per year. This is at the rate of 3 per cent a month on the unpaid balance.

In fairness to consumer finance companies, a word of explanation should be given in regard to their charges. We have referred to the charges they make as "interest." Really, only part of the charges paid by the borrower for a loan represents interest. It costs money to make a credit investigation of the applicant, put the loan on the books, and handle the monthly payments. All these expenses must be paid by the borrower in addition to the actual interest. Consumer finance companies in most of the states can make only the maximum charge specified in the law and cannot add anything for the various expenses incident to the loan. This makes the "interest" charge appear rather high. Some companies maintain that they just about break even at a 36 per cent annual rate on a small first loan to an individual consumer. Average effective interest charges (including expenses) for a consumer finance company range from 16 per cent to 42 per cent with a median under 30 per cent.

CREDIT UNIONS

A credit union is a group of people who agree to save their money together and to make loans to each other. It is organized by members of a particular group; for instance, people working for the same employer, people who belong to the same fraternal order, or people who live in the same closely knit community. It is a mutual, voluntary, cooperative organization. It is operated for the benefit of borrowers as well as savers and, in principle, these two groups are the same people. All borrowers must be members of the organization, and membership can usually be obtained by the purchase of at least one share of stock for a small sum. Management is vested in a board of trustees or directors elected by the shareholders. Officers are appointed by the board, and both the officers and the board serve without compensation.

The credit union idea originated in Germany in the middle of the last century, but its principal development in the United States came after World War I. The late Edward A. Filene, a prominent Boston merchant, was responsible for the rapid development of the credit union in this country. Credit unions may be chartered by either the state or the federal government. All states have credit union statutes, and Congress passed the Federal Credit Union Act in 1934. The state laws are generally very similar to the federal credit union law.

The statutes provide for the election by the shareholders of the credit committee, whose duty it is to pass upon applications for loans. The credit committee supervises all credit loans to members and meets regularly to approve loans. The shareholders also elect an audit committee which keeps an eye on the operation of the credit union, examines its financial affairs periodically, and reports to the membership at the annual meeting.

Credit unions obtain their funds from savings deposits (technically, purchases of shares) made by members. (The credit union as a savings institution is discussed in Chapter 6.) At the beginning of 1964, there were 21,518 active credit unions in the United States. Approximately half of these were state-chartered and the rest were federal-chartered. These credit unions had over 14 million members and in excess of $7.1 billion in deposits. $6.2 billion was outstanding in loans to members, with government bonds and cash accounts making up most of the remainder of the assets.

Nature of Operation

Credit unions lend only to their own members. The maximum unsecured loan permitted is usually from $200 to $750. For loans in excess of this amount, either a comaker's signature must be secured on the note or additional collateral must be pledged. Some state statutes limit the size of secured loans; other state statutes, and the federal statutes, do not specify a limit. Members may also borrow amounts equal to their stock investment in the credit union. There is no maximum limit on the amount of such loans. Although in the minority, the number of credit unions that grant real estate loans is increasing, but the maximum maturity specified by the various laws tends to keep down the number and size of real estate loans. The average credit union loan granted is for approximately $350; the maximum maturity of the loan is usually two to five years. Maximum maturity on loans granted by credit unions formed under the federal statute is five years. Most credit union loans include credit life insurance.

Credit unions usually operate with extremely low overhead per dollar loaned. The reason is that few, if any, expenses have to be paid by the credit union. Intimate knowledge of the various members usually eliminates the necessity for extensive credit investigation before granting loans, thereby reducing the credit union's expenses. The officers donate their services, and the employer often contributes the office space, light, heat, and stationery. Postage, fees, and a few bad debts usually constitute all the expenses of the credit union.

After paying expenses and setting up reserves, any or all remaining profits of the credit union may be paid to the shareholders in the form of dividends. Federal credit unions are not permitted to pay more than 6 per cent in dividends. The most common dividend rate paid in 1965 was 5 per cent.

Many credit unions find that only a small percentage of their capital is demanded by member borrowers. These unions invest the balance of their assets principally in bonds. Bond investments tend to yield less to the credit union than loans to members.

Borrowing Charges

Maximum interest permitted by most credit union statutes is one per cent per month on the unpaid balance. Loans are usually paid off in installments, but interest is charged only on the balance which is still outstanding. Many credit unions today are charging only one half of one per cent on the unpaid balance. This very low interest charge is due to the low overhead expenses of the credit union, the low rate (commonly 5 per cent) which the credit union pays its savers for the money it lends, and the donated services and facilities. Credit unions are, therefore, one of the least expensive places for consumers to borrow small amounts of money. Borrowing, however, is limited to members, and membership is restricted to employees or members of certain organizations. Credit unions are growing rapidly in numbers and in importance in the field of consumer lending.

OTHER SOURCES

In addition to commercial banks, consumer finance companies, and credit unions, consumers have available a number of other possible sources for borrowing money. Although these other sources are not as important in overall consumer lending volume, they may be the most desirable source of a consumer loan under given circumstances for a specific borrower.

Industrial Banks

Industrial banks came into existence at the beginning of the twentieth century to fill a need for reputable consumer lending institutions. At this time, commercial banks were lending only to government and industry. Unlike commercial banks, industrial banks have as their primary purpose the lending of money to consumers. The relative importance of industrial banks has declined in recent years with the development of consumer lending departments of commercial banks. In fact, many industrial banks have been converted into or have merged with commercial banks.

The term "industrial" is misleading because this kind of bank ordinarily does not lend to industry, but to consumers. The title probably developed from the fact that this type of lending agency was originally formed for the primary purpose of lending money to industrial wage earners. The use of the word "bank" in the title is also misleading in that most industrial banks do not accept deposits.

The leading industrial banks are the *Morris Plan* banks. Arthur J. Morris founded the first Morris Plan bank in Virginia in 1910. The Morris Plan Corporation of America, for a fee, grants the use of its name and trademark to industrial banks and holds either majority or minority stock interests in many local banks. Many industrial banks, however, are not connected with the Morris Plan system and operate throughout the country under various names.

In the early years of their development, industrial banks granted consumer loans secured only by the endorsement of two other parties on the note. In recent years, some of these institutions have been granting loans on single-name notes, and some have extended the scope of their loans to include automobile and other chattel mortgage loans. Some industrial banks even grant real estate and modernization loans and, in some cases, buy retail installment notes from dealers.

The legal status of industrial banks varies among the states. About half of the states have enacted statutes pertaining to them. In other states, industrial banks operate under the commercial banking laws. Where there are no statutes under which they may be formed and operated, industrial banks are covered by the general corporation laws. In many states, industrial banks are not entitled to use the term "bank" but rather are referred to as industrial loan companies.

Varies with States

The nature of operation of industrial banks varies according to the laws of the state in which the banks operate. Originally, and even now in some states, only installment loans were granted, but interest was charged on the whole principal for the period of the loan. In some states, installment payments are not credited directly against the loan, but rather are credited to a special non-interest-bearing account, or installment certificate account, as described above. When the borrower has built up in the deposit account or in certificates an amount sufficient to pay off the note, the account is written off against the note. In this way an effective rate of interest higher than the legal maximum rate can be legally collected. In other states, loan installment payments are credited directly against the loan balance.

higher rate is collected here

Generally speaking, industrial banks operate very much like the consumer loan departments of commercial banks. The funds for lending are obtained from stockholders, from borrowing from commercial banks, and in some cases from deposits. Effective interest charges for industrial banks range from 12 to 24 per cent per year. Typical quoted rates would be 6 to 9 per cent per year.

Pawnbrokers

Lending money that is secured by personal goods is one of our most ancient forms of loans. Down through the centuries, the symbol of three golden balls, which is said to have originated in the fourteenth century from the coat of arms of the famous Medici family of bankers in Florence, has attracted borrowers from a rather large segment of the population. Many people of some means today have at some time in the past found it necessary in an emergency to go to the "hock shop" to secure money.

In a loan of this kind, no note is signed by the borrower since the goods pledged serve as the security. The granting of the loan can be effected in a short time, and there is no need for the borrower to divulge his identity. Speed and secrecy are major assets of the pawnbroker. The pawnbroker immediately appraises the article to be pledged, and usually limits the amount of the loan to not more than half the resale value of the security. The property pledged can usually be redeemed within a year by payment of the loan and the interest due. The installment plan is not used to pay off the loan—it is payable in a lump sum.

If the loan is not repaid within the specified period, the lender has the right to sell the property pledged, either at public auction or by private sale. The borrower would have a right to any surplus left after payment of the loan and interest, but usually there is no surplus because the lender himself bids on the property for just the amount owed. If the pledged property should actually be sold to someone else for less than the amount owed, the pawnbroker has no legal right against the borrower for the deficit.

Supervision over pawnshops is usually for the purpose of recovering stolen property. There is no federal law in the United States relating to pawnshops. Most pawnshops operate under special state legislation and regulation, with very limited supervision. The size of the usual pawnbroker loan is rather small—a $10 loan is fairly common.

Interest rates charged on pawnbroker loans are usually rather high. They vary from 24 per cent to 120 per cent a year, with 36 per cent being the common rate. Of course, if the goods are never called for by the borrower, there is no need to pay the interest rate. Under these circumstances, it would generally be more desirable to sell the goods outright than to pawn them and never attempt to recover them. Since there is no installment payment in connection with pawnbroker loans, the interest charged is on the total amount of the loan for the life of the loan. In some cases, legal limits for pawnbrokers allow higher charges on small amounts and lower charges on large amounts. Pawnbroker rates are often quoted on a monthly basis. It should be kept in mind that 3 per cent per month is 36 per cent per year.

Insurance Companies

Some banks will lend money to a person on the security of his life insurance policy. Loans made on policies, however, are more commonly granted by the particular life insurance company itself. With the exception of term policies, practically all life insurance policies which have been in force for at least two years have definite loan values stated in the policy. The amount of this loan value increases with the age of the policy. Policy loans outstanding with United States life insurance companies totaled $8 billion at the beginning of 1965.

One of the advantages of having life insurance is that it is a source of money when a person may be unable to obtain it otherwise. The insurance company is compelled to make loans up to the loan value amount stated in the contract, upon proper application on the part of the insured. To prevent a run on the company, the laws of some states permit it to wait from three to six months before granting the loan. In the emergency period of the depression in the early 1930's, insurance companies temporarily had to discontinue granting loans. At the present time most insurance companies grant the loans immediately. The rate of interest charged by the leading companies today is about 5 per cent straight annual interest. This is a lower rate than can be obtained from other consumer lending agencies.

Some people feel that it is unjust for an insurance company to charge them interest on what they consider to be their own money. The policyholder should realize that the premiums he pays are calculated on the basis that the company will have the use of the premium dollars and can invest this amount in bonds, etc. If the company lends some of the money to a policyholder, it must charge him interest to cover the expense of making the loan and to offset the return which the company would otherwise be getting on this money.

Savings and Loan Associations and Savings Banks

Financing a home is discussed in a later chapter, but it is often difficult to separate home financing needs from other consumer borrowing needs. If a person owns his home clear of debt, he may mortgage the home to obtain money for other consumer purposes. In this sense, real estate finance institutions become sources of funds for consumers. Some savings and loan associations grant loans to finance home improvements under

Title I of the Federal Housing Act. The normal effective interest rate on Title I financing is approximately 9 per cent. Interest rates for borrowing under a home mortgage at savings and loan associations and savings banks range from 5 to 7½ per cent.

Savings and loan associations and savings banks will normally make loans up to the total amount of the deposit, for people who carry savings accounts at these institutions. These loans are generally called share loans, and the common interest rate is 5 to 6 per cent. Savers take advantage of these loans rather than withdraw from their account when they have need of the money for only a short period of time or when the interest charged on the loan is less than the amount of dividend or interest which would be earned on the savings account. This latter is normally the circumstance during the one or two months preceding the dividend or interest date for the association or bank. Most people who utilize share loans repay the loans from the savings account immediately following the dividend or interest date.

Remedial Loan Societies

Remedial loan societies are semicharitable organizations formed for the purpose of filling some of the demand for small loans under conditions more favorable to the borrower than those encountered in dealing with loan sharks and pawnbrokers. These institutions reached a peak in about 1915 and have been on the decline ever since. The Provident Loan Society of New York does more business than all other remedial societies combined. The development of other types of consumer lending institutions, such as consumer finance companies, has accounted in part for the decline in the relative importance of the remedial society. Interest charges of remedial societies range from 9 to 24 per cent per year.

Friends and Relatives

A considerable amount of money is loaned to consumers by friends and relatives, but no data are available on the total amount of this type of lending. Much of it is without interest, but in some cases interest charges might be extremely high. If a person needs money and can borrow it from a friend or relative without paying him any interest, or without paying him as much interest as he would have to pay elsewhere, it may be a satisfactory arrangement as far as the borrower is concerned. It must be remembered, however, that the friend or relative is not basically in the money-lending business, and that he could probably do better if he invested his money elsewhere. It is often true that the easiest way to lose a friend is to borrow money from him.

Loan Sharks

Before special laws creating the legal consumer finance business were adopted, the small borrower could look for financial aid only to his friends, relatives, pawnbrokers, or loan sharks. The usual annual rate of interest charged by loan sharks is 240 per cent. In some instances, interest of 1,200 per cent has been charged. In cases of this kind it is not surprising for the borrower to find that after making a number of monthly or weekly payments on a loan, he still owes more than the amount of the original loan.

The rates charged by these unlicensed lenders are, of course, in excess of the maximum permitted for ordinary loans, or for loans granted by pawnbrokers or consumer finance companies in states which have maximum rates set by statutes. This does not stop the loan sharks. The individuals who patronize these lenders will seldom bring the matter to the attention of the authorities. In those states which have no maximum rates, the lender is free to charge whatever he can get. In other states with maximum charges, these lenders operate outside the law. Loan sharks are most common in states which have not made special legal provision for consumer lending institutions to charge more than the maximum legal rate of interest. Therefore, legitimate lenders cannot afford to operate in these states.

In recent years a number of questionable techniques have been developed in the second-mortgage loan field which lead to extremely high effective interest rates when all fees and charges are included in figuring rates.

COMPARISON OF LENDING SOURCES

The individual who is contemplating borrowing money should study the various possible sources to determine which one best meets his need at the lowest cost. Some consumer borrowers will find only one or two sources available to them in their specific circumstances. However, many other consumers find it possible to borrow money from a large number of potential sources. In these cases, the borrower should select the source which will offer him the amount of money he needs, when he needs it, for the length of time he needs it, with payment requirements he can meet, at the lowest possible interest cost. Table 4–6 gives a comparison of the range of effective interest rates, maximum loan generally available, collateral commonly needed, maximum maturity, who is eligible, and other characteristics of the various sources of borrowing money discussed in this chapter.

Table 4–6. Comparison of Sources of Personal Loans

Lender	Range of Effective Interest Rates	Maximum Loan Generally Available	Collateral Commonly Needed	Maximum Maturity	Install-ment Payments	Credit Investi-gation	Who Is Eligible
Commercial banks—consumer loan departments	7–18%	$5,000	None, or car, or securities, or cosigner	3 years	Yes	Yes	Anyone with sufficient credit rating
Consumer finance companies	16–36%	$1,000	None or cosigner	3 years	Yes	Yes	Anyone with sufficient credit rating
Credit unions	6–15%	$750 unsecured $5,000 secured	None, or car, or personal property	3 years	Yes	No	Members only
Friends and relatives	0–120%	Unlimited	None or personal property	Unlimited	Both	No	Friends and relatives
Industrial banks	12–24%	$5,000	None, or car, or cosigner	3 years	Yes	Yes	Anyone with sufficient credit rating
Life insurance companies	5–6%	Amount of loan value of policy	Life insurance policy	Unlimited	No	No	Policyholders
Loan sharks	50–1,200%	$500	None or personal property	6 months	No	No	Anyone
Pawnbrokers	24–120%	$300	Personal property	6 months	No	No	Anyone with collateral
Remedial loan societies	9–24%	$300	None, or car, or personal property	Unlimited	Yes	Yes	Anyone with sufficient credit rating
Savings and loan associations, savings banks—real estate loans	5–10%	$30,000	Real estate	30 years	Yes	Yes	Real estate owners with sufficient credit rating
Savings and loan associations, savings banks—share or deposit loans	5–6%	Amount of deposit	Savings accounts	Unlimited	No	No	Savings account holders

QUESTIONS

1. Why do consumers borrow money? How is borrowing money related to buying on credit?
2. When is debt consolidation desirable for consumers? What advantages are normally included in debt consolidation?
3. Should you cosign loans for others? If you want to help someone else, what is a better alternative than cosigning? Why?
4. What procedure can an individual follow which would tend to eliminate the necessity for personal loans, or enable him better to meet the loan installments in case such a loan has to be obtained?
5. How should you select the lender when you need to borrow money?
6. What are the most important sources of money loans for consumers? How has their relative position changed over the years?
7. How are commercial banks regulated in relation to consumer loans?
8. What conditions led to the adoption of small-loan legislation in the United States? What is the popular name for companies which operate under the small-loan laws?
9. Indicate the nature of the small-loan laws with respect to the following points:
   (a) Maximum loan permitted
   (b) Maximum maturity of loan
   (c) Method of computing interest
   (d) Maximum rate of interest permitted
   (e) Security required
10. Do you think that the maximum rate of interest permitted by the small-loan laws of some of the states is too high? Explain.
11. Why may a consumer loan be of value to a person if he merely uses the loan money to pay off other debts?
12. Are credit unions formed under state or federal laws?
13. Describe the organizational setup of a credit union.
14. Who can borrow from a credit union? Is there any limit on the amount of a loan which may be obtained from a credit union? What is the maximum maturity usually permitted for credit union loans?
15. What is an industrial bank and why is it so named? How does it operate?
16. What do you think of borrowing your own money from an insurance company or a savings and loan association? When is this a desirable action?
17. Is a pawnshop a lending agency or a store which sells merchandise?
18. Describe the procedure for obtaining a loan at a pawnshop.
19. List all possible lending institutions for personal or consumer loans. Which of these is the least desirable and why? Which of these is the most desirable and why?
20. List the various consumer lending agencies in order of cost of borrowing from lowest to highest.

CASE PROBLEMS

1. The Security State Bank has been advertising low bank rate consumer loans at 5 per cent. This is the rate which Ted McCarthy has been earning on his savings in a savings and loan account in California. As a result, Ted has decided to borrow the $500 he needs to pay some unusual medical bills rather than withdraw money from his own savings account. Upon applying for the loan at the bank, Ted finds that there is also a service charge of $3. He also finds that the 5 per cent is deducted in advance and that he is required to pay twelve monthly equal installments into a special savings account which earns no interest. What is the effective rate of interest on this transaction? How does it compare to the cost involved in withdrawing savings from his savings account? What would it cost him to borrow against his savings account?
2. John Williams needs $300 to pay past-due bills. A newspaper advertisement tells him that the ABC Finance Company is willing to lend $300 for six months with payments of $55 per month or $30 per month for twelve months. What effective rate of interest is the finance company charging? What kind of collateral may be required of Williams? What other possibilities may he have for obtaining the needed funds?
3. Margaret Johnson missed three weeks' work due to illness. As a result, she got behind in payment of her bills. She had always paid promptly before. She now owes $150 to the doctor, $125 to a local department store, and one month's rent of $65. She is up-to-date on car payments, but has three more payments of $40 cash before the car is clear. She has checked a consumer finance company and finds she can borrow $460 to pay all bills with monthly payments of $52 for ten months. What is the effective rate of interest? Should she do this? Why?
4. Tom Davis graduated from college last year. He has held three different jobs since that time, and at the moment is employed selling vacuum cleaners door to door. He is three months behind in payments on his car, and he owes $125 on his charge account at a local men's shop. He is three weeks behind in rent on his room, and still owes a student loan he obtained in college. He is thinking of quitting his job, and wants to take a vacation in Florida before starting in a new position. He feels the vacation will give him a better attitude and help him make a success of any new position he takes. He has no money to finance a vacation. Where could Davis get the money for a vacation? What would you do if you were Davis? What should he do about his old bills? If you were the manager of a consumer finance company, would you be willing to lend him the amount he needs? Should he consolidate his bills into one loan with a consumer finance company?
5. Jack Roberts has worked for the Smith Department Store for eight years. During that time, he has used the Smith Credit Union for accumulation of savings. He has never borrowed from the fund but has withdrawn amounts over the years for various purposes. At the moment he has $640 on deposit receiving dividends of 4 per cent per annum. Roberts wants to buy a new car and needs $1,400. His old car will serve as down payment. What are the various possibilities for him in financing the $1,400? Should

he borrow from his credit union? Would it be better to borrow the full amount, or withdraw his $640 and borrow only $760? What may he need for collateral to borrow from the credit union? What are the advantages of borrowing from the credit union as compared to using the normal sales-financing channels?

6. Jane Stone is in need of $300 to pay for special dental work. She does not believe that her current salary income is sufficient to supply this amount. She has a diamond ring which she inherited from her mother and which was appraised for estate purposes at $750. She is considering pawning the ring with a pawnbroker to obtain the money. Would this be the best approach for Jane? What are her alternatives? If she does not feel that she can ever afford to repossess the ring, should she still use the pawnbroker? What are the advantages and disadvantages of obtaining money in circumstances such as this from a pawnbroker?
7. Bill and Ann Davis live in a rented house but own their own furniture and a one-year-old car. They purchased their car and most appliances on time but have paid promptly. They have two more years to pay on the car at the rate of $45 per month. By meeting bills promptly, Bill and Ann have maintained an excellent credit rating. However, they have been unable to accumulate much in savings. At the moment they have $300 in a savings and loan account and Bill has an insurance policy with a cash surrender value of $500. Bill and Ann have agreed to give $1,500 to her parents to help with an immediate personal problem. Since they do not have this amount of money, they must borrow at least part of it. How do you suggest Bill obtain the money? Should he use his savings? How should he choose between various lending agencies? List five different lending agencies which he may use and state the approximate cost connected with borrowing from each.

SELECTED READINGS

Beckman, Theodore N. *Credits and Collections in Theory and Practice,* Seventh Edition. New York: McGraw-Hill Book Co., 1963.

Consumer Finance Industry, The. Washington, D. C.: National Consumer Finance Association, 1962.

Credit Manual of Commercial Laws. New York: National Association of Credit Men. Latest edition.

Credit Union Yearbook. Madison, Wis.: Credit Union National Association. Latest edition.

Croteau, John T. *The Economics of the Credit Union.* Detroit: Wayne State University Press.

Facts You Should Know About Borrowing. New York: National Better Business Bureau. Latest edition.

Finance Facts Yearbook. Washington, D. C.: National Consumer Finance Association. Latest edition.

Foster, William T. *Loan Sharks and Their Victims.* New York: Public Affairs Committee, Inc. Latest edition.

Hawyer, Carl F. *Basic Principles in Family Money and Credit Management.* Washington, D. C.: National Consumer Finance Association, 1962.

Johnson, Robert W. *Methods of Stating Consumer Finance Charges.* New York: Columbia University Press, 1961.

Juster, Francis T. *Consumer Sensitivity to Finance Rates.* New York: National Bureau of Economic Research, 1964.

Life Insurance Fact Book. New York: Institute of Life Insurance. Published annually.

Mors, Wallace P. *Small Loan Laws,* Revised Edition. Cleveland: Bureau of Business Research, Western Reserve University, 1961.

Neifeld, Morris R. *Neifeld's Manual on Consumer Credit.* Easton, Pa.: Mack Publishing Co., 1961.

Savings and Loan Fact Book. Chicago: United States Savings and Loan League. Latest edition.

Shultz, William J., and Reinhardt, Hedwig. *Credit and Collection Management,* Third Edition. Englewood Cliffs, N. J.: Prentice-Hall, Inc., 1962.

Simpson, William H. *America's Small Loan Problem.* Columbia, S. C.: R. L. Bryan Co., 1963.

Wang, Sarah C. *Problems in Implementing Full Disclosure of Consumer Credit Cost.* Honolulu: University of Hawaii, 1962.

Woodstock, Lyle S. *Trends in Consumer Credit Legislation.* St. Louis: Liberty Loan Corp., 1961.

5

Using Your Bank

The commercial bank is the "department store" of finance. An understanding of the commercial bank, the services it performs, and its operating procedures is important, therefore, to the development of a personal financial program. You should become familiar with all of the services of your bank so that you can decide which ones you want to use.

There is evidence that the practices of safekeeping and savings banking flourished as early as 2000 B.C. Modern commercial banking as we know it evolved in Italy, Holland, and England in the early seventeenth century. As the name implies, commercial banking developed for the primary purpose of serving commerce by providing safe and reliable means of transferring money and by making commercial loans. Emphasis on offering services to individuals has developed in commercial banks only since the turn of the century. Consumer lending by banks was practically unknown until the 1930's.

Present-day commercial banking includes the acceptance of deposits for safekeeping and convenience, the granting of loans to meet the needs of individuals and business firms, the investing of funds in government and other obligations, and the creation of net additions to the effective supply of money. It is this last feature, particularly, which distinguishes the commercial bank from other financial institutions.

There are approximately 13,500 commercial banks in the United States. The Federal Reserve System is an organization, created by the federal government, to which commercial banks may belong for purposes of aid in transferring funds between different geographic areas, safe-keeping and investment of surplus funds, and a source of funds in the event of need. The Federal Reserve System serves as a secondary financial system which helps commercial banks meet their liquidity requirements in times of substantial demand. While less than half of the commercial banks in the United States are members of the Federal Reserve System, those that are members account for 80 per cent of all commercial bank assets.

Banks operate under charters conferred by either the federal government or the state in which the bank is organized. National banks—those chartered by the federal government—are examined periodically by representatives of the Comptroller of the Currency. State banks are examined by representatives of the Department of Banks of the chartering state, and by the federal government if they belong to the Federal Deposit Insurance Corporation. All national banks are members of the Federal Reserve System and state banks may be members if they meet certain requirements and so desire. The Federal Reserve System also controls and supervises its member banks. The many laws and regulations governing commercial banking are designed to protect the depositor and borrower as well as to add stability to the national financial system.

Deposits are the primary source of funds for commercial banks. Slightly more than 50 per cent of all bank assets come from demand deposits (checking accounts). In addition, more than 35 per cent of all assets are provided by time deposits (savings accounts). Investment by stockholders, reinvested earnings, and other miscellaneous sources of funds together account for less than 15 per cent of all commercial bank assets.

Funds obtained from deposits are invested in securities and in loans and discounts to businesses and consumers. Almost one fifth of commercial bank assets are kept in cash, deposits in other banks, and reserves in Federal Reserve banks. These three types of cash assets earn nothing for the bank. As a result, the commercial bank's primary sources of income are interest received on securities and loans and from discounts. A secondary source of income is service charges. These income items must be sufficient to pay interest on time deposits, cover all expenses of operation of the banking institution, pay taxes, provide reserves for future losses on securities and loans, and yield a reasonable return to the owners of the bank. Table 5–1 gives the assets and liabilities of all American commercial banks combined.

Insurance on Bank Accounts

In selecting a bank in which to open your account, the safety of your money is naturally one of the prime considerations. It is therefore desirable to select a bank which is a member of the Federal Deposit Insurance Corporation. All banks which are members of this organization are so

Table 5–1. Assets and Liabilities of Commercial Banks—June, 1964 (in millions of dollars)

Account	Amount	%
TOTAL ASSETS	$321,909	100.0
Cash assets	53,168	16.5
U.S. Government obligation	59,322	18.4
Treasury bills	9,061	2.9
Certificates of indebtedness	35	—
Treasury notes	23,141	7.2
Bonds	27,085	8.3
State and local securities	31,419	9.8
Other bonds and notes	4,975	1.5
Loans and discounts	167,713	52.1
Secured by real estate	41,388	12.9
To financial institutions	13,331	4.1
To purchase securities	8,230	2.5
Commercial and industrial loans	55,061	17.1
Personal loans to individuals	37,594	11.7
Agricultural	7,688	2.4
Other	4,421	1.4
Other	5,312	1.7
TOTAL LIABILITIES AND CAPITAL	$321,909	100.0
Demand deposits	164,639	51.1
Time deposits	120,264	37.4
Other liabilities	2,035	.6
Capital accounts	26,358	8.2
Other	8,613	2.7

SOURCE: Federal Reserve Board.

identified by signs. Over 95 per cent of the commercial banks in the United States are insured by the Federal Deposit Insurance Corporation.

A $10,000 insurance limit applies to a single depositor in a single bank. Regardless of the number of accounts a depositor may have in his own name in a given bank, his total insurance will be only $10,000. He may, however, deposit $10,000 in each of an unlimited number of banks and receive full insurance on his funds. A depositor may receive more than $10,000 in insurance in an individual bank if he takes out an account in his own name, a joint account with his wife, an account in his wife's name only, establishes trust accounts, accounts for children, etc. In order for joint accounts to be separately insured, they must include rights of survivorship. *Multiple trust accounts* allowed in some states enable a depositor to have a large number of accounts insured in the same bank. Since it is possible to use different accounts in the same bank, or to use a number of different banks, it would seem unwise for the individual to have any uninsured amounts in commercial banks.

Because of the popular misunderstandings as to the nature of deposit insurance, a word of explanation will be given. The Federal Deposit Insurance Corporation (FDIC) has been established to insure deposits in those banks which are affiliated with the organization. All members of the Federal Reserve System (thus all national banks) are required to join and other sound banks can join if they so desire. The federal government furnished part of the original capital and the Federal Reserve banks contributed the remainder. Each member bank which carries FDIC insurance must pay to the corporation an annual premium for the insurance.

There are two points which must be emphasized. One is that there is no guarantee that accounts up to $10,000 will be paid. They are merely insured. The second point is that it is the Federal Deposit Insurance Corporation, and not the federal government, which is doing the insuring. The total assets of the FDIC are equal to only a fraction of the total deposits which it has insured. In the event that all or a substantial number of the insured banks failed at or near the same time (which of course is not likely to happen), the FDIC would probably be unable to meet the claims of depositors. In this contingency it is probable that the federal government would put more money into the FDIC, but it is under no legal obligation to do so. It should be emphasized that deposits in insured institutions are substantially safer than deposits were before the FDIC was organized. Even in the event of major crisis, it is probable that the insured accounts will hold up because the federal government will undoubtedly come to the aid of the FDIC. The FDIC has paid cash to depositors in all cases of insured bank failure since its inception.

Selecting Your Bank

Since the great majority of banks which are available to the individual depositor are insured by the FDIC, the individual still has the problem of selecting a specific bank. Normally it would be advisable to pick the one which is better managed, although this is difficult to determine. The advice of businessmen on this point may be valuable. The larger institutions often are safer, due to greater diversification of risk. If the available banks have differing service charges, it might be advantageous for the individual to select the bank which would involve the least cost to him.

Convenience is another factor which should not be overlooked. You will probably be going to the bank at least weekly or monthly, so it should be near or accessible to your home or place of employment. If you are running a business, your personal account may be maintained in the same bank in which you have your business account. In some cities, one or more banks have branches located in various parts of the city to offer more convenience to the depositors. Some people, however, find it more convenient to make deposits by mail. These people may never visit their bank from one year to another. Some banks may be more convenient because they offer a wide variety of special services such as travelers' checks, United States savings bond sales, etc., which the depositor may use from time to time.

CHECKING ACCOUNTS

A *checking account* is a deposit account in a commercial bank against which withdrawals are made on demand through written orders (checks) to the bank. Today practically all business transactions are consummated with checks and an increasing percentage of personal transactions are handled in the same manner. The principal advantages of a checking account are the convenience of writing checks to pay bills and the fact that the canceled checks serve as receipts. The checking account also offers a safe place for keeping your money. There is some prestige attached to having such an account; your banking connection is normally requested when seeking employment or applying for credit.

Opening a Checking Account

Opening an account at a bank is a simple affair and requires only a few minutes' time. The depositor usually fills out a card in duplicate giving his name, address, telephone number, occupation, and signature. He will normally be given a passbook and a checkbook. The passbook gives a record of deposits made. It is not used in withdrawal—it is necessary for you to sign a check before the bank is authorized to pay money out of your account.

You may authorize others to withdraw from your account by a special authorization. This is done, in some cases, in connection with the payment of bills. An insurance company, for example, may be authorized by you to draw a monthly check on your account to pay your monthly insurance premium. This saves you the trouble of writing the check but requires you to remember the authorization and to deduct the amount withdrawn from your check stub balance each month.

Joint Account

Husbands and wives usually find it desirable to have joint checking accounts at commercial banks. In a *joint account,* either party may make deposits or withdraw funds by signing a check. If a husband and wife have separate checking accounts, the minimum monthly charge which the bank makes for an account would have to be paid by each of them. If they have a joint account, the average balance would be higher, so the monthly charge would be less, and the minimum would have to be paid only once for the family. Joint accounts make total family funds more readily accessible to either husband or wife.

A further advantage of this plan would become evident upon the death of one of the parties. Upon the death of a man who carried an account in his name only, the bank will refuse to honor any checks which the wife may attempt to write against his account. Checks written before his death, but which had not been returned to the bank for collection, would likewise not be honored. These creditors would have to look to the estate of the deceased for payment. The wife will be able to draw against the account only when she has been appointed administrator of the estate, or has been otherwise authorized by the law. If the husband and the wife have a *joint tenancy with the right of survivorship* account, although the bank will hold up payment of checks immediately after the death of one of the parties, the surviving party can have the bank request a clearance from the tax commission. This release can usually be secured immediately and will give the wife the right to draw on all or a designated part of the account.

In many states, upon the death of a joint owner of an account, the inheritance tax is applied to only half of the account balance. The federal estate tax, however, is applied to the entire amount unless the survivor can prove that he (or she) contributed to the account.

The joint account may at times result in some confusion and embarrassment. If both parties have their own checkbooks, each should deduct the checks written by the other as well as his own checks on his check stub. When two checkbooks are maintained, a tally should be made daily or weekly, or at least frequently enough to insure that one of the parties will not, by writing a check, produce an overdraft because some earlier check had not been recorded on both check stubs.

Making a Deposit

When you make a deposit in a checking account, it is necessary to fill out a *deposit slip.* Where a passbook is used, it should be given to the teller along with the deposit slip and the items being deposited. The depositor does not have to have the passbook with him to make a deposit. The deposit can be made by filling out a duplicate deposit slip, which the cashier will stamp as evidence that he has made the deposit. The next time the depositor makes a deposit and has the passbook with him, the duplicate deposit slip should be given to the cashier so that he can fill in the amount in the book. Duplicate deposit slips (automatically filled out) are used in many banks instead of passbooks.

Although all money deposited is immediately credited to the account of the depositor, the contract between the bank and the depositor provides that deposited checks drawn on other banks are subject to collection. Even though such checks are immediately recorded on the passbook of the depositor, he should not attempt to write checks against the sums they represent until the bank has had sufficient time to collect them. This time varies from two days, for checks drawn on banks in the same city, to ten days for those drawn on more distant banks.

All checks deposited in an account must be endorsed by the depositor. In addition to money and checks, money orders and bond interest coupons may also be deposited in a checking account. Some individuals arrange with their bank and employer to have their salary checks sent directly to the bank, to be immediately deposited to their account. If the bank does not notify the depositor of the receipt of the check, it would be advisable for him always to make sure the bank has received it before drawing against it.

Deposits may also be mailed to the bank. Normally it is inadvisable to mail currency or coin. Instead of enclosing the passbook, it is advisable to send in a duplicate deposit slip. The bank will stamp this and mail it back to the depositor. Some banks have arrangements that permit the depositor to leave his deposit at the bank outside regular banking hours through a night depository.

Bank Statements

At the time the account is opened, arrangements should be made regarding the return of canceled checks. It is generally advisable to obtain a statement of one's account from the bank at regular intervals—normally every month. A statement will list all deposits and all checks and other amounts charged against the account. The canceled checks will be enclosed with the statement.

Service Charges

Most banks charge for their checking account service. Usually all the banks in the same city charge the same amount. Charges tend to be higher in larger cities than in smaller ones. When charges are made, they are usually so much per check written against the account, and so much for each deposit made or for each separate check deposited. In addition to the specific charges, many banks will also add a monthly maintenance charge or will operate on a minimum charge per month regardless of the number of transactions. Sometimes charges are made only if the minimum in the account drops below a certain amount during the period. Many banks with service charges allow a credit against those charges for minimum monthly balances. Banks do not pay interest on amounts deposited in checking accounts. However, if the bank allows a credit against service charges for the amount deposited, it is in effect paying an interest on that amount. No extra amount is paid, however, if the earnings on the minimum balance are more than enough to absorb the service charges.

A typical schedule of charges and credits for banks in medium-sized cities would be as follows: 3 cents charged on each check written against the account; 10 cents for each deposit made; and a monthly maintenance charge of 60 cents. A typical credit against service charges would be 10 cents per hundred dollars of minimum monthly balance. Thus, if an individual made two deposits during a month and wrote 15 checks, his total service charge would be $1.25. If his minimum balance during the month was $410, he would receive a 40-cent credit against the charges, which would make his net charge 85 cents.

Special Checking Accounts

Some of the banks in large cities require a minimum amount ranging from $500 to $2,000 to start a regular checking account. This is more than the average person has available to put into a checking account. At the present time a number of banks have special types of checking accounts designed to meet the needs of the average depositor. A number of different titles—"Check-Master," "Special Checking Account," "Pay-As-You-Go," "ThriftiCheck" plans—are used to apply to these special accounts.

The exact nature of the special plan varies among banks, but the following is an example. At the time of making the deposit a number of blank checks are purchased. The charge made by the bank for each check is normally 10 cents, and this is paid at the time the checks are purchased. A standard book of 20 checks is also often sold. There is ordinarily no additional charge for making a deposit. Some of these accounts carry a minimum monthly charge.

These special accounts should only be used when the cost of the special account is less than the service charges on a regular account. If you are able to keep a fairly large minimum balance, a regular account is usually less expensive and, therefore, more desirable.

Overdrafts

If a depositor writes a check when his account balance is too low to cover the entire amount of the check, it is called an *overdraft*. In many states the statutes provide for a penitentiary sentence for anyone who fraudulently issues a check when there are insufficient funds in his account to cover the instrument. Subsequent payment of the bad check with cash or a good check does not necessarily release the depositor from prosecution.

If all the people who have written checks when they had insufficient funds to cover them were put into the penitentiaries, there would be no room for the real criminals. Many people overdraw their accounts through mere carelessness in failing to keep their checkbook stubs up to date. When the check comes to the bank, they will probably call the depositor by telephone and inform him that there are insufficient funds in his account. In an attempt to cut down the practice of creating overdrafts, some banks make a flat charge such as 50 cents or $1 for every overdraft. Prosecution for overdrafts is rare. Most of the overdrafts are not made with any intent to defraud, and that is realized by the parties involved. But the fact remains that a check should never be written unless there are sufficient funds in the account to cover it. Proper maintenance of check stubs is the best guard against writing overdrafts.

Stopping Payment

If for some reason the drawer of a check does not want his bank to honor a check which he has written, he may order it to stop payment. This, of course, is effective only when it is done before the bank has paid the check. The reason for such *stop-payment order* does not necessarily have to be given, but the bank will usually inquire.

There are various reasons why the drawer might not want the bank to pay the check. The goods for which he gave the check may not be what the seller guaranteed them to be, or perhaps the seller refused to turn over the goods after the check had been given. Sometimes checks given for gambling debts have payment stopped by the drawer. If a check is lost by the payee or is lost in the mails, the drawer should stop payment on it before writing a new check.

When a stop-payment order is given, the bank will usually require the drawer to sign a statement. The statement specifies that if the bank, through error, goes ahead and pays the check despite the stop-payment order, the bank will not be liable to the drawer for damages.

Certified Checks

Where the drawer of the check is unknown to the person to whom he gives or sends it, the latter may require that the check be certified. The drawer must then take the check to his bank and ask the cashier that it be certified. The bank will stamp the word "certified" on the face of the check and an appropriate officer of the bank will sign his name underneath. The bank in effect deducts the amount from the drawer's account immediately, rather than after the check is presented for payment, which would be done in the case of an ordinary check.

Such certification indicates to the person to whom the check is given that the drawer has sufficient funds to meet the check, and, furthermore, the bank by this act promises that it will pay the check. Since the bank has already deducted the amount of the check from the drawer's account, subsequent checks written by the drawer cannot jeopardize the payment of the certified check, even if these checks are presented for payment before the certified check. Banks in medium-sized cities usually charge 25 cents for certifying checks.

In contrast to ordinary checks, certified checks are not returned to the drawer after they have been paid. Since the bank assumes liability on the check as a result of its certification, it keeps the canceled check as a receipt that it has been paid.

Bank Statement Reconciliation

When the bank statement is received periodically from the bank, the depositor should immediately go over it to see that all entries are proper. The bank statement lists the amount of each check, and other charges such as bank service charges. It also gives the previous balance, deposits made, and the new balance at the end of the statement. Rarely is the statement balance the same as that recorded on the check stub for the corresponding date. One reason is that the check stub balance naturally does not give effect to the service charges. It is probable that the depositor has written some checks which were not presented to the bank for payment by the time the statement was prepared. Also, it is possible that a deposit was made at the bank after the statement was prepared. There is the possibility of error on the part of either the bank or the depositor—the latter being by far the more common.

The bank reconciliation should be made in such a manner as to indicate to the depositor the amount of funds he has on deposit at the bank against which checks can be drawn. This is normally neither the amount which the bank shows as the balance nor the amount on the check stub balance. Outstanding checks should be subtracted from the bank statement balance. Any deposits in transit should then be added to the resulting balance, and this will be the amount against which the depositor may actually write checks. If there are no errors in the check stub balance, a deduction of the amount of the bank service charges from the check stub balance should give this same amount. If the two do not balance, an error has been made somewhere along the line. If the depositor is certain that the error is not on his part, he should immediately notify the bank. When the two balances are reconciled, it is advisable to indicate when the book was balanced and the number and the amount of the outstanding checks. This makes bank reconciliation at the end of the next period less difficult.

Figure 5–1 gives an example of a bank statement reconciliation. The checks outstanding were determined by going through the canceled

Balance on bank statement		$321.14
Plus: deposit mailed in but not yet received		68.00
		$389.14
Less: outstanding checks		
no. 131	$ 6.18	
no. 139	15.00	
no. 140	45.55	
no. 141	3.09	69.82
Actual available balance		$319.32
Balance on checkbook stub		$330.34
Less: bank service charges for month		1.02
		$329.32
Less: error found in subtracting check no. 137 from check stub balance		10.00
Actual available balance		$319.32

Fig. 5–1. Bank statement reconciliation.

checks received from the bank and comparing them against the check entries in the checkbook stubs. Checks which have been written but not received from the bank are listed as outstanding. The same approach is taken in determining deposits in transit. The amount of the bank service charge is obtained from the bank statement itself and from the charge slips which most banks include with the canceled checks. If an individual does not wait too long between reconciliations, he will find that it is not a difficult task.

Reconciliation is important because bank errors may be found, but even more important is the fact that it will indicate to the depositor the exact amount against which he may write checks in the future. He would not know this if he did not reconcile his check stub balance and bank statement balance. Going through the canceled checks enables him to determine if any checks he did not write have been charged against his account. In this way forgeries and mischarges are discovered. It is also important to determine that his account has been credited with all the deposits which were actually made. It is very important that service charges and errors be entered in the check stub balance so that this balance is up to date.

Canceled checks and bank statements should be filed away, not destroyed. Canceled checks serve as receipts, and sometime in the future

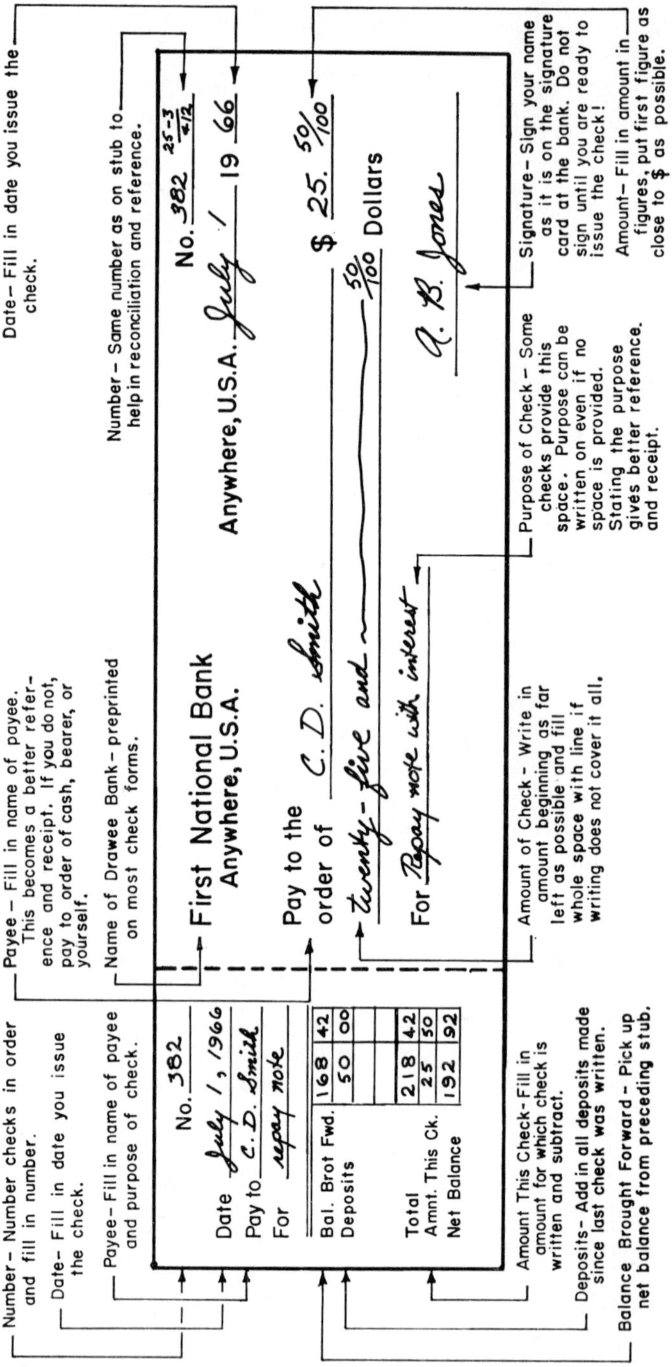

Fig. 5–2. How to write a check and fill in the check stub.

it may be necessary to produce one in order to show that a particular bill has been paid. According to the statutes of a number of states, if a creditor does not bring an action on an unwritten debt within a period of seven years from the time the debt was incurred, he loses his legal right to collect. Thus, it is advisable to retain canceled checks for at least seven years.

THE CHECK

An ordinary check is the most common kind of bill of exchange. *Bills of exchange* are written instruments drawn by one party ordering another party to pay to the order of a third party a stated amount of money. A check is a bill of exchange written by a drawer ordering his bank to pay upon demand a certain amount to the order of the payee. No printed form is necessary for writing a check. Checks may be written upon any piece of paper as long as the words include the necessary elements of a check. Commonly, banks provide check forms which can be used by the drawer in writing his checks. These may be blank, or a specific bank's name and sometimes the name of the drawer may be preprinted on the check form. Some preprinted checks have the name and number of the bank and the name and number of the depositor printed in magnetic ink, in special characters. This is for speedier check clearing and for more accurate recognition in sorting checks by bank and by accounts.

Writing the Check

Many people believe that a check has to be written in ink or filled in on a typewriter. A check may, however, be written in pencil. The danger in using a pencil—unless it is indelible—is that the amount of the check may be altered. Such a loss would not necessarily fall on the drawer of the check, unless the court held him to be negligent in using a pencil. Nevertheless, in order to make it more difficult for alterations to be made, ink should be used in writing checks. Many companies use check writers which print the name of the payee and the amount in such a way that alteration is extremely difficult.

You will note that the sample check in Fig. 5–2 has a group of numbers preprinted in the upper right-hand corner. These numbers represent the particular bank's transit number and the Federal Reserve District number. They are not necessary for the check to be transferred, but do facilitate check clearing on the part of the banks. Also preprinted is the name of the city in which the bank is located. This is the place where the check must eventually be presented for payment. Of course, the name of the bank itself is also on the form. In addition, to meet the requirement of negotiability, every check must include the words "pay to the order of."

For the convenience of the drawer these words are normally preprinted on the check form.

For the drawer's own convenience, the checks should be numbered. Banks pay no attention to this numbering, and from a legal standpoint, it is not necessary. However, it is very helpful to the drawer in reconciling his bank statement. The date the check is drawn should be stated in the space provided.

A check should not ordinarily be dated in advance (postdated) because it will not be honored by the bank, unless the bank fails to notice the date. If the bank notices the postdating, it will dishonor the check. Individuals sometimes date a check in advance to take care of some debt, asking the creditor not to cash the check until the date has arrived. This may prove embarrassing to the drawer if his deposit to cover the check cannot be made by that date and the creditor presents the check for payment. Also, the creditor is under no legal obligation to hold the check until the date given. It is better practice to postpone writing the check until the time has arrived when you are willing to have that check presented for payment. Predating a check may also result in the bank's refusing payment if the date is too long before the time of presentment.

The check should be made payable to the particular person or company to whom the drawer wishes to give payment. Although the payee (the person to whom the check is payable) could cash the check if it were made out to "Bearer," or "Cash," the drawer may want to use the canceled check as proof that he has paid this amount to a particular person. Since the payee must endorse the check exactly as his name appears on the face of the check, the drawer should use the correct name of the person or the company in making out the check. If you are withdrawing money from your checking account at the bank, you may make the check payable to "Cash," or it can be made payable to the bank itself.

In filling in the check, the amount in figures should be put immediately after the dollar sign, as close to it as possible. If a space is left between the dollar sign and the amount, some dishonest person may raise the amount by placing another number there. A decimal point can be used to separate the dollars and the cents in the amount. A check for $25.50 can be expressed in one of the following ways: $25.50; or $25 $\frac{50}{100}$; or $25 $\frac{50}{xx}$. Use of one of the latter two methods would probably make alteration more difficult. Where no cents are involved, zeros should still be filled in to prevent alteration.

The line below the one which contains the payee's name and the figures is for repetition of the amount, but here it is to be written out. The writing should begin at the extreme left-hand side of the check so that no one can raise the amount. For a check in the amount stated above, you would simply write: "Twenty-five and $\frac{50}{100}$" (the word "dollars" is printed at the end of the line). If the amount of the check is less than one dollar—50 cents, for example—it could be written "$\frac{50}{100}$" or "only fifty cents." To make it difficult for anyone to write in anything on this line a wavy line should be drawn between the end of your statement and the word "dollars."

If there is a discrepancy between the amount expressed in figures and the amount as written out, the bank probably will not honor the check, but the law provides that the amount as written out will prevail.

The drawer's signature on the check should conform to the way it appears on the card he signed at the time his checking account was opened. If a person is an officer of an organization and signs a check or other instrument for that organization, he should be careful to use the correct form of signature, in order not to render himself personally liable. The following is a correct form for such a signature:

The Standard Company
per, Robert M. Brown, Treasurer.

The word "by" could be used instead of "per." In many instances neither of these prefixes is used, but their presence indicates clearly that Robert M. Brown is signing only for the company. If the signature was merely "Robert M. Brown, Treasurer," without naming the company, and the other party did not know it was a company check, Brown could be held personally liable on the check.

The Check Stub

Most checkbooks include a stub such as the one shown in Fig. 5–2 for each check included in the book. The check stub should be filled in completely at the same time that the check itself is written. This will preclude the necessity of reliance upon memory at a future date. The check stub should clearly indicate the date, the amount of the check, and the payee. Many people also find it useful to include on the check stub a statement of the purpose for which the check was written. If a blank check is used, or if a regular check is written when the check stub or checkbook is not at hand, the depositor should remember to record the check on the stub at the earliest opportunity.

Check Endorsements

A check made payable to a particular person is referred to as an *order* instrument and the endorsement of that particular person is necessary to transfer the check. If a check is made payable to "Bearer," or "Cash," it is called a *bearer* instrument and the endorsement of the holder is not legally necessary in order to negotiate the instrument to another party.

As a practical matter, however, he will probably have to endorse it before the other party will accept it. Endorsements make the endorser liable to the holder in case the instrument is dishonored by the drawee. Any number of people may endorse a check, and the recipient of a check should always require the endorsement of the person from whom he receives the check, regardless of the way in which the check is made out. The most common endorsements are discussed below.

Blank Endorsement. If a check is drawn by A. B. Jones on the First National Bank and is made payable to the order of C. D. Smith, the latter may endorse the instrument in one of several different ways. If he does what most people do, he merely turns the check over and writes across the left-hand end "C. D. Smith." This is called a *blank* endorsement. Such an endorsement has the effect of making the check a bearer instrument and, as such, title to it can be passed from hand to hand without any further endorsements being necessary.

Restrictive Endorsement. If a check is presented or sent to the bank for deposit to Smith's account, he can endorse it as follows:

For deposit only,
C. D. Smith

This is called a *restrictive* endorsement and, as the title indicates, the endorsement limits the transfer to one purpose, that of depositing the check to Smith's account.

Special Endorsement. If Smith uses the check to pay a debt to E. F. Roberts, he can endorse it as follows:

Pay to the order of E. F. Roberts
C. D. Smith

This is called a *special* endorsement. The check remains an order instrument by this form of endorsement. Before anyone can get title to the check, it would be necessary for E. F. Roberts to endorse it; the forgery of Roberts' name would still not pass title. Such a check would be safer in Roberts' hands than if it had been endorsed in blank. Although the use of the phrase "order of" preceding the payee's name on the face of the check is necessary in order to make it a negotiable instrument, the special endorsement has the same effect when it says "Pay to E. F. Roberts" as when it says "Pay to the order of E. F. Roberts."

If Smith had used the blank endorsement, and Roberts lost the check or it was stolen from him, a finder or thief could pass good title. There is a way, however, that Roberts may protect himself, even if the blank endorsement has been used. He may convert Smith's blank endorsement into a special endorsement by writing above Smith's endorsement: "Pay to E. F. Roberts." This procedure is not considered to be an alteration of the instrument.

Restrictive and Special Endorsements. The combination of the *restrictive* and the *special* endorsements is often used when a check is being deposited. This is probably the best form to use under this circumstance. It can be made in one of the following two forms:

For deposit only Pay to the order of The Second National Bank C. D. Smith	Pay to the order of The Second National Bank only for deposit to the account of C. D. Smith

With such an endorsement no one can cash the check and appropriate the money. Business houses usually have a rubber stamp made with one of the above forms of endorsement.

Qualified Endorsement. Another form of endorsement, called the *qualified* endorsement, may be used. It is made by the addition of the words "Without recourse" to the endorsement. Following are examples of this type of endorsement:

Without recourse C. D. Smith	Pay to the order of E. F. Roberts Without recourse C. D. Smith

The purpose of using the qualified endorsement is to limit the liability of the endorser. The difference between the liability of the blank endorser, the restrictive or special endorser, and the qualified endorser will be explained in a later section.

Joint Endorsement. If the payee is two or more people as joint tenants with rights of survivorship and not as tenants in common, both parties would have to endorse the check. This is called a *joint* endorsement. If the check is payable to C. D. Smith or Susan Smith, either party could endorse the check and transfer it.

Drawer's Liability

When a drawer signs his name to a check, it constitutes an order by him to the bank on which the check is drawn (the drawee) to pay to the person indicated (the payee) or his order the amount stated. The drawer is not immediately liable on the check at the time it is issued. If the check is written in payment of a bill, the creditor cannot demand cash from the drawer of the check unless he presents the check to the bank and the bank refuses for some reason to pay the check. If the bank refuses to pay the check, the drawer becomes liable on the check after the holder gives the drawer due notice of dishonor. (What constitutes due presentment and due notice will be discussed later.)

If someone forges the drawer's name to a check, in the absence of negligence on the part of the drawer, he is not liable. Should the bank pay this check out of his account, the drawer can recover from the bank. If, however, the bank returns some canceled checks to the drawer and he does not look them over and notify the bank of the forgery, although the bank is responsible for having paid out on these checks, it is not liable on any similar forgeries occurring between the time the first canceled forged checks are returned to the drawer and the time he notifies the bank of the forgeries.

In case the endorsement on a check is forged, the law takes the attitude that parties subsequent to the forgery do not get title to the instrument. Should the bank honor a check on which the endorsement is forged, it is not permitted to charge the drawer's account; should it do so, the drawer can recover from the bank. The bank is not necessarily the loser here, because it has a legal right to recover from the person who presented the check to the bank.

It must be remembered that the most common reason for a bank's refusal to honor a check is insufficient funds. Upon receipt of due notice of dishonor of his check, the drawer becomes liable to the holder of the check. If the bank refuses to honor the check through error on its own part, the drawer is still liable after receipt of due notice of dishonor. If a bank wrongly refuses to honor a check, the drawer (not the holder) has a legal right against the bank for any damages which he may have incurred as a result of the bank's actions.

Since the drawee bank is obligated by its contract with the drawer to honor all checks signed by him which are duly presented for payment, the drawer should never put his name on a check unless he wants the bank to honor it. While the drawer has certain limited legal defenses, it is well to keep in mind that these defenses generally apply only to the payee and not to other holders in due course.

Rights of Payee

The payee (or holder in due course) naturally has the right to payment of the check by the drawee bank. The check, of course, does not have to be taken directly to the drawee bank. It may be deposited by the payee in another bank or cashed there, or the payee may endorse the check and pass it on to someone else.

If a check is not presented for payment within a reasonable length of time after it is issued, and if the drawee bank should fail in the meantime, the payee (or holder) will not be able to hold the drawer liable on the check. The law holds that if the drawee bank is in the same city as the payee, one day is a reasonable time. So long as the drawee bank does not fail, the check would be good if it is presented within the time specified within the statute of limitations in the particular state. This period, for written instruments, in many states is 15 to 21 years. Bank practice, however, is not to honor checks dated substantially before the date presented—usually three months, six months, or one year.

There is still another step which must be taken by the payee (or holder) to preserve the liability of a drawer of a check, if the bank dishonors the instrument. In addition to making due presentment of the check, the payee must give the drawer notice of dishonor within a reasonable length of time after such dishonor. Here again, one day is considered reasonable. If the payee resides in a different city, the notice must be started on its way by the next day.

Liability of Endorsers

Two types of liability are assumed by the endorser of a check: *conditional* liability, and *unconditional* liability. If C. D. Smith endorses his name in blank on the back of the check, he says, in effect, that if the check is duly presented for payment to the First National Bank (the drawee) and is dishonored, and due notice of such dishonor is given to him, he will pay the amount of the check to the holder. If E. F. Roberts endorses the check in blank, he assumes the same liability. This liability is conditioned upon due presentment, dishonor, and due notice of dishonor. The conditional liability applies to practically all reasons for dishonor of the check by the bank. In effect, an endorser who assumes the conditional liability states that he will pay the amount of the check to the holder if the bank refuses to pay. Blank, restrictive, and special endorsers are all subject to the conditional liability. Qualified endorsers are not subject to this liability.

In addition to the conditional liability, endorsers, as sellers of personal property, make certain guarantees relating to the check. These comprise the unconditional liability. Each endorser who does not qualify his endorsement makes the following warranties:

1. That the check is genuine and is in all respects what it purports to be
2. That he has good title to it
3. That all prior parties had capacity to contract
4. That the check, at the time of his endorsement, is valid.

The endorser by these warranties guarantees that the check was actually issued and that the drawer's name was not forged; that prior endorsements were not forged; that the drawer and prior endorsers were of the required legal age necessary to contract in that particular state; that there are no defenses which would prevent the payment; and that the check has not already been paid. The requirements of presentment, dishonor, and notice are not necessary to hold the endorser liable under the unconditional liabilities.

If an endorser *qualifies* his endorsement—that is, adds the phrase "Without recourse"—he relieves himself of the conditional liability. This is the reason he would use the qualified form of endorsement. But the qualified endorser still makes certain warranties in regard to the check. These warranties are the same as for the unqualified endorser, except for the fourth warranty listed above. Instead of guaranteeing that the check is valid at the time of his endorsement, he warrants that he had *no knowledge* of any fact which would impair the validity of the instrument or render it valueless. Thus, the qualified endorsement does not relieve the endorser of liability under the unconditional liabilities. The qualified endorsement is rarely used because most people will not accept a check with a qualified endorsement.

Endorsers are liable in the order in which they endorse. If the holder of the check cannot collect from the bank, he can look to the drawer or to the previous endorsers. If he sought to recover from the drawer, it would be necessary for the check to have been duly presented to the bank, and due notice given as explained above. If the holder sought to collect from the previous endorsers, there must also have been due presentment and due notice of dishonor. The rule regarding due notice is the same as that applicable to the drawer; that is, notice by the day following dishonor. However, the time element for due presentment is different. To preserve the conditional liability of the endorsers, the check has to be presented to the drawee bank within a reasonable length of time after its last negotiation. What constitutes "reasonable" depends upon the circumstances and customs of the community. It varies from a few days to a few weeks at most.

It is necessary for the holder of a check, upon due presentment and dishonor, to give notice of dishonor to whichever party he goes against not later than the day following dishonor. Thus, the safest thing to do would be to give notice to all endorsers and to the drawer. It must be kept in mind that only the preceding endorsers upon the check are liable to the holder.

Bearer Instruments

If the transferor of a *bearer instrument* does not endorse the instrument, he cannot be held liable as an endorser. In other words, he does not possess the conditional liability which attaches to the normal endorsement. But the transferor is still a seller of personal property, and as such, impliedly makes certain guarantees relating to the instrument he is transferring. The warranties he makes are exactly the same as those made by the qualified endorser, but the warranties made by the qualified endorser extend to all subsequent holders, while those of the transferor without endorsement extend only to his immediate transferee. Thus, the transferor of a bearer instrument has the liabilities of a qualified endorser to his immediate transferee but has no liability to any other recipient of the bearer instrument.

Precautions in Using Checks

Never write a check unless there are sufficient funds in your checking account to cover it. Make the check out in ink and fill all spaces on the form. Do this in such a way that it would be difficult for anyone to alter the check. Complete the checkbook stub at the same time the check is written.

It is a good policy for the average individual never to accept a check from a stranger. Business houses cannot always follow this policy, but they can require sufficient identification of the person to cut down the possibility of loss. There are a number of reasons why you should be cautious in accepting checks. The drawer's name may be forged. In this event the account of the person whose name appears as drawer cannot be charged. The only recourse for you, as the holder, would be to look to the party from whom you have accepted the check or to a prior party. Even if the drawer's signature is genuine, one of the endorsements may be a forgery. If this is the case, you do not get any title to the check. Thus, you will not be able to collect even on a check which has been properly issued by such a sound organization as the United States government. Your major recourse in a dishonored check is the party who gave you the check. Thus, it is important that you know or can reasonably identify this party. Checks which have obviously been altered in any way should not be accepted. It is not advisable to accept checks which are more than a few days old.

When you accept a check, it is advisable that you deposit it or cash it at your bank that day or the day following, rather than negotiate it to another party. The bank will present it for collection immediately, whereas another party may hold it for some time or negotiate it to still another party. If the check has been duly presented for payment and is dishonored, you, as the holder, should immediately notify all the endorsers and the drawer.

When checks are deposited in the bank you should use the restrictive or special endorsement, or a combination of these. If you receive a check which is a bearer instrument, endorsement is not legally necessary, and if the other party will accept it from you without your endorsement, it is advisable not to endorse it. When an endorsement is necessary, if the other party will accept a qualified endorsement, it may be to your advantage to use it. On the other hand, never accept a check which is not endorsed by the transferor and never accept a check with a qualified endorsement.

TRANSFERS OF MONEY

In our complex economy, transfers of value are very important. Since money in the form of coin and currency is subject to loss and theft, a complex system for the transfer of money values has been developed through the use of various types of bills of exchange. The ordinary check is the most common type of bill of exchange, but a number of others are used. Because a great majority of these money transfer arrangements can be made through commercial banks, they are included in this chapter, although some of the instruments described cannot be purchased at commercial banks.

Bills of exchange which are drawn and payable in the United States are called *domestic* bills. Those drawn here but payable in a foreign country are referred to as *foreign* bills. The term *draft* is commonly used to designate a domestic bill of exchange. A *sight* draft is one that is payable on "sight" or "presentation," and is considered to be payable on demand. A *time* draft is payable a designated number of days after date, sight, or presentation. In the latter instances the date of "sight" or "presentation" is the date of acceptance of the draft.

Bank Draft

A bank draft is a check written by one bank on its account in another bank. The rights and liabilities of the parties to a bank draft are exactly the same as in the case of an ordinary check. Many banks in cities throughout the country maintain checking accounts in banks in other cities. If a person in New Orleans wants to pay a bill to a person in New York City, he may, instead of taking the risk of sending cash through the mail, purchase a draft from his New Orleans bank which is drawn on that bank's account in a New York City bank. The need for a bank draft may arise when the New York seller demands payment in New York funds. A charge is usually made for these drafts.

Cashier's Check

A cashier's check is one which a bank draws on itself. The bank deposits a given amount in its cashier's account, and when the demand arises, the bank's cashier draws checks upon this account. On such checks the drawer and the drawee are, of course, really the same party—the bank.

Cashier's checks are more readily acceptable than ordinary personal checks. If you are not certain of the credit of the person with whom you are dealing, it is advisable to get a cashier's check or a certified check, rather than accept the ordinary check of the individual. Cashier's checks are also used at times by people who have no checking account and do not wish to run the risk of making payment in money. A common charge for a cashier's check is 25 cents.

Bank Money Order

A bank money order (Fig. 5–3) is similar to the cashier's check in that it is drawn by a particular bank on itself. It differs from a cashier's check

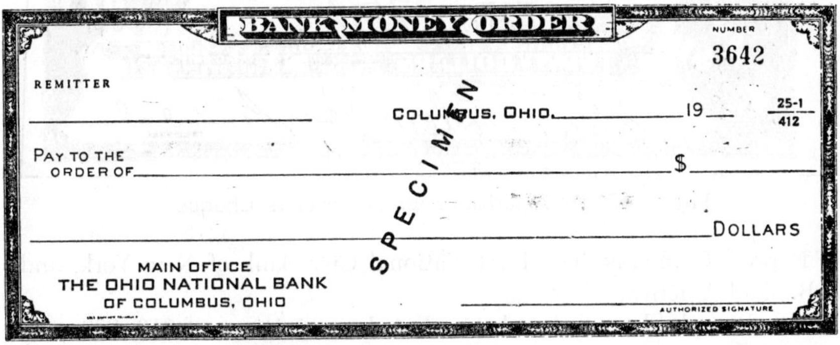

BANK MONEY ORDER

NUMBER 3642

REMITTER

COLUMBUS, OHIO. ______ 19__ 25-1/412

PAY TO THE ORDER OF ______ $______

______ DOLLARS

SPECIMEN

MAIN OFFICE
THE OHIO NATIONAL BANK
OF COLUMBUS, OHIO

AUTHORIZED SIGNATURE

Fig. 5–3. A bank money order.

in that the name of the remitter (the person buying the check) is written on the check in the space provided in the upper left-hand corner. The instrument is made payable to the person or firm that the remitter wishes to receive payment. The other important difference between this and the cashier's check relates to its form. The bank money order may have a detachable stub which shows the date, remitter's name, to whom it is payable, and the amount. The stub is retained as a receipt by the remitter. Another form of the bank money order is made out in triplicate. The first copy goes to the payee, the bank retains the third copy for its records, and the second copy is retained as a receipt by the remitter. In either case, the remitter ends up with a receipt for his payment, which he does not have for a cashier's check. Bank money orders are not available at all banks or in all cities.

Travelers' Checks

When traveling, people have need for rather large amounts of cash, but it is too risky to carry much money with them, and many strangers will not accept their personal checks. Before leaving home it may therefore be advisable to purchase travelers' checks. These travelers' checks (Fig. 5–4) may be drawn by a bank on itself, or they may be drawn on a bank in one of the larger cities. In either case they would be a form of bank draft and will usually be accepted by strangers without further identification. The most common travelers' checks are those of the Ameri-

Fig. 5–4. An American Express Travelers' Cheque.

can Express Company, The First National City Bank of New York, and the Bank of America.

Travelers' checks may be obtained in denominations of $10, $20, $50, and $100. At the time they are purchased the buyer must sign all the checks in the space provided at the top. The checks are serially numbered, and the purchaser should keep a record of these numbers for notification in case the checks are lost. When the buyer wishes to use one of the checks, he fills in the name of the city and the state where he is cashing it, the date, the name of the payee, and then signs his name at the bottom of the check.

The cost of the American Express Company Travelers' Cheques is one per cent of the total amount purchased, with a minimum charge of 50 cents. The charges for designated amounts would thus be as follows:

Amount	Cost
$ 10	$ 0.50
50	0.50
100	1.00
500	5.00
1,000	10.00

Postal Money Order

Persons wishing to send money through the mails, particularly those who have no checking account, commonly use postal money orders (Fig. 5–5). These are sold at post offices throughout the country. After filling in the specific amount, the sender writes in the name of the person to

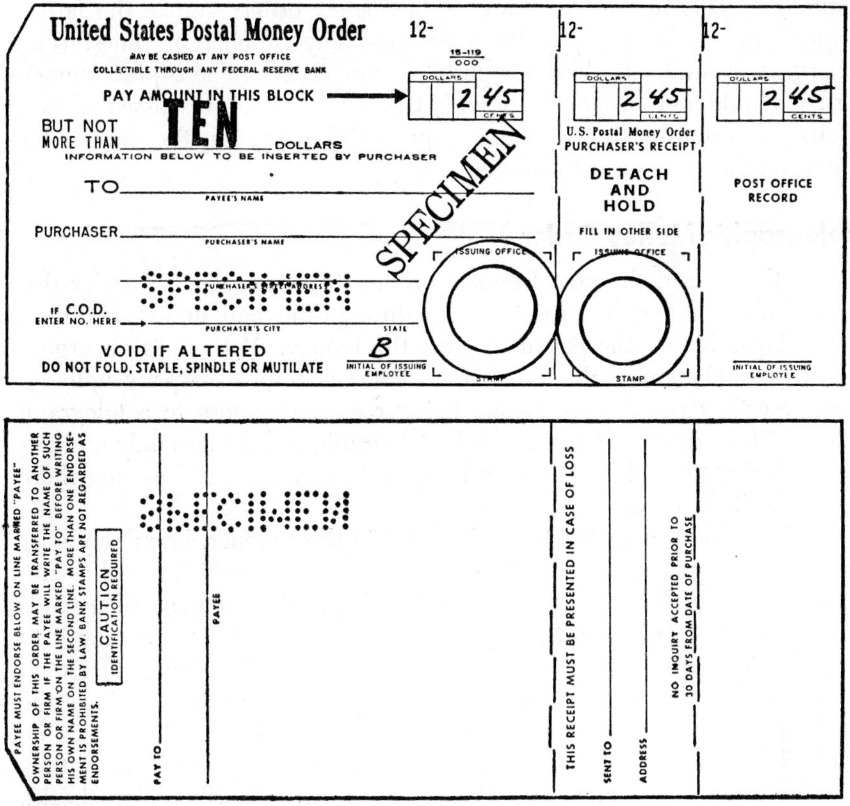

Fig. 5–5. Front (*top*) and reverse (*bottom*) sides of a postal money order.

whom he will send the order, and his own name and address. He also fills in the reverse side of the receipt stub and detaches it before mailing the order. The cost of the order varies according to its amount. Following are the rates for orders sent anywhere in the United States:

For orders from	
\$ 0.01 to \$ 10.00	\$0.25
\$10.01 to \$ 50.00	0.35
\$50.01 to \$100.00	0.40

A postal money order cannot be purchased for an amount in excess of \$100. If it is desired to send a larger amount than this, two or more postal money orders must be purchased.

Express Money Order

Express money orders are very similar to postal money orders except that they are issued on the American Express Company and are sold at express offices and various retail outlets. While express money orders are limited to $100 maximum as are postal money orders, unlike the latter, express money orders may be transferred any number of times. The charges are similar to those for postal money orders. The express money order should not be confused with travelers' checks, discussed above. Both are issued by the American Express Company, but the reasons for their purchase are usually different.

Telegraphic Money Order

In the case of the postal money order and express money order discussed above, the order or note is sent through the mail, and several days may elapse before the payee receives the money. If there is an urgent need to send money, the Western Union Telegraph Company will sell money orders payable to anyone living reasonably close to a telegraph office. These orders, of course, go by telegraph, and it takes only an hour or so during normal hours to send money to a person residing anywhere in the United States.

When a person wishes to send money in this manner, he merely goes to the telegraph office or agent. Cash for the amount which is to be sent, plus the cost of the order, is given to the clerk. The company then sends a telegram to its office in the city where the payee resides, directing it to pay the designated amount to the payee named. The receiving office then draws a check on its bank account for the proper amount payable to the order of the person to whom the money is sent. These checks will be cashed by any of the telegraph company's offices or agencies, or they can be cashed at a bank or any other place which ordinarily cashes checks.

The cost of a telegraphic money order varies according to the amount sent and, as in the case of an ordinary telegram, the distance the order is sent. The total cost of a telegraphic money order is made up of two parts: the charge for a telegram to the particular city, and the charge for the money order. In setting rates for the telegram, the United States has been divided into eight zones, and, generally speaking, the greater the distance, the larger the charge. The telegram charge to a given city is the same, regardless of how much money is sent. The charge for the money order varies according to the amount sent, but is the same for a given amount regardless of where the order is sent. The charges are considerably higher than for postal or express money orders. The telegraphic money order is the fastest way to send money.

Trade Acceptance

The term "trade acceptance" is used in this country to designate a draft drawn by the seller on the buyer and arising out of a merchandise transaction. If the seller can secure the buyer's signature, he has the buyer's written promise to pay at some agreed-upon date. This written promise to pay becomes suitable collateral for certain kinds of bank loans, which enables the seller to obtain payment for the goods from a bank while the bank in turn is paid by the buyer of the merchandise. In a trade acceptance, the drawer is the seller of the merchandise; the drawee is the buyer of the merchandise; and the payee is commonly the drawer or a bank. Trade acceptances are generally used in business rather than in personal transactions.

Transferring Money Abroad

A traveler's letter of credit, available at commercial banks, can be used by people traveling in foreign countries. Such a letter embodies the request to any foreign bank to pay to the named party or his order any sum desired that does not exceed the amount for which the letter is drawn. The foreign bank is to make proper endorsement of the amount paid, in the space provided for that purpose, so that the total sum of the amounts paid under the letter does not exceed the maximum amount of the letter. The signature of the payee accompanies the letter as a means of identification.

When it is desired to transmit money to a foreign country, international postal money orders may be used. These are similar to domestic postal money orders but the charge is somewhat higher. Bank drafts and telegraphic money orders may also be purchased to accomplish the same purpose. Travelers' checks are also commonly used by travelers in foreign countries.

SAVINGS ACCOUNTS

In addition to a checking account (demand deposit) service, most commercial banks offer a savings account (time deposit) service. Savings accounts may not be withdrawn by check, and although it is not normal practice, the bank may require an advance notice before withdrawal. Thus, savings accounts are designed for funds which the depositor does not anticipate needing for immediate use. Savings accounts are insured by the Federal Deposit Insurance Corporation under the same provisions as checking accounts.

Opening a Savings Account

The procedure for opening a savings account is practically the same as for a checking account. Some banks will accept accounts from $1 up, but others require a minimum of $100 or more. Thereafter, deposits or withdrawals of any amount may be made. The agreement between the depositor and the bank commonly states that any deposits made by minors or married women will be fully under the depositor's control. This agreement will probably also provide that no transfers or assignments of passbook or account will be recognized by the bank unless it agrees to such arrangements in advance.

Deposits and Withdrawals

According to a bank's rules, 30 or 60 days' notice may be required for withdrawals, but banks do not ordinarily insist upon this notice. In making a deposit or a withdrawal, presentation of the passbook is normally all that is necessary. Deposit or withdrawal slips must be completed and presented along with the passbook. For a checking account, presentation of the passbook is not necessary when making a withdrawal. Possession of a savings passbook, however, is evidence that the person has the right to make withdrawals from the account according to the bank's rules. There is therefore greater need to safeguard the savings passbook than the checking account passbook. If the savings passbook is lost, the bank may not issue a new one until the depositor puts up an indemnity bond to protect the bank in case it honors a withdrawal under the old book. According to the rules of some banks, any payments made upon presentation of either the original book or the duplicate will be a valid discharge to the bank. If the passbook is lost, the depositor should, of course, notify the bank immediately.

Most commercial banks will, upon request, issue a certificate of deposit on a savings account, rather than a passbook. Certificates are used when a depositor does not expect to be adding to the original amount deposited. A certificate contains a promise on the part of the bank to pay to the depositor the amount of money placed in the bank, with interest at a specified rate. This rate is often higher than the bank pays on ordinary savings accounts. The usual maturity of these certificates is six months. At the end of this period the depositor should present his certificate to the bank for payment and receive his interest. If he wants to leave the money in the bank, a new certificate will be made out. If the depositor does not present the certificate for payment on the due date, he ordinarily will not earn any interest after the maturity date.

Certificates of deposit are ordinarily made non-negotiable but in recent years a number of the larger banks have issued negotiable certificates in relatively large denominations. Some banks will issue certificates of deposit with a demand maturity date. In these cases, the bank mails to the certificate holder an interest check at the end of each six-month period. Most people prefer the ordinary savings account to the certificate of deposit because additional deposits and withdrawals may be made when they have a savings account and because interest is automatically credited to the account.

Advantages and Disadvantages of Savings Accounts

The savings account offers an excellent place for the safekeeping of funds, and there is no service charge, as in the checking account. In addition to safekeeping, the savings account pays the depositor a return on his investment. From the depression of the early 1930's to the middle 1950's, commercial banks generally paid very low interest rates on savings accounts, ranging from ½ of 1 per cent to 2 per cent. In recent years, however, many commercial banks have increased the rate paid on savings accounts so that average rates today are 3 to 4 per cent. Banks usually credit the account of the depositor, on January 1 and July 1, with the interest that has been earned during the preceding six-month period; thus the interest is compounded semiannually. The trend, however, is toward quarterly compounding. The techniques for determining the amount of the interest will be discussed in connection with savings accounts in Chapter 6.

The major disadvantages of a savings account are the inconvenience of having to appear at the bank to make withdrawals, and the possibility that the bank may require a depositor to wait a limited number of days before granting his withdrawal. Under normal conditions, commercial banks immediately pay withdrawal requests from savings accounts.

If a person has only a relatively small amount of money, he may find the savings account more desirable than the checking account. The checking account is, of course, much more convenient for paying bills, but may be rather costly to the depositor. If an individual maintains a checking account of only $100, with a maintenance charge of 60 cents per month, the account would cost him 7.2 per cent per year. In addition to this he would have to pay a certain amount for each deposit made and each check written. With a savings account, he would not have to pay a monthly service charge and would pay no charge for deposits. If he wanted to withdraw cash to pay a bill, there would ordinarily be no charge. If it were desirable to pay a few bills a month by check, he could obtain a cashier's check or bank money order from the bank for the cost of 25 cents. Many people feel, however, that the convenience of the checking account is worth the cost.

If sufficient funds are kept in the checking account so that credits against service charges cover the total service charge, additional funds in the checking account have no advantage to the depositor. These funds could readily be placed in a savings account in the same bank and would return an interest to the depositor. Many depositors maintain both checking and savings accounts—the checking account for ordinary needs and the savings account for savings funds. As far as safety is concerned, the two accounts are equal and the Federal Deposit Insurance applies to both. The checking account may be slightly more liquid than the savings account.

OTHER BANK SERVICES

In addition to checking accounts, savings accounts, and money transfer services, most commercial banks provide a number of other services to depositors and business institutions. Many banks offer different kinds of savings and Christmas clubs. Some banks give advice and offer credit references for individuals and businesses. Safe-deposit boxes are maintained in many banks. Some banks have services such as automatic deposit of salary and dividends, payment of utility bills, and clipping of coupons. Many banks sell and repurchase United States savings bonds.

Savings Clubs

Savings clubs are separate savings accounts used by the depositor for some special purpose, such as vacation or the purchase of Christmas presents. *Christmas clubs* are the most popular type. The idea is for the depositor to accumulate, by small weekly or monthly installments, enough to meet these heavy expenses when the time comes. Various forms and reminders are used in these clubs to encourage the depositor to make regular weekly deposits. Since deposits are generally small and substantial bookkeeping and other services are necessary to maintain these savings clubs, commercial banks normally pay no interest on these savings accounts. If a person can force himself to make the regular weekly deposits, there is no apparent advantage to a Christmas club over a normal savings account. The obvious disadvantage to savings clubs is that the normal savings account would pay interest on the amount of savings accumulated.

Reference and Advice

In addition to serving as a credit reference, a bank can supply a depositor with credit information about someone else. Bankers are usually good businessmen and their advice is often sought on various matters of business. Many people consult them on investment problems, and although a banker is not supposed to know everything about securities, his advice is usually sound and conservative. Even though one does not borrow from him in buying a house, his advice about real estate and its valuation may be helpful. The banker will perform these various services without cost.

Safe-Deposit Boxes

Many banks have safe-deposit boxes which are rented for an annual charge of from $3 up depending upon the particular bank and the size of the box. Unless the bank has a limited number of these boxes, they may also be rented by persons who do not maintain an account at the bank. The individual is given a key to his particular box and no one else has access to that box. Valuable papers such as insurance policies, real estate deeds and mortgages, stocks and bonds, bills of sale, or wills may be kept in a safe-deposit box. Some people also keep their birth and marriage certificates, valuable contracts, receipts, and other legal documents in the box. Individuals who do not have checking or savings accounts often keep part of their money in a safe-deposit box, and many people, although they have bank accounts, keep a little money in their boxes. Hoarding of money, however, is generally an unwise practice in our present economy both from the national and individual point of view.

Paying Utility Bills

Where it can be arranged, many people find it convenient to have their utility bills—gas, electricity, and telephone—sent to their bank, which pays the bills. The amounts are then deducted from the depositor's account and the receipts are returned along with the canceled checks when the account is balanced. In this way the depositor is relieved of the trouble of looking after the payment, and saves the expense of postage and envelopes. Furthermore, the bank never forgets to pay the bill when due. Where this is done the depositor should remember that his check stub balance will be overstated part of the time. The bank normally charges the depositor the same for paying the utility bill as for a canceled check.

Other Services

An individual may have his employer mail his checks directly to his bank for the bank to credit these deposits to his account. The bank then so notifies the depositor. This service of direct receipt of salary checks relieves the individual of the inconvenience of making deposits upon receipt of these checks and assures that the check will be deposited immediately. The same service is normally also available for dividend checks.

The depositor may ask the corporation paying the dividend to mail it directly to his bank for deposit rather than to him personally.

Most commercial banks serve as agents for the United States Government in the sale and purchase of savings bonds. Many commercial banks have trust departments which offer trust services and common trust funds such as those described in Chapter 18. Commercial banks sometimes handle estates, give investment counsel, and serve in an advisory capacity in retirement and estate planning. Sometimes there are charges for these services, but often a bank offers them as part of its overall community service program.

Instead of keeping a security in a safe-deposit box, you may give it to a bank to be serviced as well as guarded against physical loss. The bank will take care of routine details of handling securities, such as redeeming bonds, clipping coupons, receiving dividends, or reinvesting proceeds. Charge account banking (discussed in Chapter 3) is an additional banking service. Today's commercial bank is indeed a department store of finance.

QUESTIONS

1. What is the Federal Reserve System? How does it aid commercial banks?
2. Where do commercial banks obtain their funds? How do they invest these funds?
3. What does FDIC stand for? What is the difference between a government guarantee and FDIC insurance?
4. What is the maximum insurance on any one account by the Federal Deposit Insurance Corporation? How would it be possible to have more than this amount insured by FDIC?
5. What is meant by bank "service" charges? Why are they assessed?
6. Should the depositer allow any time interval to elapse between depositing other people's checks and withdrawing such credits from the bank? Why?
7. What is a joint account?
8. What are the advantages and disadvantages if a husband and wife have a joint checking account?
9. Why is it important to receive periodic bank statements?
10. When would it be advantageous to use some special checking account rather than a regular checking account?
11. What is an overdraft? What special problems are created in writing an overdraft?
12. What is meant by stopping payment on a check? When may it be necessary for you to do this?
13. List five important points to be remembered in filling in a check.
14. Why is it important to fill in the check stub at the same time the check is written?
15. Differentiate the six different possible endorsements for a check.

16. What is the difference between the conditional liability and the unconditional liability for an endorser of a check?
17. What are the advantages of using a qualified endorsement? Why is it rarely used?
18. Under what circumstances is the use of travelers' checks desirable?
19. What are the advantages and disadvantages of a savings account relative to a checking account?
20. Of what use is a safe-deposit box? How much does a safe-deposit box cost?

CASE PROBLEMS

1. Luke Myers has just moved to a medium-sized city from a small town in a nearby state. There are two national banks and two state-chartered banks in the city. One of the state banks has a branch near his home and one of the national banks is located near his office. All of the banks in the city have the same service charges. Before moving, Luke maintained his checking account in a small state bank in his previous home town. Should Luke leave his checking account in his present bank, where there are no service charges? His boss has recommended that he move the account. Why do you think the boss made this recommendation? If he moves, how would you recommend he choose from among the four banks? What factors should he consider in selecting one of the four banks?
2. Bill Edwards has just inherited $35,000. He plans to use part of this money to meet college expenses for his two children, who are now in high school. The rest of the money is to be used for retirement expenses. As Bill plans to work fifteen to twenty more years, he has decided to invest the retirement portion in long-term investments. However, he has not yet determined which types of investments he should make. In the meantime, he has deposited the entire $35,000 in his regular checking account. What would you suggest he do with the money until the children need it for college? What should he do with that portion which is to be held until he has determined which long-term investments he wants to make? Bill's wife is worried that the money is not now fully insured. How much is insured? What could Bill do to increase the amount covered by insurance? Should he worry about insurance coverage?
3. Ralph White made out a check for $10 for a donation to the Health Charities Institute. The day after he wrote the check, he discovered that this organization was not what it was purported to be. He is desirous of withdrawing his contribution. How can he go about stopping payment on the check? Is it legal to do so? What would happen if the bank went ahead and paid the check after Ralph had stopped payment? What can he do if the bank has paid the check before it receives notice of his stopping payment? Should he change his check stub balance as soon as he stops payment?
4. Susan Ronson handles the family finances and writes all checks on the Ronson family account. She stopped at the bank yesterday to deposit $90 in the account and at the same time picked up her monthly statement. She finds that there are three checks outstanding totaling $56 and that

bank charges were $2 for the month. Her check book balance is $292 but the bank says she has a balance of $236. Reconcile Miss Ronson's bank statement and checkbook for her. What entries should she make in her checkbook? Can the two figures be reconciled? If not, what may be wrong?

5. Black receives a check from Green, which was made out by White. Green has endorsed the check with a blank endorsement. Black would like to use the check in payment of his club bill. Does Black have to endorse the check? If you were the club manager, would you require an endorsement? If so, what kind? What possible endorsements can Black use in passing on the check? Did Green endorse the check in the best possible manner?
6. In the above case, the club manager accepts the check without any endorsement from Black. The club uses the check in paying a bill to Brown. In passing on the check, the club uses a qualified endorsement. Brown deposits the check at his bank, which passes it on to White's bank. White's bank dishonŏrs the check because of insufficient funds and sends it back to Brown's bank. Brown's bank charges it against Brown's account. What should Brown do now? Who can be held liable by Brown? What is a qualified endorsement? Does it relieve the club of responsibility? Can Brown go against Black? Against Green? Against White? What must Brown do to hold the previous endorsers liable? What should they do? What should Brown do to hold the drawer liable?
7. Assume the same circumstances as in the above problem except that White's bank dishonors the check because White's name was forged. The check goes back to Brown's bank, who charges it against Brown's account. What should Brown do? Can Brown hold the club liable for the check? Can Brown go against Black? Against Green? Against White? If Brown collects from the club, who can the club hold liable for the check? Is Black relieved of responsibility since he did not sign the check? Is a transferor of a check liable conditionally or unconditionally in event of a forgery?

SELECTED READINGS

Bank Terminology. Dayton: National Cash Register Co. Latest edition.

Bergh, Louis O., Conyngton, Thomas, and Kassoff, Edwin. *Business Law,* Sixth Edition. New York: The Ronald Press Co., 1964.

Beutel, Frederick K. *Beutel's Brannan Negotiable Instruments Law,* Seventh Edition. Cincinnati: The W. H. Anderson Co., 1948.

Board of Governors. *The Federal Reserve System—Purposes and Functions.* Washington, D. C.: U. S. Government Printing Office, 1963.

Bogen, Jules I. *The Changing Composition of Bank Assets.* New York: New York University Press, 1961.

Commission on Money and Credit. *The Commercial Banking Industry.* Englewood, Cliffs, N. J.: Prentice-Hall, Inc., 1962.

Craig, David S., and Howell, Rate A. *Basic Business Law—Text and Cases.* New York: The Ronald Press Co., 1959.

Credit Manual of Commercial Laws. New York: National Association of Credit Men. Published annually.

Crosse, Howard D. *Management Policies for Commercial Banks.* Englewood Cliffs, N. J.: Prentice-Hall, Inc., 1962.

Federal Deposit Insurance Corporation. *Annual Report.* Washington, D. C.: U. S. Government Printing Office. Latest edition.

Funk, Carl W. *Banks and the Uniform Commercial Code,* Revised Edition. Harrisburg: Pennsylvania Bankers Association, 1962.
Hodgman, Donald R. *Commercial Bank Loan and Investment Policy.* Urbana: Bureau of Economic and Business Research, University of Illinois, 1963.
Lusk, H. F. *Business Law: Principles and Cases,* Revised Edition. Homewood, Ill.: Richard D. Irwin, Inc., 1965.
Robinson, Roland I. *The Management of Bank Funds,* Second Edition. New York: McGraw-Hill Book Co., 1962.
Thomas, Rollin G. *Our Modern Banking and Monetary System,* Fourth Edition. Englewood Cliffs, N. J.: Prentice-Hall, Inc., 1964.
Using Bank Services. New York: American Bankers Association, 1961.

6

Investing Savings

Saving is part of the American way of life. In recent years, net personal savings in the United States have exceeded $20 billion per year. Because of the acceptance of the savings concept by Americans throughout the development of this country, individuals and corporations in the United States have accumulated a tremendous store of capital which has been channeled into productive facilities both here and abroad. This savings and capital accumulation is an important element in making this country the leading industrial nation of the world.

Since hoarding is not considered safe or practical, almost all personal savings are, in turn, invested in some way. Savings may be put directly into earning assets, such as starting one's own business, or they may be channeled to users of capital through financial institutions or other intermediaries.

REASONS FOR SAVING

The basic purpose of saving money and investing it is to help in accomplishing personal objectives for which money is necessary. These include increased income, security, deferred spending, an estate for heirs, philanthropy, and similar purposes. The setting of goals for savings and investing, in terms of both the amount to be saved and the purpose for which the savings are eventually to be used, is extremely helpful in accomplishing one's economic objectives.

The urge to save is present in most people, although they may not always analyze it as a motivation. Actually, for most people, the desire for security is an important motivating force in their lives. The quest for security involves many things, but one of its most important aspects is the search for a feeling of financial security. Complete financial security would be an assured income for the remainder of one's life, sufficient to satisfy all of one's money needs. Obviously, this complete financial security is impossible to obtain. No promise of future income completely assures one of that income, and no one knows today how much money income he will require for the remainder of his life. Because of these problems, those who search for financial security are willing to settle for a degree of security that is less than complete. One of the best approaches to financial security is through savings. The setting aside of current income to be used in the event of some future emergency gives a feeling of security proportionate to the amount of the savings so accumulated. Future emergencies which require savings fit into two major categories—unexpected major expenses and loss of expected future income. Many people maintain a "rainy day" fund to meet these emergencies.

Another common reason for saving current income is to allow for future or deferred spending. Advance saving is necessary for most people to be able to purchase large items such as furniture, automobiles, and homes. Even with our modern system of consumer credit, it is still normally necessary to make a down payment in the purchase of these major items. The down payment must, in some way, be saved in advance of the purchase.

Savings are often necessary in order to provide children with a college education or to give the family a vacation. Most people do not have an income sufficient to meet these requirements at the time the outlay is necessary. Thus they save in advance to pay for the costs of a college education for their children. Saving is not an alternative to spending, but only a device to enable an individual to spend in the future. Such deferred spending may bring much more enjoyment to an individual than immediate spending for some other items.

Both the need for financial security and the concept of deferred spending fit into a program of saving for retirement. The average American works only 40 out of his 80 years of life. Thus, if he does not want to be dependent on others, he must provide during his working years for the years in which he will not be earning. Our parents generally take care of our first 15 to 20 non-earning years, but it is up to us as individuals to provide for the years after our retirement from active work. Saving in some form is necessary for a retirement program. We plan to spend our accumulated savings during our years of retirement, to maintain our independence of others.

Another motive for saving is to provide an estate for dependents after death. The need for such savings is greater, of course, where there are small children in the family. In some instances, the estate which an individual has built up to take care of his old age is in itself adequate to provide also for his dependents. A person may be interested in providing an estate for members of his family who are no longer dependent on him, in order that their future life may be more pleasant. Obviously, he can leave an estate to others only if he saves in advance.

Savings objectives and goals vary significantly with personal circumstances. The young person is normally interested in saving to provide for his education. The newly married couple saves for various types of large outlay purchases. The family with children needs security for the children and saves for this purpose as well as for education of the children and for large durable goods expenditures. As the children grow up, saving for retirement becomes a more important objective for the parents. During their retirement years, savings are generally small but whatever is accumulated is primarily for purposes of security or for an estate to be left to the children or to charitable organizations.

Savings Patterns

Saving is important, but it is unfortunately true that many people save little or nothing. Table 6–1 indicates the amount of total savings by

Table 6–1. Percentage Distribution of Liquid Asset Holdings of Consumer Spending Units—Selected Years

Liquid Asset Holdings	1949	1954	1959	1962
Zero	29%	26%	26%	26%
$ 1–$ 199	16	15	19	31
$ 200–$ 499	13	13	14	
$ 500–$ 999	11	13	11	11
$ 1,000–$1,999	11	11	10	22
$ 2,000–$4,999	12	13	11	
$ 5,000–$9,999	5	5	5	5
$10,000 and over	3	4	4	5
Total	100%	100%	100%	100%

SOURCES: *Federal Reserve Bulletin;* and Survey Research Center, University of Michigan.

groups of individuals in the United States. While total personal savings as a percentage of personal disposable income in the United States has remained relatively constant in recent years, savings patterns of specific individuals range all the way from substantial dissaving (spending more than earning) to the saving of a very high portion of total income.

The increasing importance of savings is indicated in Fig. 6–1. Until 1951, the rise in personal savings corresponded to the rise in number of

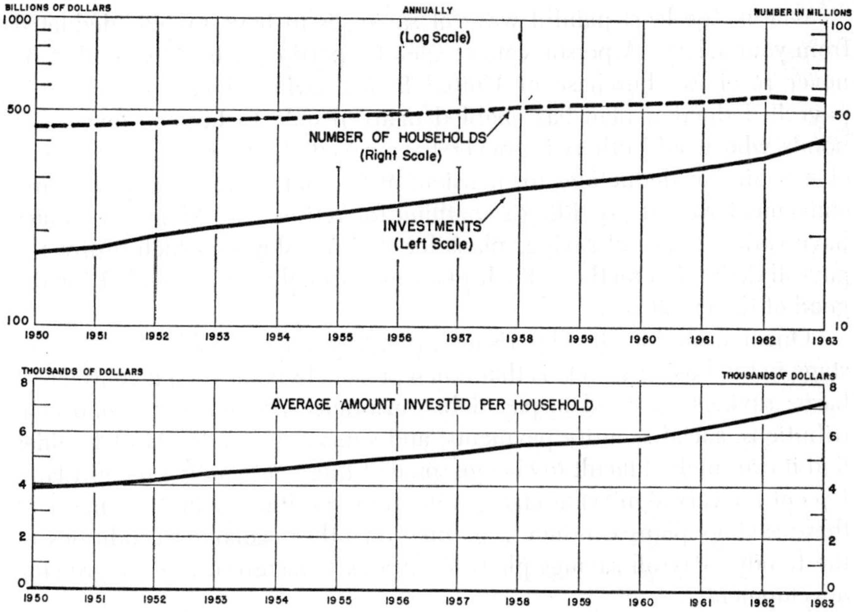

Fig. 6–1. Investments of individuals in savings accounts, life insurance reserves, and United States savings bonds, and average investment per household. (Federal Home Loan Bank Board.)

households; the average amount invested per household remained relatively constant. However, since 1951, the average amount invested in savings accounts, life insurance reserves, and United States savings bonds per household has risen steadily to a total of over $7,000 in 1964. The rise in dollar amount of savings has exceeded the eroding away of value of the dollar through inflation since 1951. With rising incomes, people should continue to save more, and the total pool of savings per family at any point in time should be greater as savings objectives in our modern society require more dollars than in the past.

Aids in Saving

It is expedient for most persons to save something, and to do so it is often necessary to have some definite plan worked out for regular weekly or monthly additions to the savings. If wages are paid weekly, then add to your savings weekly. Do not skip a week in order to buy something, intending to double the savings the following week. Regular savings of small amounts usually add up to more over a period of time than large irregular savings. Make regular savings a habit.

One of the least painful ways of saving is to have savings deducted from your salary. A person cannot spend a portion of his income that he never receives. Purchase of United States savings bonds through the payroll deduction plan has enabled many people to become owners of bonds who would otherwise never have saved the money for their purchase. Similar deductions for pensions and social security are a sure and convenient way of providing something for retirement. Many companies have various types of savings plans for their employees which utilize the payroll deduction method. Such plans are strongly recommended for the good of the employee.

One reason for steadily rising savings per household regardless of stage in the business cycle is that much personal saving is on a contractual basis: savings are used to pay debts, insurance premiums, pension contributions, social security payments, and similar demands. Most families find it extremely difficult to change some of these automatic savings plans. Except for very significant changes in family position or income, many of these savings plans continue regardless of other economic conditions of the family. Payroll savings plans of various types are a rapidly growing development.

In recent years, there has been a substantial increase in the amount of incentives offered by savings institutions. Premiums, gift certificates, special savings plans, automatic savings plans, and package savings plans have all been designed to increase the amount of personal savings. By making it easier to save and by offering special inducements for savings, the number of savers as well as the total amount of savings have increased.

INVESTMENT OF SAVINGS

The hoarding of cash is neither desirable nor practical today, and results in no return on your savings. In addition, hoarded money may be lost or stolen. Users of capital are willing to pay a return for the use of your savings until you need them. Thus, it is advisable to put your savings into some form of investment. Most people work hard for their income and it is not easy to defer present consumption in order to accumulate savings. You should, therefore, attempt to select the best investment medium for your savings in light of your purposes and objectives.

Factors to Consider

Each investment medium differs in some way from all other media. Since the selection of a specific investment medium varies with the objectives of the saver as well as with the features of the medium, certain factors should be carefully considered in making a decision on where to invest savings. The major criteria to be considered in selecting an investment for savings are:

1. *Safety.* Safety refers to the degree of risk of loss of part or all of the principal amount invested. The safest investment would be one in which there appeared to be no possible chance of loss of the original amount invested.
2. *Return.* Part of the reason for investing is to earn a return on your investment. You should be interested in safety and regularity of return as well as in its absolute amount. Generally speaking, the higher the return or the promised return, the greater the degree of risk.
3. *Liquidity.* Liquidity of an investment relates to the speed with which that investment can be converted into cash at a fair valuation. Some investments can be readily liquidated but others may require a great deal of selling effort and time.
4. *Purchasing power protection.* Safety, as defined above, is concerned with the protection of the principal in terms of original dollar amount invested. In times of substantial inflation, you could easily reacquire the dollars originally put into an investment but would be unable to purchase with those dollars as much as you could have purchased at the time the investment was made. People are generally interested in the dollar as a means of obtaining a certain amount of goods and services. Thus, you may want your investments to return you sufficient dollars to maintain your purchasing power.
5. *Convenience.* Other things being equal, you would probably select the savings medium which is most convenient for you. The concept of convenience includes the time and trouble necessary to select the proper investment and to handle the technical details of making the investment. Certain types of investments require a great deal of time for study. It is generally inconvenient for the average consumer to select and properly manage these types of investments.

The weighting of the above criteria and the selection of an investment or savings medium is dependent upon the objective which the savings are to meet. If the reason for saving is to provide financial security in the form of an emergency fund, it would appear that liquidity and safety, in that order, are the most important criteria. Potential return would be of only minor consequence. If the purpose of your saving is to plan for some specific major purchase in the near future, you would normally consider safety and then liquidity as the most important criteria. On the other hand, if the deferred consumption is in the distant future, the maintenance of purchasing power and the rate of return may also be important items. Certainly, in planning for distant retirement, maintenance of purchasing power becomes very important.

Outlets for Savings

There is a wide variety of potential investments for the person with surplus funds. These include savings accounts in banks, savings and loan associations, mutual savings banks, and credit unions; postal savings; savings through life insurance; United States savings bonds and other government securities; purchase of corporate bonds, municipal bonds, preferred stock, common stock, shares in an investment company, annuities, real estate, and mortgages; business ownership; and loans to individuals. Each of these possible investments should be judged according to how it meets the investment criteria you have established to gain the objectives of your savings program. In many instances, to have a number of different investments is the most desirable approach.

Only those savings media which are normally called savings institutions will be considered in this chapter. Other investments are covered in later chapters. Savings institutions are differentiated from other investments by their relative safety and liquidity and by the fact that they are under some type of state or federal control. In addition, their major purpose is the safekeeping of savings of individuals and institutions. As a group, savings institutions offer fixed-value investments only; that is,

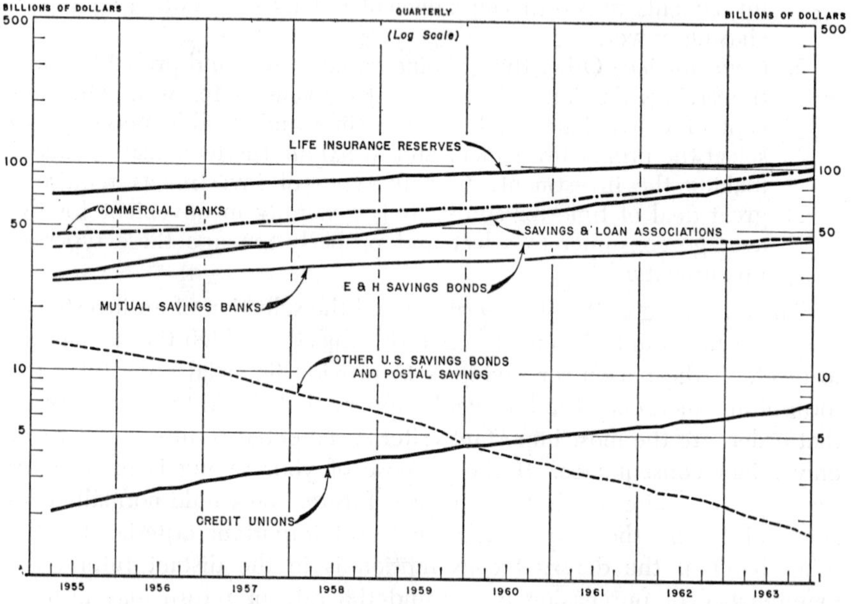

Fig. 6–2. Investments of individuals in savings accounts, life insurance reserves, and United States savings bonds. (Federal Home Loan Bank Board.)

they do not provide a hedge against the changing purchasing power of the dollar. Investments in these institutions provide for the return of a fixed number of dollars of principal regardless of the value of the dollar.

Figures 6–2 and 6–3 indicate the relative importance and growth of various institutions as outlets for personal savings. Life insurance reserves have been the primary investment for personal savings. Commercial banks superseded United States savings bonds in the early 1950's and have maintained second place since that time. Savings and loan associations have risen from fifth to third place since 1950, while United States savings bonds have fallen from second to fourth place.

In addition to the absolute position of these various institutions, Fig. 6–2 illustrates the rate of growth. It is obvious that savings and loan associations and credit unions have been growing at much more rapid rates than the other institutions listed. United States savings bonds have fallen slightly, and postal savings have fallen very substantially.

Figure 6–3 illustrates net additions each year during the time period studied. Throughout most of this period, the savings and loan associations had the largest dollar additions of these seven types of institutions. In the most recent years, with rising savings interest rates paid by com-

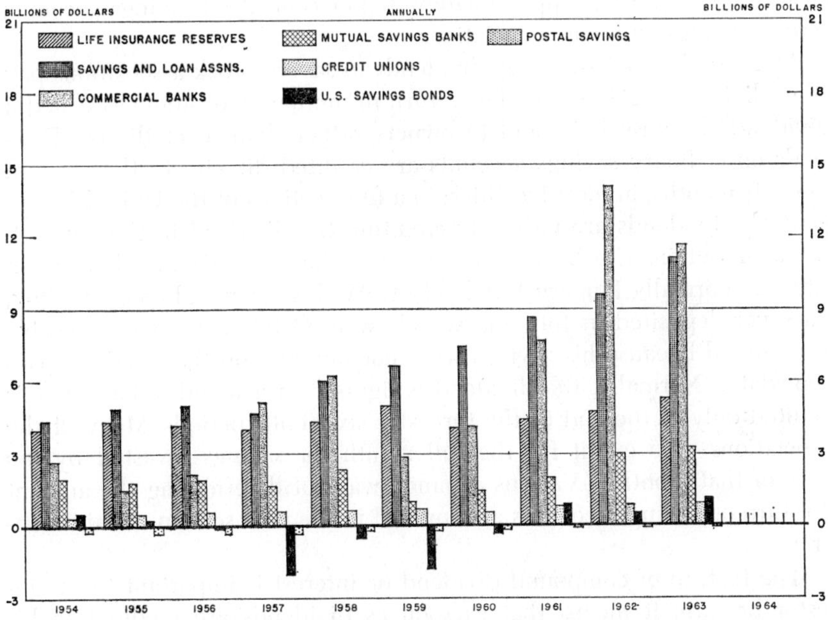

Fig. 6–3. Growth in investments of individuals in savings accounts, life insurance reserves, and United States savings bonds. (Federal Home Loan Bank Board.)

mercial banks, they have managed to grow faster in dollar volume than savings and loan associations. Additions to life insurance reserves during this time period have varied only slightly from $4 billion per year.

SAVINGS AND LOAN ASSOCIATIONS

Savings and loan associations, as the name implies, perform a double service for their customers. They are one of the most popular types of savings institutions in the United States. In addition, they furnish one of the principal sources for borrowing money for the purchase or construction of homes. Savings and loan associations are sometimes called building and loan associations, cooperative banks (in Massachusetts), or homestead associations (in Louisiana). Savings and loan associations are the most important source of funds for non-farm residential home mortgages. At the beginning of 1965, approximately 44 per cent of all non-farm one-to-four-family residential mortgage debt was held by savings and loan associations. While total savings accounts in savings and loan associations do not equal the amount held by commercial banks, in the post-World War II period the savings and loan associations have grown much more rapidly in their percentage of total United States savings accounts. At the beginning of 1965, approximately 37 per cent of all savings accounts were in savings and loan associations.

All mutual associations pay dividends to savers; stock associations pay either dividends or interest. The return in mutual associations is called a "dividend" because it is paid to owners rather than to creditors. Dividends on ordinary savings accounts are credited directly to the account every six months, in most localities; in a few sections of the United States, quarterly dividends are paid. By crediting the dividend to the account, the saver obtains the benefit of compound interest. Dividend payment dates are normally January 1 and July 1. With semiannual compounding, if a saver deposited in July and withdrew in October, he would receive no dividend because his savings were not invested on the dividend payment date. Normally, the dividend is figured on a monthly basis but is credited only at the end of the three- or six-month period. Many of the associations give credit for the full month for savings invested by the tenth of that month. (Various common ways of determining the amount of return on savings accounts are covered in the next section of this chapter.)

The feature of compound dividend or interest is important to the investor because it means that as soon as dividends are credited to his account, he begins to earn future dividends on that dividend amount. The saver does not have to go to the trouble of collecting his dividend and then reinvesting it in order to earn a return on it. If a 6 per cent dividend is compounded annually, the amount of the original investment will double in 12 years. Without compounding, it would take 17 years to double the amount of the investment by leaving in the accumulated dividend. An example of the power of compound interest is given in Table 6–2.

Table 6–2. How Long It Takes to Double Capital at Different Rates of Interest, Compounded Annually *

Rate of Return	Approximate Number of Years	Rate of Return	Approximate Number of Years
1%	70	6½%	11
2	35	7	10¼
2½	28	7½	9½
2¾	25½	8	9
3	23½	9	8
3½	20½	10	7¼
4	17½	11	6⅔
4½	15¾	12	6⅛
5	14¼	13	5⅔
5½	13	14	5⅓
6	12	15	5

* A simple way to get the approximate number of years it takes to double capital at any assumed rate of return is to divide 72 by the rate of return.

Nature of Operation

The savings and loan industry operates under a *dual* system. That is, associations may be chartered either by the federal government or by the state in which they operate. All associations with the word "Federal" in their name have federal charters. Other associations have state charters. Of the 6,248 associations at the beginning of 1965, only 1,981, or approximately 30 per cent, had federal charters (in Alaska, Florida, Georgia, Tennessee, and Wyoming, 90 per cent or more of all associations are federally chartered). However, these federal associations had more than 50 per cent of the total assets of all savings and loan associations in the country.

Most savings and loan associations are *mutual* organizations. The saving members are the owners of the association and the borrowers also become members. Although the associations are formed as corporations, permanent stock is issued only in California and in 15 other states.[1]

In the mutual associations, the persons having savings accounts are the only owners of the association. In the case of federal associations (all

[1] These states are Arizona, Arkansas, Colorado, Idaho, Illinois, Indiana, Kansas, Michigan, Nevada, Ohio, Oregon, Texas, Utah, Virginia, and Washington.

of which are mutuals) and those organized in a number of states, each member is entitled to one vote for each $100 in his savings account, with a maximum of 50 votes. In federal associations each borrower also has one vote. Thus, the savings account holders and borrowers have the right to elect the board of directors although it is appreciated that relatively few of the members of an association ever attend the annual meetings. The board of directors formulates the policies of the association and appoints the executive officers to carry out these policies.

Two major types of accounts are generally available in savings and loan associations. The most common kind of account is the *savings account.* These accounts may be opened with any amount of money and future deposits and withdrawals can be made in any amount. All transactions are recorded in the account holder's passbook. Dividends are credited to the account either quarterly or semiannually. *Investment accounts* are usually for $100 or multiples thereof. These accounts are often represented by certificates of deposit. Dividends on these accounts are generally paid quarterly or semiannually in the form of a check mailed to the saver. The dividend is normally paid on the quarterly or six-month anniversary date of the deposit rather than the beginning of the calendar quarter or six-month period, as is the case with savings accounts. Some associations offer plans whereby dividend checks are mailed to savers monthly. These plans usually require a minimum balance of about $5,000.

Except for checking accounts, many savings and loans associations today offer services similar to those of commercial banks: Christmas savings accounts, safe-deposit boxes, bank checks, money orders, collection of money on redeemed Series E savings bonds, and general investment and financial advice.

Savings and loan associations are primarily local institutions; that is, the great majority of their savings accounts come from the immediate area in which they are located, and loans are generally made within some maximum distance from the savings and loan office. However, it is possible to save in a savings and loan association through the mail regardless of its location, and an increasing number of savers are putting money in associations at a substantial geographic distance. There has been a tendency for savings accounts to move toward higher dividend rate areas.

Safety

The factors affecting the safety of a savings account are many, and vary widely among different types of savings institutions as well as among individual institutions of a particular type. In discussing the safety of a particular type of savings institution, it is possible to look into only those factors which apply to the great majority of the specific institutions of that type.

The major factors influencing the safety of a savings institution would include the type of investments made with the savers' money, the amount of the excess assets of the institution over the claims of its savers, the insurance of accounts, government and industry protections, and the quality of the management. The last point, of course, is extremely difficult to measure and tends to vary more among institutions of a given type than among different types of institutions. Management caliber, therefore, will not be discussed in our comparison of types of institutions.

Savings and loan associations invest almost entirely in first mortgages on residential real estate. Figure 6–4 shows that mortgage loans made up almost 85 per cent of total assets of all savings and loan associations in 1963. The remaining assets are kept primarily for liquidity purposes and include principally cash and United States government obligations. Thus, the safety of savings and loan associations is dependent principally upon the safety of first mortgage loans on residential real estate. History proves that this type of investment is relatively safe—particularly if there is a sufficient margin between the amount of the mortgage and the current market value of the property. The number of foreclosures on non-farm real estate properties throughout the entire United States has been very small since 1940. The substantial demand for standard residential properties makes the property fairly salable in the event the mortgagor runs into difficulties.

Over the years, savings and loan associations have left a portion of current earnings in the institution to build reserves against possible declines in value of assets in the future. These reserves represent an excess in current value of assets over claims of savers. Throughout the postwar period the ratio of reserves and undivided profits to savings accounts has been close to 7 per cent. These reserves are a necessary protection to help provide safety for the funds invested in savings and loan institutions.

Almost 70 per cent of all savings and loan associations in the United States are insured by the Federal Savings and Loan Insurance Corporation. These associations tend to be the larger institutions, so that over 96 per cent of all assets in savings and loan associations come under this insurance. The Federal Savings and Loan Insurance Corporation was chartered by the federal government in 1934 for the purpose of insuring savings accounts in savings and loan associations. All federally chartered associations must be members of the insurance corporation, and state associations which are in good financial standing may become members. For this insurance service, each savings and loan association pays to the insurance corporation an annual premium equal to $1/12$ of 1 per cent of the total deposited in its savings accounts.

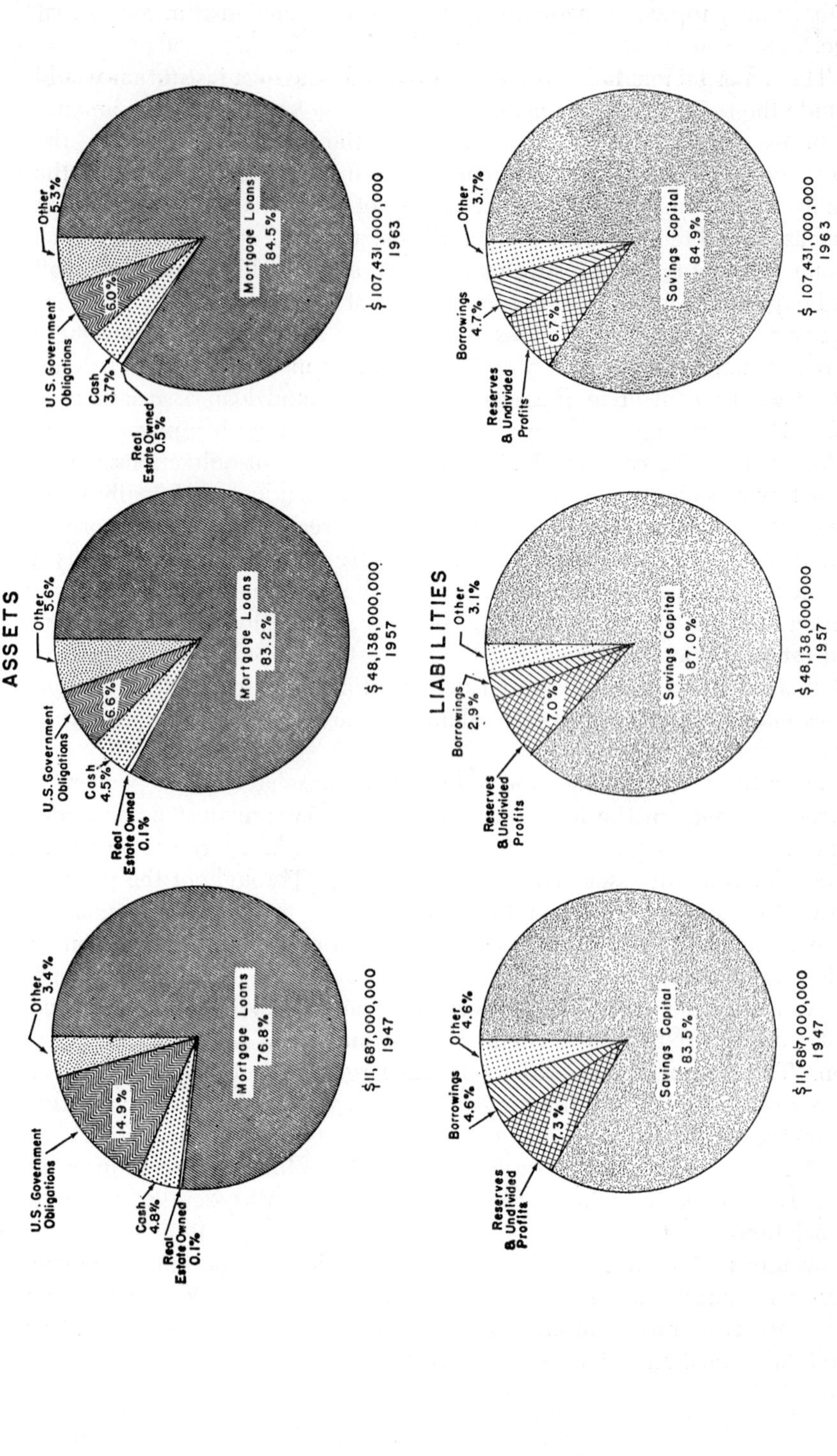

Fig. 6–4. Major classes of assets and liabilities of savings and loan associations. (Federal Home Loan Bank Board.)

As is true for the Federal Deposit Insurance Corporation, the federal government does not guarantee the accounts of savings and loan associations which are members of the Federal Savings and Loan Insurance Corporation. The maximum insurance on an account is $10,000—the same as FDIC. Joint accounts and accounts in different associations can be used by individuals to increase the amount of insured savings in savings and loan associations. In the event of default in an insured savings and loan association, the insurance corporation will either pay the account holder cash or make available to him a transferred account in another insured institution in the same community. Default does not mean inability to pay out cash on demand to savers, but, rather, is an official determination of that status by the proper authority. Since its inception, the Federal Savings and Loan Insurance Corporation has paid all savers in failing institutions the total amount of their insured savings in cash.

Government supervision and aid are additional factors in maintaining the safety of savings and loan accounts. In addition to supervision and legal requirements, Federal Home Loan Bank assistance has been established in order to help even out seasonal variations in the supply and need of savings and loan associations for funds, to provide a source of cash to the member associations in the event of a depression which would increase substantially the withdrawal requests on the member associations, and to provide a source of funds for mortgage lending in those areas where the demand for mortgage loans exceeds the local supply of funds. Almost 80 per cent of the savings and loan associations, representing over 98 per cent of the total assets of the business, are members of the Federal Home Loan Bank System. The 12 regional banks in the home loan bank system secure money from members' deposits, by selling their obligations in the open market and by borrowing from the United States Treasury. They in turn make loans to member associations.

Actual losses by savers in insured associations since 1934 have been zero, though there has been some loss by savers in non-insured associations. Because of the type of investments made by savings and loan associations, the actual loss even in the great depression was relatively small. The establishment of the Federal Savings and Loan Insurance Corporation and the Federal Home Loan Bank System has added to the safety of the savings and loan associations.

Liquidity

While savings and loan associations are not demand deposit institutions and hence cannot guarantee to pay, on demand, all requests for withdrawal of funds which their account holders may present, modern practice recognizes the growing need for sufficient liquidity to meet probable withdrawal demands. Since repayments on home mortgage loans outstanding may not be sufficient at any one time to meet all requests for withdrawal by investors, the associations carry liquid assets in the form of government securities and cash which they can use to meet withdrawal requests. The percentage of cash and United States government obligations to savings in savings and loan associations at the beginning of 1965 was 9.3 per cent. These associations had cash alone in excess of 4 per cent of savings. The Federal Home Loan Bank Board requires that insured associations must carry cash and government securities equal to 7 per cent of savings. Thus the insured associations have a substantially higher liquidity ratio than that required by the Board. Receipts from new savers and payments on mortgage loans are the most important sources of cash with which they meet the demands for withdrawal.

The Federal Home Loan Bank System is an additional liquidity aid to savings and loan associations. A savings and loan association which is a member of the system can, in an emergency, borrow up to 50 per cent of its total savings balance from the home loan bank to meet heavy withdrawals.

Except at a time of financial panic or a severe depression, the typical savings and loan association will return the saver's money on demand. But according to the laws under which they operate, prior notice can be demanded for the withdrawal of funds. The typical notice which may be required is thirty days. In practice, however, this notice is not required and the money is paid out on demand. If the savings and loan association cannot meet its withdrawal requests on demand, or at the end of a stated notice period, the procedure that it must follow is governed by the provisions in its charter or by the law and regulations under which it operates.

Typically, these provide for an orderly disposition of withdrawal requests from available cash, and receipts of additional cash from repayments of loans or from the borrowing of money from a Federal Home Loan Bank. In many instances the procedure provides for the meeting of emergency needs for cash on the part of savers and the development of a "waiting list" with people on the list receiving funds in larger amounts in rotation.

As long as the association is solvent—as long as the real value of its assets is more than the amount of the claims against it—savers must normally wait their turn for withdrawal until the association has funds available. Although this could cause a saver to wait a fairly long period of time, it has rarely been put into effect in recent years. State associations in New York are required to pay all withdrawal requests within 60 days. If they cannot do this, the Superintendent of Banks is authorized to take over the association and provide for its liquidation.

Return

Savings and loan associations receive income from interest charged on mortgage loans, interest received on government securities held, and certain miscellaneous fees and rentals. Interest on mortgages accounts for 84.5 per cent of the total income of savings and loan associations in the United States. Thus, the rate of return paid savers in savings and loan associations is closely related to the rate of interest charged on mortgage loans. In 1964 operating expenses of the associations took 20.5 per cent of their income, and interest on borrowed money and non-operating charges took another 0.2 per cent of gross income. This left approximately 79.3 per cent of gross income as earnings. In 1964, out of every dollar earned, 85 cents was paid as dividends and 15 cents was put into reserves. Reserves are income set aside as additional protection to savers in the event the association's assets should decline in value or its earnings be diminished in future years. The annual rate of return on savings in savings and loan associations varies from 3 to 5 per cent. In addition to the variation in the mortgage interest rates, the rate paid on savings varies with the general interest rate, prevailing business conditions, section of the country, and rates of competitive institutions. The associations in the West tend to pay higher rates than in other sections of the United States, because of higher prevailing mortgage interest rates. At the beginning of 1964, 77 per cent of all associations paid either 4 or 4¼ per cent.

Table 6–3 gives the total accumulation from annual savings of $100 invested at stated annual rates of interest compounded semiannually for 5 to 50 years. The worth of $1,000 invested at stated annual rates of interest compounded semiannually for 5 to 50 years is given in Table 6–4.

Table 6–3. Total Accumulation from Annual Savings of $100 Invested at Stated Annual Rates of Interest, Compounded Semiannually *

Period	3%	4%	5%
In 5 years	$ 535	$ 545	$ 560
In 10 years	1,156	1,215	1,277
In 15 years	1,877	2,028	2,196
In 20 years	2,713	3,020	3,370
In 25 years	3,684	4,229	4,874
In 30 years	4,811	5,702	6,800
In 35 years	6,118	7,500	9,264
In 40 years	7,636	9,688	12,419
In 45 years	9,396	12,357	16,459
In 50 years	11,440	15,611	21,269

* Based on the assumption that $50 is deposited at the end of each six-month period.

Table 6–4. Worth of $1,000 Invested at Stated Annual Rates of Interest, Compounded Semiannually

Period	3%	4%	5%
In 5 years	$1,161	$1,219	$ 1,280
In 10 years	1,347	1,486	1,639
In 15 years	1,563	1,811	2,098
In 20 years	1,814	2,208	2,685
In 25 years	2,105	2,692	3,437
In 30 years	2,443	3,281	4,400
In 35 years	2,835	4,000	5,632
In 40 years	3,291	4,875	7,209
In 45 years	3,819	5,943	9,228
In 50 years	4,432	7,245	11,812

COMMERCIAL BANKS

The operation of commercial banks from a demand depositor's point of view has been discussed in Chapter 5, where a brief description of the mechanics of bank savings accounts was also given. In this chapter, we discuss only time accounts deposited as savings in a commercial bank.

Safety and Liquidity

The time account in the commercial bank has the same safety aspects as the demand account. In attempting to determine the safety of savings in commercial banks as compared with other financial institutions, it is necessary to consider the type and caliber of investments which the institution makes; the insurance, if any, which is provided; the management; and the supervision and regulation. The safety record for savings in insured commercial banks since 1935 has been excellent. No saver in an *insured* account has lost his savings since that date.

Liquidity of a time account differs to some extent from that of a checking account. Commercial banks may require the saver to give the bank notice before a withdrawal can be made from a savings account. Normal notice requirement is 30 days. Ordinarily, however, the banks do not utilize this notice provision, but pay savings accounts upon demand. Withdrawal requests are paid from the bank's available cash and liquid securities, from new deposits, and from collections on loans. These sources are usually sufficient to allow for immediate withdrawal. In the event they are not, the bank may borrow money from a Federal Reserve System bank to pay depositors. Therefore, only in unusual circumstances would the bank invoke the provision for advance notice. If the bank is still unable to pay at the end of the notice period, the bank will normally go into receivership and, if it is an insured bank, the Federal Deposit Insurance Corporation will make funds available to depositors.

Return

Since commercial banks are stock companies, time depositors in commercial banks receive *interest* on their investment. The money to pay the interest comes from the earnings of the bank on its operations. The major sources of gross income to commercial banks are interest on loans, earnings on securities held, and service charges and other fees. Amounts left after paying operating expenses and setting up reasonable reserves for bad debts are available for interest payment to depositors and dividend payment to stockholders. The agreed-upon interest must be paid to depositors before stockholders can receive any dividends. Interest is usually agreed upon only for a six-month period, and new rates may be set at the end of each such period.

Commercial banks have generally paid a lower interest rate than the dividend rate on savings and loan accounts. However, in very recent years, commercial banks have substantially increased their interest payment on savings accounts. The current range of payment is from 2 to 4 per cent annually.

Interest on commercial bank savings accounts is normally credited to the account at six-month intervals and is compounded, the same as in savings and loan associations. There are a number of different ways of figuring the amount on deposit in the account for purposes of interest determination. The five most common techniques are discussed below.

1. The interest commences the first of the month following a deposit. No interest for the period is paid for amounts withdrawn before the semiannual payment date. Thus, withdrawals are charged against the first deposits or against the beginning balance of the period.
2. Interest commences at the beginning of the semiannual period and funds must be on deposit for the full six months. This means that interest is paid only on the minimum balance at any point during the six-month period.
3. Interest commences the first of the month following a deposit (in some cases, deposits made by the tenth receive interest from the first of that month) and no interest is paid on amounts withdrawn during the semiannual period. Withdrawals are charged against the most recent deposits in the current interest period, if any. This method is the technique prescribed by law for all federal savings and loan associations.
4. Interest commences at the beginning of the next calendar quarter following a deposit and no interest is paid on amounts withdrawn

during that quarter. Withdrawals are charged to the most recent deposits of the quarterly period, if any. Interest is entered and compounded every six months.

5. Interest is paid semiannually but is computed on the lowest monthly balance for each month. Interest commences the first of the month following a deposit and on amounts withdrawn ceases on the first of the month in which it was withdrawn. Interest can be earned on amounts withdrawn between the semiannual payment dates.

Where a choice of the various methods of determining interest is available to the saver, method 5 would be the most valuable and method 3 would be the next most valuable. These same methods can be used for quarterly compounding, which is increasing in importance.

MUTUAL SAVINGS BANKS

The National Association of Mutual Savings Banks has defined a mutual savings bank as a bank of deposit, without stockholders, having as its basic mission the continuous promotion of true thrift at the community level. By investment policies deliberately designed to insure liquidity for the bank, it serves people of modest means, affording them stability, safety, ready availability of their savings in full, and a satisfactory return on their money. Mutual savings banks are found in only 18 states, and 95 per cent of the assets of all mutual savings banks are in the New England and Middle Atlantic states. The total assets of mutual savings banks at the beginning of 1965 were approximately $54.2 billion. The Bowery Savings Bank in New York City is by far the largest of these institutions, with deposits of $2 billion. There are over 500 mutual savings banks, and they represent the oldest savings institution in the United States, but the relative importance of this institution outside of the northeastern states is definitely limited. Why mutual savings banks have not developed into a nationwide system is a matter of conjecture. It is certainly related to changes in commercial banks and to the development of savings and loan associations.

Nature of Operations

By definition, these institutions are of the mutual type, being owned and operated for the benefit of depositors. Historically, they have been semiphilanthropic rather than commercial in nature. All mutual savings banks are chartered by the various states rather than by an agency of the federal government. The depositors and borrowers do not possess any rights in management. Power is usually invested in a board of trustees, which is often a self-perpetuating body. The trustees are usually civic-minded individuals who have no financial interest in the institution and who serve without remuneration. They are the policy-making body of the organization. All mutual savings banks are under the supervision of their respective state banking departments.

The investments of mutual savings banks are regulated by statutes which vary among the states. Most of these institutions are permitted to purchase real estate mortgages, farm mortgages, railroad and public utility bonds, government bonds, and state and municipal bonds. Some states allow investment in industrial bonds, bank and trust company stocks, consumer loans, loans against insurance policies, and FHA Title I loans. As indicated in Table 6–5, loans are by far the most important single investment, and account for over 70 per cent of assets. Next in importance are government securities and then securities of private corporations. The variety of possible investments for mutual savings banks gives management a fair degree of flexibility in changing from one type of investment to another as conditions change.

Figure 6–5 indicates the varying importance of different assets since 1900. In 1900, corporate and other securities were more important than mortgages, to mutual savings banks. Mortgages increased until 1930 and then suffered a sharp decline to the end of World War II. By 1964, however, they were more important than ever before. Government secur-

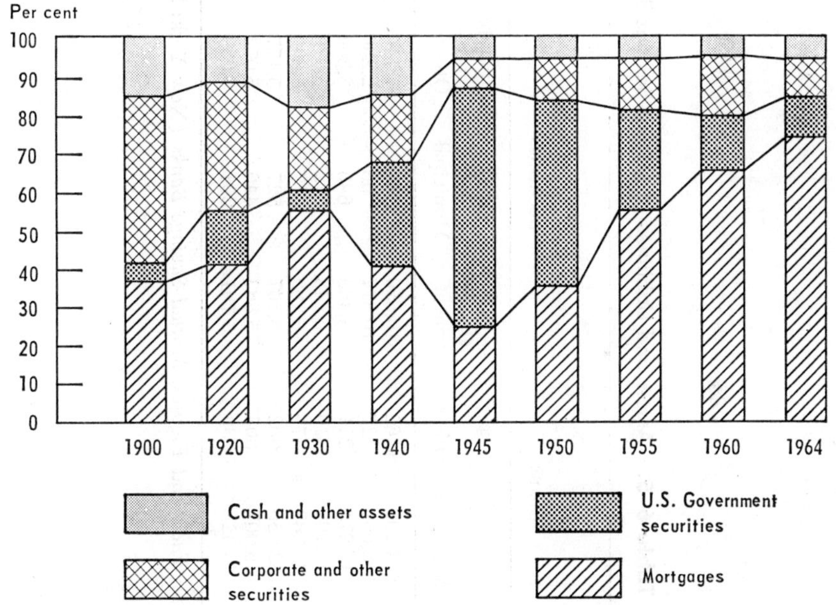

Fig. 6–5. Percentage distribution of assets of mutual savings banks, selected years, 1900–1964. (National Association of Mutual Savings Banks.)

Table 6–5. Assets and Liabilities of Mutual Savings Banks—Selected Years, 1945–1964 (in millions of dollars)

	Loans		Securities								
Year	Mortgage	Other	U. S. Govern-ment	State and Municipal	Corporate and Other	Cash	Other Assets	Total Assets – Total Liabilities and General Reserve Accounts	Deposits	Other Liabilities	General Reserve Accounts
1945	$ 4,202	$ 62	$10,650	$ 84	$1,116	$ 606	$243	$16,962	$15,332	$ 48	$1,582
1950	8,039	127	10,877	96	2,260	792	255	22,446	20,025	137	2,283
1955	17,279	211	8,463	646	3,364	966	416	31,346	28,182	310	2,854
1960	26,702	416	6,243	672	5,076	874	589	40,571	36,343	678	3,550
1961	28,902	475	6,160	677	5,040	937	640	42,829	38,277	781	3,771
1962	32,056	602	6,107	527	5,177	956	695	46,121	41,336	828	3,957
1963	36,007	607	5,863	440	5,074	912	799	49,702	44,606	943	4,153
1964	40,328	739	5,791	391	5,099	1,004	886	54,238	48,849	989	4,400

SOURCE: *Facts and Figures, Mutual Savings Banks* (New York: National Association of Mutual Savings Banks, May, 1965).

ities were particularly important during World War II and immediately thereafter, but they have declined substantially in relative importance since 1950.

Only savings accounts are accepted by mutual savings banks and there is ordinarily a maximum limit on the amount which may be deposited by any one individual. As mutual savings banks move more heavily into the residential mortgage field, they become more similar to savings and loan associations.

Safety

The safety of an investment in a mutual savings bank is dependent upon the investment policy of the bank, its supervision, its insurance, and its accumulation of surplus. Most mutual savings banks have been very prudent in their investment policy and most of them are members of the Federal Deposit Insurance Corporation. Others are covered by state insurance plans. They are generally subject to supervision by state banking authorities. In recent years the surplus accounts of mutual savings banks as a group have approximated slightly less than 10 per cent of total resources. No depositor in an insured association has suffered loss since the FDIC was established. The safety record of mutual savings banks has been very good.

Liquidity

As is true in commercial banks and savings and loan associations, most mutual savings banks pay out on savings accounts without requiring notice, under ordinary circumstances. A certain amount of cash and marketable securities are maintained for purposes of meeting withdrawal requirements. New savings receipts and collections on loans and sales of securities are also available to meet withdrawal requests.

Mutual savings banks may, by law and regulation, require from 60 to 90 days' notice for withdrawals. Since mutual savings banks were founded to encourage thrift and permanent savings, most of their investments are long-term and are not generally available to meet liquidity requirements. The treatment of savers after the notice period is similar to that in savings and loan associations.

Return

Because of their mutual nature, mutual savings banks pay dividends rather than interest. Dividends are generally not paid on amounts withdrawn between dividend distribution dates, but dividends do accrue on deposits made during that period. Since the deposits are looked upon as long-term savings, these institutions can invest in long-term obligations.

In normal times, these long-term obligations yield a relatively high rate of return and enable the mutual savings banks to pay to depositors a higher return than in the case of savings accounts in commercial banks. In recent years, most mutual savings banks have been paying between 3 and 4½ per cent annually on savings.

CREDIT UNIONS

Credit unions are cooperative associations organized to encourage thrift among members, which in turn creates a source of credit for members. Credit unions as consumer lending institutions have already been discussed in Chapter 4. We are now concerned with the saving of money through the use of the credit union. Credit union assets have increased rapidly in recent years and now exceed $8 billion.

Nature of Operation

Membership in a credit union is usually obtained by the purchase of at least one share of stock. This share normally costs $5. In some unions there is also a small membership fee of 25 cents or 50 cents. Where the employer is cooperative, a payroll deduction plan is often used for the purchase of shares. Many employees purchase shares regularly through these payroll deduction plans as a means of saving. The shares in credit unions are not transferable, but they will be bought back by the union as funds are available. Some credit unions offer life insurance to savers at no added cost. In these cases, the cost of the insurance, in effect, reduces the dividend that could otherwise have been paid.

Credit unions lend the funds of savers to other members of the organization who wish to borrow those funds. Their major use of funds, therefore, is in consumer lending. Amounts not necessary for loans to members are usually invested in government securities. The advantages of volunteer help and substantial aid from employers have already been discussed in Chapter 4.

Safety

The safety of savings in a credit union is dependent upon the lending policy of the union, the management of the union, and the position of the employer, where one is involved. Credit unions do not have the safety feature of federally sponsored insurance of accounts. There is considerably less federal or state supervision of credit unions than of other savings institutions. The safety record to date, however, has been good. Bad debt losses have been low, and in almost all instances have been adequately covered by the reserves. The advantages of lending, even unsecured, to other members of an organization have led to relatively small bad-debt loss. While credit union safety has been generally good to date in the United States, it must be remembered that the rapid development of credit unions is fairly recent. Investment in credit unions is undoubtedly not the safest form of investment. Most of the management of credit unions is not experienced in the making of consumer loans, and since most unions were formed since the crash of 1929, they have little experience in the difficulties of a severe depression with a large volume of loans outstanding. It would not normally be a wise policy to put too large a portion of total savings into this form of investment.

Liquidity

Withdrawal of savings from a credit union constitutes a repurchase, by the union, of shares in the organization. Shares are not transferable to others. They are bought back by the union as funds are available. If no funds are available, the shareholder must wait his turn for repayment. Credit unions maintain certain cash and government bond amounts for purposes of meeting ordinary withdrawals. They also use new savings and repayments on loans. They do not, however, have secondary sources to fall back upon in the event that these normal sources are insufficient. In addition, the liquidity ratios of most credit unions are not high. A saver in a credit union should be prepared to wait a fair period of time before receiving his savings.

Return

Because of their mutual nature, credit unions pay dividends. They are generally the highest paying institutions of those covered in this chapter. Because of the type investment they make—consumer loans—they have substantial income from which to pay returns to savers. Many credit unions charge an annual rate of 12 per cent on loans. After deducting expenses and setting up reserves, many unions are still able to pay 6 per cent in dividends. Those which charge less than 12 per cent on loans are able to pay 4 or 5 per cent on dividends. Where credit unions have difficulty lending the total amount of capital (less needed cash reserves) received from savers, the dividend rate is apt to be lower. Credit unions have recently paid from 3 to 6 per cent annually in dividends. The higher return available must be weighed against the safety and liquidity features of credit unions. Investment in those unions with relatively long histories of prompt payment may be desirable for a portion of one's savings.

UNITED STATES GOVERNMENT SAVINGS BONDS

The major source of financing for the federal government has been the collection of various taxes from individuals and business institutions. In many periods in our history, however, tax receipts have been insufficient to meet the current outlays necessary to maintain the program of the federal government. In such years, it becomes necessary to borrow funds. The United States Government borrows funds from a variety of sources and with various forms of instruments. In connection with the investment of savings by individuals, major interest centers in United States savings bond programs. Investing in other types of government securities is discussed in Chapter 11.

Series E Savings Bonds

Series E United States savings bonds have probably been the most popular kind of bonds ever sold. During World War II, numerous drives were conducted to stimulate the sales of government bonds, particularly the Series E bonds. Payroll deduction plans for purchasing the bonds were in effect in practically all the factories and other places of employment throughout the land.

Many companies, after the war ended, continued the payroll deduction plan for employees to purchase savings bonds. This method of buying bonds is highly recommended since it results in regular, systematic savings. Bond-a-month plans are also available through most commercial banks at no additional charge. The bank will subtract the cost of the bond from the individual's checking account at agreed-upon intervals and purchase the bond for him.

Although the savings bonds cashed in have approximately equaled the new bonds sold since 1955, the almost $50 billion still outstanding in United States savings bonds represents an important investment of the savings of individuals.

Many features of Series E savings bonds have been changed since these bonds were originally issued in 1941. Two basic changes have taken place over the years: (1) a steady increase in yield so that savings bonds could remain competitive with other possible savings investments, and (2) a change in the type of purchasers who are eligible to buy Series E savings bonds. The original bonds had a maturity date ten years from date of issue. These early bonds had a net yield to maturity of 2.9 per cent. In order to increase the net yield, the federal government has shortened the time to maturity and has left the total dollar return the same. The latest change became effective December 1, 1965, when the yield to maturity of new Series E bonds was increased from 3.75 per cent to 4.15 per cent.

Term and Redeemability. A Series E savings bond may be purchased at most financial institutions and at many post offices. The bond will be dated as of the first day of the month in which payment of the issue price is received by an agent authorized to issue the bonds. This date is called the issue date and the bond will mature and be payable at face value seven years and nine months from that date. The issue date is the basis for determining the redemption periods indicated in Table 6–6. Any bond may be redeemed prior to maturity at any time after two months from the issue date, at the owner's option, at a fixed redemption value, as indicated in Table 6–7.

Holders of Series E savings bonds are given an optional extension privilege after maturity. This means they may retain the bonds after maturity for a ten-year period known as the extended maturity period. Interest during the extended maturity period will be calculated upon the original maturity value of the bond. No special action is required of owners desiring to take advantage of the optional extension privilege. They will earn further interest merely by continuing to hold their bonds after maturity, but no interest accrues until the end of the first half-year period following maturity. The bonds will increase in redemption value at the end of each successive half-year period thereafter. Owners of bonds with issue dates of May 1, 1941, through May 1, 1949, are granted a second optional extension privilege. The redemption value of any bond at the end of the extended maturity period will be the base upon which interest will accrue during the second extension period.

Payment of a Series E bond will be made upon presentation and surrender of the bond by the owner to authorized paying agencies. These agencies include Federal Reserve banks and branches, commercial banks and other financial institutions, and the Treasury of the United States. The owner receives immediate payment of the current redemption value. A Series E bond in a denomination higher than $25.00 may be redeemed in part but only in the amount of an authorized denomination or multiple thereof. The unredeemed part will be reissued in authorized denominations bearing the original issue date. In this way, no interest is lost on the unredeemed part.

Denomination. The issue prices of the various denominations of Series E savings bonds are as follows:

Denomination	Issue Price
$ 25.00	$ 18.75
50.00	37.50
75.00	56.25
100.00	75.00
200.00	150.00
500.00	375.00
1,000.00	750.00
10,000.00	7,500.00
100,000.00	75,000.00

The $100,000 bond is available only for trustees of employee savings plans. Savings stamps in authorized denominations may be purchased at

Table 6–6. Series E Savings Bonds: Redemption Values and Investment Yields for Bonds Bearing Issue Dates Beginning December 1, 1965

									Approximate Investment Yield	
Maturity Value Issue Price	$25.00 18.75	$50.00 37.50	$75.00 56.25	$100.00 75.00	$200.00 150.00	$500.00 375.00	$1,000.00 750.00	$10,000 7,500	On Purchase Price from Issue Date to Beginning of Each Half-Year Period	On Current Redemption Value from Beginning of Each Half-Year Period to Maturity
Period After Issue Date	Redemption Values During Each Half-Year Period (values increase on first day of period shown)									
First ½ year	$18.75	$37.50	$56.25	$ 75.00	$150.00	$375.00	$ 750.00	$ 7,500	0.00%	4.15% *
½ to 1 year	18.96	37.92	56.88	75.84	151.68	379.20	758.40	7,584	2.24	4.30
1 to 1½ years	19.32	38.64	57.96	77.28	154.56	386.40	772.80	7,728	3.02	4.34
1½ to 2 years	19.70	39.40	59.10	78.80	157.60	394.00	788.00	7,880	3.32	4.38
2 to 2½ years	20.10	40.20	60.30	80.40	160.80	402.00	804.00	8,040	3.51	4.41
2½ to 3 years	20.52	41.04	61.56	82.08	164.16	410.40	820.80	8,208	3.64	4.44
3 to 3½ years	20.96	41.92	62.88	83.84	167.68	419.20	838.40	8,384	3.75	4.46
3½ to 4 years	21.42	42.84	64.26	85.68	171.36	428.40	856.80	8,568	3.84	4.46
4 to 4½ years	21.89	43.78	65.67	87.56	175.12	437.80	875.60	8,756	3.91	4.48
4½ to 5 years	22.37	44.74	67.11	89.48	178.96	447.40	894.80	8,948	3.96	4.50
5 to 5½ years	22.86	45.72	68.58	91.44	182.88	457.20	914.40	9,144	4.00	4.52
5½ to 6 years	23.36	46.72	70.08	93.44	186.88	467.20	934.40	9,344	4.04	4.57
6 to 6½ years	23.88	47.76	71.64	95.52	191.04	477.60	955.20	9,552	4.07	4.64
6½ to 7 years	24.42	48.84	73.26	97.68	195.36	488.40	976.80	9,768	4.11	4.75
Maturity value (7 years from issue date)	$25.00	$50.00	$75.00	$100.00	$200.00	$500.00	$1,000.00	$10,000	4.15	—

* Approximate investment yield for entire period from issuance to maturity.

Outstanding E and H bonds purchased before December 1, 1965 *earn 4/10 of 1% more than before for the remaining period to next maturity.* There will be lesser improvement in yields if bonds are redeemed earlier. The increase will be on a graduated scale, starting with the first interest period of five months or more which begins on or after December 1, 1965. There is no retroactive increase in interest rates for periods prior to December 1, 1965.

Interest rates on bonds entering a new extension period beginning December 1, 1965:

1. Unmatured E bonds:
   a. Issued April 1956 through April 1957 (which had not reached maturity before December 1, 1965) on which 3¾% ten-year extension had already been promised and those issued May 1957 through May 1959 on which a ten-year extension had been promised, will earn interest at an annual rate of about 4.15% for each half-year period of holding to extended maturity.
   b. Issued beginning with June 1959 have already been promised a ten-year extension privilege. Interest rates and other terms and conditions will be determined as they approach maturity.
2. Matured E bonds, issued December 1945 through May 1949 (which had not reached first extended maturity before December 1, 1965) on which a 3¾% second ten-year extension had already been promised will now earn interest at an annual rate of about 4.15% for each half-year period of holding to second extended maturity.
3. Unmatured H bonds, issued April 1956 through January 1957 (which had not reached maturity before December 1, 1965) on which a 3¾% ten-year extension had already been promised will earn interest at an annual rate of about 4.15% for each half-year period of holding to extended maturity.

Fig. 6–6. Increase in the yield of outstanding Series E and Series H savings bonds, effective December 1, 1965. (United States Treasury Department.)

Table 6–7. Examples of Improvement in Outstanding E Bonds, Effective December 1, 1965; Value of $100 Denomination Bond at Next Maturity

Issue Date	Before December 1965 Revision	After December 1965 Revision	Period to Next Maturity (years)	Length of Current Maturity Period (years)
June 1965	100.00	102.88	7¼	7¾
June 1960	100.00	100.92	2¼	7¾
June 1955	149.12	154.40	9	10
June 1950	145.88	148.48	4½	10
June 1945	201.12	208.68	9½	10

Source: Office of the Secretary of the Treasury, Office of Debt Analysis.

any post office or other agency where Series E bonds are on sale. These stamps may be used to accumulate credits for the purchase of Series E bonds. An accumulation of $18.75 in savings stamps entitles the holder to the receipt of a $25.00 savings bond. In order to increase the net yield to maturity on Series E savings bonds outstanding as of December 1, 1965, the federal government provided for payment of a slightly larger maturity value than the denomination indicated on the face of the bonds outstanding.

The limit on the amount of any Series E bonds issued during any one calendar year to any one person is $10,000 in maturity value. Co-ownership would increase this limit to $20,000. Special limitation provisions also apply to employees' savings plans. The limitations on holdings have varied from time to time in the past but those stated above are current limits.

Interest. Series E bonds are known as discount bonds. No interest as such is paid on the bonds. The return to the holder is the difference, if any, between what he pays for the bond and what he receives when he cashes the bond. If it is redeemed within six months from the issue date, the holder gets only the amount he paid for the bond. Thereafter the amount increases each six months. The rate of return on all Series E bonds of the same issue date is the same, regardless of the denomination of the bond.

A $100 Series E bond costs $75. After a period of seven years from the issue date, the bond can be redeemed for $100. This represents an increase of 33⅓ per cent for the period, which is at the rate of approximately 4.76 per cent a year. Thus, if we were to express the rate of return in terms of simple interest, we would have to say that the yield was about 4.76 per cent. But if the bond is held to maturity, since no return is paid on it until the end of the period, the purchaser does not get the use of any interest money at the end of each six-month period. If he had his money in a savings account in a bank or savings and loan association, he could either withdraw the interest (or dividend) or have it credited to his account. In the latter case his return for the next period would be computed on this new balance.

When the government states the yield on Series E bonds to be 4.15 per cent if held to maturity, it means that this is the rate of return, compounded semiannually. In other words, if the purchaser pays $75 for a Series E bond and holds it to maturity, the government allows him interest at an annual rate of 4.15 per cent for the first six months; the next six months' interest at the annual rate of 4.15 per cent is allowed not only on the $75, but on the interest which was earned for the first six months. This process is continued during the entire period. It should be remembered that this rate of interest is earned only if the bond is held until maturity. Figure 6–6 shows the increase in yield of outstanding Series E and Series H bonds, effective December 1, 1965.

It is of some interest to the investor to know the rate of return he would be earning on his money if he cashed the bond before maturity. Of even greater importance is what rate of interest he would have to earn, if he reinvested his money elsewhere, to equal or to exceed the rate he would earn on his bond, from the time he contemplated cashing it until the maturity date. Table 6–6 gives this information.

The first column under "yield" in Table 6–6 shows the yield (interest compounded semiannually) which a purchaser of a bond would get on his money from the date of issue, if he cashed the bond at the beginning of one of the various half-year periods. Thus, if a holder cashed a $100 bond after he had held it three years, he would receive $83.84. Since he paid $75 for the bond, the difference of $8.84 represents his interest return at the rate of 3.75 per cent a year, compounded semiannually.

The holder should not reason that because of this comparatively low rate of return, he should sell the bond. In fact, just the opposite conclusion should be reached. If the bond has yielded only 3.75 per cent for the first three years, and will yield 4.15 per cent if held until maturity, then obviously the rate of return for the remaining years would be greater than 4.15 per cent. The last column in Table 6–6 shows the rate of return (compounded semiannually) on the current redemption values at the beginning of each of the six-month periods to the maturity date. The person who has held the bond for three years would get $83.84 if he cashed it. But at the end of an additional four years he would get $100.00. The difference of $16.16 represents interest on the $83.84. As shown in the table, this is at the rate of 4.46 per cent for the remaining years. In other words, if you have held a Series E bond for three years, you would have to earn 4.46 per cent on your money for the next four years to equal the return you would be getting if you held your bond to maturity. If an individual has a number of different maturities, and has to cash some of them, it would be to his advantage to cash the bonds which have the longest period to run to maturity.

In addition to shortening the maturity of new bonds sold since December 1, 1965, the federal government also increased the return on all bonds outstanding at that time. This was done by offering to pay higher amounts upon redemption or maturity than originally agreed upon by contract at the time of issue.

Registration. Generally, only residents of the United States, its territories and possessions, the Commonwealth of Puerto Rico, the Canal Zone, and citizens of the United States temporarily residing abroad are eligible to invest in Series E bonds. The bonds may be registered in the names of natural persons in their own right or in the names of fiduciaries and organizations. All types of organizations, including private corporations, partnerships, unincorporated associations, and public corporations, may purchase Series E savings bonds. The only type of organization specifically excluded is commercial banks.

The bonds will be registered in the name of either an adult or a minor in one of three ways: (1) in the name of one person; (2) in the names of two (but not more than two) persons as co-owners; and (3) in the name of one person payable on death to one (but not more than one) other designated person. The address of the registered holder is stated on the bond. The following examples illustrate the types of registration in the order stated above:

(1) John H. Smith
123 Blank Street
Blankville, N. Y.

(2) John H. Smith
123 Blank Street
Blankville, N. Y.
or,
Mrs. Mary E. Smith

(3) John H. Smith
123 Blank Street
Blankville, N. Y.
Payable on death to
Mrs. Mary E. Smith

In the case of registration in the names of co-owners, as in example (2) above, it will be noticed that the two names are joined by the word "or," rather than the word "and." Perhaps it would be more correct to speak of this form of registration as "alternative ownership" rather than "co-ownership." Under this form of registration, either of the so-called co-owners could cash the bond by his endorsement without the consent or endorsement of the other. Whoever has possession of the bond would have full power over it. Although this may at times be a disadvantage, in case of death of one of the co-owners the other one would be considered the sole owner of the bond without the necessity for establishing proof of death, or having it transferred to his name.

The form of registration which indicates a beneficiary, as in example (3) above, gives the registered holder full control over the bond during his lifetime. He, and only he, can sell the bond at any time, without consulting the beneficiary. At the maturity of the bond, the money is paid to the registered holder if he is living. No change can be made in the beneficiary without his consent, as long as he lives, without cashing the bond. If the registered holder wants to eliminate the name of the beneficiary, or change the beneficiary, and cannot secure the latter's consent, he must cash the bond and have a new one issued in the form desired. This, of course, would result in a loss of interest.

Holders of bonds should always copy down the type of bond, date of purchase, and serial number of each bond purchased. This information should be kept in a place different from the bonds. In case the bonds are lost, the Bureau of Public Debt should be notified immediately, and the above-stated data given them. Payment will be made or substitute bonds will be issued to take the place of the old ones upon satisfactory proof of the loss. If the bonds have been mutilated, whatever part of them remains should be sent to the Bureau of Public Debt.

Series E savings bonds may not be used as collateral for a loan or as security for the performance of an obligation, nor can they be transferred by voluntary sale or gift, or discounted or disposed of in any manner other than through redemption as described above. The Treasury Department will recognize only the inscribed owner, during his lifetime, and thereafter his estate or heirs.

Taxability. The income received on Series E savings bonds is subject to the federal income tax. The holder can report the income in one of two ways. The increase in the redemption value may be reported as income each year, or the holder can wait until he redeems the bond and report the difference between the purchase price and the redemption value as income for that particular year. Series E bonds are also subject to the federal estate tax, and to state inheritance taxes and gift taxes, but are exempt from all other state or local taxes in respect to both principal and interest.

Safety and Liquidity. Since our entire money, credit, and business structure revolves around the federal government, securities of the federal government are considered to be minimum risk securities. The United States has never defaulted on any of its obligations. As a result, Series E savings bonds are considered minimum risk investments.

The liquidity of Series E savings bonds is also excellent. With the exception of the initial 60-day waiting period, these bonds may be cashed in at a sizable number of convenient locations without advance notice. The holder is readily assured of receiving his investment back in a very short period of time.

Return. Many Series E savings bonds were bought during World War II for patriotic reasons rather than for their investment value. On the other hand, safety and liquidity of these securities were unquestioned, and the return at that time (2.9 per cent) was competitive with other low-risk savings institutions. Following World War II, other savings media increased the rate of return available to savers. In spite of increased returns provided for in 1952, 1957, and 1965, the returns on Series E savings bonds tended to lag behind those offered by some other safe and liquid savings media. As indicated in Fig. 6–2, savings bonds

Table 6–8. Series H Savings Bonds: Checks Issued and Investment Yields for Bonds Bearing Issue Dates Beginning December 1, 1965

Face Value: Maturity Value / Redemption Value* / Issue Price	$500 / 500 / 500	$1,000 / 1,000 / 1,000	$5,000 / 5,000 / 5,000	$10,000 / 10,000 / 10,000	Approximate Investment Yield on Face Value	
Period of Time Bond Is Held After Issue Date	Amounts of Interest Checks for Each Denomination				From Issue Date to Each Interest Payment Date	From Each Interest Payment Date to Maturity **
½ year	$ 5.50	$11.00	$ 55.00	$110.00	2.20%	4.27%
1 year	9.70	19.40	97.00	194.00	3.03	4.30
1½ years	10.75	21.50	107.50	215.00	3.45	4.30
2 years	10.75	21.50	107.50	215.00	3.65	4.30
2½ years	10.75	21.50	107.50	215.00	3.78	4.30
3 years	10.75	21.50	107.50	215.00	3.86	4.30
3½ years	10.75	21.50	107.50	215.00	3.92	4.30
4 years	10.75	21.50	107.50	215.00	3.96	4.30
4½ years	10.75	21.50	107.50	215.00	4.00	4.30
5 years	10.75	21.50	107.50	215.00	4.03	4.30
5½ years	10.75	21.50	107.50	215.00	4.05	4.30
6 years	10.75	21.50	107.50	215.00	4.07	4.30
6½ years	10.75	21.50	107.50	215.00	4.08	4.30
7 years	10.75	21.50	107.50	215.00	4.10	4.30
7½ years	10.75	21.50	107.50	215.00	4.11	4.30
8 years	10.75	21.50	107.50	215.00	4.12	4.30
8½ years	10.75	21.50	107.50	215.00	4.13	4.30
9 years	10.75	21.50	107.50	215.00	4.13	4.30
9½ years	10.75	21.50	107.50	215.00	4.14	4.30
10 years (maturity)	10.75	21.50	107.50	215.00	4.15	—

* At all times, except that bond is not redeemable during first 6 months.
** Approximate investment yield for entire period from issuance to maturity is 4.15 per cent per annum.

attracted a decreasing percentage of individuals' savings. The increase in return, effective in 1965, to 4.15 per cent again made United States savings bonds competitive with many other savings media. Since 1965, some other savings media have again increased return. All bonds issued before December 1, 1965, if held to their extended maturity period, yield somewhat less than 4.15 per cent, compounded semiannually to maturity.

It must be recognized that the 4.15 per cent return on Series E savings bonds is realized only if the bond is held for seven years from issue date. As indicated in Table 6–6, the yield for any period of time shorter than seven years is less than 4.15 per cent. If the bond is held one year or less, the yield is under 2¼ per cent. These bonds must be held at least two years in order to yield 3.5 per cent. The return on Series E savings bonds is satisfactory only for longer-term holdings.

Series H Savings Bonds

Series E savings bonds appeal only to those people who are willing to wait until original maturity or longer to receive income from their investment. Many savers are desirous of receiving income currently rather than waiting until the investment is redeemed. As a result, the federal government issued Series H savings bonds, beginning June 1, 1952. Series H bonds are current income bonds; that is, the interest is paid semiannually from date of issue by check sent to the holder of the bond. On Series E savings bonds, interest is received when the bonds are redeemed and it is the amount by which redemption value exceeds the purchase price. Many of the provisions of Series E savings bonds also apply to Series H bonds. Only those provisions which are different will be included in this discussion.

Features. Series H savings bonds are issued at face or par value. As indicated in Table 6–8, the issue price, redemption value, and maturity value are all the same. Series H savings bonds may be redeemed at face value at any time after six months from issue date. One-month notice must be given for redemption. The bonds are issued only in registered form and in denominations of $500, $1,000, $5,000, and $10,000. Series H bonds may be purchased only at Federal Reserve banks and branches and at the office of the Treasurer of the United States. Customers of commercial banks and other financial institutions can arrange for the purchase of Series H bonds through such institutions. The income derived from Series H bonds is subject to federal income taxes as is that from Series E bonds; however, the holder of the Series H bonds must include interest received in his federal income tax return the year in which he receives the interest. He does not have the option of the Series E holder of paying income taxes on interest received at the time of maturity.

Series H savings bonds pay the same net yield to maturity as do Series E savings bonds; however, Series H bonds must be held ten years before they yield 4.15 per cent. Since the redemption value remains the same, the variation in yield for length of time held is obtained by paying smaller interest checks during the first year that the bond is held. After one year, the interest check is the same in amount. As indicated in Table 6–8, the approximate investment yield from issue date to redemption time increases as the bond is held to maturity (ten years). After the first year the net yield to maturity is 4.30 per cent per year.

The investment yields on all outstanding Series H bonds with issue dates prior to June 1, 1959, were increased in June, 1959, by not less than ½ of 1 per cent if held to maturity, and effective December 1, 1965, the yield was increased 4/10 of 1 per cent for the remaining period to next maturity.

Interest checks in excess of those amounts agreed upon in the original contract will be sent to the bondholders.

Series H bonds issued between June, 1952, and January, 1957, may be retained for an additional ten years with semiannual interest payments at the rate of 4.15 per cent per annum. No extension privilege has yet been announced for Series H bonds issued as of February, 1957, or later. The annual purchase limit per individual buyer is $20,000 as compared to $10,000 (maturity value) for Series E bonds. Series E bonds can be converted into Series H bonds at the option of the holder. If taxes have not been paid currently on the Series E bonds, the tax on the accumulated interest of the Series E bonds can be deferred until the Series H bond is redeemed.

Investment Status. Series H savings bonds carry the same safety features as Series E bonds. The liquidity of Series H bonds, however, is not quite as great. Series H bonds may not be redeemed until six months after issue date and one month's notice is required. This is not true of Series E savings bonds.

The return on Series H savings bonds is approximately the same as on Series E bonds with the exception that, in order to earn the maximum return, the bonds must be held ten years rather than seven years. A comparison of Tables 6–6 and 6–8 indicates that Series E savings bonds yield slightly less than do Series H savings bonds for the same period if redeemed prior to maturity. Since the lowest denomination of the Series H bond is $500, it obviously does not appeal to the very small investor. When its purchase can be afforded, the Series H bond fits those who need or want a current income.

In early 1966 the government stepped up its campaign to sell savings bonds.

OTHER SAVINGS OUTLETS

Savings and loan associations, commercial banks, mutual savings banks, and credit unions are generally classed as *savings institutions.* In addition, Series E and Series H bonds are known as *savings bonds.* There are, however, many other possible media for the investment of savings. Some of these, such as real estate, corporate stocks and bonds, municipal bonds, investment companies, and owning your own business are discussed later in the text. These are not generally classed as savings media because they are variable-value rather than fixed-value investments or because they require larger initial investment than is generally available for the average investor. The remaining savings media are life insurance, postal savings, and various employee plans.

Life Insurance

Figure 6–2 indicates that life insurance reserves are the most important type of savings investment for individuals. While the rate of growth in life insurance reserves owned by individuals is not as great as in other savings media, these reserves are still $17 billion greater than the next most important media. However, the major purpose of purchasing life insurance is not savings. Therefore, the savings feature of certain types of life insurance is considered as secondary. Our discussion of life insurance as a savings medium is covered in the next chapter in connection with the use of life insurance to combat risk.

Postal Savings

The postal savings system was started by the Post Office Department in 1910. It was founded because of the lack of availability of banks for many individuals who wanted to maintain savings accounts. Post offices were readily accessible to most people in the country and it was thought advisable by the federal government to provide a type of savings account through these facilities. Postal savings grew at a less rapid rate than savings in other financial institutions, after the establishment of federal insurance for savings institutions. In the late 1940's, postal savings accounts exceeded $3⅓ billion. By 1965, however, deposits in postal savings had decreased to just under $600 million. Many savings institutions believe that the real need for the postal savings system has long since passed and, because it is in direct competition with private savings institutions, it should be abolished.

Postal savings accounts can be opened at almost any post office, in his or her own name, by any competent person of the age of ten years or

Table 6–9. Comparison of Various Types of Investments for Savings

Investment	Safety of Dollar Principal	Rate of Return	Certainty of Return	Liquidity	Lack of Costs to Get In and Out	Inflation Hedge
Cash	Excellent	0 %	—	Excellent	Excellent	Poor
Postal savings	Excellent	2	Excellent	Excellent	Excellent	Poor
United States savings bonds	Excellent	4.15	Excellent	Excellent	Excellent	Poor
Commercial bank time account	Excellent	2½–4	Excellent	Excellent	Excellent	Poor
Mutual savings bank	Excellent	3–4¼	Excellent	Excellent	Excellent	Poor
Savings and loan association	Excellent	3–5	Excellent	Excellent	Excellent	Poor
Life insurance savings	Excellent	2½–3½	Excellent	Excellent	Excellent	Poor
Credit union	Excellent	4–5	Good	Good	Excellent	Poor
Employee plans	Excellent	Variable	Good	Poor	Excellent	Variable
U. S. Government bonds	Excellent	2–4½	Excellent	Excellent	Good	Poor
Municipal bonds	Excellent	2–4½	Excellent	Good	Good	Poor
Corporate bonds	Good	3½–5½	Good	Good	Good	Poor
Preferred stock	Fair	4–7	Good	Fair	Poor	Poor
Investment companies	Fair	3–7	Fair	Fair	Poor	Fair
Listed common stock	Fair	3–7	Fair	Fair	Poor	Good
Closely held common stock	Poor	5–10	Poor	Poor	Poor	Good
Own business	Poor	5–20	Poor	Poor	Poor	Good
Real estate mortgages	Good	5–8	Good	Fair	Poor	Poor
Rental real estate	Fair	5½–10	Fair	Poor	Poor	Fair
Unimproved real estate	Poor	0	—	Poor	Poor	Good

more. The maximum amount an individual can have to his credit, exclusive of accumulated interest, is $2,500. When deposits are made, certificates with a face value of the deposits are completed and given to the depositor. These certificates are issued in denominations ranging from $5 to $2,500.

Since postal savings are actually placed directly with the United States government through the Post Office Department, savings are fully guaranteed in respect to both principal and interest by the United States government. Thus, postal savings offer excellent safety to the investor and no loss has been experienced by any saver to date. Withdrawals can be made at any time upon presentment of the certificates to the post office.

The rate of interest paid on postal savings certificates is 2 per cent per year. Interest begins on the first day of the month following the deposit, and it is collectible for each three-month period following the date on which interest starts. On certificates issued after September 1, 1954, the interest is compounded annually on whole-dollar amounts. A 2 per cent rate of interest is considerably lower than that available from most other savings institutions. Since these other savings institutions are sufficiently safe to meet the requirements of most investors, the postal savings system is becoming relatively unimportant as a savings institution.

Employee Savings Plans

There is an almost infinite number and variety of employee savings plans. Some of these involve saving through regular institutions by payroll deduction for purchase of savings bonds or by deposit in savings accounts. Many others, however, are specialized and are included among the fringe benefits for the employees. Very often, the employee does not contribute the total amount. Various pension and profit-sharing plans involve a savings feature for employees. Total values in employee profit-sharing plans now exceed $5 billion. The very rapid growth in these funds has taken place within the last ten years. Their safety depends upon the types of investment made with the funds. No generalizations can be made. Liquidity and return to saver depend upon the features of the various plans. Social security (discussed in Chapter 18) is a type of employee savings plan.

CONCLUSIONS

Table 6–9 compares various types of investments for savings; some of those listed are discussed in later chapters. These investments are compared on the basis of certain criteria which are important in selecting savings media. Relative to types of investments discussed later, the savings investments discussed in this chapter rate excellently on safety of dollar principal, certainty of return, liquidity, and economy in buying and selling. They are all very poor hedges against inflation. The major variation among these specific investments is in rate of return. While there is some differential in degree of safety of dollar principal, certainty of return, and liquidity, all of the savings media discussed in this chapter, with the possible exception of credit unions, rate very satisfactorily for these criteria. The certainty of return in the credit union varies with the specific credit union. With the exception of life insurance and credit union savings, the other savings media discussed in this chapter are either the direct obligation of the government or are insured by an agency of the federal government. Life insurance savings rate excellently in safety, certainty, and liquidity, despite the lack of government agency insurance.

Table 6–10. Financial Assets and Liabilities of Individuals—Selected Years, 1950–1963 (in billions of dollars, as of end of year)

Assets and Liabilities	1950	1955	1959	1963
FINANCIAL ASSETS				
Total	n.a.	737.5	958.6	1,242.3
Currency	23.4	25.9	25.7	28.8
Demand deposits	49.7	55.7	56.3	62.1
Time and savings deposits	56.9	74.7	96.8	135.8
Savings and loan shares	14.9	34.5	58.2	97.7
U. S. savings bonds	49.6	50.2	45.9	48.0
Other U. S. Government securities	18.0	18.2	29.3	26.8
State and local government securities	12.9	18.7	26.3	32.9
Corporate bonds and notes	n.a.	21.6	19.8	22.9
Investment company shares	n.a.	13.8	20.7	34.2
Other corporate stocks	n.a.	262.7	372.3	487.8
Insurance reserves	57.0	76.8	92.3	111.9
Insured pension reserves	5.6	11.2	17.6	23.0
Non-insured pension reserves	5.5	15.9	30.3	51.3
Government insurance and pension reserves	39.9	57.5	67.2	79.0
LIABILITIES				
Total	58.4	117.9	169.5	245.5
Mortgage debt	37.7	79.0	118.6	174.2
Consumer debt	17.9	33.9	46.1	63.2
Securities loans	2.8	5.0	4.8	8.1
NET EQUITY				
Assets minus liabilities	n.a.	619.6	789.1	996.8

n.a. = not available

SOURCE: Securities and Exchange Commission.

Table 6–10 gives the financial assets and liabilities of individuals in selected years. Financial assets, as covered by this table, do not include all of the investments listed in Table 6–9, but do cover the great majority of them. It can be seen that the net worth of individuals has been increasing over the years. The savings media discussed in this chapter, excluding pension plans, account for 39 per cent of the total financial assets of individuals. It is obvious that the type of financial assets chosen by an individual for his savings depends on the purpose for which he is saving and his requirements for safety, return, liquidity, and purchasing power protection.

QUESTIONS

1. Why do most Americans save? What will be your reasons for saving in the future?
2. What factors should you consider in selecting a medium for investing your savings?
3. What is the primary investment for personal savings? Why do you think this is the most important?
4. Comment on the following statements:
   (a) "Savings represent postponed spending."
   (b) "A person should spend what he does not save rather than save what he does not spend."
   (c) "The bulk of the savings of most people represents forced savings."
5. How does a savings and loan association differ from a commercial bank?
6. What is meant by the "dual" system in chartering savings and loan associations?
7. Differentiate a mutual from a stock organization.
8. Comment on safety and liquidity of savings accounts in savings and loan associations.
9. What is meant by compounding of interest? Why is compounding of importance to an investor? Would you prefer annual or semiannual compounding?
10. Comment on safety and liquidity of savings accounts in commercial banks.
11. Differentiate a mutual savings bank from a commercial bank.
12. Comment on safety and liquidity of savings in a mutual savings bank.
13. Discuss trends and present amount of return on savings in savings and loan associations, commercial banks, and mutual savings banks.
14. (a) When a person invests money in a credit union, is he a creditor or part owner of the organization?
    (b) How do you account for the fact that the rate of return in the past has usually been higher than for comparable investments?
    (c) Why have the dividend rates paid by credit unions been lowered in recent years?

15. Comment on the following in regard to the new Series E savings bonds:
   (a) Denominations
   (b) Maturity
   (c) Redeemability
   (d) Rate of interest
   (e) How interest is paid
   (f) Investment status
16. A person buying a Series E bond pays $75 and gets $100 back in seven years. This $25 represents a 33⅓ per cent increase in his principal, or an increase of approximately 4.76 per cent for each year. Why is the yield advertised as only 4.15 per cent?
17. (a) Indicate the circumstances under which you would recommend the purchase of Series E bonds.
   (b) Indicate the circumstances under which you would not recommend the purchase of Series E bonds.
18. Compare Series H bonds with Series E bonds with respect to:
   (a) Denominations
   (b) Maturities
   (c) Redeemability
   (d) Rates of interest
   (e) How interest is paid
   (f) Investment status
19. Explain the advantages and disadvantages of buying United States savings bonds as compared with depositing the savings in the institutions discussed.
20. Of the various types of savings or savings accounts mentioned in this chapter, which would you prefer for yourself? Why?

CASE PROBLEMS

1. Bill Ripley graduated from college three years ago and was married last year. He and his wife were able to purchase their furniture and appliances with money they saved before they were married. Since their marriage last year, they have finished making payments on their automobile. Bill earns $600 per month, and, although they are expecting an addition to their family shortly, he feels that they can save $90 per month through careful budgeting. The credit union where Bill works will take savings by payroll deduction and is now paying 5 per cent per annum. Should they put their savings in a credit union? What other savings media are available to them? Where can they get the highest return? Where can they get the greatest safety? What besides safety and return should be considered in investing their savings? What are the advantages and disadvantages of the credit union over other savings institutions?
2. Roy Randolph was given $1,000 upon graduation from college by his grandfather. He has decided to save the money for necessary purchases after he marries. At the moment, however, he has no marriage plans and no responsibilities. He has his money in the local commercial bank in a checking account. He has been thinking of putting it into a savings account at the same bank at 3½ per cent interest per annum. He recently noticed an advertisement by a local savings and loan association that it is now

paying 4½ per cent. Should Roy move his account? If so, where? What is wrong with leaving the funds in the checking account? What are the advantages and disadvantages of the savings and loan account relative to the commercial bank? What other places should Roy consider before deciding on a depository for his funds?

3. The Scott Wilsons are thrilled at the birth of their first child—a boy. Since Scott's income is not large, they would like to start saving now toward the funds needed to send their son to college. At present-day costs, they estimate that they will need $8,000 to pay for his education at an eastern university. They would like to open some kind of account for this special purpose and start making periodic deposits in the account. What kind of account would you suggest they open? Which savings institution might best meet their needs? Why? How much will they need to set aside each year in order to have $8,000 fifteen years from now? Do you think this is a wise move for the Wilsons?
4. Glenna and Mark Hanna have been married three years and have one child. They have just been able to make ends meet living in an unfurnished apartment and paying Mark's insurance premiums. They have no savings. Glenna has now inherited $10,000 from a great aunt. What do you suggest she should do with the $10,000 inheritance? Should all or part of it go into a savings institution? Which type of savings institution might best meet her needs?
5. Alan Wright has just inherited $80,000. He has a fairly good income, is married, has three children, owns his own home, has a small savings account, and has sufficient insurance. His wife feels they should put the funds in Series E savings bonds. Wright prefers something which would give them a current income so they could increase their standard of living. He, therefore, wants to purchase Series H bonds. Do either Series E or Series H bonds meet the Wrights' needs? What would you do with the money? What other types of investment are available besides government bonds? How many Series E or H bonds could the Wrights purchase at this time?
6. Bruce Short is saving money for a car down payment. He is putting aside $15 per month toward the $350 he needs. His company's personnel officer has suggested he use the firm's bond deduction payroll plan for the accumulation of his savings. This plan allows deduction from wages for the purchase of Series E savings bonds. What advantages and disadvantages would this saving technique have for Bruce? What would you recommend?
7. Rate the desirability of Series E savings bond investment for your "rainy day" fund. Compare it to investing in a time account in a commercial bank in your area. Also compare it to a savings and loan account or mutual savings bank account in your area.

SELECTED READINGS

American Bankers Association. *The Commercial Banking Industry.* Englewood Cliffs, N. J.: Prentice-Hall, Inc., 1962.

Bogen, Jules I., and Shipman, Samuel S. (eds.). *Financial Handbook,* Fourth Edition. New York: The Ronald Press Co., 1964.

Bureau of Federal Credit Unions. *Report of Operations, Federal Credit Unions.* Washington, D. C.: U. S. Department of Health, Education, and Welfare. Latest edition.

Claycamp, John. *The Composition of Consumer Savings Portfolios.* Urbana: Bureau of Economic and Business Research, University of Illinois, 1963.

Conway, Lawrence V. (ed.). *Savings and Loan Principles.* Chicago: American Savings and Loan Institute Press. Latest edition.

Department of Health, Education, and Welfare. *The Federal Credit Union Act.* Washington, D. C.: U. S. Government Printing Office, 1963.

Facts You Should Know About Saving Money. New York: National Better Business Bureau. Latest edition.

Hanc, George. *The United States Savings Bond Program in the Postwar Period.* New York: National Bureau of Economic Research, 1962.

International Credit Union Yearbook. Madison, Wis.: Credit Union National Association. Published annually.

Kendall, Leon T. *The Savings and Loan Business.* Englewood Cliffs, N. J.: Prentice-Hall, Inc., 1962.

Mutual Savings Banking Annual Report. New York: National Association of Mutual Savings Banks. Published annually.

National Association of Mutual Savings Banks. *Mutual Savings Banking.* Englewood Cliffs, N. J.: Prentice-Hall, Inc., 1962.

Prather, William (ed.). *Savings Accounts.* Chicago: American Savings and Loan Institute Press. Latest edition.

Results of 1962 Savings Survey. 4 Vols. New York: American Bankers Association, 1963.

Savings and Home Financing Chart Book. Washington, D. C.: Federal Home Loan Bank Board. Latest edition.

Savings and Loan Fact Book. Chicago: United States Savings and Loan League. Latest edition.

Securities of the United States Government. Boston: The First Boston Corporation. Published biennially.

Statistics on the Savings Market. New York: American Bankers Association, 1964.

Survey of Consumer Finances. (Survey Research Center.) Ann Arbor: University of Michigan Press. Latest edition.

Tips for Tellers and Bond Officers About United States Savings Bonds. Washington, D. C.: U. S. Government Printing Office, 1959.

Trescott, Paul B. *Financing American Enterprise, The Story of Commercial Banking.* New York: Harper & Row, 1963.

United States Savings Bonds, Series E. Washington, D. C.: U. S. Government Printing Office, 1959.

United States Savings Bonds, Series H. Washington, D. C.: U. S. Government Printing Office, 1959.

7

Buying Life Insurance

Life insurance companies are the most important type of thrift institution for the investment of personal savings in the United States. However, the primary purpose of life insurance is not thrift—it is *protection*. Because of its importance in family protection, life insurance is discussed separately from other savings media. All life insurance policies involve some kind of protection; they do not necessarily include a savings or thrift feature.

Insurance is a social device in which a large group of persons, each of whom is subject to a similar risk, contribute to a common fund to compensate for the few who actually suffer some unusual loss. Thus, the insured person voluntarily takes a known loss—his contribution (premium) to the fund—to overcome the possibility of a much larger loss which may occur. The insurance principle requires that a large number of persons contribute and that only a few suffer unusual losses. In this way, the group bears the risk of those who actually experience the loss. Insurance of all types is based on this principle. The insurance agreement is based on the law of averages, using large numbers. Insurance changes uncertainty into certainty for the insured and his family.

Life insurance is a specific application of this insurance principle to the unexpected loss of human life. The basic hazard or loss for which life insurance is carried is the death of the insured before his average life expectancy. Life insurance varies from other types of insurance in that every insured eventually dies, whereas in the case of automobile liability insurance, for example, not every insured has an accident in which he is liable. As a result, the risk insured by life insurance is not the risk of dying, it is the risk of death before normal life expectancy. The time of death is unknown of course, but averages, using large numbers, can give very reliable estimates of time of death for the entire population based on age. The insured group pays a premium to compensate those who die early.

The basic concept of insurance also requires that the risk involve economic loss. The protection feature of life insurance is based on an economic value of the man as a living, working unit. His future earning power is important to the maintenance and well-being of his dependents. When he dies, his earning power is lost to his family. This potentially substantial economic loss is the basic hazard met by life insurance. Other economic hazards would be funeral costs, last illness expenses, expenses necessary to hire a housekeeper in the event of the death of the wife, and loss in value of business properties due to the death of the manager of the business. Many types of policies have been developed which include features other than protection of dependents in event of untimely death, but all life insurance policies, regardless of other features offered, are based on average life expectancy and include some measure of protection against an early death of the insured. Therefore, part of the premium paid on any life insurance policy goes to compensate those insureds who die before normal life expectancy.

IMPORTANCE OF LIFE INSURANCE

At the beginning of 1965, total reserves of life insurance companies (excluding National Service Life Insurance) in the United States exceeded $120 billion. This represents the value of the savings of the policyholders in the various life insurance companies. While $120 billion is larger than the savings in any other thrift institution, the figure is dwarfed by the amount of face value of life insurance in force. At the beginning of 1965, total life insurance in force in the United States (in legal reserve companies) was $800 billion, an average of approximately $13,300 per American family and approximately $16,600 per insured family. There are more than 135,000,000 policyholders in the United States. Total life insurance in force equals 26 months of disposable personal income. The amount of life insurance in the United States has increased about 100 times since 1900.

United States life insurance companies received premiums of $22,653 million in 1964. These premiums equaled 3.95 per cent of disposable personal income in that year. Total assets of life insurance companies were over $149 billion at the beginning of 1965. This makes life insurance companies, among all financial institutions, second only to commercial banks in amount of assets. Beneficiaries of life insurance policies received $10.7 billion in benefits in 1964.

Why Buy Life Insurance?

Since all types of life insurance policies involve some amount of protection in the event of untimely death, protection for dependents becomes the primary reason for the purchase of life insurance. Any person who has others dependent upon him for their financial well-being should make provision for the continued financial support of these dependents in the event of his death. Most people are unable to accumulate an investment estate large enough to provide for their dependents after their own death. This is particularly true if the insured dies comparatively young. The need for protection of dependents is based on the age and ability of the dependents rather than upon the age of the insured. The need for protection to provide for dependents is normally the greatest at the time an individual's earnings and estate are smallest in amount. The major way that such a person can have an appreciable estate for his dependents in the event of an early death is through the purchase of life insurance.

Figure 7–1 indicates the reasons given for the purchase of life insurance by individuals, in a comprehensive study in the United States. It is apparent that support for dependents was the primary factor in the minds of most people. Clean-up funds were also important—particularly when suggested by the interviewer. Clean-up funds are another way of protecting heirs. By providing burial expenses and other clean-up funds from insurance, it is unnecessary for the insured's heirs to meet these expenses from other sources. The sixth suggested reason, mortgage repayment, is also a protection for heirs and dependents. The last mentioned item, borrowing, also fits into this category. The third, fourth, and fifth reasons for purchase of life insurance are related to the savings concept. These reasons were mentioned substantially less often than those related to support for dependents or protection of estate. It is apparent that in the minds of purchasers the savings feature in most life insurance policies is secondary to the protection feature offered.

This survey of consumer attitudes toward insurance included a question regarding the chief reasons for *not* carrying life insurance. Over 50 per cent of the families who had no life insurance stated that they could not afford it. This is a highly questionable reason in many cases. What one can afford is a function of what he desires most with his available resources; very often, financial planning for low-income families indicates that they cannot afford *not* to have life insurance on the family breadwinner. Approximately 20 per cent of the respondents who did not have life insurance policies stated that they disapproved of life insurance. This reason is obviously based on some other factor and is not particularly meaningful. Eighteen per cent of those without policies were ineligible,

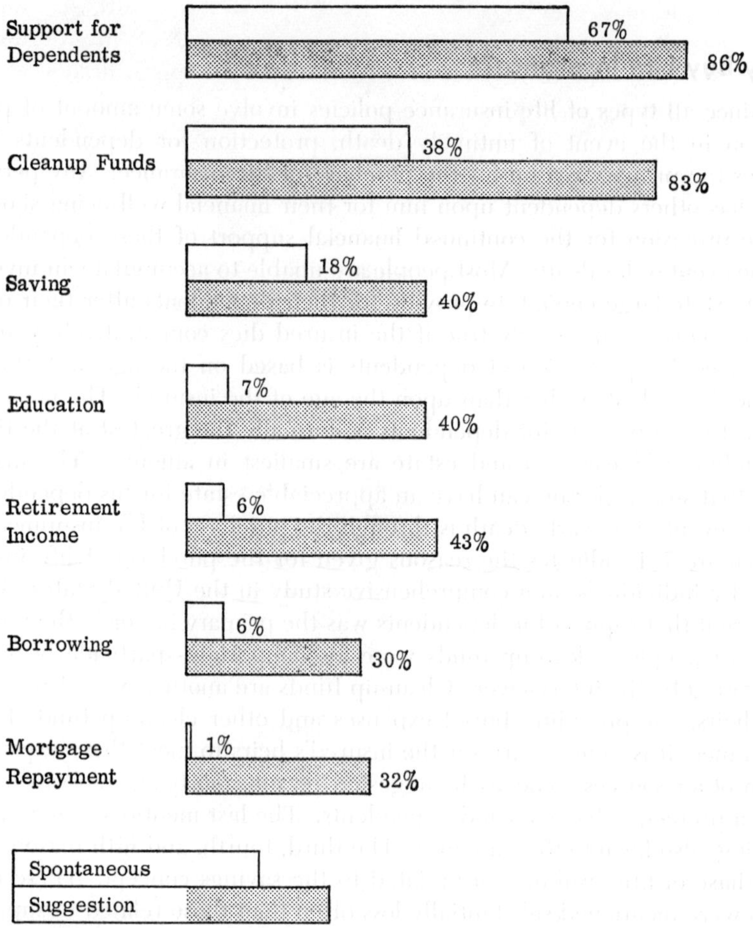

NOTE: Percentages add up to more than 100 because respondents could give more than one answer.

Fig. 7–1. Percentage distribution of reasons, given spontaneously and after suggestion, for purchasing life insurance, United States, 1955. (Reproduced with permission, from *The Life Insurance Public*. New York: Institute of Life Insurance, 1957.)

generally from a medical viewpoint. Only 14 per cent of those without life insurance stated that they did not need it. These tended to be people without dependents. Another 10 per cent preferred other ways of saving. These were probably people without dependents whose potential use of life insurance was only for savings.

Saving through insurance is useful for all of the purposes of saving discussed in the earlier chapters. Figure 7–1 indicates that retirement income is the most mentioned reason for the purchase of life insurance for savings. It is interesting to note that educational uses of life insurance savings appear to be particularly important also. The life insurance companies have done a good job of selling the American public on the ability to meet future college expenses through purchase of life insurance for children soon after they are born or in their early years. Thus, depending upon the type of policy, life insurance may be helpful in the same way as all other safe forms of liquid savings to meet the needs of unprotected old age, family misfortunes, long unemployment or business reverses, and permanent or temporary disability during the working period of life.

Insurance on Wife and Children

Life insurance as a savings medium can be useful to anyone. However, every life insurance policy involves a protection feature and a charge must be made for this feature. From the above discussion it is apparent that life insurance on the typical breadwinner in a family is extremely important. Certainly, insurance on a wife and children should not be considered at all until the breadwinner is adequately insured for the protection of the wife and children. If the death of the wife would lead to economic loss to the family, insurance on her life to make up for that loss may be considered. This would be particularly true if the wife is working and contributing to the family's support. Even if she is not working, expenses for family maintenance may arise in the event of the death of the wife. Under these circumstances, insurance on a wife may be desirable, but it is often possible for the breadwinner to meet these extra expenses without the need for insurance on his wife's life.

From a protection point of view, insurance on the life of children is even more questionable. The beneficiaries of the typical policy on a child are the parents. In most circumstances, the family would not suffer economically if the child died, or at least, would not suffer financial loss other than the cost of the funeral. Thus, life insurance on children should not be purchased with an objective of protection against financial loss except for the coverage of burial expenses. These can, in most cases, be handled out of other income of the family. Major justification for purchase of life insurance on children, therefore, is either the savings feature or the starting of an insurance program for the child in order that his insurance payments in the future, when he has definite need of insurance for protection, will be less. The first of these reasons involves savings only, and the potential purchaser should question whether there may not be more desirable ways of saving for a child's needs—particularly his education. Since part of the premium paid goes to pay the costs of protection, the total amount of the premium is not saved. A decision to start a child on an insurance program at a very young age when his payments are very low would depend upon family resources and other economic objectives.

When To Buy Life Insurance

The timing of the purchase of insurance is related to the objectives which the insurance policy is designed to meet. If the individual is buying insurance primarily for protection of his dependents, he should buy it at the time he has the greatest financial responsibility to his dependents. If life insurance is being purchased for the savings feature, the purchases would normally be made as savings become available.

It is obvious that the greatest need for life insurance comes at the beginning of the average man's working life. Each additional child born into the family is a potential financial burden on the husband's estate. As children grow older, the total amount necessary to support them until they are self-supporting becomes less. The cost of providing for a wife until her death becomes progressively less as the wife grows older. Thus, a man's insurance protection needs grow rapidly from the time of his marriage until all his children are born. At that point, the total protection need begins to decrease and continues to decrease throughout the remainder of his life. Unfortunately, most family heads do not obtain their highest earning power at the same time they have the highest protection requirements for dependents. It would be ideal if the ability to pay for insurance went hand in hand with the need for it. Unfortunately, this is not the case. In fact, just the opposite is usually true: when an individual's income is lowest, his insurance needs are generally greatest; as his income increases, his insurance needs tend to decrease.

In spite of reduced ability to pay premiums, the typical young married couple just starting to raise a family has the greatest life insurance protection requirements. The authors believe that these people would be wise to reduce other expenditures and to buy a type of life insurance which will give them the amount of protection they will need, in spite of low income at this point in their life. It takes almost $30,000 in life insurance to provide a newborn child with $150 per month until he is 21. When parents bring children into the world, they should be prepared to provide the child with financial protection in the event of their death.

The present value of future expected income is greatest for younger people. The death of a man at age 25, who would have earned $600 per month until age 65, causes a loss to a family of $288,000. If this person dies at age 45 instead, the loss to the family is $144,000. If he retires at age 65, his death at that age causes his family little financial loss, due to decreased future earning power.

Table 7–1 gives the characteristics of individuals as related to their life insurance ownership. A higher percentage of males are insured than females, and the highest percentage of the population carrying insurance, by age, are in the 35 to 44 age bracket. A higher percentage of husbands in families with children under 18 are insured than in families without children under 18. A much smaller percentage of unrelated individuals (who would tend to have fewer dependents) are insured.

When buying insurance for its savings feature, the purchase should be made as the savings become available. For the typical individual, the ability to save increases as his income grows throughout his working life, and as his children mature and are no longer financially dependent on him. It is found that the purchase of insurance *for savings* and the ability to purchase it generally move hand in hand. As a family head grows older, his reasons for owning life insurance tend to change from protection of dependents to saving for retirement or estate purposes.

Timing the purchase of life insurance is also related to the age of the insured and to his ability to pass a physical examination. The annual premium on life insurance policies increases as an individual grows older. Thus, the older a person is, the more it will cost annually to carry the same life insurance policy. It should be kept in mind that the lower annual premium for younger people is paid over a longer period of years. This (plus the mortality rates) accounts for the fact that the annual premium is lower for younger people.

A young person will usually pass the medical examination necessary for most types of policies. Many people who feel the need for insurance and have the money to pay for it regret that they did not buy a policy when they were younger and could have passed the physical examination.

In recent years, some insurance companies have offered in their life policies an additional feature called the "insurability option." For an additional premium, this entitles the purchaser of the policy to buy more life insurance as he grows older without the necessity of a medical examination. The physical examination taken at the time of the purchase of the first policy insures the purchaser of being able to buy additional amounts of insurance up to a given level at varying times in the future.

Specific points in a life cycle when the purchase of insurance should be considered are at the time of marriage, when each child is born, when substantial debts are incurred, and when savings funds are available.

How Much Life Insurance To Buy

The proper amount of insurance an individual should carry is dependent upon a great many personal factors. It is impossible to work out any formula which would give an answer for every individual to the question: "How much insurance should I buy?" The major causes for variation between the amounts of insurance required by different individuals are the objectives to be accomplished by the insurance, the amount

Table 7–1. Characteristics of Individuals and Life Insurance Ownership—1960

	Individual Life Insurance *		All Types of Life Insurance **	
	% of Persons Insured	Mean Amount Owned By Insureds	% of Persons Insured	Mean Amount Owned By Insureds
Age				
Under 6	48%	$1,263	50%	$1,280
6–13	51	1,364	54	1,362
14–17	54	1,277	57	1,273
18–24	60	2,745	67	3,562
25–29	62	4,624	74	6,840
30–34	59	5,464	73	7,651
35–44	66	6,056	78	8,786
45–54	64	4,826	75	7,180
55–64	58	3,459	70	4,755
65 or Older	42	2,444	52	2,718
All Persons	56	3,386	64	4,702
Adult–Child Status and Sex				
Males 18 or older	65	6,921	82	9,691
Females 18 or older	54	1,764	60	2,134
All adults	59	4,444	70	6,290
Males under 18	52	1,463	54	1,466
Females Under 18	49	1,144	52	1,149
All children	51	1,312	53	1,316

	Individual Life Insurance *		All Types of Life Insurance **	
	% of Persons Insured	Mean Amount Owned By Insureds	% of Persons Insured	Mean Amount Owned By Insureds
Family Status				
Heads of husband–wife families	67%	7,604	85%	$10,600
With children under 18	70	9,130	90	12,594
Without children under 18	64	5,397	80	7,637
Other family heads	58	2,616	73	3,711
Male	56	4,299	80	5,414
Female	59	2,040	70	2,964
Wives	55	1,788	59	2,098
Other household members under 18	51	1,312	53	1,316
Other household members 18 or older	56	2,184	62	2,808
Unrelated individuals	41	2,651	57	4,239
All persons	56	3,386	64	4,702

Table 7–1 (Continued). Life Insurance Ownership of Family Heads by Income Group Among Husband–Wife Families with Family Head Under Age 65—1960

	Personal Income of Family Head					
	Under $3,000	$3,000–$4,999	$5,000–$8,999	$9,000–$14,999	$15,000 or more	Total
Individual life insurance *						
Percentage of family heads insured	53%	62%	78%	88%	88%	70%
Mean amount owned by insureds	$2,757	$4,415	$ 7,189	$14,242	$50,224	$ 8,178
All types of life insurance **						
Percentage of family heads insured	71%	87%	96%	95%	94%	89%
Mean amount owned by insureds	$3,783	$6,000	$11,616	$22,042	$66,560	$11,399
Distribution of insureds by years of income covered by life insurance						
Less than 1 year	52%	46%	34%	31%	27%	40%
1 year but less than 2 years	15	29	32	27	20	28
2 years but less than 3 years	10	14	21	19	25	17
3 or more years	23	11	13	23	28	15
Total	100%	100%	100%	100%	100%	100%
Distribution of insureds by types of life insurance owned						
Individual only	51%	32%	25%	33%	22%	32%
Individual and other types	24	39	56	60	72	47
Other types only	25	29	19	7	6	21
Total	100%	100%	100%	100%	100%	100%

* Ordinary and/or industrial (but not group) life insurance with legal reserve life insurance companies.
** Individual life insurance plus group, fraternal, veterans, etc.

SOURCE: *Life Insurance Fact Book, 1964.*

of the financial responsibility for dependents, the amount of savings desired in the insurance policy, and the other assets of the insured. It is necessary to study each individual case separately in attempting to answer the above question.

Since protection for dependents is the most important single reason for the purchase of insurance, the factors which affect the amount necessary for this purpose are important in planning any insurance program. Protection of dependents includes an amount of capital necessary to meet estate clean-up expenses in the event of death, sufficient funds to provide living income for children until they are able to provide for themselves, income for the wife until her death, and amounts necessary to meet any obligations, such as a home mortgage, of the insured after his death. The major factors affecting the amount of insurance necessary for the above purposes are:

1. Present family standard of living
2. Amount of salary, other income, and property of the insured
3. Amount of income and property, if any, of dependents
4. Number and ages of dependents

The standard of living of an individual's family may, and usually does, increase as his income rises. Most family heads are interested in enabling their dependents to maintain after their death the same standard of living that was enjoyed during their lifetime. If this is the case, a larger amount of insurance is necessary as the family's standard of living increases.

If an individual owns real estate or securities from which additional income other than salary is earned, this should be taken into account in determining his insurance needs. Such income will, of course, be much more important to his dependents than his salary because it will not stop at his death. Certain types of investments may be liquidated upon the death of the insured to provide funds for his dependents. Generally speaking, the larger the personal estate of the insured, the less the need for insurance for protection purposes.

If the insured's family has, or will have, income from other sources after his death, the amount of insurance required for their protection is reduced. The wife may own property in her own name from which income may be obtained. In certain cases, children may have property inherited from grandparents which is available to support them until they are able to support themselves.

Since the primary purpose of life insurance is to give protection to dependents in event of the death of the insured, the number and age of the dependents is the most important consideration in determining the insurance needs of a particular individual. The dependency of children is normally temporary rather than permanent. The younger the child, however, the longer the period of dependency and the greater the amount necessary to provide for him until he is able to provide for himself. Obviously, the amount of insurance necessary for protection increases as the number of children increase. The amount necessary to provide an income to the wife for life decreases as she becomes older.

In speaking of protection for dependents, it should be kept in mind that we are not talking about insurance on the wife, or on the children. The insurance is carried on the life of the husband, or father. It is his death which would lessen or eliminate the family income, and therefore the insurance should be carried on him.

Analysis of the above factors leads to an estimate of the dollar amount needed at the time of death for clean-up funds and liabilities, and after death for monthly income requirements for differing periods of years in the future. These figures can then be converted into the face value of the life insurance required to meet these needs. Table 7–2 gives estimates

Table 7–2. Amount of Money Required to Provide Life Income under Various Circumstances (assumes annuity payout)

Requirements	Principal Required
$200 per month for life Woman–age 60	$ 40,600
$400 per month for 18 years, $250 per month for life Woman–age 30	112,300
$300 per month for life Woman–age 50	29,400
$500 per month for 15 years, $300 per month for life Woman–age 35	104,700

of amounts of life insurance required to meet differing circumstances. Any qualified insurance agent can determine the face amount required to meet any future dollar requirements you give him. Social security payments and funds from employee plans should be subtracted from total estimated needs before deciding how much life insurance to carry.

The amount of insurance necessary to meet the savings objectives of the insured is dependent upon what the insured plans to do with his savings. The amount of income he desires upon retirement can be determined, and, from this, the amount of insurance necessary to provide this income. If the insurance is to be used to provide a college education for children, the amount required can be determined from the expected expenditure for college.

A life insurance planning form such as the one given in Fig. 7–2 may be helpful to establish how much insurance you should buy. The problem

How Much Insurance? Use this form to estimate your needs.

Clean-up Expenses			Cash Available		
Medical care	$		Savings	$	
Funeral			Social Security		
Debts and bills			Group insurance		
Taxes			Other		
Insurance loans					
Estate settlement					
Extra family expense					Needed from life insurance
Total needed	$	Less	Total available	$	= $

Mortgage			Cash Available		
Balance outstanding, or payments pending sale	$		Savings	$	Needed from life insurance
			Other		
		Less	Total available	$	= $

Family's Monthly Expenses			Monthly Income Available		
Housing	$		Social Security	$	
Utilities and household operation			Investments		
Food			Earnings		
Clothing			Other		
Medical care					
Incidentals (car, personal, recreation)					Needed monthly from life insurance
Total needed	$	Less	Total available	$	= $

Fig. 7–2. Form for estimating insurance needs. [Reprinted by permission 1956 by The Kiplinger Washington Editors, Inc., 1729 H. Street, N. W., Wash-

of determining the amount of insurance can be resolved if the individual, in his planning, separates his protection needs from his savings needs and then decides how each need can best be met with available funds.

Savings Through Life Insurance

Life insurance is the only type of contract available which offers protection to the insured's family in the event of his untimely death. On the other hand, life insurance is only one of many possible means of saving. In deciding to save through life insurance, the individual should consider the advantages and disadvantages of this type of saving relative to other savings institutions. It is normally possible to purchase the protection feature of life insurance alone without including any savings.

Emergency Fund			Cash Available		
			Savings	$	
			Investments		
			Group insurance		Needed from life insurance
			Other		
Estimated need	$	Less	Total available	$	= $

Wife's Monthly Expenses to Age 65			Monthly Income Available		
			Investments	$	Needed monthly from life insurance
			Earnings		
Estimated budget (follow family-period headings)			Other		
	$	Less	Total Available	$	= $

Wife's Monthly Expenses After Age 65			Monthly Income Available		
			Investments	$	Needed monthly from life insurance
			Social Security		
Estimated budget (follow family-period headings)			Other		
	$	Less	Total Available	$	= $

Special Funds			Cash Available		
For	$		Investments	$	Wanted from life insurance
For			Other		
Total wanted	$	Less	Total Available	$	= $

from *Changing Times,* the Kiplinger Magazine (February 1956 issue). Copyright ington, D. C. 20006.]

The major factors considered in our discussion of financial institutions in Chapter 6 were safety, liquidity, and return. Life insurance as an investment has an outstanding safety record which has been maintained without the use of government-sponsored insurance on savings. In theory, savings in life insurance companies are no safer than the assets and reserve position of the companies. In practice, United States life insurance companies have offered excellent safety although, in recent years, there have been some failures among newly founded companies.

Liquidity of savings in life insurance companies is also very good. Only a very short time is required to borrow the loan value (equivalent to the savings feature of the policy) from the insurance company. Also, only a short period of time is required to cancel a life insurance policy and obtain the cash surrender value (also equivalent to the savings feature of the policy). The liquidity problem in life insurance is that if one does cancel his policy, he loses the protection feature which he may wish to maintain. In order to keep the protection feature and still obtain the use of one's savings, the insured has to borrow his savings from the company. This involves a payment of interest for the use of the savings.

The return on savings in life insurance has varied over the years. The current contractual rate for most United States insurance companies is 3 to 3½ per cent. Many policyholders have an opportunity to earn more than this through participating in dividends on their policies. On the other hand, the rate paid by most insurance companies is currently lower than that paid by most other financial institutions.

A major advantage of saving through life insurance is the relatively forced nature of this type of saving. Many individuals will pay life insurance premiums when they will not put funds into some other financial institution. It is much easier psychologically for most people to withdraw savings from other financial institutions than to borrow on life insurance policies or to cancel life insurance policies. A certain portion of our population finds it impossible to save in any other way than through the payment of life insurance premiums. For these people, life insurance as a savings medium is extremely important.

SELECTING A COMPANY

After you decide how much insurance to buy and when to buy it, you still must select a specific company from which to purchase the policy, and you must decide which type of policy to buy. It is hoped that the readers of this text will be more sophisticated in selecting a company from which to purchase a policy than the average individual who merely buys a policy because some insurance salesman calls upon him and sells it to him. A high degree of care should be exercised in selecting an insurance company. If you are buying a $10,000 life insurance policy, you should realize that you may have an investment of $10,000 in that particular company before you die. An investment of that much money demands proper care in the selection of the company.

Almost any insurance agent will try to get you to buy insurance in his particular company in order to earn his commission. Life insurance salesmen receive for their first-year commission from 10 to 100 per cent of the first year's premium. During the next ten years or so, if the policy is kept in force, they will receive an additional amount. Thus, if the policy is kept in force, the salesman may be receiving a total commission greater than one year's premium.

Life insurance salesmen are by no means equally informed on insurance. Those who have passed the Chartered Life Underwriters examination, and thus have the CLU designation, are capable of giving sound advice, but it does not follow that all of them give it. Many agents not possessing the CLU are equally well informed.

There are definite ways of determining the better companies, and at least some of these can be used by the average individual without much trouble. In many instances the company selected would depend upon the type of policy to be purchased. A particular company, for example, may offer a straight life policy under more favorable terms than any of the other companies, while another company may be preferred for a limited-payment life policy.

The size of an insurance company is somewhat of an indicator of the relative financial stability of the company. The very heart of insurance is the diversification of risk, and the larger the company, the greater the possible diversification. The large companies are also generally the oldest companies. The management may be better in an old company. The 15 largest life insurance companies in the United States at the present time are shown in Table 7–3. The first six companies carry approximately half of all the insurance in force in the United States today, and all 15 of them carry about two-thirds of the total. Size alone does not make a company a good one. There are a number of safe and well-managed medium-sized companies that offer life insurance on better terms than some of the large companies. The emphasis that has been placed on size here is due to the fact that the uninformed insurance buyer would probably do better in

Table 7–3. Fifteen Largest Life Insurance Companies in the United States—January 1, 1964

Company	Year Established	Insurance in Force
1. Metropolitan	1868	$106,517,192,000
2. Prudential	1873	96,606,523,000
3. Equitable Life of New York	1859	46,539,735,000
4. Travelers	1863	34,141,826,000
5. John Hancock	1862	32,833,536,000
6. Aetna Life	1850	29,204,498,000
7. New York Life	1841	28,840,579,000
8. Connecticut General	1865	14,691,868,000
9. Occidental Life	1906	13,596,879,000
10. Lincoln National Life	1905	12,701,200,000
11. Northwestern Mutual	1857	11,945,659,000
12. Massachusetts Mutual	1851	10,420,267,000
13. Mutual of New York	1842	9,392,582,000
14. Continental Assurance	1911	8,833,819,000
15. New England Mutual	1835	8,500,795,000

SOURCE: *The Spectator 1964 Life Index.*

buying from the typical large company than from the typical small one. Buyers should be particularly cautious of relatively new companies.

The individual should determine which of the better companies offers him the lowest rates. If the companies are, as far as can be determined, about equally safe, there is no reason why the insurance should not be purchased from the company offering the lowest premium rates. The following, although it is not quite accurate, is the simplest way of finding the net cost of the insurance. If the policy is *participating* (holder is entitled to dividend at year end if earnings permit), deduct the total dividends paid on this type of policy for the past 10 or 20 years from the gross premiums paid over the same period of time. From this figure deduct the cash surrender value of the policy at the end of the same 10- or 20-year period. The result is the net cost of the insurance (protection).

Mutual life
Imperial life

This method may be criticized in that the net cost of the insurance to the buyer will depend upon the amount that will be paid in dividends in the *future* while he is holding the policy. But nobody knows what that will be. Therefore, the only tangible figure that can be used is the one representing the past dividends. The prospective buyer, however, can give some weight to the trend of the dividends, and compare this with the trends in other companies.

A relatively high net cost company, however, may still be preferred because of other factors. For example, if a company allows interest at the rate of 3 per cent on money left with it, this company might be preferred over one paying interest at 2 or 2½ per cent, even if its premium rates are higher.

Although the quality of the company and the insurance cost are the most important factors to consider in selecting a company, several others should be taken into account. To some extent, the expenses of the company in relation to the insurance in force show the efficiency of the administration.

The yield which the companies make on their investments may also be compared. A high yield would be preferred if it can be obtained with safety.

Mortality experience of the companies may be compared. Generally speaking, a low rate would be favorable, but a new company would probably show a more favorable rate than an old company simply because the majority of its policyholders may not have reached the age when death is more likely to occur.

Types of Companies

Life insurance companies are either stock companies or mutual companies. The *stock* companies are owned by shareholders, and any profit the company makes goes not to the policyholders but to the shareholders.

The policyholder pays a premium of the same amount each year, which is fixed at the time the policy is issued. Efficiency of management, increased return on investment, or a favorable mortality experience may result in larger dividends to the stockholders rather than return to the policyholders. On the other hand, increased cost of operation, decreased return on investments, or a poor mortality experience will not result in larger premium requirements for policyholders. The premium charged by stock companies on non-participating policies is usually lower for the same type of policy than that charged by mutual companies. The stock companies charge these lower premiums in order to offset the dividends which policyholders in mutual companies receive. Some of the stock companies issue participating policies which have higher premiums than non-participating policies. In these policies, the insured shares the earnings along with the shareholders in the company. These policies are similar to policies in mutual life insurance companies. In making comparisons, it is probably better to compare types of policies rather than types of companies.

Mutual life insurance companies are owned by the policyholders; there are no stockholders. After setting aside certain reserves, the profits are paid to the policyholders in the form of dividends. Since there is no stock capitalization to back up the claims of policyholders, it is necessary for the mutual companies to charge higher premiums than the stock companies for the same type of policies. If the mortality experience, earnings, and expenses of the mutual company are such that all the premiums collected are not needed, part of them is returned to the policyholders in the form of dividends. These dividends can be paid to the policyholders, applied on the payment of subsequent premiums, or kept for the policyholder in the company at interest, at the option of the policyholder. From the above statements it is obvious that the mutual companies issue only the participating type policy. It is difficult to advise a prospective policyholder whether he should buy a non-participating policy in a stock company or a participating policy in a mutual company, because the dividend rates cannot be determined in advance. Excluding government insurance, about 60 per cent of the life insurance in force in the United States is carried by the mutual companies.

All of the large life insurance companies in the United States, regardless of whether they are stock or mutual companies, operate on what is called the *legal reserve* basis. Under this system the amount of the regular premium which will be paid for the particular policy is fixed in amount and can be ascertained by looking in the rate book. These premiums, judging from past experience, will be sufficient to pay the expenses of the company and to pay off the policies to the beneficiaries upon the death of the insured. Some small companies, particularly those connected with fraternal organizations, operate under the *assessment* plan. The amount of the premium is not known in advance but depends upon the expenses of the company and the amount of death claims which it had to meet the preceding year. These companies do not maintain reserves, as do the legal reserve companies, so the policies are secured only by the claims on future assessments. Generally speaking, companies operating under the legal reserve plan are recommended over assessment companies.

Regulation of Insurance Companies

Life insurance companies are among the most important financial institutions in the United States. The financial well-being of many millions of Americans is dependent upon the safety of these companies. For these reasons, the safety and integrity of life insurance company operations are basic to the American economy.

The importance of life insurance to the average individual has led to regulation of life insurance companies, agents, and salesmen. Life insurance regulation takes place at the state level. The state insurance commissioner or comparable official is charged with supervising the activities of the life insurance companies headquartered or operating within his state. He checks such things as investment patterns, reserve requirements, premiums, operating expenses, licensing of agents, types of policies issued, etc. Rules and regulations have been adopted relative to these matters by which the insurance company must abide in order to continue operating in the state. Obviously, the degree of supervision varies among the states, with the leading insurance states of New York and Connecticut setting the example for the rest of the nation. There is no federal supervision of life insurance companies other than taxation and regular interstate commerce regulation. Life insurance companies operating in more than one state are regulated by the state in which the company is incorporated but must also meet the requirements of all of the states in which they do business for that portion of their business which originates in those states.

Because the safety of a life insurance company is basically dependent upon its assets, much of the regulation of the life insurance companies is aimed at restricting the investment of their assets to safe investments. While government securities are extremely safe investments, the yields have generally been so low that life insurance companies have invested in them only a minor portion of their portfolios. Except during World War II and the immediately following years, government bonds have accounted for less than 10 per cent of the assets of life insurance companies and in recent years have accounted for less than 5 per cent. Other bonds have been more important, with public utility bonds, railroad bonds, and industrial and miscellaneous corporate bonds accounting for almost 40 per cent of assets. Mortgages have been second in importance, and with the exception of the war years have averaged more than 33 per cent of life insurance company assets. While holdings of corporate stocks have risen in recent years, they still account for less than 5 per cent of the assets.

Government Insurance

Most veterans of World War II were entitled to purchase insurance directly from the federal government. This was known as National Service Life Insurance and could be continued in force after the discharge of the veteran from the service. NSLI has been continued in force to date by periodic acts of Congress. While most servicemen and veterans, except for those with certain disabilities, are no longer eligible to purchase new or additional policies, existing policies may be continued or may be changed to other types of policies. NSLI has been lower in net cost to the insured than other sources of similar types of insurance. This is due to an excellent mortality rate, some federal government support, and lower operating expenses, including selling expenses. Those veterans who retained their NSLI policies were wise to do so, and it is recommended that these policies be continued in force in the future.

SELECTING A POLICY

The insurance buyer has a variety of types of policies and features from which to choose. He must decide the frequency of premium payments, the designation of the beneficiary, and the desired procedure for payment of proceeds. The types of policies are discussed in the next section of this chapter. Other decisions which the buyer must make are covered below.

Premium Rates

The basic principle of life insurance is based on the law of averages. Mortality tables, such as the one given in Table 7–4, have been constructed to show the number of deaths that will occur in a given group of insured people at various ages. With the use of such a table it is possible to determine how much an insurance company would have to charge people of a given age to have a sufficient amount available to pay the face value of the policy for the ones who die that year. With such a table it is, of course, not possible to determine just how long any particular person will live, but one can determine the average length of life for a group of persons at any particular age. The 1958 Commissioner's Standard Ordinary Table of Mortality (Table 7–4) has been adopted by most of the

Table 7–4. 1958 Commissioner's Standard Ordinary Table of Mortality

Age	Deaths per 1,000	Expectation of Life–Years	Age	Deaths per 1,000	Expectation of Life–Years
0	7.08	68.30	50	8.32	23.63
1	1.76	67.78	51	9.11	22.82
2	1.52	66.90	52	9.96	22.03
3	1.46	66.00	53	10.89	21.25
4	1.40	65.10	54	11.90	20.47
5	1.35	64.19	55	13.00	19.71
6	1.30	63.27	56	14.21	18.97
7	1.26	62.35	57	15.54	18.23
8	1.23	61.43	58	17.00	17.51
9	1.21	60.51	59	18.59	16.81
10	1.21	59.58	60	20.34	16.12
11	1.23	58.65	61	22.24	15.44
12	1.26	57.72	62	24.31	14.78
13	1.32	56.80	63	26.57	14.14
14	1.39	55.87	64	29.04	13.51
15	1.46	54.95	65	31.75	12.90
16	1.54	54.03	66	34.74	12.31
17	1.62	53.11	67	38.04	11.73
18	1.69	52.19	68	41.68	11.12
19	1.74	51.28	69	45.61	10.64
20	1.78	50.37	70	49.79	10.12
21	1.83	49.46	71	54.15	9.63
22	1.86	48.55	72	58.65	9.15
23	1.89	47.64	73	63.26	8.69
24	1.91	46.73	74	68.12	8.24
25	1.93	45.82	75	73.37	7.81
26	1.96	44.90	76	79.18	7.39
27	1.99	43.99	77	85.70	6.98
28	2.03	43.08	78	93.06	6.59
29	2.08	42.16	79	101.19	6.21
30	2.13	41.25	80	109.98	5.85
31	2.19	40.34	81	119.35	5.51
32	2.25	39.43	82	129.17	5.19
33	2.32	38.51	83	139.38	4.89
34	2.40	37.60	84	150.01	4.60
35	2.51	36.69	85	161.14	4.32
36	2.64	35.78	86	172.82	4.06
37	2.80	34.88	87	185.13	3.80
38	3.01	33.97	88	198.25	3.55
39	3.25	33.07	89	212.46	3.31
40	3.53	32.18	90	228.14	3.06
41	3.84	31.29	91	245.77	2.82
42	4.17	30.41	92	265.93	2.58
43	4.53	29.54	93	289.30	2.33
44	4.92	28.67	94	316.66	2.07
45	5.35	27.81	95	351.24	1.80
46	5.83	26.95	96	400.56	1.51
47	6.36	26.11	97	488.42	1.18
48	6.95	25.27	98	668.15	.83
49	7.60	24.45	99	1,000.00	.50

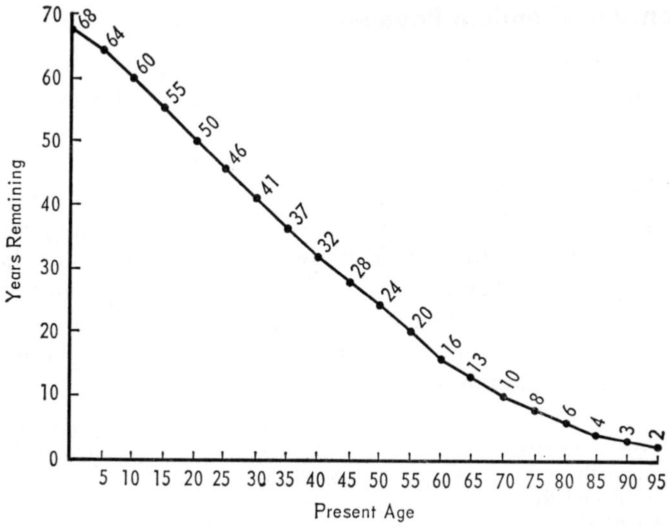

Fig. 7–3. Remaining life expectancy of individuals, by age, United States.

states for use by insurance companies in determining mortality experience and required reserves. Figure 7–3 gives the remaining life expectancy of individuals as they grow older. Since mortality rates for women are lower than for men, some companies offer lower-rate policies to women.

After determining the probability of death, the insurance company calculates what it expects to earn on its investments. The company next determines what portion of its total investment portfolio is applicable to each policy, and thereby obtains an investment return figure for each policy. The company also estimates the amount of its operating expenses and selling costs per policy. With this information it can determine what it should charge a person of a given age for premiums on a policy that gives only life protection for the period covered by the premium. The premium received plus the estimated investment income must equal a mortality payment plus the operating expenses of the company. On policies which have a loan and cash surrender value, the savings feature has to be considered in determining the premium rate. On these policies, the premiums will be proportionately higher. Some companies charge less per $1,000 for policies of $5,000 and higher than they do for policies that have a low face value.

Some companies increase the premium for special risk cases, such as pilots or miners. At least one company has a reduced premium rate for non-smokers of cigarettes, based on the assumption that a non-smoker's life expectancy is longer than a smoker's.

Frequency of Premium Payments

The basic premium rates of life insurance companies are figured on the basis of annual payments at the beginning of each policy year. If the policyholder desires, he may pay the premiums every six months or every three months, instead of annually. Some companies permit monthly payments. In industrial insurance, payments may be made weekly. When the premiums are paid oftener than on an annual basis, the policyholder is charged interest on the unpaid portion of the premium for the length of time it is unpaid. The rate of interest charged varies from 8 to 15 per cent among the different companies. The following shows the rates charged by a leading mutual company on a $5,000 straight life policy taken out on a male at the age of 25.

Premium Basis	Total Annual Premiums	Excess Over Annual Basis
Annually	$ 90.55	–
Semiannually	92.60	$ 2.05
Quarterly	94.72	4.17
Monthly	100.68	10.13

It is true, of course, that if the policyholder paid the premiums on a semiannual or quarterly basis, he would have the use of part of his premium money for part of the year, but the rate he could earn on it for this short period would undoubtedly be much less than he would have to pay in interest to the insurance company.

If it is inconvenient or impractical for the policyholder to pay the premiums annually on a $5,000 policy, for example, he can take out five $1,000 policies at different times during the year, and have each put on an annual basis. In this way the five payments would be about equal and would be staggered through the year. Some companies would charge no more for five $1,000 policies than for one $5,000 policy. Other companies would have a reduced premium for the latter policy. If the five policies are taken out at different times during the year, however, part of them will have slightly higher premiums because the insured's age, for rate purposes, changes six months before his next birthday.

A recent plan offered by some insurance companies (and approved by most banks) allows the insurance company to write a check against the insured's bank account every month for the amount of the monthly premium. This plan is usually at a lower rate than regular monthly premiums but still costs more than paying premiums annually. Some companies offer discounts for premiums paid in advance of the required payment date. Current discounts range from 4 per cent to 4½ per cent on advance premiums. In some cases, up to 20 years' premiums may be paid in advance. If this is done when the discount rate is 4 per cent, in a sense the money earns 4 per cent. However, since 1965, the savings must be reported as income for federal income tax purposes.

Designation of the Beneficiary

In most cases it is desirable to designate a beneficiary to whom the proceeds of the policy will be paid upon the death of the insured. If this is not done, the proceeds will be paid to the estate of the insured. This makes the proceeds of the policy subject to inheritance taxes and to the claims of creditors of the insured. The naming of a beneficiary may avoid these claims. In some states, however, even when a beneficiary is designated, the policy must state that it is not subject to creditors' claims, in order to escape them. A few of the states apply the inheritance tax regardless of whether a beneficiary is named. If the policy names no beneficiary, the proceeds would be taxable if paid to such an estate. The federal estate tax would also be applied in cases where a beneficiary had been indicated, if the insured at the time of his death retained any *incidents of ownership* in the policy, that is, any right or control over the policy, such as the right to change beneficiaries, the right to borrow against the policy, the right to surrender the policy, or the right to receive dividends. Despite what was said above in relation to the estate tax, it is often advisable for the insured to retain the right to change the beneficiary named in the policy. A change in marital status or other developments may make this highly desirable.

It may be advisable to name a contingent or secondary beneficiary in addition to the primary beneficiary. A married man who has no children may name his wife as the primary beneficiary, and his parents, if living, as the contingent beneficiaries. If his wife dies before he does, his parents would get the proceeds of the policy upon his death. If there are children, they can be designated as the contingent beneficiaries. If additional children are expected in the future, the policy should be worded to include them.

When a contingent beneficiary is designated, it should be noted that if the insured dies first, the proceeds of the policy are payable to the primary beneficiary, if living, and at her death the proceeds, if any are left, are payable to *her* heirs, and not to the contingent beneficiary. Thus, where there are no children and the insured's parents are named the contingent beneficiaries, if the husband (the insured) dies first, the insurance is payable to the wife. But if the wife dies before the proceeds are all paid out, *her* heirs, and not the husband's parents (the contingent beneficiaries) would be legally entitled to the proceeds. The same procedure would be followed in this case if no contingent beneficiaries had been named.

If the husband wants the proceeds of any insurance policy in which his wife is designated as beneficiary, or any other property, to go to his parents or to some other chosen party upon the death of his wife, he should have his wife make out a will to this effect.

A "common accident clause" or "common disaster clause" may be included in the policy stating who the beneficiary shall be in the event that both the insured and the primary beneficiary die within a stated period of time as a result of the same accident.

Payment of Proceeds

Upon the death of the insured, the proceeds are often paid in a lump sum to the beneficiary. Experience has indicated that certain beneficiaries, particularly children, and in some instances, wives, are not experienced in handling money and may dissipate the proceeds in a comparatively short time. It is, of course, possible to have the proceeds paid to a trustee or to some other party who will handle the estate of the beneficiary. It is also possible, however, to arrange for the proceeds to be paid to the beneficiary periodically rather than in a lump sum. Figure 7–4 gives four settlement options and the amounts which would be paid under each for a $10,000 policy.

If a policy is for an amount sufficient to pay only the funeral expenses and debts of the insured, the proceeds should be payable in a lump sum. But if the policy is for an appreciable amount, a more satisfactory arrangement would probably be to have it paid out to the beneficiary in periodic installments—usually monthly. The *lifetime income* option is an arrangement whereby the beneficiary is paid a fixed amount per month for the

Option	Settlement
The Interest Option	
Money left at interest until the family asks for it.	At 2½% interest, $250 a year until the money is withdrawn.
The Amount Option	
A regular income of as much money as you want, paid until money and interest are used up.	$100 a month for 9 years and 3 months, for example, or $200 a month for 4 years and 4 months.
The Time Option	
A monthly income to last as many years as you want, paid until money and interest are used up.	10 years income of $92 a month, for example, or 20 years income of $51 a month.
The Lifetime Income Option	
A regular income guaranteed for the person's lifetime.	$50 a month for life (for a woman 65 years old)
	$63 a month for life (for a man 65 years old)

Fig. 7–4. What $10,000 will provide under the four settlement options (interest figured at the guaranteed rate of 2½ per cent; companies will pay higher than this as earned). (Reproduced with permission, from *Decade of Decision.* New York: Institute of Life Insurance, 1964.)

remainder of his or her life (sometimes guaranteed for a given number of years regardless of an early death). The amount is based on the life expectancy of the beneficiary at the time of death of the insured and on the face value of the policy.

An *amount* option may be chosen which would pay the beneficiary a fixed amount per month until the face value of the policy and the accumulated interest were used up. A *time* option would pay the beneficiary a fixed amount per month for a given number of years. The amount per month would be based on the number of years selected and on the face value of the policy and the interest it would earn over the remaining years. In the time or amount options, a second party should be designated to receive the proceeds in the event of the death of the first beneficiary before the total amount is paid or the agreed-upon time has run out. This type of second or contingent beneficiary should be distinguished from the secondary beneficiary discussed above. (Under the lifetime income option, payments cease upon the death of the beneficiary and there is no need for a designated second party.)

Another option is the *interest* option, under which the beneficiary is paid only the interest on the money, with the face value payable to a second designated party, usually upon the death of the first beneficiary. Such an arrangement is obviously only meaningful when the amount of insurance is comparatively large. In effect, it asks the insurance company to invest the proceeds of the policy in the event of the death of the insured and to pay the income to the beneficiary until his death.

A *combination of payment* method may be desired. Under this arrangement, a certain portion of the proceeds of the policy is paid in a lump sum to meet funeral expenses and debt and the balance is paid in installments. The insured may designate a payment plan and provide that this plan is mandatory regardless of the wishes of the beneficiary, or he may indicate the particular plan he thinks is best to follow, but give the beneficiary the right to change it to another plan if desired (this can normally be done only at time of death). Giving the right to change to the beneficiary allows for circumstances that are unforeseen at the time the insured makes the decision on payment options.

Program Review

The insurance needs of a person change as time goes on. A person may marry and have children. Or, the children for whom he carried insurance protection may no longer be dependent upon him. Maybe other income-producing property has been accumulated to the extent that some of his insurance can be discontinued. His wife may now be so advanced in age that the amount of insurance needed to provide her a fixed income for life is less. Any of these possible changes would make it advisable for an individual to look over his insurance program periodically and size it up against his existing insurance needs. His program should be reconsidered whenever any changes take place which would affect his insurance needs. Even in the absence of such apparent changes, it might be a good idea for an individual to check over his insurance program every five years.

The financial objectives to be met with life insurance vary considerably over the typical life cycle. A young married couple with a growing family must emphasize protection in the event of the death of the breadwinner. As children grow older, there may be more emphasis on providing education funds for them. Once children leave home, the lost income due to death of the breadwinner becomes less important and the requirements to support the wife financially through the remainder of her life are less. More emphasis at this point may be placed upon retirement uses of life insurance.

A periodic review should include a check of benefits to which the insured is entitled. Potential new riders offered by the insurance company should be considered. Be sure that the desired beneficiary has not changed. Reconsider the dividend option alternatives and the option for the payment of proceeds in the light of circumstances as they exist at the time of the review. Consider conversion of one type of policy to another, and reconsider the total amount of insurance required and the cost of the insurance program in effect.

TYPES OF POLICIES

A wide variety of life insurance contracts are available to the individual, and they differ substantially in their relative emphasis on protection and savings. Leading insurance companies offer many types of insurance policies because the needs of individual purchasers vary considerably. No one policy meets every situation, but there is a life insurance policy to meet practically every individual's requirements.

Life insurance is commonly divided into three major classes—ordinary, group, and industrial—according to the way in which the insurance is sold. Ordinary insurance is sold on an individual basis through salesmen and agents. Premiums are paid directly to the company on a monthly, quarterly, semiannual, or annual basis. Group contracts are sold to a large number of individuals at once through their place of employment, or through fraternal and other interest groups. Industrial policies are sold to individuals but are paid on a weekly or monthly basis by having the insurance agent visit the individual to collect the insurance premium.

Another major way of classifying insurance policies is by the type of protection offered and the time period for payment of premiums. This classification includes term, straight life, limited-payment life, endowment, and combinations of these. Each of these types of policies may be available through ordinary or industrial purchases. (Group insurance is usually only of the term type.) In the discussion that follows, they will all be discussed under ordinary life insurance. The same principles are involved when the policies are purchased under an industrial or a group plan.

Almost 60 per cent of all life insurance in force in the United States is of the ordinary type. Table 7–5 indicates the breakdown by type of policy of all policies in force at the beginning of 1963. The $389.2 million in ordinary insurance represented 99 million policies. Ordinary policies are usually issued in amounts of $1,000 or more. The average size of policies outstanding is over $4,000; the average new policy sold in 1963 was $7,100. The various kinds of ordinary insurance are discussed below.

Ordinary Term Life Insurance

Term insurance is insurance payable to a beneficiary at the death of the insured provided death occurs within a specified period, such as one, five, ten, or twenty years, or before a specified age. Under the term insurance policy, the insured pays fixed premiums for a designated period, such as one, five, ten, or twenty years, or to a specified age such as 65. If he dies before the end of the period for which the policy runs, the face amount of the policy is paid to the beneficiary. If he lives beyond the life of the policy, the policy is automatically terminated at the end of the period (if not renewed) and nothing is returned to the insured. As indicated in Table 7–5, term insurance policies account for approximately 25 per cent of *all ordinary* life insurance in force, and over half of *all* types of life insurance in force.

If a person buys a one-year term policy, the contract is terminated at the end of the year. Many companies will write a one-year, renewable term policy under which the policyholder has the right to renew the policy for a fixed number of years, such as nine consecutive years, without medical re-examination. When the policy is taken out, the holder pays the premium rate for his particular age, but the rate would increase each year, upon renewal. Companies will usually not write or renew this insurance if the insured is older than 65. The one-year term policy has the lowest premium, since it is based on the age of the insured for that particular year. The contract usually provides that the policy may be converted into a level-premium term policy or any other permanent form of insurance upon the payment of the adjusted premium rates for the insured's existing age or for his age at the time the original policy was written, if the amount of the "reserve" is paid.

One of the most popular forms of term policies written today is the five-year term policy. The premiums which a person would have to pay

Table 7–5. Life Insurance in Force in the United States, by Plan (000,000 omitted)

Plan of Insurance	1950	1962
Ordinary		
Straight life	$ 55,200	$146,800
Limited payment life	37,700	65,800
Endowment	22,300	27,500
Retirement income with insurance	8,700	9,400
Regular term	6,800	19,900
Decreasing term	*	15,800
Extended term	1,800	6,400
Family policies		
Permanent	—	19,400
Term	—	14,500
Total	$ —	$ 33,900
Other combination policies		
Permanent	n. a.	26,600
Term	n. a.	37,100
Total	$ 16,600	$ 63,700
TOTAL	$149,100	$389,200
Industrial		
Straight life	$ 4,700	$ 3,100
Limited payment life	20,800	28,200
Endowment	6,200	4,300
All other	1,700	4,000
Total	$ 33,400	$ 39,600
Credit (term)	$ 3,900	$ 38,000
Group		
Regular term	$ 47,300	$203,300
All other	500	5,900
Total	$ 47,800	$209,200
Total		
Straight life	$ 60,100	$150,800
Limited payment life	58,600	70,700
Paid-up	—	23,300
Endowment	28,500	32,700
Retirement income with insurance	8,900	9,400
Regular and decreasing term		
Ordinary and industrial	6,900	35,700
Group and credit	51,200	241,300
Total	$ 58,100	$277,000
Extended term	3,200	9,700
Family policies		
Permanent	—	19,400
Term	—	14,500
Total	$ —	$ 33,900
Other combination policies		
Permanent	n. a.	$ 27,100
Term	n. a.	41,400
Total	$ 16,800	$ 68,500
TOTAL	$234,200	$676,000

* Included with Regular Term.
n. a.—not available.

SOURCE: Institute of Life Insurance. The "All other" categories in group and industrial are distributed by plan in the total breakdown.

for the next five years on a one-year renewal term policy are more or less averaged together, and the insured then pays the same annual premium for each of the five years. This is referred to as a "level premium." Some companies will write these policies with a provision providing for renewal for another five, ten, or fifteen years without medical re-examination; others will not. Regardless of whether the policy is renewable, it usually provides that the insured may, at any time during the five-year period, convert it into any of the permanent types of insurance by the payment of the adjusted premium and interest.

There is a slight reserve built up in the early years of the five-year term policy, but this is consumed by the end of the period. This kind of policy thus contains little or no investment feature. The premiums go to pay for protection only, and when the period for which the protection was obtained has passed, nothing remains for the insured.

As would be expected, the amount of the premium for term insurance is lower than for any other kind of ordinary insurance. Or, stating the same thing in a different way, you can buy more insurance under a term policy with a given amount of money than you can get with a straight life, limited-payment, or endowment policy.

The term policy is recommended where it is necessary to get maximum protection with minimum cost. At age 30, for example, a given amount of insurance can be bought with a term policy at about one seventh the cost of a twenty-year endowment policy, or one third the cost of straight life insurance. Or, with a given amount of money with which to pay premiums, the term policy will give about seven times as much insurance protection as a twenty-year endowment policy, and about three times as much as a straight life policy.

Table 7–6 shows the annual cost to the insured of the various types of ordinary insurance, for the ages indicated. For comparative purposes,

Table 7–6. Life Insurance Premiums

	Annual Premiums for $10,000 of Insurance				
Age	5-Year Term Renewable to Age 65, Convertible *	Straight Life	Limited Payment 20 Years	Retirement Income at Age 65	Endowment 20 Years
20	$ 60.40	$150.90	$274.00	$ 266.10	$468.90
25	66.30	173.10	300.90	313.80	474.60
30	73.70	200.60	332.00	376.60	482.40
35	85.80	235.30	368.40	461.80	493.90
40	107.10	279.70	411.60	583.00	511.40
45	138.90	335.30	463.10	765.40	537.50
50	187.70	409.80	526.60	1,068.60	576.80

* Five-year level premium; rates change upward every 5 years.

the rates shown are for non-participating policies, with the one exception noted. The rates are those of a leading stock company.

Term insurance would be recommended for any person who needs protection and cannot afford to get it through any other type of policy. Even when other forms of insurance can be purchased by the individual, the term policy may serve his needs just as well, and at a smaller cost. A man may have straight life insurance to protect his wife. When children are born he can take out twenty-year term policies for their protection. The children should be able to support themselves after they are from 18 to 22 years old. If straight life policies are bought for their protection, the premiums will be higher during the twenty years when the protection is needed, and they still have to be paid after the need for the protection is less or is not present at all.

It is true that the term policy does not build up any estate for the insured. But it does build up an estate for his dependents if the insured dies, and it is for the protection of dependents that the term policy is designed. Although the other forms of ordinary insurance provide protection and savings too, the savings come only from the additional amount paid in premiums. As is true of so many things we buy, we get only what we pay for.

If a person takes out term insurance, it would be to his advantage to see to it that the policy is both renewable and convertible. From the viewpoint of the insured, it would be better to have the insurance renewable and convertible without the necessity of another medical examination. The conversion feature makes it possible to exchange the term insurance for straight life or other types of ordinary insurance.

Decreasing term life insurance policies provide for a reduction of the face value of the policy over a period of time. These policies are used to meet specific decreasing needs such as payment of the remaining balance on a home mortgage in the event of the death of the insured.

Ordinary Straight Life Insurance

Both straight life and limited-payment life policies are classifications of whole life insurance. This is insurance payable to a beneficiary at the death of the insured, whenever death happens to occur. *Straight life insurance* is whole life insurance on which premiums are payable for life. Therefore, with a straight life insurance policy, the premiums are paid throughout the remaining life of the insured and the face value of the policy is paid to the beneficiary at the death of the insured. The premiums are lower than for other types of ordinary insurance except term insurance. The straight life insurance policy has some investment features in that the insured may borrow against it and it has a cash surrender value. The cash surrender value and loan value develop because the

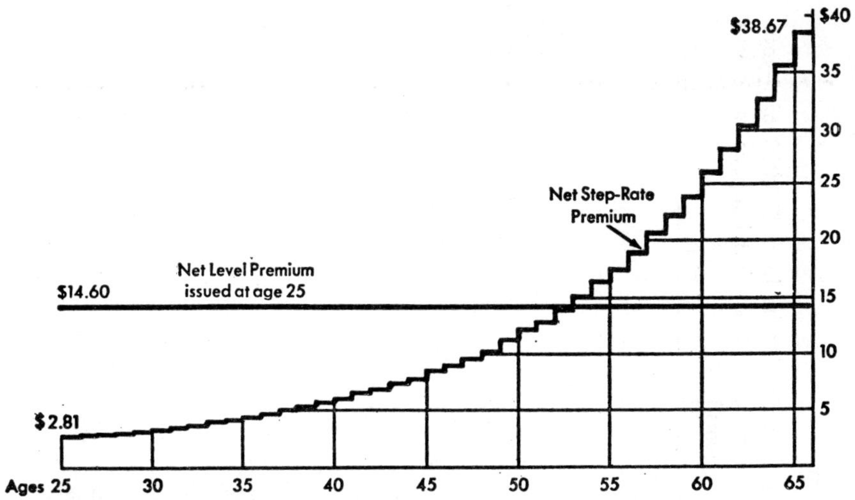

Fig. 7–5. Comparison of net premiums for $1,000 insurance. (Reproduced with permission, from *Decade of Decision.* New York: Institute of Life Insurance, 1964.)

premiums paid in the earlier years are more than the protection costs of the insurance. The amount over the protection cost is invested, and the total accumulation of these annual amounts plus earnings becomes the cash surrender value of the policy.

Figure 7–5 shows the effect of a level premium in a straight life insurance policy purchased at age 25, versus the step rate costs which would be paid for one-year term insurance each year from age 25 to age 65. The difference between $14.60 and $2.81 is not necessary to pay for protection at age 25. It is collected at this time in order to keep from paying higher premiums after age 52 and creates the savings feature in the straight life policy.

Some companies are now offering straight life insurance under a *preferred risk plan* at lower rates than for the ordinary straight life policy. This plan is available only for those whose occupation, health, and age make them better-than-average risks. It is designed particularly for business and professional people.

The straight life policy probably is more suitable to the average person than any other form of insurance contract. It should have particular appeal to people such as civil service workers and schoolteachers, whose positions are fairly secure and who may safely contemplate holding their positions until retirement. The major disadvantage of straight life relative to term insurance is the higher premium in the early years. The major advantages are the lower premium in later years and the cash surrender and loan value accumulated. A comparison of costs of a straight life and a term policy is given in Table 7–7, along with the effect of

Table 7–7. Straight Life vs. Five-Year Term

The buyer is a man just turned 30. In case "A" he buys a $10,000 straight-life policy. In "B" he buys $10,000 of 5-year term. In "C" he has the term and, in addition, banks the difference between the premiums. See what happens at various ages up to 65. (Dividends are used to reduce premiums.)

		A Straight Life					B 5-Year C & R Term		C Savings Account	
				If He Drops Policy at End of Year He Gets						
Year	His Age at Start of Year	He Pays at Start of Year	Total He Has Paid to Date	This Cash Value	Or This Much Insurance Paid Up for Life	Or $10,000 Paid Up for This Long	He Pays at Start of Year	Total He Has Paid to Date	Difference in Premiums He Deposits or Withdraws	Accumulated Savings to Date, at 3% Interest
1	30	$223*	$ 223	$ 0	$ 0	0 yrs. 0 mos.	$108*	$ 108	$115	$ 118
2		191	414	154	360	3 10	69	177	122	248
3		190	604	315	720	7 2	68	245	122	381
4		188	792	478	1,070	9 10	67	312	121	517
5		187	979	645	1,410	12 0	66	378	121	657
6	35	186	1,165	814	1,750	13 10	80	458	106	786
7		183	1,348	985	2,080	15 3	80	538	103	915
8		181	1,529	1,160	2,400	16 5	79	617	102	1,048
9		178	1,707	1,336	2,710	17 4	79	696	99	1,181
10		174	1,881	1,516	3,020	18 2	79	775	95	1,315
11	40	171	2,052	1,678	3,280	18 8	102	877	69	1,425
12		167	2,219	1,843	3,530	19 0	102	979	65	1,535
13		163	2,382	2,010	3,780	19 4	102	1,081	61	1,644
14		159	2,541	2,178	4,020	19 6	101	1,182	58	1,753
15		156	2,697	2,347	4,260	19 8	101	1,283	55	1,862

16	45	153	2,850	2,518	4,480	19	9	135	1,418	18	1,936
17		150	3,000	2,690	4,710	19	9	135	1,553	15	2,010
18		147	3,147	2,863	4,920	19	9	135	1,688	12	2,083
19		144	3,291	3,036	5,130	19	8	135	1,823	9	2,154
20		142	3,433	3,211	5,330	19	7	134	1,957	8	2,227
21	50	141	3,574					187	2,144	−46	
22		140	3,714					187	2,331	−47	
23		138	3,852					186	2,517	−48	
24		137	3,989					185	2,702	−48	
25		136	4,125	4,090	6,260	18	8	184	2,886	−48	2,323
26	55	135	4,260					243	3,129	−108	
27		133	4,393					242	3,371	−109	
28		132	4,525					241	3,612	−109	
29		131	4,656					239	3,851	−108	
30		130	4,786	4,961	7,040	17	3	238	4,089	−108	2,100
31	60	128	4,914					373	4,462	−245	
32		127	5,041					372	4,834	−245	
33		126	5,167					370	5,204	−244	
34		125	5,292					369	5,573	−244	
35		124	5,416	5,799	7,690	15	7	367	5,940	−243	1,099
	age 65	(insurance in force)	−101 (dividend due this year)					(insurance non-renewable)	−65 (final dividend due)		

Note: Cash values, paid-up values, extended-term rights, and savings-account totals are shown only at 5-year intervals after the twentieth year. There are, of course, values during the intervening years as well, but they add nothing to the comparison.

* First year's premiums include selling expenses.

Source: *Changing Times, The Kiplinger Magazine.*

depositing premium savings from the term policy in a savings account to provide for higher payment in later years. Some personal financial consultants have suggested substituting term insurance for straight life insurance and investing the premium savings in mutual funds or common stock investments. This is obviously satisfactory only if the individual is able to make the corresponding investments every period and if common stocks maintain or increase their value. A major advantage of straight life insurance over term insurance is the forced saving feature, especially for people who cannot save on their own or, if they do save, tend to dissipate their savings in a short time.

Among ordinary life insurance policies, straight life is almost twice as important as term, in the amount sold. However, as indicated in Table 7–5, for all types of insurance policies, term is almost twice as important as straight life. This occurs because practically all group and credit insurance is of the term type.

Ordinary Limited-Payment Life Insurance

Limited-payment life insurance is whole life insurance on which premiums are payable for a specified number of years or until death if death occurs before the end of the specified period. Under the limited-payment life policy, the insured pays premiums for a given number of years such as ten, twenty, or thirty, or to age 65. The face value of the policy is paid to the beneficiary when the insured dies. While premium payments stop upon reaching a specified policy date, face value is only paid in the event of death.

Slightly more than one fifth of all ordinary life insurance in force is represented by limited-payment life insurance. The amount of the premium for this type of policy is, of course, higher than for the straight life contract. The loan and cash surrender values are also greater because the amount paid in premiums is more during the early years of the contract.

The limited-payment life policy is designed for those who want to get their insurance paid for during the years of their maximum earnings. Many people want to be free of this obligation when they retire. This type of policy should appeal to a person who is in a line of work such as professional sports or the theater, where he may find it impossible to make insurance payments by the time he is 50 or 60 years old. It may also be desired by a person who will be retired on a very small income. The limited-payment life, like the straight life policy, combines protection with investment. The investment feature of the limited-payment life contract is greater than in the straight life policy. Because of the lower premium, straight life is normally preferable to limited-payment life, because considerably more protection can be obtained in the early years of life.

The extra straight life purchased in the early years can be discontinued when the need no longer exists or can be converted to paid-up insurance having approximately the same effect as limited-payment life with only slightly less coverage in later years for the same outlay.

Ordinary Endowment Life Insurance

Endowment life insurance comprises 7 per cent of the total amount of ordinary life insurance policies in force in the United States and 5 per cent of the total of all policies. On an endowment policy, the premiums are paid for a definite number of years, often twenty years, and at the end of that period the face value of the policy is paid to the insured, if he is living. If the insured should die before the end of the twenty years, the face value of the policy is paid to the beneficiary named in the policy.

In order to build up such an amount in twenty years, it is obvious that the premium would be much higher than for straight life or limited-payment life policies. The endowment policy has, of course, a higher loan value and cash surrender value than the other types. Here again, the policy combines protection and investment, but the investment feature is much greater than in the straight life and limited-payment life contracts. When the face value of the policy is paid to the insured at the end of twenty years, the policy is, of course, canceled. The person who cashes in this policy no longer has insurance protection, but does have, at least for the moment, money equivalent to the face value of the policy. If the insured does not want the entire amount at the end of twenty years, the contract usually provides alternate ways of paying it to him, such as a life income.

The endowment contract combines insurance for the protection of the insured's dependents in the event that he dies before the end of the twenty years, and savings for himself if he lives twenty or more years. With a given amount of money available to pay insurance premiums, the endowment policy provides less insurance (protection) than any of the other forms of policies. But if the insured does not need additional protection, or if he has the money to get sufficient protection with an endowment policy, this would not be a serious matter.

Although the insurance protection is gone after the face amount of the policy is paid to the insured, this is not too serious. By the time a man reaches 60 or 65, he may have few or no dependents. His children will probably be earning their own way, and his wife may be dead. If she is still living, the income from other property may well be sufficient to support her, should he die first.

Parents sometimes take out an endowment policy on their children at the time they are born, in order to insure having money for the children's college education.

The straight life or limited-payment life policies can be turned into what amounts to an endowment policy by the simple process of cashing in the policy for its surrender value. Of course, the amount obtained is less than for an endowment policy with the same face value, but the premiums also are less. In the meantime, the same amount of protection has been received at less cost.

Ordinary Retirement-Income Life Insurance

Retirement-income life insurance is similar to endowment life insurance. Among the total policies in force, it is less than half as important as endowment insurance. A retirement-income policy combines a given amount of life insurance protection with a life income payable in a given number of dollars per unit (of life insurance) per month at a selected retirement age. An accumulation of cash value above the face value of the policy is required by the time of retirement in order to provide for monthly payments during the remainder of the policyholder's life. Retirement-income policies require higher premiums than endowment policies since they build up savings faster.

A typical retirement-income policy provides that face value or cash value, whichever is higher, will be paid in the event of the death of the insured before his planned retirement age. Since the amount necessary to provide a given income for life to the insured at the time of his retirement is generally higher than the death benefit face value of the policy, these policies pay more than face value in the event of death after a given number of years and before retirement. In the event of the death of the insured after retirement, some policies provide for death benefit payments to beneficiaries; others have no death benefit after retirement payments start.

Ordinary Combination Life Insurance

When the features of two of the different types of policies discussed above are combined into one policy, it is sometimes called a *combination* policy. This usually takes the form of adding the decreasing term policy feature to one of the other types of ordinary insurance. One of the most common types of combination policy is the *family income policy.* This form of policy provides for straight (usually) life insurance of a designated face value, and a monthly income (usually one per cent of the face value of the policy) to the beneficiary if the insured dies within a designated number of years after the policy was taken out, such as, for example, twenty years. The monthly payments are not made for the period of twenty years after the death of the insured (unless he died immediately after he took out the policy), but rather the payments are made for the number of years that are left in the twenty-year period which begins from the date of the policy. The face amount of the policy is paid at the end of this same twenty-year period (and not at the time of the insured's death), provided, of course, that the insured dies within the twenty-year period.

Let us assume that Mr. Adams took out a twenty-year family income policy of $10,000 on October 15, 1965. If Mr. Adams dies on October 15, 1969, his beneficiary receives an income of $100 a month for the next sixteen years, or until October 15, 1985. On the latter date, the monthly income stops, but the beneficiary receives the face value of $10,000 (or its equivalent in income, depending upon what option is selected). If Mr. Adams lives beyond October 15, 1985, his insurance continues in force, and upon his death his beneficiary is entitled to the face value of the policy, but no monthly income is received (unless the face value is paid in installments). In other words, the straight life feature of the policy continues after the twenty-year period, but the decreasing term feature of the policy is no longer in effect.

The premiums that must be paid for the family income policy are slightly higher than would be paid for ordinary life insurance. Although the term insurance feature of the family income policy represents a type of decreasing term, the premiums on this part are usually computed on a level basis. The total premium, therefore, is usually the same amount per year for the period covered by the income provision, and thereafter the premium is slightly less.

The family income policy is highly recommended, particularly for a young family man with a limited income. Let us take the case of a man of 25 with a wife and a year-old child. Term insurance might be the only type that could give him the protection needed, but a considerable amount would be necessary. However, if the insured does not die for twenty years or more after the policy is taken out, the large amount of insurance may not be needed for the wife. Furthermore, the usual disadvantages of term insurance, discussed above, would be applicable. Ordinary life insurance would be out of the question since the large amount needed to provide the necessary income in the event of an early death would require too much in premiums. But with the family income policy, if the insured dies within twenty years, the family will be certain of an income until the child is 21. After the child is 21, and presumably no longer dependent, although the income feature will no longer be present, protection will still be afforded the wife through the straight life feature of the policy.

The family income policy features as described above may be purchased in one policy, or if a person has a straight life, limited-payment life, or endowment policy, he can usually purchase a *family income rider* for the payment of an additional premium.

Somewhat similar to the family income policy is the *family maintenance policy*. The difference between the two is that with a twenty-year family maintenance policy, if the insured dies within twenty years after the policy is taken out, monthly income is received by the beneficiary for a period of twenty years *after* the death of the insured, whereas in the case of the family income policy the monthly income is received for only the remaining twenty years dating from the time of *issue* of the policy. In both policies the income feature stops after the first twenty years, but the straight life insurance for the face value of the policy remains in effect. Premiums on family maintenance policies are higher than on family income policies, since there is a greater probability that the insurance company will have to pay the monthly benefits for a longer period of time. Of the two, the family income policy usually is more suitable to the needs of the young family man.

Another type of policy designed for the family that is buying a home on the installment plan is the *mortgage protection policy*. This is a combination of a decreasing term feature with a permanent form of insurance. A man who borrows, for example, $10,000 to purchase a home, may take out one of these policies with an initial face value of $10,000. As the installment payments are made on the loan, the amount of the life insurance (represented by the term feature) is gradually reduced, so that at the maturity of the loan the face value of the insurance will have been reduced to 20 per cent, for example, of the original face value, at which amount the insurance continues in one of the permanent forms.

Family income and family maintenance policies are not to be confused with a *family life insurance* policy, which provides life insurance on all or several family members in one contract. It is generally a whole life policy on the husband, plus smaller amounts of insurance on the wife and children including those born after the policy is issued.

Industrial Insurance

Premiums on industrial insurance are paid weekly to agents of the insurance company, who call at the home of the insured to collect. This method of paying premiums appeals to many industrial workers who receive a weekly wage, and it is because of the sale to such purchasers that it is called industrial insurance. The title used for this type of insurance is perhaps misleading, and people confuse it with group insurance because so many industries have group insurance plans. The two types of insurance are very different in almost all respects.

Approximately one third of the life insurance policies held by people in the United States are of the industrial type. Fortunately, however, the amount of such insurance in force comprises less than 6 per cent of the total amount of life insurance outstanding. Industrial insurance has been declining in relative importance in recent years. The face value of such policies is usually $1,000 or less; in fact, the average policy is for $420.

Obviously, the principal use of such insurance is to pay funeral expenses. The amount of the premium is usually less than $1; in some instances the premium is as low as 5 cents a week.

Usually the face value of the industrial policy results from the age of the individual, the kind of insurance he takes out, and the amount of the weekly premium he can afford. For this reason the amount is usually an odd figure; however, weekly rates are also quoted for a policy of a given amount such as $500. The straight life contract was the first type sold under industrial insurance, but now the limited-payment and endowment contracts are also obtainable.

The weekly premium for a $500, twenty-payment life policy for a male aged 30 would be from 35 to 45 cents. Due to the high cost and small amount of insurance carried, the medical examination connected with industrial insurance is usually a superficial affair. When the policy is for less than $500, the applicant's statement in regard to his health is usually accepted in lieu of a medical examination. Partly as a consequence of this, the mortality rate among industrial policyholders is relatively high, a fact which of course influences the rates charged.

A large percentage of what is paid in premiums goes toward the cost of the weekly collections and the large amount of bookkeeping that must be done. The fact that the amount of insurance carried is small makes the relative cost to the insured very high. The medical examination, if any, and the selling costs must be absorbed by a small policy, which also makes the relative cost high. Despite the high cost of industrial insurance, the loan and surrender values are less advantageous than can be obtained with ordinary insurance.

When we consider that about one third of all life insurance policies written are for industrial insurance, it is obvious that there is a need for this kind of insurance. Many people cannot save enough money over a period of a month to meet the premiums on ordinary insurance. If the premiums are not paid every week right after they get their wages, they will not save the money. Also, policy lapses would be much higher than they are at present if the insurance company agent did not come to the house to collect. Furthermore, most companies do not write ordinary insurance for amounts smaller than $1,000. Many people who purchase industrial insurance cannot afford to take out such a large policy. If industrial insurance were not available, most of these people would have no insurance protection whatever.

If ordinary insurance can be obtained and the premiums paid on it, such insurance is strongly recommended over industrial insurance. It would be greatly to the advantage of the individual if, instead of paying the premiums to a collector, he could save enough every week to meet the premiums every month or every three months on ordinary insurance. If the same amount of ordinary insurance is taken out, the amount which would have to be saved each week would be much less than that paid out weekly with the industrial policy.

Group Life Insurance

Group life insurance is issued on a group of persons, under a master policy. The policy is normally issued to an employer for the benefit of employees. Group insurance is usually one-year renewable term insurance. The amount of the insurance may vary according to the annual salary of the employee, years of service, or age.

Since a group policy is normally not written unless it covers ten or more people, there is a diversification of risk. Because of the group aspect, no medical examination is normally required. The premiums for group insurance are the cheapest of any form of term insurance, and term insurance is the cheapest kind of insurance. Thus, group term insurance becomes the lowest cost protection available to those individuals who have an opportunity to become members of the group. The selling cost of this type of insurance is much less than any other kind, because the insurance company usually has only one selling job to perform—"selling" the idea to the employer. Bookkeeping costs are also small, because the annual premium for all policies is usually paid in a lump sum to the insurance company by the employer. There is no medical examination expense.

In some cases the entire cost of the insurance is paid by the employer. In other instances the amount of the premium is deducted from the employee's wages, while in other cases the employer and the employee share the premium. Where the employee pays part or all of the premium, it is common practice to charge all the employees the same amount for each thousand dollars of insurance regardless of age. Unless the employer bears part of the cost, this means that the older employees are being favored at the expense of the younger ones, whose rates would be lower. In some instances where a fixed amount is deducted from the employee's wages, the difference in ages is taken into account by giving the younger employees a larger amount of insurance.

The advantages and disadvantages of term insurance which have been discussed apply with equal force to group insurance. In addition, the following considerations apply specifically to group insurance. Many people could never pass the medical examination which usually is necessary in order to get ordinary insurance. The group plan enables them to come in along with the healthy employees and secure the same insurance. This is a very desirable thing, particularly from a humanitarian or social viewpoint.

Experience of leading companies, however, has shown that the mortality rate under group insurance is approximately the same as for ordinary insurance. Of course, many people who have been insured as employees are no longer covered by the group insurance when they retire or become unable to work. The cost of the insurance for employees who are older or who are less physically fit may have to be borne, in part at least, by the employer or the youngest employees, but group insurance still gives the younger employees cheaper insurance than they could otherwise get.

Another advantage of group insurance is that people with a limited income are enabled to carry more insurance than would be possible with any other type of policy. And these may be the very people who need the protection the most. If the group insurance is paid for by a salary-deduction plan, the premiums are deducted from the employee's wages or salary before he gets paid. Salary-deduction plans, whether for insurance, retirement, or savings, are one of the least painful ways of paying out money.

In addition to the disadvantages already mentioned for term insurance, the following additional points would apply specifically to group insurance. The premium rate may be varied from year to year according to the experience of the preceding year. If the rates are not altered, the amount of the insurance may be changed according to the experience of the past. If the employee quits his job or is discharged, his insurance is terminated. He would find himself in the same position if the company discontinued the group insurance plan. Ordinarily, however, he could convert it into an ordinary life policy.

Group insurance is the cheapest form of insurance obtainable, and for the years in which the policy is carried, there is no better way to get protection. Because of the temporary nature of the insurance, however, it should be supplemented by more permanent forms. If any investment feature is desired, the individual can, of course, obtain it in some other type of insurance.

Credit Life Insurance

Credit life insurance is term life insurance issued through a lender or lending agency to cover payment of the loan, installment purchase, or other obligation in the case of death. This relieves the estate of the insured of the necessity of meeting the liability of the loan in the event of the death of the insured. Credit life insurance is the most rapidly growing form of insurance in the United States and currently accounts for 6 per cent of the value of all life insurance policies. Credit life insurance is of the term type, and the length of the term is the length of the loan being insured. It is decreasing term insurance. The beneficiaries of credit life insurance policies are creditors rather than the dependents or relatives of the insured. However, the effect is a gain for the dependents of the insured in that the insured's estate is not liable to the creditor.

Travel Insurance

A variety of special kinds of *travel insurance* are available to travelers. These policies are all term policies and insure the life of the insured only for the time he is traveling. The most common kind of travel insurance is the regular airline trip insurance. This gives $6,250 worth of insurance for 25 cents per trip with a top policy of $62,500. For travelers constantly on the move, there is an annual common carrier accident policy which gives death benefits for deaths caused by accident in travel any time during the year. The unfortunate part about all travel insurance is that it pays benefits only in the event of death due to travel. Statistics indicate that the insured is much more likely to die during the year from some cause other than travel accidents. Thus, if he counts on travel insurance as part of his regular insurance requirement, he is not sufficiently insured if his death occurs from any other cause. If he is sufficiently insured to provide all protection needs for death due to any cause, he does not really need additional travel insurance for protection of his beneficiaries in the event he is killed in a travel accident. Nonetheless, approximately $10 million is collected annually in airline trip insurance alone in the United States.

SPECIAL FEATURES OF POLICIES

Some policies contain special features which vary the amount of protection and the amount of savings from other similar policies. Most of these features are available in all types of policies with the normal exception of term policies. The insured usually has to decide whether he wants these features included in his life insurance policy. Obviously, each feature offering something additional to the insured has its added cost. Some of the more common features available in life insurance contracts are discussed below.

Disability Clause

For a small additional cost the policyholder can secure a "waiver of premium" on his policy. This means that if the insured is disabled for a period of time, the insurance company itself will pay the premiums on the policy. If such a clause were not present in the contract, many people would be unable to continue their insurance if they became disabled. This is a sort of insurance on the insurance, and it is recommended that the policyholder pay the small additional charge and secure this clause in his policy.

Additional disability features may be obtained from some companies. For the payment of a larger amount, not only will the premiums be waived, but a number of companies will pay the insured a fixed income for life if he is permanently and totally disabled.

Double Indemnity Clause

For a small extra charge, many companies will write a clause into the policy to give the beneficiary double the face value of the policy in case of accidental death of the insured. Many policyholders feel that the extra protection is worth the additional premiums, and have the clause included in their policy. The wisdom of this decision is questionable. The chances are that a person will not die by accidental death. Furthermore, the protection needed for dependents is no greater if the insured dies as a result of an accident than if he dies from some other cause. If additional protection is needed, it should be obtained in the form of additional insurance, so that the beneficiary will get the protection regardless of the cause of death to the insured. If additional protection is not needed, there is no reason why the extra premium should be paid.

Loan and Cash Surrender Value

After insurance (other than most term policies) has been in force for two or three years, loans may be obtained on the policy from the insurance company in amounts up to the cash surrender value of the policy. The amount which can be borrowed depends upon how long the insurance has been in force and the type of the policy. Table 7–8 shows the loan and cash surrender values of five types of policies, each having a $10,000 face value, at the end of various time periods, as determined by a leading company.

For the average policyholder, the insurance company may prove to be the best source of loans. The rate charged for such loans is in most

Table 7–8. Build-up of Cash Surrender Values on Various Life Insurance Policies by Age of Insured (male, policy purchased at age 20)

Age of Insured	Term	Straight Life	Limited Payment 20 Years	Retirement Income at Age 65 *	Endowment 20 Years
25	–	$ 301.50	$ 754.80	$ 799.00	$ 1,754.10
30	–	956.30	1,973.20	2,068.10	4,179.40
40	–	2,386.40	4,779.10	4,999.20	10,000.00
50	–	3,906.50	5,829.20	8,597.00	**
60	–	5,491.40	6,924.00	13,365.40	**
65	–	6,251.50	7,449.10	16,240.00	**

Note: Dividends are in addition to above if left in the company.
* Pays $100 per month for life with 10 years certain.
** Pays off at age 40.

instances about 5 per cent. This is much lower than that charged by agencies which grant personal loans. In securing the loan it is usually necessary to assign the policy to the insurance company. If the insured dies before the loan is paid, the amount of the loan will be deducted from the face value of the policy before the proceeds are paid to the beneficiary.

An individual may be able to secure a loan from a commercial bank with his insurance policy as security. In order to make sure that the bank's interests will come ahead of those of the beneficiaries, the bank may require that the policyholder make the proceeds payable to his estate, before assigning the policy. By borrowing against a policy rather than cashing it in, the insured still has the protection feature for his beneficiaries.

Conversion Feature

If a policyholder wants to stop paying the premiums on his straight life, limited-payment, or endowment policy, he may do so and have the policy converted into extended term insurance for a limited number of years at the full face value. Or he may discontinue payments and take a paid-up policy of the same type, for whatever amount the "reserve" will buy. If a policyholder discontinues paying premiums, most companies will automatically continue it as extended insurance. Some, however, will continue to pay the premiums from the loan value of the policy. If the policyholder wants to surrender the policy and not have it continued in some form, he will be entitled to the cash surrender value of the policy. The cash value might also be used for a life income.

Reinstatement Feature

A policyholder has thirty days after the due date in which to pay his insurance premium. If a premium is not paid within this time, the policy lapses. Most companies, however, will reinstate a lapsed policy within five years after it has lapsed, provided the cash value was not taken, if the policyholder pays back premiums with interest at the rate of 5 per cent, compounded annually. The policyholder must ordinarily pass a medical examination for reinstatement of his policy.

Dividend Options

If you purchase insurance from a mutual company or buy a participating policy in a stock company, you will be entitled to annual dividends in the event that the company earns more than is necessary to meet its expenses, death benefits, and reserve buildup. Five different options are generally available to the policyholder for use of his dividends. The two most common options entitle the policyholder to take his dividends in cash or to apply them to reduce the next premium. Taking either of these options simply reduces the cost of the insurance. Then the dividend can be considered as a return of an overpayment of premium.

Most companies will allow the policyholder to leave the dividends with the company to accumulate interest. If this option is selected, the value of the policy including dividends may exceed the face value of the policy as it continues to grow. This is basically a forced savings device and should be considered as an alternative to other means of savings based on the interest return and safety features discussed in Chapter 6.

Another option allows the purchaser to use the dividend each year to buy additional paid-up insurance. Generally this is insurance of the same type as the basic policy. This means that the total face value of the insurance continues to increase. It rises much more rapidly than if the dividends are merely accumulated at interest, since the dividends apply to the purchase of a policy, and depending upon the insured's age and the type of his policy, one dollar extra premium will purchase anywhere from 20 to 100 times the amount of the premium in face value. Obviously, this option should be selected only if additional insurance is desired. If additional insurance protection is really necessary to the insured's family, it is important that he purchase it whether he receives dividends from the company or not.

An additional option offered by many companies allows the annual dividends to be used to buy one-year term insurance. This purchases additional short-term protection for the insured's family and means that his policy will pay substantially more than face value if he dies during that year. This option should be considered also in the light of overall insurance needs and an overall insurance plan.

Since dividends are considered as a return of part of the premium, they are not included in "earned income," and therefore they are not to be reported as taxable income. This applies under the various dividend options. If the dividends are left with the company at interest, however, the earned interest (even though left with the company) is supposed to be reported annually for federal income tax purposes.

Coverage Limitations

Most insurance policies include certain features limiting the ability of the insured, his estate, or his beneficiaries to collect the face value of the policy. For example, many insurance policies contain a clause which stipulates that the insurance shall be incontestable after a specified period of time. This means that for the period of time that the insurance policy is *contestable,* the insurance company may void the policy. Normally a policy may only be voided if there has been a serious misstatement by the applicant. After the contestable period has elapsed, the policy may be canceled only by the insured, not by the insurance company.

Another common limitation found in many policies is the *suicide clause.* If a policyholder commits suicide within a specified period of time from the date the policy was issued (usually two to three years) the company will not honor the face amount of the policy but will return instead the premiums paid in. This clause is designed to prevent people contemplating suicide from purchasing large amounts of insurance in advance. After the period stated has expired, beneficiaries may collect the face amount of the policy even if the insured has died by suicide.

During periods of international tension or war, many insurance policies are written which include a *war clause.* This is a clause which states that the principal or face value of the policy will not be paid in the event that death results from an act of waı. The war clause is one of the major reasons that the federal government went into the life insurance business during World War I and World War II.

The above limitations may or may not appear in the insurance policies you are considering. Other restrictions or limitations may be included. One must decide how important each of these restrictions is for his own personal circumstances before deciding whether to purchase a policy which includes them. Above all, every life insurance policyholder and potential purchaser of life insurance should know what he is buying and all of its features. Only the insured can determine if the specific policy meets his requirements. It is important that every insured or potential insured read the insurance policy thoroughly before he makes his purchase. If he does not understand the terminology, he should insist upon an interpretation from some qualified and unbiased person before agreeing to purchase the policy.

QUESTIONS

1. Describe the protection feature in life insurance.
2. What is the most common reason for purchase of life insurance? What reasons may you have for buying life insurance?
3. How important is it for a family to carry life insurance on the wife? On the children?
4. When is it most important to buy life insurance? How much insurance is necessary for a typical young married man with several children?
5. What are the advantages of buying life insurance when you are young? What are the disadvantages?
6. Comment on the advantages and disadvantages of saving through life insurance rather than through the savings media discussed in the preceding chapter.
7. How should you go about selecting a company from which to purchase a life insurance policy?
8. Differentiate a mutual life insurance company from a stock life insurance company.

9. Who regulates life insurance companies? Why are they regulated?
10. How are premium rates determined on life insurance policies? Is the premium rate the same as the net cost of insurance? Explain.
11. How often should you make life insurance premium payments? Comment.
12. What is meant by designation of a beneficiary? What is a secondary beneficiary? What is a contingent beneficiary?
13. What different options are available for payment of proceeds upon death? Which option would you recommend for a wife in the event of her husband's death?
14. Why is it important to review a life insurance program periodically?
15. What is the most important type of life insurance policy in force in the United States? Why is this the most important?
16. Differentiate ordinary, industrial, and group insurance. State the advantages and disadvantages of each.
17. (a) Explain what is meant by the limited-payment life policy.
    (b) What are the advantages and disadvantages of this kind of policy?
    (c) Does the limited-payment life policy have a greater investment feature than the straight life policy? Why?
18. (a) Explain what is meant by an endowment policy.
    (b) What are the advantages and disadvantages of this kind of policy?
19. (a) What is meant by a family income type policy?
    (b) Distinguish between family income and family maintenance policies.
    (c) Under what circumstances would you recommend the purchase of a family income policy?
20. (a) Explain what is meant by group insurance.
    (b) How does it differ from term insurance?
    (c) Why is the cost for group insurance lower than for any other form of insurance?
    (d) What are the advantages and disadvantages of group insurance from the standpoint of the employee?
    (e) Does the employer gain anything by having group insurance for his employees?
21. (a) What is meant by industrial insurance?
    (b) What percentage of the life insurance policies sold are industrial policies?
    (c) What percentage of the total amount of insurance in force is industrial insurance?
    (d) Why are the premiums on this type of insurance relatively high?
    (e) Under what circumstances would you recommend the purchase of industrial insurance?
22. (a) What is meant by a disability clause in a policy?
    (b) Would you recommend that this be included in the policy?
23. Is the double indemnity clause desirable? Why?
24. (a) What is meant by the conversion feature in a life insurance policy?
    (b) In what type of policy may this feature be included?
    (c) What type of policy may be obtained on conversion?
25. What coverage limitations are commonly included in life insurance policies? How undesirable are these features for you?

CASE PROBLEMS

1. C. R. Byron is married but has no children. He is in the process of taking out a $30,000 life insurance policy to protect his wife in the event of his death. His wife is a college graduate, 40 years old, and has had little experience in handling of funds. Should Byron have the face amount of the policy paid to her in a lump sum? What other kinds of arrangements could he make? Which do you think would be best? Why? Can Mrs. Byron decide what she wants when her husband dies?

2. Mr. Robert Woodward named his wife beneficiary in his life insurance policy. He had no children, so he did not name a contingent or secondary beneficiary. Woodward died three years ago and his wife received the proceeds of the policy. His wife died recently and in her will left all her estate to her two sisters, leaving Woodward's brothers and sisters out entirely. If all the proceeds of the policy had not been paid out, who would receive them? Are Woodward's brothers and sisters entitled to any of the life insurance proceeds? What should Woodward have done if he wanted them to share in the policy after his wife's death? If a secondary beneficiary is named and if the primary beneficiary dies after the insured, will the remaining proceeds from the policy be paid out to the secondary beneficiary or to the heirs of the primary beneficiary?

3. Wynthrop Fellows is married and has two children. He is 56, his wife is 58, their children are 32 and 30. Both children are married and have children of their own. Wynthrop carries $60,000 in straight life insurance and another $40,000 in term insurance. His term policy is up for renewal this year. Should Wynthrop renew the policy? What goals should his insurance program meet? What would be the advantages and disadvantages of renewing the term versus converting to straight life policies? Should he consider dropping the policy in total?

4. Homer Smith has a $10,000 straight life policy. His income has been $4,000 a year to support himself, his wife, and their three small children. Smith believed that $10,000 was all the life insurance he could afford. He has recently been given more responsibility at work and is to receive a $1,000 per year raise. He feels that he should apply part of this raise to another $10,000 insurance policy on himself. His wife disagrees as she believes that she and the children should each be covered by life insurance, and wants him to take out a $2,500 policy on each of them instead. What reasons could she have for her point of view? What is his reasoning? Which one is right? What would you do under similar circumstances?

5. Jim Black has just started work at the ABC Manufacturing Company. The company has a group insurance plan which Black can join if he so desires. He plans to be married next month and has no insurance at the moment. The company does not pay any of the premiums in the group policy, but it does handle the collection on a weekly deduction plan. Everyone under the plan is covered with $5,000 term insurance. Weekly deductions would be about 80 cents. Black has been thinking of taking out an insurance policy with a savings feature after he is married. Should he join the group plan? Does this insurance involve a savings feature? What are the ad-

vantages of group insurance? If Black does take out a private policy, would he have any need for the group policy also?

6. Penny Mount is a career woman, aged 40. She has no responsibilities other than herself. She has a $10,000 term life insurance policy and about $1,000 in savings in the bank. She will be forced to give up her job at age 60. Her only income after that time will be social security. Is Miss Mount utilizing her insurance and savings money properly? Is she properly insured? Does she need any life insurance? If not, what should she be doing with her extra funds? If so, what kind of life insurance would suit her needs?
7. Bill Green is 32 years old, and has four dependents. His youngest child is three. Green has several hundred dollars per year that he can put into life insurance. An insurance agent has been trying to talk him into a $10,000, twenty-year, family income policy. Green has been thinking more along the lines of a limited-payment life policy, but his wife feels term insurance would best suit their needs. What seems to be the best solution to the problem? What is the advantage of a family income policy over limited-payment life? What is the advantage of a family income policy over term insurance? Would a family maintenance policy be better than a family income policy? Why or why not?

SELECTED READINGS

Athearn, James L. *Risk and Insurance.* New York: Appleton-Century-Crofts, 1962.

Blanchard, Ralph H. *Risk and Insurance.* Lincoln: University of Nebraska Press, 1965.

Cohen, Jerome B. *Decade of Decision.* New York: Institute of Life Insurance, 1964.

Denenberg, Herbert S., *et al. Risk and Insurance.* Englewood Cliffs, N. J.: Prentice-Hall, Inc., 1964.

Eilers, Robert D., and Crowe, Robert M. *Group Insurance Handbook.* Homewood, Ill.: Richard D. Irwin, Inc., 1965.

Facts You Should Know About Life Insurance. New York: National Better Business Bureau. Latest edition.

Greene, Mark R. *Risk and Insurance.* Cincinnati: Southwestern Publishing Co., Inc., 1962.

Gregg, Davis W. *Group Life Insurance,* Third Edition. Homewood, Ill.: Richard D. Irwin, Inc., 1962.

———. *Life and Health Insurance Handbook,* Second Edition. Homewood, Ill.: Richard D. Irwin, Inc., 1964.

Handbook of Life Insurance. New York: Institute of Life Insurance. Latest edition.

Huebner, S. S., and Black, Kenneth, Jr. *Life Insurance,* Sixth Edition. New York: Appleton-Century-Crofts, 1964.

Life Insurance Fact Book. New York: Institute of Life Insurance. Latest edition.

Magee, John H., and Bickelhaupt, David L. *General Insurance,* Seventh Edition. Homewood, Ill.: Richard D. Irwin, Inc., 1964.

Policies for Protection. New York: Institute of Life Insurance, 1965.

Russell, George H., and Black, Kenneth, Jr. *Human Behavior and Life Insurance.* Englewood Cliffs, N. J.: Prentice-Hall, Inc., 1963.

Spectator Insurance Year Book—Life Insurance. Philadelphia: The Spectator. Latest edition.

Wherry, Ralph H., and Newman, Monroe. *Insurance and Risk.* New York: Holt, Rinehart and Winston, Inc., 1964.

Williams, C. Arthur, Jr., and Heins, Richard M. *Risk Management and Insurance.* New York: McGraw-Hill Book Co., 1964.

8

Hospitalization, Medical, Illness, and Disability Insurance

While life insurance protects dependents from loss of income due to the death of the family breadwinner, it does not protect the family from loss of income due to the breadwinner's illness or disability. In many cases, ill health or disability can create greater financial burden for dependents than the death of the head of the family. Illness or disability involves not only loss or depletion of income, but also hospital and medical expenses.

The rapid growth in the number of people protected by various types of health and accident insurance plans and the emphasis on Medicare (discussed in Chapter 17) are evidence of the recognition by individuals, families, employers, and government of the value of planning in advance against the financial hazards of accident or illness. More than three fourths of the American population is covered by some form of health or accident insurance. It is impossible to compute the total economic costs in medical expenses and wages lost in the United States due to accident and sickness, but some indication is given by the fact that over $7.8 billion in insurance benefit payments was paid out in 1963. These policies do not reimburse all losses from ill health and accident, and not all persons in the country are covered. Therefore, the actual loss involved is substantially greater than $7.8 billion. The possible financial effects of injury or illness include the loss of family income, expenditure of family savings accumulated over a long period of time, and increase in family debt or an inability to make use of the medical service needed, due to shortage of funds.

The purpose of buying health and accident insurance is to protect yourself or your family, or both, against the financial hazards of unpredictable illnesses or accidents. There are many types of health and accident insurance protection available and a variety of agencies offer policies. No one type of policy protects against all potential losses. It is important, therefore, that the average individual have an understanding of the many types of policies available and that he carefully determine which of these is important to his financial well-being.

Health and accident insurance operates on the same insurance principle as life insurance: the spreading of risk of an unknown loss among large numbers. In health and accident insurance, the risk insured against is the risk of having to pay *unusual* medical, hospital, and surgical bills and/or the risk of loss of income due to *unexpected* illness or disability. The premiums paid under various health and accident plans must be sufficient to pay the benefits to all those persons experiencing unexpected losses. The premium paid is a known outlay for medical costs, which is paid in lieu of potentially incurring some much larger medical outlay. Inherent in the insurance principle is the fact that some people will receive benefits much less in amount than the sum paid in premiums while others will receive benefits far in excess of the amount spent.

Insurance is purchased to take care of medical expenses rather than other types of consumer expenses such as housing and food, because of

Table 8–1. Ratio of Personal Consumption Expenditures for Medical Care to Disposable Personal Income—United States, Selected Years, 1948–1963 (in billions of dollars)

Year	Personal Consumption Expenditures for Medical Care *	Disposable Personal Income	Ratio
1948	$ 7.7	$189.3	4.1%
1950	8.7	207.7	4.2
1952	10.1	238.7	4.2
1954	11.9	256.9	4.6
1956	14.3	292.9	4.9
1958	16.7	317.9	5.3
1960	19.6	349.9	5.6
1961	20.7	364.4	5.7
1962	21.9	384.4	5.7
1963	23.7	402.5	5.9

* Includes expenses for health insurance.

SOURCE: *Source Book of Health Insurance Data.*

the inability to predict the amount of medical expenses which will be required in the future and because these expenses can be extremely high relative to income. Table 8–1 gives the total personal consumption expenditures for medical care in the United States from 1948 to 1963. The rapid rise in these expenditures is clearly indicated.

In recent years, personal consumption expenditures for medical care have risen much more rapidly than disposable personal income. The ratio of medical care expenses to income rose from 4.1 per cent in 1948 to 5.9 per cent in 1963. There is every expectation that expenditures for medical care will continue to rise relative to personal income in the future. Because of the variability of medical costs based on individual circumstances, it becomes apparent that many people spent much less than 5 per cent of their income on medical care and that others spent 100 per cent or more.

MEDICAL CARE—DEMAND AND COST

More than 25,000,000 persons in the United States were admitted to non-federal short-term hospitals during 1963. This was an increase of almost 1,000,000 over the previous year. One out of every eight Americans became a hospital patient in 1963 compared to one out of nine in 1955 and one out of every ten in 1949. The average daily population of hospitals in 1963 was 530,000 persons or 2.8 per 1,000 population. Over 69,000 persons entered hospitals each day in 1963. By the end of 1963, there were 698,000 hospital beds available for an average of 3.7 beds per 1,000 population. A special study from July 1, 1962, to June 30, 1963, indicated that during this period employed Americans lost a total 260.4 million workdays or 3.8 days per employed person due to illness and disability.

Women require approximately twice as many surgical procedures each year as men. Respiratory ailments are the primary cause of lost workdays. More persons over 45 lose workdays than persons under that age. The average length of hospital stay in 1963 was 9.4 days per person. A survey conducted by the Health Information Foundation showed that the American economy lost an estimated $13.6 billion in wages and salaries because of absence from work due to illness or injury in one year. This represented about 2.8 per cent of the gross national product and 5.3 per cent of the total civilian payroll for the period studied. The Health Information Foundation reported in 1960 that there were 843,000 patients in long-term hospitals. This represents one out of every 200 persons in the United States in this type of institution each day of the year.

Medical care costs include much more than hospitalization. The cost of physicians' services exceeds the total cost of hospital services in the

United States. The average female in the United States visits a doctor 5.1 times per year and the average male sees a physician 4.0 times per year. The number of visits per year is highest for those under age 5 and over age 65.

The financing of adequate health care concerns all Americans. Table 8–2 indicates the number of people who have approached this problem

Table 8–2. Number of Persons with Various Types of Health Insurance Protection—United States, 1940–1963 (000 omitted)

Year	Hospital Expense Insurance	Surgical Expense Insurance	Regular Medical Expense Insurance	Major Medical Expense Insurance	Loss of Income Insurance
1940	12,312	5,350	3,000	—	n. a.
1945	32,068	12,890	4,713	—	n. a.
1950	76,639	54,156	21,589	—	37,793
1955	107,662	91,927	55,506	5,241	39,513
1960	131,962	121,045	87,541	27,448	42,436
1963	145,329	134,908	102,177	42,010	46,956

n. a.—not available.

SOURCE: *Source Book of Health Insurance Data.*

through various types of health and accident insurance. Hospital expense plans protected more than 145,000,000 persons by the beginning of 1964. This was a 50 per cent increase in the percentage of the population covered since 1950. More than three fourths of all Americans are covered by such plans today. In addition, 70 per cent of Americans are covered by surgical plans and over half of all Americans are covered by general medical plans. While only slightly over 20 per cent are covered by major medical insurance, this type of health and accident insurance has had the highest percentage of increase in coverage. As late as 1954, only approximately one per cent of the population was covered by such policies.

Types of Medical Care

There are two major types of medical care. The first is the care necessary to treat existing illnesses or disability. The second is more often overlooked but is certainly equally important and from a planning point of view can be much more important. This is *preventive* medical care and it can do much to reduce the problems of illness or disability. No figures have been collected on relative expenditures for preventive medical care versus care for existing illnesses. However, it is obviously much smaller. Nonetheless, it can be extremely important in personal financial planning.

The data on expenditures given in Table 8–3 break down personal consumption expenditures for medical care into types of care by the provider of the service. It is not possible to tell from these data what portion

Table 8–3. Personal Consumption Expenditures for Medical Care*—United States, Selected Years, 1948–1963 (in billions of dollars)

Year	Total Medical Care **	Hospital Services	Physicians' Services ***	Medicines and Appliances	Dentists	All Other Medical Care †
1948	7.7	1.9	2.6	1.9	.9	.4
1950	8.7	2.3	2.7	2.2	1.0	.5
1952	10.1	2.8	3.0	2.6	1.1	.6
1954	11.9	3.5	3.6	2.8	1.4	.7
1956	14.3	4.2	4.1	3.7	1.6	.7
1958	16.7	4.8	4.8	4.3	1.9	.9
1960	19.5	5.8	5.6	5.0	2.0	1.1
1961	20.5	6.3	5.9	5.2	2.0	1.1
1962	22.1	6.8	6.5	5.4	2.2	1.1
1963	23.7	7.6	6.8	5.6	2.3	1.3

* Includes expenses for health insurance.
** In some cases will not add to total due to rounding.
*** Includes osteopathic physicians' services.
† Includes other professional services and nursing home care.

SOURCE: *Source Book of Health Insurance Data.*

is preventive. The rapid rise in personal consumer expenditures for medical care of all types is clearly illustrated by Table 8–3. Total medical care expenditures more than doubled from 1953 to 1963. Each of the classifications of expenses also doubled in this same time period.

While all consumer prices have increased in recent years, the greatest percentage increase was in medical care: the consumer price index for medical care increased 40 per cent during the 1953–1963 decade. This compares to an increase in the overall consumer price index of 14 per cent and an increase of 10 per cent in the food price index. During the same period of time, hospital room rates, which comprise about 25 per cent of total medical care expenditures, increased 84 per cent.

Costs of Medical Care

The average cost per patient day, average length of stay, and average cost per patient stay in non-federal, short-term hospitals in the United States are given in Table 8–4. While the cost per patient day has risen

Table 8–4. Average Costs and Length of Stay in Non-federal, Short-Term, General, and Other Special Hospitals—United States, Selected Years, 1946–1963

Year	Average Cost per Patient Day	Average Length of Stay (days)	Average Cost per Patient Stay
1946	$ 9.39	9.1	$ 85.45
1948	13.09	8.7	113.88
1950	15.62	8.1	126.52
1952	18.35	8.1	148.64
1954	21.76	7.8	169.73
1956	24.15	7.7	185.96
1958	28.27	7.6	214.85
1960	32.23	7.6	244.95
1961	34.98	7.6	265.85
1962	36.83	7.6	276.91
1963	38.91	7.7	299.61

SOURCE: *Source Book of Health Insurance Data.*

substantially (to an average of $41.58 in 1964), the length of stay has decreased slightly so that the average cost per patient stay has slightly more than doubled from 1952 to 1963. Nonetheless, the trend is alarmingly upward and has led to increasing interest in health and accident insurance policies.

TYPES OF POLICIES

Health and accident insurance provides two major types of protection. One of these is protection against the incurring of large medical costs. A second type offered is protection against loss of income due to ill health or injury. *Medical insurance* does not include reimbursement for this loss of income. *Health or disability insurance* is carried primarily for the purpose of providing income to take the place of salary or wages lost due to illness or accident. This latter type of insurance is rarely sold without inclusion of medical insurance whose primary purpose is to pay medical and hospital bills. Medical expense insurance, however, is often sold alone. A great majority of policies in the health and accident category are designed primarily to meet medical costs rather than loss of income.

Table 8–2 indicates the number of people covered by various types of health and accident policies. Hospitalization, surgical, medical, and major medical policies all deal with medical costs. It is apparent that loss-of-income policies are carried by a much smaller percentage of the population than medical care policies. It is further apparent that the loss-of-income policies are the only type that is not rapidly expanding in its percentage coverage of the population. Nonetheless, approximately one fourth of all people in the United States are covered by loss-of-income health and accident insurance.

Many insurance policies which are not classified as health and accident insurance policies carry some medical features or loss-of-income provisions. The disability income feature included in certain life insurance policies is a type of loss-of-income insurance. Some travel insurance policies include payments for different types of disability and dismemberment as well as payments for general medical expenses. However, the major purpose of these policies is generally protection in the event of death and they are therefore classed as life insurance rather than medical insurance. Many automobile liability insurance policies include a medical payments clause which will pay certain medical costs in the event of an automobile accident. These policies are discussed in the following chapter.

Loss-of-Income Insurance

Loss-of-income insurance policies provide benefits to help replace an insured person's wages when they are stopped as a result of illness or accident. Protection against loss of income resulting from injury or illness is the oldest form of voluntary health insurance. Approximately 25 per cent of all people in the United States are covered by some type of voluntary loss-of-income insurance program.

Involuntary plans to replace lost income, at least partially, have been developed nationally and by many states. These plans are generally called *workmen's compensation.* While only a small portion of the accidents and illnesses each year are covered by workmen's compensation, this insurance is a highly important part of the effort to meet the losses resulting from injuries or illnesses. The premiums on workmen's compensation insurance are paid by the employer and, therefore, this insurance comes at no direct cost to the employee. It is important to know whether a job is covered by workmen's compensation. If so covered, the employee should be sure to file for benefits in the event of a work-related injury or illness. However, workmen's compensation applies only to certain industrial accidents and occupational diseases and does not provide full protection against loss of income caused by injury or illness.

Income lost due to working days missed because of illness and accident amounts to billions of dollars each year. Table 8–5 gives the number of workdays lost and the average days lost per currently employed person. To many people, the loss of a day's work due to illness also means the loss of a day's income. While only 25 per cent of the population is covered by loss-of-income policies, there is obviously a much higher per-

Table 8–5. Total Number of Workdays Lost, and Days Lost per Currently Employed Person for Selected Acute Conditions—United States Civilian Population, July, 1962 to June, 1963

Sex; Acute Conditions	Number of Workdays Lost * (in millions)			Days Lost From Work Per Currently Employed Person *		
	All Ages 17+	17–44	45+	All Ages 17+	17–44	45+
Both Sexes						
All acute conditions	260.4	145.8	114.6	3.8	3.6	4.2
Respiratory conditions	121.9	67.1	54.8	1.8	1.7	2.0
Injuries	69.6	38.7	30.9	1.0	1.0	1.1
All other conditions	68.9	40.1	28.9	1.0	1.0	1.0
Male						
All acute conditions	158.7	86.8	71.9	3.6	3.3	4.0
Respiratory conditions	69.6	36.3	33.3	1.6	1.4	1.8
Injuries	54.1	32.4	21.8	1.2	1.2	1.2
All other conditions	34.9	18.1	16.9	.8	.7	.9
Female						
All acute conditions	101.8	59.0	42.7	4.4	4.3	4.5
Respiratory conditions	52.3	30.8	21.6	2.2	2.2	2.3
Injuries	15.4	6.3	9.2	.7	.5	1.0
All other conditions	34.0	22.0	12.0	1.5	1.6	1.3

* In some instances will not add to total due to rounding.

SOURCE: *Source Book of Health Insurance Data.*

centage of the working population who could suffer lost income due to illness and accident.

Waiver of premium clauses in life insurance policies offer a partial compensation for a loss of income due to illness or injury. These clauses (discussed in Chapter 7) provide only for payment of life insurance premiums during the period of disability, but they do not provide for other very important needs. The waiver of premium clause in life insurance policies does not, therefore, substitute for other loss of income protection. Some life insurance policies include a *disability* clause which does provide for a periodic payment to the insured in the event of disability.

Loss-of-income policies are not usually sold to persons who are in poor health or who are engaged in hazardous occupations. Rates will sometimes vary with occupations. Or, if rates are the same, the restrictions or benefits may be less for certain types of occupations than for others. A *commercial policy* is issued to persons engaged in selected or preferred occupations, such as businessmen, professional men, and clerical

Table 8–6. Cost of $100 per Month Income in Health and Accident Insurance

Age of Insured When Policy Is Issued	Amount of Annual Premium											
	Payments for a Maximum of Ten Years				Payments for a Maximum of Five Years				Payments for Life for Accidents and to Age 65 for Illness			
	Waiting Period (in days)				Waiting Period (in days)				Waiting Period (in days)			
	14	30	60	90	14	30	60	90	14	30	60	90
25	$29	$24	$21	$18	$ 44	$ 38	$31	$27	$ 63	$ 57	$ 54	$ 50
35	37	31	26	24	57	49	41	36	82	74	71	65
45	50	43	37	34	79	69	57	53	108	99	94	86
55	84	72	63	58	125	109	93	83	146	134	127	118

workers. A *semicommercial policy* is intended for persons in any insurable occupation, but usually it is written on wage earners engaged in manufacturing, agriculture, or transportation. The commercial policy gives liberal benefits with few restrictions. The semicommercial or industrial policy is usually for smaller amounts and has lower limits. Some companies will not sell loss-of-income insurance to women. Other companies generally charge women a higher rate than men and often limit their policies to age 55. Premium payments may be made monthly, quarterly, semiannually, or annually.

Most disability policies include a "waiting period." This is the time which elapses between the commencement of the disability and the beginning of income payments under the policy. This waiting period does away with claims for short-term periods of disability which the insured can afford to finance without reliance upon insurance payments. Generally speaking, the shorter the waiting period, the higher the premium costs for the policy. The waiting period is an important factor in adapting a policy to the needs of the insured. A salaried person who would not lose income from illnesses shorter than a one-month period could well afford a thirty-day waiting period. A person whose income falls off immediately when work is missed should consider a shorter waiting period in his policy. Some policies provide for a waiver of the waiting period if the individual is admitted to a hospital.

Upon conclusion of the waiting period, weekly or monthly payments are made to the insured for some given period of disability—usually up to 52 or 104 weeks. Some policies provide for payment for life, in the event of total disability. Others pay only to age 60 or 65. It is important to watch for the distinction between ability to return to *your occupation* as compared to ability to return to *any occupation*. Those policies which consider a person disabled as long as he is unable to perform his own specific occupation have more expensive premiums. Partial disability exists when the insured is unable to perform at least one important duty of his occupation but can attend to some of his usual work activities. When this situation arises, the insurance company often pays a portion of the weekly or monthly indemnity for a stated period of time or until the partial disability no longer exists.

Health and accident policies with a loss-of-income provision are normally written to cover only some fraction of normal income. The amount of loss-of-income protection sold will generally not exceed 75 per cent of one's anticipated income. The features offered in connection with loss of income, and the conditions under which payments are made, vary so substantially between policies that it is difficult to compare rates or costs. As indicated in Table 8–6, annual premium rates may vary from \$18 to \$146 for a monthly indemnity of \$100, depending on the features included and the number of months of payment. It is important to study the loss-of-income provisions in any health and accident policy to make certain they will cover anticipated needs and meet the requirements of your personal situation.

Under certain types of disabilities, loss-of-income provisions are met by lump-sum payments rather than by weekly or monthly payments over a period of time. For example, a person may receive a lump sum equal to 100 weeks of indemnity for the loss of one hand or one foot. He may receive a sum equal to 200 weeks for the loss of the sight of both eyes. These lump-sum payments are made in lieu of the continuing weekly indemnity.

Less than half of the policies provided coverage for a maximum of 13 weeks. An additional one third of the policies have coverage for 26 weeks and only 20 per cent of the policyholders are protected by plans providing benefits for as long as one year. The plans provide for benefit payments beginning on the first day of an accident and on the eighth day of sickness in almost three fourths of the plans. Half of the plans call for maximum weekly benefits of between $35 and $54. Approximately one fourth of the plans have benefits under $35 per week, and one fourth provide for benefits in excess of $55 per week.

Most people have some *involuntary* loss-of-income insurance. Social security will pay to a worker and his family a given amount for life, after six months, if he has been totally disabled. Workmen's compensation has been discussed above. Many companies have sick leave or salary continuation plans. Disability benefits are available under certain circumstances to veterans. And a life insurance policy may include some loss-of-income benefits. All of these involuntary loss-of-income benefits should be considered in deciding how much is required in a voluntary loss-of-income insurance program.

In buying loss-of-income insurance, there are a number of factors to consider carefully. The definition of total disability varies substantially among policies. The more liberal the definition of total disability, the better for the insured. Some loss of income policies are *cancelable* at the option of the company. If this is the case, the policy could be canceled to reduce the amount of lifetime benefits received in the event of illness or accident. A *non-cancelable* and guaranteed renewable policy is definitely preferred. Since many policies are issued for short periods of time, a renewable feature is important so that the insured can continue his coverage even though he has contracted an illness before the expiration date of the old policy.

Most policies say that the company will not pay benefits for disability due to attempted suicide (within a specified period after the policy is issued), or self-inflicted injury, or to war or military service. Other policies have different exclusions. Circumstances under which the policy pays benefits vary among policies. Be sure that your policy pays benefits in the circumstances in which you may need them. Also be cautious about restrictions on existing illnesses in the payment of benefits after the policy is purchased. If there is such a restriction, be sure you do not have an "existing" illness.

Hospitalization

Almost all health and accident policies carry provision for payment of hospital expenses. Insurance benefits can be provided to help meet part or all of hospital charges for room, board, X ray, medicines in the hospital, physical therapy, and all other services incidental to medical care and treatment which are furnished by the hospital. Depending on the type of policy, cash benefits may be paid directly to the patient, or the patient may assign the benefits to the hospital. In the latter case, the insurance company pays the hospital directly.

Under most insurance plans for hospital expense, a certain amount is allowed per day for hospital room and board, up to a maximum number of days—usually 90 or 120. In addition there is usually a lump-sum amount available to cover other hospital expenses. These policies are designed to pay only expenses, so that if the payments are made directly to the insured, they cannot exceed the cost of the hospitalization to him. The premiums for hospitalization insurance vary, depending upon the locality covered and the services provided. Employee group plans paid through payroll deduction arrangements are very numerous and tend to have lower premium rates.

At the beginning of 1964, over 145 million people had private hospitalization expense protection through some type of insurance. Hospitalization insurance is the most prominent type of health and accident insurance. Sixty per cent of the people insured through private hospitalization plans are covered by plans issued by insurance companies. The remaining 40 per cent have various types of cooperative and independent plans such as Blue Cross and Blue Shield.

While the largest number of people are covered by hospitalization insurance under the various types of health insurance, it is the authors' opinion that this type of protection is not as important to the average family as major medical insurance or loss-of-income insurance. A typical family may pay from $50 to $300 per year for hospitalization insurance. Since almost every family experiences some hospital charges during its lifetime, premiums must be high to pay all the people who collect under the policy. The maximum amounts payable are restricted under all hospitalization policies, so that this insurance does not insure against a very unexpected major catastrophe, which could be most damaging to a family's financial situation. Hospitalization insurance comes close to being a prepayment of a known outlay which will be incurred in the future. For many people who find it difficult to save funds to meet emergencies, hospitalization insurance is very important, but it should not be thought of in lieu of major medical or other types of health insurance.

Surgical Insurance

Surgical insurance is the second most common form of protection in the field of health and accident insurance in the United States. Benefits from surgical insurance are usually paid according to a predetermined schedule of fees which states the maximum payment for each type of operation. Fees for office calls made before and after the operation are included in this maximum. If an operation costs more than the sum provided specifically in the policy, the company pays the stated maximum and the patient pays the remainder. The cost of the policy, of course, bears a direct relationship to the maximums which the company agrees to pay for each type of surgery. The fees fixed are maximums, and if the cost of the operation is less than the maximum, only the actual cost is paid as a benefit. Cash payments from surgical insurance may be paid to the patient or they may be assigned to and paid directly to the surgeon involved.

The comments made above, concerning the relative value of hospitalization insurance, also apply to surgical insurance which has relatively low maximum benefit payments.

Regular Medical Expense Insurance

This type of insurance provides protection for non-surgical and non-hospital expenses. Office and home treatments, examinations, medications, and periodic health examinations may be included. Over 100 million people in the United States are covered by this type of insurance. The maximum number of physicians' calls for each sickness or injury is usually specified in the policy so that the patient will not unduly utilize the physician's services. The amount of the benefit is also usually restricted to a stated amount per call. Payments may be made directly to the insured or assigned to and paid to the physician. As practically everyone incurs some general medical expense, and the maximum benefits under these policies are small, this type of insurance is less important to an overall health insurance plan than hospitalization and surgical insurance. General medical expense insurance can also be considered a type of prepayment or periodic payment of an expected outlay.

Major Medical Insurance

Major medical expense insurance is designed to meet the large or catastrophic costs of serious accident or prolonged illness and to pay a major share of the cost of all normal treatment prescribed in connection with these prolonged illnesses. While many people covered by hospitalization or surgical expense insurance will probably collect something under that insurance policy, only a small portion of those covered by major medical expense insurance will actually receive or need benefits under the policy. In this sense, those persons who are fortunate enough to remain in reasonably good health help pay, through their premiums, the costs of those who suffer from prolonged illnesses.

Major medical expense insurance was developed to take up where the basic health plans leave off. This insurance is designed to pay the major share of all the costs involved in connection with a major accident or illness, including hospital, surgical, other medical treatment, and physicians' expenses. Major medical expense insurance differs from other medical expense insurance in that it has very high maximum limits, it usually involves a co-insurance clause, and it includes a deductible provision. There is usually a maximum amount of benefit stated for each policy, and this maximum may range as high as $10,000 or $20,000. This maximum may apply to any one illness or the total may apply to all payments within a policy year.

The co-insurance feature provides that the insurance company will pay only a portion of the total cost incurred in connection with the illness. The policyholder, therefore, has to pay part of the total bill. A normal co-insurance percentage would be 75 or 80 per cent of costs insured by the insurance company. In addition, since these policies are designed primarily to meet catastrophic medical outlays, a basic deduction is also included. The deductible amounts would commonly range from $100 to $500. This amount may be covered by other forms of insurance or must be paid by the insured. Most of the major medical insurance in force is under group plans.

Table 8–7 illustrates the types of expenses which may be reimbursed and the application of the deductible provision and the co-insurance clause. Because of the deductible feature and the co-insurance clause, major medical insurance is not expensive. The premium varies with the amount of the deductible provision and with the co-insurance percentage, as well as with the maximum amount, the size of the family, and other features.

Major medical insurance was practically unheard of prior to 1950. Since that time, over 42 million Americans have purchased major medical

Table 8–7. A Claim Collection Determination for Major Medical Insurance *

Expenses	
Hospital room and board	$ 520
Special nurses' fees	400
Physicians' fees	300
Surgical fee	600
Anesthetist's fee	50
Medicines	320
Transfusions	60
Oxygen	120
Ambulance	30
Total expenses	$2,400
Claims	
Expenses	$2,400
Less deductible amount	300
	$2,100
20 per cent co-insurance paid by insured	420
Collectible amount	$1,680
Payments	
By insurance company	$1,680
By insured	$ 720

* $10,000 major medical policy with $300 deductible and an 80 per cent co-insurance clause.

expense insurance policies. While this is a smaller number of people than are covered by other types of medical insurance policies, major medical insurance is the most rapidly growing type of health insurance. A principal reason for its rapid growth in recent years is its importance in personal financial planning.

The authors believe that major medical expense is the most important of the health and accident insurance policies. The major medical policy comes into operation only when a catastrophe occurs. That may be several times in a lifetime or never. But if it does occur, the typical family is completely unable to meet the financial requirements of such a catastrophe. For the amount of its potential coverage, the cost of major medical insurance is extremely low. The high deductible amount forces the policyholder to handle the smaller expenses himself and his insurance premium goes to pay for only those unusually high expenses of major medical difficulties.

In hospitalization, surgical, and general medical insurance, the policyholder is in a sense trading dollars with the insurance company. The average policyholder pays a regular premium and gets a large portion of it back in claims. In effect, he is paying the insurance company to do his medical expense budgeting for him.

The authors strongly recommend major medical insurance with at least a $10,000 face value for all families. Only those families who are unable to accumulate emergency resources need to purchase other types of medical cost insurance. The $10,000 major medical policy on a family with two children, with the husband and wife both aged 30, will cost from $30 to $60 per year.

Comprehensive Medical Insurance

Comprehensive medical insurance policies are designed to give the protection offered by basic hospitalization and surgical and medical policies, as well as a major medical policy. Comprehensive policies tie together all other types of medical policies into a one-package policy. Comprehensive plans cover both short-term illnesses and long-term catastrophes. They are usually characterized by low deductible amounts, low co-insurance features, and high maximum benefits. The features of these policies are similar to a combination of the features of basic and major medical policies. A typical comprehensive medical expense policy covers all illnesses and accidents, in and out of the hospital, with benefits up to $15,000, for a five-year term for each family member. The maximum amount payable in any one year is $7,500; but a "re-instatement" clause provides that if part or all of the $7,500 benefit is used in one year, and total physical recovery is proven, the maximum $7,500 limit is restored for the next year, though the $15,000 overall limit during the life of the policy still applies. Cost varies with age and number of family members. A husband and wife, both aged 45, with two teen-age children, would pay approximately $300 per year. To qualify for a comprehensive policy, other types of hospital and medical coverage must be dropped to prevent making illness "pay off."

Over 10 million American families were covered by comprehensive medical insurance policies at the beginning of 1964.

Group Medical Policies

In addition to classification by type of coverage, health and accident insurance policies may be classified by type of sale—to groups or individuals. *Group* health insurance differs from *individual* health insurance in the same way that group life insurance differs from ordinary life insurance. Group policies are much more important in health insurance than in life insurance. Less than 25 per cent of all health and accident insurance policies are sold on an individual basis.

TYPE OF INSURER

A number of different types of insurers offer some or all types of health and accident insurance policies. These policies are available through insurance companies, hospital approved plans, medical association approved plans, and various independent plans. Most insurance companies offer health and accident insurance on either a group or an individual policy basis. Other insurers generally offer only group insurance. In some of the hospital, medical, or independently sponsored plans, a person may become a member of the group merely by living in a certain locality.

Table 8–8 gives the numbers of persons covered for hospitalization, surgical, and general medical insurance by type of insuring organization. The importance of Blue Cross in hospitalization insurance and Blue Shield in surgical insurance is clearly indicated.

Table 8–8. Persons Covered for Specified Health Insurance Service, by Types of Insuring Organization—1963 (in millions of people)

Health Insurance Service	Number of People
Hospitalization expense	
Insurance companies	
Group	60,547
Individual policies	38,065
Blue Cross and Blue Shield	61,659
All other plans	7,221
Surgical expense	
Insurance companies	
Group	60,944
Individual policies	33,745
Blue Cross and Blue Shield	52,474
All other plans	8,562
Medical expense	
Insurance companies	
Group	42,066
Individual policies	11,884
Blue Cross and Blue Shield	49,302
All other plans	8,647

Note: Not adjusted for duplication of people having more than one policy.
SOURCE: *Source Book of Health Insurance Data.*

Insurance Companies

Insurance companies sell health and accident insurance to cover all types of medical expenses ranging from loss of income to major medical expense and hospital, surgical, and general medical expense. Most companies sell either individually or through a group plan. Cash benefits of most insurance policies may be paid directly to the insured or assigned by him to a hospital or doctor. Private insurance companies selling health and accident insurance may be general life insurance companies or may specialize in health insurance. The discussion of life insurance companies in the preceding chapter would generally apply to health insurance companies also.

Blue Cross

The Blue Cross Hospital Service Plan is a cooperative, non-profit group hospital plan for paying the hospital bills of its members. Blue Cross plans are sponsored by the American Hospital Association and by groups of local hospitals. In each community, the Blue Cross plan is administered by a local management appointed by a board of trustees composed of civic-minded residents of the community. Each separate Blue Cross plan has locally administered rates and benefits. The national office of the Blue Cross Commission is mainly advisory and educational. Most Blue Cross plans have a working arrangement whereby a subscriber to one plan may transfer his benefits to hospitals in another community or he may transfer his subscription to another plan upon moving to a new community.

The benefits in coverage to be derived from Blue Cross membership depend upon the particular kind of contract purchased and the features offered by the local Blue Cross association. Ordinarily, the contract will provide for part or all of a hospital bill for some limited period of time—21 days to 120 days. Some plans provide for additional partial payments for longer periods in the hospital. Normally only semiprivate or ward plans are sold. The semiprivate plan pays the standard price for a semiprivate (two-, three-, or four-bed) room in standard hospitals in the area. The ward plan pays the lower ward rates charged by the hospitals. The premium for the ward plan is, of course, less. The maximum amounts paid per day for room and board are stated in the contract.

In addition to the cost of room and board, the typical standard contract will also cover the cost of the following: general nursing service in the hospital, special diets, operating room, laboratory work done in the hospital, drugs and medicines, vaccines, serum, dressings, biologicals, oxygen, plaster casts, and intravenous preparations. Hospital bills in connection with some types of operations, which may be needed at the time the contract is purchased but may be put off, such as a tonsillectomy, adenoidectomy, or hysterectomy, are not covered until a lapse of nine months after the insurance is purchased. Maternity benefits also are covered only after a period of nine months from the date of the contract, and the coverage is limited to ten days. These benefits are provided only in the "family" policy. This type policy covers all members of the family, including unmarried children from the age of three months to 18 years.

In addition to the standard policy, some plans provide for comprehensive coverage. These cover hospital bills in connection with all types of operations, but with the same maternity benefit limitations stated above. The policy covers children from time of birth to 19 years. The comprehensive contract may also provide for benefits up to 70 or 120 days. Also, these benefits may be received for more than one time during the contract year, provided there is a lapse of at least 90 days since the last discharge from the hospital. Naturally the premiums paid for these contracts are higher than those paid for the standard contract. Some plans provide for a $25 deductible contract. The holder of such a policy stands the first $25 of the bill and Blue Cross pays the balance, within the limitations of the policy. The deductible feature lowers the cost of the contract.

It should be emphasized that Blue Cross covers only the *hospital* bills within the limitations stated above. It does *not* cover the charges, if any, made by private physicians or surgeons for calls in or out of the hospital.

The Blue Cross plan is essentially a *group* hospitalization plan. There are three different circumstances under which a person may become a member of Blue Cross:

1. If a person is employed at a place where there are five or more employees, it is necessary to join on a group basis at the place of employment. In some instances the employer pays the bill; in others the insurance premiums are deducted from the employee's pay. When the employee must stand the bill, it is necessary, in some instances, for him to send the money directly to the local Blue Cross office.
2. If the entire county or city has been designated as a group by the Blue Cross, then a person who is employed at a place where there are less than five persons employed can join on a group basis. Farmers or professional men would come within this category. If a person is working where five or more are employed, however, to become a member he must join through a group plan at his place of employment.
3. If ineligible to join under one of the two circumstances stated above, a person can join on a *non-group* basis, provided he is under 65 years of age. (When joining as a group member under either of the circumstances mentioned above, there is no limitation as to age.) Unemployed persons as well as employed ones may become non-group members. Maternity benefits are not covered under the non-group contracts. All forms of membership are open to both men and women.

Of particular interest to many people is the fact that a medical examination is not necessary for membership in Blue Cross. A person who could never pass a medical examination for a policy in a private company is on an equal footing with his healthier fellow workers. Another point of importance is that once a person has qualified for membership, his contract will be continued as long as he pays his membership fees. In many private insurance companies, if a person becomes afflicted with some illness or injury that necessitates hospital treatment, his policy will not be renewed unless he signs a waiver for that particular affliction.

The cost of Blue Cross membership is low and easily within the means of most workers. Table 8–9 shows the cost of the standard semiprivate

Table 8–9. Monthly Cost of Blue Cross Membership

Type of Contract	Group	Non-Group
Individual	$ 4.50	$ 6.00
Family	12.00	14.00

contract for cities of moderate size. In the very large cities, slightly higher rates are charged.

Blue Shield

The Blue Shield plan provides surgical rather than hospital expense insurance. It is sponsored by groups of local doctors and is organized and operated in a manner similar to the Blue Cross plan. In many communities, the Blue Cross organization handles the details of selling, billing, and collecting for Blue Shield. Like Blue Cross, Blue Shield is essentially a group plan, but in many communities, non-group membership may be obtained. The procedure for becoming a member is practically the same as for Blue Cross.

The coverage and benefits of Blue Shield vary among the states and communities, and according to the particular type of contract purchased. Practically all of the plans cover surgical charges. The amount that will be paid for each type of operation is set forth in the schedule. For an appendectomy, for example, the allowance ranges, among the various plans, from $50 to $150, with $100 being the usual amount. For the standard policy the maximum paid on the more difficult operations is usually $300. Some of the plans, however, provide for a higher premium contract which will pay up to $500 on certain operations. Surgical benefits usually cover operations not only in the hospital, but also in a doctor's

Table 8–10. Surgical Benefits and Amounts Under Blue Shield Preferred Contract

Description of Surgery	Maximum Allowances	
	Surgical	Anesthesia
Appendectomy	$125.00	$20.00
Childbirth (vaginal)	50.00	None
Fractured collar bone, simple	35.00	10.00
Gall bladder removal	175.00	25.00
Hernia repair, single	100.00	17.50
Kidney removal	250.00	35.00
Stomach removal	300.00	40.00
Tonsillectomy (over age 12)	60.00	12.50

SOURCE: Ohio Medical Indemnity, Inc.

office or at home. Maternity benefits are paid only after a waiting period of from nine to twelve months. Table 8–10 gives some standard payments for certain types of surgery.

Limited medical benefits may also be obtained under most plans through the payment of a higher premium. In practically all of the plans, benefits are paid only for a doctor's hospital calls. The allowance is usually $3 to $5 a call, but covers not more than one call a day, and it is limited to 21 or 30 days. A few of the plans cover limited medical charges for house and office calls. Some of the plans also provide allowances up to $50 when a separate charge is made for the services of an M.D. in administering anesthesia.

In the areas covered by about three fourths of the plans, the following arrangements are typical. A great majority of the physicians in the area agree to not charge members of Blue Shield any more than the schedule of benefits set forth in the contract, provided the annual income of the member does not exceed a specified amount, for example, $4,000 or $6,000. In these cases the doctor is paid directly by Blue Shield. If the member's income is in excess of this amount, the doctor may charge more. Blue Shield would then either pay the member the amount specified in the contract and let him take care of the bill, or the insured would pay the doctor the difference between the amount of the bill and the allowance provided for in the contract, and Blue Shield would pay the doctor the amount set forth in the contract. If a doctor does not agree to participate in the plan, Blue Shield pays the allowances provided in the contract directly to the member.

The cost of Blue Shield membership varies according to the community in which a person lives and the type of policy he buys. The

Table 8–11. Monthly Cost of Blue Shield Group Standard Surgical and In-Hospital Medical Services

Type of Contract	Cost
Individual	$1.40
Family	3.90

charges in Table 8–11 are typical of medium-sized cities in the United States for group surgical and limited in-hospital medical contracts. These charges are for the standard contract, which provides a maximum of $300 for the most difficult operations. The in-hospital medical benefits are $10 a day for the first day, and $5 a day for the next three days of each hospital confinement, and $4 a day thereafter, to a maximum of 120 days in any one year.

Other Insurers

Independent hospital or medical benefits plans are sponsored by industries, communities, trade unions, private clinics, or other organized groups, or by a group of physicians joined together. These plans involve an association with some type of health center, clinic, hospital, or group of physicians. The plans primarily involve a direct payment to a doctor or hospital, but a number of them offer cash indemnity payments instead. Benefits vary extensively, depending on the type and location of the plan.

Private carriers usually offer broader coverage than the mutual community plans. They tend to have a wider selection of plans, to fit particular needs and to give greater freedom in the selection of the hospital and more flexibility on the type of accommodation. However, if more complete coverage or greater flexibility is obtained, the cost of the policy is normally higher than for the community sponsored plans.

Examples of independent plans are the health insurance plans of Greater New York, the Detroit Health Community Association, and the Trans-Canada Medical Plan.

FACTORS TO CONSIDER

Because of the tremendous variety of health and accident insurance contracts, it is important for each buyer to study carefully the contract he is considering, before he purchases it. In fact, a wise buyer will take time to compare the values of several similar policies. He should be sure that he is getting exactly what he needs and wants. In addition, he should be careful to buy only from a reputable company or through a reliable agent. The buyer should read the policy carefully so that he knows the exact extent of coverage and the benefits provided. He should not only *read* the contract provisions, he should understand them.

The buyer will generally find that group policies are cheaper than individually purchased policies. However, he may not be eligible for participation in a group, or the group may not offer the kind of policy he desires. In addition, if group insurance is obtained through his place of employment, the buyer may lose it if he leaves his job.

In the past, it has been difficult for people over 65 to acquire private health insurance. (Medicare became effective in 1966.) Today, there are a large number of private plans available for people in 65-plus age brackets—regular medical and surgical policies, as well as major medical policies. Because of the wide variety of policies, the senior citizen must choose carefully. The cost of policies is often higher for people over age 65.

In buying health and accident insurance it would be advisable to acquire a policy while you are young and in good health. It is desirable that the policy be guaranteed renewable and non-cancelable for life (not just to age 65). In planning your insurance purchase, however, it is most important to guard against the worst possibilities first. It is easier for the average individual to shoulder the smaller, more predictable expenses than to meet major medical catastrophes. The major medical coverage would, therefore, appear to be the most important for the average individual to carry.

In planning your hospitalization and surgical insurance coverage, keep the benefits of Medicare in mind so that you do not double-insure after age 65 (see Chapter 17).

QUESTIONS

1. How much does medical care cost the average family in the United States?
2. Why have medical care costs been rising both absolutely and relatively?
3. What is preventive medical care? Why is it important?
4. What risk is insured against in regular medical insurance? In major medical insurance? In loss-of-income insurance?
5. Describe loss-of-income insurance.
6. Does the ordinary health and accident policy start paying from the first day of illness? Would you advise the purchase of a policy which did start then? Why or why not?
7. In addition to paying so much a week or month in event of illness, what other types of payments are often made under health and accident policies?
8. Is a medical examination necessary in order to purchase a health and accident policy?

9. Differentiate between hospital and surgical insurance.
10. What is general medical insurance?
11. Why is major medical insurance particularly important for many people?
12. What are the common features of a major medical policy?
13. How is the amount of proceeds determined in major medical insurance?
14. Describe comprehensive medical insurance.
15. Differentiate group from individual health insurance policies.
16. How do private health insurance plans tend to differ from community or association sponsored plans?
17. Who sells medical and health insurance?
18. (a) Indicate the nature of the Blue Cross plan.
    (b) Indicate the benefits which are received by members of this organization. Are any benefits paid for maternity cases? Under what conditions?
    (c) Indicate specifically who can become members of the Blue Cross.
    (d) Describe the different types of contracts offered by the Blue Cross.
    (e) Is a medical examination necessary for Blue Cross membership?
    (f) If a person contracts a disease or has an accident which may necessitate frequent hospitalization in the future, can the Blue Cross cancel his membership or refuse to renew his membership?
    (g) Explain how the Blue Cross may benefit the following:

The individual	The taxpayer
Hospitals	Society
Doctors	

19. Ascertain whether your state or community has the Blue Shield plan, and if so, indicate the nature of the following features:
    (a) Who can become members of the plan?
    (b) What different types of contracts are available?
    (c) What is the amount of the monthly membership dues?
    (d) What are the benefits received under the plan?
    (e) Are "waiting periods" provided for any types of operations?
    (f) Are any medical, as distinguished from surgical, benefits obtainable by members?
    (g) Who benefits from the plan in your community?
    (h) What are the doctor's obligations?
20. What factors should you consider in selecting a medical or health insurance policy?

CASE PROBLEMS

1. Bill and Betty Maxy are newlyweds. In setting up their budget, how much should they allow for medical care expenses? How should they provide the funds to meet these expenses? Why? How will their medical care expenses change through the years?
2. Ralph Asbury is married and has three children. He is considering the purchase of hospitalization insurance from a private company for monthly premiums of $9.00. A friend has suggested he purchase major medical insurance instead. The major medical policy would cost only $4.00 per

month. Which should he purchase? What benefits will he potentially receive from each policy?

3. John Brant fell and broke his hip last year. Surgery was required to set it properly. John was in the hospital for 2½ months and required care at home for 2 months more. He incurred the following expenses: surgeon $200, physician $250, hospital bill, $1,800, nurses $700, anesthesia $50, wheelchair rental $40, ambulance $30, and drugs $75. John had a major medical policy with a $600 deductible clause and 80 per cent co-insurance. How much will John collect from his policy?
4. In the above case, if John had had Blue Cross and Blue Shield instead, how much would the accident have cost him personally? (Assume Blue Cross pays all hospital related expenses for thirty days and Blue Shield pays all surgical expenses.) What other policies would have offered John additional protection?
5. Charles Bates has taken a job as an explosives researcher for a small company. He is worried about the physical hazards of his job in the event of an accident. The company provides him with Blue Cross, Blue Shield, and a major medical policy. He also is covered by workmen's compensation. Charles is married and has three small children and very little savings accumulated. He is considering purchasing a $100,000 term life insurance policy. Will this cover all his needs along with the company programs? Would you recommend other insurance? Why?
6. Ray Jenks is starting his first job after graduation from college. He will earn $375 per month. Jenks is planning to be married in a few months. Neither he nor his future bride has ever carried health and accident insurance. Both were covered by Blue Cross hospitalization under a family plan taken out by their parents. Jenks has to decide whether he wants to join the group Blue Cross plan at his new place of employment. He also has the opportunity to join the group Blue Shield plan. If he does not join now, he will have to wait a full year before he has the opportunity again. Should he join Blue Cross? Blue Shield? What are the advantages and disadvantages of each? What difference may a one-year wait make? If he joins, will the policies cover all his medical expenses? If not, what will not be covered?
7. Set up a hospitalization, medical, illness, and disability insurance plan for yourself for the future.

SELECTED READINGS

Angell, Frank J. *Health Insurance.* New York: The Ronald Press Co., 1963.
Athearn, James L. *Risk and Insurance.* New York: Appleton-Century-Crofts, 1962.
Cohen, Jerome B. *Decade of Decision.* New York: Institute of Life Insurance, 1964.
Dickerson, O. D. *Health Insurance,* Revised Edition. Homewood, Ill.: Richard D. Irwin, Inc., 1963.
Eilers, Robert D. *Regulation of Blue Cross and Blue Shield Plans.* Homewood, Ill.: Richard D. Irwin, Inc., 1963.
Follmann, J. F., Jr. *Medical Care and Health Insurance.* Homewood, Ill.: Richard D. Irwin, Inc., 1963.
Greene, Mark R. *Risk and Insurance.* Cincinnati, Ohio: Southwestern Publishing Co., 1962.
Gregg, Davis W. *Life and Health Insurance Handbook,* Second Edition. Homewood, Ill.: Richard D. Irwin, Inc., 1964.

Handbook of Health Insurance. Cincinnati, Ohio: The National Underwriter Co. Latest edition.
Magee, John H., and Bickelhaupt, David L. *General Insurance,* Seventh Edition. Homewood, Ill.: Richard D. Irwin, Inc., 1964.
Margolis, Sidney K. *A Consumer's Guide to Health Insurance Plans.* New York: Public Affairs Committee, 1962.
Mayerson, Allen L. *Introduction to Insurance.* New York: The Macmillan Co., 1962.
Source Book of Health Insurance Data. New York: Health Insurance Institute. Latest edition.
Your Health and Recreation Dollar. Chicago: Money Management Institute of Household Finance Corp. Latest edition.

9

Property, Casualty, and Automobile Insurance

In addition to life and health and accident insurance, many types of insurance are available to protect against a wide range of possible losses or catastrophes. Only those forms of property and casualty insurance which are of primary interest to the individual or his family are discussed in this chapter. Other than losses due to death and accident and illness, the two major categories of insurable losses are the potential loss of value of property due to fire, theft, and acts of God, and the potential loss of property due to legal claims of others brought on through some legal liability on the part of the insured. Since legal liability usually occurs in connection with the ownership of some physical asset, property and casualty insurance are considered together.

Because legal liability usually accompanies property ownership, the discussion of property and casualty insurance in this chapter is based on type of property rather than type of potential loss. Automobile insurance is treated separately from other forms of property and casualty insurance because of its importance and its special features.

The importance of property and casualty insurance is indicated by the fact that property and liability insurance companies in the United States wrote premiums in 1963 of approximately $17 billion and paid losses in that year of approximately $10 billion.

REAL ESTATE AND PERSONAL PROPERTY INSURANCE

Think for a moment of the amount of physical property which a couple accumulates during their lifetime. This may include not only a home and one or two automobiles, but a large amount of furniture, clothing, jewelry, linens, dishes, utensils, household equipment, and innumerable other items. The cost of replacing some of this physical property in the event of fire or other types of destruction could be very great. In many cases, available emergency funds or current income would not be sufficient to replace the loss. Therefore, it seems important to be insured against the loss of possessions through an unexpected catastrophe.

The most valuable possession of most people is their home. The great majority of homes in this country are insured against loss resulting from fire and other catastrophes, but many people do not realize how much their other belongings are worth. If the loss of other belongings would be substantial to an individual or a family, insurance should be carried on them just as on a house.

It is important to guard against the loss of physical property through unexpected catastrophes, but it is also important to protect oneself against liability which ownership of this physical property may create. Home ownership carries with it a potential liability to anyone using the property, including guests, tradesmen, neighborhood children, and servicemen. All of a person's real estate and personal property—in fact, all of his assets—stand behind any personal liability which he may incur. Thus, a liability to someone else could mean loss of his real estate or personal property through their claims in court action. Liability to others could also result in claims upon his future income. Liability to others may be incurred by his children and his pets or by himself in a manner unrelated to the ownership of physical property. It is important, therefore, to be insured against claims upon property and future income because of this potential liability due to actions of people for whom an individual is responsible or to his ownership of property.

Fire Insurance

A large amount of value is lost each year in the United States because of fire. More than $1 billion per year has been lost in each of the last six years. The cumulative loss in the past ten years exceeds $10 billion. The amount of loss per year has increased rather steadily since 1935. Part of this rise is due to increasing population and consequently more ownership of property. The 1955 fire loss was $5.39 per capita, and by 1963 the loss per capita had increased to $7.48. These figures indicate that a substantial amount of fire loss does occur and that property owners must absorb this loss in some way.

The insurance principle applies in fire insurance in that the premiums paid by a large group of people are used to reimburse the few experiencing loss due to fire. In spite of the large amount of loss per year, it is still small relative to the total value of property insured. Therefore, fire insurance premiums are relatively small per dollar of value covered. The typical property owner cannot afford *not* to be insured for loss due to fire.

Fire insurance will reimburse the insured for the actual *value* (giving due consideration to the amount of the insurance carried) of the property which is destroyed. The owner should not expect to get back the actual *cost* price of the property which is destroyed. Actual value normally takes into consideration depreciation on the property over the time it has been held and used. Thus, if a $20,000 (original cost) house burned entirely to the ground, and if the house was ten years old, the fire insurance would normally reimburse only some portion of $20,000 even though it would require $20,000 to rebuild exactly the same house. However, this example assumes no increase in prices. If prices have risen, it is possible to collect more than the original cost of the house. If the house mentioned above would cost $30,000 to replace, it may have a depreciated value of $22,500 and the insured could collect this amount in a total fire. Of course $22,500 would not replace the house with a similar new one. In certain cases, it is possible to insure for *replacement* value rather than *actual* value. This, of course, involves an added premium. In some states, the value of the property is agreed upon in advance of loss, at the time the policy is written.

The amount written on the face of the policy is the maximum amount which the insurance company would pay as a result of a fire. Real estate values have increased greatly in recent years, and people who were carrying the proper amount of fire insurance in the past but have not recently increased their coverage are underinsured.

Fire insurance is rarely taken out for the full value of the real estate, for two reasons. First, the lot itself will not be damaged by fire or other catastrophe, and second, the house is rarely completely destroyed.

If a fire occurs, the individual should make every effort to control it. If possible, he should also remove the furniture or whatever other property is threatened. If fire insurance is carried on the furniture, it will cover any losses, except theft, which may be experienced as a result of moving the furniture to a safe location. This coverage normally extends for a period of only five days, after which time the individual should apply for a continuance of the coverage in that location.

Fire insurance policies are ordinarily written for a term of one, three, or five years. The longer the term of the insurance, the less the annual cost, so it is advisable to get at least a three-year policy. If the property is sold, or if for any other reason the individual wants to cancel the policy, he may do so at any time, and a portion of the premium will be returned to him.

The amount of the premium varies according to the type and construction of the house, the number of families living in it, the location, and other factors. A typical annual premium in a medium-sized city is $1.20 per $1,000 coverage for an ordinary frame house. If a three-year policy is taken out, the annual cost per $1,000 would be only $1.00.

An individual should read his fire insurance policy carefully in order to ascertain what is covered and what is not covered by the policy. Fire insurance normally also covers damage due to lightning. Property may be damaged by heat, steam, or smoke, but such damage is not covered by the policy unless there is actually a *fire*. Unless specifically included in the policy, fire losses resulting from public disorder are not ordinarily covered. Theft of property often occurs at the time of a fire, but this is not covered in the fire insurance policy. If it can be proved that the individual himself set the property on fire, the insurance, of course, would not be operative. The insurance company is also not liable for loss or damage directly or indirectly resulting from the negligence (negligence is difficult to prove) of the insured to use reasonable care to save the property when there is a fire or when the property is threatened by a fire.

If the policy is purchased from a reliable company, the provisions of the contract will be fairly well standardized. Nevertheless, the policy should be read in order that the individual will know exactly what he has and what steps should be taken to preserve the insurance. Most policies state the conditions which will render the contract void. The following are among the more important acts which may void the policy:

1. Willful concealment or misrepresentation of any material fact or circumstance concerning the insurance.
2. Increasing the fire hazard by storing explosives or other combustible materials in the house.
3. Moving property from the location specified in the policy, unless it is done to prevent damage.
4. Lack of an insurable interest in the property.
5. Changing title to the insured property.

Extended Coverage

Straight fire insurance policies cover losses resulting from fire or lightning. There is also need for protection from acts of God and acts of individuals. By the payment of an additional amount of premium, coverage for damages resulting from other catastrophes may be obtained. Most property owners carry "extended coverage" in connection with their fire insurance policies—in fact, *straight* fire insurance policies are rarely written today. In addition to loss due to fire and lightning, *extended coverage* covers losses resulting from damage by windstorm, hail, explosion, riot, aircraft damage, vehicle damage, and smoke damage. These seven extra coverages can normally be purchased only as a unit at a fixed additional cost to the insured. It is not normally possible to exclude one or two of them and apply for a lower premium.

Extended coverage insurance on an ordinary frame dwelling may cost an additional \$0.60 to \$1.00 per \$1,000 on an annual policy, and \$0.50 to \$0.83⅓ per \$1,000 annually on a three-year policy. The total cost of fire and extended coverage on an ordinary frame house in a medium-sized city in the United States might be \$1.80 per \$1,000 on an annual policy, and \$1.50 per \$1,000 annually on a three-year policy. If the house has wood shingles or other fire hazards, or is located where there is inadequate fire protection, the cost would, of course, be higher.

Most fire insurance companies have available an additional coverage beyond extended coverage. This is usually called *additional extended coverage* or "twenty perils insurance" and protects the property of the insured from damage due to a variety of actions not covered in normal extended coverage. This would include such things as damage from vandalism and malicious mischief, glass breakage, freezing, falling trees, water damage from plumbing and heating systems, and collapse. This additional extended coverage may cost from 40 to 50 cents per \$1,000 of protection for one year. The majority of extended and additional extended coverage policies are sold only with a deductible clause—usually \$50 deductible. In some areas, it is not possible to insure against loss caused by certain acts of God. Flood insurance is normally unobtainable in areas regularly subject to floods.

Losses to property for catastrophes covered by "extended coverage" insurance have exceeded a quarter of a billion dollars each year since 1954. This indicates the importance of extended coverage insurance to property owners in the United States; these figures do not include uninsured losses or losses from hazards covered by additional extended coverage.

Co-Insurance

Some fire insurance policies include a *co-insurance clause*. If there is no co-insurance clause, the insured would be paid for any fire damage up to the face value of the policy. If a co-insurance clause, such as 80 per cent co-insurance, is included in the contract, it means that the insured agrees to carry in fire insurance at least 80 per cent of the current value of the property in order to be paid in full for fire losses. If loss should occur in a property covered by insurance with a co-insurance clause, and the insured does not have a policy with a face value of 80 per cent of the current value of the property, the insured will collect only a pro rata portion of the loss. The purpose of co-insurance is to encourage property owners to carry a reasonable amount of insurance on the property. A policy with the co-insurance feature would be available at a much lower premium than the same face value policy without this feature.

If a property with a current value of $10,000 is covered by an 80 per cent co-insurance policy, the insured would have to have a policy with a face value of $8,000 in order to collect the full loss in the event of a fire causing damage of $8,000 or less. Should the insured have only a $6,000 policy, he would collect only 75 per cent of the losses up to $6,000. With a $5,000 loss, he would collect only $3,750. Had there been no co-insurance feature, he could have collected the full $5,000 in the event of loss. A formula for determining the amount collectible under a co-insurance clause is as follows:

$$\frac{\text{Amount of insurance carried}}{\text{Amount of insurance required under co-insurance clause}} \times \text{Amount of loss} = \text{Amount collectible}$$

Even if there is no co-insurance clause, it is not desirable to underinsure one's property. While the chance of a complete loss of property due to fire is small, the cost of extra fire insurance is also small, and should loss occur, it is important to most people to be fully covered. On the other hand, it does not help to overinsure your property. If the property is worth only $10,000 and you insure for $15,000, the most you could collect under a complete loss would be $10,000. The premium paid for the extra $5,000 coverage would be wasted.

Theft Insurance

While real estate is not normally subject to loss through theft, a large amount of personal property is annually lost in this manner. For this reason, it may be important to carry some type of theft insurance upon valuable personal property which is likely to be stolen.

Theft insurance on personal property is available under two major types of contracts. *Personal theft* is a more limited form of theft policy: it covers only burglary, robbery, and larceny. Jewels and furs must be listed and insured separately. There are a number of exclusions in the policy such as property left in unattended cars.

In a *broad form* personal-theft policy the exclusions are much more limited, jewelry and furs need not be separated, different amounts may be purchased for protection on the premises and away from the premises, and, most importantly, this policy covers *mysterious disappearance* and theft damage as well as burglary, robbery, and larceny. The broad form policy is more expensive than the more limited personal-theft policy.

Because of the variation among different property theft policies, it is important to select a policy carefully and to be certain that it insures against the conditions that may cause loss. Not all property is protected against theft under all circumstances. There may be a variation in a policy between theft occurring on the premises and off the premises. Theft from secondary locations and theft from children away at school may or may not be covered. The policy's face value indicates the total amount that can be paid out by the company due to theft, but the amount for the theft of specific items may be less than the amount of the face value. Mysterious disappearance may or may not be covered.

Personal Property Floater

Personal property floater policies include much broader coverage than fire and theft policies alone. They are the most comprehensive form of insurance available for personal property, providing in one contract all the personal property insurance protection an individual would ordinarily require for his belongings. Loss away from home as well as on the premises is covered.

This policy insures personal property against all risks of loss or damage, with a few minor exceptions such as moth damage. Loss of cash and unscheduled (not listed separately) jewelry and furs is generally limited in amount. All items of personal property may be covered in this policy without specific listing. There is no co-insurance feature in this policy. Only animals and automobiles and other conveyances are generally excluded from the property covered under this type of policy. While certain perils are excluded, almost every type of unexpected loss is covered. The major exclusion applies to normal wear and tear. Of course, the personal property floater is substantially more expensive than fire and theft policies combined. It is bought ordinarily with a $25, $50, or $100 deductible clause, at a reduction in premium.

Special floater policies may be obtained for specific personal articles which are scheduled separately. They are necessary for items which may exceed in value the general limit per item stated in the personal property floater policy. Such items would normally be jewelry and furs, but could also include fine art, silverware, and collectors' items of varying kinds. The insured is normally required to exercise "ordinary care" in protecting his property. Like fire insurance policies, personal property floater policies may be purchased on a three-year basis at a lower annual premium than for the purchase of a one-year policy.

Personal Liability Insurance

Personal liability insurance protects against risk of legal claims if an individual's actions or negligence involve bodily injury or property damage to someone else. A comprehensive personal liability policy has an all-inclusive insuring clause under which the company promises to pay for the insured the obligations imposed upon him as a result of legal liability, including employer's liability, and the liability of others assumed by him under a written contract relating to his premises. It covers both bodily injury and property damage sustained by anyone under which legal liability is incurred.

The comprehensive insurance includes the insured and his family and normally any animals which he might own. The policies do not normally include liability related to ownership and use of motor vehicles or other means of transportation. Besides covering the liability of the insured in connection with owned premises or rented residence, the policy covers all of his personal acts and those of his family. The comprehensive policy covers the liability of the resident-owner or tenant toward people employed by him in connection with the residence.

Most policies contain a medical payment provision under which up to $250 or $500 in medical expenses will be paid to anyone injured while on the premises with the insured's permission. This provides protection for guests or others who may not have a legal claim against the insured. The standard limit in a comprehensive personal liability policy is $10,000 per accident per person with a maximum of $20,000 per accident for bodily injury and $5,000 in property damage. Annual premiums range from $8 to $15 for this type of policy. Its very low cost is well worth the expenditure when the effects of possible liability are considered. *Excess personal liability* policies are now issued with maximum coverage up to $1,000,000. These policies generally carry large deductible amounts such as $10,000 to $50,000.

Owning and maintaining a home carries the constant risk of liability. There are a wide variety of conditions which can cause accidents for which the homeowner may be held responsible. In addition to business visitors, delivery people, and guests, the homeowner may even be liable to trespassers. Personal liability insurance, therefore, is particularly important to all homeowners. It can also be important to people who do not own homes but can be held liable for actions against others under given sets of circumstances.

Homeowner's Policy

A recommended type of insurance called a homeowner's policy covers in one package all of the normal property and liability insurance needs of the homeowner. This policy would normally meet all of the insured's insurance needs with the exception of those relating to his life, his health, and his automobile. A comprehensive homeowner's policy would include fire and extended coverage and additional extended coverage on the insured's home. In addition, it might cover up to 10 per cent of the face value of the policy for fire and extended coverage and additional extended coverage perils to outbuildings. For personal property, such a policy would usually include theft and unusual damage coverage up to 50 per cent of the value of the dwelling for items stolen or damaged on or off the premises. The same coverage for personal property stolen or damaged off the premises may be included or it may be as low as 10 per cent of the value of the dwelling. Additional living expense during dislocation due to fire or damage is commonly covered for up to 20 per cent of the value of the dwelling.

Comprehensive personal liability with a maximum of $25,000 may be included along with $500 in medical payments whether liability is involved or not. Physical damage to property of others may be covered up to $5,000. This type of policy is, of course, more expensive than an individual fire policy or a separate theft policy. On the other hand, it may be substantially less expensive than purchasing all of these coverages in separate policies. It may be found that by using a homeowner's policy, the insured can obtain additional coverage for no more cost than he is currently paying for fire and extended coverage and some theft coverage on his personal property.

AUTOMOBILE INSURANCE

Next to a home, an automobile is the most expensive piece of property which most people own. As a result, protection against loss of an automobile from fire, theft, or collision is important. Of much more importance, however, is protection against the kinds of liability which owning and/or driving an automobile could create. An automobile is an instrument of great power which can cause substantial harm to people and to property. There is no practical limit to the amount of liability which the ownership and use of an automobile can cause an individual. The total financial resources of most people are insufficient to meet the potential demands of liability actions arising from automobile use or ownership. All property owned, as well as expected future income, can be taken to satisfy liability claims. The major types of insurance available for automobile drivers and owners are bodily injury and property damage, fire and theft, collision, and medical payments.

Economics of Automobile Insurance

According to the National Safety Council, a traffic death occurs every twelve minutes in the United States. This represents 43,600 traffic deaths per year. A traffic injury occurs every nine seconds and a traffic accident occurs every three seconds. There are more than 11 million traffic accidents each year. More casualties are caused by traffic in a single year than were suffered by the armed forces during all the years of World War I and World War II combined.

The economic loss from traffic accidents is indicated in Fig. 9–1. There has been a steady rise in economic loss (with the exception of the years of World War II, when there was much less driving) to a total of over $9 billion per year in 1964. This figure includes both insured and uninsured losses and is the total required to pay for property damage, for legal, medical, surgical, and hospital costs, for loss of income from absence

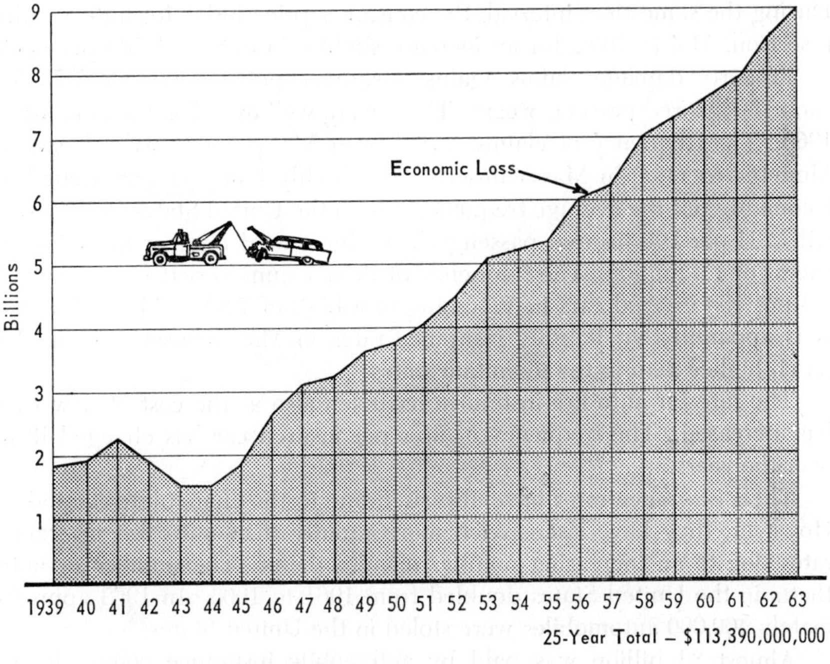

Fig. 9–1. Economic losses from traffic accidents in the United States, 1939–1963. (Reproduced with permission, from *Insurance Facts, 1964.* New York: Insurance Information Institute.)

from work, and for the administrative costs of insurance. This is equal to a bill of $7.42 for every man, woman, and child in the nation.

Automobile insurance rates have been rising more rapidly in recent years than the rate of population increase. The frequency of traffic accidents has risen, but the most important cause of rising rates is the increasing economic loss involved in each accident. The average incurred claim cost for property damage in 1939 was $42 per accident. By 1962, this average had risen to $179 per accident. The average incurred claim cost for bodily injury per accident in 1939 was $450. By 1962, this average had risen to $1,150. The bodily injury claims average rose 156 per cent during this period and the property damage claims rose 326 per cent. Inflation has accounted for part of the increase in property damage claims. The increasing complexity of automobiles and "extras" on cars have also contributed to this increase. The rising cost of living has only partially accounted for increased claim cost for bodily injury insurance. Another factor has been the tendency of juries to award larger amounts to claimants in the event of physical injury or death.

The consumer price index for new automobiles rose from 42.4 in 1939 to 101.5 in 1963. Thus, the cost of new cars increased almost 250 per cent. During the same time interval, the consumer price index for auto repairs rose from 51.4 to 109.2 for an increase slightly in excess of 200 per cent.

Property damage claims against insurance policies average 7.78 for each 100 insured passenger cars. There were well over 5 million claims in 1963. The frequency of claims varied from 5.00 per 100 insured cars in Montana to 11.96 in Massachusetts. The bodily injury claims occur less frequently but the average frequency rate in the United States in 1963 was still 2.34 per 100 insured passenger cars, for a total number of claims in excess of 1.6 million. The frequency of these claims varied from a low of .74 per 100 insured cars in Wyoming to a high of 7.82 in Massachusetts. It is apparent that liability insurance rates in Massachusetts should be much higher than in the mountain states.

The rate for auto fire insurance has risen also as the cost of new cars has increased. The frequency of fires per insured car has changed little over the years.

Theft insurance rates have also risen due to the changing price index. However, they have risen much more rapidly than auto fire insurance rates due to an increasing number of auto thefts. The number of auto thefts in the United States doubled from 1961 to 1963. In 1963 approximately 400,000 automobiles were stolen in the United States.

Almost $4 billion was paid by automobile insurance companies to cover losses in 1963 (Table 9–1). These companies had gross premiums of $6.8 billion in that year. Over 40 per cent of the premium income and the losses paid were in connection with bodily injury insurance. These

Table 9–1. Automobile Insurance Premiums Written and Losses Paid—1963

Type of Coverage	Premiums Written	Losses Paid	Per Cent Losses Paid of Premiums Written
Auto liability–bodily injury	$3,464,446,528	$1,798,820,956	51.9%
Auto liability–property damage	1,362,281,258	792,901,419	58.2
Physical damage (fire, theft, collision, and comprehensive)	2,481,471,648	1,369,177,895	55.2
Total	$7,308,199,434	$3,960,900,270	54.2%

SOURCE: *Insurance Facts, 1964* (New York: Insurance Information Institute).

figures indicate the importance of automobile insurance and potential losses and liability due to automobile operation.

A few states require that an individual carry automobile liability insurance before he can legally operate an automobile. Many other states have financial responsibility laws which require that an individual carry a minimum amount of insurance or post a bond in the event that he has an accident involving liability. This type of law does not apply to a person until he has already had an accident. Regardless of whether liability insurance is required by law, every individual should carry such insurance for his own financial protection. When buying a car on the installment plan, the organization financing the purchase of the automobile will require that fire and theft and collision insurance be carried. Many people think that they are properly covered by insurance when purchasing automobiles on installment. In order to be fully covered, the individual buyer must add bodily injury and property damage insurance to the insurance which the finance company requires him to purchase.

Bodily Injury Liability Insurance

Bodily injury insurance covers claims from injury, sickness, or death of others for which the insured may be legally liable, up to the limits of his policy. Every car owner should carry bodily injury insurance. The minimum bodily injury policy is the so-called "five and ten." In some states, the minimum is "ten and twenty." Such a policy covers personal injuries up to $10,000 for one person, and a total limit of $20,000 for personal injuries in one accident. The maximum amount which may be collected from the insurance company by any one individual is $10,000. This insurance covers awards made for death as well as injuries.

The cost of this type of policy varies widely, according to the locality. In congested cities where accidents are more likely to happen, the rates are, of course, higher. Higher limits than those stated above may be obtained for a small additional cost. For example, if the policy is written for a limit of $20,000 for injuries to one person, and $50,000 for injuries to more than one person, the cost would be only 15 per cent greater. Wealthy individuals, who may be made the targets for damage suits, should carry a large amount of this insurance.

It is recommended that the average motorist take out at least a $25,000–$50,000 policy. Many people are now carrying $100,000–$300,000 limits. The cost of the insurance varies not only according to locality, but also according to the type of company from which it is purchased. The agency companies—those companies which sell through local agents—usually charge higher rates than the companies which sell directly to the motorist. Some mutual direct-selling companies charge lower premiums than the direct-selling stock companies. In addition to the cost, however, the prospective purchaser should determine the exact nature of the insurance being sold, and the reputation of the companies or agencies for service and paying claims.

Table 9–2. Rates Charged for Automobile Insurance

Maximum Coverage	Annual Premiums Charged
Bodily Injury Insurance	
$ 10,000–$ 20,000	$31.60
25,000– 50,000	36.80
50,000– 100,000	39.80
100,000– 300,000	42.60
Property Damage Insurance	
$ 5,000	25.40
10,000	28.00
25,000	30.60
50,000	32.00
Medical Payments Insurance	
$ 500	6.00
1,000	8.00
2,000	10.00
5,000	12.00
$50 Deductible Collision Insurance	
First year	46.60
Second and third years	38.60
Fourth year and beyond	32.60
$100 Deductible Collision Insurance	
First year	38.00
Second and third years	31.60
Fourth year and beyond	26.60

All of the automobile insurance rates in Table 9–2 apply when the car is for non-business use only, and where there are no car operators under 25 years of age in the family. Table 9–2 gives the rates charged for bodily injury insurance in a medium-sized city in the United States by a large mutual company. From the figures it can be seen that substantial amounts of bodily injury insurance may be carried for only a few dollars more than would be paid for a much smaller coverage.

In addition to the protection afforded against liability claims, bodily injury insurance meets the requirements of the financial responsibility laws of most states. Also, and very important, the insurance company will, at its own expense, handle the legal problems arising from an accident for which its policyholder is liable. The insurance companies have considerable experience in the handling of liability cases and are generally able to bring them to reasonably successful conclusions. If the insured had to provide his own defense or hire his own legal counsel, the costs could be very substantial. With the insurance company handling the legal problems, all the insured need do is to file the proper forms and make himself available for appearance in court if necessary. Most policies pay all legal costs as well as bail bond premiums, defense of all suits, court fees, and other costs.

Property Damage Insurance

Property damage insurance covers loss to the property of other persons rather than to that of the insured. Bodily injury insurance may be obtained without property damage insurance, but the latter is rarely purchased without bodily injury insurance. Most people buy policies which include both types of insurance in the same contract. Companies at the present time usually will not write a policy for less than $5,000 property damage coverage. The rates vary throughout the country according to location and use of car. In very large cities the cost of bodily injury and property damage insurance is considerable. Most people who have property damage insurance carry the $5,000 limit, but an increasing number are raising it to $10,000. The latter limit costs only a few dollars more than the $5,000 policy. Table 9–2 gives the rates charged by a company in a medium-sized city.

Medical Payments Insurance

An increasing number of motorists are carrying *medical payments* insurance. This insurance applies to medical, hospital, or funeral expenses incurred within one year as a result of accidents in, upon entering, or while alighting from an automobile. The basic medical payments policy covers the husband and wife and all passengers in their own automobile, and also the husband and wife when driving or riding in another automobile. Extended medical payments coverage may also be obtained for a slight additional premium covering the following: children of the insured riding in other automobiles; husband, wife, and children riding in buses, taxis, or trucks; husband, wife, and children if struck by an automobile while riding bicycles, motor bikes, roller skating, sledding, etc., or while a pedestrian. Most of the companies now write only a policy which covers both basic and extended coverage (this is also referred to as the *broad form*).

The minimum amount of medical payments insurance that may be purchased is $500, and the maximum is $5,000. This refers to the amount of coverage for *each* person injured as a result of an accident. Table 9–2 gives the rates charged for the broad form by a leading company in a medium-sized city.

Collision Insurance

Collision insurance (also called physical damage insurance) covers the damage done to one's own car as a result of a collision or upset. This type of insurance is less necessary than bodily injury and property damage. A person never knows what amount in damages will be awarded against him as a result of personal injuries to others, or damage to their property. But he does know that the maximum loss which he can incur as a result of damage to his own car is the value of the car at the time of the accident. This ordinarily would not be in excess of a few hundred to a few thousand dollars. The individual may be able to stand this loss himself, and accordingly will not take out collision insurance. But if a person is not able to stand such a loss, he may want to carry this type of insurance.

Collision insurance may be purchased in two general forms: full coverage, and deductible. In the full coverage policy, the insurance company will pay the full amount of the damage resulting from the collision or upset. Many people are constantly bumping their fenders, etc., so minor accidents are numerous and the cost of investigation and settling of claims makes this type of policy very expensive. Furthermore, an individual can stand the cost of repairs from minor accidents. For these reasons, a person should rarely buy the full coverage policy and few companies sell it.

The deductible policy is the one that should be purchased when collision insurance is desired. With this type of policy a fixed initial amount of the cost of the damage must be borne by the insured, and the insurance company will stand all the expense over this stated amount. The usual policy is $50, $100, or $250 deductible. With a $50 deductible policy, the cost of any accident involving $50 or less must be borne by the individual himself. If an accident cost $125, the insured would absorb the first $50, and the insurance company would pay for the additional $75 damage.

The actual cost of collision insurance varies according to location, kind and age of car, and its use. The rates shown in Table 9–2 are charged in a medium-sized city for a new eight-cylinder standard four-door sedan in one of the lower-priced lines. Rates decrease after the first and third year of ownership.

Instead of writing a deductible policy of the type just described, some companies sell collision insurance policies in which the insurance company will stand a specified percentage of the claim, such as 80 per cent, and the insured must absorb the other 20 per cent. Upper limits are, of course, also specified.

Fire and Theft or Comprehensive Insurance

Fire and theft insurance policies cover the damage or loss resulting from fire or theft of the insured's car. When both these forms of insurance are obtained, they are always written in the same policy. Fire insurance alone can be obtained, but theft insurance is never written without fire insurance.

The fire policy includes loss from lightning. Any damage to the body, equipment, or machinery resulting from a fire is covered, but damage to robes, clothes, or other articles which happen to be in the car is not covered by a fire policy unless specifically included in the particular policy.

Insurance companies commonly charge a minimum premium of $5 on fire policies. If the actual premium happens to be less than this amount, the individual may be able to secure theft or tornado, or some other kind of insurance, without the payment of any additional amount.

Many people buy what is known as comprehensive coverage. This covers not only fire and theft, but all kinds of damage to the car, whether resulting from tornadoes, windstorm, hail, water, riot, falling airplanes—in fact, about every kind of damage except that covered by collision insurance. The cost of this type of policy is slightly higher than the standard fire and theft policy.

As is true of collision insurance, the rates for fire and theft or comprehensive insurance vary according to locality, age, and type of car. Thieves usually steal lower-priced cars because they are more easily disposed of; the rates for theft insurance for these cars are usually higher than for more expensive cars. The annual premium for a comprehensive policy on a new lower-priced automobile in a medium-sized city in the United States is $14, declining to $10 by the fourth year.

Preferred Risks and Assigned Risks

A preferred risk is a person who has an excellent safety record in driving. Certain companies sell policies to preferred risks only. Normally, the cost of these policies is lower than the ordinary risk policies sold by standard companies. Many standard automobile insurance companies have "safe driver" plans in which they offer insurance at lower premium rates to people with good driving records. To be a preferred risk, a person would have to have a certain number of years of driving without an accident.

The assigned risk, on the other hand, is one with a very poor driving record who finds it difficult or impossible to obtain insurance coverage from regular companies. Standard companies may refuse to write automobile policies for certain persons because of age, traffic convictions, or driving record. Insurance companies cannot be compelled to accept applicants, and they may refuse to write policies for certain people. In many states, the insurance companies band together to operate an assigned risk plan whereby persons who cannot obtain insurance directly with standard companies may obtain insurance from this agency for a substantially higher premium. Each insurance company, as a member of the plan, agrees to accept its proportionate share of the poor risks. In some cases, a person's driving record may be so bad that he will find it impossible to obtain insurance even under the assigned risk plan.

Uninsured Motorist Protection

Bodily injury and property damage liability insurance covers losses resulting from liability to others. The normal insurance policy protects the insured for his own losses only to the value of his car, under collision insurance, and for the maximum amount of medical payments, if there is a medical payment provision. Through no fault of his own, the insured or members of his family may be seriously hurt or property other than his automobile may be lost through the fault of others. While the person responsible for the accident may be legally liable, he may be uninsured and have no property or wages from which to collect. Many insurance companies, for an added premium, will give protection against bodily injury due to inability to collect where uninsured persons are liable. In some states, this problem is met by compulsory insurance for all automobile drivers but in many states it cannot be assumed that the other person has liability insurance.

Automobile Insurance Coverage

Questions often arise as to whether automobile insurance covers situations where persons other than the insured are driving the insured's car, or where the insured or members of his family are driving other people's automobiles. The standard contract now provides that bodily injury (sometimes called public liability), property damage insurance, and collision insurance cover the insured in the event another person is driving the insured's car. The other person will also be covered if he is driving the car with the permission of the insured. The insurance also covers the insured when he or his spouse (provided she is living in the same household as the insured) is driving another person's automobile.

Everyone should read his automobile insurance policies thoroughly to understand just what the insurance covers. The statement above relates to the "standard contract," but not all policies follow the same form. Even though a policy ordinarily covers a particular situation, it may be rendered void because of some act of the insured or his representative. Any of the following circumstances may render the policy ineffective, depending upon the exact wording of the policy:

1. Operation of the car outside the United States, its territories or possessions, and Canada.
2. Failure to correctly notify the insurance company of an accident as soon as is practicable.
3. Failure to cooperate with the insurance company in connection with the settlement of claims.

The Combined Policy

While the various types of automobile insurance policies are discussed separately above, the normal way to purchase such insurance is in a policy which combines all of these types of insurance. Table 9–3 gives a summary of the costs of the types of automobile insurance discussed above. These rates represent those charged to an ordinary driver in a medium-sized city, and are for a new automobile in the lower-priced field. If the collision insurance were $100 deductible instead of $50 deductible, the amount would be reduced by $8.60.

If a person has a collision and his car upsets and burns up, some question may be raised as to how much should be paid out by the company in which collision insurance, if any, is carried, and how much by the one which wrote the fire policy. It is common today to obtain all types of automobile coverage in one insurance policy from one company. This reduces the selling costs involved and reduces the question of which company will be responsible under a given set of circumstances.

In addition to the type of automobile, its age, and its cost, auto insurance rates vary with the size of the city and its accident experience, the repair rates in a given locality, state regulatory requirements, age of driver, and types of company. Rates are highest in those cities which have a high accident experience. Automobile insurance is much cheaper in rural areas with little traffic.

Most insurance companies charge more if one of the normal drivers of the car is a single male under age 25. The reason for this is that the accident experience rate for male drivers under 25 is much higher than for male drivers over 25 or for female drivers. In fact, the rate is so much higher that the typical insurance company increases its rates from 100 to 150 per cent if there is a single male driver under age 25 covered by the policy. If the male driver under 25 is the primary driver of the automobile, rates are still higher. Rates for female drivers under 25 are much less. However, one company increases the premium for bodily injury and property damage by 25 per cent over regular rates with no change in other portions of the coverage for a single female driver under age 25 who is not the primary driver of the automobile.

Table 9–3. Rates Charged for Automobile Insurance

	Annual Premiums Charged		
Insurance	No Single Male Driver Under 25	A Single Male Driver Under 25	Primary Driver Single Male Under 25
Bodily injury ($10,000–$20,000)	$ 31.80	$ 69.00	$111.00
Property damage ($5,000)	25.40	55.60	85.40
Collision ($50 deductible)	46.60	93.20	139.80
Comprehensive	14.00	14.00	14.00
Medical payments ($500)	6.00	6.00	6.00
Total	$123.80	$237.80	$356.20

Table 9–3 gives premium charges for a family policy with a single male driver under 25 and for a single male under age 25 who is the primary driver. A 15 per cent reduction on these rates is given if the driver has taken and satisfactorily completed a driver training course. This saving amounts to $32.67 per year for the occasional driver and $50.43 per year for the primary driver. Obviously, this is a large amount of saving for the nine years from age 16 to age 25. Driver training courses are strongly recommended, not only for the saving in insurance premium, but also for the safety feature of better driving. Because of a better

accident record for young people who have taken driver training, insurance companies are able to offer these large reductions in premiums.

Some companies give reduced rates if two cars in the same family are insured with the same company. This reduction is commonly 10 to 20 per cent off on the normal premium for the second car. In the past, some companies offered reduced premiums for compact cars but these reductions are gradually being removed. In spite of lower values in the compact cars, recent accident experience has not been any better than for regular cars as physical damage tends to be more extensive and more bodily injury is involved in compact car accidents.

Insurance rates vary also with the specific company offering a policy. A *direct-selling* company is one in which the policy is sold by a representative employed directly by the company. *Agency* companies are those which sell their policies through independent agents. An independent agent is in a position to help the buyer of insurance select from a number of possible companies in choosing an automobile insurance policy. When insurance is purchased from a direct-selling company, the insurance agent contacted sells the insurance of only that company. Direct-selling companies have been increasing in importance in recent years.

Automobile insurance premium rates have risen substantially in the past twenty years, due to the increasing rate of accidents, rising repair costs, rising costs of automobiles, and increase in settlements in liability cases. Settlements in excess of $100,000 per accident are no longer uncommon. Larger settlements to injured persons and the higher costs of property repair cause all drivers to pay higher insurance rates. All drivers should encourage safety practices and demand only reasonable liability settlements, in order to keep automobile insurance rates at a manageable level for the average family.

Settlement of Claims

The reputation for ease and speed in settling claims varies among different insurance companies. As a potential claimant against your own policy, you would desire a company which is reasonable in its settlement of claims in both the amount paid as benefits and the time it takes to collect the payment. As a person potentially liable to others, it is important that the insurance company you select offers you good legal advice and is willing to represent you properly in any liability case. The reputation of a company in claims settlement is generally developed over a period of time based on policyholders' experiences in settling claims with the company under consideration.

QUESTIONS

1. What are the two major categories of insurable losses in connection with property ownership?
2. What is the greatest hazard that confronts the property owner? Can this risk be insured against?
3. Does fire insurance lessen the risk, or only shift it from the property owner to the insurance company? Explain.
4. Mr. Adams says that he has owned a house for thirty years and never had a fire, so that proves that he does not need fire insurance. Comment on this statement.
5. If property which is covered by fire insurance is destroyed by fire, will the insurance company pay the owner the actual cost of the property destroyed?
6. For what period are fire insurance policies written? What period do you recommend to the purchaser? Why?
7. What is extended coverage and additional extended coverage?
8. Describe the co-insurance feature and how it works.
9. What is the broad-form personal-theft policy?
10. Describe the personal property floater policy.
11. Does a non-homeowner need personal liability insurance other than in connection with his car? Explain.
12. What are the advantages of the homeowner's policy?
13. (a) Explain the nature of bodily injury and property damage insurance.
    (b) In addition to the payment of damage suits, what other advantage is there in having this kind of insurance?
    (c) What is meant by a "five-and-ten policy"?
    (d) Do you think wealthy people should carry more or less of this kind of insurance than other people? Why?
14. Does bodily injury insurance cover the following?
    (a) Guests riding in insured's automobile.
    (b) Members of family riding in insured's automobile.
15. (a) Explain the nature of collision insurance.
    (b) How much of this kind of insurance should an automobile owner carry?
    (c) Distinguish between a "full coverage" and a "deductible" policy. Which would you recommend? Why?
16. (a) Can a person buy theft insurance on his automobile without buying fire insurance?
    (b) Does automobile fire insurance cover articles which are in the automobile?
17. What is meant by a "comprehensive" coverage policy on an automobile? Would you recommend it? Why?
18. Explain the nature of "medical payments" insurance.
19. Which kind of automobile insurance is most important? Why?
20. What is the assigned risk plan?

CASE PROBLEMS

1. Ralph and Linda Boles have just purchased a home. The savings and loan association which is financing the purchase requires them to carry fire and extended coverage insurance. The only property or casualty insurance they have at the moment is a comprehensive automobile policy. A work associate of Ralph is a part-time insurance salesman. He has suggested a homeowner's policy but this policy costs more than fire and extended coverage. Should Ralph and Linda buy the homeowner's policy? What advantages does it have? What disadvantages? If they do not buy the homeowner's policy, should they purchase other insurance in addition to the fire and extended coverage policy?
2. Bill and Peggy Bryan have just purchased a new frame five-room house for $14,500. A number of fire insurance salesmen have called on Mr. Bryan trying to sell him fire insurance or extended coverage on his new house. Should he buy a straight fire policy or obtain extended coverage? How about additional extended coverage? How much fire insurance should he take out on his new home? Why? Should he buy a one- or a three-year policy? Why? Is fire insurance worth the premium that must be paid since there are so few fires that are total losses these days?
3. Bob Warner, a college sophomore, has just purchased a used car (1959 Chevrolet) on time. He was required by the sales finance company to carry insurance on the car. The finance company purchased the insurance for him. What kind of insurance do you suppose the finance company purchased for Bob's car? Why? Is this sufficient insurance? What would you do if you were Bob?
4. Clayton Jones is moving from Sheridan, Wyoming, to New York City. In contacting his insurance agent about the move, he finds that his automobile rates will rise substantially. Can he keep his policy in Wyoming and obtain the lower rates? Why does insurance cost more in New York City? Since the cost is higher should he reduce the amount of insurance carried? Is he getting more for his money in Wyoming than in New York City?
5. Jim Phelps was driving his brother's car when he skidded into a parked car. Jim's brother's car suffered a dented fender and bent bumper but the parked car had $450 worth of damage. Jim's brother carried no insurance, but Jim had a $25 deductible collision policy on his own car and a $5,000–$10,000 bodily injury policy and a $5,000 property damage policy. Does it cover the damage to the parked car? What kind of policy should Jim's brother have to cover all damage in this accident? If Jim's brother, rather than Jim, had had the two policies, what damage would have been covered? If you were the owner of the parked car, would your liability policy do you any good in this case? Would your collision policy do you any good in this case?
6. Belle Robbins accidentally ran over a small child who was playing in the street. There is some question as to who was at fault. The child suffered a broken back and will be crippled for life. Belle had a $5,000–$10,000 bodily injury policy and a $5,000 property damage policy. Will this insurance cover all Belle's liability in the accident if the court rules she was at fault? What is the maximum this policy will pay? If Belle is not at

fault, is there any advantage of her in having this policy? What should Belle have done immediately after the accident even if she was not at fault? Why?

7. Set up a complete property and casualty insurance program for yourself.

SELECTED READINGS

American Mutual Insurance Alliance. *Property and Casualty Insurance Companies.* Englewood Cliffs, N. J.: Prentice-Hall, Inc., 1962.

Athearn, James L. *Risk and Insurance.* New York: Appleton-Century-Crofts, 1962.

Brainard, Calvin H. *Automobile Insurance.* Homewood, Ill.: Richard D. Irwin, Inc., 1961.

Denenberg, Herbert S., *et al. Risk and Insurance.* Englewood Cliffs, N. J.: Prentice-Hall, Inc., 1964.

Gordis, Philip. *Property and Casualty Insurance,* Eleventh Edition. Indianapolis: Rough Notes Co., 1964.

Hedges, Joseph E., and Williams, Walter. *Practical Fire and Casualty Insurance,* Seventh Edition. Cincinnati: National Underwriters Co., 1961.

Heins, Richard N. *Fundamentals of Property and Casualty Insurance,* Revised Edition. Philadelphia: American College of Life Underwriters, 1960.

Long, John D., and Gregg, Davis W. *Property and Liability Insurance Handbook.* Homewood, Ill.: Richard D. Irwin, Inc., 1965.

Magee, John H., and Bickelhaupt, David L. *General Insurance,* Seventh Edition. Homewood, Ill.: Richard D. Irwin, Inc., 1964.

Magee, John H., and Serbein, Oscar N. *Property Insurance,* Fourth Edition. Homewood, Ill.: Richard D. Irwin, Inc., 1965.

10

Home Ownership

The purchase of a home is the most important single purchase in the lifetime of most Americans. Home ownership is becoming increasingly common in the United States in spite of the large purchase prices involved. Home ownership is a reality for most middle-income families and is even possible for many relatively low-income families. This is one of the things which differentiates the American economic system from those of foreign countries.

The 1960 Census of Housing indicated that approximately 33,000,000 or 62 per cent of all American families owned their own homes. This represented an increase from 55 per cent in the 1950 Census. In the past, home ownership was a rare privilege which only a minority of families could afford. Today, with higher incomes and better and easier financing available, home ownership is within the grasp of the average American family.

In a survey conducted in 1963, the United States Savings and Loan League found that the typical single-family conventional-loan purchaser of a home in metropolitan areas in the United States was approximately 41 years of age with median annual income of $7,000. He had two dependents, was most likely to be employed as a skilled laborer or white-collar worker, and had been employed on his main job for approximately seven years. He purchased a home for approximately $16,000 and borrowed between $11,000 and $12,000 to finance the transaction. His monthly payment for principal and interest came to approximately 15 per cent of his total income. With insurance and real estate taxes added to this total, monthly fixed charges ran to approximately 20 per cent of income. While the median buyer was 41 years of age, this included buyers of all homes and for many this was the second or third purchase. Other studies indicate that the average age of first-time home buyers is closer to 30 than 41.

Home ownership is not a strictly financial decision. People buy homes to satisfy a number of different individual desires. Some buy homes merely to meet an ideal of home ownership rather than for any specific economic reason. Others find that home ownership gives a sense of independence and security which cannot be obtained through renting. Desirability of home ownership includes intangible factors as well as the economics of the situation.

In planning for housing needs, space should be allotted for every member of the family. Home should be a place where each person can find relaxation, a chance for self-expression, and pleasant group living. While many people settle for something less than they desire in a house, the amount invested will produce the most if the tenant or buyer first considers the type of living space required and the related costs, and then judges values and makes his decision. This is true whether housing is obtained through rental or ownership.

OWNING VERSUS RENTING

While some families have such low incomes that home ownership is out of the question, most American families give considerable thought to the relative merits of renting housing versus owning a home. Many people conclude that owning a home is cheaper than renting because there is no rent to pay. An individual whose thinking goes no further than this should reconsider the question because he may often find that renting is cheaper than owning. However, there are a number of factors other than economic which every family should consider in determining whether to own or rent.

Advantages of Owning

The homeowner, as long as he continues his payments, need not worry about where he is going to live. The renter is not always sure of obtaining a suitable place to live, and, if he does secure a house or apartment, he is not sure that he can remain there. A potential homeowner often has a wider choice of location and housing arrangements than does a potential tenant. The individual who builds his own house can choose his own location, provided there is a lot available, and can plan his housing arrangements to meet his exact needs. Even in buying an existing house, a wider variety of locations and arrangements is generally available than in renting.

When a person buys a house, he knows what the loan payments will be, and that the amount of these payments will remain constant. Also, he can ascertain with some degree of certainty the amount that must be paid in taxes, insurances, and maintenance. The renter who does not have any lease, or who has a short-term lease, has no assurance of the amount of his rent and other housing payments in the future.

There is a probability of greater savings on the part of the homeowner because in order to buy or build a house, most people have to cut down on other expenditures. The homeowner is really investing part of his money rather than spending it. Most people who purchase homes are, in the long run, better off financially. If owning a house results in fewer unnecessary expenditures, the greater savings may more than offset the possible additional cost of owning a home versus renting one.

The ownership of a home is a fairly safe investment. The average individual does much better investing in his own home than buying stocks or making other kinds of business investments. Real estate which is purchased in a good residential section of a growing community has a fair chance of increasing in value. Although this increase in value will not be realized unless the property is sold, the homeowner's costs are no greater; the renter may have his rent raised when real estate values increase. If the homeowner wishes to sell his house and buy another one after prices have gone up, the profit he makes will offset in part the increased price of the new house. When a person who has been renting buys a house, he has no such profit to apply on the purchase price. It is realized, of course, that the buyer of a house stands to lose from any decrease in real estate value, but this does not really matter as long as he continues to live in the house.

Greater personal enjoyment is undoubtedly the most important advantage of owning a home. The pride of ownership and security which is felt by the average homeowner is a real factor to consider, and may offset the additional cost in terms which cannot be expressed by a dollar amount. Homeowners are more likely to remain in one location for a longer period than renters. Children will not be forced to change schools and make new friends so often. More interest will be taken in civic and community affairs by the homeowner, and this broadens his enjoyment. The feeling of security possessed by the homeowner who can meet his payments or who has paid off the loan on his house is important. This peace of mind is worth the many sacrifices which may be necessary to attain it.

Advantages of Renting

It may be a surprise to many people, but renting is often cheaper than buying. The comparative costs of renting and owning are discussed later in this chapter.

Buying a home involves the outlay of more money than any other purchase for the average family. If the property is sold in the future, the price that will be obtained for it depends not upon the cost price but upon the supply and demand for houses at that particular time, the cost of real estate at that time, and the urgency of the sale. Aside from the fluctuations in the real estate market, the sale price may be less than cost because of depreciation. Thus, the buyer of a home who thinks in terms of investing in his home is taking a risk in changing market values and in declining value due to depreciation.

Further, since most people must borrow money in order to buy a house, they have the risk of meeting payments on the house or losing it and wiping out their equity in times of difficulty. Unfortunately, it is when prices are falling or have fallen that many people are unable to continue payments on their mortgages and are forced to sell their houses or allow them to be foreclosed. They may then lose not only the down payment and the installment payments made on the loan, but, if the property sells for less than the balance due on the note, they may also be liable on their notes for this difference. In renting, there is no potential loss on investment and no commitments for payment on a mortgage should conditions change.

Renting tends to be more flexible than home ownership. If an individual is renting a house and his income is cut or his expenses increase, he may be able to find a house which rents for a lower amount. Or, if rents decline, he may profit from a reduction in rent. If he owns a house and is making payments on it, he ordinarily cannot have the amount of the payments reduced if his net income is reduced or if rents decline in general. If the renter's place of employment changes, he can ordinarily pack up and move to another house nearer his work. The owner of a home may face a difficult burden if he is forced to move to another city. Even without moving, family needs change through the years. The renter can move to a larger or smaller house or apartment as required, but the owner finds it more difficult to change.

Costs of Home Ownership

Many real estate advertisements point out that you can buy a house on the installment plan and pay no more per month than you are now paying in rent. They further remind you that you will end up owning the house, instead of paying rent during all the years and still not owning the house! It sounds convincing. But why should anyone want to sell a house if he can get just as much out of it per month by renting it and still retaining ownership of the house?

Sometimes a home can be purchased on a long-term loan for monthly payments only slightly in excess of the amount that would have to be paid in rent for a similar house. But the would-be homeowner should think further before jumping to conclusions.

When an individual buys a home, his annual expenses are much greater than the monthly installments of principal and interest. He must pay the taxes and insurance on the property, in addition to such items as repairs, painting, papering, etc. When renting, these expenses, and the problem of depreciation, are the landlord's responsibilities.

Maintenance is something which the homeowner ordinarily cannot ignore. This is another way in which depreciation makes itself felt. Usually, the older the house, the greater the amount which must be spent for maintenance. Regardless of how well constructed a house may be, it will need painting and papering at fairly regular intervals. The homeowner is also inclined to make changes in the house—improvements and additions—and these cost money. The homeowner should realize that, as time goes on, his property deteriorates even when there is proper maintenance, and that this depreciation will usually cause the value of the property to fall.

Another item which many homeowners or would-be homeowners do not take into account is interest on their investment. The renter can earn interest on the money which the homeowner uses as the down payment on a house. If this money is used in buying a home, the return on it will be lost.

It is possible to arrive at the approximate investment cost of owning a home under a given set of circumstances by the use of (more or less) average expense figures. For example, assume that a house costing $17,500 is purchased with a down payment of $3,500. The remaining $14,000 is borrowed on a monthly direct-reduction twenty-year loan at 6 per cent interest. The average annual interest which would have to be paid on this loan would be approximately $503. [Annual payments are approximately $1,203 (see Table 10–4); subtracting from this the average annual payment on principal of $700 leaves $503, which is the average annual interest charge.] The amount paid for taxes would vary in different localities, but 1.8 per cent of the market value would be about average. Property insurance would be about ¼ of 1 per cent. If more complete insurance coverage were obtained, the insurance cost would be more. Utility costs vary substantially from one locality to another. An average cost of $30 per month for utilities and services is assumed here. Assume average maintenance costs to be 2 per cent. The rate of depreciation would vary somewhat according to the type of house. In this example, a life of forty years is assumed. As the value of the lot will not depreciate, only 80 per cent of the total value of the property will be written off.

With $3,500 cash paid down on the property and the entire $17,500 to be paid at the end of twenty years, the average investment during the twenty-year period is $10,500 ($3,500 plus $17,500, divided by 2). At the present time 4½ per cent can be obtained on an investment in savings accounts, so it is assumed that this is the rate of return which is lost by investing the money in a home. Actually the interest lost is lost on the amount of the down payment plus the amount by which the cash outlays for home ownership exceed the cash outlays for renting. In this example, it is assumed that this amount is equal to the increase in investment in the property.

With the above assumptions, the annual investment costs of owning a home would be as follows:

Average Annual Investment Costs During Life of Mortgage

Interest on mortgage (average at 6 per cent)	$ 503
Taxes (1.8 per cent of $17,500)	315
Property insurance (½ of 1 per cent of $14,000)	35
Utilities and services	360
Maintenance (2 per cent of $17,500)	350
Depreciation (2½ per cent of $14,000)	350
Interest cost (4½ per cent of average investment of $10,500)	473
Average annual cost	$2,386
Average monthly cost	$ 199

From the above figures it can be seen that, if a person could rent a house similar to the one described above for less than $199 per month, including utilities, it would be cheaper to rent than to buy. Naturally, if the expenses were less than those stated above, or if less than 4½ per cent could be obtained on investments, or if a mortgage loan of less than $14,000 were required or if it could be secured at less than 6 per cent, the cost of home ownership would be less than indicated by the above figures. If these items are higher, the cost rises. If the depreciation expense item were eliminated in the above computation, the annual cost would be reduced to $2,036 and the monthly cost to $170. However, depreciation is a very definite cost of home ownership and should be included in the computation. It is not realistic to assume that a property will maintain a constant value over a long period of time. Obviously, any house declines in value due to physical deterioration.

In spite of the high monthly cost of the described property, it is conceded that the intangible values accruing from home ownership may more than justify buying this house even though a similar house could be obtained more cheaply through renting. In many cases, it is impossible to rent a house similar to the one a person may want to buy. It should be noted that the above computations are for the life of the mortgage only. If it is assumed that the owner would own the house and live in it for forty years, the total annual cost and the average monthly cost would be less. However, studies indicate that the typical resident lives in a house for an average of seven years only. The above costs should apply any time during the twenty-year mortgage period.

Perhaps more people are interested in the current outlay of cash necessary to purchase a home than in the investment cost as determined above. Assuming the same factors stated above, the annual cash costs or current outlay would be as follows:

Average Annual Cash Outlay During Life of Mortgage

Interest on mortgage (average at 6 per cent)	$ 503
Amortization of loan (average for 20 years)	700
Taxes (1.8 per cent of $17,500)	315
Property insurance (¼ of 1 per cent of $14,000)	35
Utilities and services	360
Maintenance (2 per cent of $17,500)	350
Average annual outlay	$2,263
Average monthly outlay	$ 189

Of the total outlay of $2,263, only $1,563 should be considered as housing costs because the $700 amortization of the loan represents a saving, although due consideration should be given to depreciation. Again, recognize that the above figures are based on a twenty-year period of time. After twenty years, the cash outlay is reduced by $1,203 per year. This reduces total cash outlay to $1,060 but it is likely that maintenance and other expenses would increase to make up part of this differential. If the loan runs for a longer period than twenty years, the *annual* cash outlay during the time the loan is being paid off would naturally be less than that indicated above but the *total* cost would be more because of the additional interest.

Income Tax Considerations

In the above examples of the investment and cash costs of owning a home, no consideration has been given to the income tax savings which are enjoyed through home ownership. The $315 annual tax bill and the average interest payments of $503 are deductible from the individual's income before applying the personal tax rate. These deductible expenses total $818.

In addition, if this individual did not own his home, the money invested in the home would probably be invested in taxable income property. If we assume that the average investment of $10,500 were invested in savings accounts which yield 4½ per cent, then the annual taxable income from this investment would be $473. Adding this to the $818 deduction mentioned above would make a grand total of $1,291. If we assume the individual's top income bracket is 22 per cent, then the annual savings in income taxes would amount to $284, or about $24 per month. For comparative purposes, therefore, the *net* after-tax cost of home ownership is $24 a month less than that shown in the above examples.

Conclusions

The decision to own or rent housing depends upon personal circumstances. Before you reach a decision on this matter, it would be advisable to study the various aspects of your situation. Consider your personal inclinations, the permanence of your position, your income, the size of your family, your health and that of your family, how much time you spend in your home, and what your home means to you and your family. It would appear desirable to rent in most circumstances if you are single and live alone or if your work involves constant transfer. You may also prefer to rent if your family is grown and you wish to lighten your responsibilities. Low-income families will generally find it more economical to rent. After weighing the relative advantages and disadvantages of renting and owning a home, it may be apparent from the above discussion that the authors believe the advantages of owning a home far outweigh the disadvantages for the average family. It is in the intangible values of greater happiness and enjoyment that the greater part of the difference lies.

OWNING AN APARTMENT

Many people prefer apartment living to living in a one-family residence. This is particularly true for older people and for large-city dwellers who prefer to live near the downtown area but find only apartments available. Even though they prefer living in apartments, many of these people want the pride and advantages of ownership. As a result, in recent years there has been an increase in the number of apartment projects in which the apartments are owned by the people living in them. The two most common approaches to this are cooperative apartments and condominiums.

Cooperative Apartments

Cooperative apartment ownership is popular in major metropolitan areas. In a cooperative arrangement, people buy proportionate interests in multifamily dwelling units. The purchaser of a cooperative apartment or unit acquires many of the advantages of home ownership without some of the personal responsibilities for upkeep of the property. Usually he pays monthly for upkeep and maintenance (and possibly some utilities). The amount paid for these services is normally less than rent on a similar apartment because it is a cooperative venture. However, in addition to the payment for these services he will also have payments on his financing, or he will have to invest a substantial amount of money from which he receives no cash income.

Before buying into a cooperative building, it would be important to determine the legal liability to which one may be committing himself as an owner of that building. It is also important to have an agreement relating to the building management and the types and costs of services to be included in the monthly fee. Provisions for subletting or reselling should be included in the agreement. Buying a cooperative apartment involves most of the problems of buying a single residence and certain others in addition.

Condominiums

The condominium is a cross between a cooperative apartment and a privately owned home. The purchaser actually owns his individual apartment with a title deed to show for it. The common areas of the building such as halls and lobbies are jointly owned with other apartment owners. Like a cooperative apartment owner, the condominium owner pays a maintenance charge, but only for his share of maintaining the common area. Therefore, the charge would usually be considerably less than a monthly bill in a cooperative apartment, which includes taxes and mortgage interest on the building as a whole. The condominium owner pays interest charges on his own mortgage and his own real estate taxes on his apartment. Since the condominium owner buys the apartment on his own, he has freedom to negotiate his own mortgage terms, which could mean a larger down payment to reduce interest charges or a cash outlay with no down payment at all, or he could choose to speed up payments and retire a mortgage early. In a cooperative project, there is no such flexibility. The condominium owner has no worry about taking on the burden of the charges for any vacant apartments in the building. This is sometimes a burden in cooperative apartments during a recession.

The major advantage of the condominium is that it is a separate piece of real estate salable on the open market. In the typical cooperative apartment, the cooperative corporation has the first choice or approval rights on any new buyers. In a condominium, the outright ownership of the apartment allows the owner to sell as he sees fit, at any price he can obtain. Thus, the condominium owner becomes more like an owner of a single residence than the cooperative apartment owner, who is in many ways like a tenant. In recent years, a number of states have passed laws providing for condominium ownership. It is expected that most other states will follow suit in coming years.

RENTING AN APARTMENT OR HOME

Renting involves an agreement between a tenant and a landlord. Commonly, the agreement is formally written and is called a lease. However, even without a lease the tenant and the landlord have certain rights and duties; these are summarized in Fig. 10–1.

Whether there is a formal written lease or merely a verbal agreement, certain things must be clearly understood by both parties. The formal written lease is generally more satisfactory. The agreement must establish how long the lease runs, the amount of the rent, and if, when, and by what amount it can be increased. The length of notice required before moving should be understood, as well as responsibility for the rent should the tenant move before his lease expires. The question of what happens to prepaid rent at the expiration of the lease or in the event of moving should be agreed upon, along with the determination of who is responsible for upkeep, maintenance, and utilities. A fairly drawn and well-understood lease is an important asset to both tenant and landlord.

BUYING OR BUILDING

If a family has decided to own its own home, the next question is whether it should build a new house or buy one which has already been constructed. If they plan to buy a ready-built house, they must decide whether to select a new house or an older one. In addition, the amount which the family can afford to pay for the house must be determined. Finally, there is the important task of selecting an existing house or the plans and lot for a new one.

Advantages of Buying a Ready-Built House

The majority of home buyers, when they decide to purchase a house, look over existing houses and give little or no thought to building a new one. Generally speaking, it is cheaper to buy an existing house than to build a new one. One reason for this is that a ready-built house decreases in value over a period of time due to deterioration. The buyer, therefore, may not necessarily be getting a bargain, but the lower-priced depreciated house may serve his needs just as well as a more costly new one. A house which has just been completed and therefore has not depreciated may be cheaper than building a new one because of the advantages of large-scale construction by builders who build new houses for speculative sale. Also, in a buyers' market in housing, many ready-built new and old houses offered for sale must be sold regardless of what they originally cost to build. In many instances, a discriminating buyer can buy a new

For owner and renter: a give-and-take proposition

TENANT'S RIGHTS

- to have possession and quiet enjoyment of the property without disturbance by the landlord
- to use any other part of the landlord's property necessary for the enjoyment of the leased part
- to cease paying rent if the property becomes uninhabitable through no fault of his own so long as he also leaves the premises
- to sublet, but only with the consent of the landlord

LANDLORD'S DUTIES

- to refrain from unlawful entry or trespassing
- to furnish the necessities for habitation as set out in the lease (such as heat, lights on common halls and stairways, elevator service)
- to keep the premises safe from hidden defects and free of rodents and other household pests
- to make major—or structural—repairs
- to pay real estate taxes and assessments
- to keep immoral persons out of the building

TENANT'S DUTIES

- to pay rent on time
- to make minor repairs
- to inform the landlord of necessary major repairs
- to practice reasonable alertness in seeking out dangerous building defects before moving in
- to use the premises for lawful purposes only and only for purposes set out in the lease if they are specified
- to surrender the property promptly at the end of the term unless renewal is agreed upon

LANDLORD'S RIGHTS

- to evict a tenant for failure to perform his duties under the lease or for just being objectionable as a tenant
- to assign his interest in the property to someone else without the tenant's consent
- to claim as his own any permanent improvements made by the tenant and any installations that are permanently affixed to the building
- to consider the property abandoned and to terminate the lease if the tenant fails to take possession

Fig. 10–1. Rights and duties of tenants and landlords. [Reprinted by permission from *Changing Times,* the Kiplinger Magazine (April 1964 issue). Copyright 1964 by The Kiplinger Washington Editors, Inc., 1729 H. Street, N. W., Washington, D. C. 20006.]

house for less than it would cost him to build the same house, because the seller is willing to sell at a sacrifice.

A family may be able to move into a ready-built house immediately, without incurring additional expenses for such things as landscaping, porches, weather stripping, storm doors, etc., which the person who builds may have to pay for in addition to the contractor's bill. The street, water, and sewer assessments may have been paid in full on the ready-built house, and the purchase price may not be any higher because of it.

Another advantage of buying a ready-built house is that the purchase price is fixed. The person who builds cannot be certain of the final cost—in fact, building usually costs more than originally estimated. After a house is completed, the owner may find it necessary to spend additional money on items which were not included in the contract.

Where immediate occupancy is essential, usually buying rather than building is the solution. The person who decides to build normally has to wait a period of time before his house is completed. Shortages in materials or strikes may slow up construction. It is rather common experience to find that building a house takes longer than originally planned and in many cases may exceed a one-year period from the time of the decision to build until the family can move into the new house.

Disadvantages of Buying a Ready-Built House

The major reason for building a new house rather than buying a ready-built one is the difficulty of finding a ready-built house that fits an individual's taste and needs. He may have unusual ideas which he would like to see incorporated into his house that are not available in existing houses. In existing houses, the buyer must take what is for sale even though he is not completely satisfied with the design or layout of the house.

In addition, the buyer of an existing house may not have as broad a choice of locations as one who is willing to build, although the reverse of this may also be true. In building his own home one may be able to be more certain of the workmanship and quality of materials than he would be of those in an existing house.

Buying a New House Versus an Older One

The major advantage of buying a new house is that everything inside and outside the house will be new and should be in top condition. In addition, the new house buyer normally has the opportunity to choose certain interior decoration for the completion of the house. New houses tend to offer the latest modern conveniences and are generally designed for better utilization of space. A new house offers the opportunity to landscape the property to individual tastes, but involves the expense of so doing.

Older homes are generally purchased because more space is available for the money. Also, they may be structurally more substantial than newer houses. Some flaws in new houses may not show up for from one to ten years after the house is completed. In buying a new house or buying one which is not very old, the owner cannot always be certain that the proper materials were used, or that the house will not settle too much. The presence or absence of such flaws can be detected in an older house.

There are more older houses available than new houses, thus a wider choice is offered in the purchase of older houses. The property is normally fully improved and completely landscaped. Older homes are frequently available in established neighborhoods. When buying a new house, it may be difficult to determine the ultimate quality or makeup of the neighborhood.

Many older houses are not modernized. This is more serious to some prospective buyers than to others. The absence of modern improvements generally results in the price of the house being lower than if it were modern throughout. People who want a house in a good neighborhood, but cannot afford to pay a very high price for it, may find something suitable in an older house. Modernization may be accomplished in the future as money becomes available. Before buying an older house, the prospective buyer should have it looked over by a competent person in order to determine if any extensive repairs are needed immediately or will be needed in the near future.

Conclusions

It is impossible to draw a conclusion that new houses are better than old ones or that buying a house is better than building a house or vice versa. The final decision depends upon available properties, available money, and the desires of the potential homeowner. The latter are most important, for people who desire originality can generally find it only in homes they build themselves. Others are willing to pay more for a new house because of non-economic considerations; still others desire the most space for their money and are willing to settle for an older house in order to get it.

MOBILE HOMES

According to the 1960 Census of Housing, 766,565 mobile homes were occupied as living units in 1960. Of these, 82,000 were on permanent foundations and the remainder were on wheels. (The census did not count unoccupied mobile homes as housing units. Also, if a room had been added to what was originally a mobile home, the housing unit was counted as a house rather than a mobile home.) It has been estimated that, in 1965, three million people lived in mobile homes or homes that were once mobile. Recent annual production of mobile homes has exceeded 125,000 units per year. Thus the mobile home is an important element in housing in the United States and it is continuing to grow in importance.

The early mobile homes were designed to be "mobile"; that is, they were on wheels and were of such a size that they could be readily transported from one place to another. A normal family car can pull a mobile home up to a size of 8 feet by 29 feet. It takes special trucks to pull larger mobile homes, and as a result they are not moved very often. In this discussion of mobile homes, we are not including camping trailers or mobile homes which are used as temporary rather than permanent housing by families. A large number of mobile homes serve as second houses for many families.

A modern mobile home can be a rather substantial residence. Some are as large as 12 feet by 60 feet with pull-out rooms which can add another 70 square feet. Some of these homes include three bedrooms, a bathroom, a living room, and a dining and kitchen combination. A modern mobile home is fully equipped with modern furnishings and includes such items as garbage disposal units and dishwashers. While the number of square feet is small relative to permanent houses, the many built-in features provide for very efficient uses of space.

A mobile home is no longer the cheapest way to live. The average price for mobile homes is in excess of $5,500, with a range of from $3,500 to $15,000. This price includes furniture and equipment but it does not include a lot. To compare to standard housing, a lot price would have to be added and the cost of furnishings and equipment subtracted. Mobile homes are probably no less expensive per square foot than certain standard housing without a lot.

The above price quotations are for new mobile homes. With good maintenance, a well-built mobile home may last 15 to 20 years or longer. Since there is a large drop in market value after the first year, good buys can often be found in used mobile homes. Buying either a new or used mobile home requires careful study on the part of the buyer. Over 400 firms produce mobile homes, so there is substantial quality variation among the homes on the market. In addition, there is a wide variety of sizes and types. The buyer should be careful of packaged prices and price variations.

In considering the cost of a mobile home, the buyer must take into account the cost of the place on which he parks his home as well as the cost of moving the home. Many rural people already have land and can place a mobile home on a portion that is not being used otherwise. Thus they would have relatively little expense for a lot. However, for urban dwellers (who are the major users of mobile homes) rent for a lot may range from $25 to $125 per month. The rent for the lot commonly includes water and utility installations. In some places lots may be purchased for mobile homes, but it is much more common to rent the space by the month. Adding lot rental to the cost of financing and the depreciation of the mobile home may make it as expensive as many other types of housing.

Financing mobile homes is considerably different from financing standard housing. Commonly, the dealer arranges the financing but does not actually finance the mobile home himself. He generally places it through a bank or a finance company. Mobile homes have not gained acceptance by financial institutions to the same level as standard housing. Thus, the rates on mobile home financing are higher and the terms less flexible. Typically, there is a five- to seven-year maximum term on mobile home financing. In addition, 25 to 30 per cent must be paid down. Interest is commonly from 6 to 8 per cent discounted but figured on the original balance so that the effective rate ranges from 12 to 17 per cent. Financing mobile homes is handled in the same way as auto financing rather than standard home financing. Therefore, it is much more costly to the buyer.

Consumers should consider mobile homes when there is a substantial cost advantage to buying one and when the consumer would like this kind of living. Many people do not enjoy a large amount of room; others like to be more mobile in their living and to take their house with them. Even though modern mobile homes are not readily transported, they can be moved when the occasion arises. Mobile housing is particularly useful to people such as construction workers, who move often from one temporary site to another. Anyone who likes built-in features and an efficient floor plan with a small amount of space may be very happy in a mobile home.

The above discussion of mobile housing has been from the point of view of a homeowner. Relatively few mobile homes are for rent. In the 1960 Census, only 90,000 units were tenant-occupied. This represented less than 15 per cent of the total mobile homes in the country.

WHAT TO LOOK FOR IN HOUSING

The value of real estate is influenced by location, nature of the neighborhood, design and layout of the house, type of construction, type of materials used, landscaping, age of house, and the supply and demand for real estate at a particular time. In addition to these factors, the price which must be paid depends on the eagerness of the seller to sell and the buyer to buy.

An appraisal may be made of the value of the property based upon the amount it would cost to reproduce the particular house. From this would be subtracted the depreciation which has taken place since the time of construction. This appraisal approach is called *reproduction value.* The *market value* of a house at any particular time can, to some degree, be determined by ascertaining, if possible, the price at which recent sales of comparable houses in the same community were made. This is perhaps the most practical approach to appraisal, but, of course, the market value of a specific house at any time is the price at which it can be sold regardless of the price at which others were sold. A third approach to appraisal is determining the amount for which the house could be rented and then capitalizing this at some return figure. This is called the *earning power* or *income* approach.

Since a home is probably the most important purchase which a family will make, it is advisable to approach the selection of a home wisely. They should select the house which best meets their requirements within the funds they have available. Most of all, their home should satisfy their desires—not the desires of others. Unless they anticipate moving in the near future, their home is really a consumption item and should not be purchased strictly as an investment. Thus, the appraisal value determined by others becomes only one factor to consider in a personal decision to buy a house. The major use of appraised values is to protect against an inability to sell a house at a reasonable value should its sale be required.

Location

If the individual has any choice in the matter, it is desirable to acquire property in a good neighborhood of a growing community. Locations which have strict building codes are preferred. The adequacy of transportation is important. If major transportation will be by automobile, the location should be such as to facilitate reaching various destinations easily. Many new developments are growing in close proximity to freeway systems in major cities. If there is any need for public transportation, the location should have public transportation available within walking distance.

The location is more desirable if it is close to community facilities. For people with children, or who expect to have children, location near or accessible to a good school is important. In addition to schools, proximity to shopping, churches, health services, playgrounds, and fire and police protection should be considered. A good neighborhood is quiet, safe, well-zoned, well-kept, congenial, and generally peopled by homeowners rather than tenants.

It is generally more desirable to buy homes in a neighborhood which was not developed as a tract, that is, where the homes were built by different builders according to a wide variety of plans. However, in many cases, much more value can be received by buying a house in a tract or project. This is particularly true for young married couples purchasing their first home. When buying a tract house, they should be sure that there is enough differentiation among the houses in the neighborhood and that there is potential for further differentiation as various owners eventually make modifications in their housing.

Taxes, Assessments, and Maintenance

Systems of valuation for tax purposes and the tax rate vary among communities. The prospective builder or buyer should ascertain this information in order to be able to determine his total costs. He should also look up the amount, if any, due for street, sewer, and any other special assessments which may be owing. These assessments are usually paid for on an installment basis every six months along with the taxes. The owners of some lots and houses have paid these special assessments in their entirety either in a lump sum or through the installment plan. Changing tax rates can be important in certain areas. This is particularly true of new suburban developments with growing school populations.

Maintenance costs will vary from one home to another. Older homes particularly will require substantial maintenance outlays. The type of construction also influences future maintenance costs. Unpainted brick or stone is cheaper to maintain than frame, stucco, or painted brick. A well-insulated house costs less to heat and cool than a poorly insulated one. An experienced real estate man, appraiser, or maintenance man can usually discover weaknesses in construction, wiring, plumbing, heating, or roofing before a home is purchased. If these items are in good condition at the time of purchase, immediate maintenance costs should be less.

When Building

The first step in building a new house is selection of a lot. It is important to make certain that the soil is suitable for building and that proper drainage can be obtained. The lot must be of sufficient size to handle properly the house that is considered and to allow for the amount of outdoor living desired. Care should be taken not to put too expensive a house on too cheap a lot, or too cheap a house on an expensive lot. Either procedure may result in loss of resale value of the property. In general, the value of the lot should be about one fifth of the total value of the property.

Guard against special real estate promotions. In recent years, large numbers of lots have been sold to people on a high pressure basis. Many of these purchasers have later been dissatisfied because they discovered that the location was not all that it was claimed to be or that improvements were not available. It is particularly important to be cautious in buying real estate at a distance. A great many people approaching retirement buy property in Florida, California, or Arizona without ever seeing the land they are purchasing.

Housing Checklist

Whether building, buying, or renting, there are certain features to look for in choosing a home. The number of rooms and baths available, closet space, storage space, traffic patterns, heating and cooling, electrical circuits, lighting and windows, styling—all are important factors which should meet an individual's requirements. He must judge whether the house meets his probable future needs as well as his present needs. The house should be suitable in layout, design, and appearance. Figure 10–2 is a checklist for renting or buying. There are a large number of factors to be considered in obtaining desirable housing.

Resale Value

While an individual's home should primarily meet *his* requirements, it is generally worthwhile to consider its potential resale value. Certain typical features are expected in a home; if a home does not include these features, resale may be more difficult. While he may not be planning on reselling his home, an owner does not know when circumstances may arise which will require this transaction.

USING PROFESSIONAL PEOPLE

Anyone planning to build or buy a home will undoubtedly use professional people in connection with the purchase. In building a new home, the services of an architect and a contractor will often be needed. In buying an existing home, the purchaser would normally utilize the services of a realtor, a lawyer, an insurance agent, and someone representing a financial institution. It is important, when one deals with professional people, to select practitioners who are reliable and who know their profession. The clients of a professional person must have trust in his ability and must be able to communicate well with him.

The Architect

The major basis on which an architect is selected is study of his prior work. The first step is to look at other houses which he has designed and to contact purchasers of these houses to determine their degree of satisfaction. It is also important to hold exploratory discussions with a potential architect to get to know him and to be sure that he understands particular needs and requirements. If desired, it can be determined whether he is a member of the American Institute of Architects. In addition to planning a house, the architect will often advise in the selection of a builder; if requested, he will supervise the construction of the house to be sure it is built according to his specifications.

The Contractor

The selection of a contractor is similar to the process for selecting an architect: look at his prior work and determine the degree of satisfaction of prior purchasers. In addition, it is important to determine whether the contractor is solvent and whether financial or labor difficulties may delay your construction. The builder should be willing to give a warranty relative to construction and materials in the house. Be sure to select a builder who takes pride in building a house and who is anxious to maintain a reputation for good work.

The Realtor

In most purchases of real estate, it is important to consult a reputable real estate broker. He can be extremely helpful in making a selection and may often save the purchaser time, trouble, and money. A good real estate broker knows the properties which are for sale in the community and is in a position to give expert advice and to answer questions. He can supply information on values, zoning, taxes, transportation, assessments, and utility services. He may also be helpful in obtaining finances.

It is important to note that the commission of the real estate broker is paid by the seller, not the buyer. A good real estate broker attempts to represent both the buyer and the seller, but the buyer should be cautious of buying through some real estate brokers. A purchaser should be sure that the real estate broker who helps him buy a home is willing to show him properties which are listed by other companies and to help him find the property he needs regardless of whether it is listed with him. Multiple listing services in many cities enable a real estate broker to obtain a commission on a sale of property almost anywhere in the community, not just on properties which were originally listed with him.

Other Professional People

Financing a home requires dealing with financial institutions. This is discussed later in this chapter. At the time a house is purchased, it is important that proper insurance be arranged. Dealing with insurance agents has already been covered in Chapter 9.

It is generally well worth the expense to be represented by a lawyer at the time of purchase of property. He knows how the legal documents

CHECKLIST FOR

In looking at either apartments or houses to rent or buy, there are both general and specific points to consider (such as those included in the checklist below) to help you decide whether the facilities will meet your requirements. Answers to many of the questions can be found through careful inspection, trying out equipment and plumbing, and by asking questions of the occupant, owner, or other person in charge. Questions of a technical nature to which you would like the answers may require the help of an expert. *To use the checklist,* make a check opposite each point that is adequate for your needs, omitting

Exterior

- Is the character of the community:
  - to your liking? ______
  - convenient for your activities? ______
- Is the style of the dwelling:
  - attractive? ______
  - in keeping with others in the area? ______
- Is exterior construction in good condition? ______
- Are major views pleasant? ______

  Is there sufficient:
  - daylight? ______
  - sunlight? ______
- If there is a yard, is it large enough for:
  - a play area? ______
  - outdoor living? ______
  - a garden? ______
- If it is a house, is it located to take best advantage of:
  - sun? ______
  - wind? ______
  - shade? ______
- Is property fenced in or enclosed with shrubs for children's safety? ______
- Are the dwellings far enough apart to provide the privacy you want on either side, as well as at the back of the house? ______
- Is yard landscaped, with lawn and shrubs in good condition? ______
- If there is a well instead of a public water system, are the following adequate:
  - depth of well? ______
  - quantity of water? ______
  - flow of water? ______
- If there is a septic tank instead of a municipal sewer system, is it:
  - adequate in size for your family? ______
  - properly installed? ______
- Are there improvements on the lot, such as:
  - sidewalks and streets? ______
  - grading? ______
  - utility connections? ______
- Are there parking facilities, such as:
  - a garage or carport? ______
  - 24-hour parking on street or in an alley? ______

Entrance

- Are entrances well lighted? ______
- Is there a side or rear entrance for deliveries? ______
- Is there an outside entrance for fuel deliveries? ______
- Is the entrance to inside hallway kept locked? ______
- Are there locked mailboxes? ______
- Are there facilities for accepting packages when you are away? ______
- Are hallways and stairways well lighted and clean? ______
- Is there elevator service that eliminates climbing steps to the apartment? ______
- Are there adequate fire escapes? ______

Interior

- Are the following in good condition:
  - windows and doors? ______
  - floors, walls, and ceilings? ______
  - roof and gutters? ______
  - porches, including railings? ______
  - steps? ______
- Is insulation adequate? ______
- Are walls and floors insulated against noise? ______
- Are electric outlets where you will need them for:
  - lamps? ______
  - radio and television? ______
  - large appliances? ______
  - small appliances? ______

Fig. 10–2. Tenants' and homeowners' checklist for evaluating an apart-
Shelter Dollar. Chicago: Household Finance Corp., 1963.)

RENTING OR BUYING

those which do not apply to the property at which you are looking. Then evaluate the importance to you of the points you have left unchecked. You probably will not find any one location that will measure up to your standards in all respects, but if the features most important to you are included, perhaps you can afford to overlook the less important items. Applying this checklist to each house or apartment in which you are interested may give you a basis for making an intelligent decision, and may save you from dissatisfaction and unnecessary expense later on.

- Is the current adequate for all purposes and appliances? ______
- If there is a basement, is it:
  - well ventilated and dry? ______
  - well lighted? ______
  - without hazards, such as low beams, exposed pipes and wires? ______

Equipment

- If needed, are the following provided for all windows:
  - shades or blinds? ______
  - storm windows? ______
  - screens? ______
- Are the following adequate and in good condition:
  - plumbing? ______
  - heating unit? ______
  - kitchen appliances? ______
  - laundry appliances? ______
  - water heater? ______
  - Are all of the above operating satisfactorily? ______
- If needed, is there a place for storing:
  - screens? ______
  - storm windows and doors? ______
  - outdoor furniture? ______
  - garden and yard tools? ______
- Are there facilities for disposal of garbage, such as:
  - an incinerator? ______
  - disposer in kitchen sink? ______
  - city garbage collection? ______
- Is there telephone service? ______
  Must you have a telephone installed? ______
- May you have an outside aerial for television? ______
- Is there a charge for plugging into a common aerial? ______

Arrangement of space

- Can the rooms be adapted to your needs? ______
- Are rooms and wall spaces large enough for your furniture? ______
- Is amount and arrangement of work space in kitchen satisfactory? ______
- Is there space for laundry purposes? ______
- Is placement of bathroom convenient to all areas of house? ______
- Are closets, cabinets, shelves and all other storage spaces adequate for your needs? ______
- Are windows well placed for satisfactory ventilation in all rooms? ______
  If not, are there fans or an air conditioning system? ______

Responsibility for maintenance when renting

- Is the person responsible for upkeep and taking care of complaints easy to get in touch with? ______
  Is he:
  - the owner? ______
  - an agent? ______
  - a representative of a management firm? ______
- What maintenance costs are included in the rent, such as for:
  - electricity? ______
  - gas? ______
  - water? ______
  - telephone? ______
  - repairs and replacement? ______
  - decorating? ______
- If needed:
  - will the landlord make repairs? ______
  - decorate completely before you move in? ______
- Is window washing taken care of by the management? ______
- Are you offered a written lease? ______

ment or house. (Reproduced with permission, from *Money Management, Your* should be drawn for proper protection, and can make sure that the financing and purchase provisions are in the purchaser's best interest. He can also interpret contracts so that the buyer has a clear understanding of his rights and obligations. The failure to be represented by a lawyer has cost many purchasers sizable subsequent amounts.

HOW MUCH CAN YOU PAY?

When building or buying a house, an individual should stay within his means. Some relationship should exist between the size of an individual's income and the maximum amount he spends for a house. This is assuming that most of the money to acquire the house must be borrowed. If sufficient cash is available to acquire the house, this relationship between size of income and cost of house would not be applicable. But even here some thought should be given to the amount which will have to be paid in taxes and upkeep. The number of dependents, the amount of outstanding debts, if any, and the security of employment must all be taken into account when acquiring a house.

What Others Spend

Table 10–1 indicates what amounts families have spent on housing relative to their monthly income before taxes. There are a number of common rules of thumb which can be stated. First, the down payment should be as large as possible. The larger the down payment, the smaller the monthly and annual requirements thereafter. In addition, the faster the payoff, the lower the total carrying charges. While monthly and annual payments will be higher during the life of the loan, the total cost will be substantially less if a shorter-term mortgage is acquired. A fifteen-year 6 per cent mortgage loan for $10,000 requires total payments of $3,500 less than the same amount borrowed for twenty-five years.

If most of the money must be borrowed, the total cost should not exceed the buyer's annual (before tax) income multiplied by two. In addition, the total monthly carrying charges—including the amortization of the mortgage, interest, taxes, and insurance—should not exceed 25 per cent of his monthly take-home pay. These rules of thumb are of course averages and should, therefore, be considered as only very general guides. Individual circumstances vary from one purchaser to another.

Family size and living expenses have a great deal of influence on the amount which any specific family can afford to pay for housing. Stability of income, other savings requirements, and other debt commitments will influence the amount a family can afford to pay for a home. Table 10–2 indicates the amount of a mortgage which may be financed at given per-

Table 10–1. What Others Spend on Houses

Monthly Income Before Taxes	In Actual Dollars: Mortgage Payment*	In Actual Dollars: Other Expenses**	In Actual Dollars: Total House Expense	As Per Cent of Income: Mortgage Payment*	As Per Cent of Income: Other Expenses**	As Per Cent of Income: Total House Expense
New Houses						
Less than $300	$ 58.76	$18.21	$ 76.97	22.5%	7.0%	29.5%
$300–$349	68.14	20.18	88.32	20.9	6.1	27.0
$350–$399	73.58	21.87	95.45	19.7	5.8	25.5
$400–$449	78.86	22.65	101.51	18.7	5.3	24.0
$450–$499	84.43	23.54	107.97	17.9	5.0	22.9
$500–$549	88.98	24.42	113.40	17.1	4.7	21.8
$550–$599	93.00	24.92	117.92	16.3	4.3	20.6
$600–$649	96.54	25.36	121.90	15.6	4.1	19.7
$650–$699	99.45	26.16	125.61	14.9	3.9	18.8
$700–$749	103.10	26.63	129.73	14.3	3.7	18.0
$750–$799	105.86	27.15	133.01	13.8	3.5	17.3
$800–$849	111.30	28.12	139.42	13.6	3.4	17.0
$850–$899	111.83	28.13	139.96	12.9	3.2	16.1
$900–$999	113.78	28.47	142.25	12.1	3.1	15.2
$1,000 or more	123.62	30.51	154.13	10.0	2.5	12.5
Old Houses						
Less than $300	$ 56.24	$20.56	$ 76.80	21.0%	7.7%	28.7%
$300–$349	66.06	22.15	88.21	20.2	6.8	27.0
$350–$399	71.56	22.85	94.41	19.1	6.2	25.3
$400–$449	76.68	23.47	100.15	18.2	5.5	23.7
$450–$499	81.83	24.19	106.02	17.4	5.1	22.5
$500–$549	86.14	24.98	111.12	16.6	4.8	21.4
$550–$599	90.07	25.58	115.65	15.8	4.4	20.2
$600–$649	93.67	26.28	119.95	15.1	4.3	19.4
$650–$699	96.98	26.74	123.72	14.5	4.0	18.5
$700–$749	100.22	27.13	127.35	13.9	3.8	17.7
$750–$799	104.29	27.59	131.88	13.6	3.6	17.2
$800–$849	109.07	28.00	137.07	13.3	3.4	16.7
$850–$899	111.98	29.12	141.10	12.9	3.3	16.2
$900–$999	116.71	30.12	145.83	12.4	3.1	15.5
$1,000 or more	127.73	31.83	159.56	10.4	2.6	13.0

* Includes principal, interest, insurance, taxes.
**Includes maintenance, repair, heat, utilities.

SOURCE: *Changing Times, The Kiplinger Magazine.*

centages of interest for indicated monthly and annual incomes available for housing. To use this table, add the amount of the expected down payment to the total value of the mortgage, based on income available for housing. This is the amount that can be afforded for a house. For example, if a purchaser plans to pay $4,000 down with 6 per cent financing

Table 10–2. Amount of Mortgage Which May Be Financed by Amount of Monthly and Annual Income Available for Housing, by Interest Rate and Maturity of Mortgage

Income for Housing		At 4¾ Per Cent			At 5 Per Cent			At 5½ Per Cent			At 6 Per Cent		
Monthly	Annual	10 yr.	15 yr.	20 yr.	10 yr.	15 yr.	20 yr.	10 yr.	15 yr.	20 yr.	10 yr.	15 yr.	20 yr.
$ 40	$ 480	$3,265	$4,210	$4,850	$3,245	$4,140	$4,800	$3,180	$4,035	$4,615	$3,115	$3,935	$4,485
50	600	4,080	5,265	6,060	4,055	5,170	6,000	3,975	5,040	5,770	3,895	4,920	5,605
60	720	4,900	6,315	7,275	4,865	6,205	7,200	4,770	6,050	6,920	4,675	5,900	6,730
80	960	6,530	8,420	9,695	6,485	8,275	9,600	6,360	8,070	9,230	6,235	7,870	8,970
100	1,200	8,165	10,525	12,120	8,110	10,345	12,000	7,950	10,085	11,540	7,790	9,835	11,215
125	1,500	10,205	13,160	15,150	10,135	12,930	15,000	9,935	12,605	14,425	9,740	12,295	14,020
150	1,800	12,245	15,790	18,180	12,160	15,520	18,000	11,920	15,125	17,310	11,690	14,755	16,820
175	2,100	14,285	18,420	21,210	14,190	18,105	21,000	13,910	17,650	20,190	13,635	17,215	19,625
200	2,400	16,325	21,050	24,240	16,215	20,690	24,000	15,895	20,170	23,075	15,585	19,670	22,430
225	2,700	18,365	23,685	27,270	18,245	23,275	27,000	17,880	22,690	25,960	17,530	22,130	25,235
250	3,000	20,405	26,315	30,300	20,270	25,860	30,000	19,870	25,210	28,845	19,480	24,590	28,035

Note: Taxes have been estimated at $18 annually, insurance at $3 annually, for every $1,000 loaned on the home.

for twenty years, with monthly income of $100 available for housing, he could purchase a home valued at $15,215.

What You Should Spend

Since no two families are alike, the ability to pay a certain price for a home depends on a number of things. Table 10–3 gives home ownership costs and family income required, assuming an expenditure of 20 per cent of gross income on housing. The ability to pay 20 per cent or more of one's income depends on the steadiness of employment, amount of savings, personal desires for other expenditures, number of children, and do-it-yourself ability.

To find out how much of *your* income you can devote to buying a home, list your monthly or yearly expenses and income aside from expenses relative to housing. (Income should be take-home pay rather than gross and a wife's income should be omitted if it may prove temporary.) Expenses to be subtracted include savings requirement, food and clothing, recreation, utilities, transportation, life insurance, and miscellaneous expenses. Subtracting these non-housing expenses from net take-home pay gives the amount which is available for housing. This amount can be compared to the monthly carrying costs in Table 10–3 to determine the selling price that can be paid, assuming that you are able to make a 20 per cent down payment. If you can make a higher down payment, a more expensive house can be purchased. The required annual income given in Table 10–3 is gross income, not net take-home pay.

Table 10–3. Home Ownership Costs and Family Income Required

Selling Price	Down Payment *	Monthly Carrying Costs **	Annual Income Required †
$10,000	$2,000	$110.33	$ 6,620
12,500	2,500	131.58	7,895
15,000	3,000	158.00	9,480
17,500	3,500	179.33	10,760
20,000	4,000	205.58	12,335
25,000	5,000	248.25	14,895
30,000	6,000	295.92	17,755
40,000	8,000	381.17	22,870

* A 20 per cent down payment was used.

** Monthly costs were based on a 25-year, 6 per cent mortgage with taxes of 1.8 per cent, insurance at .25 per cent, and maintenance at 2.0 per cent of selling prices. Utilities and services were varied from $25 per month for the $10,000 house to $40 per month for the $40,000 house.

† Based on assumed expenditure of 20 per cent of gross annual income for housing.

FINANCING HOME OWNERSHIP

The safest way to buy a home is to pay cash. If a mortgage is placed on a house, the inability to make the payments in the future may result in loss of both the house and the amount paid on it. However, the majority of homes are purchased with mortgages because most families are not able to accumulate sufficient amounts to pay cash for their homes. This is particularly true of younger families.

Mortgaging a Home

When buying a home on mortgage, the borrower must sign a note for the amount of the loan. A mortgage on the house is given as security for the loan. Thus, in addition to the mortgaged property, the borrower's general credit is behind the loan. If the borrower is not able to keep up the payments on the loan, the lender can foreclose on the house. In event that the sale of the house to pay the note does not bring enough to pay off the loan in its entirety, the borrower is liable, on the note, for the difference between what the house brought and the amount of the loan.

If a buyer can pay only an exceedingly small amount down, such as 5 or 10 per cent, it may be necessary for him to get two loans against the house. The lender under the first mortgage may lend him only 60 or 70 per cent of the purchase price, and the balance may have to be obtained by placing a second mortgage against the property. Since the risk of the loan under the second mortgage is greater, the rate of interest charged would be much higher than for the first mortgage. Builders sometimes will accept the second mortgage in part payment for a house.

Many young married couples, desiring to purchase homes before they have had a chance to accumulate down payments, often borrow the down payment from parents, other relatives, or friends. If the amount is borrowed from parents, there is no particular problem. However, if a person cannot obtain sufficient money under a first mortgage to finance a house, and he is considering financing the down payment by a second mortgage through a lender who will enforce terms, it is generally recommended that the purchase be postponed until sufficient money has been accumulated to obviate the use of the second mortgage. In the discussion which follows, it will be assumed that only one mortgage is used.

Down Payment

It is usually advisable to make the down payment as large as possible. The buyer, however, should not use all his money, as he would then have no reserve to fall back upon if extraordinary expenses arise in the future, or if his income is reduced.

When the loan comprises a large percentage of the purchase price, the interest rate is usually higher than otherwise. If the down payment is small, the installment payments on the loan may be too heavy for the purchaser and may result in the loss of the property, the down payment, and the amount paid on the loan.

With a loan of a given amount, the price that can be paid for a home varies according to the amount of the down payment. If a purchaser can afford $100 per month for housing, on a 6 per cent twenty-year mortgage, he can borrow $14,000. A $6,000 down payment would allow him to purchase a $20,000 home. A $3,000 down payment would allow him to purchase only a $17,000 home. Down-payment requirements vary from one source of mortgage funds to another. They also vary between types of loans. Obviously, one cannot pay more down than he has available. The most common limiting factor in home purchase is the amount of the down payment.

In recent years it has been possible to purchase certain types of housing with no money down. People who buy with no money down restrict themselves to houses available in this category. It may be better to accumulate a down payment and have a wider choice in selecting a house for purchase. In December, 1963, the Federal Home Loan Bank Board estimated that down payments on new houses with conventional loans averaged 26 per cent and the down payments on previously occupied houses averaged 28 per cent. If FHA and GI loans had been included in the study, the average down payment would have been significantly less.

Figure 10–3 illustrates the advantage of larger down payments. With a down payment of $5,000 on a $10,000 house financed on a 6 per cent fifteen-year loan, total interest paid over the life of the loan would be

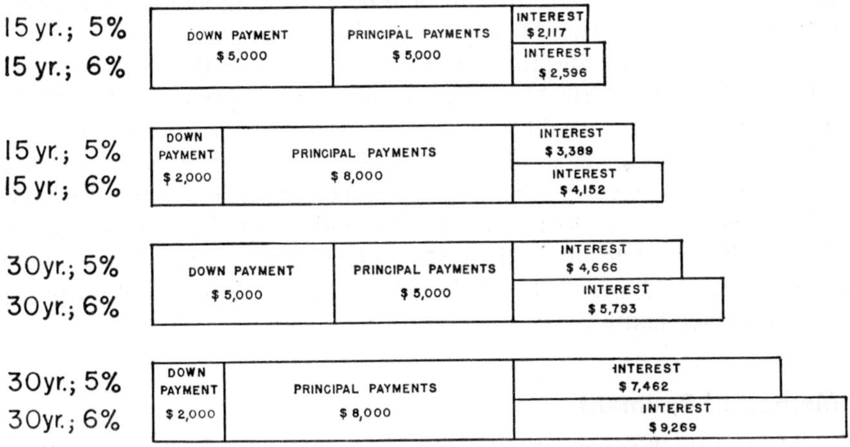

Fig. 10–3. Variation in dollar interest paid in eight methods of financing a $10,000 house.

$2,596. If only $2,000 is paid down on the house, the interest requirement becomes $4,152 over the life of the loan, or 60 per cent greater.

Interest Rate

The rate of interest charged is not the same for all loans. Generally speaking, the rates charged in the South and West are higher than those charged in the East. Some institutions charge a higher rate as the percentage of the loan to the appraised value increases. For example, at the present time some institutions will grant loans up to 50 per cent of the appraised value at 5½ per cent, loans of from 50 to 65 per cent of the appraised value at 6 per cent, and those from 65 to 75 per cent of the appraised value at 6½ per cent. A person with a high credit rating can often obtain a loan at a lower rate of interest than other individuals.

The stage of the business cycle and the condition of the money market naturally influence the rate of interest charged. At the present time the rates charged for home loans range from 5 to 8 per cent. It should be appreciated that a rate of 7½ per cent is not 2½ per cent greater than 5 per cent, but rather is 50 per cent greater.

Other conditions being equal, it is naturally to the advantage of the borrower to secure the loan from the lending agency which offers the lowest rate of interest. Should interest rates fall after a loan has been obtained, the borrower should try to persuade the lending agency to lower the rate for the remaining period of the loan. If this cannot be readily accomplished, and if the borrower has the right according to the contract to pay off the loan, then the threat to pay off the loan may induce the lending agency to accede to his demands. Should this not be successful, a loan may be obtained from some other lending agency at a lower rate, and the proceeds used to pay off the old loan.

Figure 10–3 illustrates the importance of obtaining the lowest interest rate possible. On a $5,000 loan for fifteen years, a 5 per cent interest rate instead of 6 per cent would save the borrower $479. On an $8,000 thirty-year loan, the borrower would save $1,807. These figures are based on a one percentage point variation; the difference between a 7 per cent and a 4½ per cent rate on these same loans would be much more substantial. Average interest rates in 1965 on conventional loans on new houses were approximately 5.8 per cent and the rate was almost 6 per cent on previously occupied houses.

Method of Payment

Most of the loans granted in recent years have been of the *amortized* type. Under this plan the borrower pays a fixed amount, usually monthly, to the lending institution. Part of this payment goes to pay the interest due, and the balance is immediately used to pay off part of the principal amount of the loan. When the amortized plan is used, the principal is usually reduced monthly.

In some lending institutions, the amount of the monthly payment which is in excess of the interest due is not credited directly against the principal, but is credited to a share account in the name of the borrower. When the amount paid into this account, plus the dividends or interest credited to the account, equals the principal amount of the loan, then the account is used to pay off the entire loan. It should be realized by the borrower that, when this plan is followed, the amount of the loan remains at the original figure, despite the fact that monthly payments in excess of the interest due are being made over a period of years. Thus the amount being paid monthly for interest does not decrease over the years.

The best type of loan, and the one which the borrower should insist upon, is the *direct-reduction* plan. Under this method the borrower pays a fixed amount at regular intervals, usually monthly. Part of this amount goes to pay the interest due, in the same manner as in the above discussed plan, but the balance of the payment is immediately credited against the loan. The principal amount of the outstanding loan is thus cut down with every payment, and therefore the amount which the borrower has to pay in interest each month is reduced.

Since the amount of the monthly payment is fixed, this means that a larger portion of it is applied on the principal as time goes on. Under this method the borrower knows exactly how long it will take him to pay off the loan. At the end of the period for which the loan was granted, the entire principal amount and interest will have been paid off. This method is cheaper for the borrower because the part of the monthly payment which is applied against the principal reduces the base on which the rate of interest is computed.

Table 10–4 shows the monthly payments necessary to pay off a $1,000 monthly direct-reduction loan in from five to twenty-five years, with interest rates of from 5 to 6½ per cent.

Table 10–4. Monthly Payments to Amortize a $1,000 Loan in from 5 to 25 Years, with Interest at from 5 Per Cent to 6½ Per Cent per Year

	Interest Rates					
Length of Loan	5%	5¼%	5½%	6%	6¼%	6½%
5 years	$18.87	$18.99	$19.10	$19.33	$19.45	$19.57
10 years	10.61	10.73	10.85	11.10	11.23	11.35
15 years	7.91	8.04	8.17	8.44	8.57	8.71
20 years	6.60	6.74	6.88	7.16	7.31	7.46
25 years	5.85	5.99	6.14	6.44	6.60	6.75

The monthly payments necessary to liquidate a loan of any amount may readily be obtained from Table 10–4 by multiplying the monthly payments shown by the number of thousands borrowed. The amounts of the payments shown in the table do not appear to be much greater as the rate of interest increases, but it should be remembered that these represent monthly payments for each thousand dollars borrowed. For example, for a fifteen-year loan of $1,000 at 6 per cent interest, the borrower would pay only $.53 per month more than if he obtained the loan at 5 per cent interest. But if the loan was for $5,000, this would be $2.65 per month, or $31.80 per year more. For the entire fifteen years he would thus have to pay a total of $477 more than if he were able to obtain the loan at 5 per cent.

Size of the Loan

The size of the loan which may be obtained depends upon two factors—the value of the property being mortgaged and the credit standing of the borrower. The laws of the various states and the practices of lending institutions differ as to the maximum percentage of valuation which can be borrowed. On conventional home loans (those not insured or guaranteed by the federal government), federal savings and loan associations may lend up to 90 per cent of the appraised value under special circumstances. They may make loans approved by the Federal Housing Administration (FHA loans), however, up to 97 per cent when the appraised valuation is not more than $13,500. Loans granted under the Servicemen's Readjustment Act of 1944 (GI loans), as amended, may be made up to 100 per cent of the valuation, up to $12,500. Banks and insurance companies usually lend from 50 to 66⅔ per cent of valuation on conventional loans.

Regardless of appraised valuation, the borrower has to be able to meet the required payments in order to obtain the loan. Figure 10–4 gives an

Regular wages, salary, or commissions	$8,000 × 1 =	$ 8,000
Variable income from employment	300 × ⅓ =	100
Income from second job	900 × ⅓ =	300
Income from investments	200 × ½ =	100
Wife's earnings if 32 to 40 years old *	3,600 × ½ =	1,800
Wife's earnings if over 40	— × 1 =	—
Total weighted annual income		$10,300
Less annual installment payments		1,300
Net available weighted income **		$ 9,000

* No credit if wife is under 32.

** Annual mortgage payments plus taxes and insurance should not exceed 25% of this figure.

Fig. 10–4. Income computation form for eligibility for a mortgage loan.

example of an income computation form for eligibility for a mortgage loan on a personal residence. The weights are based on the experience of lenders regarding permanence of these sources of income to most home buyers. The total income available places a limit on the amount which can be paid for housing and this in turn determines the monthly figure which may be required by the mortgage. In the example given, annual mortgage payments plus taxes and insurance should not exceed 25 per cent of \$9,000 or \$2,250. If taxes and insurance consume \$250 per year, \$2,000 is available for the mortgage payment (principal and interest) annually or \$167 per month. In this example, the potential buyer could not borrow more than \$15,300 for ten years at 5½ per cent, or \$15,000 for ten years at 6 per cent, or \$24,000 for twenty years at 5½ per cent, or \$23,400 for twenty years at 6 per cent. (See Table 10–4.)

Maturity of the Loan

The most important factor to consider in connection with the maturity of a loan is that it is sufficiently long not to impose too heavy a burden on the borrower. The amount of the loan must, of course, be considered along with the maturity in determining the ability of the borrower to pay it off. The tendency in recent years has been to increase materially the maturity of real estate loans. Loans which were formerly made by banks and insurance companies for from one to five years are now being made for ten years, and in some instances for fifteen years and twenty years. National banks can lend up to 75 per cent of the appraised value of the property for a period of twenty years, if the entire loan is amortized during the twenty-year period. Savings banks and savings and loan associations will give conventional loans for up to twenty or twenty-five years.

The length of the loan has a significant bearing on the total cost. This is because interest must be paid on the money borrowed for a longer period of time. In addition, a much larger portion of early payments is for interest only, and therefore the principal goes down more slowly and the required dollar interest is increased. In addition, some institutions will grant short-term loans at lower rates of interest than long-term loans. But even with the loan at the same rate of interest, the longer the maturity of the loan, the higher will be the total interest cost.

A \$5,000 loan at 4½ per cent can be paid off in ten years by the payment of \$621.60 a year. Over the ten-year period the borrower would thus be paying a total of \$6,216. The total interest cost would, therefore, be \$1,216. But if the loan ran for twenty years, he would have to pay back a total of \$7,596. Subtracting from this the amount of the loan proper (\$5,000) we get \$2,596, which represents the total interest charges on the loan. Thus a twenty-year loan would cost the borrower \$1,380 more than the ten-year loan. And it will be noted that we are assuming that the same *rate* of interest is charged on both loans. If a higher rate of interest were charged for the long-term loan, it would add more to the total cost of the loan.

Figure 10–3 illustrates the effect of maturity on interest costs. A fifteen-year $5,000 loan at 6 per cent requires interest of $2,596 over the life of the loan. A thirty-year $5,000 loan at 6 per cent requires total interest of $5,793. While the maturity is exactly twice in the thirty-year loan, the amount of interest paid is more than 100 per cent greater. Similar differences are illustrated for an $8,000 loan with a fifteen-year versus a thirty-year maturity. Table 10–5 illustrates the effect of varying

Table 10–5. Monthly Mortgage Payments and the Total Amount of Interest To Be Paid on a 15- and a 25-Year Loan (based on a home costing $15,000 and a mortgage rate of 6%)

Down Payment	Total Loan Required	Payment per Month for Interest and Principal—15-Year Maturity	Approximate Total Cost of Interest Only—15-Year Period	Payment per Month for Interest and Principal 25-Year Maturity	Approximate Total Cost of Interest Only—25-Year Period
10% or $1,500	$13,500	$113.93	$7,007	$86.99	$12,597
20% or 3,000	12,000	101.28	6,229	77.32	11,196
30% or 4,500	10,500	88.61	5,450	67.66	9,798
40% or 6,000	9,000	75.95	4,671	57.99	8,397

down payments and maturity dates. On a 6 per cent loan of $12,000 for fifteen years, monthly payments would be $101.28. For twenty-five years, monthly payments would be only $77.32. However, since in the latter loan, 120 more payments are made than in the fifteen-year loan, the *total* interest paid in the twenty-five-year loan is $11,196 versus only $6,229 in the fifteen-year loan. In other words, it costs the borrower almost $5,000 more to finance for twenty-five years rather than for fifteen years. It is thus apparent that the interest paid on fifteen-year loans at 6 per cent for the life of the loans equals slightly more than half of the amount borrowed. On twenty-five-year loans, the total interest paid over life is almost as much as the amount borrowed.

Table 10–6 illustrates the declining principal amount based on years to maturity of the loan. As interest is paid on only the unpaid balance, it is obvious that the shorter maturity leads to a very significant reduction in total interest over the life of the loan. It takes ten years of payments on a thirty-year loan to reduce the principal to the same level to which one year's payments would reduce it on a five-year loan. Figure 10–5 illustrates the balance due on a mortgage versus the depreciated value of a $15,000 property with varying term mortgages. If this property were financed for forty years with a 10 per cent down payment, the homeowner would owe more on his mortgage than the property was worth during twenty of the forty years. This is obviously an unsatisfactory situation.

Table 10–6. Loan Progress—Dollar Balances Remaining on a $10,000 Loan at 6 Per Cent

Age of Loan (in years)	Original Term in Years					
	5	10	15	20	25	30
1	$8,230	$9,250	$9,580	$9,730	$9,820	$9,880
3	4,360	7,600	8,650	9,150	9,430	9,610
5	—	5,740	7,600	8,490	8,990	9,300
7		3,640	6,420	7,740	8,490	8,960
9		1,280	5,090	6,900	7,930	8,570
11		—	3,590	5,960	7,300	8,140
13			1,900	4,890	6,590	7,650
15			—	3,690	5,780	7,090
17				2,330	4,880	6,470
19				810	3,860	5,760
21				—	2,710	4,970
23					1,410	4,080
25					—	3,070
27						1,940
29						660

In 1963, conventional home loans in major cities averaged twenty-five years in maturity for new houses and twenty years for previously occupied houses.

In determining the maturity of the loan, it is important that the lending agency not be able to call for payments in excess of those amounts specified or to call for payment before the time specified in the contract. If the lending agency could demand payment as it sees fit, it would be difficult for the buyer to plan his future financial program.

It is of interest to the borrower to have a provision in the contract which gives him the right to pay off the loan at a more rapid rate than that specified in the contract. This is called the "prepayment" provision. Some home finance contracts include a penalty for prepayment. This is to the disadvantage of the buyer, who may be forced to move to another location due to the requirements of his work. A penalty for prepayment on his mortgage would mean an additional cost in selling his home.

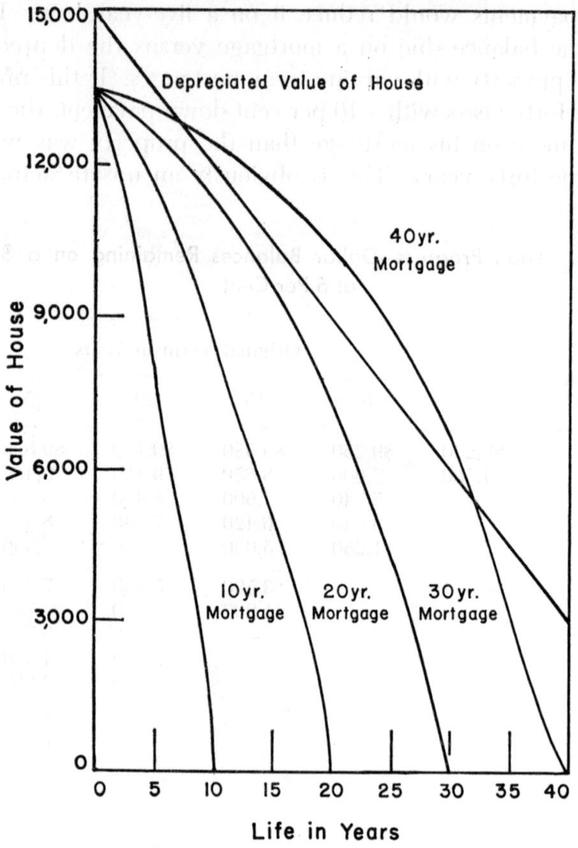

Fig. 10–5. Depreciated value of a $15,000 property (including a $3,000 lot) with a forty-year life, compared to remaining balances on various-maturity 6 per cent mortgages (assuming a 10 per cent down payment).

Closing Costs

Regardless of the home financing plan used, there are a number of initial cash outlays arising at the time the loan is made. These fees are known as closing costs and may be substantial—ranging from a minimum of $25 up to several hundred dollars. The costs of closing the loan are normally paid in cash at the time of closing but in some cases they may be included in the loan itself. Some of the more common closing costs include appraisal fees, mortgage recording fees, legal fees, title insurance, initial service charges, documentary stamps, prepaid taxes, prepaid interest, and insurance fees. Property insurance is normally paid in advance and if there is no transfer of insurance from the seller to the buyer, the buyer will have to acquire his own insurance and pay the premium at the time of closing.

The mortgage service charge (sometimes called organization charge or closing percentage) can be the most important of the closing costs. It is presumably designed to compensate the lender for clerical work and costs involved in making the loan. During a time when mortgage money is difficult to get, this cost will tend to be high. In times of surplus funds for lending institutions, there may be no fee of this type. The closing cost charged may vary among institutions at any one time. One should attempt to obtain the lowest closing cost possible as well as the lowest rate of interest. Figure 10-6 is an example of possible closing costs in connection with a loan. In this case, the total closing costs were equal to almost 3 per cent of the loan.

Costs in connection with construction loans (loans obtained to finance the building of the house before the owner can occupy the residence) may vary substantially from costs on normal loans. For example, some institutions will charge the borrower interest on the total amount of the construction loan even though the borrower does not withdraw the total amount for the entire time period of the construction loan. A closing cost of 1 per cent on a construction loan lasting six months would be the equivalent of paying 2 per cent extra in interest rate. Lending institutions may charge extra service charges in connection with construction loans for periodic inspections of the house and for handling the paper work.

Attorney fees	$ 50.00
Credit report	3.00
Recording fee and stamps	15.00
Appraisal fee	25.00
Title insurance	175.00
Mortgage service charge	150.00
Prepaid hazard insurance	30.00
Total	$448.00

Fig. 10–6. Loan closing costs on a $15,000 mortgage for 20 years at 6 per cent. (*Note:* This is a hypothetical example. Figures would vary significantly based on circumstances.)

Sources of Funds

A number of financial institutions provide funds on a mortgage basis for the purchase of residential real estate. Leading institutions in this field are savings and loan associations, life insurance companies, commercial banks, and mutual savings banks. Individual lenders also provide funds for this purpose as do certain governmental agencies and pension funds, charitable organizations, and educational institutions.

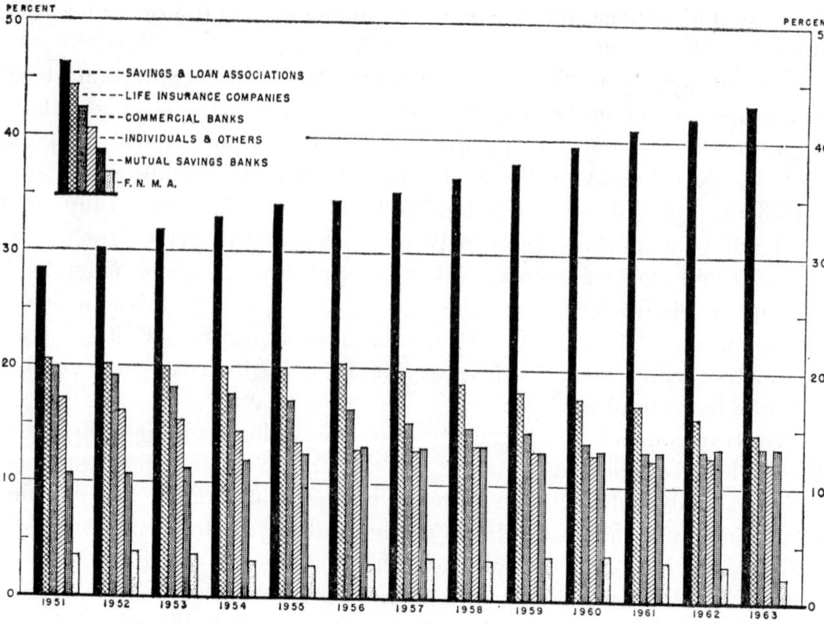

Fig. 10–7. Mortgage debt by type of lender, 1- to 4-family non-farm homes, at end of year, 1951–1963. (Federal Home Loan Bank Board.)

Figure 10–7 illustrates the relative importance of these various institutions in the residential real estate mortgage field. Savings and loan associations have increased significantly in importance over the past twenty-five years while individuals and other lenders have substantially decreased in relative importance. Savings and loan associations are now more than twice as important as the next most important lender. In recent years, they have accounted for more than 40 per cent of all residential mortgage recordings.

Mortgage bankers are not included in the above listing of institutions because they serve primarily as middlemen in the field. While they originally grant the loans and provide the initial money, it is their general purpose to resell the mortgage to some financial institution such as a life insurance company or mutual savings bank or pension fund. As a result, they serve as a channel of distribution rather than as providers of mortgage funds. In recent years, mortgage bankers have been growing significantly in importance. They provide an important function in channeling mortgage money from geographic areas of surplus to areas where money is needed for residential home finance.

While it is difficult to generalize about financial institutions, it can be said that life insurance companies have generally concentrated their conventional mortgages on homes with higher down payments. As a result, they have generally charged lower rates of interest than other institutions. Commercial banks have stressed shorter-term mortgages with higher down payments and therefore their interest rates tend to be somewhat lower also. Savings and loan associations and mutual savings banks have covered the spectrum in conventional lending in maturity and down payment required. As a result, these institutions have financed the majority of conventional loans with low down payments and long maturity, and have, therefore, charged higher rates of interest than would be the case on other types of loans.

Types of Loans

Three basic types of loan plans are available to the average buyer: the conventional loan, the FHA loan, and the VA loan. The conventional loan is the most important of the three.

Conventional Loan. A conventional loan is a transaction between a borrower and a lending institution in connection with the purchase of residential real estate and does not involve any federal government backing. The lending institution advances its own funds to the borrower at its own risk. If any loss results from the borrower's failure to repay his loan, the mortgage lender must absorb the loss. In recent years, some conventional lenders have insured certain mortgages against loss through private insurance companies. From the point of view of the lender, these insured conventional loans become similar to government guaranteed or insured loans.

Conventional loans are normally written for a period not to exceed twenty-five years. The maximum loan is usually limited to 80 or 90 per cent of appraised (not market) value of the property, but 60 to 70 per cent is most common. Conventional-loan interest rates in the postwar period have varied from 4½ per cent to 8 per cent. The typical conventional loan is an amortized direct-reduction loan.

Some conventional loans include in the mortgage a package-provision feature which enables the home purchaser to finance the purchase of appliances and other specified equipment at the time of the purchase of the home, along with the purchase of the home. A prepayment without penalty clause is normally also included. Another possible feature of the conventional loan is the *open-end* privilege, which is discussed later.

FHA Loans. In FHA loans, the federal government, through the Federal Housing Administration, insures the lending agency against any loss if the borrower fails to meet the payments on the loan. The borrower must pay the lending agency, and it in turn pays the government a premium for this insurance of ½ of 1 per cent, computed monthly, on the outstanding balance of the loan for the full term of the loan. This premium is in addition to the interest paid by the borrower. It should be noted that, although the borrower pays the insurance premium, the insurance runs in favor of the lending institutions. FHA home loans are granted by private lending agencies, and not by the federal government. The Federal Housing Administration will appraise the house and approve or disapprove the loan.

The statutes and regulations governing FHA loans have been changed a number of times in recent years. At the present time the maximum rate of interest charged on FHA loans is 5½ per cent. This is in addition to the ½ of 1 per cent insurance premium charge for a total charge of 6 per cent. According to the law, home loans may be made for a maximum period of thirty-five years, but in no case may the loan run for a period in excess of three fourths of the remaining life of the house. Despite the thirty-five-year maximum, many lenders will not grant an individual FHA loan with a maturity in excess of twenty years. FHA loans may be granted up to a maximum of 97 per cent of a $15,000 property, 95¼ per cent of a $20,000 property, and 90¼ per cent of a $30,000 property. The maximum home loan is $30,000.

The FHA home loans are amortized over the life of the loan, with the borrower paying the same amount per month. The interest and insurance charges are based on the unpaid balance of the loan. FHA loans may be paid off faster than the original contract provides, if the borrower desires to do so.

The total of the 5½ per cent interest charge and the ½ of 1 per cent insurance fee is not excessive at the present time. In fact, the borrower may find that he would have to pay in excess of this for a conventional loan. Some lending agencies are more anxious to grant FHA loans because they are insured against loss by the government.

VA Loans. GI loans, which is the popular title, may be made to any man or woman who has served 90 days or more in the active military service during World War II or the Korean War, and who has been discharged or released from service under conditions other than dishonorable. Veterans who served in other periods of time are eligible for special loans (reduced down payments) under the FHA program.

The VA loans are made by private lending institutions such as savings and loan associations, banks, and insurance companies, or they can be made by individuals. They are not made by the government. The loans can be made up to 100 per cent of the purchase price of the property (up to $12,500), provided this does not exceed the valuation placed on the property by an appraiser approved by the Veterans Administration. If the price of the property is more than the valuation set by the appraiser, then the lending institution is not permitted by the Act to lend anything on the property. Amounts above $12,500 are not subject to the guaranty and are handled on whatever loan percentage terms the lender agrees to.

The maximum rate of interest which may be charged on these loans is 5½ per cent per annum. Loans made with a first mortgage on residential real estate as security may be made up to thirty years.

On GI loans which are properly granted, the Veterans Administration will guarantee the loan up to 60 per cent, but in no event can the amount of the guaranty for any one veteran exceed $7,500. As the principal of the loan is reduced by payments, the amount of the guaranty is proportionately reduced. For example, if an $8,000 loan, 60 per cent of which is guaranteed, is reduced to $6,000, the amount of the guaranty is reduced from $4,800 to $3,600.

After the veteran has used up the $7,500 guaranty permitted him by the Act, he is not entitled to any more GI loans. But if he took out a $6,000 loan, which is guaranteed for $3,600, he would in the future be entitled to $3,900 more in guaranties. This might enable him to get a subsequent loan.

Refinancing Your Home

Since a house is the most important asset that most people own, it is a potential source of funds to a homeowner who has paid a large down payment on his mortgage or who has paid on his mortgage for a number of years. If the house is worth substantially more than the amount of the mortgage balance, it may be refinanced so that the homeowner can obtain additional cash. Obviously, this requires additional interest and should be considered only when the homeowner has important requirements for funds. If he has been paying for ten years on a 6 per cent twenty-year mortgage on a $12,000 house with a $2,000 down payment, he may bring his mortgage back to $10,000 and receive in excess of $3,500 by refinancing with a new 6 per cent mortgage for twenty years. Monthly payments would remain the same but they would be paid for an additional ten years. Refinancing mortgages to obtain money for consumer spending has been gaining rapidly in recent years as a source of consumer rather than real estate credit. The interest cost is often substantially less than other sources of consumer credit.

The *open-end* provision in many mortgages is advantageous to the borrower in the event that he needs refinancing. This provision entitles the borrower to increase the amount of his mortgage after it is paid down over a period of time in order to acquire additional funds. With an open-end provision, refinancing can be done without processing a new mortgage or obtaining a completely new loan. Thus, the cost is lessened.

The FHA has a home improvement loan program. Under this program, homeowners may borrow for permanent improvements to their home from a lending institution and have the loan insured to the lending institution by the Federal Housing Administration. Home improvement loans run up to a maximum of thirty-six months and are amortized loans. However, they are not direct-reduction loans. The interest rate charges are for the total amount of the loan for the entire life of the loan regardless of the fact that monthly installments are paid. While the quoted rate of interest on home improvement loans is 5 per cent, the effective rate of interest is approximately 9 per cent. Therefore, if the homeowner could refinance his home for the amount required for home improvements, he would generally find it much less expensive than to take out a home improvement loan.

SELLING A HOUSE

Regardless of plans at the time of purchase, many people find it necessary to sell the home they have purchased. Some people sell in order to move into a newer or larger home, others sell as their families grow up because they no longer require as much room. Many people are forced to sell their homes because of a requirement to move to a new area. In any case, it is advisable to approach the selling of a house as carefully as the purchase.

Some people attempt to sell their own houses with the thought that they can save the real estate agent's fee. This fee normally ranges from 5 to 6 per cent of the selling price of the house. The seller pays the real estate commission. However, many people who have attempted to sell their homes themselves have found that they were unable to do so. Or, if they were able to sell their house, there is a question as to whether they obtained the highest price possible. It may be that the buyer is the one who saved the real estate commission rather than the seller, through paying a lower price for the house. Unless he is willing to devote a fair amount of time to the project, it would generally be advisable for a seller to hire someone to sell his house for him.

The real estate broker gives experience, contacts, financial and legal resources, and sales know-how in return for his commission. He generally has a list of potential buyers who are looking for certain types of houses. In addition, he can spread his advertising costs over a number of houses which he is selling and thereby get more advertising for the same dollar expenditure. In many cases, real estate brokers belong to multiple listing services whereby they exchange knowledge of homes for sale with all other brokers in the area. All of this saves the seller a substantial amount of time and trouble.

Pricing a house is a difficult problem. Many people approach pricing by determining how much they paid for the house and adding to it the amounts they have spent in improving the house. If they can sell at this price, they will have lived in the house rent-free since their purchase. Remember that properties depreciate in value from time and use and that one cannot normally expect to sell a property for the price paid for it. The safest thing to do in pricing a house is to have the house appraised by a competent real estate appraiser. The real estate agent can be very helpful in suggesting current market prices for a particular type of house. The value of the house to the seller is not necessarily the value to anyone else. He, of course, wants to obtain as high a price as possible, but over-pricing may cause the house to stay on the market for a long period of time and make eventual sale at a reasonable price even more difficult. Proper pricing, based on current market conditions, generally leads to a satisfactory sale.

LEGAL ASPECTS OF HOME OWNERSHIP

It is not necessary for people to know real estate law when they buy and sell real estate. But because the acquisition of a home involves the outlay of a considerable amount of money, it is advisable to know something of the nature of the law pertaining to real estate. Despite the amount of legal knowledge which a layman may acquire, it is recommended that he engage a competent attorney when he purchases or sells real estate.

When a person buys a piece of land he gets not only the soil or surface of the earth, but his ownership extends down to the center of the earth and upward to the heavens. Thus the owner gets any minerals, oil or gas which may be beneath the surface of the land. However, he may sell the oil and gas to someone else, usually through means of a *lease,* and retain ownership of the surface, or he may sell the latter and retain ownership of the minerals. Growing trees, shrubbery, and crops go along with the land unless otherwise indicated. The right of the owner to the air above his land has had to be reconsidered in view of the development of air travel. So long as airplanes fly at sufficient altitude not to frighten or endanger people or livestock, they have a right to use the air space without charge.

The acquisition of land carries with it any permanent improvement such as a house or garage which has been constructed on the land. Difficulties arise, however, when movable personal property such as carpeting, stoves and refrigerators, washers and dryers, and similar appliances are attached or semiattached to the house, and the real estate is sold without mention of such specific items. If the item is considered to be a fixture, title to it passes to the buyer of the real estate. A *fixture* is personal property which is installed in or attached to the house or property in a more or less permanent manner. Kitchen linoleum which is cemented to the floor and built-in stoves and refrigerators would probably be considered fixtures. Door keys are not permanently attached to the house but they would undoubtedly be considered fixtures since it would probably be intended that they go with the house.

The Contract to Purchase

It is common practice for real estate brokers to ask for a deposit and a binder agreement when a buyer decides upon a particular house. In general, it would be best to wait until a formal sales contract is signed before paying a deposit. In many cases, the deposit will not be returned if the buyer decides not to go through with the sale, and, in certain cases, the binder could turn out to be a sales contract.

Because of the uncertainty of financing arrangements, a buyer does not normally buy a house immediately but, instead, contracts to purchase. Because the seller withholds his house from any other potential buyer, he normally requires a signed contract of purchase. This contract should include the sale price of the house. It would be best for the price to be fixed rather than including "escalator" clauses which permit the builder or seller to increase the price because of other price increases. The contract should include the amount of the deposit and any other cash payments which would be expected of the buyer. It should require the seller to deliver the property on or before a given date in satisfactory condition. In the case of new properties, the contract should state the responsibility which the builder assumes toward the buyer and should also define completion. It is important that a clause be provided protecting the buyer against defective title and, in the case of new construction, against mechanics' liens.

Deeds

When a person purchases real estate, the title is conveyed or transferred to him by means of a written document called a *deed*. The law relating to deeds varies among the states, but the following are the usual requirements for a valid deed:

1. Must be in writing
2. Competent grantor (seller)
3. Grantee (purchaser)
4. Words of conveyance
5. Recital of consideration
6. Description of the property

7. Signature and (in some states) seal of grantor
8. Attestation by witnesses (in some states)
9. The completed deed must be delivered to the grantee.

Recording the Deed

All the states have laws relating to the filing and recording of real estate deeds and mortgages. They are filed with a designated public official such as the County Recorder, Recorder of Deeds, or Registrar of Deeds.

It is to the advantage of the buyer or mortgagee always to have the deed or mortgage recorded immediately. Since the laws provide for the recording of real estate deeds and mortgages, when this is done it is assumed that any subsequent purchaser or mortgagee has *constructive notice* of the sale or mortgaging of the property, and if he buys property or lends money on it without first looking up the title, he does so at his own peril. Likewise, it is only fair to the subsequent purchaser or mortgagee that if the deed of the prior sale or a prior mortgage was not recorded, he should get good title or lien despite the prior sale or mortgage.

Kinds of Deeds

There are four different kinds of deeds which may be used in a real estate sale. The *warranty deed* is the one ordinarily used. In it, the grantor guarantees that the deed conveyed a good and unencumbered title. If it later develops that some prior party still had title to the land or a mortgage claim against it and the grantor did not have clear title, the grantee may, if he is dispossessed or suffers loss, sue the grantor for damages under his warranties.

In the *special warranty* deed, the grantor merely guarantees that he has not executed a deed or placed a mortgage or other encumbrance on the property not mentioned in the deed. If it later develops that some party prior to this grantor had a claim on the property, the grantor would not be liable under this kind of deed. Obviously, this deed is not generally desirable to the purchaser.

A *quitclaim* deed is one which conveys whatever interest, if any, the grantor has in the land at that time. It is generally used to extinguish the grantor's title or claim rather than to transfer the real estate itself. If the grantor, however, had title to the property, the quitclaim conveys that title to the grantee. The grantor makes no guarantees whatsoever in regard to title. In normal purchases, the buyer receives a warranty deed from the seller and a quitclaim deed from anyone else who might have an interest in the property.

A deed of *bargain and sale* is one which recites a consideration and which conveys the land to the grantee. It may convey no warranties, in which case it would be similar to a quitclaim deed. Or it may contain one or more warranties as agreed upon by the parties. It would not, however, contain the number of warranties which are found in the warranty deed.

Evidences of Title

Although the deed conveys whatever title the seller has, the purchaser of real estate wants some assurance that the seller has title. The four different kinds of evidence of title are abstract, certificate of title, Torrens Certificate, and title insurance.

Abstract. The most common evidence of title used in the United States is the abstract. This consists of a history of the title to a particular piece of land. It describes the property and in a very abbreviated form traces the sales from the original governmental grant down to the present time. Not only are all sales recorded, but all mortgages, mortgage release deeds, liens, etc., which have affected the property in the past are also shown.

The lawyer for the seller (or an abstract company) takes the abstract to the recorder's office and by looking up the recorded deeds, mortgages, mortgage releases, etc., stated in the abstract, determines if there are any liens or claims outstanding against the land. He then certifies in the abstract what records he has examined, and states any liens, mortgages, or claims which are outstanding against the land.

The abstracter does not guarantee title. As long as he uses due care in his work—in other words, as long as he is not negligent—he cannot be held liable if some lien holder later asserts his rights to the property. But if the abstracter fails to note a mortgage or lien outstanding against the property and the seller suffers as a result, the seller (assuming that he hired the abstracter) could sue him for damages. In most states the abstracter's liability extends only to the person who hired him.

Certificate of Title. In some instances the abstract has become lost and then a certificate of title is used in its place. In some localities, the certificate of title is commonly used instead of the abstract. This is merely a certificate issued by the attorney which states his opinion of the nature of the title which is possessed by the seller. It is prepared after the attorney has examined the recorder's records dealing with the transfers and liens and releases which have affected the property. Here again, the attorney does not guarantee title, and he can be held liable for damages only when he is negligent.

Torrens Certificate. The Torrens Certificate system is mostly confined to large cities such as New York, Chicago, and Boston. Where it is authorized, the landowner has the option of using either the Torrens System or other ordinary methods of searching title and recording deeds.

To register land under the Torrens System, the landowner obtains from the abstract a list of persons who may have an interest in the land. He then files these along with his application for registration of the title. This application acts as a lawsuit against the named persons. The latter are sent notices of the filing of the application, and if they wish to contest the owner's claim of title they may do so. If it is not contested, then the court orders the recorder to register the title in the name of the applicant. A certificate is then made out in duplicate showing that the applicant is the owner of the land. The original copy is retained by the public official and a duplicate is given to the owner.

If the owner after registering the land wants to sell it, he makes out a deed to the purchaser. But in this case the delivery of the completed deed does not transfer title to the purchaser. Before the latter gets good title he must present the deed to the recorder's office and get a new certificate of title made out to him. The deed is not returned to the purchaser, but is retained by the recorder.

Title Insurance. If an owner or purchaser of real estate wants greater assurance of good title, he may purchase title insurance from a private company. These companies examine the title carefully and if they think the title is clear, they will, for the payment of a fee or premium, issue to the owner a title insurance policy insuring him against loss from any defects in the title which are not stated in the policy. Furthermore, the insurance company agrees to handle at its own expense any lawsuits which attack the title they have insured. This latter feature is of some practical importance because, even though a person may have good title, it may cost him a considerable amount to defend himself in the event that lawsuits are brought attacking the title. Title insurance companies also issue title policies to companies which lend money on the security of real estate mortgages. Unlike other types of insurance, the premium is not paid annually—it is paid only once, at the time the policy is granted.

Land Contracts

When a buyer has little or no cash for a down payment, he will usually be unable to finance the purchase of a home through normal methods. The seller in this case may sell the property to the buyer on a *land contract.* A written contract is entered into between the buyer and the seller in which the buyer agrees to pay a fixed amount on the contract, commonly by installments, and when this fixed amount has been paid, or when the unpaid balance of the purchase price is reduced to a designated figure, the seller agrees to deliver to the buyer the deed to the property. During the life of the land contract, title stays with the seller. If the amount paid on the land contract is not equal to the purchase price of the property at that time, the buyer may finance the remainder elsewhere or the seller would retain a purchase money mortgage on the balance due on the property.

The legal status of the land contract is somewhat cloudy in many states; some hold that, although the buyer of the contract does not get legal title to the land, he does acquire an interest in the land which is called *equitable title.* While recording of land contracts is not required, the buyer should generally see that this is done.

Co-Ownership of Real Estate

Several people may own a particular piece of land. They are referred to as co-owners. In addition to community property, which is described later in the chapter, three different types of co-ownership should be distinguished:

1. Tenants in common
2. Joint tenants
3. Tenants by the entireties.

Tenants in Common. When land is conveyed to two or more persons who are not husband and wife, and the deed does not state anything further in regard to the character of the ownership, the grantees become *tenants in common.* It is not necessary that tenants in common acquire their title by the same deed, nor is it necessary that they acquire their title at the same time. The ownership need not be equal. Each tenant is free to sell his interest to someone else, or he can mortgage his share. Their interests are also subject to lien of judgment creditors. Income from the property and expenses are shared according to the interests of the co-owners.

An important point in regard to tenants in common relates to the disposition of a co-owner's share upon his death. In this event the share goes to the heirs of the deceased co-owner, and not to the other co-owners. In event of a will, the share would go to the beneficiaries under the will.

Joint Tenants. If the property is conveyed to two or more persons "jointly" or as "joint tenants," then the owners become not tenants in common, but, as the term indicates, *joint tenants.* It is generally necessary that the following four requirements be met in order to create a joint tenancy.

1. The interests of the joint tenants must stem from the same deed or conveyance.
2. The interests of the parties must begin at the same time.
3. All the joint tenants must have the same and similar interest in the property.
4. All the tenants must be entitled to the entire possession of the property at all times.

An important legal difference of the joint tenancy, as compared to the tenancy in common, is that in event of the death of a joint tenant, his interest in the property automatically goes to the surviving tenants. Some states have enacted laws, however, which purport to abolish this right of the surviving joint tenants and which provide that the deceased tenant's interest shall go to his heirs or to the beneficiary of his interests under his will. Even in these states, however, if the deed expressly provides that the title to the property shall be vested in the joint tenants "or the survivor of them" (or similar words), then the right of survivorship continues to exist.

Tenants by the Entireties. *Tenancy by the entireties,* which applies only to husband and wife, is a form of joint tenancy. In a number of states, when property is deeded to a husband and wife and nothing further is stated as to the nature of their interests, it will be held that they acquired title as tenants by the entireties. This is similar to the joint tenancy in that, upon the death of either, the surviving spouse automatically acquires the interests of the deceased spouse. It differs from joint tenancy in that neither the husband or the wife may sell his interest or mortgage it without the signature of the other spouse. Tenancy by the entireties is not recognized in all states.

Interest in Land

When a person is the sole owner of a piece of land and no one else has any legal interest in it, he is said to be the owner *in fee,* or *in fee simple.* There are, however, a number of different kinds of interest which a person may have in land other than owning it in fee simple. The following are the more important of these interests:

1. Leasehold estate
2. Life estate
3. Trust estate
4. Dower
5. Curtesy
6. Homestead
7. Community property

Leasehold estates are quite common in practice. For example, if Adams leases property, which he owns in fee simple, to Brown for a period of twenty-five years, Brown is said to have a leasehold estate in the land. He would have the right to occupy the land and use it according to the terms of the lease.

A *life estate* is created when someone has the right to use the land only for the period of his life. For example, Adams may will his property to his wife during her life, and at her death to designated children. The wife is said to possess a life estate in the land. She cannot sell the land, nor is she permitted to do anything which would injure the property, but she can occupy and use the property, or she can rent it and collect the rents for herself.

A person may by will leave his property or estate to a trust company, to be administered by it for the benefit of his family or heirs. The trust company would have a *trust estate* in the property. A similar situation exists when a person makes his life insurance payable to a trustee or trust company for the benefit of his family, who are referred to as the *beneficiaries.*

In a number of the states the statutes provide that a widow has a life estate in one third of all real estate owned by the husband at the time of his death. This interest of the widow is called her *dower* right. In a few states the right extends to one half of all the real estate owned. Although the dower right exists during the husband's lifetime, it really becomes operative only after his death. During his lifetime, the wife cannot sell or mortgage her dower right in the real estate. Should the husband, however, sell or mortgage the land without the wife's releasing her dower right and the husband precedes the wife in death, her dower right will be superior to the title obtained by the purchaser or the lien obtained by the mortgagee. The dower right merely gives the wife a *life estate* in the property. Release of dower is ordinarily accomplished by having the wife sign the deed or mortgage as grantor or mortgagor, and having it acknowledged along with the husband. If the wife obtains a divorce, the dower right is thereby terminated.

Some of the states have statutes which give a husband a life estate in all the real estate owned by the wife. This is referred to as *curtesy.* In a few of these states the couple must have a child before this right exists. It is to be noted that curtesy extends to *all* the real property of the wife, whereas dower extends usually to only *one third* of the husband's real property. In other respects curtesy is similar to dower.

For the protection of the family, a number of the states have laws which give the wife or husband and minor children certain rights called *homestead rights* in property which is owned and occupied as a home. For such rights to apply, it is necessary that there be a family consisting of two or more persons, such as husband and wife, or wife and child, or son and dependent mother, etc. The value of homestead laws lies in the protection they give the family against creditors or even against the actions of the head of the family. The homestead cannot be sold or mortgaged without the consent of both the husband and wife. Also, its sale cannot be forced in order to pay creditors' claims. The widow is usually given a life estate in the property, and the children can usually claim homestead rights until they become of age. These rights will be observed in almost all the states, even if the head of the family attempts to distribute the property otherwise in his will.

The Spanish influence has left its mark in certain states which have the *community property* system. Under this system, the property of the husband and wife is legally divided into two classes: *separate property* and *community property*. The separate property consists of the property which the husband or wife owned at the time of their marriage, and any property that they acquire during the marriage by gift, inheritance, or will. The community property consists of property acquired other than by gift, inheritance, or will, by either the husband or wife during their marriage. In most of the states having community property laws, the spouses may, by taking prescribed steps, dissolve their community holding of the property and divide it. If they become divorced, the court will usually divide the property. Upon the death of either the husband or wife, one half of all the community property goes to the surviving spouse. This would be true even if a will indicated a different disposition. The other half of the property, in the absence of a will stating otherwise, goes to the heirs of the deceased spouse according to the laws of descent, and these laws vary widely among the states. If the deceased spouse had a will, this half of the property would be distributed according to the will.

REAL ESTATE AS AN INVESTMENT

The discussion throughout this chapter has been from the point of view of a homeowner who would live in the home he purchased. Therefore, the house becomes a consumption item rather than an investment. However, many people also invest in real estate for income purposes. Investment in vacant land is highly speculative and depends upon future uses of the land. Investment in real estate for specialized commercial businesses such as motels, hotels, stores, factories, or gasoline stations depends upon the future of the business and is also a relatively high risk. The usual real estate investment for small investors is residential property.

Most people have found that it does not pay to own one single-family residence for investment purposes. Problems of management are great and the potential rental values are generally not sufficient to justify the investment. However, a great many small investors own duplexes or four-family units. They commonly live in one of the units and use the return on the other units as income on investment. Large apartment projects are becoming increasingly popular as investments. High land values and a growing population of young married couples and older people explain the continuing boom in apartment houses. However, vacancy rates have also been rising and one cannot assume that an apartment project will automatically be successful. It is only successful if the vacancy rate is kept low.

In analyzing investment real estate property, it is most important to estimate future income. This income estimate should include an allowance for expected vacancies. All landlord expenses should be subtracted from estimated income. These include repairs, taxes, and insurance. Depreciation should also be subtracted in determining a net return on investment. The net expected income after deducting expected expenses gives the return. This net return can be capitalized at a reasonable rate (from 10 to 13 times) to determine the amount of investment which the potential investor could make in the property. To this can be added an amount which can be financed if the interest on the financing has been included as one of the expenses subtracted from expected gross income.

A major difficulty with real estate as an investment for small investors is that it does not provide for diversification. The typical small investor is unable to own more than one or two properties and these are generally located in the same city and subject to the same economic risk. If proper diversification can be obtained, residential real estate can become a highly desirable investment. Investment real estate is commonly not as marketable as other possible investments for small investors. This means that the investor should only consider putting long-term investment money into investment real estate. In recent years, a number of real estate syndicates and real estate investment trusts have been organized which offer to the real estate investor a means of obtaining diversification and marketability.

QUESTIONS

1. Why is home ownership increasing in popularity in the United States?
2. Indicate the relative advantages of renting as compared to owning a home.
3. Some people say that "you can buy a home on the installment plan and pay no more per month than you would have to pay in rent." How would you reply to such an argument to convince someone that the statement is probably erroneous?
4. What "costs" of home ownership are often not actually given any attention by the homeowner or prospective homeowner when comparing the relative costs of home ownership and renting?
5. Does the homeowner have any advantage over the renter in respect to income taxes? Can a person list depreciation on real estate as an expense before arriving at his net taxable income?

6. List the advantages of building a new house as compared to buying an old one.
7. Differentiate cooperative apartment ownership from condominium ownership.
8. What different methods may be used to determine the value of a particular piece of property? Which of these do you think is the best?
9. Indicate some of the factors which should be considered in selecting the location for a home.
10. Would you recommend that a person pay cash for a home when it is possible to do so? Why? If a family has insufficient cash to buy a home outright, would you recommend that they wait until they have the necessary amount before buying the home? Explain.
11. Can a purchaser acquire a home for a smaller price if he can pay the entire amount in cash? Explain.
12. If the prospective buyer does not have sufficient money to acquire a home but does have other investments, such as securities and savings accounts, would you recommend that all such investments be liquidated before any money is borrowed?
13. What is the minimum down payment which a person should make on a house? Explain.
14. When a person borrows money to acquire a home, what is the security behind the loan?
15. Assume that you borrowed $5,000 to acquire a home. After you have made payments on the principal of the loan to the amount of $1,000, you are unable to keep up the payments, the lending agency forecloses on the property, and it is sold at court sale for $3,000. Are you liable for anything? Explain.
16. (a) What is meant by a straight loan? Would you recommend this type of loan to the buyer of a home? Why?
    (b) What is meant by an amortized loan? What are its advantages?
17. Indicate why a short-term loan is usually less expensive than a long-term loan.
18. (a) What is the range of interest rates for home loans at the present time?
    (b) What is the maximum rate permitted for FHA loans?
    (c) What is the maximum rate for GI loans?
19. What type of institutions lend money for the purchase of a house? Would you have any preference as to which you would rather do business with?
20. What are closing costs? Are they important? Why?
21. Should you use a real estate agent in selling your house? Why or why not?
22. Explain definitively the differences in the following kinds of deeds and indicate when each would be used:
    (a) Warranty deed
    (b) Special warranty deed
    (c) Quitclaim deed
    (d) Deed of bargain and sale
23. What is meant by an abstract? Of what importance is it to the purchaser of real estate? Is the abstract necessary to get title?

24. Differentiate tenancy in common from joint tenancy and tenancy by the entireties.
25. Explain what is meant by each of the following:
    (a) Leasehold estate
    (b) Life estate
    (c) Trust estate
    (d) Dower
    (e) Curtesy
    (f) Homestead right
    (g) Community property

CASE PROBLEMS

1. Bill and Mary Short have been renting a house for the past eight years. Mary has always wanted to buy a house but Bill says that if you own a home you are tied down to one job or one locality all of your life. He feels that home ownership would consequently cause him to miss opportunities for advancement. Bill is a programmer for computing equipment. Since getting out of the service four years ago, he has had three jobs in two different cities. Mary feels they can afford to buy a house and if they need to move for Bill's advancement they can sell the house and buy in the new location. Comment on Mary's arguments. What do you think of Bill's arguments? Should they buy a home or not? Why?
2. Keith Dawson is being transferred by his employer to San Juan, Puerto Rico. Keith has been in San Juan on business on several occasions. On his last trip there, he looked into the housing market in light of his potential move to that city. Upon accepting his transfer, he informed his wife, Sally, that it would probably be best for them to buy a condominium apartment in San Juan. Sally is highly opposed to this idea; she has been used to private home ownership. Keith has tried to convince her that home ownership is very expensive and that, since not many apartments are for rent, they need to buy a condominium. Sally thinks it would be a mistake to purchase only a part of a building. She worries about her neighbors, about building upkeep, about tax payments, about liability for actions of other occupants of the building, etc. What are the potential problems in owning a condominium? What arguments could Keith use in convincing Sally that they should purchase a condominium? Would a cooperative arrangement be better than the condominium arrangement? Why or why not?
3. Don Martin applied for a $10,000 home loan with a local savings and loan association. The loan officer recommended a fifteen-year loan. With a 5 per cent interest charge, which was more or less agreed upon, the monthly payments would be $79.10. This seemed rather high to Martin, particularly since he knew that the monthly payments of one of his neighbors was less than this, and he suspected that the neighbor had borrowed more than $10,000. The loan officer explained that probably the neighbor was taking longer than fifteen years to retire the loan. Martin thereupon asked the loan officer how much his monthly payment would be for a twenty-five-year loan. The officer told him $58.50. The latter sounded much better to Martin than the $79.10 figure. What arguments would you give to sell him on the idea that the fifteen-year loan would be to his advantage?

4. Edwin Collins was anxious to buy Ted Frey's house at the asking price of $12,000. Frey bought the house as an investment, but wanted to sell at the present time because he thought real estate prices had reached their peak. Collins had only $1,500 to pay down on the house and he found that local savings and loan associations would not lend in excess of $9,000. Indicate two or three different "arrangements" which may be made between Collins and Frey under which the "sale" might possibly be made at the present time at the price stated above.
5. For some years Mrs. Jean Smith had been using the argument on her husband, without success, that owning was cheaper than renting since you have to pay rent all your life and still never own a house. The Smiths for some time had been paying $65.00 a month rent. Mrs. Alton Jones, who lived on the north side of Mrs. Smith, had told the latter that they bought their home and that the payments were only $64.40 a month. The two houses appeared to be worth about the same. After some persuasion from his wife, Mr. Smith finally asked Mr. Jones about his home deal. It was found that Mr. Jones had paid $13,500 for the property. His down payment had amounted to $3,500 and he had borrowed $10,000 from a local financial institution. The interest rate being charged was 6 per cent, and the loan had a maturity of twenty-five years. The loan payments did not include insurance and taxes. If you were in Mr. Smith's shoes and did not wish to buy property, how would you explain to Mrs. Smith what it was costing the Jones family to own their own home?
6. Assume that Joe Williams buys a home for $15,000 (value of the lot alone is $3,000) with a down payment of $4,000. He borrows the balance at 5 per cent interest on a twenty-year, monthly direct-reduction loan. Based on the expense percentages stated in this chapter, compute the following:
   (a) Monthly investment cost of owning the home
   (b) Average monthly cash outlay for the first twenty years
   (c) Average monthly cash outlay after the first twenty years
7. Mr. and Mrs. William Dawson own their home as joint tenants. Dawson and a business associate, Robert Roberts, own a storeroom as tenants in common. Upon Dawson's death who would be legally entitled to his interest in the properties? If Dawson provides in his will for a different disposition of his interests, would the above rights apply, or would the provisions of the will take precedence? Explain.

SELECTED READINGS

Anatomy of the Residential Mortgage. Chicago: United States Savings and Loan League, 1964.

Bergh, Louis O., Conyngton, Thomas, and Kassoff, Edwin. *Business Law,* Sixth Edition. New York: The Ronald Press Co., 1964.

Beyer, Glenn H. *Housing and Society.* New York: The Macmillan Co., 1965.

Brown, Robert K. *Real Estate Economics.* Boston: Houghton Mifflin Co., 1965.

FHA Home Mortgage Insurance. Washington, D. C.: Federal Housing Administration, 1964.

FHA Home Owner's Guide. Washington, D. C.: Federal Housing Administration.

Hebard, Edna L., and Meisel, Gerald S. *Principles of Real Estate Law.* New York: Simmons-Boardman Publishing Corp., 1964.

Hoagland, Henry E., and Stone, Leo D. *Real Estate Finance,* Third Edition. Homewood, Ill.: Richard D. Irwin, Inc., 1965.

Housing Yearbook, The. Washington, D. C.: The National Housing Conference. Latest edition.

Kahn, Sanders A., Case, Frederick E., and Schimmel, Alfred. *Real Estate Appraisal and Investment.* New York: The Ronald Press Co., 1963.

Kratovil, Robert. *Real Estate Law,* Fourth Edition. Englewood Cliffs, N. J.: Prentice-Hall, Inc., 1964.

Lusk, Harold F. *Law of the Real Estate Business,* Revised Edition. Homewood, Ill.: Richard D. Irwin, Inc., 1965.

Maisel, Sherman J. *Financing Real Estate.* New York: McGraw-Hill Book Co., 1965.

Rogers, Tyler S. *The Complete Guide to House Hunting.* New York: Charles Scribner's Sons, 1963.

Savings and Loan Fact Book. Chicago: United States Savings and Loan League. Latest edition.

Story of Modern Home Financing, The. Chicago: United States Savings and Loan League. Latest edition.

Unger, Maurice A. *Real Estate Principles and Practices,* Third Edition. Cincinnati: Southwestern Publishing Co., 1964.

What You Should Know Before You Buy a Home. Chicago: United States Savings and Loan League. Latest edition.

Your Shelter Dollar. Chicago: Money Management Institute, Household Finance Corp., 1963.

11

Investing in Securities

Previous chapters have discussed the investment of money in savings accounts, United States savings bonds, life insurance, and real estate. In this and the two following chapters the nature of bonds (other than United States savings bonds) and stocks, the relative merits of these types of securities, and the procedures relating to their purchase will be explained. Preceding this, however, we will consider briefly the general subject of investing in securities.

Successful investing in securities calls for a high degree of intelligence, careful study, a knowledge of general business conditions, and the ability to determine with some degree of accuracy the probable course of future business trends. How many people possess these qualities?

A large part of a person's life is spent in working, so that he can meet his expenses and have a little left for investment. Considerable time and money are spent in securing an education or training for a particular trade or profession. But when it comes to investing the savings which have been accumulated over the years, many people squander them on some worthless stocks without first taking time for a proper investigation of the particular securities. Most people are much better at earning money than at either saving or investing it. It is surprising that so many individuals, who have spent many years learning their particular trades or professions, but have given no thought or study to the problem of investing, do not realize that successful investing calls for education, training, and experience in a manner somewhat similar to their own business. In fact, some professional people are the easiest targets for high-pressure securities salesmen. People who are inexperienced at investing should consult reliable and competent individuals before purchasing securities.

Make Other Investments First

If a person wants to purchase stocks or bonds, he should first have a reserve fund in government bonds or in a savings account, or both, adequate to carry him over a considerable period of illness or unemployment. If he is buying a home on the installment plan, it may be advisable to have the mortgage substantially paid off before purchasing corporate securities.

Annuities are another type of investment which should be considered along with stocks and bonds. There is no assurance of what, if anything, a commitment in stocks will return in the future, but an investment in an annuity in a reliable company assures a definite future return.

Be Able To Assume Risk

Before purchasing *speculative* securities, a person should be financially able to stand the loss of part or all of his principal without seriously affecting himself and his family. This means that he should have his house substantially paid for, as stated above. Also, he should have a steady income so that he will not have to worry in the future if his security investments do not turn out well.

Only people with steady incomes or people of some wealth can afford to take the risk involved in buying speculative securities, but paradoxically, it is often found that the wealthy class purchases the more conservative type of bonds, while people of more limited financial means often buy the more speculative securities.

DIVERSIFICATION

The old adage, "Don't put all your eggs in one basket," is probably more applicable in the investment or speculation field than in any other place. Although Andrew Carnegie said that you should put all your eggs in one basket and then watch that basket, it was found, upon his death, that he owned securities in more than fifty companies. To be certain as to the outcome of any single investment would require a look into the future, and no one on earth has as yet been gifted with this power.

This is a dynamic world. Business trends are constantly changing, economic and social philosophies are altered, new political factions have their day and then fade away, corporations are prosperous, expand, and then maybe die of old age. No one can select a particular stock or bond today and be sure that it will turn out to be a good investment twenty to thirty years from now. Careful study should be given to any security before purchasing it, but the best minds are often wrong when it comes to anticipating the future.

Various Forms of Diversification

Diversification may take different forms. An individual may purchase securities in different types of industries, such as public utilities, industrials, and investment trusts, and in state, municipal, or government bonds. Factors which adversely affect one may have no effect on some of the other industries. Another type of diversification is to purchase different types of securities in either the same or different companies, in either the same or different industries. Thus various kinds of bonds, or preferred stock, or common stock may be acquired. In certain phases of the business cycle, good bonds and common stocks usually move in opposite directions, so that each may serve as a hedge at different periods of the cycle. The "right" well-bought common stocks offer a hedge against inflation, whereas good bonds are a hedge against deflation. Diversification by industry, company, and type of security are the principal forms observed in practice, but other types also are sometimes followed.

Geographical diversification is sometimes observed. Securities issued by companies located in different sections of the country, or in foreign countries, are sometimes purchased as a hedge against adverse factors which may develop in one section of the country, or in one country. The purchase of a single issue in one company, however, such as the American Telephone and Telegraph Company, which does business in all parts of the country, would really give geographical diversification. So far as foreign securities are concerned, the authors believe that diversification should not be followed if it means buying inferior securities—and many foreign securities are of inferior quality.

The tragedy of this whole thing is that the people who need diversification the most are the least able to get it. With the exception of United States government bonds and some state and municipal bonds, it is a wise policy not to invest more than 5 per cent of your total investable surplus in any single issue. The face value of bonds issued by private companies is usually \$1,000 (in some instances \$500) so, unless they can be acquired at less than their face value, a person would need at least \$20,000 (or \$10,000) in order to follow a *conservative* investment policy in buying bonds.

If stocks instead of bonds were purchased, a wider diversification program could be followed on even less money because most stocks sell for less than \$100 a share. However, since stocks as a class are much more speculative than bonds, it would be advisable to carry diversification further.

Diversification could, of course, be carried too far, with the result that too many different securities are held to permit adequate supervision.

FACTORS OF SELECTION

Qualities of a Good Investment

In purchasing any stock or bond, an individual should be primarily concerned with the *safety of the principal* amount invested. There are other qualities, of varying importance according to the particular circumstances, but they are subordinate to the cardinal principle of protecting the money invested. Next in order is the *certainty and regularity of income* on the principal amount invested. These factors are closely related. Generally speaking, securities which offer the greatest safety usually also offer greater certainty and regularity in respect to the return paid on them. If part or all the principal invested is lost, the income will necessarily cease, so safety of principal is essential for certainty and regularity of income. The rate of return on an investment usually varies inversely to the safety of the principal. The safer the investment, the lower the return.

Safety of the principal refers to the safety of the *number of dollars* invested, and not to the maintenance of the *purchasing power* of the particular sum of money invested. It is realized that an investor in some of the safest bonds in the world—United States government bonds—may lose in purchasing power as a result of inflation. Safe bonds which offer certainty and regularity of income, furthermore, do not pay the investor any more dollars in interest per year when inflation becomes rampant. The addition of high-grade common stocks to the bond investment portfolio may be the answer to inflation. More will be said about this later when common stocks are discussed.

The safety of principal of existing securities may be affected also by changes in the market rate of interest (money rate). If existing market rates of interest generally increase, the price of outstanding high-grade bonds would be expected to decline. Aside from factors affecting the particular company or business in general, price-level changes, and fluctuations in general rates of interest, the price that might be obtained from a particular security depends upon the general market conditions prevailing at the time. Thus, looking at safety from the converse side—the risk involved—we can classify the kinds of risk as follows:

Types of risks in buying securities

1. Business
2. Price level (or purchasing power)
3. Money rate
4. Market

It is unfortunate that people with small investable surpluses often feel that it is necessary for them to get a high rate of return on their investments because it is the only way that they hope to be able to get an appreciable return. These individuals (and there are many of them) argue that wealthy people can afford to invest their money at low rates of interest because of the larger size of the fund, or because they are not dependent upon the return from their investments. Wealthy people are content with a low rate of return on their money, but too many individuals of limited financial means unwisely attempt to secure too high a return on their investments and thus subject the principal to too much risk.

Other qualities to consider in selecting an investment would be *marketability, tax position, maturity date,* and *denomination,* but none of these is nearly so important as safety of principal, certainty and regularity of income, and maintenance of purchasing power. A high degree of *marketability* is usually desirable in most forms of investment. Bonds come due at a specified time, but unforeseeable future events may make it necessary for an individual to sell them before the maturity date. Inability to sell, or a limited market resulting in a low sales price, would reflect adversely on the investment position of a bond. Stocks do not come due at any time, so the market must always be depended upon for the liquidation of this type of security.

The position of stocks is enhanced by listing on one of the organized exchanges, particularly the New York Stock Exchange. Generally speaking, a higher price must be paid for a stock which is listed on the New York Stock Exchange than for a comparable one which is not listed. But it is, of course, likewise true that one can get more from the listed stock when he sells it. Banks will lend a larger percentage on listed stocks than on those which possess a more limited market.

With the high tax rates in effect, the *tax position* of securities is important. By tax position is usually meant whether or not the particular security is exempt in whole or in part from the federal income taxes. State and municipal bonds are entirely exempt from these taxes, and certain United States government bonds issued prior to 1941 are either wholly or partially exempt. A tax-exempt bond may be preferred by a person who is in the higher tax brackets. Such persons bid up the price of tax-exempt bonds to such a price that the yield is too low to make them attractive to the average investor.

The *maturity dates* of bonds may or may not be of importance to individual investors. If a number of different bonds are purchased, it would be desirable that they have different maturity dates so that the problem of reinvesting all the funds at a time when circumstances are unfavorable would be averted. Banks must purchase large amounts of short-term obligations and this, among other reasons, causes such securities to sell on a comparatively low-yield basis. It might therefore be inadvisable for the average individual to purchase short-term securities.

Long-term obligations fluctuate more in price than short- or medium-term securities, and the possibility of having to sell them at a loss is greater, so they are generally not recommended for the ordinary individual investor. Bonds with maturities of from ten to twenty years would be more suitable for the average bond investor. Stocks, of course, have no maturity date, but so long as they can be readily sold in the market, this is not a serious drawback.

Selecting a Safe Investment

The word "safe" is used here in a relative sense. There is no security which offers 100 per cent safety. As we have emphasized, the future course of events has much to do with the determination of the degree of risk present in any security, and these events cannot be foreseen. The study of past trends and present conditions is useful insofar as it may shed some light on the probable future trends, but there is no assurance that the past trends will continue. In any event, it takes experience and wisdom to interpret properly all available data. Following are the more important factors which should be considered in determining the safety of an investment.

Type of Security. Bonds constitute a debt of the issuing corporation or agency, and contain a promise to pay interest at a fixed rate on specified dates, and to pay the principal on the maturity date. As a class, therefore, they are a safer investment than stocks which merely represent ownership in the corporation, and on which there is no promise to pay dividends or to repay the principal amount. Bonds are always a safer investment than stocks of the same corporation, but the stock of one company might be a safer investment than the bonds of another company. First mortgage bonds are safer than second mortgage bonds issued by the same company.

The Issuing Company or Agency. The credit standing of corporations and of states and nations varies in the same way as does that of individuals. After deciding what type of security is desired, the first thing a prospective investor should do is to select the particular company which in his mind offers the safety or other qualities which he demands. The bonds issued by sound governments and states, which can be paid off through the collection of taxes, offer greater safety than the bonds which are sold by private corporations.

Railroad securities were formerly considered the best type issued by private companies, but in recent years they have lost favor because of lower earnings. Because of the nature of the business and their relatively steady income, public utility securities are generally considered to be safer than those issued by industrials.

The age of the company is of importance. Securities issued by new companies are more speculative than those sold by well-established concerns, and seasoned issues of the latter are generally safer than new issues. Care should be exercised, however, to avoid purchasing securities of companies which are in their declining years.

The size of the company should be considered along with the other factors. Small concerns should generally be avoided, as the death rate among them is usually higher than for large companies. Furthermore, the securities issued by small companies do not enjoy the same degree of marketability as those sold by the larger companies.

The nature of the industry is of paramount importance. Some industries, such as woolen textiles, have been declining for many years, while new ones, like rocket fuels and electronics, are expanding. Although new industries may offer greater speculative possibilities, some seasoning is necessary in order to secure a high degree of safety. Thorough study should be made before selecting any security, but if an individual does not do this, he may minimize his losses by selecting the leading companies in the leading industries.

Importance of Management. In selecting the company in which to buy securities, considerable weight should be placed upon its management. In the case of new companies it is difficult to judge the probable efficiency of the management, but a knowledge of the connections and past performance of the personnel is useful. Investors, however, should usually stay away from new companies. For established companies, the record speaks for itself. Although past earnings figures may not continue in the future, it is a consolation to know that the management which produced those earnings is still in the saddle. The efficiency of management can be seen in its ability to meet competition, introduce new products, follow proper expansion and financing policies, maintain good labor relations, cope with new situations, and earn money for its stockholders.

All the past management records of a particular company may be favorable, but, if this is due primarily to the efforts of one man, it may be wise not to purchase any of the company's securities. This would be true particularly if he were now an old man. Another point to observe is whether or not the existing management is following a proper policy of training the qualified younger men for executive positions. There are some companies that have been very successful in the past, but the founders, who are still active in the business, are old and have done little in the way of training younger men to take over the management after they are gone. Although their children may be legally entitled to their stock, they may not be capable of managing the business.

A shift in public demand may cause a decline in sales, but well-managed companies keep abreast of changes.

SPECULATION AND INVESTMENT

Most people make some distinction between speculation and investment. But these terms have different meanings to different people. Some base the distinction on the quality of the security purchased. Thus, the purchase of United States government bonds would be considered an investment, while the purchase of some risky common stock would be a speculation. Other people look to the intent of the purchase, and say that if an individual bought a security primarily for the purpose of deriving income from it, this would be an investment, while if he purchased it chiefly on the chance of appreciation in the market price, it would be a speculation. According to this idea, one person might invest in United States government bonds while at the same time another individual might purchase them as a speculation.

Although the above two are the principal distinctions made between speculation and investment, there are several others. The purchase of stocks for the "quick turn" is often considered speculation, while if the same stock were purchased with the intent of holding it for a long period of time, it might be considered an investment. Marginal buying is quite commonly classified as speculation, although it does not follow that all outright purchases would be considered as investments. Some would say that if a person makes a thorough analysis of all the pertinent factors, and makes the purchase with complete knowledge of the risks involved, this would be investing, whereas if he bought securities without making a complete analysis, he would be speculating.

Most of us would probably agree with several of these ideas. The purchase of relatively safe bonds for the primary purpose of deriving regular income from them would undoubtedly be considered an investment, while the purchase of a relatively risky stock on the chance of appreciation in the market price within a short period of time would be regarded as speculation.

Although a fixed and regular income is sometimes listed as a requisite of an investment, reinvesting the earnings in the corporation instead of using them for dividend purposes would make the stock safer, and thus it may be considered a better investment. An individual may thus invest in a relatively good stock with the intent of deriving his income from the appreciation in the market price resulting from the reinvestment of earnings in the corporation. A stock of a company which cannot pay dividends would be too risky to put in the class of investments. From the last statement it can be seen that the authors believe any commitment involving a relatively high degree of risk must be considered a speculation. Whether the commitment is an outright purchase or a marginal transaction is not conclusive. Most marginal transactions, however, are speculations.

After giving due consideration to the above views, it seems fair to say that if a competent person makes a thorough analysis of the particular security and reaches the conclusion that the security offers a relatively high degree of safety and a satisfactory return, his purchase of this security would be regarded as an investment. If a thorough analysis is not made, or if the security does not meet the above-stated requirements after such an analysis is made, its purchase would be considered a speculation.

We sometimes hear the statement that so-and-so gambles in the stock market. Is there any difference between speculation and gambling? Textbook writers commonly make this distinction: speculation is the assumption of existing risks, while gambling involves the creation of risks which were not previously existing. By this definition, buying and selling stocks is not gambling. The distinction is, of course, from the social viewpoint. As far as the individual is concerned there commonly is little difference.

BONDS

Bonds represent a promise on the part of the issuer to pay to the holder thereof a sum certain in money at a fixed time with interest payable, usually semiannually, at a fixed rate. They are the same as notes except that they have a maturity of five years or more. (The term "note," however, is used for any length of maturity when the entire loan is obtained from only one creditor, such as a bank or life insurance company.) When a person buys a bond he is lending the issuer a definite amount of money. The issuer is the debtor and the bondholder the creditor.

If a corporation wishes to borrow $100,000,000 on the security of its property, it is highly probable that it will be unable to find one individual or institution which could or would lend this amount. It may be necessary to borrow from thousands of lenders in order to get this amount of money, but issuing a separate mortgage to each of thousands of lenders would be cumbersome and impractical. Instead, the corporation will execute a mortgage in favor of a trust company, which will serve as trustee for the various lenders. Separate bonds are issued to each of the individuals or companies which lend money to the corporation, and all of these bondholders, through the trustee, will have a claim or lien on the mortgaged property.

If the bond interest is not paid when due, the principal amount will, according to the agreement, become due. If the principal is not paid when due, the *indenture,* which is the elaborate agreement relating to the bond issue, will provide the steps which the bondholders can take in order to have the trustee foreclose on the property in the case of secured bonds, or to secure a lien against the property in event that the bonds are not secured by a specific claim on property. Receivership, however, is usually resorted to before the trustee can foreclose on the property, and the bondholders then must take their turn and get whatever settlement is forced upon them in the reorganization.

Denomination of Bonds

Most corporate bonds and those issued by states and municipalities have a denomination of $1,000 ($500 in some instances) or higher. Depending upon the rate of interest stated on the bond and the condition of the money market, bonds may originally sell for a slight premium over, or discount from, the face value. In addition, accrued interest, if any, from the day the bonds are dated may have to be paid by the original purchaser. With the exception of the Series E and H United States savings bonds, the price of a bond, after its issuance, depends upon the market.

Upon maturity of the bond, the face value is paid to the holder. If a bond is callable by the issuer before the maturity date, it may, according to the terms of the agreement, be payable at its face value, or at a slight premium. The interest payable on bonds is expressed in percentage, and the face value is the figure on which this percentage is based.

Registered vs. Coupon Bonds

Bond issues are usually sold in both registered and coupon form. If a holder has either one of these forms, he may exchange it for the other. In the case of the *registered* bond, the holder's name is recorded on the issuer's books. Interest and principal are paid directly to him in the form of a check. The advantage of this form of bond lies in its safety. If the bond is not endorsed by the owner and is lost or stolen, no subsequent holder can get good title to the bond. A further advantage is that the holder has no coupons to clip. The principal disadvantage of the registered bond is that transfer is a little more difficult and time-consuming. The new owner must get the bond transferred to his name on the issuer's records before he will be recognized as the owner. Because of this trouble in getting it transferred, the registered bond often sells for slightly less than a coupon bond after it has once been issued. In case the registered bond is used as collateral for a loan, the owner will have to complete an assignment form before the bank will accept the bond.

The *coupon* bond is payable to the bearer, and the issuing agency has no record of the owner. The bond has attached to it a series of coupons which, as the interest becomes due, are detached by the holder and presented to a bank for collection. When the principal becomes due, the bond is presented for payment. Banks ordinarily make a slight charge for collecting them. In a few instances corporate bonds are registered as to principal, but bear coupons for collecting interest.

The advantage of the coupon bond is that title to it can be passed by delivery. No endorsement is necessary, and the transferee gets title without the necessity of having it transferred to him on the records of the issuing agency. Coupon bonds are more readily acceptable as collateral for a loan. The disadvantage of the coupon bond is that it is not as safe as the registered bond, because if it is lost or stolen, an innocent purchaser for value will get good title to the bond. For this reason greater care should be exercised in the case of the coupon bond.

TYPES OF BONDS

All bonds constitute debts of the issuing corporation or state, and are therefore secured by the general credit of the issuer. In addition, they may be secured by a mortgage on specific property. The latter are usually called *secured bonds,* while the former are commonly referred to as *unsecured bonds.* If a corporation which has a number of plants issues a mortgage bond, the investor cannot take for granted that the mortgage is on all the plants. It is necessary to read carefully the indenture accompanying the issue in order to ascertain the exact property which is mortgaged. If the mortgage is on only one of the plants, then the mortgage bonds will have no specific lien on the other plants.

Secured Bonds

There are a number of different kinds of secured bonds, but only the more common ones will be mentioned here. The reader is referred to standard books on corporation finance or investments for a more detailed description of secured bonds.

First Mortgage Bonds. As their title indicates, these bonds have a first lien on the particular property. First mortgage bonds are commonly called *senior* bonds. Being more secure, the yield on such bonds is lower than on the other bonds of the same company.

Second Mortgage Bonds. These bonds are issued against the equity possessed by the issuing corporation on property on which a first mortgage has already been issued.

Since the risk is greater on second mortgage bonds, they have a higher yield than first mortgage bonds of the same company. In any particular case the degree of risk depends, among other things, on the amount of first mortgage bonds issued, the value of the property, and the earning power of the company.

Issuing corporations realize that the term "second" is not received well by the investing public, so some other title is usually used. They may be called *general mortgage bonds,* or if part of the proceeds is being used to retire another bond issue, the title *refunding mortgage bonds* may be used. When used to consolidate several bond issues, or when part of the proceeds is to be used to effect a consolidation, they are sometimes called *consolidated mortgage bonds.* Second, third, etc., mortgage bonds are referred to as *junior* bonds in practice.

Mortgage bonds of any kind may be *open-end* or *closed-end.* In the case of open-end mortgage bonds, more bonds may be issued under the same mortgage, while in the case of closed-end bonds, no more bonds having the *same lien* can be issued against the property without the consent of the holders of a designated percentage of the bonds. A second mortgage bond may, however, be issued against property which is security for a closed-end first mortgage bond issue. The closed-end feature tends to benefit the investor.

Mortgage bond issues may or may not have the *after-acquired-property* clause in the agreement. Where this clause is present, any future property of the kind described in the indenture will, when acquired by the corporation, come under the claim of the particular mortgage bonds. The presence of this clause tends to strengthen the bonds, so it may benefit the investor.

Collateral Trust Bonds. These bonds are issued with the security, not of real property, but of stocks or bonds usually of other companies. They are commonly used by holding companies.

Equipment Trust Obligations. These are issued by railroads to help finance the acquisition of rolling stock. When issued in the same way as ordinary mortgage bonds, they are called *equipment mortgage bonds.* When issued under the Philadelphia Plan, they are termed *car trust certificates.* Under the latter plan, title to the equipment is held by a trust company for the benefit of the certificate holders. The property is leased to the railroad, and the rental payments are used in part to pay interest or dividends on the certificates, and in part to retire a portion of the certificates. When the certificates have all been retired, title to the rolling stock is transferred to the railroad. Such a method of financing avoids the immediate effects of an after-acquired-property clause in an old bond issue.

The obligations are ordinarily retired serially. They are quoted on a yield basis, which will be explained later in the chapter. Due to the low yield and relatively short maturities, they are ordinarily not purchased by individuals.

Real Estate Securities. Several different types of securities are found in real estate financing. Valuable land in the larger cities is frequently sold through the use of the *land trust certificate.* Ownership of the land is divided into units, each of which is represented by a $1,000 land trust certificate. Title to the land is held by a trust company for the benefit of the certificate holders. The land is then leased to a company which probably erects a building. The land trust certificates, which are really certificates of beneficial interest in the land and the lease, have first claim against the building for ground rent. The investment quality of the certificate depends upon the use to which the land is put.

A *real estate mortgage bond* is really a participation certificate either in a large real estate mortgage or in a number of mortgages. These bonds are usually issued in $1,000 denominations, but in some instances they have been put as low as $100.

A *leasehold mortgage bond* is usually issued to finance a building which is constructed on leased land. Although these bonds have a first claim on the leasehold (the lease and the building), the claim of the landowner for ground rent comes ahead of their claim. The land may have been financed through the issuance of land trust certificates.

Unsecured Bonds

This is rather a misnomer, because all bonds are really secured by the general credit of the issuer. The term is used, however, to apply to those bonds which are not secured by a mortgage on real property or by a lien on securities. Another term, *debenture bond,* is commonly used as the title for this type of bond. If a corporation issues both a first mortgage bond and a debenture bond issue, from the standpoint of safety of principal the mortgage bonds will be the better investment. But we cannot conclude that debenture bonds, in general, are a weak type of obligation.

All United States Government bonds, which are the best in the world today, and those issued by the states and municipalities, many of which are very good investments, are debenture bonds. Many corporations which have a good credit standing can borrow money without placing a mortgage on their properties. So, we find that, generally speaking, the safest bonds happen to be debenture bonds.

If a corporation issues debenture bonds, and has no mortgages against its properties, in event of default in the bonds, the bondholders, through the trustee, can get judgment against the issuing corporation and have the property attached. Thus, in final analysis the debenture bonds may end up the same as first mortgage bonds. In the event, however, that some other creditor secured a lien on the properties first, the story would be different.

The general credit of the issuing corporation, which is the security for debenture bonds, is also behind its mortgage bonds. Every mortgage bond is similarly secured in this respect, and, in addition, has the pledge of specific property. The general promise to pay embodied in the mortgage bond may really be better security than the specific property which is mortgaged. The worth of any business property, together with the management, is expressed in the earning power of the company. The specific property mortgaged is of little value if the company is unable to use it in such a way as to earn money. For this reason, in buying debenture bonds or mortgage bonds, the general credit of the issuing corporation should be carefully considered.

Subordinated Debenture Bonds. In recent years many companies have issued subordinated debenture bonds. The indenture of such bonds provides that in the event of insolvency of the issuer, the claim of these bonds is subordinated not only to the debentures, notes, and bank loans that were outstanding at the time the subordinated debentures were issued, but also to debt in the form of debentures, notes, and bank loans contracted after the subordinated debentures are issued. The future borrowing power of the issuer is improved rather than imperiled by the issuance of such a security, in a manner comparable to the issuance of preferred stock. But being a bond, the face rate of interest would be lower than the preferred stock dividend rate. Furthermore, interest on the bonds is tax deductible for income tax purposes, whereas dividends on the stock are not deductible. Although the subordinated debentures are not as strong an obligation as ordinary bonds, they still have an advantage over preferred stock, with respect to both the income and principal amount of the bonds.

Convertible Bonds. As the term is ordinarily used, a convertible bond is one which may, at the option of the holder, be converted into a specified amount of the stock—usually common stock—of the company, within a specified period of time. Usually the conversion may be made at any time during the life of the bond. Although some convertible bonds are secured bonds, in most instances they are debentures. Industrial companies issue them much more frequently than do companies in other fields. Subordinated debentures are often made convertible.

The amount of stock that may be obtained from converting a bond is expressed either in the number of shares of stock which may be obtained from the conversion of one $1,000 bond, or in terms of the price per share that must be paid for the stock. In the latter instance the exchange value of a bond is equivalent to its face value. For example, the indenture may provide that one $1,000 bond is convertible into 20 shares of stock. This would mean the same as if the indenture provided that the bond could be converted into stock at $50 a share.

It would be immediately profitable for a bondholder to convert whenever the value of the stock obtained would exceed the value of the bond. The "break-even" price of the stock may be found with the following formula:

$$\text{Break-even price of stock} = \frac{\text{Market price of bond}}{\text{Number of shares of stock obtained}}$$

To illustrate the use of this formula, let us assume that a $1,000 bond purchased at $1,050 is convertible into stock at $50 a share. We will assume that the stock is now selling for $45 a share. Would it be profitable to convert now? At the conversion price of $50, it is obvious that one bond ($1,000 face value) could be converted into 20 shares of stock ($1,000 divided by $50). Substituting in the formula we get the following:

$$\frac{\$1{,}050}{20} = \$52\tfrac{1}{2}, \text{ break-even price of stock}$$

This shows that it would not be profitable to convert until the stock went above $52½ a share (assuming the bond price remained at $1,050). We can easily test the accuracy of the formula. It obviously would not be profitable to convert until the market value of the 20 shares exceeded $1,050, the price of the bond. To just equal the market price of the bonds, the shares would have to sell at $52½ a share. If conversion was made when the stock was selling for $45, the bondholder would get only $900 in stock. He would thus lose $150 by converting.

Another way to determine the break-even price is to multiply the conversion price of the stock by the market price of the bond expressed in percentage of its face value:

$$\text{Break-even price of stock} = \begin{array}{c}\text{Market price of the bond (expressed in per}\\ \text{cent)} \times \text{Conversion price of the stock}\end{array}$$

Substituting the above figures in the formula we get the following:

$$105 \text{ per cent} \times \$50 = \$52\tfrac{1}{2}, \text{ break-even price of stock}$$

It is also of importance to be able to determine what the *conversion* value of the bond would be when the stock was selling at a particular price. This can be computed as follows:

$$\begin{array}{c}\text{Conversion value of bond}\\ \text{(expressed in per cent)}\end{array} = \frac{\text{Market price per share of stock}}{\text{Conversion price of stock}}$$

Assume that the stock in the above example was selling for $65 a share. By substituting in the formula we get the following:

$$\frac{\$65}{\$50} = 130 \text{ (per cent of face value), conversion value of bond}$$

If the bond was selling for 130 per cent of its face value, that means a price of $1,300. We can get the same result by the obvious roundabout method. Since 20 shares of stock can be obtained from the conversion of one bond, with a market price of $65 a share, the bondholder would get $1,300 in stock. Thus, this would represent the conversion value of the bond.

A convertible bond tends to sell at a price which reflects its value as a credit instrument (or slightly higher because of the possibility of the stock's increasing in price) until the stock approaches the break-even price, at which time the bond will increase in price in anticipation of the stock going still higher in price. After the stock has advanced beyond this point the price of the bond will reflect its convertible value. Thus, it will go up and down with the price of the stock. But if the stock price drops drastically, the bond will level off at a price which reflects its value as a credit instrument. Thus, the convertible bond offers the security of a credit instrument when business conditions and the financial position of the company are such as to require security. But if the stock price increases, the bondholder can profit by converting his bond. It is also apparent that a convertible bond may offer some hedge against inflation.

If it appears that the equity of the existing shareholders will be diluted unduly by the future conversion of the bonds, however, the issuing company will probably exercise the call feature. The bondholder would be given the right to convert for a short time after the call was issued, but he must then convert or take the call price. This dims somewhat the attractiveness of a convertible bond. Many companies that issue convertible bonds do not have top credit ratings or otherwise it would not be necessary to add the convertible feature in order to sell the bonds, but there are a number of notable exceptions.

Income Bonds. In the past, these bonds usually arose in a railroad reorganization. Interest on such bonds is not a fixed charge and need not be paid unless the issuing company has earnings sufficient to pay the interest. In addition to their use by railroads, income bonds have been used frequently in real estate company reorganizations.

Income bonds are frequently called *adjustment* or *adjustment mortgage bonds.* In recent years several solvent railroads have issued income bonds to retire a preferred stock issue. The tax savings on the interest was a principal reason. A number of solvent industrial corporations have used income bonds to raise new capital. Some of these issues have been subordinated income debentures.

CLASSES OF BONDS

United States Government Bonds

Series E and Series H United States savings bonds were discussed in Chapter 6. In terms of dollars the largest segment of the federal debt is in the form of *United States Treasury bonds.* These are issued in various maturities ranging from five to forty years. Most of the issues are callable at their face value from two to five years before the maturity date. The lowest denomination is usually $500 or $1,000. Most issues are available in either coupon or registered form. They are fully negotiable and thus may be bought and sold in the regular market at the prevailing price, or used as collateral for a loan.

The face rate of interest on Treasury bonds is set at such a figure that the bonds on original issue will sell for approximately their face value. Face rates of interest on outstanding Treasury bonds range from 2½ per cent to 4¼ per cent.

Since all federal bonds issued since March 1, 1941, are subject to the federal income tax, the interest on all outstanding Treasury bonds is fully subject to the federal income tax. The bonds are taxable also under the federal estate and gift tax laws and the state inheritance, estate, and gift taxes, but they are exempt both as to principal and interest from all other state and local taxes.

Institutional investors, rather than individuals, are the principal buyers of Treasury bonds. An individual may purchase them if their yield at a particular time is higher than on the Series E and Series H savings bonds, or if he has already bought his limit of savings bonds for the year, or if he wants a short-term investment. (Even if the maturity is some distance away, the Treasury bonds may be sold in the market at any time.)

United States Treasury notes are similar to the bonds except that they have a maturity of from one to five years. *United States Certificates of Indebtedness* are bearer instruments, have a maturity of one year or less, and carry one coupon providing for the payment of interest at maturity. *United States Treasury bills* are issued in bearer form with a maturity of usually from three to six months. They are issued (and sold) on a discount basis (and thus have no interest coupons attached). All of these federal obligations have the same tax status as the Treasury bonds. Because of their relatively short maturities, the yield on these obligations is usually lower than on the Treasury (and savings) bonds and for this reason they are rarely purchased by individuals.

Table 11–1. Tax-free Yield Equivalents

Individual—Taxable Income Brackets (000)	Tax Bracket Rates (%)	Joint—Taxable Income Brackets (000)	Tax-exempt Interest (%) 1.00	2.00	2.25	2.50	2.60	2.70	2.80	2.90	3.00	3.10	3.20	3.30	3.40	3.50	3.60	3.70	3.80	3.90	4.00
			Equivalent Taxable Return (%)																		
$ 2 to $ 4	19	$ 4 to $ 8	1.23	2.47	2.78	3.09	3.21	3.33	3.46	3.58	3.70	3.83	3.95	4.07	4.20	4.32	4.44	4.57	4.69	4.81	4.94
4 to 6	22	8 to 12	1.28	2.56	2.88	3.21	3.33	3.46	3.59	3.72	3.85	3.97	4.10	4.23	4.36	4.49	4.62	4.74	4.87	5.00	5.13
6 to 8	25	12 to 16	1.33	2.67	3.00	3.33	3.47	3.60	3.73	3.87	4.00	4.13	4.27	4.40	4.53	4.67	4.80	4.93	5.07	5.20	5.33
8 to 10	28	16 to 20	1.39	2.78	3.13	3.47	3.61	3.75	3.89	4.03	4.17	4.31	4.44	4.58	4.72	4.86	5.00	5.14	5.28	5.42	5.56
10 to 12	32	20 to 24	1.47	2.94	3.31	3.68	3.82	3.97	4.12	4.26	4.41	4.56	4.71	4.85	5.00	5.15	5.29	5.44	5.59	5.74	5.88
12 to 14	36	24 to 28	1.56	3.13	3.52	3.91	4.06	4.22	4.38	4.53	4.69	4.84	5.00	5.16	5.31	5.47	5.63	5.78	5.94	6.09	6.25
14 to 16	39	28 to 32	1.64	3.28	3.69	4.10	4.26	4.43	4.59	4.75	4.92	5.08	5.25	5.41	5.57	5.74	5.90	6.07	6.23	6.39	6.56
16 to 18	42	32 to 36	1.72	3.45	3.88	4.31	4.48	4.66	4.83	5.00	5.17	5.34	5.52	5.69	5.86	6.03	6.21	6.38	6.55	6.72	6.90
18 to 20	45	36 to 40	1.82	3.64	4.09	4.55	4.73	4.91	5.09	5.27	5.45	5.64	5.82	6.00	6.18	6.36	6.55	6.73	6.91	7.09	7.27
20 to 22	48	40 to 44	1.92	3.85	4.33	4.81	5.00	5.19	5.38	5.58	5.77	5.96	6.15	6.35	6.54	6.73	6.92	7.12	7.31	7.50	7.69
22 to 26	50	44 to 52	2.00	4.00	4.50	5.00	5.20	5.40	5.60	5.80	6.00	6.20	6.40	6.60	6.80	7.00	7.20	7.40	7.60	7.80	8.00
26 to 32	53	52 to 64	2.13	4.26	4.79	5.32	5.53	5.74	5.96	6.17	6.38	6.60	6.81	7.02	7.23	7.45	7.66	7.87	8.09	8.30	8.51
32 to 38	55	64 to 76	2.22	4.44	5.00	5.56	5.78	6.00	6.22	6.44	6.67	6.89	7.11	7.33	7.56	7.78	8.00	8.22	8.44	8.67	8.89
38 to 44	58	76 to 88	2.38	4.76	5.36	5.95	6.19	6.43	6.67	6.90	7.14	7.38	7.62	7.86	8.10	8.33	8.57	8.81	9.05	9.29	9.52
44 to 50	60	88 to 100	2.50	5.00	5.63	6.25	6.50	6.75	7.00	7.25	7.50	7.75	8.00	8.25	8.50	8.75	9.00	9.25	9.50	9.75	10.00
50 to 60	62	100 to 120	2.63	5.26	5.92	6.58	6.84	7.11	7.37	7.63	7.89	8.16	8.42	8.68	8.95	9.21	9.47	9.47	10.00	10.26	10.53
60 to 70	64	120 tc 140	2.78	5.56	6.25	6.94	7.22	7.50	7.78	8.06	8.33	8.61	8.89	9.17	9.44	9.72	10.00	10.28	10.56	10.83	11.11
70 to 80	66	140 to 160	2.94	5.88	6.62	7.35	7.65	7.94	8.24	8.53	8.82	9.12	9.41	9.71	10.00	10.29	10.59	10.88	11.18	11.47	11.76
80 to 90	68	160 to 180	3.13	6.25	7.03	7.81	8.13	8.44	8.75	9.06	9.38	9.69	10.00	10.31	10.63	10.94	11.25	11.56	11.88	12.19	12.50
90 to 100	69	180 to 200	3.23	6.45	7.26	8.06	8.39	8.71	9.03	9.35	9.68	10.00	10.32	10.65	10.97	11.29	11.61	11.94	12.26	12.58	12.90
100 and over	70	200 and over	3.33	6.67	7.50	8.33	8.67	9.00	9.33	9.67	10.00	10.33	10.67	11.00	11.33	11.67	12.00	12.33	12.67	13.00	13.33
Corporations																					
Under $25	22		1.28	2.56	2.88	3.21	3.33	3.46	3.59	3.72	3.85	3.97	4.10	4.23	4.36	4.49	4.62	4.74	4.87	5.00	5.13
Over $25	48		1.92	3.85	4.33	4.81	5.00	5.19	5.38	5.58	5.77	5.96	6.15	6.35	6.54	6.73	6.92	7.12	7.31	7.50	7.69

Foreign Bonds

The question of foreign securities can be disposed of in quick order by saying that the average investor should never buy any securities issued either by foreign governments or by private companies within foreign countries.

There are enough securities issued in the United States, both by the government and by private companies, for people to buy without resorting to foreign issues. The average investor is not well enough acquainted with conditions in foreign countries to warrant the purchase of their securities.

State and Municipal Bonds

The realm of state and municipal finance is quite complicated, and only those who have studied or had experience in this specialized field should feel competent to pass judgment on state and municipal bonds.

State and municipal bonds are wholly exempt from all federal income taxes. This, plus the fact that the bonds of the particular state may be exempt from local taxation as well, and that they qualify as legal investments for fiduciaries in the state, has resulted in the bonds of many states being sold on a lower yield basis than United States Government bonds. The same reasons account for the fact that many municipals sell on a lower yield basis than the best bonds issued by corporations.

Due to this favored position, the bonds issued by states and municipalities sell on a much lower yield basis than is warranted by the degree of risk present. Their purchase by corporations and by persons who are in the high tax brackets may be justified, but the average investor should not buy them.

Table 11–1 shows the yields (before federal income taxes) that must be received by individuals filing both a separate return and a joint return (the latter for married couples) in taxable income brackets (after exemptions and deductions) ranging from $2,000 to over $200,000 to be equivalent (after taxes) to yields ranging from 1 to 4 per cent on tax-exempt bonds. It can be seen from the table, for example, that if a single person who has a taxable income of from $18,000 to $20,000 (or a married person with a taxable income of from $36,000 to $40,000 who files a joint return) buys a stock or taxable bond, he would have to obtain a yield (return) before taxes of 6 per cent to be equivalent (after taxes) to a yield (return) of only 3.3 per cent on a tax-exempt bond. It is apparent that the higher the income of the individual, the greater is the tax saving from buying tax-exempt bonds. The table is based on the tax rates that became effective January 1, 1965. In making up tables of this kind, it is always assumed that the income from investments is taxed at the highest income bracket. Actually this is the case because if the individual chose the tax-exempt bond he would eliminate the top part of his taxable income figure. Comparable yields for corporations are given at the bottom of the table.[1]

Corporate Bonds

Corporate bonds are classified into three groups: public utility, railroad, and industrial. The latter embraces the various types of industries which are not included in the other two groups. Generally speaking, as a class, public utility bonds are considered the safest type of corporates, while industrials are, as a class, the most speculative. It must of course be realized that there are a number of different types of public utilities and of industrials, and that the quality of the companies within each type varies greatly. The bonds of some industrials would therefore be considered better investments than the bonds of some utilities.

The degree of risk to the bondholder varies according to the ability of the corporation to pay interest when due and the principal at the maturity of the bond. This can be determined with a fair degree of accuracy by a thorough examination of the nature of the company and the products it manufactures or processes, its age, its size and development, its management, its outlook for future sales and profits, and similar factors. We will briefly discuss only two items relating to this—interest coverage and bond ratings.

Interest Coverage. The margin of safety behind a corporate bond issue can be determined in part by ascertaining how many times the company earned the interest on all of its bonds. Since bond interest is deducted before arriving at the base on which income taxes are computed, the "earnings" figure used would be before the interest and taxes have been deducted. We are of course interested in the ability of the company

[1] If a person wants to ascertain the equivalent taxable yield of a tax-exempt yield not specifically stated in the table, he can do so by multiplying the equivalent taxable yield for his taxable income bracket, shown in the Tax-exempt Interest column headed "1%," by the particular tax-exempt yield with which he is concerned. For example, if a person in the \$22,000 to \$26,000 taxable income bracket (\$44,000 to \$52,000 for joint return) is contemplating buying a 3¼ per cent tax-exempt bond, his equivalent taxable yield would be 6½ per cent (2.00 × 3.25).

If a tax equivalent table is not available, the equivalent taxable yield can be found through the use of the following formula:

$$\frac{\text{Tax-exempt yield}}{1 - \text{Top tax rate}} = \text{Equivalent taxable yield}$$

Substituting the above figures in the formula,

$$\frac{3.25}{1 - .50} = 6\tfrac{1}{2}$$

to pay the interest in the future, but since future earnings are an unknown quantity, we use an average of past earnings to give some indication of the amount of probable future earnings. The more speculative the type of business, the greater should be the number of times the interest is earned in order to qualify the bonds as good investments. Thus, the investor would want an industrial bond to earn its interest a greater number of times than a public utility bond. One authority[2] recommends that to provide the necessary margin of safety the earnings (before taxes) for the past seven to ten years should cover the bond interest the following number of times at a minimum:

Industry	Minimum Number of Times Interest Earned
Public utilities	4
Railroads	5
Industrials	7

In addition to meeting the requirements just stated, it would add to the attractiveness of the bond if the earnings trend were up, the profits for the current year satisfactory, and the earnings in each of the years more than enough to meet the interest for that year. If a company has several bond issues outstanding, the interest on all the issues should be covered the number of times stated above.

BOND RATINGS

The leading financial services rate bonds on which they are able to get adequate information. These ratings are on the basis of the quality of the bonds. Changes in the ratings are made by the services when-

Moody's		*Standard & Poor's*	
Symbol	Explanation	Symbol	Explanation
Aaa	Highest grade	A1+	Highest grade
Aa	High grade	A1	High grade
A	Higher medium grade	A	Upper medium grade
Baa	Lower medium grade	B1+	Medium grade
Ba	Somewhat speculative	B1	Lower medium grade
B	Speculative	B	Speculative
Caa	Very speculative	C1+	Outright speculations
Ca	Highly speculative	C1	
C	Little prospects	C	Best defaulted issues
		D1	In default
		D	In default, little value

[2]Benjamin Graham, David L. Dodd, and Sidney Cottle, *Security Analysis*, Fourth Edition. New York: McGraw-Hill Book Co., 1962, p. 348.

ever they believe it is warranted. It is realized that none of the services can predict the future, but certainly they are more qualified and experienced in the determination of the investment worth of bonds than is the average investor. The latter would undoubtedly benefit from weighing the ratings rather heavily in the selection of his investments. These bond ratings are respected in banking circles. Illustrated are the bond rating symbols of Moody's and Standard & Poor's. Although the language used in the interpretation of the symbols by the two services is not exactly the same, the comparable symbols have practically identical meanings. Abbreviated explanations for the symbols are given.

The rating should not be the sole criterion for selecting a bond, but it should be considered along with many other factors. Bonds with relatively low ratings sometimes turn out to be better investments than some of those which are given a higher rating. In view of the shortcomings of any system of rating and the different status of investors, it is difficult to say what rating a bond should have before it should be purchased. But if something definite is desired by the reader, it is suggested that only those bonds with a rating of "A" or above be bought by the average investor. People with steady income and considerable wealth can afford to buy the higher-yielding bonds with lower ratings, but the small investor should be very conservative.

The cost of the manuals and services in which the bond ratings are contained is prohibitive to the small investor. However, almost all commercial banks, brokerage offices, and bond houses, and many libraries, have one or more of these services, which are accessible to the individual without cost.

The financial services ordinarily do not rate small bond issues, or those of real estate companies, investment companies, and other financial corporations, and government and municipal bonds (the latter, however, are rated by Moody's).

PRICE QUOTATIONS ON BONDS

Corporate bonds are quoted in terms of percentage of the face value. Thus, a quotation of 101¼ for a bond with a face value of $1,000 would mean a price of $1,012.50. The lowest spread between the bid and ask price for a corporate bond is ordinarily ⅛ of a point, or, in other words, $1.25 on a $1,000 bond. United States Treasury bonds are also quoted in percentage of face value, but the figure to the right of the decimal point indicates thirty-seconds. For example, a quotation of 103.24 means $103\frac{24}{32}$, or a price of $1,037.50 for a bond with a face value of $1,000. Because of their greater stability, and also because sales are usually in relatively large blocks, dealers are willing to trade in Treasury bonds in thirty-seconds instead of in eighths.

Except in the case of most income bonds and those which are in default, bonds are quoted "and accrued interest." This means that in addition to the quoted price, the purchaser must pay to the seller the amount of interest which has accrued since the last interest payment date (the issue date in the case of a new issue). In computing accrued interest on all except certain United States Government bonds (on which the 365-day-year basis is used), a 360-day year, or 30 days a month, is assumed, regardless of the actual number of days in the particular month. The purchaser pays the accrued interest up to, but not including, the day of delivery.

"Regular way delivery" on the New York Stock Exchange requires delivery on the fourth day following day of sale. If on February 12, a person bought a 5 per cent corporate bond on which interest is payable January 1 and July 1, for regular way delivery on February 16, at 96½, he would pay the seller a total of $971.25. The quoted price of 96½ would mean $965. The buyer must pay accrued interest for one month and a half (the whole month of January and 15 days of February) at the rate of 5 per cent per annum. This would amount to $6.25. Adding the two figures would give us a total of $971.25. Regular way delivery on United States Government bonds is the day following the sale.

No accrued interest is added to the quoted price of most income bonds or bonds which are in default. This type of quotation is called "flat," and is the way in which stocks are quoted.

Serial Bond Quotations

The price quotation for serial bonds is commonly expressed in terms of yield for the average maturity. Equipment obligations are practically always quoted in this way. In the case of a serial bond issue, part of the issue matures each year until the entire amount is paid off. Short maturities usually sell at a different price (or yield) than long-term maturities. Even if this were not the case, if the bonds were selling at a discount or at a premium, the varying maturities would result in different discounts or premiums. If the face rate of interest is the same on all the maturities, then, for the two reasons just stated, a different price quotation would be necessary for each maturity. In order to give only one price quotation, investment dealers sometimes quote the price of the average maturity. In other instances, they quote the average price for all the maturities. Anyone interested in the price of a particular maturity will have to inquire further.

The price quoted for the serials is in terms of yield rather than in terms of dollars. For example, if a person asked the price of a particular 4 per cent bond that matured in twenty years, the dealer might give him the following quotation:

Bid 4.0
Ask 3.9

When the dealer bids 4, he is saying that he will pay such a price for the bond that his yield will be 4 per cent. Since the face rate of interest on the bond is 4 per cent, this means that the dealer is bidding 100 ($1,000 for the ordinary bond). The ask price of 3.9 means that the dealer will sell the bond at such a price that the yield to the purchaser will be only 3.9 per cent to maturity. Obviously, the dealer is asking a premium for the bond. Consulting the bond tables (these will be explained later in the chapter) for the price one would have to pay for a twenty-year, 4 per cent bond to yield 3.9 per cent to maturity, you find it is 101.38 ($1,013.80 for the ordinary bond). It was stated above that equipment obligations are practically always quoted in terms of yield. The quoted bid and ask prices are an average for all the maturities, unless each maturity is quoted separately. The bid and ask prices printed in the newspapers are for the close of the preceding day. The price quotations for listed bonds indicate the actual sales price. Serial obligations are not listed on the stock exchanges.

COMPUTING YIELDS ON BONDS

Current Yield

Bonds bear a fixed rate of interest, sometimes called the face rate, or nominal rate. This rate is stated on the bond. To determine the amount of interest which will be paid annually on the bond, the face value of the bond is multiplied by this stated rate. Thus, a $1,000, 4 per cent bond will pay interest of $40 a year, regardless of what amount is paid for the bond. Most bonds pay interest semiannually, so the holder of this bond would receive $20 interest every six months. If the purchaser pays more than $1,000 for the bond, the yield will be less than 4 per cent, and if he pays less than $1,000, the yield will be more than 4 per cent. For example, if he pays $1,035 (this would be a quoted price of 103½) for the bond, he would get a *current yield* of a little over 3.86 per cent ($40 divided by $1,035) on his money.

The current yield computation is used when the bond is to be held for a relatively short period.

Yield to Maturity

With the exception of a few isolated instances, all bonds mature at some time in the future. Except in cases of default, the bondholder will be paid the face value of the bond at its maturity. Taking the example stated above, if a person paid $1,035 for a bond, the current yield would, as computed above, be 3.86 per cent. But the *yield to maturity,* which is also called the *net yield,* would be less than this because, when the bond matures for $1,000, the purchaser will have lost the amount of $35, which is the *premium* he paid on the bond. Just what the yield to maturity would be in this case depends upon how long the bond has to run to maturity. The closer the maturity, the less would be the yield on a premium bond.

To compute the exact yield to maturity on bonds which are purchased at a premium or discount, it is necessary to use a complicated algebraic formula. Since bond tables have been worked out to show the exact yields for bonds bearing different rates of interest and maturing at different times, almost all bankers and security dealers have forgotten the formula. The reader would probably do likewise, so the formula will not be given. A page from each of two bond table books will, however, be given and explained later.

In the meantime, a method of computing the approximate yield to maturity, without use of the complicated formula or bond table, will be stated. Let us assume that the 4 per cent bond, which was purchased for $1,035, has twenty years to run to maturity. The premium of $35, which will be lost over the twenty-year period, is at the rate of $1.75 a year. As the holder gets $40 a year interest, we will deduct the annual amortized premium of $1.75 from this, which gives us a net annual return of $38.25. (This is really an understatement of the current return, because the holder gets the use of the entire $40.) Since $1,035 was paid for the bond, and it matures at $1,000, the average cost price would be $1,017.50 ($1,035 plus $1,000, divided by 2). (This is really an understatement of the cost, and using it in the next computation tends to overstate the yield. This understatement of cost balances the understatement of yield in the previous computation.) Dividing the net annual income of $38.25, computed above, by the average cost of $1,017.50, gives us a net yield to maturity of 3.759 per cent. Reference to the bond table (Table 11–2) indicates that the exact yield in this case would be 3.75 per cent. Thus, using this inexact but simple method of computing yields to maturity gives a yield slightly in excess of the actual yield for bonds selling at a premium.

Table 11–2. Bond Table—20 Years—Interest Payable Semiannually

Per Cent per Annum	Face Rate of Interest						
	3%	3½%	4%	4½%	5%	6%	7%
2.90	101.51	109.06	116.60	124.15	131.70	146.80	161.89
3.	100.00	107.48	114.96	122.44	129.92	144.87	159.83
3.10	98.52	105.93	113.34	120.75	128.16	142.98	157.81
3⅛	98.15	105.55	112.94	120.33	127.73	142.52	157.31
3.20	97.06	104.41	111.75	119.09	126.44	141.13	155.82
3¼	96.34	103.66	110.97	118.28	125.59	140.21	154.83
3.30	95.63	102.91	110.19	117.47	124.75	139.30	153.86
3.35	94.93	102.17	109.42	116.66	123.91	138.40	152.89
3⅜	94.58	101.81	109.04	116.27	123.49	137.95	152.41
3.40	94.23	101.44	108.66	115.87	123.08	137.51	151.93
3.45	93.54	100.72	107.90	115.08	122.26	136.62	150.98
3½	92.85	100.00	107.15	114.30	121.45	135.74	150.04
3.55	92.17	99.29	106.41	113.52	120.64	134.87	149.11
3.60	91.50	98.58	105.67	112.75	119.84	134.01	148.18
3⅝	91.16	98.23	105.30	112.37	119.44	133.58	147.72
3.65	90.83	97.88	104.94	111.99	119.04	133.15	147.26
3.70	90.17	97.19	104.21	111.24	118.26	132.30	146.35
3¾	89.51	96.50	103.50	110.49	117.48	131.46	145.44
3.80	88.86	95.82	102.78	109.74	116.70	130.63	144.55
3⅞	87.90	94.81	101.73	108.64	115.56	129.39	143.22
3.90	87.58	94.48	101.38	108.28	115.18	128.98	142.78
4.	86.32	93.16	100.00	106.84	113.68	127.36	141.03
4.10	85.09	91.86	98.64	105.42	112.20	125.76	139.32
4⅛	84.78	91.54	98.31	105.07	111.84	125.37	138.90
4.20	83.87	90.59	97.31	104.03	110.75	124.19	137.63
4¼	83.27	89.96	96.65	103.35	110.04	123.42	136.80
4.30	82.68	89.34	96.00	102.66	109.33	122.65	135.98
4⅜	81.80	88.42	95.04	101.65	108.27	121.51	134.75
4.40	81.51	88.11	94.72	101.32	107.93	121.14	134.35
4½	80.35	86.90	93.45	100.00	106.55	119.65	132.74
4.60	79.22	85.72	92.21	98.70	105.19	118.18	131.16
4⅝	78.94	85.42	91.90	98.38	104.86	117.82	130.77
4.70	78.11	84.55	90.99	97.43	103.86	116.74	129.61
4¾	77.57	83.98	90.39	96.80	103.20	116.02	128.84
4.80	77.02	83.40	89.79	96.17	102.55	115.32	128.08
4⅞	76.22	82.56	88.90	95.24	101.59	114.27	126.95
4.90	75.95	82.28	88.61	94.94	101.27	113.92	126.58
5.	74.90	81.17	87.45	93.72	100.00	112.55	125.10
5.10	73.86	80.09	86.31	92.53	98.76	111.20	123.65
5⅛	73.61	79.82	86.03	92.24	98.45	110.87	123.29
5.20	72.85	79.02	85.19	91.36	97.53	109.87	122.22
5¼	72.34	78.49	84.64	90.78	96.93	109.22	121.51
5.30	71.85	77.97	84.09	90.21	96.33	108.57	120.81
5⅜	71.11	77.19	83.27	89.36	95.44	107.60	119.77
5.40	70.87	76.94	83.01	89.07	95.14	107.28	119.42
5½	69.90	75.92	81.94	87.96	93.98	106.02	118.06
5⅝	68.72	74.68	80.64	86.59	92.55	104.47	116.38
5¾	67.57	73.46	79.36	85.26	91.15	102.95	114.74
5⅞	66.43	72.27	78.11	83.95	89.78	101.46	113.13
6.	65.33	71.11	76.89	82.66	88.44	100.00	111.56

This same method of computing the approximate yield to maturity can be used if the bond is purchased at a discount, but then the accumulation of the annual discount will be added to the annual interest received. The following example will illustrate the method. Assume that a twenty-year, 4 per cent bond is purchased for $960. In this case the purchaser will get $1,000 at the maturity of the bond, but that is $40 more than he paid for the bond. If we spread this income over the twenty-year period, it would be at the rate of $2 a year. This $2, plus the interest of $40, gives a net annual return of $42. Dividing this $42 by the average cost price of $980 gives us a yield to maturity of 4.285 per cent. According to the bond table, the actual yield to maturity would be 4.30 per cent. This simple method thus slightly understates the yield for bonds purchased at a discount. Following is the formula for this method of computing the approximate yield to maturity.

$$\frac{\text{Annual interest} - \text{Annual amortized premium (or, + Discount)}}{(\text{Cost price} + \text{Maturity price}) \div 2} = \begin{array}{c}\text{Approximate}\\ \text{yield to}\\ \text{maturity}\end{array}$$

Bond Tables

It was stated above that bond tables have been worked out to show the actual yield to maturity of bonds of different maturities, bearing various rates of interest and selling at different prices. Specimen pages from two different types of bond tables are shown in Tables 11–2 and 11–3. The difference in construction of the two tables is apparent after a few minutes' study. In the case of Table 11–2 the yields and prices of all twenty-year maturities are stated on the same page, whereas Table 11–3 contains the prices and yields of only a 4 per cent bond, and for maturities of from seventeen to twenty years.

With the use of the tables it is a simple matter to find the yield on a bond when the face rate and maturity are known, or to find the yield when the purchase price and maturity are known. Let us refer to the first table to find the yield to maturity of the twenty-year, 4 per cent bond purchased for $1,035, which we discussed above. The percentage figures across the top of the table represent the face rate of interest of the bond. Since this is a 4 per cent bond, we will go to the column headed "4%." Then going down this column we find the figure "103.50." Since this figure, the same as bond quotations, is a percentage of the face value of the bond, then this figure is for the bond costing $1,035. Now following across the line on which the figure of 103.50 is contained, we find in the extreme left-hand column the figure "3¾." (The heading of this column is "Per cent per Annum.") So this figure of 3¾ per cent represents the yield to maturity of this particular bond.

Table 11–3. Bond Table—Interest Payable Semiannually

4% per Annum	Maturity in Years						
	17	17½	18	18½	19	19½	20
2.00	128.70	129.41	130.11	130.80	131.48	132.16	132.83
2.25	124.61	125.20	125.78	126.36	126.93	127.50	128.06
2.50	120.67	121.16	121.64	122.11	122.58	123.04	123.50
2.60	119.14	119.58	120.02	120.46	120.89	121.31	121.73
2.70	117.63	118.04	118.44	118.83	119.22	119.61	119.99
2.80	116.14	116.51	116.88	117.23	117.59	117.94	118.28
2.85	115.41	115.76	116.11	116.45	116.78	117.11	117.44
2⅞	115.04	115.39	115.72	116.05	116.38	116.70	117.02
2.90	114.68	115.01	115.34	115.66	115.98	116.30	116.60
2.95	113.96	114.27	114.58	114.89	115.19	115.49	115.78
3.00	113.24	113.54	113.83	114.12	114.40	114.68	114.96
3.05	112.53	112.81	113.08	113.36	113.62	113.89	114.15
3.10	111.82	112.09	112.34	112.60	112.85	113.10	113.34
3⅛	111.47	111.73	111.98	112.22	112.47	112.70	112.94
3.15	111.12	111.37	111.61	111.85	112.08	112.31	112.54
3.20	110.43	110.66	110.88	111.10	111.32	111.54	111.75
3¼	109.74	109.95	110.16	110.37	110.57	110.77	110.97
3.30	109.05	109.25	109.44	109.63	109.82	110.01	110.19
3.35	108.37	108.55	108.73	108.91	109.08	109.25	109.42
3⅜	108.03	108.21	108.38	108.55	108.71	108.87	109.04
3.40	107.70	107.86	108.03	108.19	108.35	108.50	108.66
3.45	107.03	107.18	107.33	107.48	107.62	107.76	107.90
3½	106.37	106.50	106.64	106.77	106.90	107.02	107.15
3.55	105.71	105.83	105.95	106.07	106.18	106.29	106.41
3.60	105.05	105.16	105.27	105.37	105.47	105.57	105.67
3⅝	104.73	104.83	104.93	105.02	105.12	105.21	105.30
3.65	104.40	104.50	104.59	104.68	104.77	104.85	104.94
3.70	103.76	103.84	103.92	103.99	104.07	104.14	104.21
3¾	103.12	103.19	103.25	103.31	103.38	103.44	103.50
3.80	102.49	102.54	102.59	102.64	102.69	102.74	102.78
3.85	101.86	101.90	101.93	101.97	102.01	102.04	102.08
3⅞	101.55	101.58	101.61	101.64	101.67	101.70	101.73
3.90	101.23	101.26	101.28	101.31	101.33	101.36	101.38
3.95	100.61	100.63	100.64	100.65	100.66	100.68	100.69
4.00	100.00	100.00	100.00	100.00	100.00	100.00	100.00
4.05	99.39	99.38	99.37	99.35	99.34	99.33	99.32
4.10	98.78	98.76	98.74	98.71	98.69	98.67	98.64
4⅛	98.48	98.45	98.42	98.39	98.36	98.34	98.31
4.15	98.18	98.15	98.11	98.08	98.04	98.01	97.98
4.20	97.59	97.54	97.49	97.45	97.40	97.36	97.31
4¼	97.00	96.94	96.88	96.82	96.76	96.71	96.65
4.30	96.41	96.34	96.27	96.20	96.13	96.07	96.00
4.35	95.83	95.74	95.66	95.58	95.51	95.43	95.36
4⅜	95.54	95.45	95.36	95.28	95.20	95.11	95.04
4.40	95.25	95.15	95.06	94.97	94.89	94.80	94.72
4.45	94.67	94.57	94.47	94.37	94.27	94.17	94.08
4½	94.10	93.99	93.88	93.77	93.66	93.55	93.45
4.55	93.54	93.41	93.29	93.17	93.05	92.94	92.83
4.60	92.98	92.84	92.71	92.58	92.45	92.33	92.21
4⅝	92.70	92.56	92.42	92.29	92.16	92.03	91.90
4.65	92.42	92.27	92.13	91.99	91.86	91.73	91.60
4.70	91.87	91.71	91.56	91.41	91.27	91.13	90.99
4¾	91.32	91.15	90.99	90.84	90.68	90.53	90.39
4.80	90.77	90.60	90.43	90.26	90.10	89.94	89.79
4.85	90.23	90.05	89.87	89.70	89.53	89.36	89.20

The other table is used in the same way. Taking the above example of the twenty-year, 4 per cent bond purchased at $960, we find the sample page is for a 4 per cent bond. The figures across the top of this table represent the number of years to maturity, so go down the column headed "20" until you find the figure 96.00, and then on the same line in the left-hand column you find the yield to be 4.30 per cent. If the yield and maturity are known, the price can easily be found by looking to the right on the same line as the yield, to the figure in the column headed by the proper maturity.

Computing Yields of Callable Bonds

Many bonds are made callable before their maturity date. If a bond was selling, and continued to sell, at its face value up to the time of call or maturity, no problem would be encountered because the yield to call date and maturity date would be the same. But very few bonds ever sell in the market at their exact face value. Furthermore, with the exception of United States Treasury bonds, which are callable at their face value, most corporate bonds, when callable, are callable at a premium over the face or maturity value. This further complicates the problem of determining the yield on the bond.

When a bond is callable before maturity, the long-term investor has the problem of deciding whether to figure the yield to the call date or the maturity date. To be conservative, he should use whichever basis gives him the lower yield. Thus, if a bond is purchased at a discount, the longer it runs the lower will be the yield to the investor, so in this case he should compute the yield to the maturity date. Looking at it from the standpoint of the issuing corporation, if the bond sells at a discount it is indicative of the fact that the corporation's current borrowing rate is in excess of the face rate on the bond, so it would be more costly for it to refund the bonds on the call date. For the same reasons, if the bond is purchased at a premium and is callable at par, the yield would be lower if figured to the call date, so this is the date which should be used by the bondholder. The fact that the bonds sell at a premium indicates that the corporation would be able to save some interest if it calls the bonds and issues a refunding issue at a lower rate of interest.

If a bond is callable at a premium, the yield should be computed to the maturity date if the bond is purchased at a discount, or at par, as this method gives the lower yield. If, however, it is purchased at a premium and it is also callable at a premium, the investor will need to compute the yield to both the call and maturity dates in order to determine which gives the lower yield, and thus which method should be used. United States Government bonds, when callable, are callable at face value.

The types of bond tables shown here can be used only when the yield is being computed to the maturity date, or to the call date when the bonds are callable at par. Special tables are available to compute the yield to the call date when the bonds are callable at a premium.

Bonds Selling at Large Discounts

We previously stated that, in the case of bonds selling at a discount, the yield should be computed to the maturity date rather than the call date. If, however, a bond is selling at a discount large enough to make it appear questionable whether the bond will ever be paid at par, even at maturity, the investor would be more conservative if he uses the *current yield* rather than the yield to maturity. The amount of the discount will never be income to the bondholder if he does not get it.

Accrued Interest

It has also been pointed out above that bonds, except those in default and income bonds, are quoted "and accrued interest." When the total amount paid by the purchaser includes something for accrued interest, the amount of such accrued interest should be deducted from the total amount paid, to arrive at the real cost of the bond proper. It is this latter figure which is used as a base in the computation of yields. Any commissions and taxes paid in connection with the purchase of a bond may, at the option of the purchaser, be included in the price on which the yield is computed.

Bond Prices and Maturity Dates

The price of bonds selling at a premium or a discount approaches the face value as the maturity date approaches, if it appears probable that they will be paid. Likewise, if a bond is presently selling above its call price, it will go down in price to the call price as that date approaches. In fact, if the call date is somewhat close, the bond will probably not rise above the call price.

Bond Prices and Interest Rates

The rate of interest which a corporation must pay on its bonds is determined chiefly by the credit rating of the particular company, the maturity of the bonds, and the supply and demand for money at the particular time. The condition of the money market is expressed in the rates of interest prevailing at the time. Although the market interest rates for short-term commercial loans and long-term investment loans tend to move together, the short-term rates follow the business cycle more closely and go to greater extremes in both directions than do the long-term investment rates.

When interest rates in general are high, people want to continue to get the relatively high rate for a long time, so they compete with each other for long-term bonds. This forces the price up and the yield down. If an individual purchased his bond sometime in the past at par, for example, his yield remains the same, of course, regardless of how high or low the bond price may go. In 1920, when interest rates were relatively high, two-year high-grade bonds sold on a yield basis of 9½ per cent, while thirty-year bonds sold to yield only 5¼ per cent. But in 1940, when interest rates were relatively low, the yield on two-year bonds had fallen to about 1 per cent, while that on thirty-year bonds had gone to only 2⅝ per cent. This results from the fact that when interest rates in general are low, investors do not want to tie up their money for long periods, so they demand short-term obligations. This forces the price up, and thus the yield is forced down. By 1960 interest rates had gone up to the point where there was little difference between the yield on long-term and short-term bonds. By 1965 a similar situation existed, with long-term interest rates only slightly higher than short-term rates. The investor is more interested in the long-term investment rate on high-grade bonds than the short-term rates.

Although yields on long-term bonds are relatively more stable than on short-term obligations, the price fluctuations in the bonds caused by changes in the market interest rates are greater. For example, an increase from 2 to 3 per cent in interest rates, which is really a 50 per cent increase, would cause a 2 per cent, two-year bond to fall from 100 to only 98.07. But if at another time, a ten-year, 2 per cent bond was selling in the market at par, an increase in the market rates from 2 to 3 per cent for this maturity would cause a drop in the price of the bond from 100 to 91.42. This is due to the fact that in buying discount bonds in the market, people will give less for the bond as the length of maturity increases, because part of the yield for each year results from the discount.

It should be observed that different times were assumed for the two examples just mentioned. This was due to the fact that two-year and ten-year bonds would probably not be selling in the market at the same time on a 2 per cent yield basis. Furthermore, an increase of one point, or an increase of 50 per cent in the market rate for two-year bonds, would probably not be accompanied by the same, or the same proportionate, increase in the market rate for ten-year bonds.

The price of bonds in the market fluctuates according to the yield demanded by investors. The face rate of two comparable bonds with similar maturities may be different, but the one bearing the higher face rate of interest may not be preferred by the investor due to the fact that its price would be so much higher than the other bond that the yield to maturity would be no greater. For example, if a 3 per cent and a 4 per cent bond with ten years to run to maturity were both bought on a 4 per cent yield basis, the 3 per cent bond would cost only 91.82, but, of course, it would be necessary to pay 100 for the 4 per cent bond.

As stated above, when bonds are bought to yield different rates than the face rate of interest, the longer the bond has to run to maturity, the greater will be the premium or discount. The following example illustrates this fact:

Maturity in Years	Price of a 3% Bond in a 4% Market	Price of a 4% Bond in a 3% Market
5	95.51	104.61
10	91.82	108.58
20	86.32	114.96
30	82.62	119.69

It is assumed in the above example that the bonds are not callable before maturity. The reader should not interpret the above figures to be the prices of different maturities of the same issue of bonds. If a 5-year maturity of a serial issue were selling in the market on a 4 per cent yield basis, it is probable that the longer maturities would not be selling on the same yield basis. The above example merely shows the different prices for the various maturities *if* they were purchased on a given yield basis.

If a person buys a bond at its face value, regardless of how much the bond fluctuates in the market, he will still get a yield equal to the face rate of interest if he holds the bond to maturity. But if the market rate of interest rises after he has purchased the bond, he has lost the opportunity to invest his money at the higher rate. The prices of high-grade bonds move in response to changes in interest rates more than do the prices of junior bonds.

If the price of a bond drops to the extent that the yield is increased, for example, from 4.50 per cent to 4.60 per cent, it is said that the yield increased 10 "basis points."

BONDS AND THE SMALL INVESTOR

Most of this chapter has been devoted to the subject of bonds. We have felt this was necessary in order that the student of personal finance would have some knowledge of this important type of security. But the typical small investor probably will find it advisable not to invest in corporate bonds. There are several reasons for this. Corporate bonds ordinarily come in denominations of not less than $1,000. The small investor does not have sufficient investable surpluses to diversify properly in this type of security. Also, the average person does not have sufficient information at hand to judge properly the safety of corporate bond issues. Furthermore, he will probably not go to the trouble of acquiring this information. When United States Government bonds can be obtained on only a slightly lower yield basis than the best corporate bonds, which has been the situation in recent years, it is suggested that if the small investor wants to purchase bonds, he confine himself to United States Government bonds. The Series E and Series H savings bonds are generally recommended since the redemption price of these bonds is fixed regardless of how high interest rates may go. It should be realized of course that bonds, even United States Government bonds, offer the investor no hedge against inflation. The interest rates remain fixed and upon maturity the investor receives only the face value of the bond.

QUESTIONS

1. (a) Do you think there is any correlation between a person's ability to earn money and his ability to invest it successfully? Explain.
   (b) Do you think that an educated person would ordinarily be a more astute investor than one who is uneducated? Why?
2. Indicate the types of investments a person should make before he buys corporate bonds or stocks.
3. (a) Indicate the importance of diversification in an investment program.
   (b) Indicate several different types of diversification. Which of these types do you think is most important to the average person?
   (c) What is meant by the statement that the people who need diversification most are the least able to get it?
   (d) With a given sum of money, can greater diversification be obtained in buying stocks or bonds?
   (e) Is greater diversification advisable when buying stock than when buying bonds?
4. (a) Indicate the qualities which should be sought in a good investment.
   (b) Do safety of principal and amount of the income vary directly or inversely? Do changes in the purchasing power of money affect the safety of the principal of an investment?
   (c) What are the different kinds of risks encountered in investing in securities?
   (d) Should people who have little money, or those who have to work hard for their money, be entitled to a higher return on their money than those who have a large amount of wealth?
5. Why is the return on a bond usually more certain than the return on a stock?
6. (a) Explain how the factor of "marketability" is of importance to an investor. Are "marketability" and "safety" synonymous?
   (b) Does listing stock have any effect on its market value?
   (c) Explain definitely why a listed stock has greater marketability than a farm.
   (d) Why do bankers prefer to lend money with listed stocks as collateral?

7. (a) What is meant by a "tax-exempt" bond?
   (b) What bonds are tax-exempt? Are United States Government bonds tax-exempt?
   (c) Should the average person buy tax-exempt bonds? Why?
8. Are long-term bonds more speculative than short-term ones?
9. Is there such a thing as a "safe" investment?
10. List the most important factors which should be considered in determining the safety of a security.
11. Explain the difference, if any, between "speculation" and "investment."
12. Explain the nature of a bond. How does it differ from a note?
13. In event of default in the payment of interest on a bond, does the principal become due? When the principal becomes due and the issuing company does not pay it, what steps can be taken by the bondholders in order to obtain payment?
14. Distinguish between the terms "indenture" and "debenture."
15. (a) What denominations do corporate bonds generally have?
    (b) Do you think that this high denomination forces many people into buying stocks when they otherwise would buy bonds?
16. Indicate the advantages and disadvantages of a registered bond as compared to a coupon bond. Which would you prefer to buy? Why?
17. (a) Explain specifically the security behind a mortgage bond.
    (b) Does a mortgage bond have a superior claim over a debenture bond on all the issuer's property?
    (c) Which gives greater value to a mortgage bond: the mortgaged property, or the general promise of the issuer to pay?
    (d) Comment on the following statement: "The safest bonds in the world today are unsecured."
18. Explain the nature of each of the following kinds of bonds:

    (a) First mortgage bonds
    (b) Senior bonds
    (c) Second mortgage bonds
    (d) Open-end bond
    (e) General mortgage bonds
    (f) Collateral trust bonds
    (g) Equipment trust obligations
    (h) Real estate mortgage bonds
    (i) Leasehold mortgage bonds
    (j) Land trust certificates
    (k) Debenture bonds
    (l) Subordinate debenture bonds
    (m) Convertible bonds
    (n) Income bonds.

19. Distinguish between open-end and closed-end mortgage bond issues. Which would you prefer to buy?
20. (a) Explain what is meant by the "after-acquired-property" clause.
    (b) Would the presence of this clause add more to an open-end or a closed-end issue of bonds? Explain.
21. (a) How do United States Treasury bonds differ from the Series E savings bonds?
    (b) Explain the features of the following kinds of United States Treasury obligations: notes, bills, and certificates of indebtedness.
22. Why are state and municipal bonds not recommended for the average investor? Why are their yields usually relatively low?
23. Indicate the minimum interest coverage on public utility, railroad, and industrial bonds in order to qualify them as investment securities. Is this the interest coverage on the particular bonds in question, or on all the bonds of the company?

24. Explain in general the systems of bond ratings used by Moody's and Standard & Poor's. Do these ratings give any indication as to whether a bond is a good buy at a particular time?
25. Explain how bonds are ordinarily quoted in the market. Are serial bonds and equipment trust obligations ordinarily quoted this way? Explain.
26. Under what circumstances should a person figure his yield on a current basis rather than to the call or maturity date?
27. In computing yields on bonds should the amount, if any, of accrued interest paid be included in the purchase price? Why or why not?
28. What is the importance of figuring yields in bond investment?
29. What effects do current interest rates have on the price of outstanding bonds? On new bond issues?
30. (a) If interest rates are relatively high, will short-term bonds sell on a higher or lower yield basis than long-term bonds? Explain.
    (b) If interest rates are relatively low, will short-term bonds sell on a higher or lower yield basis than long-term bonds? Explain.
31. If interest rates in general were to go up, what effect would this have on the price of high-grade bonds? Would the price of long-term, or short-term bonds fluctuate more? Explain.
32. Comment on the following statement: "A bondholder need not be concerned with the fluctuation on the price of his bonds because his yield remains the same."
33. Is a relatively higher yield on a bond adequate protection for the greater degree of risk?
34. Why are corporate bonds ordinarily not recommended for the average investor?

CASE PROBLEMS

1. Indicate by using the words High, Low, or None (or practically none, or not directly affected) the degree of each of the following kinds of risk as applied to United States Treasury bonds and industrial common stocks:

Kind of Risk	*United States Treasury Bonds*	*Industrial Common Stocks*
Business		
Price level		
Money rate		
Market		

   Assuming that you confine your investment to the particular type of securities stated, indicate how you might go about providing a hedge, or partial hedge, against the particular kind of risk.
2. P. J. Morgan, who has a sizable amount invested in common stocks, has decided to invest in corporate bonds as a means of securing a hedge against deflation. He is considering buying either Bethlehem Steel-4½s90 at the quoted offer of 99½, or Philip Morris 4⅞s79 at 100. Expressed in dollars, how much would he have to pay for each of these bonds? When do they mature? Which bond yields more? Judging from the yield and maturity date, which bond appears to be safer? What disadvantage may be experienced in buying a bond which does not mature until 1990?

Could he secure a better deflation hedge in another type of bond? Explain.

3. Assume that you purchased a 4½ per cent debenture bond of The Industrial Corporation for $1,020. (Face value of bond is $1,000.) This bond is convertible into the common stock of the company at any time at $20 per share. When you purchased the bond the stock was selling for $14 a share.
   (a) If you converted immediately how much would you lose?
   (b) If the price of the bond remained constant, to what price would the stock have to go in order that you would merely break even by converting?
   (c) If the stock should go to $28 a share what would be the convertible value of the bond? Do you think its actual market price would be this amount, or would it be higher or lower than its conversion value? Why?
   (d) If the bond was selling for $1,600, what would be the "break-even" price of the stock? Do you think the actual market price of the stock would be this figure, or higher or lower than that amount? Why?
4. ABC Company 3s, which mature in ten years, closed last night at 78. Guy Webster is thinking of purchasing a $1,000 bond in this company but feels that 3 per cent is too low a return. His broker tells him that the return is greater than 3 per cent and that this bond has a satisfactory yield consistent with the risk involved. What is meant by yield? How could the bond give a greater return than 3 per cent when it was a 3 per cent bond? What is the yield on this security? What would happen to the yield if the price of the bond rose to 84¾? What is the price of this bond in dollars? How should Webster go about determining whether the yield is satisfactory in comparison with the risk involved?
5. Lew Henry purchased "regular way" on the New York Stock Exchange an ordinary 4 per cent corporate bond on November 12 at the quoted price of 102¼. Interest on this bond is paid June 15 and December 15, and the interest is not in default. How else could Henry purchase this bond besides "regular way"? Compute the exact amount in dollars and cents that he would have to pay for this bond. What would it mean if this bond had been quoted "flat"? Under what circumstances are bonds generally quoted flat?
6. Harry Burke is considering the purchase of a twenty-year, 4 per cent corporate bond for $1,100 (interest has just been paid). Compute the current yield on this bond. Compute approximate yield to maturity without the use of bond tables. Compute the actual yield to maturity. If Burke were paying a price that yielded 3.425 per cent to maturity, how much would the bond cost in dollars? If this bond were callable in ten years, would it change your yield computations? If so, how?
7. Mr. Alright and Mr. Brady are both considering the relative merits of purchasing a tax-exempt state bond that yields 3 per cent to maturity and a taxable United States Government bond which yields 4¼ per cent to maturity. After subtracting deductions and exemptions, Mr. Alright has a taxable annual income of $7,000 (top tax rate is 19 per cent), and Mr. Brady a taxable annual income of $26,000 (top tax rate is 36 per cent). On a yield basis only, which bond would you recommend for Mr. Alright? For Mr. Brady? Why? Would you take any other factors into consideration in your decision? Explain.

SELECTED READINGS

Amling, Frederick. *Investments: An Introduction to Analysis and Management.* Englewood Cliffs, N. J.: Prentice-Hall, Inc., 1965.

Badger, Ralph E., Torgerson, Harold W., and Guthmann, Harry G. *Investment Principles and Practices,* Fifth Edition. Englewood Cliffs, N. J.: Prentice-Hall, Inc., 1961.

Ball, Richard E. (ed.) *Readings in Investments.* Boston: Allyn and Bacon, Inc., 1965.

Barnes, Leo. *Your Investments.* Larchmont, N. Y.: American Research Council. Latest edition.

Bellemore, Douglas H. *Investments: Principles and Practice,* Second Edition. New York: Simmons-Boardman Publishing Corp., 1960.

Bogen, Jules I. (ed.). *Financial Handbook,* Fourth Edition. New York: The Ronald Press Co., 1964. Sections 7, 11, 14, 27.

Clendenin, John C. *Introduction to Investments,* Fourth Edition. New York: McGraw-Hill Book Co., 1964.

Dowrie, George W., Fuller, Douglas R., and Calkins, Francis J. *Investments,* Third Edition. New York: John Wiley & Sons, Inc., 1961.

Fredrikson, E. Bruce (ed.). *Frontiers of Investment Analysis.* Scranton, Pa.: International Textbook Co., 1965.

Freund, William C., and Lee, Murray G. *Investment Fundamentals.* New York: American Bankers Association, 1962.

Graham, Benjamin. *The Intelligent Investor,* Third Revised Edition. New York: Harper & Row, 1965.

———, Dodd, David L., and Cottle, Sidney. *Security Analysis: Principles and Techniques,* Fourth Edition. New York: McGraw-Hill Book Co., 1962.

Hayes, Douglas A. *Investments: Analysis and Management.* New York: The Macmillan Co., 1961.

Jordan, David F., and Dougall, Herbert E. *Investments,* Seventh Edition. Englewood Cliffs, N. J.: Prentice-Hall, Inc., 1960.

Plum, Lester V., Humphrey, Joseph H., and Bowyer, John W. *Investment Analysis and Management,* Revised Edition. Homewood, Ill.: Richard D. Irwin, Inc., 1961.

Sauvain, Harry. *Investment Management, Second Edition.* Englewood Cliffs, N. J.: Prentice-Hall, Inc., 1959.

Securities of the United States. New York: The First Boston Corp. Latest edition.

Wu, H. K., and Zakon, A. J. *Elements of Investments: Selected Readings.* New York: Holt, Rinehart and Winston, Inc., 1965.

12

Buying Stocks

Most male adults in the United States have savings accounts of one kind or another and carry some form of life insurance. Also, the majority of them either own or have a substantial equity in their homes. Many own United States savings bonds. These are, of course, the types of investments that should be made first. But there is another form of investment that should be considered by people with sufficient capital and earning power—stocks. To the well-informed, prudent investor, stocks (often called *equities*) offer an attractive medium for investment.

The statement is often made that more people lose money than make money in stocks. Perhaps that is true. The reasons are not difficult to find. In the first place, the typical person does not have sufficient capital to invest in this medium. Stock prices will continue to fluctuate in the future. If the stock buyer does not have sufficient capital or earning power, he may be forced to liquidate his securities at a time when stock prices are relatively low. Furthermore, the average person is not temperamentally suited to buy stocks. Many people just cannot stand to see the price of their stocks decline. Such declines at one time or another are almost inevitable. When the first major decline comes some investors will dump their stock on the market—commonly at a loss. For these two reasons alone the typical person is probably doomed to failure when it comes to buying stocks.

Even if the investor does not fall into one of the two classes just mentioned, he may lose money because of other factors. The typical person does not know enough about the various industries and the companies within these industries to select the "right" stocks. Security analysts, advisory services, and others, however, have developed various techniques which aid materially in the selection of stocks. It is hoped that the reader will be able to improve his own ability in this respect from what is said in this chapter and in the three succeeding chapters.

Even if a "good" stock is bought, it may be bought at the wrong time. Timing is important in security buying, and particularly so in connection with speculation. No one knows what the future course of the market—either short run or long run—will be. The so-called experts are often wrong in their predictions. But judging from the past it is apparent that if the "proper" stocks are bought, the long-term secular trend in the price of the stock may bail out the investor even if he purchased the stock at what was at the time a relatively high price. Certain techniques, such as dollar averaging (see pages 483–484), have been developed to prevent the investor from tying up too large an amount in stocks at relatively high prices.

The final problem—and a common pitfall—for the stock buyer is the determination of the proper time to sell. Perhaps this is the most difficult one to solve. Much money can be lost if good investment securities purchased at the right time are sold at the wrong time. One way of solving the problem is to attempt to buy stocks that will continue to be good investments in the indefinite future—then the decision in regard to selling will not have to arise. This, of course, is more difficult to do than to say. Many people who have been in and out of the stock market for many years have realized that in many instances, perhaps most instances, they would have been better off today if they had continued to hold their stocks rather than follow the practice of trading in the stocks.

Some persons have been able to build up sizable estates through the purchase of common stocks. The stocks of well-managed growth companies have paid large dividends over a long period of years, and the prices of many of them have advanced greatly. It is probable that the stocks of well-managed growth companies that carry on extensive research will continue to advance in the future as the population increases and new products and techniques are developed. The average person should confine his program to investment rather than speculation. Attempting to buy and sell for quick-turn profits will probably prove to be disastrous. Successful investment in stocks can be enjoyed by those who select a well-diversified list of the more promising common stocks, and who hold on to them for a long period of time, such as ten or twenty years. Good stocks may be purchased with the intention of never selling them (except under unusual circumstances). They can be an important part of an estate left to a family upon the death of the investor. During and since World War II there has been a prolonged period of inflation. A well-executed program of common stock investments has proved, for many people, to be a good hedge against such inflation.

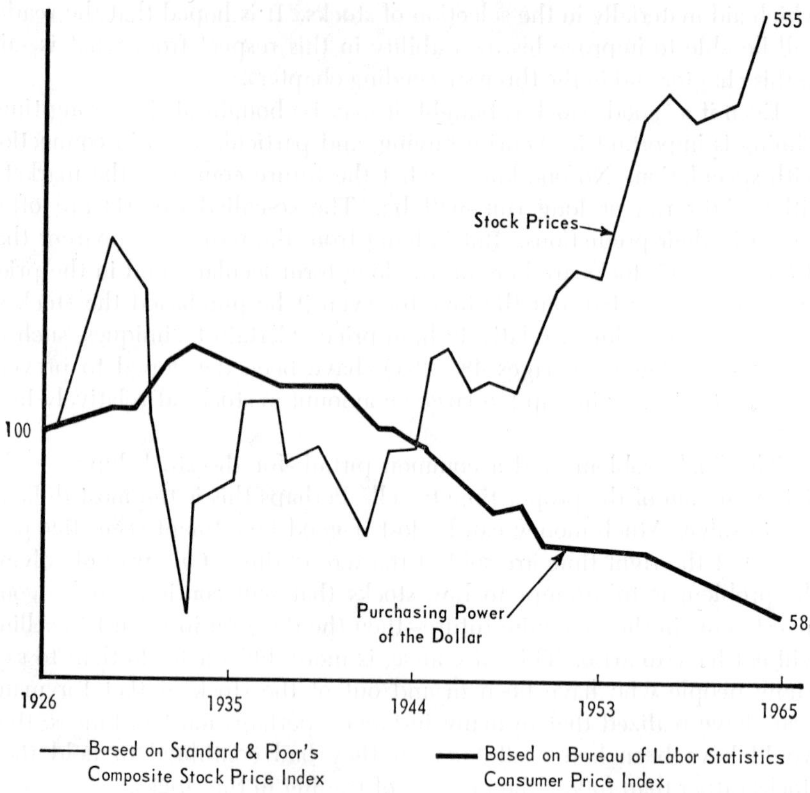

Fig. 12–1. How investing in common stocks can help protect the purchasing power of the dollar. (Reproduced with permission, from *Monthly Investment Plan.* New York: Merrill Lynch, Pierce, Fenner & Smith Inc.)

Figure 12–1 shows that the purchasing power of a dollar in 1926 had declined to only 58 cents in 1965, but during this time the price of stocks, as measured by the Standard & Poor's Composite Stock Price Index, increased from $1.00 to $5.55. Thus, the increase in stock prices was much greater than the decline in the purchasing power of the dollar.

Who Owns the Stock?

According to the latest study by the New York Stock Exchange,[1] in 1965 there were 20,120,000 people in the United States who owned stock in publicly held corporations. This represented an increase of 18 per cent over the 1962 figure, and more than three times the number of shareowners in 1952. The 1952 study showed that only one adult in each sixteen owned stock, but by 1962 this had increased to one in each six adults

[1] *1965 Census of Shareowners* (New York: The New York Stock Exchange, 1965).

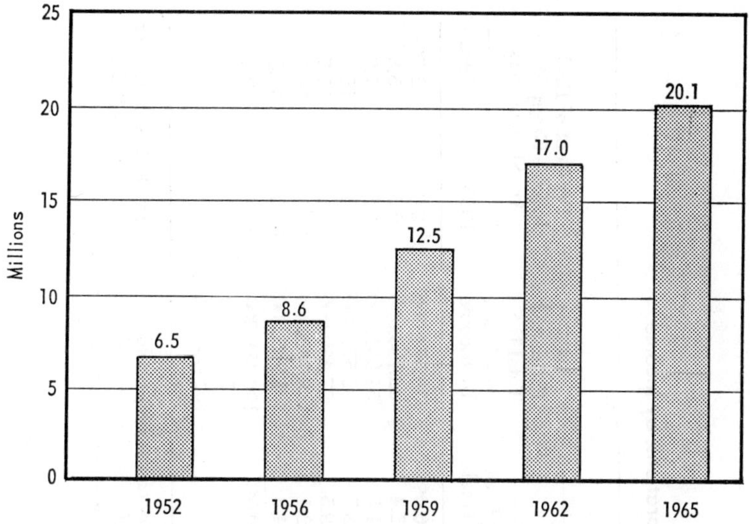

Fig. 12–2. Number of shareowners in publicly owned companies. (Reproduced with permission, from *The Exchange*. New York: The New York Stock Exchange, July, 1965.)

—and the same proportion prevailed in 1965. Figure 12–2 shows the increase in shareowners from 1952 to 1965.

The 1965 study showed that women slightly outnumber men as shareholders—51 per cent to 49 per cent. (This proportion has not changed much since 1952.) This has resulted from several factors. A wife who is the same age as her husband will on the average outlive her husband by about five years. Furthermore, men commonly marry women younger than themselves. So, the usual thing is for a wife to inherit her husband's estate. Some men carry much of their personal property in their wife's name in order to escape possible loss of the property from action on the part of their business creditors. Wealthy men often transfer part of their stock holdings to their wives in order to escape the heavy federal estate taxes (this is discussed in Chapter 19). Many husbands have transferred some of their stock to their wives in order to gain an added $100 dividend exclusion for federal income tax purposes (this is discussed in Chapter 16). An increasing number of working wives are also now investing part of their savings in stocks. In terms of the number of shares held, however, men own approximately 33 per cent more stock than women.

Table 12–1 breaks down the number of shareholders in 1965 and 1962 according to income groups. It is interesting to note that 54½ per cent of all shareholders in the United States had family incomes of less than $10,000 in 1965.

Table 12–1. Total Shareowners of Public Corporations, by Income

Reported Household Income *	Individual Shareowners 1965 Number	Individual Shareowners 1965 Per Cent of Total	Individual Shareowners 1962 Number	Individual Shareowners 1962 Per Cent of Total	1965 Estimated Total U.S. Population by Income	Per Cent of Each Income Group Who Are Shareowners 1965	Per Cent of Each Income Group Who Are Shareowners 1962
Under $3,000	1,087,000	5.5%	1,002,000	6.0%	36,574,000	3.0%	2.5%
$3,000–$5,000	2,096,000	10.6	2,072,000	12.4	32,193,000	6.5	5.8
$5,000–$7,500	3,223,000	16.3	3,592,000	21.5	51,051,000	6.3	7.9
$7,500–$10,000	4,369,000	22.1	3,959,000	23.7	32,573,000	13.4	12.6
$10,000–$15,000	5,199,000	26.3	3,258,000	19.5	27,430,000	19.0	17.7
$15,000–$25,000	2,649,000	13.4	2,021,000	12.1	8,762,000	30.2	39.3
$25,000 and over	1,147,000	5.8	802,000	4.8	1,905,000	60.2	45.3
Subtotal	19,770,000	100.0%	16,706,000	100.0%	190,488,000	10.4	9.4
Not classified by income	350,000		304,000		7,012,000		
Total	20,120,000		17,010,000		197,500,000		

* "Household Income" is the total combined income before taxes of all members of the household. If, for example, a shareowner had $8,000 income and a non-shareowner member of the same household had $4,000, the shareowner's household income is $12,000. On the other hand, if both are shareowners, each is considered to have $12,000 household income.

SOURCE: *1965 Census of Shareowners,* The New York Stock Exchange, 1965.

Table 12–2. Adult Shareowners of Public Corporations, by Education

Last Year of School Completed	Individual Shareowners 1965 Number	1965 Per Cent of Total	1962 Number	1962 Per Cent of Total	1965 Estimated Total U.S. Population by Education	Per Cent of Each Education Group Who Are Shareowners 1965	1962
3 years high school or less	3,106,000	16.8%	3,007,000	18.5%	55,375,000	5.6%	5.2%
4 years high school	5,344,000	28.9	4,828,000	29.7	35,198,000	15.2	15.8
1 to 3 years college	4,012,000	21.7	3,284,000	20.2	11,322,000	35.4	34.2
4 years college or more	6,028,000	32.6	5,137,000	31.6	10,200,000	59.1	60.9
Subtotal	18,490,000	100.0%	16,256,000	100.0%	112,095,000	16.5	15.3
Minors	1,280,000		450,000		78,393,000		
Others not classified by education	350,000		304,000		7,012,000		
Total	20,120,000		17,010,000		197,500,000		

SOURCE: *1965 Census of Shareowners,* The New York Stock Exchange, 1965.

Table 12–3. Adult Shareowners of Public Corporations, by Occupation

	Individual Shareowners						
	1965		1962		1965 Estimated Total U.S. Population by Occupation	Per Cent of Each Occupation Group Who Are Shareowners	
Occupation	Number	Per Cent of Total	Number	Per Cent of Total		1965	1962
Professional and technical	3,136,000	17.0%	2,682,000	16.5%	8,393,000	37.4%	35.9%
Clerical and sales	2,903,000	15.7	2,959,000	18.2	13,300,000	21.8%	23.3%
Managers, officials, and proprietors	2,330,000	12.6	2,276,000	14.0	7,490,000	31.1%	32.3%
Craftsmen and foremen	924,000	5.0	927,000	5.7	8,845,000	10.4%	10.6%
Operatives and laborers	647,000	3.5	439,000	2.7	14,915,000	4.3%	2.9%
Service workers	414,000	2.2	423,000	2.6	7,876,000	5.3%	5.6%
Farmers and farm laborers	64,000	0.3	65,000	0.4	3,748,000	1.7%	1.4%
Housewives and non-employed adult females	6,416,000	34.7	5,462,000	33.6	37,440,000	17.1%	15.1%
Non-employed adult males (including retired persons)	1,656,000	9.0	1,023,000	6.3	10,088,000	16.4%	14.7%
Subtotal	18,490,000	100.0%	16,256,000	100.0%	112,095,000	16.5%	15.2%
Minors	1,280,000		450,000		78,393,000		
Others not classified by occupation	350,000		304,000		7,012,000		
Total	20,120,000		17,010,000		197,500,000		

SOURCE: *1965 Census of Shareowners,* The New York Stock Exchange, 1965.

Table 12–2 shows the number of shareholders in 1965 classified according to education. Although college graduates comprise slightly less than 10 per cent of the adult population, it is noted that they make up 32.6 per cent of the total shareowners in the United States.

As was true of previous surveys, the 1965 study showed that as far as occupations of shareowners are concerned, housewives still are at the head of the list. Table 12–3 shows that housewives and non-employed adult females comprise approximately 35 per cent of the total number of adult shareowners. But it is also to be noted that they also make up about 35 per cent of the adult population.

The New York Stock Exchange studies referred to above included only those large corporations whose stock is held by the public. It must be realized that many people, although they may not own any stock of these large companies, do hold stock in privately owned companies. In addition, there are millions of people in the United States who are indirect shareowners in that they are investors in pension funds, trust funds, and other financial corporations, which in turn own corporate shares.

WHAT STOCK IS

Stock represents ownership in a corporation. When a business incorporates, the owners receive stock to represent their equity in the company. This stock is divided up into units, or *shares*. A stock *certificate* is given to represent the number of shares held. The certificate may be made out for one share or a number of shares. Where a large number of shares is acquired by one person, the certificates are commonly made out for 100 shares each. These certificates are not the stock. They are merely evidence of the stock ownership. Should the certificate be lost or destroyed, a new one can be obtained. The owner's name appears on the stock certificate and is recorded on the stock books of the issuing corporation. A specimen of a stock certificate is shown in Fig. 12–3.

Stocks and Bonds Contrasted

It was pointed out in the previous chapter that bonds represent debts of the corporation. The bondholder is a creditor. Legally the corporation must pay the bondholder interest on the date due, and the principal amount of the loan at its maturity. If these are not paid when due, legal steps can be taken to force their payment. The obligation to pay is not contingent upon earnings.

Stocks are quite different from bonds. When a person buys stocks, he does not lend the corporation anything—he merely buys a part ownership in the business. The amount he pays will not be paid back to him by the corporation—it never comes due. (Many preferred stocks, however, are callable by the issuing corporation.) There also is no obligation on the part of the corporation to pay him dividends. In fact, the law will not permit the payment of dividends unless there is a profit or surplus of sufficient amount.

If there are profits, it does not follow that the stockholder will receive dividends, for the board of directors must decide whether or not dividends should be paid. All expenses, including bond interest and income taxes, must be deducted from the income of the corporation before arriving at the profits available for dividends.

Par and No-Par Stock

Formerly, all stocks had a par or nominal value which was usually $100 per share. Later the laws were amended to permit lower per share par values. Today, par values of $1, $5, $10, and $25 are the most popular. This par value is stated on the stock certificate, and the aggregate of the par values of the total shares of the corporation is the amount which is shown as the capital stock of the corporation in the balance sheet. If a person buys par value stock directly from the issuing corporation and does not pay the full par value, he may be made to stand the difference be-

Fig. 12–3. Specimen of a stock certificate of the American Telephone and Telegraph Company.

tween what he paid and the par value of the stock in the event that the corporation cannot meet the claims of its creditors.

If a corporation's stock is selling in the market for less than its par value and the corporation wants to sell additional stock, people will naturally not pay par for the new stock when they can get the old stock in the market for a lower price. In most states, except under special circumstances, a corporation could not sell the new issue as full-paid stock if it was sold below the par value. As a practical matter this means that the corporation would either not secure the money needed, or it might be forced to issue bonds at a time when this type of obligation probably should not be issued.

Another disadvantage of par value is that many people believe a par stock was originally worth par, or that it should be worth par, or that it will eventually be worth par value. If a corporation issued $1,000,000 in par stock for its properties, and half of the properties are destroyed by fire overnight, the book value of the stock is immediately reduced to $500,000. If the stock had a par value of $100 per share, the book value per share would thereby be reduced to $50 a share. To say that the stock will eventually be worth its par value is no more warranted than to say that it would eventually be worth $200 if the fire had not taken place.

It would be more practical to speak of the relationship between stock values and earnings, rather than book values of the property. If a corporation is earning such an amount as to make its stock sell at the par value, and the earnings decrease by 50 per cent, the real value of the stock would actually be only half the par value. If the earnings never go back up, there is no reason why we should expect the actual value of the stock to go back to its par value.

Because of the above-stated shortcomings of par value stock, a number of the states have, since 1912, amended their laws to permit the issuance of no-par stock. In many of the states a so-called "stated value" is given to the no-par stock either in the charter of the corporation, or it is determined from time to time by the directors. The latter method is practically always followed. If the corporation wants to sell additional stock, the directors can always place a stated value on the stock at, or even below, the existing market price. In this way there is no chance for stockholder liability after the stated value has been paid.

The stated value, however, does not appear on the stock certificate. Thus, the stockholder will not think that his stock should be worth a fixed amount, as is the case many times when par value stock is issued. The stock certificate merely states the number of shares which it represents. It is argued that the shareholder will thus look to the corporation's balance sheet or earnings statement in order to arrive at a valuation for his stock. Since a stock is worth what you can get for it, a person should look at the existing market price of the stock to determine its worth, regardless of whether it is par value or no-par value stock.

The above explanation has been given merely to indicate the difference between par and no-par stock. The average stock buyer, especially the speculator, probably does not know whether the particular stock he is buying is par or no-par. And, as a practical matter, it does not make much difference which it is. Par and no-par stock represent exactly the same thing: ownership in the corporation. The difference between the two is more a matter of form than of substance.

PREFERRED STOCK

When a corporation issues only one class of stock, it is necessarily common stock, and in practice is often called "capital stock." In order to appeal to a wider market, or for other reasons, many corporations issue a *preferred stock* in addition to their common stock. To ascertain just how this preferred stock ranks with the common, it is necessary to refer to the statutes of the state, the articles of incorporation, and the preferred stock certificate.

Types of Preferences

One right or preference which is always given preferred stock is the preference as to dividends. It should be kept in mind, however, that preferred stock is only stock, and that the preferred dividends need not be paid. They can be paid only from the surplus or earnings of the corporation, and then the declaration of the dividends is left to the discretion of the board of directors. The advantage of the preferred over the common stock is that no dividends can be paid on the common for a particular year until the dividends, at the rate stated in the contract, have been paid on the preferred. They may be paid on the preferred, however, without paying dividends on the common.

The preferred stockholder may thus reason that, if the earnings are sufficient to pay dividends to only one class of stock, he will receive the dividend while the common stockholder will go without. This, however, does not necessarily follow. If the profits are so low that dividends cannot be paid both classes of stock, the directors might decide that in view of the low earnings the total amount should be retained by the corporation.

This raises the question as to whether the dividends not paid the preferred in any one year accrue into subsequent years and must be paid before any dividends can be paid on the common. The answer depends upon whether the stock is *cumulative*. If it is cumulative, then the dividends in arrears must be paid in subsequent years before the current dividends can be paid on the common. If it is not cumulative, then no claim for dividends passed in any year can be made by the preferred. The courts hold that where a stock has been issued with a stated preferential rate of dividends, it is cumulative, unless a contrary intention is expressed.

The investor should not attach too much importance to the cumulative feature. A corporation can pay dividends only if its earnings permit, regardless of the provisions contained in the preferred stock contract. If the dividends accumulate for a number of years, the probability is that they will not be paid, or at least not paid in full. Such a situation adversely affects the credit of the corporation and the market price of its stock, and the corporation often arranges a compromise settlement with the preferred stockholders. In many instances, of course, the corporation fails and there is nothing left with which to pay the accrued dividends. Despite what has just been said, it is nevertheless to the advantage of the preferred stockholder that his stock be cumulative.

Another point of interest to the preferred stockholder is whether or not his stock participates with the common in the distribution of earnings after the preferred has received its stated rate and the common a similar or specified rate. If nothing is said in the contract on this matter, there is some difference of opinion as to whether the stock is participating. The Supreme Court of Pennsylvania has, on several occasions, very definitely held that the stock should participate equally with the common in the distribution of such dividends. But according to the weight of authority, the stock is non-participating. It should be kept in mind that we are here speaking of court interpretations in the absence of definite contractual provisions. If the contract states that the stock is participating or non-participating, that will govern.

Unless specifically stated, preferred stock does not have a preference over the common in respect to assets upon dissolution of the corporation. It is quite common in practice, however, to give the preferred a preference over the common up to the par value of the stock, or the par value and accrued dividends. In some instances, the contract specifies a premium. A higher premium may be stated for voluntary than for involuntary dissolution.

This preference should not be given much weight by the preferred stockholder. As long as the issuing company operates, the preference on dissolution never comes into play. If the company dissolves, it will probably be due to the inability of the company to meet the claims of creditors. The creditors must, of course, be paid in full before anything can be returned to the stockholders. In many instances the assets of the corporation are insufficient to meet even the creditors' claims. In the case of large corporations, particularly, reorganization rather than dissolution follows failure. The security holders are then asked to accept new securities in exchange for their stocks and bonds. It is doubtful if the preference as to assets feature gives the preferred stockholders much of an advantage in a reorganization.

Preferred stockholders have the same voting rights as the common unless the contract states otherwise. It is quite usual in practice, however, to take away the voting rights of the preferred stock, and to provide that it shall vote only if dividends are in arrears for a specified number of consecutive quarterly periods. The voting right is of little interest to the average stockholder. Even where the stockholder has the right to vote, in most instances he will either complete the proxy giving the designated officials the right to vote the stock for him, or he will not even bother to send in the proxy. The number of shares of common stock outstanding is usually much greater than the number of preferred shares, so even if the preferred stock has voting rights, the common stockholders can control the corporation. In some instances, however, each class of stock voting as a group (class voting) is entitled to select a specified number of directors. Also, occasionally one class of stock is given more than one vote per share (plural voting).

Investment Position of Preferred Stock

Preferred stock is similar in some ways to bonds and in other ways to common stock. But in final analysis we must remember that preferred stock is stock, and that it lacks the advantages of credit instruments. The principal advantage of preferred stock over common is the preference as to dividends. But the bond interest must always be paid ahead of the preferred dividends. Interest constitutes a fixed charge which legally must be paid, regardless of whether the company has any earnings. Dividends on the stock can be paid only from the earnings or surplus, and then they are paid only at the discretion of the directors. The claim of the bondholders for interest thus has greater superiority over the right of the preferred stock for dividends than has the right of the preferred over the common in respect to dividends.

Preferred stock is usually non-participating. Thus the maximum dividends which preferred stockholders may get are fixed in amount. The rate of such dividend would, however, ordinarily be larger than the rate of interest paid on bonds issued by the same company. Thus the preferred stock, when non-participating, lacks the advantage of the common in that it will not participate in any large earnings which the corporation may experience. It is because of these features that it is sometimes said that preferred stock possesses the weakness of both bonds and common stock without having the advantages of either.

The disadvantage of the fixed rate of dividends on the preferred stock arises not only from the inability of preferred stock to share in abnormal profits of the company, but also from the fact that, when prices are rising, the purchasing power of the fixed dividends declines. A similar disadvantage is, of course, suffered by the bondholder. Although the price of some preferred stocks may rise during a period of prosperity, due to the greater assurance of receiving dividends, the increase in price is usually not nearly so great as that which occurs in the price of common stocks. The prices of high-grade preferred stocks tend to follow bond prices rather than prices of common stocks.

The dividends received by a corporation on the stock of another corporation are subject to an 85 per cent credit before applying the income tax (to lessen the double taxation of the same dollar of income), but the entire amount of bond interest received by a corporation is subject to the income tax (because the corporation paying the bond interest can deduct the interest as an expense before computing its income tax). Thus with a 48 per cent corporation federal income tax, a corporation pays a tax of 48 per cent on its interest income, but a tax of only an effective 7.2 per cent on the dividends received on its preferred (and common) stock investments. This results in corporations bidding up the price of preferred stocks, as compared to bonds, and thus lowering the yield from what it otherwise would have been. Individuals, however, are not entitled to a dividend credit, so the entire dividend (less the exclusion of $100 per person) is subject to their respective tax rates. Thus, considering the existing price of a particular preferred stock (due in part to the corporate demand for it), it may, after giving effect to the degree of risk involved, not return the individual an adequate after-tax yield.

People discount the future some months ahead in buying common stocks. The price of the stock is run up so high that the dividend yield based on existing market prices of common stocks may be lower than on preferred stocks during a period of prosperity. But considering the greater appreciation in the price of the stock, the common stockholder may gain more during a period of prosperity than the preferred stockholder.

From what has been said it is apparent that the common stock of a company, and not the preferred, stands to gain from inflation. Many industrial companies, however, make their preferred stock convertible into common. The discussion on convertible bonds in Chapter 11 applies also, in general, to convertible preferred stock. The addition of the conversion feature tends to remove some of the weaknesses of preferred as compared to common stock and offers the preferred a means of hedging against inflation.

Preferred stock is often made callable by the corporation, usually at a slight premium. When this is done, the market price of the preferred will usually not go above the call price. The stock will, of course, be called when it is to the advantage of the corporation to do so, and this will ordinarily be when the preferred stockholder is more desirous of holding it.

When the corporation pays dividends on both the preferred and the common, there would be no advantage in having the preference as to dividends. The real advantage of the preferred would appear to be when the corporation can pay dividends on only one class of stock. But experience shows that when a depression occurs, many companies, perhaps a majority of them, either reduce the amount of the preferred dividend or eliminate it entirely within a year or so after they reduce or eliminate the common dividend. In these cases the preferred would not be considered very much superior to the common stock. The advantageous position of the bondholder at such times is readily apparent, unless the situation is so serious that interest on bonds also cannot be paid.

Although it is said that preferred stock occupies a position somewhere between bonds and common stocks, it is difficult to say just who should purchase it. If the investor cannot afford to assume much risk, he should buy bonds and not preferred stock. If he can take the risk and wants a chance to make large profits, he should purchase common stock rather than preferred stock.

It is difficult to generalize on any type of securities. The particular company and the time of purchase are all-important. The common stock of one company might be a safer investment than the preferred stock, or even bonds, of another company. In comparable companies the common stock of one which does not have any preferred stock or bonds outstanding might be a safer investment than the preferred stock of another company which has bonds outstanding.

The discussion above has been somewhat critical of preferred stocks, due in part to the fact that many people rate them too highly. Many preferreds are, of course, regarded as high-grade investment securities. Included in these are the following (arranged alphabetically; the dollar figure is the annual dividend):

Boston Edison	$4.25	General Motors	$3.75
Chesapeake & Ohio	$3.50	Honeywell	$3.00
Cincinnati Gas & Elec.	$4.00	Ingersoll-Rand	$6.00
Consumers Power	$4.50	Norfolk & Western Ry.	$ .60
Corning Glass Works	$3.50	Pacific Tel. and Tel.	$6.00
du Pont (E. I.) de Nemours	$4.50	Procter & Gamble	$8.00
Duquesne Light	$2.00	Standard Oil of California	$3.30
General Mills	$5.00	U. S. Gypsum	$7.00

A leading authority [2] states that the same minimum standards should be required for a company's total preferred stock as are required for its

[2] Benjamin Graham, David L. Dodd, and Sidney Cottle, *Security Analysis*, Fourth Edition. New York: McGraw-Hill Book Co., 1962, p. 384.

bonds. Interest on bonds, however, is deducted as an expense before arriving at the base on which income taxes are computed. But the taxes are figured before there is any distribution of dividends. With an income tax rate of 48 per cent, a company must earn its dividend almost twice (for simplicity's sake we will call it twice) before taxes in order to have enough left after taxes to meet the dividend requirement once. If it is accepted that an industrial company should earn its preferred dividend seven times in order for the proper margin of safety to be attained, then it should earn the dividend almost fourteen times before taxes.

If a company has bonds outstanding it would be misleading, to say the least, to consider the coverage for preferred dividends by taking the earnings figure after interest has been subtracted. All the interest must be earned before there are any earnings available for the federal government and the preferred stock. The ability of a company to pay its preferred dividend then can best be determined by the number of times it earns (before taxes) its combined interest charges plus twice its preferred dividends. From what has been said previously, it follows that the following minimum standards (approximate) be met in order to establish the proper margin of safety:

Type of Company	Times Combined Fixed Charges and Twice Preferred Dividends
Public utility	4
Railroad	5
Industrial	7

Preferred Stock Ratings

Some of the financial services assign quality ratings to the leading preferred stocks. The Standard & Poor's ratings are based primarily on

Standard & Poor's Preferred Stock Ratings

Rating	Explanation	Rating	Explanation	Rating	Explanation
AAA	Prime	BBB	Medium Grade	C	Sub-marginal
AA	High Grade	BB	Low Grade		
A	Sound	B	Speculative		

Value Line Stock Ratings

Rating	Explanation
A+ and A	Highest
A− and B+	Above Average
B	Average
B− and C+	Below Average
C and C−	Lowest

the stability of the dividend yield, but Value Line's ratings reflect mainly stability in price for the past ten years and growth of cash earnings. The ratings do not indicate whether the particular stock may be an attractive buy or sell. For example, the stock may carry a high quality rating, but it may be so overpriced in the market that its purchase would not be advised.

Standard & Poor's uses a different set of ratings for preferred stock than for common stock, but Value Line uses the same symbols for both preferred and common. Common stock ratings are discussed in Chapter 15.

OTHER TYPES OF STOCK

Guaranteed Stock

These stocks, like guaranteed bonds, are usually found in the railroad field and originate in connection with a lease. When one railroad leases the properties of another road, the former commonly guarantees the interest and dividends on the bonds and stocks of the latter company. The stock may be common or preferred, or both. Since the guaranty constitutes a fixed charge, these stocks rank equal with the debenture bonds of the guaranteeing company with respect to the income. The value of the property of the issuing company is also of importance because, if it constitutes an important part of the lessor's system, the guaranty will be more highly regarded. Because of the greater safety, the yield on the better guaranteed stocks is low.

Various Classes of Stock

Some corporations issue more than one class of preferred stock. They may issue a *first preferred* and a *second preferred.* The former has a preference over the latter in respect to dividends. The rate of dividends is usually different. Sometimes the term *prior preferred stock* is used instead of first preferred. Several companies have issued *debenture stock,* which is given a preference over the preferred stock in respect to dividends. The term *debenture stock* is commonly used in England to refer to a bond, and in some instances it is used in this country to apply to a bond issued by a state or municipality. It should be kept in mind that the term *debenture* as ordinarily used in this country refers to a bond which is not secured by the pledge of specific property.

Some corporations have issued *Class A* and *Class B* common stock. The Class A is usually non-voting, and may or may not have a preference over Class B in respect to dividends. It may or may not participate with the Class B in the distribution of dividends in excess of the stated rate. Classified preferred stock is also issued.

Treasury Stock

Stock which has once been issued by a corporation and then reacquired by it, either through purchase or gift, and is not canceled is called *treasury stock.* Treasury stock may also be acquired by a corporation through forfeiture from stockholders for payment of amounts due on the stock and through purchase from individual stockholders or on the open market. It may be either common or preferred, but is usually common stock.

COMMON STOCK

The nature of common stock was more or less explained at the beginning of the chapter, and when preferred and common stock were contrasted. The common stockholders are sometimes called the residual owners of the business. That is, upon dissolution of the company, they would get what is left, if anything, after all the creditors and preferred stockholders (assuming they have a preference as to assets) have been paid in full. As a practical matter, when a corporation reaches the stage of dissolution there is usually nothing left for the common stockholders—and often nothing for the preferred stockholders either.

Since the preferred stock is often non-participating, non-cumulative, or non-voting, the common stock in particular instances may really be the "preferred" stock to buy. There is some chance that the stockholder will lose regardless of whether he buys preferred or common stock. The possibility that the preferred stock of a particular company may be a good investment, and the common stock a poor investment, is very remote. If the preferred stock proves to be a good investment, probably the common would be as good as, or even better than the preferred. With common stock, the investor takes a chance on reaping large rewards in those instances when the company is outstandingly successful.

Nature of Common Stock Investment

The worth of common stock is more difficult to determine than the value of bonds or preferred stock. It is likewise more difficult to measure the degree of risk involved in purchasing common stock as compared to buying bonds or preferred stocks.

After the corporation has deducted all expenses from the earnings, and paid the bond interest, income taxes, and preferred dividends, the amount left is considered the earnings on the common stock. This amount, when divided by the total number of shares of common outstanding, gives the *earnings per share* on the common stock. The earnings per share is a significant figure. It should be immediately noted that the earnings per share is not what the stockholder gets in dividends, but it is from these earnings that dividends on the common are paid.

Since the common stockholders are the residual owners in the business, all of the earnings on the common are considered the property of the common stockholders, regardless of whether or not they are paid out to them in the form of dividends. Thus, if a corporation earns \$6 per share on its common in a particular year, but pays out only \$4 per share in dividends, the undistributed earnings of \$2 per share is considered to be the common stockholders' property. By retaining part of the current earnings, the corporation may be able to increase its earnings. Also, the retained earnings may make it possible for the company to pay dividends on the common stock in some subsequent year when earnings may be small or nil. As a practical matter, however, the undistributed earnings will probably be invested in fixed property and will be unavailable for the payment of dividends in subsequent years. Experience has shown that most corporations reduce or eliminate the dividends on their common stock soon after their earnings decline, regardless of how much of the stockholders' earnings had been retained in previous years.

It should be appreciated, however, that the undistributed portion of the earnings is reinvested in property which in all probability will make the future earnings larger than they would have been, had all the earnings been paid out in the form of dividends. The common stockholders may thus get larger dividends in the future. If the corporation can make a larger return on the money than the stockholder can through another investment possessing a comparable degree of risk, in the long run the stockholder may be further ahead if the corporation retains part of his earnings. And if the corporation cannot make more on his money than the investor can, probably he should sell his stock and reinvest the money.

The common stockholder need not wait for future dividends in order to profit from the corporation's retaining part of his earnings. If part of the profit is not distributed in the form of dividends, the price of the common may advance because of the greater equity behind it. This has been particularly true in the past with new companies which have proved successful.

Common stockholders stand to gain more during a period of prosperity than do bondholders or preferred stockholders for two reasons: (1) the value of property increases during a period of prosperity, and since common stock represents ownership of this property, the value of the stock increases, and (2) profits are larger at this time and therefore dividends are usually increased. The latter point should be given much more weight than the first. In contrast to the position of the common stockholder, the bondholder may actually suffer during a period of prosperity. The interest which he gets is fixed in amount, and as prices rise, purchasing power of this fixed income declines. Also, interest rates usually advance during a prosperous period. For these reasons the price of high-grade bonds usually goes down during a period of prosperity.

The purchasing power of the common stockholder's dollar, of course, also declines, but since he gets larger dividends and the price of his stock advances, his gain usually more than offsets the decline in the purchasing power of the dollar. Preferred stockholders suffer from the fixed income in a manner similar to bondholders, but, because of the greater assurance of dividend payments, the price of preferred stock will usually advance with the common, although it will not go as high.

In a period of depression, just the reverse of the above will be true. The position of the holder of high-grade bonds may actually improve, while the common stockholder will suffer a reduction or loss of his dividends and a drastic decline in the price of his stock. During the course of the business cycle, the price and income of bonds are the most stable of all types of securities, preferred stocks less so, while the price and income of common stock are subject to the most violent fluctuations. Good common stocks, we repeat, offer a hedge against inflation, while good bonds provide a hedge against deflation.

DIVIDENDS

Dividends on stock may be paid only from the earnings of the company or from its surplus. Companies with a steady record of dividend payments will sometimes pay dividends from the accumulated earnings of the past when they have no current earnings. When there are current earnings the shareholders cannot ordinarily compel the directors to declare dividends. In the older, well-established, successful companies, shareholders can expect to be paid cash dividends quarterly. But the rate of dividends may vary according to the amount of the earnings. Some companies follow a practice of paying out approximately 50 per cent of the earnings in dividends and reinvesting the balance in the business. For the typical successful company, the pay-out ratio approximates 60 per cent. Some companies have more or less established by practice a fixed rate of dividends per share, although the fixed rate may be increased as future earnings increase. A company may pay a "regular" dividend for the first three quarters of the year and then in the fourth quarter, after the earnings for the full year have been established, it may pay an "extra" dividend in addition to the regular.

Who Gets the Dividend?

The procedure of paying dividends is as follows: The directors meet, for example, on January 25, and declare dividends to shareholders of record February 10, with the dividend payable on February 25. When stock is bought or sold near the record date the question often arises in the minds of the parties concerned as to whether the buyer or the seller gets the particular dividend. The rule established for this grows out of the rule relating to delivery on the stock. The New York Stock Exchange rules provide that all stock sold *regular way* shall be *delivered* on the fourth day (business day) following day of sale. Thus stock sold regular way on Monday will be delivered on Friday. Let us assume that the record date of February 10 is Friday. Since a person buying the stock on the preceding Monday is entitled to delivery of stock on Friday, he should be entitled to the dividend. Thus, stock purchased (or sold) on Monday would be said to be selling *dividend-on*, or *cum-dividends*. But if a person bought the stock on the following day—Tuesday—he would not get delivery until the following Monday, so he would not be entitled to the dividend. Tuesday morning, therefore, the stock will open *ex-dividends*, or as it will be marked in the stock quotation sheet of the newspaper, "xd." The Tuesday seller of the stock will therefore get the dividend since he is a stockholder of record on Friday—the record date.

Referring to the hypothetical example above, it would make little difference to the buyer or the seller whether the sale took place on Monday or on Tuesday. Stocks sell "flat." This means that any accrual or anticipation of the dividend is reflected in the quoted price of the stock. Let us assume that during a particular period a stock, which pays a quarterly dividend of $1.50, tends to sell ex-dividends at $100 a share. During the next three months (if the market on the stock otherwise remains about the same) the price of the stock would tend to work up to $101.50 a share because of the dividend expected or declared on the stock. Using the above example the buyer would have to pay $101.50 (the cum-dividend price) for the stock on Monday, but he will collect (really from his broker) the dividend paid on the stock for the preceding three-month period. The seller does not get the dividend that was earned on his money for this period, but he gets reimbursed for the dividend in the price received from the stock. If the sale took place on Tuesday, the seller would be sent the dividend, so he would be willing to sell the stock ex-dividends at $100. If the directors take a different dividend action than was anticipated, then the price of the stock would abruptly reflect this action.

Yield

The *yield* on a stock, which is expressed in percentage, is found by dividing the annual dividend (expressed in dollars) by the price of the stock. The *current yield* is found by dividing the current market price of the stock by the dividends paid during the past year (past four quarters). If, however, the regular dividend has been changed during the year, the new dividend figure is used.

Since stock prices usually reflect or discount the amount of the expected dividend for the current year (and even some years in the future), if the amount of the dividend during the current (or even the next) year can be estimated with a fair degree of accuracy, [illegible]haps this should be used instead of the dividends for the past four [illegible]s.

The *actual yield* that a person gets on h[illegible]k is, of course, determined by dividing the *cost* of the stock into [illegible] current dividend. Thus, fluctuations in the price of the stock (as[illegible] that the dividend rate is not changed) do not affect his actual [illegible] but emphasizing actual yield can be misleading and may result [illegible] shareholder's missing out on improving his income position.

Assume that you bought Sto[illegible]k [illegible]or $50 a share. It pays an annual dividend of $3. Your yield is [illegible]ent. Over a period of time the price of the stock advances to $1[illegible]0 [illegible]ause the investing public is expecting increased future earnings [illegible] B, which pays a dividend of $4 is now selling in the market a[illegible] You believe that Stock B offers the same prospects for increase[illegible]ngs, etc., as Stock A (which may not be the opinion of other pe[illegible]ce Stock B is selling on a higher current yield basis), and that [illegible] it is as safe an investment as Stock A. But you hesitate to sell y[illegible]ock A and buy Stock B because you say that Stock A is yielding you 6 per cent on your money, whereas Stock B would yield only 4 per cent. But it is apparent that if you made the switch your annual income would be increased from $3 to $4, which is actually an increase of 33⅓ per cent. So, in comparing investment opportunities it would be better for you to use the current yield basis of 3 per cent for your Stock A, rather than the actual yield of 6 per cent.[3]

[3] In this example we have ignored the capital gains tax that may have to be paid if Stock A is sold. The amount of such tax would reduce the amount that you could invest in Stock B. But you still would be ahead by making the switch. Assume that Stock A had been held for more than six months and that your top income tax rate is, for example, 19 per cent. You would report half of the $50 gain, or $25, and this would be taxed at the rate of 19 per cent, or a tax of $4.75. Subtracting the latter from $100.00 leaves $95.25 that could be invested in Stock B. Dividends of 4 per cent of this would be $3.81, which is 27 per cent more than your $3 dividend. Even if you paid the maximum tax of 25 per cent on your long-term gain of $50, it would take only $12.50. This would leave $87.50 to be invested in Stock B at 4 per cent—

It is often said that the yield or return on an investment varies inversely with the degree of safety involved. That is, the safer the investment, the lower the yield. But for high-grade stocks particularly, it often does not turn out this way, especially in the short run. Despite the fact that bonds are a safer investment than stocks, and therefore they should yield less than stocks, during most of the time since 1958 the yield on high-grade stocks (as measured by recognized indexes) has actually been lower than on high-grade bonds. Several factors account for this.

Many people believe that inflation is a factor that must be taken into consideration in their investment program. Good common stocks have in the past provided a fairly good hedge against inflation, and it is thought that they will continue to do so. So investors are buying, and thus bidding up the price, of common stocks with the result that the current yield is relatively low.

Since the shareholders are the owners of a corporation, they stand to gain not only with respect to the dividend paid, but also with respect to the profits which are retained in the business. But the retained earnings are not immediately reflected in the yield of a stock.

People buy stocks not because of the dividend being paid currently, but rather in anticipation of larger dividends that may be paid in the future. Hence the current yield may be relatively low.

With the favored tax treatment accorded capital gains (gains realized from appreciation in the price of the stock), and considering the relatively high tax bracket of many people, the prices of many stocks, particularly growth stocks, are run up by people who are more concerned with the possible increase in the price of the stock than they are with the current dividends being paid. Extremely low yields, or no yields at all, may not deter them in purchasing the particular stock.

In recent years, high-grade common stocks that offer a fair chance of future growth have been selling on a current yield basis of approximately 3 per cent. But on many of these stocks, people who bought them sometime in the past are enjoying an actual yield of, for example, 6, 8, or 10 per cent on their money.

From what has been said it should be obvious that yields are only one factor to be considered in buying common stocks. Rather than deterring people from buying a stock, a low current yield may be indicative that investors believe the earnings of the company, and possibly the dividends, will be increased in the future. It is therefore necessary to give effect to the possible appreciation in the price of the stock, along with the yield,

---

which would return you $3.50 (which is 16⅔ per cent more than you would be getting on Stock A). And by making the switch the capital gains tax that you may have to pay in the future would be less since the cost basis of your investment is now $100 (or $100 minus the taxes) and not $50.

in selecting stock investments. Conversely, a relatively high yield may make the stock unattractive since it is an indication that the investing public may be expecting that the earnings of the company are or will be declining in the future, and possibly the dividend will be reduced or even omitted. These events would probably also result in the price of the stock going still lower in the future. So, the possible loss in market value must be considered along with the yield in purchasing stocks.

Studies of Common Stock Yields

The Center for Research in Security Prices, at the University of Chicago, is carrying on, with the use of a computer, a series of studies relating to common stocks.[4] In the first release in 1963,[5] it was reported that an investment of an equal sum of money in each company having one or more common stock issues on the New York Stock Exchange showed a rate of return of 9 per cent per year for the period 1926–1960. This assumed the reinvestment of dividends *and included the gain from the appreciation in value of the stocks.* Table 12–4 shows the yield for various periods between 1926 and 1960 for tax-exempt holders and for persons in the $10,000 and $50,000 income tax brackets in 1960. The same research organization in a study released in 1965, "Outcomes for 'Random' Investment in Common Stocks Listed on the New York Stock Exchange,"[6] found that the typical—or median—rate of return (*including capital appreciation*) on a random selection and sale of common stocks on the New York Stock Exchange for the period 1926–1960 was 9.8 per cent per year.[7]

People should not get carried away with the idea of earning a relatively high rate of return on their money simply because of the results of the above studies. During most of the years covered by the studies, stock prices were rising. No one knows what the future course of stock prices

[4] The studies are being financed largely from contributions from Merrill Lynch, Pierce, Fenner & Smith, Inc., and also from the Ford Foundation and the National Science Foundation. Summaries of the studies may be obtained free from Merrill Lynch, Pierce, Fenner & Smith, Inc., New York, N. Y. 10005.

[5] Lawrence Fisher and James H. Lorie, "Rates of Return on Investments in Common Stocks."

[6] A detailed report on the study appears under this title in the April, 1965, issue of *The Journal of Business* (University of Chicago), written by Professor Lawrence Fisher, who conducted the study, and a summary of the study appears in the May 27, 1965, issue of *The Commercial and Financial Chronicle.* A reprint of the latter is available in pamphlet form from Merrill Lynch, Pierce, Fenner & Smith, Inc.

[7] This assumed the payment of a 1 per cent brokerage commission on purchases and sales, and the reinvestment of all dividends; taxes, however, were ignored. If small groups of stocks instead of a single stock were purchased, there was an even chance that the rate of return would be higher than 9.8 per cent. In making the study a computer was used to select a purchase date in any month within the twenty-five-year period, and a sales date in any subsequent month in the period. The results of the study came from more than 56 million different hypothetical common stock investments.

Table 12–4. Rates of Return on Investment in Common Stocks Listed on the New York Stock Exchange With Reinvestment of Dividends * (per cent per annum compounded annually)

	Income Class					
	Tax Exempt		$10,000 in 1960		$50,000 in 1960	
Period	Cash-to-Portfolio **	Cash-to-Cash †	Cash-to-Portfolio	Cash-to-Cash	Cash-to-Portfolio	Cash-to-Cash
1/26–12/60	9.0	9.0	8.4	8.2	7.4	6.8
1/26– 9/29	20.4	20.3	20.4	20.3	20.3	19.4
1/26– 6/32	−16.5	−16.8	−16.5	−16.8	−16.5	−13.4
1/26–12/40	2.4	2.3	2.4	2.4	2.2	2.4
1/26–12/50	6.8	6.8	6.3	6.1	5.5	5.1
9/29– 6/32	−48.4	−48.8	−48.4	−48.8	−48.2	−40.6
9/29–12/40	−3.0	− 3.1	− 3.0	− 2.9	− 3.0	− 2.3
9/29–12/50	4.9	4.8	4.3	4.1	3.5	3.2
9/29–12/60	7.7	7.7	7.0	6.8	5.9	5.4
6/32–12/40	21.3	21.1	21.2	20.8	20.8	19.5
6/32–12/50	18.6	18.6	17.8	17.5	16.5	15.5
6/32–12/60	17.4	17.3	16.5	16.2	15.0	14.1
12/50–12/52	12.5	12.0	11.1	10.0	9.0	7.1
12/50–12/54	17.9	17.6	16.6	15.3	14.4	11.6
12/50–12/56	17.0	16.8	15.8	14.8	13.7	11.4
12/50–12/58	16.5	16.4	15.4	14.6	13.4	11.4
12/50–12/60	14.8	14.7	13.8	13.1	12.0	10.3
12/55–12/56	6.4	5.4	5.7	4.6	4.0	2.8
12/55–12/57	− 3.7	− 4.2	− 4.4	− 4.0	− 6.0	− 4.2
12/55–12/58	13.0	12.6	12.2	11.1	10.5	8.2
12/55–12/59	14.0	13.7	13.3	12.2	11.6	9.2
12/55–12/60	11.2	10.9	10.5	9.6	8.9	7.2

* The data underlying this table have been exhaustively checked. Any subsequent refinement or adjustment will do no more than change an occasional figure after the decimal point.

** "Cash-to-Portfolio" means the net rate of return which would have been realized after paying commissions and taxes (if any) on each transaction but continuing to hold the portfolio at the end of each period.

† "Cash-to-Cash" means the net return which would have been realized after paying commissions and taxes (if any) on each transaction including the sale of the portfolio at the end of each period.

SOURCE: The Center for Research in Security Prices, Graduate School of Business, University of Chicago, 1963. A summary of the study is available from Merrill Lynch, Pierce, Fenner & Smith, Inc.

and yields will be. It is probable, however, that over long periods of time, stock prices will continue to advance; also, stock prices will generally advance in more individual months and years than they decline. The typical investor pays higher commission rates than were assumed in the study. Furthermore, the small investor will have to pay the odd-lot differentials, which are explained in the following chapter. The studies were based on investments of the same dollar amount when stock prices were low as when they were high, and on sales being made in months of high stock prices as well as in months of low ones. Many people do their buying only when stock prices are relatively high, and too many of them panic when stock prices drop and they sell out at a loss. The studies assumed the reinvestment of all the dividends. The typical investor must pay taxes on these returns and therefore can invest only a part of the dividends. Furthermore, the average investor does not reinvest the dividends left after taxes.

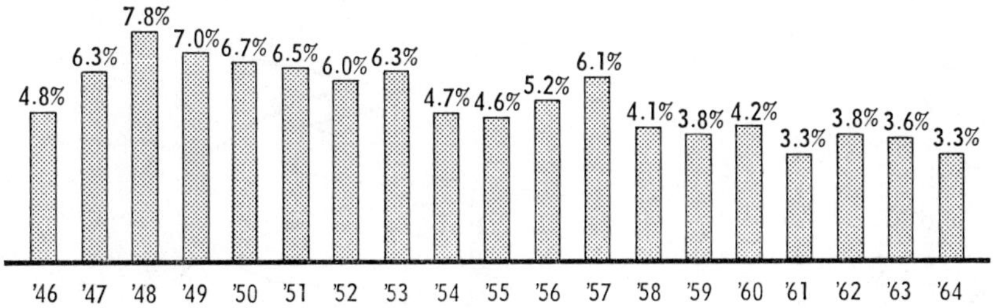

Fig. 12–4. Median yield on dividend-paying common stocks listed on the New York Stock Exchange at year end, 1946–1964. (Reproduced with permission, from *Fact Book, 1965.* New York: The New York Stock Exchange.)

Figure 12–4 shows the median yield (capital gains *not* included) on dividend-paying common stocks listed on the New York Stock Exchange at year end for the period 1946–1964. Table 12–5 shows the eight companies listed on the New York Stock Exchange which have paid dividends every year for over 100 years. The lower part of the table shows the dividend-paying record for all the common stocks listed on the Exchange.

Figure 12–5 shows the yield on common stocks from 1870 to 1965. The yields are based on the Standard & Poor's 500 common stock index (described in Chapter 15), and on the Cowles Commission Study for the period preceding the inception of the Standard & Poor's Index. Also shown on the chart is the price-earnings ratio (price of the stock divided by the annual per share earnings of the company; this ratio is further discussed in Chapter 15) for the same period.

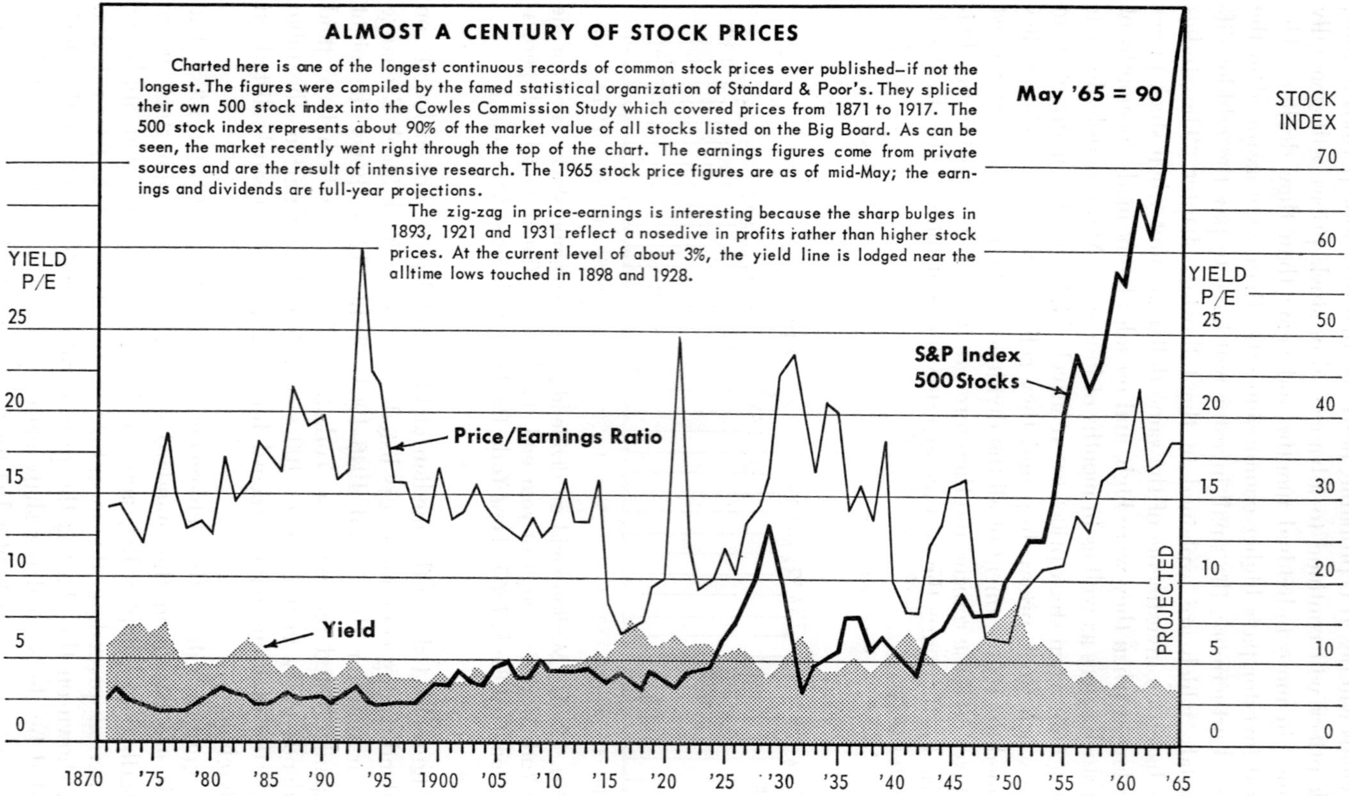
ALMOST A CENTURY OF STOCK PRICES
Charted here is one of the longest continuous records of common stock prices ever published—if not the longest. The figures were compiled by the famed statistical organization of Standard & Poor's. They spliced their own 500 stock index into the Cowles Commission Study which covered prices from 1871 to 1917. The 500 stock index represents about 90% of the market value of all stocks listed on the Big Board. As can be seen, the market recently went right through the top of the chart. The earnings figures come from private sources and are the result of intensive research. The 1965 stock price figures are as of mid-May; the earnings and dividends are full-year projections.
The zig-zag in price-earnings is interesting because the sharp bulges in 1893, 1921 and 1931 reflect a nosedive in profits rather than higher stock prices. At the current level of about 3%, the yield line is lodged near the alltime lows touched in 1898 and 1928.
May '65 = 90
STOCK INDEX
YIELD P/E
Price/Earnings Ratio
S&P Index 500 Stocks
Yield
PROJECTED
25
20
15
10
5
0
70
60
50
40
30
20
10
1870 '75 '80 '85 '90 '95 1900 '05 '10 '15 '20 '25 '30 '35 '40 '45 '50 '55 '60 '65

Fig. 12–5. Record of common stocks, 1870–1965. (Reproduced with permission, from *Investor's Reader,* June 2, 1965. Copyright 1965 by Merrill Lynch, Pierce, Fenner & Smith Inc.)

Table 12–5. Companies That Have Paid Dividends for Over a Century, and Date of First Consecutive Payment

Pennsylvania Railroad	1848
Washington Gas Light Co.	1852
Cincinnati Gas & Electric Co.	1853
Continental Insurance Co.	1853
Scovill Manufacturing Co.	1856
Pennsalt Chemicals Corp.	1863
Singer Co.	1863
American News Co.	1864

All NYSE Listed Common Stocks

Number of Consecutive Years Dividends Paid	Number of Stocks	
	Quarterly Record	Annual Record
100 or more	1	8
75 to 99	5	22
50 to 74	71	126
25 to 49	308	464
20 to 24	116	100
20 yrs. or more	501	720
10 to 19	275	195
Less than 10 *	451	312
Total	1,227	1,227

* Includes non-payers and stocks with no quarterly records.
SOURCE: New York Stock Exchange *Fact Book,* 1965.

Stock Dividends

Instead of, or in addition to, a cash dividend, a company may pay its shareholders a dividend in the stock of the same company. This, of course, is called a *stock dividend.* The stock dividend results in the capitalization of the surplus in an amount equivalent to the dividend. Let us assume that the net worth section of the balance sheet of a particular company shows the following:

Capital stock	$10,000,000	(100,000 shares of $100 par value)
Surplus	20,000,000	
Total net worth	$30,000,000	

If this company paid a 100 per cent stock dividend the above would be changed to the following:

Capital stock	$20,000,000	(200,000 shares of $100 par value)
Surplus	10,000,000	
Total net worth	$30,000,000	

It is obvious that the stock dividend does not take any money or other property out of the company and thus the total net worth remains the same. But there are now twice as many shares outstanding as formerly. Before the stock dividend was paid the book value (net asset value) of the stock was $300 per share, but after the dividend the book value per share is reduced to $150 per share—but each shareholder has two shares for each original share. Thus, the shareholder did not directly gain anything from the stock dividend. A company that has need for the retention of its earnings in the business might pacify its shareholders with a stock dividend instead of a cash dividend, or in addition to a relatively small cash dividend.

A dividend paid in stock is not taxable under the income tax laws.[8] The stock dividend reduces the cost basis of the stock for the purpose of computing the capital gains tax when the stock is sold. For instance, in the above example, if the shareholder paid $100 per share for his stock, the 100 per cent stock dividend would reduce the cost basis of his stock to $50 per share. If he subsequently sold a share for $180, he would have a capital gain of $130. The taxation of capital gains is discussed in Chapter 16.

Stock Splits

A *stock split* (or *split-up*) results in a company giving its shareholders a larger number of shares without disturbing the surplus of the company. Thus a company may effect a 2-for-1 split by exchanging two new shares for each old share (actually it will probably let the shareholder retain his old share and send him a new one). The par value per share of the stock would be reduced, but the aggregate par value of all the stock would remain the same. If the company in the hypothetical example above had a 2-for-1 split instead of a 100 per cent stock dividend, the total figures would remain the same:

Capital stock	$10,000,000	(200,000 shares of $50 par value)
Surplus	20,000,000	
Total net worth	$30,000,000	

If one new share was exchanged for each two old shares it would be referred to as a *reverse stock-split*, or a *split-down*.

The new shares received in a split are not subject to income tax. The effect of the split is to lower the cost basis of the shares in the

[8] This is because the stock dividend is not considered as income. If, however, a shareholder has the option of taking either cash or stock, the dividend is taxed even if he elects to receive the stock. A dividend paid in stock to the preferred shareholders in lieu of their cash dividend for the current or preceding year is also taxable.

computation of the capital gains tax when the stock is sold, in the same manner as was stated above for stock dividends.

Companies generally have a large stock dividend or split in order to reduce the market value per share. Generally speaking, the higher the price of a stock, the narrower the market. If a company's stock gets to $100 or $200 per share it may declare a large stock dividend or split to bring the price down to $40 or $50. This may be done particularly if the company is going to bring out a new issue of stock. The lower market price will result in an easier sale of the stock, and it may even be sold on a lower yield basis because of this. The split or stock dividend also would reduce the per-share earnings (the dividends per share may also be reduced by the company) so that it will not appear to union leaders, possible competitors, customers, and possibly the government that the company is making too much in profits.

The lower price of the stock and the wider market may result in the shareholder's experiencing an actual increase in the aggregate value of his stockholdings in the company. In some instances the dividends are not reduced in proportion to the increase in the number of shares, with the result that the yield to the shareholder on his future cash dividends may be higher.

STOCK "RIGHTS"

According to the common law and according to the statutes in many of the states, a common shareholder is entitled to subscribe to new common stock issued by his corporation before it may be offered to the public. (The statutes and charter frequently place restrictions or limitations on the pre-emptive right.) This pre-emptive right is given the shareholder in order to enable him to maintain his relative degree of control and his relative equity in the surplus of the company. Aside from legal compulsion, in many instances the sale of new stock to the old shareholders may be the best and the cheapest way to sell the stock.

Mechanics of Privileged Subscription

Sale of stock to the old shareholders is carried out under what is called a *privileged subscription.* The amount of new stock offered is always less than the amount of stock then outstanding—the ratio may be, for example, one new share for each four, eight, or ten old shares held. The subscription price is practically always less than the market price of the old stock at the time the new is offered. The board of directors will specify the date as of which stockholders of record will be entitled to subscribe to the new stock. The shareholders will be given several weeks within which to sell their rights to the stock or to subscribe to the new stock.

Computing Value of Rights

Stockholders entitled to subscribe to the new stock will receive pieces of paper called *warrants* which evidence the number of *rights* they are entitled to. One right is given for each old share, but it will require four, eight, or ten rights—the exact number depending upon the ratio of old stock to the new—to subscribe for one new share. Some stockholders look upon the privileged subscription as a scheme to sell them more shares and accordingly throw away their rights. When they do this they are in effect throwing away part of the old shares. The shareholder should either exercise his rights and purchase the new stock, or he should sell his rights in the market. The following example will explain the reason.

We will assume that the net worth section of a company's balance sheet appears as follows:

Capital stock	$10,000,000	(100,000 shares of $100 par stock)
Surplus	8,100,000	
Total net worth	$18,100,000	

The company offers its shareholders the right to subscribe at par to one new share for each eight old shares owned. After all the new stock is issued the company's net worth will be changed to the following:

Capital stock	$11,250,000
Surplus	8,100,000
Total net worth	$19,350,000

Before the new stock was sold, the *book value* per share of the old stock was $181 per share ($18,100,000 divided by 100,000). After the new stock is issued the book value per share has been reduced to $172 per share ($19,350,000 divided by 112,500). In other words the book value per share has been reduced by $9. Thus, a shareholder who does not subscribe to the new stock or who does not sell his rights would lose $9 on each share of stock he owned. In addition, his degree of control in the corporation would be lessened.

A person would give approximately $72 for the privilege of subscribing at $100 per share to stock which will be worth $172. In other words, the value of the *rights* necessary to subscribe to one new share should be approximately $72. Since it takes eight rights to get one new share, the value of the single *right* should be approximately $9. As we saw above, this is the amount that each old share would decline in value from the privileged subscription. Thus, a person subscribing to the new stock would lose in the value of his old shares the amount he gained in the value of the new share or shares. He would merely break even by subscribing. In actual practice he would probably gain by subscribing to the new stock because the stock values later tend to rise in price after the diluting effect has worn off. This would be the case particularly if the company continued the old dividend rate on the stock.

If the shareholder does not have the amount of money necessary to buy the new stock, or if he believes that he should not tie up any more money in the particular company, he should sell his rights in the market rather than let them expire. A person owning eight old shares could sell his rights for $72, which would just offset the loss in the value of his old shares. If a person owned, for example, only five shares of stock and wanted to subscribe to a new share, he could purchase three additional rights in the market.

In this example we have assumed that the market price of the stock was the same as its book value. This was done in order that the effect of the privileged subscription could be better understood. In actual practice, rarely would the two be the same. When they are different, the market value rather than the book value should be used to determine the value of a right. The value of a right in any situation may readily be calculated through the use of the following formula:

$$\frac{\text{Market price of old share} - \text{Subscription price of new share}}{\text{Number of old shares necessary to get one new share} + 1} = \text{Value of a right}$$

Substituting the figures in the hypothetical example given above, we get the following:

$$\frac{\$181 - \$100}{8 + 1} = \$9, \text{ value of a right}$$ [9]

Taxation

In the typical case, stock rights are not taxable under the federal income tax at the time they are received by the shareholder (or at the time the rights are exercised). The following discussion pertains to this type of rights. If a shareholder allows valuable stock rights to expire without exercising them, no tax loss may be taken with respect to either the rights or the stock.

Rights Valued at Less Than 15 per cent of Stock Value. If at the time the stock rights are received by the shareholder they have a

[9] After the stock has gone "ex-rights" the "1" in the denominator of the formula is dropped. The stock is said to sell "ex-rights" on the first day that the new purchaser is not entitled to the "right." If he bought the stock before this date he would be buying it "rights-on."

market value of less than 15 per cent of the value of the stock (selling ex-rights) on which the rights were issued, which is the case in the example given above, the shareholder has an election in determining the cost basis of the rights and the stock for tax purposes. He may elect to consider the cost basis of the rights to be zero, or he may elect to allocate the cost of the stock over both the stock and the rights in the manner described in the next paragraph. If it is decided to treat the cost basis of the rights as zero, then the following is the tax treatment. If the rights are sold, the entire proceeds (less commissions, etc.) are considered to be a capital gain. In determining whether the gain is a short- or a long-term gain, the holding period begins on the date when the stock on which the rights were paid was acquired. (Taxation of capital gains is described in Chapter 16.) If the old stock is sold, its cost basis remains the original cost. If the rights are used to subscribe to the new stock, the subscription price is the cost basis for the new stock.

Rights Valued at 15 per cent or More of Stock Value. When this is the situation the shareholder must apportion the cost basis between the stock and the rights in the ratio that the market value of each bears to the total market of both. The following example will clarify this. A company offers its shareholders the right to subscribe to one new share at $10 for each three old shares held. Assume that the "rights-on" value of the share is $30. Applying the formula stated above, a right should be worth $5, and "ex-rights" price of the stock should be $25 per share. (Right value is thus more than 15 per cent of stock value.) Assume you hold three old shares which were acquired several years ago at $20 per share.

Market value of stock	$75
Market value of rights	15
Total market value	$90

$\frac{75}{90} \times \$60$ (cost of old stock) = $50, cost basis allocated to stock (which is $16⅔ per share)

$\frac{15}{90} \times \$60$ = $10, cost basis allocated to rights (which is $3⅓ per right)

If you sold your three rights for a total of $15, a long-term gain of $5 would be realized. If you sold the three old shares for a total of $75, a long-term gain of $25 would be realized. (The gain would be $30 if the old shares were sold for $30 each "rights-on.") If you subscribed to the one new share, its cost basis would be the subscription price of $10 plus the cost basis of the three rights of $10, or a total cost of $20. If you sold this share for $25 you should report a capital gain of $5. The holding period (to determine whether gain is short- or long-term) for the new share begins on the date the rights were exercised.

WARRANTS

The term *warrant* is applied to the piece of paper that evidences a right to purchase stock of a particular corporation according to the terms expressed in the warrant. There are several different types of warrants which are issued under different circumstances. The type we are now interested in is the kind which is often referred to as the *stock purchase warrant.*

Mechanics of Issue

Stock purchase warrants usually come into existence in connection with a reorganization or are issued in connection with the sale of bonds or preferred stock as an inducement to get people to buy the securities. The warrants call for the purchase of common stock (usually) at a price above the existing market price of the stock at the time the warrant is issued. In some cases the price that must be paid for the stock increases as time goes on. The life of the warrant may be limited to a few years or it may be perpetual. In some instances the warrant is non-detachable from the security with which it was issued, but in other cases it is detachable and has a market separate from the particular security.

A larger profit (or loss) may be made with a given amount of money through the purchase of warrants than by purchasing the stock itself. The following actual example will illustrate the point. The Tri-Continental Corporation had perpetual warrants outstanding which permitted the holders thereof to purchase 1.27 shares of the common stock at $17.76 per share for each warrant owned. Thus, the warrant would have no immediate exercisable value until the stock price excceded $17.76 per share. In actual practice, however, the warrants possessed a market value when the stock was selling below this figure, due to the fact that speculators would give something for the warrants in anticipation of a further increase in the price of the stock in the future. On June 30, 1951, for example, the stock sold for only $10¾, but the warrants had a market value of $2¾.

On June 15, 1965, the stock closed at $45¼ and the warrants at $36⅛. If a person had invested $10,000 in the stock on June 30, 1951, he could have purchased a total of 930 shares. If the same amount of money had been invested in the warrants on the same day it would have purchased a total of 3,636 warrants. On June 15, 1965, the 930 shares of stock were worth $42,082. This is a profit of $32,082, or 321 per cent on the original $10,000 investment. But the 3,636 warrants on June 15, 1965, were worth a total of $131,350. Thus, the investor would have made a profit of $121,350 on the warrants, which represents a 1,214 per cent return on the original investment.

When Tri-Continental split its common 2 for 1 in late 1965, the warrant provisions were changed to permit warrant holders to buy 2.54 shares of the common for each warrant held at $8.88 per share.

In addition to Tri-Continental Corporation, perpetual warrants have also been issued by Alleghany Corporation and by Atlas Corporation. The warrants of these three companies are traded on the American Stock Exchange, whereas the stocks of these companies are listed on the New York Stock Exchange.

Protection Against Dilution

In purchasing warrants or securities to which they are attached, the investor should see to it that adequate protection is given to him in event the company has a large stock dividend or stock split. The effect of the latter would be to reduce the per share value of the stock. The contract should provide that in event of these actions the provisions of the warrant contract should be changed to prevent loss to the warrant holders. The Tri-Continental situation, stated above, is an example.

Taxation

Gains (or losses) made on the sale of purchased stock purchase warrants are treated as capital gains (or losses) and handled in the same manner as in the case of stock, which is discussed in Chapter 16. The cost of purchased stock purchase warrants which are used to acquire another security is added to the purchase price of the new security to obtain the cost basis of the latter for capital gains tax purposes. For the tax handling of profits realized on the sale of warrants which are acquired along with another security, the sale of the latter after the holder has sold the warrants, and the sale of stock acquired under special options such as restricted and qualified stock options, and those acquired under employee stock purchase plans, it is suggested that the Internal Revenue Service be consulted.

COMMON STOCK RATINGS

Standard & Poor's and Value Line (financial services, which are discussed in Chapter 15) have a system of quality ratings for common stocks. Generally speaking, they rate only the larger corporations, and where sufficient data are available. Standard & Poor's does not rate the stock of financial corporations.

The reliability of common stock quality ratings should really not be compared with that of bond ratings (or even preferred stock ratings) due to the residual nature of common stock. Earnings and prices of common stocks fluctuate widely, and even dividend returns may be subject to some variation. Asset values behind common stocks have little meaning when it comes to judging common stocks.

The Standard & Poor's ratings are found in their monthly publication, the *Security Owner's Stock Guide*, which is available in libraries, brokerage offices, and similar service agencies. These ratings are based on the stability and growth in earnings for the past eight years, and the dividends for the past twenty years, with increased weight being given in each case to the more recent years. The ratings and their explanations are as follows:

Standard & Poor's Common Stock Ratings

Rating	Explanation	Rating	Explanation	Rating	Explanation
A+	Excellent	B+	Average	C	Lowest
A	Good	B	Below Average		
A−	Above Average	B−	Low		

The Value Line quality ratings are determined mainly by the stability in the price of the stock over the past ten years and by the growth of the company's earnings. The symbols and their explanations are the same as for preferred stock, discussed earlier in the chapter. The Value Line ratings are found in the *Value Line Investment Survey* in connection with the analysis of the particular company. These ratings are then kept current in Value Line's *The Weekly Summary of Advices and Index*. Leading libraries and many brokerage offices subscribe to these services.

As noted in our discussion of preferred stock, the ratings are an attempt to judge the quality of the stock independently of the market price at a particular time. A stock bearing a low rating may be a speculative buy at a particular time due to its extremely low market price, whereas a stock having a high quality rating may be a poor buy at the time because of its relatively high price.

COMMON STOCK INVESTMENT IN THE VARIOUS INDUSTRIES

Railroads

Prior to 1920, railroads had the transportation business mainly to themselves, and railroad securities were regarded as top quality investment securities. Then, as the automobile industry developed and good roads were built, trucks, buses, and private automobiles started making serious inroads on the rail business. Pipelines also added to its woes. Later, the development of the airplane and the airlines took a large chunk of the passenger business that had been going to the railroads.

With the losses in revenues, many railroads found it impossible to meet their heavy fixed expenses and interest on their outstanding bonds. In the 1930's a number of roads, including several large ones, went through bankruptcy and reorganization. During World War II and the immediate postwar period, their business increased somewhat, but the future was not very bright for the industry as a whole. During 1957 to 1962, while the economy in general was enjoying unparalleled prosperity, fifteen of the leading twenty railroads had a declining revenue trend. Then Wall Street took a more favorable attitude toward rail stocks. For some months after the 1962 market low was reached, rail stocks actually advanced faster than industrials. Railroad earnings also started to rise. The shift of industry and population to the South and West has improved the prospects for railroads in those areas. The more liberal depreciation rules and the tax cuts in 1964 and 1965 have helped the situation. Also, the start made in 1964 against expensive featherbedding, which has plagued the industry for so many years, should materially reduce future operating costs.

Despite the improvement in recent years, most railroad stocks must be regarded as speculative. Purchases should be confined to only leading roads which are in a sound financial position and have a satisfactory record of earnings and dividends. The following, arranged alphabetically, are considered among the best railroads:

Atchison, Topeka and Santa Fe
Norfolk and Western
Southern Pacific
Union Pacific

Public Utilities

Public utilities as a class have taken the place formerly occupied by railroads as the safest investment among private companies. The holding company device has been developed more fully in the public utility field than in any of the other industries. In general the securities of the better operating companies are safer investments than those of the holding companies.

The degree of risk involved in the purchase of public utility securities varies not only among the different companies within the same field, but also among the various types of utilities. Brief descriptions of the different types of utilities follow.

Electric Light and Power. Within the field of public utilities the electric light and power companies are the most important, when measured by the amount of securities outstanding and investment interest. Since the turn of the century, tremendous developments have taken place in this field and the future appears equally favorable. Although electricity was at first used for illumination only, its principal use now is as a source of power. In recent years it has been used to an increasing extent for heating and air-conditioning purposes. There is really no substitute for electricity in the illumination field, and its importance as a source of power has been steadily increasing. With greater mechanization in manufacturing, its use as power will increase in the future. More and more electrical appliances and conveniences are being developed and sold to the consumer.

Growth of the electric utilities is expected to do somewhat better than the growth in the Gross National Product. A growth of 5 per cent per year in the per-share earnings on the stock has been typical of the industry since the end of World War II. A somewhat similar growth pattern is expected in the immediate future. The internal generation of cash, particularly through the more liberal depreciation charges, has been relatively high and this is expected to continue into the future. Although the cash demands for new equipment will be high, many of the large companies expect to be able to finance their needs until at least 1970 without resorting to the sale of additional common stock. Dividend pay-out of between 70 and 75 per cent of net earnings is expected to continue in the future.

Although the reductions in corporate tax rates in 1964 and 1965 have been enthusiastically received by industry in general, many electric utilities have passed on the tax savings to the consumers in the form of lower rates. Thus, the shareholders of many companies have not received any benefits from the reduction in the corporate tax rate, except to the extent that the lower rates may stimulate more business.

The following are included among the best electric light and power operating companies:

Baltimore Gas and Electric
Boston Electric
Cleveland Electric Illuminating
Commonwealth Edison
Consolidated Edison Co. of New York
Consumers Power
Detroit Edison
Duke Power
Florida Power & Light
Hartford Electric Light
Houston Lighting & Power
Pacific Gas and Electric
Philadelphia Electric
Tampa Electric

Natural Gas. The natural gas industry is one of the oldest among the utilities. Its principal use in the past was illumination, but electricity has taken over the great bulk of this market. The principal market for gas at the present time is for heating and cooking. This is a steady market and it will probably continue to increase along with the population growth. In most parts of the country, gas has a strong competitive position in price as compared to other types of fuel. In recent years, air-conditioning equipment has made an additional market for gas. New industrial processes are also utilizing gas. A possible future industrial market may be the use of gas turbines to generate electricity "on-site."

The tremendous development of pipelines in recent years has resulted in a situation where most of the markets are now being served by gas. It is therefore thought that the rate of growth of the gas industry will slow down considerably, although it will undoubtedly expand along with the development of business and the increase in population. The following are included among the leading natural gas operating companies:

- Baltimore Gas & Electric (principally electricity)
- Brooklyn Union Gas
- Consolidated Edison Co. of New York (principally electricity)
- Consolidated Natural Gas
- National Fuel Gas
- Northern Illinois Gas
- Pacific Gas and Electric (principally electricity)
- Pacific Lighting
- Peoples Gas Light and Coke

Telephone. The telephone business in the United States is dominated by the American Telephone and Telegraph Company, which, through its ownership of stock of subsidiary companies of the Bell System, controls 82 per cent of the telephone business of the country. The company also owns long-distance connecting lines, suboceanic transmission cables, and the stock of Western Electric Company, which manufactures the telephone equipment which is sold to the company and its subsidiaries. Substantial stock interest is held also in other operating companies, including the Bell Telephone Company of Canada. AT&T is the largest public utility enterprise in the world. The number of shareholders in the company is in excess of 2,250,000.

The company through its subsidiaries and research laboratories has been a pioneer in the development of communications by means of satellites. In 1962 it successfully completed and put "Telstar" into orbit. The company is the largest single stockholder in the Communications Satellite Corporation ("Comsat"). Later, other similar satellites were put into orbit, and the company will undoubtedly continue to be a leader in the development of satellite communications.

American Telephone and Telegraph has long been considered one of the best investment stocks obtainable. From 1922 to 1959 the company paid a regular dividend of $9.00 a year ($2.25 quarterly). Thus, the stock appealed to people who were interested in a steady dividend of a fixed amount. But for the individual who was in the high-income tax bracket and who was seeking a return through capital gains, the stock was not very appealing. With the increased use of telephones resulting from the business expansion, the increase in population, and the development of electronics, AT&T stock by 1959 had become also a growth stock.

In 1959, AT&T stock was split 3 for 1 (the par value per share was reduced from \$100 to \$33⅓), and the annual per-share dividend rate was set at \$3.30. This was increased to \$3.60 in 1961. In 1964, the stock was split 2 for 1 (the par value per share was reduced to \$16⅔), and the annual dividend was established at \$2.00 per share (50 cents quarterly). Thus, a shareholder who owned one share of AT&T in 1958, and held on to his stock, would now have six shares. His annual dividend return would have been increased from \$9 to \$12. In addition, the market value of his holding would have increased considerably. In the past, AT&T shareholders have benefited also from the receipt of valuable rights to subscribe to new shares and convertible bonds on advantageous terms.

General Telephone & Electronics Corporation controls the largest group of telephone properties in the United States outside the Bell System. It has thirty subsidiary operating companies located in thirty-two of the states. The company also owns subsidiary manufacturing companies in the United States, Europe, Latin America, and Japan which are engaged in the telephone equipment business, lighting, electronics, chemicals, and nuclear components. In recent years, an increasing emphasis has been placed on the manufacturing end of the business. Both the company and its stock have shown rapid growth since World War II, and there are favorable prospects for continued growth in the future.

Telegraph. All the telegram business of the country is handled by the Western Union Telegraph Company, except for some teletype and wire services carried on by AT&T. The company furnishes wire telegraph and microwave radio throughout the United States and by ocean cable between the United States and foreign countries. It also carries on an extensive telegraphic money order business. In recent years progress has been made in increasing its private wire and facsimile services. The competition offered by AT&T, however, has been severe and this will probably continue in the future. The stock can be considered to be of only fair investment quality.

Industrials

Industrials comprise all companies which are not railroads, public utilities, or financial organizations. Thus, extractive industries, manufacturing of all kinds, and the distributive industry covering all forms of wholesale and retail selling are included in the category of industrials. Obviously, great differences exist among the various types of companies and industries. The problems and risks involved in mining are much different from those encountered in the automobile industry or the mail-order business. Some industries are considerably more speculative than others and great differences exist among companies within any one industry.

It is thus difficult to make general statements about industrial securities which would apply to the various types of industries within the group. Industrial securities, as a group, are more speculative than securities issued by public utilities. The essential character of the service furnished by utilities, the monopoly conditions under which they operate, and the relative stability of their earnings give utility securities a higher investment standing. Industrial companies are subject to keen competition and their earnings fluctuate widely as business conditions change. In many industries there is overcapacity, and in some the saturation point for their products has been reached. Since there is little regulation or control over their operations, the factor of management is of prime importance. Because of these things it is evident that a very thorough analysis should be made before purchasing industrial securities. Such an analysis, however, is more difficult to make than in the case of railroads or public utilities.

In addition to some of the general comments which have been made in regard to selecting investment securities, the purchaser of industrial securities should pay particular attention to the nature of the product manufactured or service rendered by the company. Integrated companies are preferred over those which must depend upon others for their raw materials and the sale of their product. Companies selling to the domestic trade offer greater stability of earnings than those which do business abroad, although foreign trade offers a means of increasing sales when the domestic market has reached the saturation point. The imposition of trade barriers may greatly reduce foreign sales. The dependence, if any, of the company on protective tariffs should be considered. The advisability of selecting leading companies in the leading industries has been mentioned several times above.

Other things being equal, stocks of companies which have no bonds outstanding are safer than those that have bonded indebtedness. Common stocks have a better chance of receiving dividends if there are no preferred issues ahead of them. The presence of preferred stock, however, would not be regarded as seriously as an issue of bonds. Some good industrial companies, however, such as the United States Steel Corporation, for example, have both bonds and preferred stock outstanding.

The common stock should have a record of steady dividends for the preceding ten years, and no more than twenty times average earnings should be paid for it. A price-earnings ratio of about twelve to fifteen times would be better. The leading industrial common stocks are listed in the next chapter.

FOREIGN STOCKS

Some people are attracted to foreign stocks in the hope that they may make a larger profit than could be made through the purchase of domestic securities. This is a possibility, but it is doubtful if the average investor will have this success.

Many foreign nations are only beginning to go through the industrial expansion which occurred in the United States many years ago. Many of their markets are just being tapped. Some foreign companies will enjoy large profits; others will fall by the wayside. Risks are encountered in buying any securities, domestic or foreign, but additional problems and risks are usually experienced in dealing with foreign securities. Included in these are the following:

1. Economic and political uncertainty
2. Possible devaluation of the currency
3. Changing rates of exchange
4. Additional taxes
5. Inconvenience and cost of buying and selling the securities
6. Lack of adequate government and securities exchange regulation
7. Inadequacy of financial reporting

In 1964, Congress, in order to help curtail the outflow of gold from the United States, enacted the popularly called "interest equalization" excise tax (retroactive to mid-1963) of 15 per cent on the purchase price of new or existing issues of foreign stocks by United States residents *from persons other than the United States residents.* The tax does not apply, however, to new issues of Canadian securities, or to securities originating in underdeveloped countries. It is expected that this tax will put a damper on the purchase of foreign stocks by United States residents, unless they can be purchased from other United States residents.

Aside from the purchase of some English and Japanese securities, the principal interest of American investors in foreign securities at the present time is in Canadian and Western European stocks, so these will be briefly discussed.

Canadian Stocks

For some years, an increasing number of American investors have been buying Canadian stocks. Many believe that the industrial development in the United States has reached an advanced stage, whereas that in Canada is merely beginning. Canada today leads the free world in the production of pulpwood, newsprint, nickel, and asbestos. It is also a major producer of aluminum, copper, uranium, and many other important metals. The production of oil and natural gas in Canada has increased tremendously in recent years and the extent of the reserves, although unknown, appears to be enormous.

As is true in the early stages of the development of any country which appears to be promising, many fraudulent and extremely speculative promotions have been undertaken. This is particularly true in the oil and mining fields. In most promotions of the latter type in recent years, the only thing tangible the companies owned was the claim to many acres of land. The chances of making any money out of such promotions are exceedingly rare. In a few instances people have been able to make a profit only because someone else paid them a higher price for the stock than they paid for it. The promoters and stock salesmen usually are the only ones who profit from such companies. In fact, in many instances all, or practically all, of the money obtained from the sale of the stock goes to the promoters and their stock salesmen. Of course, a few of the very speculative ventures will be successful, and the buyers of their stocks will reap large returns, but the chances of picking one of these companies in its early development are extremely remote.

Despite what has just been said, it must be admitted that the prospects for many Canadian stocks, over the long run, look good. It is suggested, however, that the investor or speculator confine his purchases to those companies which are large and well-established. Companies which have met the exacting listing requirements of the New York Stock Exchange would appear to be safer than those which are not listed. Exception, however, must be made for many excellent stocks which are ordinarily not listed, such as bank and insurance company stocks. More Canadian stocks are listed or traded in on the American Stock Exchange than on the New York Stock Exchange, but generally speaking, they are more speculative.

Table 12–6. Canadian Common Stocks Listed on the New York Stock Exchange

Company	Dividends Paid Every Year Since	Company	Dividends Paid Every Year Since
Aluminium Ltd.	1939	Granby Mining	1963
Campbell Red Lake Mines	1952	Hudson Bay Mining & Smelting	1935
Canada Southern Railway	1887	International Nickel	1934
Canadian Breweries	1945	McIntyre Porcupine Mines	1917
Canadian Pacific Railway	1944	Pacific Petroleums	—
Distillers Corp.–Seagrams	1937	Walker (Hiram)	1936
Dome Mines	1920		

Table 12–7. Selected List of Canadian Common Stocks Listed or Traded in on the American Stock Exchange

Company	Dividends Paid Every Year Since	Company	Dividends Paid Every Year Since
Asamera Oil	–	Dominion Tar & Chemical	1946
Banff Oil	–	Ford Motor of Canada	1933
Bell Telephone of Canada	1881	Imperial Oil	1912
Brazilian Traction, Lt. & Pwr.	–	Imperial Tobacco of Canada	1912
British American Oil	1909	Massey-Ferguson	1946
Canadian Javelin	–	Power Corp. of Canada	1936
Canadian Marconi	1964	St. Lawrence Corp.	1951
Consolidated Mining and Smelting	1924	Simpson's Ltd.	1946
		Steel Co. of Canada	1916
Dominion Bridge	1912	Union Gas Co. of Canada	1949

A more conservative way to profit on the future development of Canada is to purchase the stock of United States companies which have substantial holdings of Canadian properties or stocks of Canadian companies. Practically all the major United States oil companies have sizable holdings of Canadian oil lands or stocks of Canadian oil companies. The Standard Oil Company of New Jersey, for example, owns 70 per cent of Imperial Oil, which is the leading Canadian oil company. International Paper Company owns the Canadian International Paper Company, which is Canada's leading newsprint producer.

Canadian law requires that Canadian companies withhold a tax equivalent to 10 per cent of the dividends paid to non-residents of Canada, provided that the company is at least 25 per cent Canadian-owned. If the company is less than 25 per cent Canadian-owned, the withholding tax is 20 per cent. This tax, however, may be credited against the federal income tax owed by a resident of the United States, provided he files special Form 1116. Dividends received from Canadian corporations (or those formed in any other country) are not subject to the dividend exclusion, which is discussed in Chapter 16.

Western European Stocks

The lifting of national barriers and the formation and development of the European Common Market during the past decade has opened up a vast trading area of nearly 300 million people. The rate of economic development there during the past ten years has surpassed that of almost anyplace else in the world. The large common market has been conducive to the development of large-scale production. The introduction of modern machinery and the utilization of relatively cheap labor (although the cost of labor is increasing) have made it possible for local industry to turn out modern products at a relatively low cost.

Although tariff walls are disappearing within the Common Market countries, they are erecting stiff ones on the importation of goods into the bloc. This, plus the relatively high labor and transportation expenses, is making it more difficult for American industry to compete successfully with the European producers. The result has been stimulated interest among investors in the stocks of Western European companies.

The problems and risks involved in buying and selling foreign stocks, listed at the beginning of this section, apply to European stocks to a much greater extent than they do to Canadian stocks. Some of the physical difficulties involved in the buying and selling of foreign stocks, and in collecting dividends on them, have been alleviated by trading in the stocks through foreign branch offices of American brokerage firms, listing of the stocks on the New York Stock Exchange or the American Stock Exchange, and through the use of American Depositary Receipts (ADR's).

American Depositary Receipts are issued by the larger New York banks against the deposit of the actual stock certificates. The purchaser then buys these, rather than the stock directly, and makes payment in American dollars. He likewise sells the ADR's for dollars. Meanwhile, the dividends paid by the foreign companies to the banks which hold the stock certificates are converted into dollars and passed on to the holders of the ADR's. Another advantage of the ADR's is that in the event of the death of the holder, the ADR's are not subject to any foreign inheritance tax.

The following European stocks (listed alphabetically) are among those which are favored by institutional investors in the United States (NYSE indicates listing on the New York Stock Exchange):

Dresdner Bank (W. Germany)
Farbenfabriken Bayer A.B. (W. Germany) (NYSE)
Farbwerke Hoechst (W. Germany)
Hoogovens (Holland)
Montecantini (Italy) (NYSE)
Olivetti (Italy)
Pechiney (France)
Philips Lamp Works (Holland)
Photo-Products Gevaert (Belgium)
Royal Dutch Petroleum (Holland) (NYSE)
Siemens & Halske (W. Germany)
Unilever N. V. (Holland) (NYSE)

If the investor wants to reap some of the possible benefits arising from the European Common Market, but does not want to withstand the greater risk that is usually associated with foreign stocks, he may invest in stock of American companies which do an appreciable amount of business in that region of the world. To compete more successfully with foreign companies in the Common Market, many American companies are organizing or acquiring foreign subsidiaries to carry on their business in those particular countries. Information on these companies may be secured through the financial services and from brokerage offices.

AVOIDING INFERIOR STOCKS

Earmarks of Inferior Stocks

The securities laws of the various states and particularly the federal legislation—the Securities Act of 1933 and the Securities Exchange Act of 1934—and the regulations set forth by the Securities and Exchange Commission have been of tremendous help in eliminating fraud and misleading statements in connection with the issuance and subsequent sale of securities. It is difficult, however, to regulate or check on everything that a securities salesman may say. The prospective investor should shy away from any stocks for which the following statements or arguments are used:

1. Promise of absolute safety
2. Promise of high return
3. Use of the ground-floor argument
4. Inflating-the-ego method
5. High-pressure selling
6. Appeal to the avaricious instinct
7. Use of irrelevant material

A Few Suggestions

Money can be lost in the purchase of any security, but the individual will lose less if he follows the additional suggestions below.

Don't Buy Securities of a New Company or Industry. A comparatively few individuals have made tremendous profits by buying stock of new companies in established industries or new companies in new industries. Most new companies fail, and most of those that fail do so within a short time after they are promoted. So, by the law of averages, an investor is apt to lose if he buys securities of a new company. Furthermore, in the case of most of the companies which are successful, after their investment banker's support is withdrawn, their stocks will sell for less in the market than the original offer price. Even if there is no banker support, it is probable that stocks or bonds of the new company can be acquired later at a lower price. There are so many securities of well-established and successful companies which can be purchased on the market, any day, that it seems foolish for the average individual to take a chance on a security of a new and untried company.

Don't Buy Securities of Small Companies. There is a greater chance of loss in buying securities of small companies than in purchasing those issued by the larger organizations. Many small companies are not strong financially and cannot stand the strain of competition. Large companies are often better managed and can attract bank support in the sale of securities. Furthermore, they can afford to carry on extensive research which may lead to the introduction of more profitable processes and products. They also have an advantage in advertising and foreign sales promotion.

Don't Buy Securities of Local Companies. This would not always apply, but in most instances it is good advice. Most local companies are small organizations, so the arguments stated above would be applicable here. Pressure is sometimes put upon an individual to buy stock in some local enterprise in order to get it to locate in the community, or to prevent its moving to another city. The selling argument is that more employment will thus be available to the local residents, and the added payroll will increase the prosperity of the community. Many local shoe factories, brick plants, and similar enterprises have been promoted in this way. Should the venture be successful, the arguments are valid, but if the industry fails, the community, and particularly the people who purchased the stock, would have been much better off if the promotion had never been started. If a person is an executive in a local company there is more reason why he should purchase stock in the new organization. Nevertheless, when it comes to investing his money, an individual should be primarily concerned with his own well-being, rather than that of the community.

Don't Buy Unlisted Stocks. The stocks of most small and local companies are not listed on the New York Stock Exchange, hence the last two points mentioned above would be applicable here. Before a particular stock can be listed on the big board (New York Stock Exchange), the issuing company must be established and have proper distribution of its stock. Listing increases the marketability of the stock and makes it more readily acceptable as collateral for a loan. Many corporations whose stock is listed on the Exchange are not very successful, but there are undoubtedly more unsuccessful companies whose stocks are not listed. While much money is lost by buying the listed stock of good companies and selling it at a price lower than the purchase price, the same thing occurs with unlisted stocks. The Exchange requires those companies whose stocks are listed to furnish considerable information about their organization and security issues, and regular financial statements must be sent to the stockholders. Listing on the American Stock Exchange or the exchanges of the leading cities in the United States does not carry the same weight as listing on the New York Stock Exchange. Stocks of insurance companies and banks, many of which are considered good investments, are ordinarily not listed on the stock exchanges.

Listing is not so important for bonds as for stocks. In fact, most bonds, including some of the highest type, are not sold on the organized exchanges but are marketed through investment bankers and bond houses in what is called the *over-the-counter* market.

STOCK GIFTS TO MINORS

In the past it has generally been impractical to make gifts of stock to children. A guardian would have to be legally appointed to hold the stock and sales of such stock and the reinvestment of the proceeds must follow the strict letter of the law. To facilitate the procedure the New York Stock Exchange developed a model or uniform law and this with some modifications has been adopted in all the states. Two general forms of the law are in effect, the Uniform Gifts to Minors Law, which has been adopted by most of the states, and the Model Law, which is in force in the other states. The principal difference between the two types of laws is that the Uniform Law provides for gifts of money as well as of securities (stocks and bonds), whereas the Model Law provides for gifts of securities only (except in Georgia where it includes money).

How the Law Works

A permanent and irrevocable gift of the stock (or other securities) is made to the child. The stock is registered in the name of a designated adult relative of the child (sometimes the donor, who ordinarily would be the father of the child) as custodian for the designated child. The custodian may thereafter sell the stock, if he deems it advisable, and reinvest the proceeds in "such securities as would be acquired by prudent men of discretion and intelligence who are seeking a reasonable income and the preservation of their capital." Income from the account may be invested in the same manner. If the child dies before reaching 21, the custodian property will be paid to the child's executor or administrator. Upon reaching 21 the property is turned over to the child. The custodian should maintain detailed records of all transactions.

Tax Status

Stock gifts to minors qualify for the annual gift tax exclusion of $3,000 ($6,000 for a married couple), and the lifetime exemption of $30,000 ($60,000 for a married couple). (Gift taxes are explained in Chapter 19.) If the donor or custodian dies before the child reaches 21, the custodian property is not subject to the federal estate tax. (Estate taxes are discussed in Chapter 19.) But if the donor and custodian are the same person and this person dies before the child reaches 21, the property would be subject to the estate tax.

Income from the custodian account is considered to belong to the child. Thus, the child would not have to report this for federal income tax purposes unless his total income amounted to more than $600. Even if the amount was in excess of this, the tax rates on it would begin with the lowest tax bracket. Had the donor (the father) retained the stock in his own name, he might have been paying a tax of 50 or even 70 per cent on it. But if some of the custodian account income is used to meet the parents' obligation to support the child, this amount must be included in the parents' taxable income.

QUESTIONS

1. Why do so many people lose money when they buy and sell stocks?
2. Explain what corporate stock is. Why may it be of practical value to distinguish between the stock and the stock certificate?
3. Explain the different ways in which common stock differs from corporate bonds.
4. What other term is sometimes applied to corporate stock?
5. Explain why a bond of a particular company is considered a safer investment than the common stock of the same company. What types of risks, however, are inherent in the bond that are not present in the stock?
6. Does a stockholder feel the effects of the federal income taxes more than the corporate bondholder? Explain.
7. Should stocks yield more or less than bonds? Do they? Explain.
8. Why may a corporation prefer to issue no-par stock rather than par-value stock? Would you as a buyer prefer one over the other? Explain.
9. Indicate reasons why it could be said that the term "preferred stock" is misleading.
10. Contrast the rights—common law, statutory law, or contractual—of common and preferred stock.
11. What are the usual preferences and limitations set forth in the typical industrial preferred stock contract?
12. Of what practical importance are the cumulative, participating, voting, and preference as to assets features of preferred stock?
13. Why is it sometimes said that preferred stock has the weakness of common stock without its advantages, and the weakness of bonds without their advantages?
14. Indicate in some detail the investment position of preferred stocks.
15. What are some preferred stocks that are generally regarded as good investments?
16. Indicate what is meant by each of the following:
    (a) Guaranteed stock
    (b) Debenture stock
    (c) Classified stock
    (d) Treasury stock
    (e) Prior preferred stock
17. If a friend is contemplating buying some stocks, would you recommend that he buy preferred stocks or common stocks, or diversify between these two types of stock?

18. Indicate to what extent the "plowed back" earnings belong to the common stockholders. Do these earnings constitute a reserve out of which dividends may be paid in lean years?
19. Indicate how common stockholders, preferred stockholders, and bondholders are affected by inflation.
20. Several studies made in the past have showed that a diversified group of common stocks have proved to be better investments over a period of years than a commitment of a similar amount of money in bonds. Even if similar results were to be experienced in the future, why are bonds rather than common stocks recommended for the average investor?
21. When a stock is sold near the time of the "record date," who gets the dividend—the buyer or the seller? Explain.
22. How is the "yield" on a common stock determined? Why is the "current yield" a better figure to use for comparative purposes than the actual yield?
23. Distinguish between stock dividends and stock splits and their effects on the balance sheet.
24. Are stock dividends taxable? Why or why not?
25. Explain the procedure of selling stock through the privileged subscription method.
26. Why may a person prefer to speculate in the stock purchase warrants of a company rather than in the stock which may be purchased with the warrants?
27. Why is the inexperienced stock buyer sometimes advised to buy stocks of the largest companies in the leading industries?
28. Indicate the investment position of railroad common stocks.
29. Indicate the investment position of public utility common stocks.
30. What features of American Telephone and Telegraph Company's common stock make it a highly favored investment stock?
31. Why are industrial stocks generally considered more speculative than those issued by public utilities?
32. Explain the principal features of the Uniform Gifts to Minors Law and the tax status of gifts made under the law.

CASE PROBLEMS

1. The Space Age Company was organized on April 15, 1964, and shortly thereafter sold $1,000,000 of 6 per cent preferred stock and $2,000,000 of common stock, both having a par value of $100 per share. The stock was sold at its par value and the company had no paid-in surplus. Net earnings after taxes for the first four years were as follows:

Year	*Earnings*
1964	$ 0
1965	60,000
1966	120,000
1967	210,000

Assume that all the earnings were paid out in dividends each year, and that you owned one share of the preferred and one share of the common. Indicate the amount you would receive in dividends on each share in each of these years if the preferred stock was one of the following.

(a) Non-cumulative and non-participating
(b) Non-cumulative and participating
(c) Cumulative and non-participating
(d) Cumulative and participating
(e) If the statutes of the state and the contract (except to the extent indicated) were silent as to cumulation and participation.

2. Assume that the preferred stock in the preceding question was by contract entitled to par and accrued dividends ahead of the common in the event of dissolution, and that the company sold out at the end of 1967 (after paying the dividends from earnings) and obtained cash of $6,000,000 which was distributed to the shareholders as a liquidating dividend. Indicate how much would be paid on one share of preferred and one share of common.
3. Ruth Wells has $800 to invest in common stocks. She is looking for a conservative investment but knows little about corporate stocks. A number of friends have made suggestions to her. She has narrowed the list down to the ABC Railway Company, the DEF Electric Power Company, and the GHI Manufacturing Company. All three companies have paid dividends for the past thirty years and the yield is approximately the same for each company. In which company would you suggest Ruth purchase common stock? Why? Does the type of industry make a difference in selecting a security? What are the major differences in investing in companies in these three fields? If Miss Wells were looking for price appreciation, would your choice of a security for her be different? Why? What other data should she consider in making her choice besides the information given above?
4. John and Mary Turner have been married two years. They rent an unfurnished apartment. Because they have been buying furniture and a car, they have been unable to set aside any savings. John carries a $10,000 straight life insurance policy. They have one child. Mrs. Turner has just inherited $500 from an uncle and wants to invest the money in government bonds. Mr. Turner wants to put it into some common stock as he believes the return on such a small amount in government bonds is too low to bother with. He also says that since this is all they have to invest, they should put it somewhere where it will grow rapidly. What do you think of his reasoning? Why? Do you think that Mrs. Turner has the right approach? What would you do with the funds? Will common stock investment give the greater return that Mr. Turner wants, along with rapid growth of the investment?
5. Dick Smith started setting aside about $25 per month in 1941 to provide for his retirement. He invested all his savings in Series E savings bonds. Dick reaches retirement next year and is thinking about cashing his bonds. He had allowed all those coming due previously to be extended. He is disappointed in his bond investment because he claims that the $25 original maturity value on a bond will buy him less than the $18.75 he invested. He claims he would have been better off spending the money when he earned it rather than buying government bonds. He is sorry that he did not invest in corporate stocks and is thinking of doing so now when he cashes the bonds. He has seen many of his friends make a lot of money in the rising stock market after 1962. Should Dick cash his bonds and buy stocks? Why? Should he have bought stocks instead of bonds in 1941

and thereafter? Comment. What would you have done? Are stock investments good in inflationary periods? Why? Since we had inflation after 1939, why buy bonds instead of stocks?

6. Doug Wilson owns 4 shares of common stock of the Rapid Electronics Corporation which he purchased some years ago at $50 a share. The net worth section of the company's balance sheet showed the following:

Capital stock	$50,000,000	(1,000,000 shares of $50 par stock)
Surplus	40,000,000	

The company's stock is selling in the market for $90 a share. The company has announced a privileged subscription of one new share at par for each four old shares held.

(a) Under what circumstances would you advise him to subscribe to the new stock?
(b) If he did subscribe to the stock what would be the value of his investment in the company?
(c) Assuming that the rights and the stock "ex-rights" sold for their theoretical values, what amount would be subject to federal income tax if he:
  (1) Sold the four rights?
  (2) Sold the four old shares "rights on"?
  (3) Subscribed to the new share and then sold it?

7. Vin Ellis was considering purchasing some preferred stock issued by the American Electric Power Company. His investment banker had advised him that the company should be earning the sum of its bond interest and twice the preferred stock dividend (before taxes) at least four times before he should consider the stock. Mr. Ellis found that the bond interest amounted to $2,500,000 per year, and the preferred stock dividend was $3,000,000. What should be the minimum annual earnings (before taxes) of the company in order for it to meet the test set up by the investment banker? Mr. Ellis indicated to the banker that he could understand the margin of safety afforded by requiring that the company earn its interest charges and preferred dividends four times, but he said he did not understand why the preferred dividend requirement was first multiplied by two. Explain why this should be done.

SELECTED READINGS

Amling, Frederick. *Investments: An Introduction to Analysis and Management.* Englewood Cliffs, N. J.: Prentice-Hall, Inc., 1965.

Barnes, Leo. *Your Investments.* Larchmont, N. Y.: American Research Council. Latest edition.

Bellemore, Douglas H. *Investments: Principles and Practice,* Second Edition. New York: Simmons-Boardman Publishing Co., 1960.

Bernhard, Arnold. *The Evaluation of Common Stocks.* New York: Simon and Schuster, Inc. Latest edition.

Bogen, Jules I. (ed.) *Financial Handbook,* Fourth Edition. New York: The Ronald Press Co., 1964. Sections 13 and 18.

Clendenin, John C. *Introduction to Investments,* Fourth Edition. New York: McGraw-Hill Book Co., 1964.

Donaldson, Elvin F., and Pfahl, John K. *Corporate Finance–Policy and Management,* Second Edition. New York: The Ronald Press Co., 1963. Chapters 5, 6, 9, 13, and 26.

Engel, Louis. *How to Buy Stocks*. New York: Bantam Books. Latest edition. Paperbound. (Single copies may be obtained free from any office of Merrill Lynch, Pierce, Fenner & Smith.)

Fisher, Philip A. *Common Stocks and Uncommon Profits,* Revised Edition. New York: Harper & Row, 1960.

Fried, Sidney. *The Speculative Merits of Common Stock Warrants.* New York: R. H. M. Associates. Latest edition.

Gifts of Securities or Money to Minors—A Guide to Laws in 50 States. New York: Association of Stock Exchange Firms. Latest edition.

Graham, Benjamin, Dodd, David L., and Cottle, Sidney. *Security Analysis: Principles and Techniques,* Fourth Edition. New York: McGraw-Hill Book Co., 1962.

Merritt, Robert D. *Financial Independence through Common Stocks,* Seventh Edition. New York: Simon and Schuster, Inc., 1963.

Moody's Handbook of Widely Held Common Stocks. New York: Moody's Investors Service. Latest edition.

13

The Stock Market

To the uninformed, the stock market is a mysterious thing, and is approached with a great deal of timidity and skepticism, or, unfortunately, in some instances, in a blind and unwonted manner which is almost certain to result in financial disaster. But to the person who will take the time and make the effort to learn the intricacies involved and to apply accepted standards of sound investment policies, it offers an intriguing experience which can be quite profitable.

When the term "the stock market" is used, probably most people think of the activities of buying and selling stock on the New York Stock Exchange, but the meaning of the term is broader than this. Perhaps a clearer picture of the true meaning of the term would be had if the term "the market for stocks" were used instead.

Primary Distribution

When stocks are first issued by a corporation, the sale is referred to as the *primary distribution* of the stock. Small, close (stock held by a few investors) corporations directly exchange their stock for the cash or other property given by the investor. Large corporations commonly sell their stock to large investment bankers, who in turn sell the stock to other investment bankers, institutions, and the investing public. In some instances a large, established company will undertake the direct sale of a new issue of stock to its present shareholders. Public offerings in interstate commerce of issues in excess of $300,000 must conform to the requirements of the Securities Act of 1933. This federal legislation requires that a very detailed *registration statement* be filed with and approved by the Securities and Exchange Commission before the issue may be sold. The registration statement must contain all the essential and pertinent information relating to the company and its issue. The company's officers and directors and the investment bankers handling the issue are subject to penalties for any misstatement of material facts or for the omission of any material facts in the registration statement. Each prospective purchaser must be given or shown a *prospectus* relating to the issue before his order may be solicited. The prospectus contains information similar to the registration statement but in an abbreviated form.

Secondary Distribution

After a security has been issued by a corporation, any sale by a stockholder to another person is referred to as a *secondary distribution.*[1] Such resales of securities may be made on an organized securities exchange, such as the New York Stock Exchange, if the securities are listed there, or they may occur in the over-the-counter market.

Over-the-Counter Market

This market has no particular place where buyers and sellers meet. It consists, rather, of the system of security dealers and brokers who are connected with each other by means of the telephone and teletype. In fact, the term "over-the-telephone" might be more descriptive of the market than "over-the-counter." This market is both local and national in scope and consists of some 2,500 securities houses with over 1,500 branches scattered over the country.

The National Quotation Bureau, which collects and publishes over-the-counter securities prices, daily quotes prices on 8,300 over-the-counter stocks, and 1,900 over-the-counter bonds. In the course of one year the Bureau will quote prices on 26,000 stocks, and 14,000 bonds—all over-the-counter.

Since small issues of securities cannot be listed on an organized exchange, the over-the-counter market constitutes their trading place. Practically all of the trading in United States Government bonds (even though some are listed on the New York Stock Exchange), state and municipal bonds, bank and insurance company stocks, and railroad equipment trust obligations takes place in this market. An appreciable amount of trading in listed stocks and bonds occurs in the over-the-counter market by persons who are not members of the organized exchanges. The over-the-counter market accounts for about 80 per cent of the total bond business

[1] The term *secondary distribution* is also used in a more restricted, narrower sense to refer to an *off-the-board* offering of a large block of securities which are listed on an organized stock exchange.

of the country and for about 33 per cent of the total stock business. In addition to the resale of securities, the original sale of new security issues through investment bankers takes place in the over-the-counter market. Large blocks of listed stocks are also sold in the over-the-counter market through the secondary distribution plan.

Table 13–1 shows the favorite over-the-counter industrial and utility stocks with some 435 investment companies.

THE NEW YORK STOCK EXCHANGE

Although only about 2 per cent of all domestic corporations whose stock is in the hands of the public have their common stock listed on the New York Stock Exchange (NYSE), these companies employ approximately 21 per cent of all civilian workers in the United States; they own about 30 per cent of the total business capital; and their net income represents about 65 per cent of the total of all corporate profits. In terms of the dollar volume of all stocks sold on organized stock exchanges in the United States, the NYSE accounts for about 83 per cent (about 73 per cent of total share volume).

A total of 1,247 companies have 1,227 common stock issues and 379 preferred stock issues listed on the NYSE. The aggregate market value of this stock is approximately $474,322,000,000.[2] Figure 13–1 shows the number of common and preferred issues and shares listed on the NYSE since 1900, with estimates extended to 1980. A total of 485 companies and agencies have 1,186 different bond issues listed on the NYSE which have a total market value of approximately $127,724,813,000.

The NYSE is an unincorporated association consisting of 1,366 members. With prior approval of the Exchange, a member or members may combine with other individuals to form a partnership or a corporation to engage in the securities business. Such firms are referred to as member organizations. No one may become a partner or a stockholder of a member organization without the approval of the Exchange. Only the Exchange member of the firm may personally transact business on the floor of the Exchange. There are 656 member organizations–518 partnerships and 138 corporations. Of the 1,366 members of the Exchange, 1,116 are associated with member firms.

Memberships (often referred to as "seats") are acquired through purchase from another member or his estate–subject, of course, to the approval of the Exchange. The price paid for membership in the NYSE since 1929 has ranged from a high of $495,000 (1929) to a low of $17,000 (1942). In 1965 the price was approximately $200,000.

[2] Most of the data in this chapter relating to the NYSE are as of January 1, 1965.

Table 13–1. Vickers Over-the-Counter Favorites—Industrials and Utilities

Rank by $ Value			Stocks	Industry	$ Value (mil.)	No. Inv. Cos. Hldg.	Number Shs. Held	% Outst. Stk. Held by Inv. Cos.	Approx. Range * 1965		
June 1 1964	Dec. 31 1964	June 1 1965							Hi	Lo	Last **
8	4	1	Pabst Brewing Co.	Beverage	37.8	19	1,002,500	21.1	39	31	38
2	2	2	Eli Lilly & Co. "B"	Drugs	33.1	12	436,300	2.7	82	61	76
3	3	3	Tampax, Inc.	Consumer Gds.	30.3	17	291,300	10.3	115	94	104
14	8	4	American Express Co.	Finance	24.3	21	391,700	8.9	70	49	62
33	19	5	Ethyl Corp. "B"	Chemical	24.2	9	567,200	6.4	45	34	43
45	38	6	Anheuser Busch, Inc.	Beverage	20.2	11	463,600	4.8	47	32	44
10	7	7	Transcontinental Gas Pipe Line	Gas Pipe Line	14.6	12	598,600	3.2	26	20	24
5	6	8	Pioneer Natural Gas Co.	Utility	14.4	10	722,000	10.1	23	20	20
15	13	9	Beneficial Corp.	Finance	11.9	8	334,300	8.0	36	32	36
11	10	10	Roadway Express	Trucking	11.9	12	303,900	12.4	41	33	39
9	9	11	A. C. Nielsen Co.	TV Ratings	10.4	12	163,800	5.2	71	62	63
20	25	12	Houston Natural Gas Corp.	Natural Gas	10.1	6	220,900	5.7	46	39	46
16	20	13	American Greetings "A"	Printing	9.9	16	262,900	11.9	39	32	38
13	11	14	Tucson Gas & Electric	Utility	9.7	13	470,800	8.8	25	21	21
6	14	15	Dun & Bradstreet, Inc.	Publishing	9.7	7	295,100	2.9	36	30	33
19	12	16	El Paso Electric Co.	Utility	9.4	12	460,800	7.2	22	20	21
21	18	17	Marsh & McLennan, Inc.	Ins. Agency	9.1	9	209,500	8.1	45	37	43
78	60	18	Swank, Inc.	Consumer Gds.	8.9	6	259,800	11.8	34	15	34
32	27	19	Thrifty Drug Stores Co. (new)	Drug Chain	8.4	8	344,600	7.6	25	20	25
12	21	20	Wyandotte Chemicals Corp.	Chemicals	8.2	8	238,200	8.2	39	34	34
70	48	21	Fieldcrest Mills, Inc.	Household Gds.	8.1	6	223,000	7.0	37	31	36
23	43	22	Transcontinental Bus System	Transportation	8.0	5	207,300	10.4	44	38	39
18	15	23	Public Svce. Co. of New Mexico	Utility	8.0	8	232,900	7.0	38	34	34
24	23	24	Shulton, Inc.	Cosmetics	7.8	6	185,100	6.5	43	32	42
55	16	25	Southern Union Gas Co.	Gas Pipe Line	7.6	7	266,000	6.4	34	29	29
1	1	26	Christiana Securities Co.	Finance	7.5	4	29,700	0.3	315	245	254
26	24	27	Grinnell Corp.	Fire Eqpt.	7.5	10	59,600	4.3	141	98	126
67	44	28	Wolverine Shoe & Tanning	Apparel	7.3	4	225,300	7.5	36	22	32
48	34	29	State Loan & Finance "A"	Finance	7.2	10	339,000	8.4	22	20	21
54	35	30	Mid-America Pipeline	Propane Gas	7.0	6	[illegible]	[illegible]	[illegible]	[illegible]	[illegible]

37	17	31	Aztec Oil & Gas Co.	Oil & Gas	6.9	5	413,900	11.0	23	17	17
60	46	32	Electrolux Corporation	Vacuum Clnrs.	6.7	12	136,300	5.5	51	40	49
17	22	33	United Nuclear Corp.	Uranium Mng.	6.7	10	348,200	7.9	26	19	19
29	30	34	Liberty Loan Corp.	Finance	6.5	3	207,500	9.5	32	28	31
27	26	35	Central Louisiana Electric	Utility	6.2	12	140,100	4.8	47	43	44
30	37	36	Western Publishing Co.	Publishing	6.1	10	217,300	6.0	29	23	28
41	51	37	Genuine Parts Co.	Auto Eqpt.	5.6	4	177,400	6.9	32	21	32
39	36	38	Russell Stover Candies	Candy	5.4	13	152,200	9.0	39	34	35
49	45	39	Hanna Mining Co.	Mining	5.3	8	99,700	2.3	57	52	53
28	31	40	Sierra Pacific Power	Utility	4.8	7	205,600	5.4	27	23	24
38	55	41	Beryllium Corp.	Beryllium	4.7	7	271,300	18.4	21	14	18
56	54	42	Smith & Wesson, Inc.	Arms & Missiles	4.7	4	99,300	35.2	–	–	48
34	40	43	Sanders Associates "A"	Electronics	4.7	14	311,900	17.2	21	15	15
–	33	44	Federal Natl. Mortgage Assn.	FHA & VA Mtges.	4.7	9	54,200	5.9	88	84	86
47	58	45	Potash Co. of America	Potash Prods.	4.6	8	96,000	7.6	51	48	48
51	53	46	Rich's, Inc.	Dept. Store	4.3	3	107,900	4.1	44	39	40
69	59	47	California Liquid Gas	Propane Gas	4.2	4	213,400	17.4	22	18	20
44	47	48	Philadelphia Suburban Water	Utility	4.2	2	142,200	5.8	32	30	30
42	50	49	Savannah Electric & Power	Utility	4.2	5	167,500	8.4	25	22	25
–	78	50	Itek Corp.	Photocopying	4.1	8	84,600	7.0	62	35	49
36	42	51	Taylor Instrument Cos.	Electronics	4.1	7	160,800	10.9	30	24	26
–	57	52	Southwest Gas Corp.	Utility	4.0	6	134,500	6.5	35	30	30
73	63	53	Northwest Natural Gas	Utility	3.9	2	225,600	4.6	19	16	18
52	56	54	Hugoton Production	Natural Gas	3.9	4	76,000	4,5	54	50	51
77	65	55	General Waterworks	Utility	3.9	2	90,900	5.5	43	38	43
			Totals		$516.9		14,484,400 Shs.				

REPLACED – LISTED: Boise Cascade Corp. – Grolier, Inc. – Jostens, Inc. "A" – Ludlow Corp. – A. H. Robins Co. – Texas Oil & Gas
DISPLACED: Baystate Corp. – Longview Fibre Co. * Fractions Omitted ** As of June 1, 1965

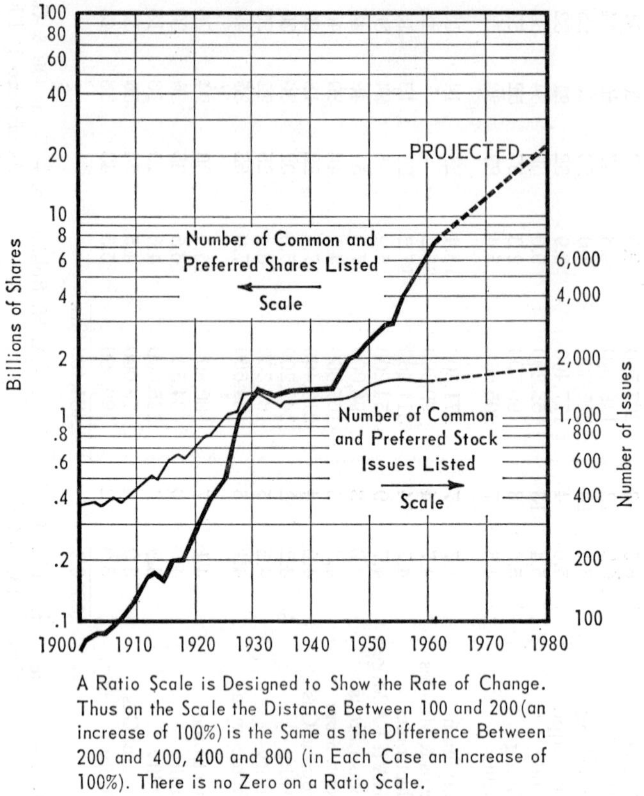

Fig. 13–1. Number of stock issues and shares listed on the New York Stock Exchange. (Reproduced with permission, from *The Exchange,* July, 1964. New York: The New York Stock Exchange.)

Types of Members

Membership on the NYSE is acquired for one of three reasons: (1) to enable the member (a broker) to transact his customers' business on the floor of the Exchange without the payment of any commissions, (2) to enable the member to have his orders executed by other members of the Exchange at reduced commission rates, and (3) to enable the member to transact his own personal business on the floor without the payment of a commission.

Commission Brokers. About half (665) of the total Exchange members are commission brokers. They execute orders received from the public through their offices throughout the United States (and branch offices in many foreign countries). They do not take title to the securities which they purchase for their customers—hence they are referred to as *brokers.*

Bond Brokers. Although commission brokers may take orders for bonds as well as stocks, there are fifteen members of the Exchange who specialize in bonds on the floor of the Exchange. They are known as *bond brokers.* Several of these operate as dealers (they take title to the bonds).

Specialists. About one fourth (382) of NYSE members are specialists. As the term indicates, they specialize in one or more stocks. In the case of some of the more active stocks, several specialists will be assigned by the Exchange to the same stock. Subject to the rules and regulations of the Securities and Exchange Commission and the NYSE, the specialist may act as either a broker or a dealer in a particular transaction (of course, not as both in the same transaction). Although he charges a commission (lower than that charged the public by commission brokers) when acting as a broker, he cannot charge one when he is acting as a dealer. The specialist "makes" the market for the stock. About half of all orders to buy or sell stocks on the NYSE are executed by the specialist, acting either as a broker or a dealer. Of all orders given to the specialist, about three fourths are filled by the specialist acting as a broker, and in the other fourth, he is acting as a dealer. Most of the "limited" and "stop" orders (explained later) are given to the specialist. The latter also practically always "opens" the stock each day. Strict rules govern the specialist to prevent him from profiting personally (as a dealer) at the expense of other brokers (for whom he is acting as a broker). The specialist never deals directly with the public.

Odd-Lot Dealers and Brokers. In the case of most of the stocks listed on the NYSE the smallest number of shares that technically may be bought or sold on the floor is 100 shares (referred to as a "round lot"). Two odd-lot houses, Carlisle & Jacquelin and De Coppet & Doremus, however, will buy or sell any number of shares from 1 to 99. These two odd-lot houses together own 22 memberships on the NYSE. In addition 106 other NYSE members are hired by these two firms as "associate" members to help them handle the odd-lot business that is sent to them by the commission brokers. Two odd-lot men operate at Post 30 (where 10 shares constitute a round lot).

Floor Brokers. Floor brokers execute orders for other members at reduced commission rates. They are used by commission brokers when they have too many orders to handle efficiently at any one time. As of January 1, 1965, there were 110 floor brokers, but as is true of other types of members, the exact number varies from time to time.

Floor Traders. Although other types of members of the NYSE may occasionally buy and sell for their own account, the floor trader is one who makes a business of trading for his own account on the floor of the Exchange. Such strict rules relating to his activities have been adopted by the Securities and Exchange Commission and the NYSE (to protect the public whose orders are filled by other members) that it is difficult for the floor trader to make a living. There are only 20 such members operating today.

Listing

The NYSE is interested in listing the stock only of large, successful corporations whose securities have a wide public following. Many requirements must be met by the corporation, and it must agree to keep its stockholders and the Exchange informed of all important developments. An initial listing fee must be paid and an annual fee for a period of fifteen years. Each listing application is considered on its own merits, but in general a company must meet the following requirements in order to be listed:

1. Demonstrated earning power under competitive conditions of $2 million annually before taxes and $1.2 million after all charges and taxes.
2. Net tangible assets of $10 million, but greater emphasis will be placed on the aggregate market value of the common stock, where $12 million or more applicable to publicly held shares at the time of listing is looked for.
3. One million shares outstanding, of which at least 700,000 common shares are publicly held among not less than 1,700 round-lot shareholders, and a total of 2,000 shareholders of record.
4. The company must be a going concern, or be the successor to a going concern.

Although bonds as well as stocks are listed on the NYSE, the principal interest of the public is in stocks, so this discussion will be confined to this type of security. Much of what is said, however, applies with equal force to bonds.

Value to Corporation. As noted above, it is only after a corporation has sold its stock to the public that it may be listed on the NYSE. The resale of the stock on the NYSE does not bring any money to the issuing corporation—the money goes to the selling shareholder. But the listing of its stock does result in a number of benefits to the issuing company. These may be summarized as follows:

1. It provides a ready, continuous market for the stock, thus making the stock more attractive to investors.

2. It helps to determine a fair price for the stock.
3. It results in more stockholders.
4. The stock tends to sell on a lower yield basis.
5. Future financing costs will probably be lower.
6. It aids in the sale of rights issued under a privileged subscription.
7. The publicity resulting therefrom, and the larger number of shareholders, may result in better sales for the company's products.

Value to Investor. Although listing may result in a stock selling on a lower yield basis, most people when buying ordinary corporate shares prefer those that are listed, for one or more of the following reasons:

1. Assurance that the company met all the listing requirements.
2. The stock may be bought or sold within a matter of minutes.
3. Immediate quotations and sales figures are available.
4. The price paid or received for the stock is fair.
5. The stock will have a higher collateral value.
6. The issuing company is compelled to issue prompt and complete financial information.
7. Lower commissions are charged for buying and selling the stock.

THE AMERICAN STOCK EXCHANGE

The American Stock Exchange (formerly called the New York Curb Exchange) is the second largest stock exchange in the United States. The organization and rules of the American Exchange are patterned very closely after those of the New York Stock Exchange, but there are several important differences.

Membership on the American Stock Exchange (ASE) is of two types: (1) regular members, the number of which in 1965 was 600, who can trade on the floor of the Exchange, and (2) associate members, of which there are 278. Associate members are not permitted on the floor, but may have their orders executed by regular members for a smaller commission than is charged non-members. The associate memberships are largely held by members of the New York Stock Exchange. The price of regular membership has ranged from $3,600 in 1923, to $254,000 in 1929.

The purpose of the American Exchange is to provide a market for seasoned securities which meet the listing requirements, and a market for the securities of new corporations which cannot meet the listing requirements of the New York Stock Exchange. Many corporate stocks now listed on the latter exchange served their apprenticeship on the American Exchange.

The listing requirements for the ASE are somewhat similar to those of the NYSE, but are not so rigid. Although the following are not inflexible requirements for listing a security on the American Stock Exchange, they are generally accepted as guidelines for companies (effective February 1, 1965):

1. Net tangible assets of at least $1,000,000.
2. Net earnings of at least $150,000 after all charges, including federal income taxes, in the fiscal year immediately preceding the filing of the listing application, and net earnings averaging at least $100,000 for the past three fiscal years.
3. Minimum public distribution of 250,000 shares (exclusive of the holdings of officers and directors and other concentrated holdings or family holdings) among not less than 750 holders, including not less than 500 holders of lots of 100 shares or more.
4. Aggregate market value of publicly held shares of at least $1,250,000. (In the case of issues selling below $5 per share the aggregate market value of the publicly held shares must be substantially in excess of $1,250,000. Generally, this will be interpreted on the basis of requiring 100,000 more publicly distributed shares for each 50 cents below $5 per share at which a stock is selling at the time the listing application is filed.)

Unlike the New York Stock Exchange, where all issues traded are listed, the American Exchange permits trading in both listed and unlisted securities. Securities which were admitted for unlisted trading privileges prior to 1934 may be continued in that category. No new issues, however, have been accepted for unlisted trading privileges since that date. As

Table 13–2. Number of Issues and Market Value of Securities Traded in on the American Stock Exchange—as of June 25, 1965

	Common Stock	Preferred Stock	Total Stock	Bonds
Number of issues listed	838	64	902	76
Unlisted	105	29	134	19
Total	943	93	1,036	95
Market value listed			$12,876,549,157	$ 971,006,554
Unlisted			15,343,445,931	295,817,088
Total			$28,219,995,088	$1,266,823,642

would be concluded from Table 13–2, the principal activity on the American Stock Exchange relates to stock, particularly common stock. The American Exchange accounts for approximately 9 per cent in value of all stocks traded in on all the organized stock exchanges in the United States (19 per cent of total share volume).

THE REGIONAL STOCK EXCHANGES

The Securities and Exchange Act of 1934 required that all organized securities exchanges be registered with the Securities and Exchange Commission unless exempt. (Four small exchanges have been exempt.) Also, all stocks traded in on the registered exchanges must be registered with the SEC. In addition to the NYSE and ASE, there are twelve registered regional exchanges throughout the United States. Listed in the order of their importance, they are as follows:

Midwest Stock Exchange (located in Chicago, with branches in Cleveland, New Orleans, and St. Louis)
Pacific Coast Stock Exchange (located in Los Angeles and San Francisco)
Philadelphia–Baltimore Stock Exchange (offices in Philadelphia, Baltimore, and Washington, D. C.)
Detroit Stock Exchange
Boston Stock Exchange
Cincinnati Stock Exchange
Pittsburgh Stock Exchange
Spokane Stock Exchange
Salt Lake City Stock Exchange
San Francisco Mining Exchange
National Stock Exchange (New York City)
Chicago Board of Trade

All of the regional exchanges combined do only about 8 per cent of the total dollar value business of all the registered exchanges. The original purpose of having the regional exchanges was to provide an organized market for local and regional stocks which could not be listed on the NYSE or the ASE. In the meantime many of the stocks that are listed or traded in on the NYSE and the ASE have, with the approval of the Securities and Exchange Commission, been given unlisted trading privileges on one or more of the regional exchanges. Today, on most of the regional exchanges, more than half of all the trading is in stocks that are listed or traded in on the NYSE and the ASE.

In addition to the registered regional exchanges, there are small stock exchanges located in Colorado Springs, Honolulu, Richmond, and Wheeling, which have been exempt from registration by the SEC. All the regional exchanges are patterned somewhat after the NYSE, but on a much smaller scale. The discussion on stock exchanges which follows will have direct application to the NYSE but most of it will apply also to the ASE and only to a much lesser extent to the registered regional exchanges.

BUYING AND SELLING LISTED STOCKS

It is fundamental to the understanding of the organized securities markets to realize that the stock exchanges themselves do not buy and sell the securities which are traded in on their floors. And it will be repeated here that the issuing corporation never sells any of its stock on the exchanges. Listed stocks are bought and sold on orders from the public or from professional members of the exchanges. The exchanges merely provide the physical facilities for the execution of orders, take care (in some instances) of the clearing of the stocks, and provide the rules and regulations under which their members may operate.

When a person gives a buy or sell order to a broker, it is telegraphed to the broker's home office or correspondent house in New York City (if the stock is listed there). From there the order is telephoned to the house's member broker on the floor of the Exchange. Upon receipt of the order this broker goes to the "post" at which the particular stock is traded, and if it is a market order, he executes it immediately. From the time the order is given by the purchaser until he receives a confirmation that the order has been executed may take only a few minutes. If the stock is bought "regular way," it will be delivered on the fourth day following the date of purchase, although it may be several weeks before the new stock certificate is received.

TYPES OF ORDERS

Market and Limited Orders

In buying or selling stocks, two types of orders may be given to the stockbroker; namely, (1) market orders, and (2) limited orders. If a market order to buy is given, it will be executed immediately at the lowest price at which sellers are willing to dispose of their stock. On the organized stock exchanges, bid and ask prices are continuously being given for stocks. The market order to buy would, of course, be executed at the lowest ask price. A market order to sell would be executed at the highest bid price.

The limited order is one in which the buyer or seller sets a definite price at which he wants the order executed. Naturally the order would not be executed until the market price reached the price specified in the order. A limited order to buy would be placed below the market, while a limited order to sell would be set above the existing market. Unless otherwise specified, a limited order, if not executed, will be automatically canceled at the end of the day on which it is given. If the customer does not want it canceled that day, he can indicate to the broker that he wants the order "open." Or he may state that it is to be open until a certain specified time.

In placing a market order the customer is sure that the order will be executed, and executed immediately. Thus, if he wants to be sure of getting into the market or getting out of the market, he accomplishes this with the order "at the market." The disadvantage of the market order is that the price paid or received may not be as satisfactory as if the limited order had been used. This is particularly true if the stock in question is inactive. On such stocks the spread between the bid and ask prices is usually relatively large. The bid and ask prices on an inactive stock may, for example, be 42 and 46, respectively, while those on an active stock may be 44 and 44⅛. A market order to buy the inactive stock would be executed at 46, and a market order to sell, at 42.

The advantage of the limited order can be seen from what has just been said. If an order to buy the inactive stock—on which the bid and ask prices were 42 and 46, respectively—were put in at about 44, there is a fair chance that it might be executed at that price almost immediately. This would be a saving of $2 per share as compared to the person who puts in a market order.

A similar gain may be made by using the limited selling order under these circumstances. The limited buy order is also used for active stocks when the customer believes that the particular stock is too high, or that the market in general is too high. He may place an open order at the price which he believes is justified for the particular stock, and then wait until the stock drops to that price. A seller may feel that he can get a higher price for his stock than the existing market price, so he puts in an open order to sell at a price above the market. In either of these instances the customer could wait until the market reached the particular price, and then place a market order. But the market may reach the point or price he has in mind, and then go back in the other direction before he gets his order in, or it may not be convenient for him to watch the market closely.

The disadvantage of the limited order is that the market price may never reach the price specified in the order, and it accordingly would not be executed. A buyer, for example, may place an order to buy at 43, when the market price is 46. The market may drop to 43¼ and then start back up and keep going up for several years. But all of this rise does him no good if he does not own the stock. The person putting in a market order at the same time would have his stock and be enjoying the rise. Before deciding on the price at which a limited order will be placed, the individual should not only study the general market thoroughly, but he should also be well acquainted with the normal fluctuations in the price of the particular stock.

The Stop Order

Aware of the many pitfalls which exist in the market, many speculators use devices or methods to limit their losses. One of these devices is the stop order (also called "stop-loss order"). At the same time that an individual buys a stock at 60, for example, he may place a stop order to sell it at 58. If he has misjudged the market and it goes down, the stop order will become a market order when the market price reaches 58. The speculator, therefore, is assured that his maximum loss will be approximately $2 per share. He may then be able to rebuy the stock at a price much lower than 58. It is also true, of course, that he may wait for the stock to go still lower, while in the meantime it may climb back up to 58 or 60 or even more, and he may find himself paying more than 60 for the stock.

The stop order can similarly be used to protect a gain. If a stock is bought at 60 and advances to 68, a stop order to sell at 66 might be given in order to protect part of the paper profit. If the stock goes higher, the price at which the stop is to be executed can be accordingly raised.

There is a psychological aspect here which is worth noting. When the average person owns stock and the price of this stock drops, he will hesitate to sell because he feels that *his* stock is almost certain to go back up. If the stop order gets him out of the market, he can look at the stock and the market from a more detached viewpoint. He may then see that the stock was not a good one, or that he had misjudged the trend of the market. With the exception of those who were forced to sell in order to pay their loans at the broker's, about the only people who got out of the market near the peaks in 1929 and 1937 were those who had stop orders in. The stop order, properly handled, may prove to be of value to the speculator.

There are two points which should be observed in connection with stop orders. The order should not be placed too close to the existing market price. Even if the market in general is relatively stable, individual stocks will fluctuate within a certain price range. Generally speaking, the higher the price of the stock, the wider will be the fluctuations. Also, the prices of inactive stocks will cover a wider range than those which are active. The stop order for these types of stocks should be placed at a greater number of points away from the market. If the sell stop order price is placed too close to the market, it may be touched off by the normal fluctuation in the price of the stock even though the market is not headed down. The past experience of the particular stock should be carefully studied before setting the price at which the stop order is to be executed.

The other point to be observed is this: after the stop order price has been set, if the market starts going down, do not change the price at which the order is to be executed. For example, stock is bought at 60, and the buyer decides that 58 is the proper price for the stop order. If the stock goes to 59, the stop order price should not be lowered to 57. If the market reaches 58 he is sold out, which is exactly the position he wished to be in at this point at the time he bought the stock. Many people keep lowering the price of the stop order as the stock declines. When this is done the stop order ceases to be a stop order.

When stocks advance in price, however, it would be advisable to keep moving up the price of the sell stop order, since the higher a stock goes, the greater is the probability of a drop. We are here speaking of speculation—where the individual is in the market to make a profit on the short swing. The person who buys for the income return or for the long-time trend would either not use the stop order, or he would use it only to limit a loss. The use of the stop order by the short seller will be mentioned in connection with short selling later in the chapter.

ODD-LOT TRANSACTIONS

With the exception of some 279 inactive stocks (the exact number of which will be found to vary from time to time), which include a number of preferred issues, the smallest number of shares which may be bought or sold on the floor of the New York Stock Exchange is 100 shares, which is called a "round lot." The smallest unit for the 279 inactive issues is 10 shares. An individual may purchase or sell less than a round lot of stock, but his order will be executed by one of the representatives of an odd-lot house. In addition to paying brokers' commissions, the buyer or seller of odd lots has to pay the odd-lot house a differential of ⅛ of a point (stocks selling at $40 a share and above have a differential of ¼ of a point) for handling the order. (This applies to the 100-share round lots.) The odd-lot houses buy stock on the floor of the Exchange in 100-share units, and then split them into smaller units for the odd-lot purchasers.

A market order for odd lots is executed at ⅛ of a point (for stocks selling below $40) away from the next sale of a round lot after the order reaches the odd-lot house representative. For example, assume that a market order to buy 10 shares of a particular stock (round lot assumed to be 100 shares) is placed with the broker. If the first sale of a round lot following receipt of this order by the odd-lot broker was at 20, the purchaser would have to pay 20⅛ for the stock. If it had been a sell order he would get 19⅞ for the stock.

If, instead of being a market order, it had been a limited order to buy at 20, the market price would have to fall to 19⅞ before the order would be executed. The buyer, however, would pay 20 for the stock. If the order had been to sell at 20, round lots of the stock would have to sell for 20⅛ before the order would be executed. The seller would get only 20.

Since stocks do not necessarily move by eighths or quarters in the market, a rule is needed for those instances in which the stock may go more than an eighth or a quarter point through the limit. The New York Stock Exchange rule on this is as follows: for stocks selling below 40, the seller gets the price specified in his order, or ½ point less than the round-lot sale which made his order effective, whichever is more favorable to the seller. For example, if the next sales, after his order to sell at 20 reached the floor, were at 19 and 21, the latter would make his odd-lot order effective, and the seller would get either 20 (the price specified) or 20½ (½ point below the effective sale price), whichever is greater. The seller would thus get 20½ in this case. If the stock is selling for more than 40, the rule is that the seller gets the price specified in his order or *one* point below the effective sale price, whichever is more favorable to him.

A similar rule applies to purchase orders. Using the above example in which a buy order was placed at 20, assume that after the order reached the odd-lot broker the next successive sales of round lots were as follows: 20½, 20, 19. The sale at 19 would make the odd lot effective, and the buyer would pay 19½ (½ point above the market), since this is more favorable to him than paying 20. If the stock is selling for more than 40, one point instead of ½ point is used in the computation. An exception to the rules just stated is that, if the effective sale is the very next sale after the order reaches the odd-lot dealer, or is the opening sale for the day, only an eighth (or a quarter in the case of stocks selling at $40 and above) is added to (in the case of a buy order) or subtracted from (in the case of a sell order) the price of the effective sale. For example, if an odd-lot order to buy at 20 is placed, and the very next sale of a round lot is at 19, the odd-lot buyer will pay only 19⅛.

In the case of stop orders for odd lots, the order is executed ⅛ point away from the next sale of a round lot that makes the stop order effective. Thus, if a stop order to sell at 20 was given when the market was 20⅛, the odd-lot broker would wait until the sale of a round lot at 20 occurred, at which time the sell order would become effective. The seller would then get 19⅞. If the market dropped from 20⅛ to 19½, the order would then become effective and the seller would get 19⅜.

If a stop order to buy an odd lot at 21 is given when the market is 20½, for example, the odd-lot broker will wait until a sale of a round lot takes place at 21, at which time the buy order becomes effective. The buyer would then pay 21⅛ for the stock. If the market goes from 20½ to 21½, the buy order would then be effective, and the buyer would pay

$21\frac{5}{8}$. The stop order to buy is used by the short seller, which will be explained later in the chapter.

About one fourth or one third of all buy and sell orders on the New York Stock Exchange are for odd lots, but this accounts for only about one tenth of the total share volume of business. Although an individual is able to enter the market with a smaller amount of capital and is better able to diversify as a result of odd-lot orders, it should be realized that he pays an eighth or quarter more and gets an eighth or quarter less than the person who deals in round lots.

COMMISSIONS AND TAXES

Brokers' Commissions

The New York Stock Exchange sets minimum commission rates which member brokers must charge for the purchase and sale of stocks for customers. Member brokers in practice charge these commissions. The minimum commission rates in Table 13–3 are for round-lot shares selling at $1 per share and above.

Table 13–3. New York Stock Exchange Commission Rates of Stocks Selling for $1 per Share and Above

Money Value of 100-Share Unit	Commission Charge for 100-Share Unit
If less than $100.00	As mutually agreed (usually 6%)
$100.00 to $399.99	2% of money value + $3
$400.00 to $2,399.99	1% of money value + $7
$2,400.00 to $4,999.99	½% of money value + $19
$5,000.00 and above	1/10% of money value + $39

It is to be noted that the commission rates are computed on the money value of a 100-share unit. Assume, for example, that a person bought 200 shares of stock at $20 per share. First we ascertain what the money value would be for 100 shares. Obviously, this would be $2,000. The commission on this would be $27 (1 per cent of $2,000 plus $7). Since the order was for 200 shares, the total commissions would be two times $27, or $54. If the transaction involves an odd lot, the commissions are $2 less than that set forth in the table. For example, the commission to buy (or sell) 10 shares (100-share round-lot stock) of stock at $30 (odd-lot differential included) per share would be $7 (2 per cent of $300 plus $1). If an order consists of, for example, 150 shares, it would be treated as a round lot for 100 shares and an odd lot for 50 shares.

The given schedule of commission rates is subject to some minimums and maximums when the amount involved in the transaction is $100 or more. The commission cannot exceed $1.50 per share or $75.00 per transaction (of 100 shares), but in any event it cannot be less than $6 per single transaction. A few examples will be given to illustrate these rules.

Transaction	Commission	Rule Applicable
5 shares, $400 per share	$7.50	$1.50 maximum per share
200 shares, $500 per share	$150.00	$75.00 maximum per 100 shares
100 shares, $1 per share	$6.00	$6.00 minimum per transaction

The above-stated commission rates are applicable both when a stockholder buys and when he sells. Generally speaking, the larger the amount of money involved in the order, the lower the percentage of commission, as the following indicates:

Money Value of 100 Shares	Commission	Commission (per cent)
$ 100	$ 6.00	6.00
500	12.00	2.40
1,000	17.00	1.70
10,000	49.00	.49

Commission rates for the American Stock Exchange are quite similar to those for the NYSE. They tend to be somewhat higher on the regional exchanges.

Stock Transfer Taxes

All sales of stock are subject to a transfer tax in four states: Florida, New York, South Carolina, and Texas. The transfer tax is paid by the seller of the stock. The New York stock transfer tax is of particular interest since all stocks sold on the NYSE and the ASE are subject to the state tax regardless of where the seller lives. The New York tax is as follows:

Per-Share Selling Price of Stock	Tax per Share
Less than $5	$0.01
$5 but less than $10	0.02
$10 but less than $20	0.03
$20 or more	0.04

The federal stock transfer tax was eliminated, effective January 1, 1966.

Securities and Exchange Commission Fee

The SEC charges the registered exchanges an annual fee on the amount of all sales made on the exchanges for the year. The exchanges pass this fee on to the seller of the stock. The amount of the fee is 1 cent for each $500 or fraction thereof of money value involved.

Total Cost

To illustrate the total costs involved in buying and selling an odd lot, we will assume that a person bought 10 shares of stock when a round lot sold for 29⅞ (so the odd-lot buyer paid $30 per share), and later he sold the stock when round lots were selling for 29⅞ (so the odd-lot seller received $29.75 per share).

	Total	Per Share
Buying Costs for		
Odd-lot differentials	$1.25	$0.125
Commission	7.00	0.700
Total cost	$8.25	$0.825
Selling Costs for		
Odd-lot differentials	$1.25	$0.125
Commission	6.95	0.695
New York tax	0.40	0.040
SEC fee	0.01	0.001
Total cost	$8.61	$0.861

Thus, the total cost for buying and selling would amount to $16.86, or $1.686 per share. So, the stock would have to go up approximately $1.686 per share before the buyer would be "even with the board" (after giving effect to the selling costs, but not adjusting for the higher commissions and taxes based on the higher market value of the stock).

MARGINAL TRADING

Purchasing on margin means that the customer or trader puts up only part of the money needed to buy the stock, and borrows the balance from the broker. (The margin required varies from time to time; see page 476.) For example, suppose Mr. Smyth has $5,600 with which he wishes to purchase a stock selling for $8 per share. If he buys the stock outright, he can acquire only 700 shares. If this stock goes up in price to $15 a share, he can sell out with a total profit of $4,900 (less his costs). But if he uses his $5,600 as a 70 per cent margin, and borrows $2,400 from his broker, he will be able to buy 1,000 shares of stock instead of only 700. If the stock goes up to $15, he can sell out and make a profit of $7,000 (less interest on the money borrowed and other costs) instead of only $4,900. Thus, he has made 125 per cent on his own money instead of only the 87½ per cent which he would have made if he had bought the stock outright.

If Mr. Smyth bought the 1,000 shares on margin and sold out when the stock hit $15, a total of $15,000 would be obtained from the purchaser. After paying off the broker's loan of $2,400, Mr. Smyth would have $12,600 cash left (commissions and taxes ignored). He may put this up as a 70 per cent margin and buy a total of 1,200 shares of the stock at $15 per share. This is 200 more shares than he originally had. His account would then stand as follows:

Margin on 1,200 shares	$12,600
Loan from broker	5,400
Cost of stock	$18,000

Should the stock advance further he will gain $1,200 for every dollar that the stock goes up, instead of only $1,000 (if he had kept only the 1,000 shares). Of course, if he had originally bought the 700 shares outright, he would stand to gain only $700 for every point the stock advanced. If the stock continues to go up in price, he may buy still more shares in this way without having to put up any more cash with the broker.

This doubling up as the stock advances is called "pyramiding" in the market. As a practical matter, it is not necessary to sell out each time the stock advances, as part of the paper profit can be used as margin for the purchase of additional shares. In the above illustration sale and repurchase were assumed because that procedure is much easier to understand.

Pyramiding has its dangers too, as does any situation where large profits are possible. In the example above, which involves buying on margin and then pyramiding, Mr. Smyth stands to lose $1,200 (some of which would be his paper profits) for every point (one dollar) the stock drops (instead of $1,000 or $700). To illustrate the point, we will assume that the broker would not call for more margin, and that the stock dropped in price to $5 a share. If Mr. Smyth sold out now, the 1,200 shares would bring only $6,000. After paying off the broker's loan (referred to as the debit balance) of $5,400, he would have only $600 left out of his original investment of $5,600. So he would lose all of his paper profit and $4,800 of his original cash (a loss of approximately 89 per cent of his original investment). Had Mr. Smyth bought the 1,000 shares on margin and not pyramided, and sold out at $5 a share and paid off the broker's loan of $2,400, he would have $2,600 left. This is a loss of only $3,200 on his original investment (approximately 57 per cent). But if he had bought the 700 shares outright his loss would be only $2,100 (a loss of approximately 37 per cent).

As a practical matter, the broker would call for more margin long before the stock got down to $5, as he would want to be sure that there is at all times sufficient equity to enable him to pay off this loan, the money for which he probably secured from a bank. (The minimum maintenance margin is discussed later in the chapter.) The call for more margin may force Mr. Smyth to cash in his insurance policies, sell all his marketable property, or try to borrow from his relatives. His attitude may be that if he is sold out now he will lose, but if he can secure some money for more margin he can hold on until the stock comes back. The fallacy of this is that the stock may never go back up, or it may be several years before it starts up, and then it may never go back up to the old high.

The inherent danger of pyramiding can be illustrated by using the analogy of the dice game of "shooting craps." Many people, when they are playing this old game, double their bets when they win, and go back to the original bet when they lose. That is one of the reasons why most people lose at this game. If the original bet is 25 cents, and the shooter wins, he may bet 50 cents, and then if he wins that he might bet $1. By the law of averages he must lose sometime, and when he does, he will lose everything he has made. This is the same as pyramiding in the stock market. If, on the other hand, he retained his original bet on wins, but doubled his bets on losses, he would probably come out ahead. For example, if he lost 25 cents, he could then shoot 50 cents, and if he loses this, he could shoot $1, etc. If he has enough cash, and if the other players stay with him, according to the law of averages he must win sometime, and when he does he will recoup all his losses. Then he could go back to the 25-cent bet.

It is not intended that the above be interpreted as a tip in shooting craps, and the authors want to make it very clear that they do *not* recommend that the speculator in the stock market try to double up on his losses. *That would be more disastrous than ever.* The above example was used only to illustrate the dangers inherent in a speculator's using his profits as margin for the purchase of additional shares.

The Securities Exchange Act of 1934 gives the Federal Reserve Board the power to set the minimum marginal requirements, and since 1934 it has varied between 40 and 100 per cent of the market value of the stock at the time of purchase. The Board will raise the minimum margin requirement when it believes that too much credit is being used in the stock market, or that an inflationary threat is present, or when it is believed that stock prices are rising too fast or going too high in view of the existing situation. Likewise, the Board will lower the margin requirement when it believes that stock buying should be stimulated in an effort to

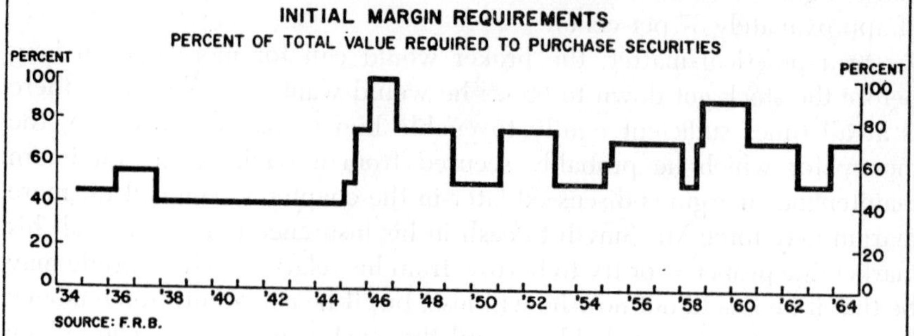

Effective	Rate	Effective	Rate	Effective	Rate
10/15/34	45%	2/ 1/47	75%	1/16/58	50%
2/ 1/36	55	3/30/49	50	8/ 5/58	70
11/ 1/37	40	1/17/51	75	10/16/58	90
2/ 5/45	50	2/20/53	50	7/28/60	70
7/ 5/45	75	1/ 4/55	60	7/10/62	50
1/21/46	100	4/23/55	70	11/ 6/63	70

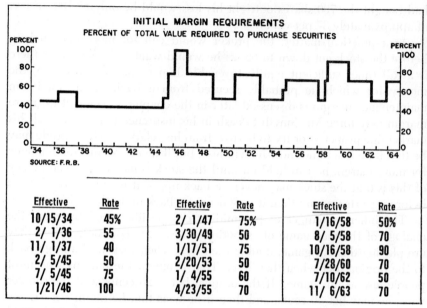

Fig. 13–2. Effective dates for initial margin requirements—1934–1963. (Reproduced with permission, from *Fact Book, 1965.* New York: The New York Stock Exchange.)

prevent a recession or depression. Figure 13–2 shows the margin requirements that have been in force since 1934, together with the dates on which changes in the margin requirement became effective.

The Federal Reserve Board establishes the minimum *initial* margin—the lowest margin on which stocks can be purchased or sold short. When this margin requirement is raised, the new margin requirement applies only to *new purchases,* and not to the stocks held in accounts existing at the time. The Board does not specify what minimum margin must be maintained after the original purchase. The New York Stock Exchange, however, sets minimum margins which must be maintained by customers of the exchange members. The minimum *maintenance* margin at the present time is 25 per cent on long accounts (purchases). If a person purchased a stock on a 70 per cent margin, the member broker must call for more margin if the stock drops more than 60 per cent, as can be seen from the following example. Assume that $70 is put up as margin to buy a share of stock selling for $100. If the stock drops 60 per cent, it would fall to $40. This decline in price of $60 would reduce the margin by a like amount, so the margin would then be only $10. This latter amount is just 25 per cent of $40, the existing market price of the stock. The broker, of course, could call for more margin before the stock had dropped the full

60 per cent. The New York Stock Exchange regulations also provide that a margin account cannot be opened with an initial margin of less than $1,000.

SELLING SHORT

One phase of stock market operations which is rather confusing to most individuals is the practice of short selling. When a person sells short, he sells stock which he does not own. The question that naturally arises is: How can a person sell something which he does not own? As we look about us we can see numerous examples of people selling things they do not have. For example, when a magazine company takes a year's subscription in advance, it is really selling the magazine short.

Speculators buy stock when they expect the price to rise. If they are successful, they sell out at a higher price. They sell stock short when they expect the price to decline. Then if the price trend is favorable to them, they buy at a lower price to cover the short sale. The short seller, in contrast to the person who buys stock expecting it to go up, makes the sale before the purchase. Since the person who buys when the short seller sells will expect delivery of the stock, it is necessary for the short seller to borrow the stock from someone and deliver it to the buyer. The following is a summary of the steps involved in short selling.

Assume that Mr. Adams believes that the price of a particular stock is too high at 70, and he expects the price to fall in the future. He sells 100 shares of the stock short at 70, and puts up the required margin of $4,900 (70 per cent). We will assume that Mr. Brown buys the stock, and pays Adams, or his broker's representative, $7,000. Adams' broker then borrows 100 shares of the stock from Mr. Clark and delivers it to Mr. Brown. This raises the question: Why would Mr. Clark lend the stock? The reason he does this is because Mr. Adams lends Mr. Clark the $7,000 which was received from Mr. Brown. Mr. Clark may need the cash in order to purchase some other stocks, and in this way he is able to borrow money for that purpose. Mr. Clark may pay Mr. Adams interest on the money borrowed at a rate similar to the call loan rate, in New York. Mr. Adams' broker, however, usually keeps this interest as compensation for his services in handling the transaction.

If short selling in the stock is so great that a relatively large number of people want to borrow the stock, then individuals like Mr. Clark might lend it only on condition that they would not have to pay any interest on the money borrowed. Under such a condition the stock would be said to loan "flat." If the supply of loanable stock becomes very scarce, Mr. Clark may not only insist that he pay no interest on the money borrowed, but he may also demand a "premium" from Adams for the loan of the stock. In recent years practically all stocks have been lending flat. Either the lender or the borrower can terminate the loan at any time upon reasonable notice to the other party.

If the price of the stock goes up to 72, for example, Mr. Clark can demand an additional loan of $200 from Mr. Adams. And likewise, if the stock goes down to 67, for example, Mr. Clark would be required to return $300 of the loan to Mr. Adams. The amount of money borrowed is thus kept even with the existing market price of the stock Adams has borrowed.

Suppose the price of the stock goes down to 64. Mr. Adams decides that this is about the low point for the swing and that he wants to take his profit. He accordingly puts in an order to buy 100 shares of the stock. If he gets the stock at 64, he will thus pay $6,400 for it. Mr. Adams then, upon due notice, returns the 100 shares of the stock to Mr. Clark, and the latter pays off the $7,000 loan, less whatever amount he had already paid as the stock declined. This purchase on the part of Mr. Adams is called "covering." The net effect of the short sale is that Mr. Adams sold the stock for $7,000, and bought it for $6,400, so his profit on the transaction is $600. His net profit would, of course, be a little less than this because he must pay brokers' commissions, taxes, and maybe a premium for the borrowed stock. Mr. Adams must also account to Mr. Clark for any dividends paid on the stock during the period.

If the price of the stock had advanced rather than declined, Mr. Adams would sustain a loss if he covered at a higher price than he received for the stock. In order to keep from losing any of his own money on the deal, Mr. Adams' broker would require that Mr. Adams put up a margin at the time the short sale was made. The minimum initial margin on short sales, as determined by the Federal Reserve Board, is the same as that required for buying. If the price of the stock goes up, the broker can call on Mr. Adams for additional margin. The minimum *maintenance* margin on short sales, which is fixed by the New York Stock Exchange, is 30 per cent of the existing market price. The short seller can use a stop order to buy in the same way and for the same reasons that an owner of the stock may use the stop-loss order to sell.

Over the years there has been considerable criticism of the practice of short selling, both in this country and abroad. But after thorough studies of its effects, it has been allowed to continue. The Securities and Exchange Commission has the power to regulate the practice, and even to eliminate it. A chief criticism of short selling has been that it causes a falling market to go down faster and further than it otherwise would. A rule adopted by the Commission and now in effect provides that short sales can be made only at a price higher than the last sales price, or at the same price as the last sale, provided the last sale price was higher than the last different price that preceded it. If the preceding sales of the stock occurred at the following prices: 70, 69⅞, 70, 70, then a short sale of the stock could be made at 70 or higher. If the price movement had been 70, $69\frac{7}{8}$, the short sale could be made only at 70 or above. Thus, a short sale cannot be made when the immediate trend of the market is down. No one will buy the stock from the short seller when he can buy it for less from someone else.

Short selling should never be attempted by anyone who is not thoroughly acquainted with the market in general and the stock in particular. The following may be a little theoretical, but it emphasizes the point. If a person buys a stock outright, the most that he can lose is his entire investment in the stock, because the lowest price the stock can go is zero. But if he sells short there is theoretically no limit to the amount of money which he may lose, because there is no top limit to which the price of the stock may go.

By the law of averages, a person who buys stock will lose less (or gain more) than the short seller, because advances in prices cover a larger number of months or years than do the declines. The price advances occurring during a number of years of prosperity may be wiped out in a year or two by a precipitous decline.

Naturally, a person should not sell short if the market or particular stock is expected to advance in price. His profit comes from a decline in price, so he would sell short only when he expects the price to fall. But determining when the price of a particular stock is going to fall is as difficult, if not more so, than figuring when it is going to advance. It takes more courage to sell short than to purchase stock. Most people are optimistic and expect stock prices to go up most of the time (which they do). The successful short seller must be able to see the unfavorable indications and have the nerve to sell when most people feel that they should hold on to their stock, or buy more.

WHEN TO BUY AND SELL

The problem of when to buy and when to sell securities is almost as important as that of determining what to buy. For the speculator it is probably even more important.

To some people the question of timing their investments presents no problem. They buy the securities when they have the money, and sell them when they need the money. This commonly results in a policy of buying high and selling low. The income, if any, received from the investment may be more than offset by the loss taken when the securities are sold.

The workings of business cycles have a profound effect on the prices of securities, and in some periods of the cycle the prices of stocks and bonds generally do not move in the same direction. Stocks are relatively low in price during a period of depression. When recovery gets under way, the prices of both stocks and bonds will advance. The increased earnings, or prospect for increased earnings, will increase the ability of the company to pay dividends and at the same time improve the safety of the bonds and the ability of the issuing company to meet the bond interest. When the recovery advances into prosperity, stocks continue to increase in price because of the increased earnings and the prospect for larger dividends. Bonds, on the other hand, particularly high-grade bonds, will usually decline somewhat in price because of the higher interest rates then prevailing, and also because of the shifting of investors from bonds to stocks. After the peak has been reached and a recession sets in, the prices of both stocks and bonds will usually fall, but stock prices will fall much faster because stocks are usually greatly inflated during the period of prosperity. When the turn comes, bonds will usually lead stocks in the decline, although this is not always the case. During a depression stock prices will usually continue downward because of the lower earnings and dividends and the pessimistic outlook for the future. The prices of good bonds, however, strengthen at this time, due in some instances to the prevailing lower interest rates and to the shift from stocks to bonds. The price patterns of stocks and bonds in the late 1940's and early 1950's did not conform to that just described, because of the governmental support of bond prices.

From what has just been said, a person might conclude that stocks should be bought at the bottom of a depression and sold when the peak of prosperity is reached. Later on, the money may be invested in bonds until the bottom of the depression is reached, at which time a shift could be made from bonds to stocks. Such an interpretation is not intended by the authors. No one knows when a peak has been reached until the economy is past it.

In a period of depression it takes more courage to buy stocks than it does to buy bonds. Furthermore, when stock prices are rising, it is difficult to make the decision to sell. It should be remembered that a person should not attempt to sell out at the peak—he never knows what that will be or when it will occur. If he sells, and the market continues to rise, he may be inclined to go back into the market and buy the stock back at a higher price, and he is just as likely not to sell out until after the turn has occurred. In fact, he may hold on so long that he finally sells out at a price lower than he paid when he re-entered the market. This is only one of the dangers which faces a person who tries to buy low and sell high.

The investor usually buys for the income derived from the investment rather than for the chance for a profit in resale. Even so, it is certainly desirable to buy at a time when the prices of securities and interest rates are such that a relatively high yield can be obtained. If good bonds are being purchased, they should be acquired during periods of relatively high interest rates, as the price will then be lower. When bond prices strengthen, it would be more conservative to hold on to the bonds rather than switch into stocks.

Difficulty is encountered in attempting to make an investment policy fit the business cycle, because it is not always easy to determine just what period of the cycle we are in at any particular time. Or, if it is known, there is no one who can accurately predict the length of a prosperous phase, or the severity of a depression phase of the cycle. A period of prosperity is characterized by abnormally heavy building construction, large iron and steel production and freight car loadings, high stock prices, low unemployment, and high interest rates. When the recession sets in, production activities, stock prices, and interest rates decline, and unemployment increases. As these trends reach extremes, depression is upon us. A reversal in the trends signals the beginning of a recovery movement, which finally flowers into another prosperous era.

In recent years some economists in the United States have been asserting that the old-fashioned business cycle is a thing of the past. It is argued that the built-in controls, and the improved ability of businessmen and governmental officials to predict ahead and to take proper steps in the right direction, can head off a recession or depression before it becomes serious. Time alone will tell. It must be admitted that the prosperity following World War II continued through the 1950's and on into the 1960's, with only a few relatively minor recessions. But throughout this period it has been noticed that one industry may be enjoying record sales and profits while another is in the doldrums. Furthermore, some companies within a particular industry are prospering when at the same time others in the same industry are experiencing declining sales. So, the problems of timing purchases and sales, and of the selection of the right industry and the best company within the particular industry remain with us.

TECHNICAL POSITION OF THE MARKET

In looking at the financial pages of the newspapers, one can see that on some days the prices of most stocks advance, while on other days they decline. And this goes on regardless of whether the general trend of the market is up or down. The general market trend, which lasts generally from one to five years, is determined by fundamental conditions such as the period of the business cycle, earnings, condition of the money market, prospects for the future, etc. But the movement in stock prices, which lasts for from one to eight weeks, or from a few hours to a few days, and is superimposed on the general trend, is caused by technical factors within the market itself.

Stock prices always appear to go too far in one direction, correct themselves, and then go too far in the opposite direction. Technical factors cause these corrective movements in the market. After stocks have gone down in price for some weeks, the market is said to be in a strong technical position. The downward trend may have resulted in part from a large volume of short selling. After a decline the short interests will start buying in to take their profits. Many of them will have stop orders to buy placed slightly above the market. When the buying starts and advances the price slightly, the stop orders to buy become market orders and are executed. Furthermore, after a decline has taken place, the weak-margined accounts will have been closed out, and additional forced selling will not be necessary. All of these factors are considered technical in nature, and the ones just mentioned result in a rise in stock prices even though the general trend of the market may be down.

Technical factors can also result in a decline in stock prices. After prices have gone up for some weeks, the bulls (those expecting prices to rise) will have overbought. Their margins may have become too thin, and their credit overextended. During a rise in the market, stocks are distributed or sold by the professional traders to the public. Thus the stock passes from strong into weak hands. A slight drop in prices will bring selling on the market. Some are forced to sell because of weak margin accounts, some because they want to take their profit or prevent a loss. After a rise has taken place, stop orders to sell are commonly placed just beneath the market in order to protect the gain. Thus when the market is relatively high it is said to be in a weak technical position, because the factors just mentioned will result in prices starting down, and once started a cumulative effect is produced. This temporary movement downward may, of course, take place when the primary trend is either up or down.

It is very difficult to predict the minor movements in the market which result from the technical factors. Only those who have had a considerable amount of experience and are close to the market should ever attempt to speculate on the minor swings.

STOCK PURCHASE PLANS

Certain stock purchase plans are available to the investor to aid him in the difficult problem of investing his money in securities. None of these is foolproof. Some of these can be used under certain circumstances, whereas others cannot be used. Not all of them would fit the needs of the particular investor. Space will not permit a detailed discussion of the relative merits of the various plans but a brief description of several types will be given.

Stock–Bond Plan

If a person has sufficient capital he may want to split his investments between stocks and bonds in order to avoid the shortcomings inherent in the purchase of either class of securities alone. The plan offers some hedge against both inflation and deflation. Many people unconsciously follow this plan without realizing it. For example, they may have some of their money invested in United States Government bonds, savings accounts, life insurance, and annuities—"fixed dollar" investments, which offer a hedge against deflation—and the balance invested in a home or other real estate, and stock, which may provide a hedge against inflation. Following are several types of stock–bond plans.

Constant Dollar Plan. A predetermined fixed dollar amount, such as $5,000, is invested in stocks and the balance is put into bonds or other fixed dollar investments. If the value of the stock investments increase, stocks are sold to bring the amount down to the $5,000. Should stock prices decline, some of the bonds are sold to enable the investor to purchase additional stocks to bring the total stock value up to the $5,000.

Constant Ratio Plan. The total investments may be divided 50–50 between stocks and bonds. If the stocks advance in price to the point where their value exceeds 50 per cent of the total, some stock is sold and bonds are purchased to bring the ratio back to 50–50. In event the value of the stocks declines and brings the stock value below 50 per cent, some bonds are sold and the proceeds invested in stock to bring the ratio back to 50–50.

Variable Ratio Plan. At the time the plan is started, the investment might be split 50–50 between stocks and bonds. But if stock prices increase by a predetermined amount (in points or percentage as measured by some stock average or index) the ratio of stock value to bond value will be reduced to 40–60, 30–70, etc., according to how high stock prices advance. On the other hand, should stock prices decline from the level existing at the time the plan was started, bonds will be sold and stocks purchased to bring the ratio of stocks to bonds up to 60–40, 70–30, etc.

Dollar Averaging Plan

In order to overcome the errors of judgment in buying and selling stocks mentioned above, the *dollar averaging* or *dollar cost averaging* plan of purchasing stocks has been devised. Under this system a fixed amount of money is invested in a diversified group of stocks at fixed intervals of time. For example, $40 or $100 or more might be invested on a given day monthly, quarterly, or annually. Over a period of years some stocks will have been purchased when prices were high, some when they were low, and some at more or less normal prices. By investing a fixed amount of money each period, however, few shares are purchased when stock prices are high and many shares when prices are low. The result is that the average *cost* per share to the investor will be less than the average *price* of the stock during the period, as may be seen from the following hypothetical example:

Investment Period	Amount Invested	Price per Share	Number of Shares Purchased
1	$ 40	$40	1
2	40	30	1⅓
3	40	20	2
4	40	10	4
5	40	20	2
6	40	30	1⅓
Total	$240		11⅔

From the above figures it can be seen that, although the average *price* of the stock during the purchase periods was $25, the average *cost* per share was only approximately $20½ ($240 divided by 11⅔).

If the dollar averaging plan is adopted, it should be adhered to regardless of the level of stock prices. There is a natural temptation to invest more money during prosperous times and less during periods of depression. This would defeat the objective of the dollar averaging plan. It is realized, of course, that in many instances a person may not be financially able to invest the fixed amount during a depression when prices are low, even if he desired to do so.

A number of open-end investment companies, described below, have "a cumulative investment program" which permits people to invest a fixed amount of money at regular intervals and thus secure the advantage of dollar averaging.

Monthly Investment Plan for NYSE Stocks

A Monthly Investment Plan (MIP) for stocks listed on the New York Stock Exchange is available through many brokers who are members of the Exchange. A person may invest any amount from $40 and up every three months, or at more frequent intervals, in any listed stock. A separate plan or agreement is arranged for each stock selected. The buyer is credited immediately with the number of shares or fractional shares which his money, less the commissions, will purchase. On a commitment of $40, for example, $37.74 is applied on the purchase of stock, and the balance of $2.26 pays the commissions (6 per cent on amounts of $100 or less)

Table 13–4. Amounts Invested and Commissions under the Monthly Investment Plan for Periodical Investments of Specified Amounts

Payment	Amount Invested at Odd-Lot Prices	Commission *	
		Amount	%
$ 40	$ 37.74	$ 2.26	6.0
75	70.75	4.25	6.0
100	94.34	5.66	6.0
200	194.00	6.00	3.1
300	293.14	6.86	2.3
500	490.10	9.90	2.0
1,000	985.15	14.85	1.5

* Commission may be less on high-priced stocks, but in all cases the 6% minimum below $100 and the $6 charge above $100 must be maintained.

Table 13–4 shows the amount actually invested and the amount of the commissions for periodic investments of amounts ranging from $40 to $1,000.

If a particular stock is selling for $100 a share (to purchasers of odd lots), the buyer would be credited with .3774 of a share (share fractions are carried out to the fourth decimal place). If the company paid a dividend of $2 a share, the owner of .3774 of a share would be entitled to 75 cents in dividends. The dividends are either paid the buyer in cash or applied to the purchase (less commissions) of additional stock, depending upon the instructions given by the buyer at the time the plan was adopted. Dividends are automatically reinvested in about 95 per cent of the plans in force.

The Monthly Investment Plan was started in January, 1954. The purchaser can drop out of the plan at any time without incurring any type of penalty. The share certificates are delivered to the buyer at the time the plan is terminated.

During the first ten years the MIP was in existence, investors bought over 7,424,571 shares under the plan. This represented an investment of over $304 million. The following, in the order listed, are the most popular stocks with MIP investors:

1. American Telephone and Telegraph
2. General Motors
3. General Telephone & Electronics
4. International Business Machines
5. Tri-Continental
6. Radio Corp. of America
7. Sears, Roebuck

Table 13–5. The Monthly Investment Plan in Retrospect—January, 1955 to January, 1965

How an investor would have stood on December 31, 1964, if he had invested $100 each month in any of the twenty stocks presently most popular with Merrill Lynch's MIP investors. Starting in January, 1955 (the month the MIP was inaugurated) and continuing through December 31, 1964, the performance of the present twenty most popular stocks is shown below.

These stocks are not necessarily all presently suggested for purchase. Those stocks that Merrill Lynch, Pierce, Fenner & Smith does suggest for long-term investment are listed in the latest issue of "20 Stocks for Long-Term Growth."

Stock	Without Reinvestment of Dividends				With Reinvestment of Dividends		
	Total Invested	Shares Owned	Market Value	Total Dividends Received	Total Invested	Shares Owned	Market Value
American Telephone & Telegraph	$12,000	278.44	$19,004	$3,491	$16,142	355.74	$24,280
Dow Chemical	12,000	182.15	13,935	1,420	13,521	203.82	15,592
Eastman Kodak	12,000	173.49	24,029	2,323	14,543	199.11	27,577
General Electric	12,000	164.75	15,363	1,854	14,040	190.55	17,769
General Motors	12,000	232.85	22,790	3,916	16,672	305.82	29,932
General Telephone & Electronics	12,000	594.28	22,434	2,765	15,141	717.60	27,089
Gulf Oil	12,000	337.76	19,759	2,341	14,600	398.16	23,293
International Business Machines	12,000	80.02	32,768	1,344	13,404	85.20	34,890
International Harvester	12,000	257.32	19,460	3,472	16,126	332.76	25,165
Minnesota Mining & Manufacturing	12,000	325.49	18,024	1,419	13,496	353.53	19,577
Pacific Gas & Electric	12,000	523.09	17,916	2,970	15,427	647.12	22,164
Pfizer (Charles)	12,000	436.95	21,629	2,507	14,780	509.44	25,217
Phillips Petroleum	12,000	239.91	12,835	2,301	14,593	289.26	15,475
Radio Corporation of America	12,000	783.49	26,541	1,862	14,043	893.07	30,253
Safeway	12,000	726.42	27,114	3,306	15,711	870.99	32,553
Scott Paper	12,000	425.68	14,420	1,878	14,058	487.83	16,525
Sears Roebuck	12,000	257.93	33,338	2,500	14,780	299.59	38,722
Standard Oil of California	12,000	249.24	18,288	2,446	14,774	301.24	22,103
Standard Oil of New Jersey	12,000	212.83	19,182	2,855	15,313	266.66	24,033
Tri-Continental	12,000	315.66	15,428	2,976	15,498	398.73	19,488

The above table shows for each stock the number of shares an investor would have owned at December 31, 1964 and the market price of such shares on that day (1) if dividends had not been reinvested and (2) if dividends had been reinvested. Dividends received and dividends reinvested are before deduction for income taxes. Brokerage commissions on all purchases have been deducted.

The table illustrates how an investment through MIP can work out over a period of years. It is, of course, no indication as to future performance of any of the 20 stocks or of any other stock which might be purchased under MIP. Accordingly, the investor should take into account his financial ability to continue purchases through periods of low price levels. An investor should understand that he will incur a loss if he discontinues his purchases or sells when the market price of his shares is less than his average cost and that the MIP does not protect against loss in value in declining markets. The Monthly Investment Plan is designed to take advantage of temporary fluctuations in the market price and its advantages depend upon continuous, regular investment.

Table 13–6. A Special Investor's Account in Retrospect—January, 1955 to December, 1964

How an investor would have stood on December 31, 1964, if he had invested $1,000 in any of the twenty stocks presently most popular with Merrill Lynch's MIP investors. The investment figures below show what would have happened if an investor had either had his dividends paid out to him, or had his dividends reinvested in the particular stock shown.

These stocks are not necessarily all presently recommended for purchase. Those stocks that Merrill Lynch, Pierce, Fenner & Smith does recommend for long-term investment are listed in the latest issue of "20 Stocks for Long-Term Growth."

	Without Reinvestment of Dividends				With Reinvestment of Dividends		
Stock	Total Invested	Shares Owned	Market Value	Total Dividends Received	Total Invested	Shares Owned	Market Value
American Telephone & Telegraph	$1,000	34.0800	$2,326	$706	$1,931	54.1134	$3,693
Dow Chemical	1,000	23.7790	1,819	313	1,345	28.8373	2,206
Eastman Kodak	1,000	31.4692	4,358	585	1,671	39.3642	5,452
General Electric	1,000	21.0027	1,959	419	1,484	27.5026	2,565
General Motors	1,000	29.1262	2,851	771	2,011	46.4556	4,547
General Telephone & Electronics	1,000	125.1290	4,724	900	2,090	173.2259	6,539
Gulf Oil	1,000	57.7895	3,381	601	1,699	75.4232	4,412
International Business Machines	1,000	20.9651	8,585	437	1,465	23.0814	9,452
International Harvester	1,000	25.9771	1,965	584	1,759	41.0753	3,106
Minnesota Mining & Manufacturing	1,000	68.9655	3,819	402	1,435	78.4533	4,344
Pacific Gas & Electric	1,000	64.7297	2,217	591	1,736	94.3494	3,231
Pfizer (Charles)	1,000	74.7353	3,699	609	1,714	96.5743	4,780
Phillips Petroleum	1,000	26.3234	1,408	468	1,564	37.5165	2,007
Radio Corporation of America	1,000	91.2893	3,092	377	1,440	118.9075	4,028
Safeway	1,000	131.2526	4,899	847	2,015	177.1418	6,614
Scott Paper	1,000	48.3492	1,638	373	1,432	62.7929	2,127
Sears Roebuck	1,000	39.5004	5,105	550	1,648	51.1418	6,610
Standard Oil of California	1,000	31.1668	2,287	528	1,636	43.8869	3,220
Standard Oil of New Jersey	1,000	26.9058	2,425	633	1,788	40.3408	3,636
Tri-Continental	1,000	35.7332	1,746	605	1,779	55.9403	2,734

The above table shows for each stock the number of shares an investor would have owned at December 31, 1964 and the market price of such shares on that day (1) if dividends had not been reinvested and (2) if dividends had been reinvested. Dividends received and dividends reinvested are before deduction for income taxes. Brokerage commissions on all purchases have been deducted.

The table illustrates how an investment can work out over a period of years. It is, of course, no indication as to future performance of any of the 20 stocks or of any other stock which might be purchased. An investor should understand that he will incur a loss if he sells when the market price of his shares is less than his cost and that a Special Investors Account does not protect against loss in value in declining markets.

SOURCE: Merrill Lynch, Pierce, Fenner & Smith, Inc.

8. General Electric
9. Minnesota Mining & Mfg.
10. Standard Oil Co. (N.J.)

In addition to the "forced savings" which result from following the MIP it forces the investor into dollar averaging, which has proved to be a very worthwhile procedure. Table 13–5 shows what an investor's position would have been with the MIP if he had started it in January, 1955, when the MIP was inaugurated, and continued it for a ten-year period to January, 1965. Investment of $100 a month in each of twenty popular stocks is assumed. Table 13–6 shows the results for the same ten-year period of making a lump-sum investment of $1,000 in each of the twenty stocks in January, 1955.

Investment Clubs

Many people would like to buy good stocks to augment their investment in savings accounts and government bonds, and to serve as a hedge against inflation, and would like to be able to invest in stocks regularly in order to obtain the advantage of dollar averaging, discussed above. But the trouble is that the average person does not have sufficient savings to do this. Either he could not purchase a whole share of stock regularly, or if he could, the commissions would be prohibitive. One solution is the *investment club.*

A group of from ten to twenty people who have a common interest in the purchase of stocks may get together and form an investment club. Presumably the people would be good friends or have some common tie such as working at the same place, or belonging to the same social club, or being neighbors. The investment club could be incorporated, or if the group feels that the taxes would be too high to operate as a corporation, they could carry on as a partnership. Although the latter form of organization gives unlimited liability to the members, the possibility of any liability is very remote.

Each member of the club would contribute a fixed amount per month, such as $10. The total contributions would then be used monthly to purchase stocks selected by the members. A committee, or several committees, could be appointed by the officers to report on the desirability of buying certain stocks at the monthly meeting. After a thorough discussion of the relative merits of the stocks suggested, the members would vote on which should be purchased. In some instances the purchase may be delayed a month in order to reduce the commission percentage. It is suggested, however, that the members not attempt to postpone buying for a prolonged period "waiting for the market to come down." This will result in speculation rather than investment. Also, the members should overcome the temptation to sell when they see a profit in the stocks. If they attempt to "buy cheap and sell dear," the members will be speculating and trading, and before they know it, they may find that they are buying back in at a higher price than that at which they sold. Perhaps they should decide to buy the stocks as an investment, for a relatively long period, such as, for example, five years. At the end of this period, the members can appraise the situation and determine their future course.

The number of investment clubs in the United States has increased tremendously in recent years. People have found that, in addition to serving as a means of investment, the investment club procedure also enables an individual to acquire a considerable amount of knowledge about various industries, and companies, and in general about business and the field of investments. Those interested in forming an investment club can get helpful information from the National Association of Investment Clubs, Detroit, Michigan.

THE INVESTOR'S DILEMMA

When it comes to the stock market, people are usually confronted with at least five questions. The first is, "Should I buy stocks?" If this can be answered in the affirmative, the remaining questions are: "How much should I put into stocks?" "When should I buy?" "What stocks should I buy?" "How long should I hold on to the stocks?" No definite answer to these questions can be given to any particular person, to say nothing of the impossibility of attempting to answer all these questions in such a manner that they would apply to everyone. A few general answers, however, can be given.

Before undertaking the purchase of stocks the typical person should first have an adequate life insurance program to protect his family in the event of his early death. He should own his own home, or have a home within his means that is at least half paid for. He should have savings accounts or United States bonds sufficient in amount to cover a crisis or emergency or illness of normal duration when his income may be temporarily suspended. If a person purchases stock without such an emergency fund he may find it necessary in the future to sell his stocks—possibly at a loss—to carry him over. A final statement on the point: *Some people should never buy stocks.* Some stocks are almost certain to fall in price, at some time or other, below that paid for them. Many people are not temperamentally constituted to stand this. They rush in to sell when this happens. It is apparent that these people should never buy stocks since they are almost certain to lose money.

The smaller the person's estate, the larger the percentage which should be invested in relatively safe fixed-dollar investments such as life insurance, savings accounts, and United States savings bonds. As more investable funds become available, a larger amount, as well as a larger percentage, may be invested in stocks. A person or family in moderate financial circumstances may plan to have approximately half of their assets (exclusive of their home) in stocks, or in stocks and rental real estate combined. This half of the estate will provide a hedge against inflation and enable the owner to profit from the long-term secular growth which may be experienced in this country. The other half will provide security and a hedge against deflation.

The extreme difficulty of properly timing the purchase of stocks has already been mentioned. One way of solving the problem is to "dollar average" the purchases as described above. This can be done by the person acting alone, but because of lack of the proper self-discipline, some organized plan or procedure is recommended. These would include the Monthly Investment Plan, an investment club, or a cumulative or savings plan offered by one of the leading mutual funds, which is described in Chapter 14. If a person is confronted with the problem of investing a sizable amount of money at one time, he may split it evenly between fixed-dollar investments and stocks. Or, most of the money may be invested in savings accounts or United States savings bonds, and a relatively small amount invested in stocks. Then each six months thereafter part of the fixed-dollar investments may be liquidated and the proceeds invested in stocks until the desired ratio between the two types of investments is reached. In this way the investor may avoid the shortcoming of investing a sizable amount of money in stocks at a time which later events proved to be a high point in the market.

Comment on the next point raised—what stocks to buy—will be given after something has been said about the question of deciding when to sell. The shortest—and perhaps the best—answer that can be given to this is: Don't sell! In most instances the only time a person suffers a loss on a listed stock is when he sells it. (Of course he may have a "paper loss" before that time.) If people buy stocks only under the circumstances stated above, they will not be forced to liquidate their holdings. Their decision to sell then results from one of the following: to prevent a loss, or to prevent a further loss; to take a profit; to get the funds in order to invest in something else. Any stock that is purchased may go down in price. Sale at that time naturally results in a loss. But if the "right" stock is purchased it will probably be higher five years from now and ten years from now, even though its price may have declined at various times during the period. The temptation to take a profit by selling may be great. But the sale of stock at a profit necessitates the payment of the capital gains tax, which thereby depletes the fund by amounts up to 25 per cent of the amount of the gain. The retention of the stock means retention of the entire 100 per cent invested. Furthermore, the factors that have given a paper profit in the stock may still be present and will produce further gains in the future. If the stock is sold, the seller may find himself in the future going back into the stock at a still higher price (and with the principal reduced by the capital gains tax). In fact, people who sell at a loss often see their stock advance in price not only beyond that at which they sold, but even higher than the price they paid for it. And some of these same people decide they made a mistake by selling, and they buy back the stock at this higher price. This process may be repeated a number of times over a period of years. A person should not allow himself to be whipsawed in this fashion. He should *invest*, not trade.

The switching from one stock to another may result in the same shortcomings as trading back and forth in the same stock. Here again, if the stock has been well selected it should prove to be as attractive over a long period as some other stock. Furthermore, the capital gains tax that must be paid on any increases in the market price thereby reduces the amount of capital that may be invested in another stock. In addition, odd-lot differentials and the double commissions—those for selling and those for buying—further reduce the size of the investment fund.

It must be admitted that there may come a time when it would be desirable to sell a particular stock. Unforeseeable future events may cause a particular industry or particular company to start the downhill path toward obscurity or failure. It is observed, however, that the better managed companies tend to adjust their policies and operations to cope successfully with changing conditions. So the conclusion remains that, generally speaking, the average investor should attempt to select the best stocks and hold on to them for the long-term pull. Stock market trading should be confined to the professionals or to those who have sufficient capital to be able to stand the losses that might follow.

SELECTING THE RIGHT STOCKS

When a person has decided at a particular time to invest some money in stocks, he is immediately confronted with the problem of what particular stock or stocks to buy. Here again, no solution can be given which would apply to all individuals alike. Investment programs must be tailored to fit the need of the particular investor. If a person has such a small amount of money available that he can purchase the stock of only one company, perhaps he should give serious consideration to the buying of stock of an investment company—these are discussed in Chapter 14. This is the only way he can get diversification with a small amount of money. If a person already owns stock in a number of different companies in various industries, stocks can be recommended that will provide him with a wider diversification.

In addition to the factors mentioned above, no recommendation can be made until the particular objective of the investor is known. If a person has only a small amount invested in stocks or can invest only a relatively small sum of money, and if his other investments are relatively small and his income is of modest amount, he cannot afford to take a chance. Thus, he should stick to stocks which offer a relatively high degree of safety of principal and assurance of a fair income return. It is a general principle of investments that the degree of safety and the rate of return vary inversely. That is, the safer the principal, the lower the rate of return. For the small investor, particularly, the safety should not be sacrificed for a high rate of return.

Table 13–7. Selected List of Top-Grade Industrial Common Stocks

Company	Standard & Poor's Rating	Value Line Rating	Dividends Paid Each Year Since
American Home Products	A+	A−	1919
Avon Products	A+	A+	1919
Borden	A+	A−	1899
Bristol-Myers	A+	A	1905
Campbell Soup	A+	A−	1902
Chesebrough-Pond's	A+	A	1883
Consolidated Cigar	A+	A	1937
du Pont (E.I.)	A+	A−	1904
Eastman Kodak	A+	A	1902
General Electric	A+	B+	1899
General Foods	A+	A	1922
Hershey Chocolate	A+	A	1930
International Business Mach.	A+	A	1916
Kellogg	A+	A	1922
Merck	A+	A−	1935
Minnesota Mining & Mfg.	A+	A−	1916
National Biscuit	A+	A	1899
National Dairy Products	A+	A−	1924
Procter & Gamble	A+	A	1891
Sears, Roebuck	A+	A−	1935
Smith, Kline & French	A+	A	1923
Standard Oil of N. J.	A+	B+	1883
Texaco	A+	A−	1903

Leading top-quality railroad, public utility, and communications common stocks have been listed in the preceding chapter. Table 13–7 contains a list of top-quality industrial stocks, all listed on the New York

Stock Exchange, together with their Standard & Poor's and Value Line ratings, and the year in which regular dividends began.

Table 13–8 contains data similar to those in Table 13–7 for selected common stocks listed on the New York Stock Exchange which, according to at least one of the rating agencies, do not quite meet the standard of top-quality, but nevertheless would be considered high-grade common stocks. It should be appreciated, of course, that the quality of a particular stock may change over a period of time, and when this occurs, the rating agencies will accordingly change the rating on the stock. The ratings given in the accompanying tables were applicable July 2, 1965.

Table 13–8. Selected List of High-Grade Common Stocks

Company	Standard & Poor's Rating	Value Line Rating	Dividends Paid Each Year Since
Associated Dry Goods	A	A−	1943
Beatrice Foods	A	A−	1935
Beech-Nut Life Savers	A	A−	1902
Coca-Cola	A	A−	1893
Consolidated Foods	A	A	1946
Federated Department Stores	A	A−	1931
General Motors	A	B+	1915
Ginn & Co.	A	A−	1949
Helme Products	A−	A	1912
Macy, R. H.	A	A−	1927
Plough, Inc.	A+	A−	1931
Quaker Oats	A	A−	1906
Reynolds Tobacco	A+	A−	1901
Safeway Stores	A	A−	1927
Standard Oil of Calif.	A+	B+	1912
Sunshine Biscuits	A	A−	1927
Walker, Hiram	A−	A	1936
Warner-Lambert	A	A−	1934
Winn-Dixie Stores	A	A−	1934

The stocks listed in Tables 13–7 and 13–8 would all qualify as *blue chip* stocks. This term is applied to the stock of those leading companies which have experienced no losses for a relatively long period of time and which have had a steady record of earnings and dividend payments. Blue chip stocks are sometimes referred to as *heirloom* stocks, or stock market *aristocrats.* Because of the long and successful record of these companies, their stocks have been in great demand on the part of investment companies, trust companies, pension and profit-sharing plans, investment clubs, and the public in general. As a result, the price that must ordinarily be paid for them is relatively high in relation to the current earnings and dividends. Many of the blue chip stocks have qualified as growth stocks.

Growth Stocks

A great deal of emphasis in the stock market today is put on growth stocks. A *growth* stock is one on which the earnings have been constantly increasing at a faster rate than the typical company and such increase is expected for some years into the future. The rate of growth is greater than would be expected from the population increase. Although growth companies may fall back somewhat in a business recession, they usually do not suffer to the same extent that the typical company does. Furthermore, they snap back faster and reach higher earnings peaks in succeeding cycles.

It is easy to look back and see what have been the growth stocks of the past. But the past earnings benefited the former and present owners of the stock. Generally speaking, the buyer of the stock today will benefit only from the future earnings of the company. Confusion exists when past experience is projected into the future. Although the past is surely an important factor in attempting to predict the future, it does not follow that the growth stocks of the past will be the growth stocks of the future.

Growth stocks are found in growth companies within growth industries. What are the growth industries of the future? Time alone will tell. But here are some things the experts tell us. There has been a large increase in the population in recent years, and this will continue in the future. This will result in a greater demand for articles purchased for or by children and teen-agers: sporting goods, clothing, textbooks, and school facilities. People are living longer than formerly. A larger percentage of our population will be in the "old" category. This will increase the demand for vitamins and other drugs, housing facilities for the aged, etc. Pressure will continue for higher wages. This will result in more automation and mechanization. Furthermore, labor-saving devices will be needed since a smaller proportion of the population will be in the working-group age bracket. In addition, workers will be putting in a shorter work week. The greater leisure time of the working group, plus the increase in both the youngsters and oldsters, will result in a greater demand for goods used in leisure-time activities. These would include bowling alleys, boating, fishing, sporting goods, do-it-yourself tools, etc. A shift in population to Florida and the Southwest will result in increased earnings for electric and gas utilities and telephone companies located in these particular areas. More money will be spent on public works, schools, and interstate highways. The federal government may be forced to spend more money for defense purposes. The electronics and space industries offer almost unlimited possibilities for future development.

After the investor has determined which, in his own mind, will be the best growth industries in the future, he is confronted with the problem of selecting the particular company or companies which he believes will do the best. This is a difficult matter. Like judging the industry, one approach is to determine which companies have done the best in the past in increasing their earnings per share, and then try to determine whether this experience will carry forward into the future. One factor to look at is the percentage of the sales dollar that is going into research and development. Generally speaking, those companies which have put the largest percentage of their income into research and product development have been able in the past to show the best growth. Those which have used the money for *new* product development as well as improvement of present products have done better in general than those which have expended the funds for old product development alone. The development of new industries or the demand for new products causes many new companies to rush into the field. Many of these companies are small, poorly financed, and do not have the amount of money needed for research and development. Furthermore, many of them are organized and operated by inexperienced management. They cannot successfully compete with the large, well-established, well-financed, and well-managed companies which also take on the manufacture and sale of the new products that are in demand. A larger percentage may be made on money invested in the small new companies that *later* prove to be successful than in the large established ones, but the chances of picking an embryo General Motors or International Business Machines are slim.

Following is a list of what would at the present time be considered long-term growth stocks. Some of these are high-quality blue-chip stocks and were included in the above lists of top-quality and high-grade stocks. Some of them, however, have to date never paid a cash dividend, and would be considered speculative stocks.

Selected List of Long-Term Growth Stocks

Addressograph-Multigraph
Aerojet-General
American Electric Power
American Home Products
American Hospital Supply
Avon Products
Bristol-Meyers
Coca-Cola
Chesebrough-Pond's
Conn. General Life Ins.
Consolidated Cigar
Continental Casualty
Control Data
Corn Products
Eastman Kodak
Federated Dept. Stores
Florida Power
Florida Power & Light
Franklin Life Insurance
General Foods
General Tel. & Electronics
Honeywell

(*Continued on next page*)

Int'l Business Machines	Procter & Gamble
Jefferson Standard Life Insurance	Scott Paper
Kellogg	Sears, Roebuck
Kerr-McGee Oil	Smith, Kline & French
Litton Industries	Standard Brands
Magnavox	Texaco
McDonnell Aircraft	Texas Utilities
Minnesota Mining & Mfg.	Transamerica
Norwich Pharmacal	Warner-Lambert
Pfizer (Chas.)	Winn-Dixie
Philips Lamp Works	Xerox
Polaroid	Zenith

Having selected the growth industries and growth companies, the investor must then decide whether the price of the stock is so relatively high that all of the foreseeable growth in the stock has already been discounted. Growth stocks are characterized by high price-earnings ratios (high market price in relation to earnings per share), and extremely low (or non-existing) yields (dividend per share divided by the price per share).

The price-earnings ratio (stock price divided by annual earnings per share) may vary from 30 to 50, or in some instances even to 100. Yields may be less than 1 per cent. (In some instances the particular company may be classed as a growth company but the stock may no longer be a growth stock.) However, should the earnings per share continue to increase in the future, the relatively high prices may be justified. Particularly would this be the case if investors continued to value the stock at the same (or even higher) price-earnings ratio. So long as the company can plow back the earnings and earn much more on them than the stockholder can, then the investor may profit in the long run. The investor can, of course, profit from a successful growth stock in two ways: retain the stock and enjoy receiving increased dividends as time goes on or sell the stock and make a profit over his cost price. Tables 13–9 and 13–10 show selected lists of growth stock.

Favorites of Institutional Investors

Institutional investors refers to the large professional investors such as endowment funds, mutual funds, closed-end investment companies, insurance companies, pension funds, and trust funds. Collectively they own slightly in excess of 20 per cent of all stocks listed on the New York Stock Exchange. These institutions are managed by experienced people who are professionals when it comes to investing. Although their investment needs and requirements may differ from those of an individual, it is still of considerable interest to a person to know what stocks are preferred by these large institutional investors. Table 13–11 shows the fifty stocks listed on the New York Stock Exchange which are favored by institutional investors; the stocks are ranked according to the number of institutional stockholders.

Table 13–9. 20 Stocks for Long-Term Growth

Name of Stock	Approx. Price 6/18/65	Current Annual Div. Rate	Yield %	Consec. Years Divs. Pd.	1965 Price Range * High	Low
Aluminium Ltd.	27	\$0.80[a]	3.0[a]	27	32⅛	26⅝
Chesebrough-Pond's	26	0.60	2.3	83	29¼	21½
Corn Products	52	1.50	2.9	47	58¾	49½
Du Pont	236	5.75[g]	2.4[g]	62	261	232¼
Eastman Kodak	79	1.40[e]	1.8[e]	64	84⅝	69⅛
FMC Corp.	67	1.20	1.8	31	71¾	59¾
Firestone	45	1.20	2.7	42	50¼	43¼
General Electric	97	2.20	2.3	67	106¾	91
General Foods	80	2.00	2.5	44	86	78⅛
General Tel. & Electronics	40	1.00	2.5	30	43⅛	36
Insurance Co. of North Amer.	88	2.00	2.3	92	98¾	84⅜
IBM	462	6.00	1.3	50	491½	404
Merck	56	1.00[e]	1.8[e]	31	59¾	48½
Pacific Gas & Electric	36	1.20[b]	3.3[b]	47	40⅜	33⅞
RCA	34	0.70[c]	2.1[c]	26	37½	31
Safeway Stores	36	1.00	2.8	39	42¼	33⅜
Scott Paper	35	0.90	2.6	51	38⅞	33⅝
Sears, Roebuck	69	1.00[e]	1.4[e]	31	77	62¾
Standard Oil of California	69	2.20	3.2	54	76¼	67⅜
Texaco	77	2.30[c, f]	3.0[c, f]	63	87½	72½

* Adjusted for stock splits and stock dividends of 10% or more.
[a] In U.S. funds subject to applicable Canadian non-residents tax.
[b] Dividends expected to be partially exempt from Federal income taxes.
[c] Including extra.
[e] Excluding extra.
[f] Plus stock.
[g] Estimated.

SOURCE: Merrill Lynch, Pierce, Fenner & Smith, Inc., June, 1965.

Figure 13–3 shows the percentage increase in holdings of NYSE stocks by types of institutional investors for the years 1956–1964. Pension funds represent the largest single type of owner at the present time. Their relative importance has been constantly increasing, and it is expected that this increase will continue in the future. "Non-insured" pension funds are those which are not administrated by insurance companies. Pension

Table 13–10. Growth Stocks

Annual Per-Share Growth Rates (percentages)					Per-Share Earnings						
Revenues	Earnings	Dividend	Stock Price		Est. 1965	1964	Indicated Dividend	1963–1965 Price Range	Recent Price	Current Yield	Ratio of Price to Est. 1965 Earnings
6.9	7.8	4.0	14.1	Abbott Laboratories	$ 1.90	$ 1.71	$1.00	50 - 24½	46	2.2%	24.2
1.6	5.9	6.0	11.7	Borden	2.05	1.84	1.11	47¼– 28½	44	2.5	21.5
10.3	8.6	8.0	11.9	Delaware Power & Light	2.60	2.40	1.68	64½– 46¼	59	2.8	22.7
5.1	7.6	10.2	15.9	* General Foods	3.70	3.44	2.00	93¼– 77½	80	2.5	21.6
16.1	21.7	30.4	16.9	IBM	13.50	12.30	6.00	494 –307¾	467	1.3	34.6
9.3	7.8	7.6	11.3	Chas. Pfizer	2.50	2.27	1.25	60⅜– 44¼	55	2.3	22.0
5.3	8.0	19.7	30.3	** Procter & Gamble	3.05	2.99	1.85	86½– 69⅝	74	2.5	24.3
6.2	8.2	8.1	14.1	Virginia Electric & Power	1.95	1.72	1.20	51⅞– 38¾	47	2.6	24.1

* Fiscal years end March 31 of following years.
** Fiscal years end June 30.

SOURCE: *Moody's Stock Survey* (July Stock Selector), July 12, 1965 (New York: Moody's Investors Service).

Table 13–11. Stocks Most Widely Held by Institutional Investors

Stocks are ranked according to the number of institutional holders in DATA DIGESTS' survey. Latest ranking reflects an increased number of portfolios surveyed as well as changing preferences mainly of investment companies.

Number Institut'ns Holding Stock As Latest Reported		Price Per Com. Share May 17, 1965	Common Stocks Favored By Institutions	Rank By No. of Institutions (Varied Kinds**) Holding This Stock—In Order of Latest Indicated Preference			
Invest. Cos. Only*	Varied Kinds**			Most Recent	3 Mos. Ago	1 Yr. Ago	2 Yrs. Ago
182	1329	106¼	General Motors	1st	1st	1st	1st
176	1235	78⅜	Standard Oil (N. J.)	2nd	2	2	2
117	1155	69	American Tel. & Tel.	3rd	3	3	3
109	1061	104¼	General Electric	4th	4	4	4
187	1027	474½	Int'l Business Mach.	5th	5	6	7
141	979	78¾	Texaco Inc.	6th	6	5	6
80	887	252¼	Du Pont (E. I.)	7th	7	7	5
91	837	a68⅛	Union Carbide	8th	8	8	8
107	735	82	Socony Mobil Oil	9th	9	9	9
108	704	56¼	Gulf Oil	10th	10	10	11
72	651	71¼	Sears, Roebuck	11th	12	14	17
79	647	a82¼	Eastman Kodak	12th	11	11	12
102	613	58⅝	Ford Motor Co.	13th	13	13	16
44	595	53⅛	Phillips Petroleum	14th	14	12	10
70	577	69¾	Standard Oil Calif.	15th	16	15	13
106	572	92½	Monsanto Co.	16th	18	18	27
76	566	34⅞	Internat'l Paper	17th	17	17	18
41	561	b58¼	First Nat'l City Bank	18th	15	15	15
53	545	76⅛	National Lead	19th	19	21	22
59	513	44	Amer. Electric Pr.	20th	21	18	19
30	510	82⅛	General Foods	21st	20th	20th	24th
31	504	78	American Cyanamid	22nd	22	22	25
65	494	42¾	Standard Oil (Ind.)	23rd	24	23	20
64	486	76⅝	Dow Chemical	24th	23	24	21
44	467	40⅞	South'n Calif. Edison	25th	25	26	26
62	445	63¼	Texas Utilities	26th	26	28	29
57	436	56⅛	Goodyear Tire & Rub.	27th	30	38	45
33	432	66⅝	Chase Manhattan Bk.	28th	29	31	31
49	431	53½	Allied Chem. Corp.	29th	28	27	30
24	426	56¾	Commonw'th Edison	30th	27	29	27
25	424	77¾	Penny (J. C.)	31st	31	32	36
55	418	62⅝	Minnesota M. & Mfg.	32nd	32	39	46
68	409	68¾	Southern Co.	33rd	33	34	32
68	406	41⅛	Gen'l Telephone & El.	34th	43	65	63
50	402	49⅝	Virginia Elec. & Pr.	35th	35	37	38
14	399	96	Nat'l Dairy Prods.	36th	34	33	41
22	388	59⅞	Consumers Power	37th	37	34	34
57	383	46⅝	Caterpillar Tractor	38th	40	51	52
48	383	57⅛	Merck & Co.	38th	40	41	44
64	378	73	Continental Oil	40th	39	46	37
30	378	38⅞	Pacific Gas & Elec.	40th	42	42	42
50	375	51½	U. S. Steel	42nd	35	25	14
56	374	50¼	Cent. & South West	43rd	45	45	43
119	374	92¾	Int'l Nickel of Can.	43rd	44	36	33
57	373	53¾	Westinghouse Elec.	45th	38	30	23
21	370	55⅛	Corn Products	46th	49	47	54
25	366	46⅞	American Can	47th	48	40	40
33	365	74⅛	Procter & Gamble	48th	45	47	58
34	361	70⅜	Amer. Home Prods.	49th	51	52	68
22	358	109⅜	Morgan Guaranty Tr.	50th	47	44	34

* Indicates how many out of a total of 420 investment companies hold this stock.

** Indicates how many out of a total of more than 2,100 financial institutions (insurance companies, investment companies, common trust funds, etc.) hold this stock.

Note: a and *b* refer to footnotes elsewhere in the *Digest*.

SOURCE: *Monthly Stock Digest,* June, 1965 (New York: Data Digests, Inc.).

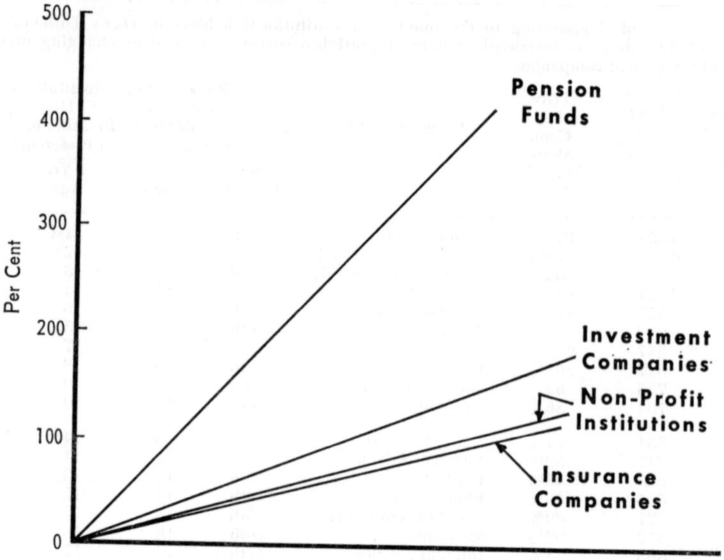

Fig. 13–3. Percentage increase in holdings of New York Stock Exchange stocks, 1956–1964. (Reproduced with permission, from *The Exchange*, March, 1965. New York: The New York Stock Exchange.)

funds that have been insured by insurance companies are included in the figures for insurance companies.

QUESTIONS

1. Explain what is meant by the "stock market." Are both primary and secondary distributions of stock included within the meaning of the term? Explain.
2. (a) List the types of sales that occur in the over-the-counter market.
   (b) List the kinds or types of securities that are bought and sold in the over the-counter market.
3. How does a securities exchange market differ from the over-the-counter market? What functions are performed by the securities exchanges?
4. The following questions pertain to the New York Stock Exchange:
   (a) How would a person acquire membership on the Exchange?
   (b) Check through recent issues of *The Wall Street Journal* to determine at what price the last sale of a membership took place.
   (c) Indicate the different types of membership and explain the functions of each.
   (d) What advantages accrue to a person owning a membership on the Exchange?
   (e) Does the Exchange buy and sell stocks? Explain.
   (f) Does the Exchange determine the prices of listed stocks?
   (g) Do you believe the Exchange should determine the minimum commission rates members can charge their customers? Why or why not?

5. Assume that Adams in New York City placed a buy order for 100 shares of General Motors at the market with a broker who is a member of the NYSE. Explain how the order would be filled.
6. (a) Explain what is meant in financial circles by a "specialist."
   (b) Do you think that he is in a position to take advantage of the buying or selling public? Explain.
7. (a) What is meant by "floor trading" on the part of members of the New York Stock Exchange?
   (b) Do you think that it should be prohibited? Explain.
8. Indicate the advantages which accrue to the issuing corporation and to investors and speculators from listed stock on the New York Stock Exchange. What are the NYSE listing requirements?
9. Do you think that "Wall Street" controls the prices of stocks listed on the New York Stock Exchange? Explain.
10. (a) What is the difference between the New York Stock Exchange and the American Stock Exchange?
    (b) Distinguish between the regular and the associate members of the American Exchange.
    (c) Are all stock issues traded in on the floor of the American Exchange listed? Is this true of the NYSE?
11. Is the limited order an open order? Explain.
12. What disadvantage might be encountered through the use of the stop order?
13. (a) What is the smallest unit of shares which can be bought and sold on the floor of the New York Stock Exchange?
    (b) Explain how a person can buy and sell "odd lots" of listed stocks.
    (c) What determines the price at which a market order for odd lots is executed?
    (d) Explain the price which the odd-lot buyer pays or the odd-lot seller gets when a limited odd-lot order is executed.
    (e) Explain when a stop order for odd lots is executed, and the price which the buyer pays or the seller gets.
    (f) What is the relative importance of odd-lot orders on the New York Stock Exchange?
14. In view of the commissions and differentials, can it be said that "the cards are stacked" against the small stock buyer even before he enters the market? Explain.
15. Who sets margin requirements? What are the present margins?
16. Criticize the "doubling up on losses" analogy that has been stated in this chapter.
17. Assume that you sell 100 shares of a stock short at 40 and cover when the price reaches 30. Outline all the steps which would be taken in connection with this transaction.
18. (a) What margin is required on short sales at the present time?
    (b) Do you think that short selling is more dangerous for the speculator than buying stock? Explain.
    (c) Does short selling tend to depress the prices of stocks? Does it ever tend to increase them?

(d) Do you think it is right for a person to sell something which he does not own?

19. Is the speculator who sells short doing anything worse than the speculator who buys stock?
20. Why is selling short never used for investment purposes?
21. Comment on the following statement: The way to make money in the stock market is to buy low and sell high.
22. Should the stock speculator buy for the minor swings or only for the major movements?
23. (a) How do "technical" factors in the stock market differ from "fundamental" factors?
    (b) Explain how the market may be fundamentally strong but technically weak.
    (c) Should the small investor pay any attention to the technical condition of the market when he buys and sells? Explain.
24. Explain briefly several different types of stock–bond ratio plans.
25. Explain the advantage to the investor of following the dollar-averaging plan.
26. Explain the details of the Monthly Investment Plan. What are its advantages?
27. What are the advantages to the small investor of belonging to an investment club?
28. Explain several reasons why it might be better for the average investor to buy good stocks and hold on to them rather than sell.
29. Distinguish between blue chip stocks and growth stocks. Under what circumstances would each be recommended?
30. Indicate the reasons for and against an individual's buying the stocks that are most popular with institutional investors.

CASE PROBLEMS

1. Carl Dempsey purchased 50 shares of Stock A some years ago at $75 a share. The price per share is now $100 and the stock is paying an annual dividend of $4. Carl's friend Jim Baker, who is a retired banker, has recommended that he buy Stock B, which is currently selling for $50 a share and pays a $2.50 annual dividend. Stocks A and B appear to have equal prospects for the future despite the higher current yield on Stock B. If Carl bought Stock B it would be necessary for him to sell his Stock A. Carl thought that it would be unwise to sell his Stock A since, as he said, he is enjoying a yield of 5.3 per cent on his purchase price whereas Stock B yields only 5 per cent. But Jim told him this was erroneous reasoning, and that he should for comparative purposes figure his yield on Stock A on a current basis, which was only 4 per cent. Who was right? Should he make the switch? Explain.
2. Carl Dempsey, in the above problem, consulted his broker, who agreed with Jim. But the broker added that in considering the switch, Carl should give proper attention to the commissions (both stocks were traded in round lots of 100 shares on the NYSE), the odd-lot differentials, the New

York stock transfer tax, and the loss of principal through the payment of federal taxes on the gain from the sale of Stock A. Carl's top income tax rate was 22 per cent. Compute the amount of principal left after the sale and payment of the taxes, and the number of shares of Stock B that could be purchased. (No fractional shares can be bought, but any balance of cash can be put in a savings and loan association at 4 per cent.) Would you recommend the switch? Explain.

3. In a discussion at the bar in the City Country Club, Jess Way said that he thought Control Data was a good stock and that he was going to buy some of it the next day. Bill Jenkins volunteered the information that he was holding some of the stock at a loss and that he would not buy any more of it. Ward Benton said that any stock which was not a buy was a sell. Jon Balou said he owned some of Control Data and that the stock has been good to him and he thinks he may buy more of it. Comment on the wisdom of these statements.

4. Compute the amount of the broker's commissions and transfer taxes that you would have to pay to sell the following on the New York Stock Exchange. (Each is a separate transaction, and a round lot of each stock consists of 100 shares.)
   (a) 300 shares at $15 per share
   (b) 10 shares at $50 per share
   (c) 5 shares at $350 per share
   (d) 100 shares at $400 per share
   (e) 100 shares at $1⅛ per share

5. Joe Brown wants to buy 100 shares of ABC Corporation common stock. He finds out from his broker that the last sale was at 48 and that the stock is now quoted 47¾ bid and 48 ask. If Brown puts in a market order, at what price will he buy? What is the advantage of a market order? If he puts in a limited order, what price should he specify? What is the advantage and disadvantage of a limited order as compared to a market order? If he buys at 48 and then puts in a stop order, at what price should this order be placed? If the price of the stock falls to 45, should he change his stop order? If the price of the stock rises to 60, should he change his stop order?

6. You give an order to your broker to purchase 10 shares of XYZ common (round lot is 100 shares) at the market. You note that the next sale on the ticker tape is at 36½. At what price did you purchase the stock? From whom did you purchase it? If someone else sold 10 shares at the same time, at what price did he sell? What would be the total cost of this transaction to you? Which transfer taxes would you pay and when? If you later sold this stock for 41, what would your net profit be? Should an investor buy and sell odd lots? Should a speculator? Why or why not?

7. Phil Phillips believes that the price of PDQ common is too high at the moment. He decides to sell 100 shares of this stock short. The last sale before his sell order is at $25⅛. Sales take place at $25, $24¾, $24½, $24¾ afterward. Which of these could have been his short sale? What is meant by selling short? Is this a speculative move for Phil? Why? If he later covered his sale at $20 per share, what would be his profit or loss (ignoring commissions and taxes)? If the price of the stock rose to $30 and he

covered, what would be his profit or loss (assuming that he did not cover at $20)?

SELECTED READINGS

Barnes, Leo. *Your Investments.* Larchmont, N. Y.: American Research Council. Latest edition.

Bogen, Jules I. (ed.). *Financial Handbook,* Fourth Edition. New York: The Ronald Press Co., 1964. Section 10.

Cooke, Gilbert W. *The Stock Markets.* New York: Simmons-Boardman Publishing Corp., 1964.

Encyclopedia of Stock Market Techniques. Larchmont, N. Y.: Investors Intelligence, Inc., 1963.

Engel, Louis. *How to Buy Stocks.* New York: Bantam Books. Latest edition. Paperbound. Single copies may be obtained free from any office of Merrill Lynch, Pierce, Fenner & Smith, Inc.

Granville, Joseph E. *New Key to Stock Market Profits.* Englewood Cliffs, N. J.: Prentice-Hall, Inc., 1963.

Jenkins, David. *How to Profit from Formula Plans in the Stock Market.* Larchmont, N. Y.: American Research Council, 1961.

Leffler, George L., and Farwell, Loring C. *The Stock Market,* Third Edition. New York: The Ronald Press Co., 1963.

Loll, Leo M., and Buckley, Julian G. *The Over-the-Counter Securities Markets.* Englewood Cliffs, N. J.: Prentice-Hall, Inc., 1961.

Merritt, Robert D. *Financial Independence through Common Stocks,* Seventh Edition. New York: Simon and Schuster, Inc., 1963.

Newsbook: The Stock Market. Princeton, N. J.: Newsbook, The National Observer, 1965.

Odd Lots. New York: Carlisle & Jacquelin. Single copies may be obtained free by writing to the firm.

Report of Special Study of Securities Markets of the Securities and Exchange Commission. Washington, D. C.: U. S. Government Printing Office, 1963. Parts 1–5.

Shultz, Birl E., and Squier, Albert P. *The Securities Market and How It Works,* Revised Edition. New York: Harper & Row, 1963.

Vickers Guide to Investment Company Portfolios. Vickers Associates, Inc., Huntington, N. Y. 11743. Latest edition.

NEW YORK STOCK EXCHANGE PUBLICATIONS AND FILMS

Fact Book. Published annually.

Investment Facts. Concise booklet answers such questions on common stocks as: who owns them, how much it costs to invest, and how to open an account. Lists statistical data on over 500 common stocks that have paid quarterly cash dividends for 20 to 100 years.

How to Get Help When You Invest. New primer for prospective and new investors combining basic information on investing with a description in clear, non-technical language of the services of New York Stock Exchange member firms.

How to Invest on a Budget. Describes how the Monthly Investment Plan works, how to start, and what it costs. Includes most recent list of fifty stocks favored by MIP investors—with price, dividend, and yield information.

Investment Clubs . . . What Are They . . . How Are They Started? Information on the organization and operation of investment clubs.

Understanding the New York Stock Exchange. Comprehensive and easy-to-read description of the functions of the Stock Exchange and member firms.

Understanding Financial Statements. Has seven "keys" to help make annual reports more meaningful. Especially prepared to aid those who want to make their own studies of financial statements.

Understanding Preferred Stocks and Bonds. An explanation of the investment characteristics of senior securities and their role in a balanced investment program.

The Language of Investing, A Glossary. Definitions of stock market terms.

Now, About the Specialist. Tells about the activities and responsibilities of the specialist, and Exchange regulations and policies governing his operations.

The Modern Auction Market. A guide for institutional investors.

1965 Census of Shareowners.

Requests for free single copies of publications should be sent to:
New York Stock Exchange, Publications Division, New York, New York 10005

Subscription Publications:

The Exchange. Monthly magazine of the NYSE provides, in everyday language, facts, figures, and articles of current interest to present and potential shareowners.

New York Stock Exchange Monthly Review. A compilation of current securities markets financial statistics, including record highs and lows for each series.

Films:

The Lady and the Stock Exchange. An amusing drama. Emphasizes the right versus the wrong way to start investing. (27 minutes)

Your Share in Tomorrow. A documentary on the role of the shareowner in the past, present, and future. (27 minutes)

What Makes Us Tick. An animated Technicolor short about the investment process, the NYSE, listed corporations and their stockholders. (12 minutes)

Working Dollars. A cartoon film in full color, showing how Fred Finchley puts his dollars to work through MIP. (13 minutes)

(Requests for these films should be sent to the local office of any member firm of the NYSE or to: Modern Talking Picture Service, with offices in major cities. Only cost is postage.)

The Big Board (13 minutes); *Bid and Asked* (15 minutes); and . . . *At the Market* (22 minutes). Designed for the professional investment manager. In color.

(Available, free of charge, through any member firm, or contact: Institutional Investor Information Office, New York Stock Exchange, New York, New York 10005.)

14

Mutual Funds and Other Types of Investment Companies

It is probably apparent to the reader by now that the average person who is seeking a suitable stock investment is faced with several serious problems. In the first place, he probably is in a quandary as to what stock to buy. If he solves this dilemma, he is immediately faced with the decision as to when to buy it. Quite frequently a person keeps watching a particular stock that he wants, but in view of all the current data relating to the stock, he feels that the price at any particular time is too high. So he puts off buying it.

If the problems of what to buy and when to buy can be solved, many investors are still faced with the realistic situation that they have too little to invest to secure proper diversification, which they realize is extremely important when it comes to buying stock. Even if a solution to all these problems can be found, the investor still faces another dilemma. How long should he hold the securities? How can he ascertain when to sell them? In an effort to solve some or all of these problems more and more people in the United States are buying the shares of *investment companies, investment trusts,* or *mutual funds,* as they are variously called.

Nature of Investment Companies

Investment companies originated abroad many years ago. Their main development was in England, The Netherlands, and Scotland. They were not generally formed in the United States until after World War I, and their main development here came in the late 1920's and after World War II.

The theory behind investment companies is good. They sell their stock in small denominations to the public and invest the proceeds in securities of many companies. In this way small investors are able to buy a part ownership in the securities of a number of companies and thus get diversification. Furthermore, the investment companies have, or are supposed to have, expert management, better qualified to select securities than is the average investor. They pay dividends to their shareholders from the dividends and interest received from the company's investment portfolio and from the capital gains realized from the sale of securities from the portfolio.

Types of Investment Companies

Under the Investment Company Act of 1940, investment companies are divided into three different types: *face-amount certificate companies, unit investment trusts,* and *management companies.* The face-amount certificate companies issue certificates with a face or maturity value of a fixed amount, such as $1,000. They are paid for in installments, and any dividends paid are credited against the unpaid balance. Such a method of payment involves more expense to the company, and the investor, accordingly, usually has to pay a higher price for the certificates. Generally speaking, the securities of a face-amount certificate investment company are not recommended for the investor. (These companies are relatively unimportant today.)

The unit or fixed investment company issues its shares against the deposit of a fixed list of securities which cannot be changed except under the few circumstances stated in the agreement. Although this type of investment trust was popular in the late 1920's, the drastic decline in security values in the early 1930's resulted in its becoming unpopular. There are relatively few securities of unit investment companies outstanding today.

By far the greatest percentage of the investment company field is now represented by the management companies. In this type of company the management, subject to the provisions of the Investment Company Act and any special provisions in the contract, is free to buy and sell securities for the company. Management companies, which will be discussed later in the chapter, are of two classes:

1. *Open-end companies*
2. *Closed-end companies.*

TYPES OF PORTFOLIO

The *portfolio* of an investment company refers to the securities owned by the company. Some companies invest only in bonds, some only in preferred stocks, some in bonds, preferred stocks, and common stocks, but most of the companies confine their investments almost entirely to a broad list of diversified common stocks. In the following classification it is usual to refer to the investment companies as "funds."

Bond Funds

Only a few companies confine their investments to bonds. For those persons who want to invest in bonds, the bond companies offer broad diversification and expert management, the same as other types of investment companies. An example of bond funds are the Keystone Custodian Funds: B–1 (high grade), B–2 (medium grade), B–3 (low priced), B–4 (discount bonds). Most people, however, are interested in investment companies' shares which offer a chance for larger dividend return, capital gains, and a hedge against inflation.

Recently a new type of bond fund was put on the market. The fund's capital is invested only in tax-exempt state and municipal bonds. Dividends paid by the fund are tax-free to the fund's shareholders. This type of fund would appeal to persons in the high tax brackets. An example is the Nuveen Tax-Exempt Bond Fund.

Preferred Stock Funds

The preferred stock funds usually return a higher yield than the bond funds. Like the bond funds, however, they are not popular with the average fund buyer because they lack the appeal of common stock investments, and only a few of them remain today. An example is the National Securities Preferred Stock Series.

Balanced Funds

Balanced funds invest in both bonds and stocks. The latter may consist of both common and preferred stock. In some instances, a portion of the bond investment may be in government bonds. As of January 1, 1965, 22.9 per cent of the assets of all open-end companies were owned by the balanced funds. The balanced fund, which is sometimes called a *bond-stock* fund, offers the investor a relatively safe fixed return from the bond portion of the fund, and the chance to earn relatively larger dividends and capital gains from the part of the fund that is invested in stocks, particularly common stocks. The bond investments give protection against deflation while the common stock portion of the fund offers protection against inflation. Thus, the investor is hedged if the economy goes either way. In their personal investment program, most people attempt to balance their investments somewhat between the fixed dollar investments, such as bonds, savings accounts, etc., and equities, such as common stocks and real estate that provide a hedge against inflation. A balanced fund's stock offers the investor one security which provides the balance between fixed dollar investments and equities.

The percentage of the total fund invested in bonds or stocks varies from time to time. When common stock prices get relatively high, the managements of the balanced funds tend to work out of stocks somewhat and invest more in bonds. After common stock prices have declined, some of the bonds may be sold and additional common stock purchased with the proceeds. Generally speaking, a balanced fund provides a more conservative investment than the common stock funds. The following are among the largest balanced funds (all are open-end companies, which are discussed later in the chapter):

Balanced Funds

Axe-Houghton Fund B
Boston Fund
Commonwealth Investment Co.
Diversified Investment Fund
Eaton & Howard Balanced Fund
George Putnam Fund of Boston
Incorporated Income Fund
Investors Mutual
Keystone Custodian Fund—K-1
Loomis-Sayles Mutual Fund
Massachusetts Life Fund
Puritan Fund
Scudder, Stevens & Clark Balanced Fund
Wellington Fund

Diversified Common Stock Funds

In terms of net asset values, the diversified common stock funds are more important than all the other types of funds combined. On January 1, 1965, they held 63 per cent of the assets of all types of open-end companies combined. Some of the common stock funds may from time to time have a small portion of their portfolio in preferred stock or government or corporate bonds, but the bulk of the investment is in common stocks. The specific investment objectives of the common stock funds vary among the different companies. Some invest primarily in the stocks of the large and well-known companies whose equities have come to be known as blue chips. Others go in for growth company shares. Some specialize in low-priced stocks which it is thought may have a better opportunity for advancement in price than the average stock. In some of the companies the emphasis is on dividend return, while in others it is on appreciation in the price of the securities.

In view of the size and the large number of companies in the diversified common stock group, it is evident that this is the type of investment company that appeals to most fund buyers. The typical investor has holdings of United States savings bonds, savings accounts in banks and savings and loan institutions, life insurance, and perhaps annuities or interest in company pension plans. He also is probably receiving or will be receiving social security benefits. All of these are fixed-dollar investments, which provide no hedge against inflation. The average investor is becoming more and more conscious of the effect of inflation on these fixed-dollar investments and wants, therefore, to purchase common stocks as a means of attempting to provide some hedge against this inflation. Due to the relatively greater risk, diversification is more essential in common stock investment than in any of the other media of investment. But the typical investor does not have sufficient funds to give him this diversification. Furthermore, the management of a common stock portfolio is more difficult than in the case of other types of securities. The diversified common stock fund offers the solution to this problem for many investors. With the investment of even a relatively small amount of money in the fund, the investor secures a broad diversification and expert management.

Practically all of the bond funds, preferred stock funds, and balanced funds are of the open-end variety. But both open-end and closed-end companies (discussed later) are found in the diversified common stock fund field. The following companies are among the largest diversified common stock funds:

Diversified Common Stock Funds

Open-End

Affiliated Fund
American Mutual Fund
Broad Street Investing Corp.
Dividend Shares
Dreyfus Fund
Fidelity Fund
Financial Industrial Fund
Fundamental Investors
Hamilton Funds—Series H-DA
Incorporated Investors
Investment Co. of America
Investors Stock Fund
Investors Variable Payment Fund
Massachusetts Investors Growth Stock Fund
Massachusetts Investors Trust
National Investors Corp.
National Securities—Stock Series
Putnam Growth Fund
United Accumulative Fund
United Income Fund

Closed-End (all listed on the New York Stock Exchange)

Adams Express Co.
General American Investors Co.
General Public Service Corp.
Lehman Corp.
Madison Fund
Tri-Continental Corp.
U. S. & Foreign Securities Corp.

Illustration of a

$10,000 Assumed Investment 1955-1965

with capital gain distributions accepted in additional shares

This chart covers the period from January 1, 1955 to March 31, 1965, one of generally rising common stock prices. The results shown should not be considered as a representation of the dividend income or capital gain or loss which may be realized from an investment made in the Fund today.

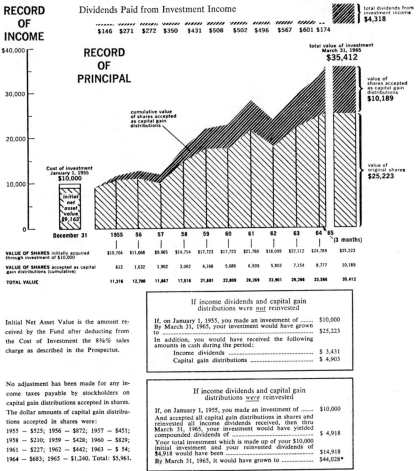

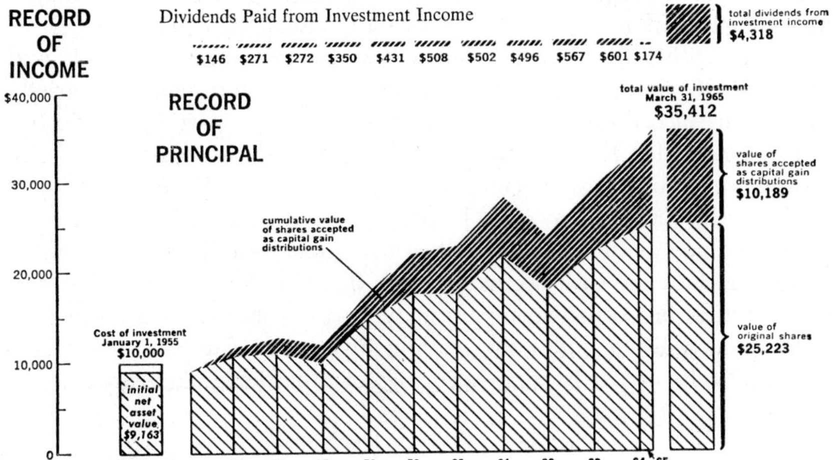

December 31	1955	56	57	58	59	60	61	62	63	64	65 (3 months)
VALUE OF SHARES initially acquired through investment of $10,000	$10,704	$11,068	$9,965	$14,754	$17,723	$17,723	$21,760	$18,099	$22,112	$24,789	$25,223
VALUE OF SHARES accepted as capital gain distributions (cumulative)	612	1,632	1,902	3,062	4,168	5,086	6,509	5,802	7,154	8,777	10,189
TOTAL VALUE	11,316	12,700	11,867	17,816	21,891	22,809	28,269	23,901	29,266	33,566	35,412

Initial Net Asset Value is the amount received by the Fund after deducting from the Cost of Investment the 8⅜% sales charge as described in the Prospectus.

If income dividends and capital gain distributions were *not* reinvested

If, on January 1, 1955, you made an investment of	$10,000
By March 31, 1965, your investment would have grown to	$25,223
In addition, you would have received the following amounts in cash during the period:	
Income dividends	$ 3,431
Capital gain distributions	$ 4,903

No adjustment has been made for any income taxes payable by stockholders on capital gain distributions accepted in shares. The dollar amounts of capital gain distributions accepted in shares were: 1955 – $525; 1956 – $872; 1957 – $451; 1958 – $210; 1959 – $428; 1960 – $829; 1961 – $227; 1962 – $442; 1963 – $ 54; 1964 – $683; 1965 – $1,240. Total: $5,961.

If income dividends and capital gain distributions *were* reinvested

If, on January 1, 1955, you made an investment of	$10,000
And accepted all capital gain distributions in shares and reinvested all income dividends received, then thru March 31, 1965, your investment would have yielded compounded dividends of	$ 4,918
Your total investment which is made up of your $10,000 initial investment and your reinvested dividends of $4,918 would have been	$14,918
By March 31, 1965, it would have grown to	$44,028*

**2,049 shares which includes 518 shares acquired through reinvestment of $6,707 in capital gain distributions.*

Fig. 14–1. Illustration of a $10,000 assumed investment, 1955–1965, in Dreyfus Fund, Inc. (Reproduced with permission, from Dreyfus Fund, Inc., Quarterly Report, March 31, 1965.)

Figure 14–1 shows the results that would have been experienced over the ten-year period, 1955–1965, through a $10,000 investment in one of the leading open-end diversified common stock funds.

Specialized Common Stock Funds

Some investment companies confine their investments to securities within a particular industry, such as aviation, chemicals, electronics, financial, etc. In most instances they purchase only common stock of companies within the industry, but a few also purchase preferreds and bonds. Most of the specialized companies are of the open-end variety, but some are closed-end. If the investor expects that a particular industry, such as electronics, for example, will do well in the future, he may desire to purchase a stock of some company in that industry. He may not know which particular company's stock to buy. Furthermore, he may realize the importance of diversifying among a number of different companies, but he may lack the cash necessary to do this. The purchase of shares of an electronics investment company may be the solution to the problem. The following list includes the leading investment companies that specialize entirely, or partly so, in securities of a particular industry.

Specialized Common Stock Funds

Open-End	*Closed-End*
Atomics, Physics & Science Fund	Petroleum Corp. of America
Capital Life Insurance Shares & Growth Stock Fund	Standard Shares
Century Shares Trust	United Corp.
Chemical Fund	
United Science Fund	

One of the reasons why people buy investment company shares is to gain *broad* diversification. In a specialized investment company, however, anything adversely affecting the particular industry may cause a decline in all the stocks held by the investment company. This would naturally cause a sharp drop in the price of the investment company's shares. The typical fund buyer, hence, would probably prefer to buy shares in investment companies that invested in stocks of many different types of industries.

"Special Situation" Funds

Some investment companies specialize in buying into so-called "special situations." They may buy up controlling stock interest in particular companies and take an active part in the management of the companies. When a favorable opportunity arises they may sell their entire holdings in the companies. In some instances the stock purchased may be that of a reorganized company, or a company that stands to gain from a contemplated merger or a sale of the assets. The largest special-situation investment company is Equity Corporation, which is traded on the American Stock Exchange.

Although technically a holding company rather than an investment company, Alleghany Corporation operates in a manner similar to a closed-end non-diversified investment company and a special situation fund. Of the total assets of this company, 53 per cent represents the shares of Investors Diversified Services, and the latter controls a number of open-end investment companies. In addition, Alleghany Corporation has controlling or substantial stock interest in several railroads. In addition to common stock, Alleghany has notes, preferred stock, and warrants outstanding.

OPEN-END COMPANIES

Open-end investment companies are also called *mutual companies* or *mutual funds.* The Investment Company Act of 1940 permits these companies to issue only one class of securities—common stock. (A few formed before 1940 have senior securities outstanding.) These shares are purchased directly from the issuing company, usually through selling agents or brokers. If a holder wants to sell his open-end shares, the company stands ready at all times to purchase them back. The company will also sell new shares to investors at any time. Thus, the capitalization of the company is "open" and they are known as "open-end companies." From what has just been said it is apparent that the shares issued by open-end companies cannot be listed on any of the stock exchanges. All of the different types of investment portfolios described above are found among the open-end companies. In terms of the value of their assets, however, the diversified common stock funds and the balanced funds are the most important kinds of open-end companies.

Price Paid for Shares

For stocks listed on the exchanges or those sold in the ordinary way in the over-the-counter market, the price of a particular stock depends upon the law of supply and demand. In other words, the stock sells for the price agreed upon between the buyer and the seller. The price paid for open-end investment companies' shares, however, is determined as follows: twice daily at 1:00 P.M. and 3:30 P.M., New York time, the investment company determines the market value of its entire portfolio—in other words, the value of its entire assets. From this is subtracted any liabilities owed by the company. The resultant figure, which is the total net asset value, is divided by the total number of shares the investment company has outstanding at that particular time. This gives the *book* value, or the *net asset* value of the share. The price paid by the investor (referred to as the "asked" or "offer" price or quotation) for open-end shares is the book value per share plus, in most instances, a *loading* or *selling* charge equivalent to from 8.11 to 9.59 per cent of the book value.

The loading charge is not expressed as a percentage of the book value but rather as a percentage of the selling price. With a few exceptions, the lowest stipulated selling charge of open-end companies is 7½ per cent (charges of 8 or 8½ per cent are more common). This means that an amount equivalent to 7½ per cent of the selling price constitutes the selling charge, and thus the book value per share is only 92½ per cent of the selling price. For example, assume that the book value per share of the open-end company is $18.50. The selling agent will offer the stock to investors at a price which will give the issuing company the full book value and permit the selling agent to keep an amount equivalent to 7½ per cent of the selling price. Since the book value of $18.50 represents 92½ per cent of the selling price, the selling price (100 per cent) would be $20.00. Thus, the load in this case would be $1.50 per share (7½ per cent of $20.00). The $1.50 represents a charge of approximately 8.11 per cent of the book value of the share. This selling charge is relatively high as compared to the regular commission rates paid to buy shares of closed-end companies.

Most of the leading open-end companies sell their shares through wholesale distributors who in turn sell the shares through local brokers and agents to the public. Where this system of distribution is used, the wholesaler will usually get one third of the selling charge and the "retailer" will get the other two thirds.

Nearly all of the leading open-end companies reduce the (percentage) selling charge as the amount of the purchase increases. Massachusetts Investors Trust, for example, charges 8½ per cent on orders of less than $25,000; 5¾ per cent on orders of from $25,000 to $50,000; 4 per cent on orders of from $50,000 to $100,000; 3¼ per cent on orders of from $100,000 to $250,000; and 2½ per cent on orders of $250,000 and over.

In some of the mutual companies an investor need not purchase a large number of shares at the same time in order to get the reduced rate. The investor may sign a *letter of intention* to purchase a stipulated amount in the mutual shares over a period of usually 12 or 13 months. In the meantime the regular charge is made on each purchase. If the investor fulfills his agreement, an adjustment is made in the cost of the last purchase so that the total selling charge for the entire amount purchased is the same as if the total amount had been purchased at one time. There is no penalty if the investor does not fulfill his agreement to purchase the stipulated amount within the stated period—except that he will be paying the higher charges for each separate purchase. Some of the open-end companies also offer a reduced selling charge rate on certain cumulative contractual plans, which are discussed later.

Some of the mutual fund managers or sponsors have several different funds or series under their control. Some of these will permit a shareholder in one of the funds or series to "convert" his shares for those of another fund or series without the payment of any load. In other instances the load is reduced approximately 50 per cent. In other cases a small flat fee is charged regardless of the amount involved. Nevertheless, the conversion is treated by the Internal Revenue Service as a sale, and therefore subject to a tax on any capital gains involved.

No-Load Funds

A relatively small number of open-end companies sell their shares directly to the public without the use of dealers or brokers, and do not add a selling charge. The investor pays the net asset value for the shares. In most instances these companies were formed and are managed by an investment advisor firm. The latter makes its profit from the fee charged to manage the investment company. (Management fees are also charged in the case of the companies which have a selling charge.) The following are included among the larger no-load companies:

No-Load Funds

American Investors Fund
De Vegh Mutual Fund
Dodge & Cox Balanced Fund
Energy Fund
Guardian Mutual Fund
Johnston Mutual Fund
Loomis-Sayles Canadian & International Fund
Loomis-Sayles Mutual Fund
Northeast Investors Trust
One William Street
Penn Square Mutual Fund
Rittenhouse Fund
T. Rowe Price Growth Stock Fund
Scudder, Stevens & Clark Balanced Fund
Scudder, Stevens & Clark Common Stock Fund
Stein Roe & Farnham Balanced Fund
Stein Roe & Farnham International Fund
Stein Roe & Farnham Stock Fund

Price Obtained for Shares

If an investor wants to sell his open-end shares, the issuing company will buy them back (in practically all instances) at any time at the then existing book (net asset) value. Thus he does not have to pay a commission or charge to sell the shares. A few funds, however, including several no-load funds, charge a redemption fee of either 1 or ½ per cent (of the net asset value).

In the case of a few of the large open-end (load) funds, some brokers have established an over-the-counter market for the shares, and they will buy the shares from the investor at slightly more than the net asset value.

Accumulation Plans

Nearly all of the open-end companies offer the investor a plan whereby he can invest a fixed amount of money in the company's shares at regular intervals. Most of the plans require a minimum initial purchase of a fixed amount, such as $100, $200, or $250, although the amount varies among the companies from $10 to $1,000. Minimums are also usually required for the subsequent regular purchases. This is usually not less than $25 or $50.

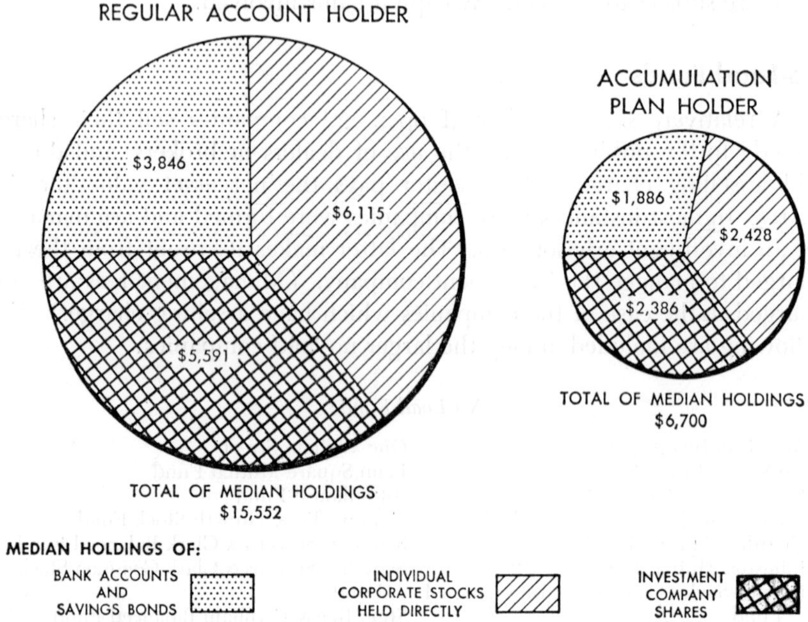

Fig. 14–2. Financial assets of shareholders, open-end investment companies. (Investment Company Institute.)

Figure 14–2 shows the median holdings of bank accounts and savings bonds, individual corporate stocks, and investment company shares both for regular account holders and accumulation plan holders. Figure 14–3 shows the occupations of both regular account and accumulation plan holders.

The accumulation plans offered by the various companies fall into one of three types.

Contractual Plan With Penalty. Under this type of plan the investor signs up to purchase a specified amount in shares, usually over a given period of time, for example, $10,000 over a period of ten years. Half of

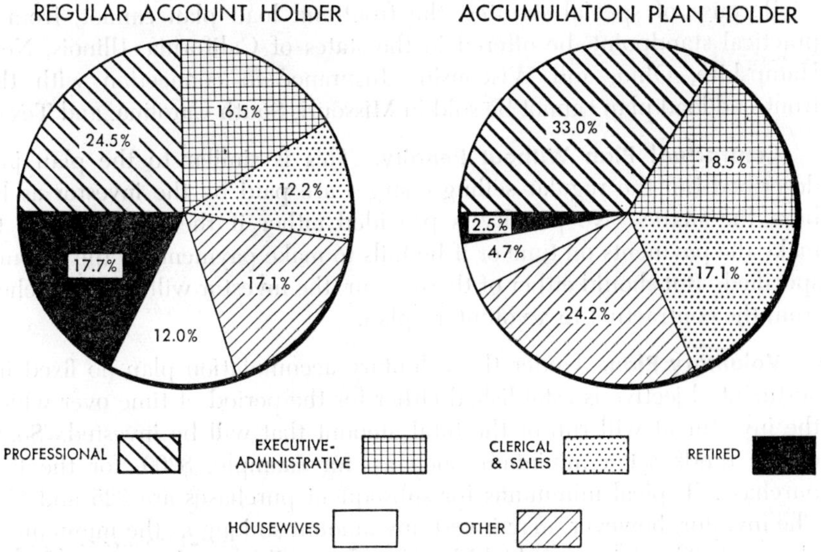

Fig. 14–3. Occupations of shareholders, open-end investment companies. (Investment Company Institute.)

the load or selling charge on the entire amount of shares to be purchased is taken out of payments made during the first year. The balance is spread evenly over the remaining part of the particular period. This type is referred to as the "prepaid charge," or "front-end load." If the investor drops out of the plan during the early years, he will have lost a substantial amount of what has been paid in. Because of this, generally speaking, an investor should not sign up for this type of plan. But if the prepaid load will force an investor to continue with the plan it is not so objectionable.

There has been considerable criticism of the front-end load plan, particularly in the Wharton School Report on Mutual Funds published in 1962. In 1964, a front-end load plan was filed with the Securities and Exchange Commission which provided for a deduction of only 20 per cent of the load during the first year, 18 per cent during the second and third years, and smaller deductions thereafter. (This was apparently done to meet the provisions of a new law in Michigan.)

Some of the companies offer, along with the contractual plan, a declining term life insurance policy with a face value equivalent to the unpaid balance of the intended investment goal specified in the contract. If the investor dies before he has paid in the entire amount specified in the contract, the insurance proceeds are paid to the trustee or custodian and he will invest the money in the mutual shares. When such insurance is taken out, failure to make the exact payments on time will lapse the insurance.

Because of special statutes, the front-end load plan cannot, from a practical standpoint, be offered in the states of California, Illinois, New Hampshire, Ohio, and Wisconsin. Insurance in connection with the front-end load plan cannot be sold in Missouri, South Carolina, and Texas.

Contractual Plan Without Penalty. This is similar to the plan just described but the regular selling charges are paid by the investor as he buys the shares. No penalty is provided either if the investor fails to make the payments on time or if he fails to make payments in the amount specified. But should either of these occur, the investor will have switched from the contractual to a voluntary plan.

Voluntary Plan. Under the voluntary accumulation plan no fixed investment objective is established either for the period of time over which the investment will run or the total amount that will be invested. Some of the funds set a minimum, such as, for example, $200, for the first purchase. Typical minimums for subsequent purchases are $25 and $50. The investor, however, may invest any amount so long as the minimum is observed. The dates on which the payments will be made are specified in the plan. These are commonly monthly or quarterly.

In passing, it should be noted that the voluntary plan discussed above is one of the *accumulation* plans. An investor can purchase any number of shares (so long as the minimum payment is made) in practically all of the open-end companies at any time through the regular channels without having first signed up for an accumulation plan.

When an investor puts a fixed amount of money at regular intervals into a mutual fund under one of the accumulative plans discussed above, he is following the principle of *dollar averaging*, or *dollar cost averaging*, as it is sometimes called, which was described in the preceding chapter.

Reinvestment of Dividends

Arrangements may be made with practically all of the open-end companies for the automatic reinvestment of dividends in the companies' shares, regardless of whether or not the investor is buying the shares under an accumulation plan. Unless the investor needs the dividend return this procedure is recommended, since it has the same effect as compounding interest.

With some exceptions the mutual funds will reinvest *capital gains* dividends (dividends paid from profits arising through the sale of securities) at the book value of the shares. Thus, no load or selling charge is made on shares sold to investors through the reinvestment of capital dividends. But nearly half of the mutual funds charge their regular commissions on shares sold through the reinvestment of *ordinary income* dividends (dividends paid from interest or dividends received on portfolio).

Figure 14–4 shows the results that would have been attained during the period 1950–1964 by the investment of $100 a month in one of the leading open-end diversified common stock funds.

PRODUCTIVE INVESTMENT RESULTS

Here are the tangible dollars and cents benefits from investing in the Trust during the past fifteen years.

All illustrations assume that capital gain distributions were taken in shares. Common stock prices generally were higher at the end of the period than at the beginning. Results shown should not be considered as a representation of the dividend income or capital gain or loss which may be realized from an investment made in the Trust today.

Monthly Investments
With Dividends Invested

If you had followed a program of gradual accumulation by investing, say, $100 each month and had automatically invested all dividends, here is how you would stand today:

SUMMARY

Monthly Investments since January 1, 1950....	$18,000
Income Dividends for Period — Invested......	8,723
Total Cost — Including Invested Dividends....	$26,723
Value of Investment December 31, 1964.......	$48,252

DETAILED ILLUSTRATION

	COST				CUMULATIVE VALUE OF SHARES ACQUIRED				
Year Ended 12/31	Cumulative Monthly Investments	Annual Dividends Invested	Cumulative Dividends Invested	Total Cost Including Invested Dividends	Through Monthly Investments +	As Capital Gain Distributions =	Sub-Total +	From Investment of Dividends =	Total Value
1950	$ 1,200	$ 47	$ 47	$ 1,247	$ 1,246	$ —	$ 1,246	$ 46	$ 1,292
1951	2,400	110	157	2,557	2,568	80	2,648	155	2,803
1952	3,600	174	331	3,931	3,930	145	4,075	334	4,409
1953	4,800	239	570	5,370	4,874	139	5,013	543	5,556
1954	6,000	332	902	6,902	8,339	400	8,739	1,123	9,862
1955	7,200	439	1,341	8,541	10,974	810	11,784	1,732	13,516
1956	8,400	528	1,869	10,269	12,776	1,055	13,831	2,320	16,151
1957	9,600	601	2,470	12,070	11,636	1,144	12,780	2,438	15,218
1958	10,800	643	3,113	13,913	17,317	1,770	19,087	4,017	23,104
1959	12,000	719	3,832	15,832	19,197	2,256	21,453	4,856	26,309
1960	13,200	823	4,655	17,855	19,258	2,538	21,796	5,367	27,163
1961	14,400	829	5,484	19,884	23,888	4,302	28,190	7,109	35,299
1962	15,600	938	6,422	22,022	21,550	4,464	26,014	6,969	32,983
1963	16,800	1,070	7,492	24,292	25,822	5,910	31,732	8,972	40,704
1964	18,000	1,231	8,723	26,723	29,987	7,108	37,095	11,157	48,252

The total cost figure represents the cumulative total of monthly investments of $100 per month plus the cumulative amount of income dividends invested, and includes a distribution charge on all shares so purchased, as described in the Prospectus. No adjustment has been made for any income taxes payable by shareholders on capital gain distributions accepted in shares and income dividends invested. The dollar amounts of capital gain distributions accepted in shares were: 1951 — $75; 1952 — $56; 1954 — $171; 1955 — $337; 1956 — $192; 1957 — $262; 1958 — $206; 1959 — $409; 1960 — $406; 1961 — $1,311; 1962 — $750; 1963 — $811; 1964 — $504; Total — $5,490.

A program of regular monthly investments does not assure a profit nor protect against depreciation in declining markets.

Fig. 14–4. Investment results of an investment of $100 per month for the period 1950–1964, in Massachusetts Investors Trust—reinvestment of all dividends and capital gains distributions. (Vance, Sanders & Co., Inc.)

Systematic Withdrawal Plans

Many investors, after retirement, feel the need for some kind of a plan whereby they may be able to receive regularly a fixed amount of money for a certain period of time from their stock investments, even if it involves the return of part of their principal. A majority of the mutual funds now provide for a systematic withdrawal plan.

The details of the plans vary. One common requirement, however, is that the investor have at least $10,000 (or other specified amount) invested in the fund's shares, or that he purchase this amount in shares. An arrangement may be made for the investor to receive a fixed amount, such as $50 or $100 per month or per quarter. After giving effect to the dividends currently due the investor, the company will sell whatever number of shares may be necessary in order to provide the cash to pay the specified amount. Naturally, this reduces the principal on which dividends are paid in the future, so that more and more shares will have to be sold as time goes on. The investor, of course, runs the risk of outliving his money.

A "conservative" type of arrangement, used by some, is to withdraw annually an amount equivalent to 6 per cent of the original principal investment. If the company earns 3 per cent on its investments, and if the value of the fund's investments does not fluctuate, the investor receives his regular fixed payments for a period slightly in excess of twenty-three years, before the principal has all been exhausted. Of course the investor may figure that he will not live that long, and furthermore, he may have the need for a larger amount monthly.

The retired investor may, of course, sell all his shares in the fund, as he could do with any other type of investment, and buy a life annuity (or some other form of annuity) with his money.

Figure 14–5 shows how the systematic withdrawal plan would have worked out for the years 1955–1965 for Group Securities Common Stock Fund, an open-end diversified common stock fund whose objective is about equally divided between low risk, current return, and possibilities for growth of principal and income. An investment of $10,000 is assumed, and withdrawals of $50 a month (6 per cent a year) are made. It should be noted that this record was achieved during an extended period of rapidly rising stock prices.

Figure 14–6, which is taken from the 1965 edition of Johnson's Investment Company Charts,[1] shows the 1955–1964 results of an original investment of $10,000 in Affiliated Fund, Inc., an open-end diversified

[1] Hugh Johnson & Company, Buffalo, New York 14203. Reproduced with permission.

ILLUSTRATION OF AN ASSUMED INVESTMENT OF $10,000

Based On Initial Net Asset Value of $9,150 With $50 as the Amount Withdrawn Each Month

The table below covers the period from December 1, 1954 to May 31, 1965. It is assumed that shares were purchased at the beginning of the period at a cost of $10,000 and that $50 was planned to be withdrawn each month. This was a period during which common stock prices fluctuated, but were generally higher at the end of the period than at the beginning. The results reflect the operation of a plan under the terms of which all investment income dividends (and any capital gain distributions) necessary for the planned payments in the following quarter are held in cash until needed to meet a withdrawal payment, such payments being made first from these sources to the extent available and then by liquidation of shares to the extent necessary to provide for such payment. Continued withdrawals in excess of current income will eventually exhaust principal, particularly in a period of declining market prices. The results shown should not be considered as a representation of the dividend income, capital gain or loss, or amount available for withdrawal from an investment made in the fund today. Only that portion of the total amount withdrawn designated "From Investment Income Dividends" should be regarded as income; the remainder represents a withdrawal of principal.

$10,000 Assumed Investment — $50 Withdrawn Monthly

	AMOUNTS WITHDRAWN*				VALUE OF REMAINING SHARES*		
Year Ended 11/30	From Investment Income Dividends	From Principal	Annual Total	Cumulative Total	Value of Remaining Original Shares +	Value of Shares Acquired Through Capital Gain Distributions† =	Total Value of Shares Held at Year-End
1955	$ 324	$276	$ 600	$ 600	$9,855	$1,001	$10,856
1956	460	140	600	1,200	9,290	1,568	10,858
1957	515	85	600	1,800	8,168	1,817	9,985
1958	527	73	600	2,400	10,209	2,526	12,735
1959	528	72	600	3,000	10,104	3,095	13,199
1960	536	64	600	3,600	9,418	3,161	12,579
1961	559	41	600	4,200	11,447	4,749	16,196
1962	530	70	600	4,800	9,522	4,291	13,813
1963	557	43	600	5,400	10,349	5,163	15,512
1964	581	19	600	6,000	11,792	6,527	18,319
5/31/65	305	—	305	6,305	12,089	6,693	18,782
	$5,422	$883	$6,305				
RESULTS IF PLAN HAD COMMENCED JUNE 1, 1964							
6/1/64 to 5/31/65	$238	$362	$600	$600	$9,427	$268	$9,695

†Capital gain distributions accepted in shares: 1955, $987; 1956, $624; 1957, $418; 1958, $234; 1959, $578; 1960, $266; 1961, $878; 1962, $308; 1963, $478; 1964, $636; total, $5,407. For the one-year period ending May 31, 1965: $265.

*This illustration assumes that withdrawals were made first from income, then from principal. Any cash balance remaining at the year-end which was required for payments in the first quarter was assumed to be part of "Total Value of Shares Held at Year-End." Withdrawals from principal representing the sale of shares were assumed to have been in the order shares were acquired.

No adjustment has been made for any income taxes payable by shareholders on investment income dividends and capital gain distributions or on any net capital gains realized on the liquidation of shares in connection with periodic withdrawals.

Fig. 14–5. Illustration of withdrawal of $50 per month from an investment of $10,000 in Group Securities Common Stock Fund, 1955–1965. (Distributors Group, Inc., sponsor of Group Securities, Inc.)

common stock fund whose objective is long-term growth of capital and income. The liquidating value line assumes no withdrawals, except ordinary income dividends. Figures shown above the graph (and the "With. Plan Liq. Val." figures at the extreme bottom of the chart), however, show what would have resulted from withdrawals of $50 a month for the period. The examples given do not give effect to any income taxes that the investor would have to pay on ordinary income or capital gains.

AFFILIATED FUND, INC.

January 1, 1955—December 31, 1964

Objectives: Long-term growth of capital and income.

Policy: Diversified common stocks. Borrowed capital may be used to provide leverage.

Withdrawal Plan Illustration

$10,000 investment, $50 per month withdrawal

	10 Years Ended 12/31/64	One Year 1964
Withdrawn from income	$ 3,983	$ 221
Withdrawn from principal	2,017	379
Total	$ 6,000	$ 600
Asset value original shares	$11,514	$ 9,740
Capital dists. reinvested	6,680	415
Liquidating value	$18,194	$10,155

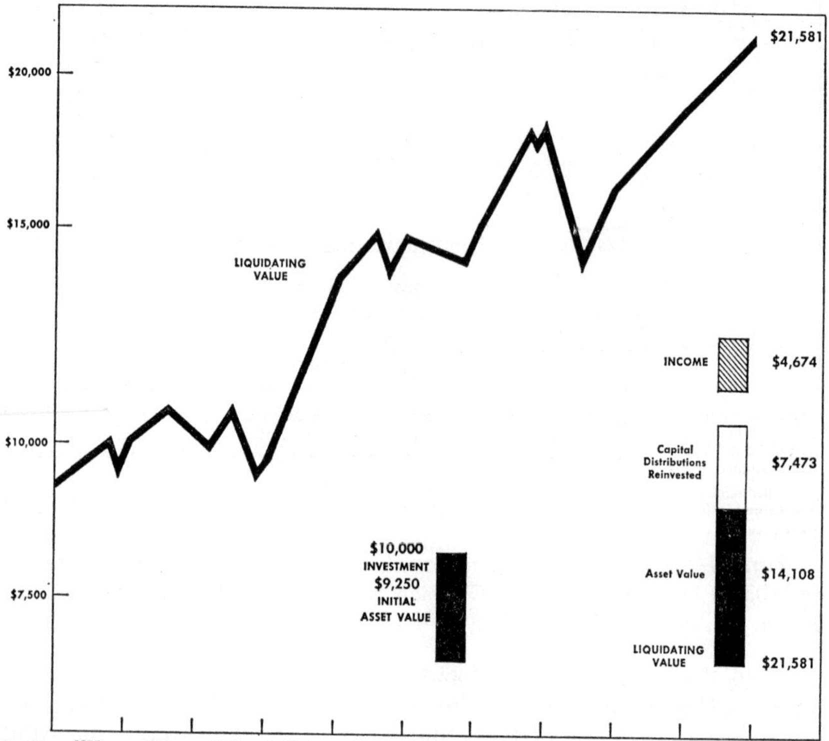

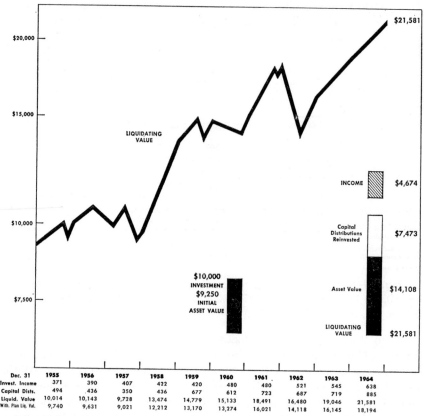

Dec. 31	1955	1956	1957	1958	1959	1960	1961	1962	1963	1964
Invest. Income	371	390	407	422	420	480	480	521	545	638
Capital Dists.	494	436	350	436	677	612	723	687	719	885
Liquid. Value	10,014	10,143	9,728	13,474	14,779	15,133	18,491	16,480	19,046	21,581
With. Plan Liq. Val.	9,740	9,631	9,021	12,212	13,170	13,274	16,021	14,118	16,145	18,194

Fig. 14–6. Results of an original investment of $10,000 in Affiliated Fund, Inc., from January 1, 1955, to December 31, 1964, and effect on investment of withdrawal of $50 per month. (Reproduced with permission, from *Johnson's Investment Company Charts, 1965.* Buffalo, N. Y.: Hugh Johnson & Co.)

In the illustration in Fig. 14–6 the initial asset value was less than the $10,000 because of the deduction of selling charges.

Retirement Use for Self-Employed

In 1962, Congress passed the Self-Employed Individuals Tax Retirement Act (also called the Smathers–Keogh Act, or the Keogh Act) which provides for tax-saving retirement plans for professional people and the self-employed. The details relating to this Act are stated in Chapter 18. Mutual funds are specifically mentioned in the Act as agencies with which such retirement plans may be invested. The leading mutual funds now have "approved" plans available to qualified persons.

CLOSED-END COMPANIES

The closed-end investment company has a more or less fixed amount of stock outstanding. It does not constantly sell new shares to investors, nor does it stand ready to redeem the shares held by investors. In this respect it is similar to ordinary commercial or manufacturing companies such as General Motors or General Foods. If a person wants to buy some shares of a closed-end company he buys them from other shareholders in the over-the-counter market or possibly on one of the stock exchanges.

Table 14–1. Investment Company Assets (Beginning of Year)—Selected Years, 1941–1965

Year	Mutual Funds	Closed-End Companies	Total
1965	$29,116,254,000	$3,523,413,000	$32,639,667,000
1964	25,214,436,000	3,217,936,000	28,432,372,000
1963	21,270,735,000	2,783,219,000	24,053,954,000
1962	22,788,812,000	3,205,277,000	25,994,089,000
1961	17,025,684,000	2,083,898,000	19,109,582,000
1951	2,530,563,000	871,962,000	3,402,525,000
1941	447,959,000	613,589,000	1,061,548,000

From: *Investment Companies 1965.* Published by Arthur Wiesenberger & Co., Members of the New York Stock Exchange.

Likewise, when an investor wishes to sell his closed-end company shares he sells them in these markets through his regular broker. The leading closed-end companies are listed on the New York Stock Exchange. As already indicated, open-end company shares are never listed on the exchanges. The relative importance of closed-end as compared to open-end companies can be seen from Table 14–1.

Leverage

We have seen that open-end investment companies have only one class of securities outstanding—common stock. Some of the closed-end companies, however, have both preferred stock and bonds outstanding in addition to common stock. A few also have warrants outstanding, and some have bank loans. When they have senior securities outstanding, they are referred to as leverage companies. The presence of senior securities can be an advantage to the holders of the common shares at one time and a disadvantage to them at another time. When the investment company earns a higher rate of return on the preferred stockholders' or bondholders' money than it pays for the use of this money, the extra earnings usually benefit the common shareholders in the form of additional dividends. But when the company's earnings decline drastically, the payment for the use of the senior capital may prove to be a burden to its common shareholders.

In recent years practically all the companies which had bonds outstanding have paid them off. None of those listed on the New York Stock Exchange now has any bonds outstanding. Only two of those listed on the NYSE have preferred stock outstanding: General American Investors and Tri-Continental Corporation.

Market Price of Shares

The market price of closed-end investment companies' shares is determined in the same way as that of ordinary business corporations, by the law of supply and demand. The common shares of the closed-end companies typically sell at discounts below the net asset value of the shares. This discount may vary from time to time from 1 to approximately 50 per cent in a few instances. Generally speaking, the discount rate narrows as the stock market in general goes up and increases when the market is headed down. The shares of a few closed-end companies, such as Lehman Corporation, in the past have generally sold at slight premiums over the net asset value (book value).

The prima facie reason for the typical discount is, of course, that the investor will not pay the full book value for the shares. This results from the fact that the investor will receive only part of the income earned by the investment company; the balance is used to pay the management fees and other expenses incident to running the company. It is true, of course, that the open-end company must pay similar management fees and expenses, but the investor pays the full book value for the shares, plus in most instances, the loading charge. Table 14–2 shows the discount below book value at which the closed-end company shares listed on the New York Stock Exchange were selling at the beginning of each year, 1961–1965.

Table 14–2. Discounts (Percentage Below Net Asset Values) at Which Closed-End Investment Companies Listed on the New York Stock Exchange Were Selling at Beginning of Each Year, 1961–1965

Company	1965	1964	1963	1962	1961
Diversified Companies					
U.S. & Foreign Securities	26%	24%	19%	16%	22%
Tri-Continental	24	21	15	13	23
General Public Service	16	15	8	P12	13
Abacus Fund	16	11	4	P2	2
Dominick Fund	12	9	5	4	17
American International	12	6	4	1	14
Adams Express	10	9	4	3	14
Carriers & General	6	8	7	2	12
General American Investors	6	3	P1	10	19
Lehman Corp.	6	P1	P4	P5	P1
Niagara Share	0	6	3	P6	12
Madison Fund	P3	P13	P26	P23	2
Non-Diversified and Specialized Companies					
Japan Fund	32	15	34	started in 1962	
Hanna (M.A.) Co.	28	20	30	24	31
Eurofund	19	24	23	7	20
United Corp.	19	12	3	5	4
American Research & Devel.	15	P6	21	P7	12
American-South African	10	34	35	39	30
National Aviation	10	2	P2	3	P2
Petroleum Corp.	3	6	5	0	0

P—Indicates premium over net asset value.
From: *Investment Companies 1965.* Published by Arthur Wiesenberger & Co., Members of the New York Stock Exchange.

While it is to the advantage of the investor to be able to purchase an investment company's shares at a discount, assuming no unusual circumstances to account for the discount, it should be realized that if and when he sells the shares, he probably will have to dispose of them also at a discount. Of course, the amount of the discount could be larger or smaller than when he purchased the shares. In the meantime, however, the discount favors the investor because his yield is based on his purchase price.

Commissions for Buying Shares

The investor pays a broker the same commission rates to buy closed-end investment company shares as for the shares of ordinary business corporations, such as Anaconda Copper or General Dynamics. Generally speaking, the rates for listed stocks vary according to the amount of money involved in the transaction and whether the purchase involves a round lot or an odd lot of shares. In Table 14–3 the commissions for purchasing an odd lot of a closed-end investment company listed on the New York Stock Exchange are shown, together with selling charges for buying an equivalent amount of the typical open-end investment company shares. The amount of the purchase is assumed to be the book value of the shares.

Table 14–3. Selling Charges and Commissions for Purchasing Specified Amounts of Open-End and Closed-End Investment Company Shares

Amount of Purchase (book value)	Open-End Company		Closed-End Company	
	Selling Charge	Per cent	Commission	Per cent
$ 50	$ 4.05	8.108	$ 3.00	6.00
100	8.11	8.108	6.00	6.00
200	16.22	8.108	6.00	3.00
250	20.27	8.108	6.00	2.40
300	24.32	8.108	7.00	2.33
400	32.43	8.108	9.00	2.25
500	40.54	8.108	10.00	2.00
1,000	81.08	8.108	15.00	1.50

It will be recalled that open-end company shares are quoted at their book value plus a selling charge, which is typically at least 7.5 per cent of the selling price (approximately 8.108 per cent of the book value). So, if open-end shares with a book value of $500.00, for example, were sold to an investor, they would be quoted at $540.54. In Table 14–3 it was assumed that the closed-end investment company shares were purchased at their book value. The typical closed-end share would actually be selling at a discount of approximately 10 to 15 per cent below the book value. Thus, for example, if the book value of closed-end shares was $500.00, the shares may be selling for only $425.00. The commissions on this would amount to only $9.25. Adding this to the price of $425.00 would give a total of only $434.25 for the closed-end shares as compared to $540.54 for the open-end shares. It should again be pointed out, however, that most open-end companies will buy back their shares at the book value without any charge being added, whereas the investor must pay the same commission rates to sell the closed-end shares as when he purchased them.

But if the shares are not sold this would not be a consideration. In the meantime, if other things are equal, the investor should enjoy a higher yield on closed-end shares. For example, assume that the companies in the above example paid dividends equivalent to 4.00 per cent of the book value of the shares. The holder of the closed-end shares would enjoy a yield of 4.83 per cent while the investor in the open-end shares would get only 3.70 per cent.

It should be clearly understood that the yield on the closed-end shares would be higher than on the open-end shares only if the two companies are paying the same rate of dividends on the book value of the stock, and provided the total price paid for the closed-end was less than that paid for the open-end. The yield on some open-ends is higher than that obtained on some closed-end companies. In some instances a higher yield may be obtained on a closed-end only because of the leverage present. But the presence of leverage ordinarily makes the shares more speculative.

Cost to Reinvest Dividends

With some exceptions, closed-end investment companies make no provision for the reinvestment of dividends with the company. If the investor wants to withdraw the dividends and then reinvest them he may, of course, do so, but the regular broker's commission must be paid to acquire the new shares. This constitutes a disadvantage as compared with the open-ends, practically all of which have provisions for the reinvestment of dividends. But of course the full book value must be paid for the new open-end company shares purchased with capital gains dividends, and in about half the cases the book value plus the regular selling charges must be paid for the shares purchased with ordinary income dividends.

Four of the closed-end companies now have provision for the automatic reinvestment of dividends. They are Consolidated Investment Trust (over-the-counter market), Lehman Corporation, Niagara Corporation, and Tri-Continental Corporation (the latter three are listed on the NYSE). In some instances, a small nominal charge is made for this service. In addition to these, a number of closed-end companies now give their shareholders the option of taking the customary year-end capital gains dividend in cash or stock. In some instances the final annual dividend from regular income may also optionally be paid in cash or stock.

No Accumulative Savings or Systematic Withdrawal Plans

Only one closed-end investment company—Consolidated Investment Trust (traded over-the-counter)—has an accumulative savings plan. But an investor can use the Monthly Investment Plan, which was discussed in the preceding chapter, for any of the closed-ends that are listed on the New York Stock Exchange. This would be very similar to the accumulative plan of the open-ends. Ordinary brokerage commissions would have to be paid for the regular purchase of shares and the reinvestment of dividends. Most of the time, however, practically all of the closed-end shares can be purchased at a discount below the asset value. None of the closed-ends has a systematic withdrawal plan.

GOVERNMENT REGULATION OF INVESTMENT COMPANIES

Investment companies are subject to the Securities Act of 1933 and the Securities Exchange Act of 1934, the same as other types of corporations. In addition they are governed by the provisions of the Investment Company Act, which was enacted by Congress in 1940. The Securities and Exchange Commission administers these acts.

All investment companies must register as such with the Securities and Exchange Commission. They must have a minimum capital of $100,000 before they may sell securities to the public. Open-end companies formed since the passage of this legislation may issue only one class of securities —common stock. Closed-end companies may issue also one class of preferred stock and one class of bonds, but the bonds must be covered three times by assets, and the preferred stock must be covered twice. The preferred stock must be voting stock.

A registration statement must be filed with the Securities and Exchange Commission showing a description of the investment company, the method of operation, and a statement regarding the investment policy which the company intends to follow. The prospectus which must be offered to every prospective purchaser of the company's securities contains similar data. In connection with the investment policy, it must be clearly stated whether the company intends to have a balanced portfolio, whether it plans a diversified common stock investment program, whether its primary purpose of investment is for income or for capital growth, etc. The investment policy cannot be changed without the consent of the security holders.

TAXATION

Corporations whose shares are owned by investment companies must pay the regular corporation taxes to the federal government and in some states a state income tax is also levied. Subject to the exception noted below, the investment company itself must pay the corporate tax on the dividends and interest received from the securities which it holds (except tax-exempt bonds). But, as in the case of all corporations, the investment company is entitled to a credit equivalent to 85 per cent of the dividends received. In other words, only 15 per cent of the dividends are taxed. To this extent, double taxation has resulted. The investor who owns the investment shares must pay his personal income tax on the dividends received from the company. Now we have triple taxation to the extent noted.

Regulated Investment Companies

All investment companies are "regulated" by the Securities and Exchange Commission under the Securities Acts and the Investment Company Act. But to obtain special tax relief, an investment company, either open- or closed-end, may (if it meets the proper requirements) register with the Internal Revenue Service as a *regulated investment company.* The principal requirements of a regulated investment company are as follows:

1. It must pay out in dividends at least 90 per cent of its net income, exclusive of capital gains, every year.
2. At least 90 per cent of its gross income for any taxable year must be from dividends, interest, and gains from the sale of securities.
3. Not more than 30 per cent of its gross income may be derived from gains on securities held for less than three months.
4. Not more than 5 per cent of its assets may be invested in the securities of any one company.
5. Not more than 10 per cent of the voting securities of any company may be acquired.

Once an investment company has registered as a regulated company, it must continue the same status every year thereafter.

Tax Benefit to Regulated Company

A regulated investment company, as defined above, does not have to pay any federal corporate income tax on that portion of its net income, whether obtained from ordinary income or from capital gains, which is paid out in dividends to its shareholders. On any portion of the net income which is retained, the company pays the regular corporate income tax (subject to the credit of 85 per cent on dividends received). Any retained income arising from long-term capital gains is of course subject to the capital gains tax of 25 per cent.

Tax Status of Regulated Company's Shareholder

The shareholder of a regulated investment company pays his regular personal income tax on dividends received from the company. In most instances the dividends from ordinary income will be subject to the dividend exclusion.[2]

Any part of the dividend received by the investment company's shareholder which represents a long-term capital gain is taxed as a long-term capital gain. On any realized long-term capital gain which the investment company *retains,* it will pay the regular long-term capital gains tax of 25 per cent. The company will notify the shareholder as to the amount of such gain which is applicable to his shares, and the shareholder will report this capital gain on his personal income tax return. The shareholder, however, can then take credit for his share of the tax which was paid by the company. If the 25 per cent paid by the company exceeds the amount of taxes that would be applicable to the particular shareholder's capital gains, figured at his top bracket rate, he can apply the balance of the credit against other gains, or he can apply for a refund. The amount of the retained capital gain (less the 25 per cent tax paid by the company) is added to the cost basis of the stock for the purpose of determining capital gains or losses upon sale of the shares by the shareholder.

State Taxation of Capital Gains

Although the federal government treats dividends paid by investment companies from long-term capital gains as long-term capital gains to the shareholders (regardless of how long the stock has been held by the shareholder), a number of the states that have income tax laws treat it otherwise. The following sixteen states (and the District of Columbia) treat such capital gains dividends as ordinary income regardless of whether they are distributed in stock or in cash: Alabama, Arizona, Arkansas, California, Louisiana, Maryland, Mississippi, New Mexico, North Carolina, Oklahoma, Oregon, South Carolina, Tennessee, Utah, Virginia, and Wisconsin.

The following fifteen states follow the federal law and consider *all* long-term capital gains dividends as long-term capital gains to the shareholders: Alaska, Colorado, Georgia, Hawaii, Idaho, Indiana, Iowa, Kansas, Kentucky, Minnesota, Missouri, Montana, New York, North Dakota, and West Virginia.

The following three states tax capital gains dividends as ordinary income if they are paid out in cash, but do not tax them when the distribu-

[2] If the dividends *received* by an investment company, however, constitute less than 75 per cent of its gross income (capital gains excluded), the portion that is entitled to the dividend exclusion is computed as follows:

$$\frac{\text{Dividends received by investment company}}{\text{Investment company's gross income (excluding capital gains)}} \times \text{Dividends received from investment company}$$

tion is made in stock: Delaware, Massachusetts, and Michigan. The states not specifically mentioned above do not have a state income tax.

Special Tax Benefits

Some investors who are in a high tax bracket may be interested in a few domestic investment companies whose dividends may be partially or completely exempt from taxation. If an investment company owns securities which have a current market value that is less than the original cost of the securities, the sale of these securities will produce a loss which can be used to offset current income. Any dividends paid by such a company that year may be partially or entirely a return of capital rather than constituting income, and to that extent need not be reported by the shareholder as income for that year. Such dividends, to the extent that they constitute a return of capital, are used to write down the cost basis of the stock. When such stock is sold, any capital gain realized would thereby be larger, or any capital loss smaller, than would otherwise be the case. The following are among the investment companies which may have this special tax advantage:

Abacus Fund
Standard Shares
United Corporation

CANADIAN AND OTHER FOREIGN INVESTMENT COMPANIES

A number of investment companies have been formed to invest in the stocks of Canadian and other foreign companies in order to reap the benefits that may accrue from the expansion of business in new or underdeveloped countries, or to invest in older countries which are adopting modern industrialized methods, or to gain special tax benefits that may be enjoyed. Many of these investment companies are formed in a particular foreign country and the principal market for their securities is in that country. Generally speaking, the American investor is advised to bypass these companies because of their speculative nature, the inability to secure adequate financial information relating to them, the difficulty of buying and selling their securities, the rates of exchange, taxation and other considerations.

In the past, the principal interest of American investors in investment companies specializing in foreign stocks has been those companies which invest in Canadian securities. At first these companies were formed in the United States. Then there was a trend toward the formation in Canada of a "non-resident-owned" (NRO) investment company in order to secure special tax benefits. Subsequent legislation, however, eliminated the favored tax treatment. Since then several of the NRO companies have reformed in the United States. Also, some of the investment companies which specialized in Canadian securities are now branching out and buying securities of other foreign companies.

For companies formed in Canada there is a Canadian withholding tax on dividends paid to non-residents of 20 per cent (if the company is less than 25 per cent Canadian owned; otherwise the tax is 10 per cent). The American investor reports the full amount of the dividend on his federal income tax form, but by filing special Form 1116 he can deduct the entire amount of the Canadian withholding tax from his income taxes. Dividends received from foreign companies are not subject to the dividend exclusion. Most of the investment companies formed in the United States qualify as regulated investment companies and are therefore taxed in the manner described previously.

In 1964, Congress enacted a flat tax of 15 per cent of the purchase price of new and existing foreign stock bought by a United States resident from foreign issuers or owners. The tax, however, does not apply to United States residents who buy foreign stock from other United States residents. It does not apply to new issues of Canadian securities or to securities originating in underdeveloped countries.

The following are among the largest domestic open-end investment companies specializing in Canadian and other foreign securities:

Canada General Fund
Canadian Fund
Investors Inter-Continental Fund
Loomis-Sayles Canadian & International Fund
Stein Roe & Farnham International Fund

Listed on the New York Stock Exchange are the following closed-end investment companies which specialize in foreign securities:

American-South African Investment
Eurofund
Japan Fund

In most instances the investment companies which specialize in foreign securities would be classified as diversified common stock funds. Generally speaking, they would be considered more speculative than funds which confine themselves to securities issued by United States companies.

BUYING A TAX LIABILITY

The typical investment company in the United States has been in existence for a number of years. Included in its portfolios are a number of securities in which it has an appreciable unrealized capital gain. This of course increases the book value of the investment company's shares. In buying the open-ends the investor pays the full book value for the shares plus the selling charge. In the case of closed-ends the increase in the value of portfolio also causes the market value of the investment company's shares to rise. Thus, part of the purchase price paid for investment company shares represents an unrealized capital gain. If the company should sell part of its portfolio at a profit and retain the gain, it would have to pay a tax of 25 per cent on this gain. If, in the case of a regulated company, the capital gain is distributed to the company's shareholders, the latter must pay the capital gains tax. Thus the investment company shareholder would be paying a tax on the return of part of his purchase price (the return of part of his capital). It is for this reason that an investor may be better off buying the shares of a new investment company organized by experienced and successful management than purchasing the shares of an older company. The new company would be purchasing its portfolio at the existing market prices and thus not have an unrealized capital gain on its books.

FACTORS TO CONSIDER IN BUYING

Companies Not Comparable

The average person who buys open-end investment company shares does so because he is sold on the idea by a salesman. The particular shares he buys are those issued by the company or companies which the salesman represents. Needless to say, this is not the best way to proceed. An alternative would be for the prospective investor to investigate the various investment companies and purchase the shares of the one that looks best to him. But this takes time and effort and the investor may not be qualified to interpret the data properly.

One of the difficulties encountered in comparing one company against another is that in many instances the companies are not comparable. Another is that the prospective investor probably does not have a clear picture in his mind as to just what kind of investment company shares he wants. A person should attempt to decide whether he wants shares in a balanced fund, a diversified common stock fund, an income fund, a growth fund, etc. After having done this, a comparison may then be made of different companies within the particular class of the type of fund desired. A decision is still difficult, because within the same type of trust, companies vary according to age, size, past management performance, selling charges, flexibility of savings and withdrawal options, etc.

Open-End vs. Closed-End

Perhaps enough has already been said about the relative merits of open- and closed-end companies. Other things being equal, it would practically always be to the advantage of the investor to buy a closed-end company at a discount of 15 per cent below the net assets value of the shares plus a commission of 1 or 2 per cent, than to buy an open-end at the full net asset value plus a selling charge of 8.108 per cent. But a general statement that it is better to buy a closed-end than an open-end cannot be made. Some open-ends have in the past proved to be better investments than some closed-ends, and vice versa. The fact that discounts on closed-ends tend to increase as the stock market goes down may result in some investors taking a larger loss on the sale of their shares than that experienced by a holder of open-end shares. The flexibility of accumulated savings plans and systematic withdrawal plans offered by some of the open-ends may appeal to some investors. The prospective investor should consider the past performance of the particular companies and their probable future performance rather than deciding the issue on whether the companies are open- or closed-end.

Age of Company

Age is perhaps not too important, but generally speaking the older the company the more experienced the management. In the case of open-ends the older companies may be larger since they have been continuously selling new shares over a long period of time.

Size

Generally speaking, the larger companies should be preferred. This is particularly true of the open-ends. The larger companies can practice diversification to a greater extent than the smaller companies, and their expense ratios tend to be lower. Also, the fact that an open-end company has reached large-scale size is some expression of investor confidence, although in some instances it may merely indicate aggressive selling.

Expense Ratios

The principal expense of the typical investment company is the management fee. The customary fee in the past has been an annual charge of ½ of 1 per cent of the average assets for the period (sometimes expressed as $\frac{1}{8}$ of 1 per cent a quarter). This is still the amount of the fee for medium- and small-sized companies. As the size of individual companies has increased over the years, the total amount of such a fee has become enormous for large companies. But if the size of a particular investment company doubled, the work or responsibility of the management would not double. A few years ago several large companies reduced the percentage fee as the size of the companies' assets increased. In very recent years, due undoubtedly to stockholders' suits and threatened suits, a number of the large companies have reduced their management fees. Most of these follow the practicc of charging $\frac{1}{2}$ of 1 per cent on the first hundred or two hundred million of the assets, and then reducing the fee to $\frac{3}{8}$ of 1 per cent on the next bracket of assets and to $\frac{1}{8}$ of 1 per cent on the balance.

The other operating expenses would include office expenses, brokerage commissions, custodian fees, (some) taxes, and in some instances, investment advisory fees. These other expenses approximate $\frac{1}{4}$ of 1 per cent of the average assets for the typical company. Thus, the total expenses (all expenses except interest and taxes) for a medium-sized company would approximate $\frac{3}{4}$ of 1 per cent of the average asset value. For some of the large companies it will approximate $\frac{1}{5}$ of 1 per cent, while for smaller companies it may run as high as 1 or 2 per cent, and in the case of very small companies, it will go in a few instances to 3 per cent.

The ratio of expenses to average asset value does not mean much to the investor until he knows what percentage the company is averaging on its investments. Funds stressing income currently earn a much higher percentage than companies which are stressing long-term growth. Between 3 and 4 per cent would be typical for the average diversified common stock and balanced fund. The ratio of total expenses to investment income of the larger funds will run from a low of 6 per cent for several of the largest funds to a high of 20 or 25 per cent. In the case of some of the smaller funds it will run to 50 (and even 100) per cent. Expense ratios for the various companies can be found in Wiesenberger's *Investment Companies, Johnson's Investment Company Charts,* and the *Forbes* annual survey.

Other things being equal, it is of course advisable to buy into a company with a relatively low ratio of expenses to average assets and investment income. This can be found only in the larger companies.

The selling charge or "load" of a mutual company is not treated as an expense of running the company. This charge goes to the salesman and selling organization. So far as company expenses are concerned, the no-load funds have the same types of expenses as the load funds. The same goes for closed-end investment companies.

Investment Performance

The best way to judge the past success of any investment company is to ascertain the relative earnings experienced by the company and the growth in the book value of the company's shares over a period of years. Two companies may show similar results in these respects but one would show a much better yield to the investor because of the fact that his shares were purchased at a smaller percentage of the net asset value than the other. This can be compensated for by determining the yield for the year based on the market price or offer price of the shares at the beginning of the year. Capital gains paid out are usually excluded in this computation.

The income yield itself, however, does not show the whole picture. The company may have had substantial capital gains, both unrealized and realized, and part or all of the latter may have been paid out in dividends to the shareholders. Perhaps the best way of showing the investment performance of an investment company is to add all dividend payouts, both from ordinary income and capital gains, to the increase in the price of the share (offer price or market price), and express this as a percentage of the price per share at the beginning of the period under consideration.

The investor who depends upon the dividend return from his investment company shares for his living would be interested in a company that can show a good yield on the stock. Another investor, particularly one who is in the high income-tax bracket, would probably be interested in a company which could show good growth in the value of its shares.

It was stated above that the *past* performance of an investment company could be determined in the manner just discussed. Any investor is interested in the probable *future* success of a company, not the past, since it is only through the future performance of the company management that he can profit. But no one can accurately predict the future. The past record of the management performance is perhaps the best way to judge the probable future performance. If the average record for the past ten years, the past five years, and the immediate past year or two is good, it is a good sign that the company has a better than average chance of showing good results in the future.

Reinvestment of Dividends

To some investors an important consideration is whether or not the company will reinvest the dividends, both from ordinary income and from capital gains. With some exceptions, only the open-ends do this. If reinvestment of the dividends may be done, then the question as to whether or not the company exacts a selling charge for reinvesting the ordinary dividends or the capital gains dividends would be of importance.

Accumulation and Withdrawal Plans

We discussed accumulation and withdrawal plans above. Only the open-ends provide these. The exact nature of the particular company's plans would be of interest to the investor. The minimum initial investment and the minimum periodic investment would be an important factor to many investors. Some would be interested in life insurance in connection with an accumulation plan. A majority of mutual funds are now offering some type of systematic withdrawal plan.

GETTING INFORMATION ON INVESTMENT COMPANIES

A wealth of information is available on various types of investments. Data on the leading investment companies may be obtained from the standard financial services discussed in the next chapter, such as Moody's, Standard & Poor's, and Value Line Investment Service. The advice of brokers and investment dealers can be sought, but if they are selling a particular open-end company's shares, it is probable that their advice will not be unbiased. Many investors will give their advice freely, but although they may be acting entirely honestly, they will usually advise only the particular company that they have invested in; they probably are not acquainted with the many other investment companies.

Following are suggested publications that deal exclusively with investment companies or which regularly include some information relating to these companies.

Sometimes referred to as the "bible" of investment companies is a book called *Investment Companies,* published annually by the firm of Arthur Wiesenberger & Co., New York, N. Y. 10006. The book is available in the leading libraries and in most brokerage and investment dealers' offices. This book contains recent and past information on all of the leading investment companies, both open- and closed-end. The general nature of the various companies is stated and the type of investment policy followed is explained. The past management performance is shown by figures on the percentage increase in the net asset value per share plus dividend payouts for the past ten years. Charts showing this performance are provided for the leading companies. Overlays are provided for comparison with the leading averages and indexes.

A special type of book dealing only with open-end companies is *Johnson's Investment Company Charts.* This is a looseleaf book published annually by Hugh Johnson & Company, Buffalo, N. Y. 14203. The book is generally available in many brokerage and investment dealers' offices, and in some libraries. Tables are included showing twenty pertinent facts about the leading mutual funds: the funds which have had the greatest capital appreciation, those which have paid the largest dividends, and those which have best resisted market declines. As the title would indicate, the principal feature of the book is a series of charts on each of the leading mutual funds showing by a line graph how much the shares would be worth today, including all capital gains distributions, on a $10,000 investment in the particular fund ten years ago. Dividends paid from ordinary income are shown separately. Transparent plastic overlays

JOHNSON STOCK FUND AVERAGE

January 1, 1955—December 31, 1964

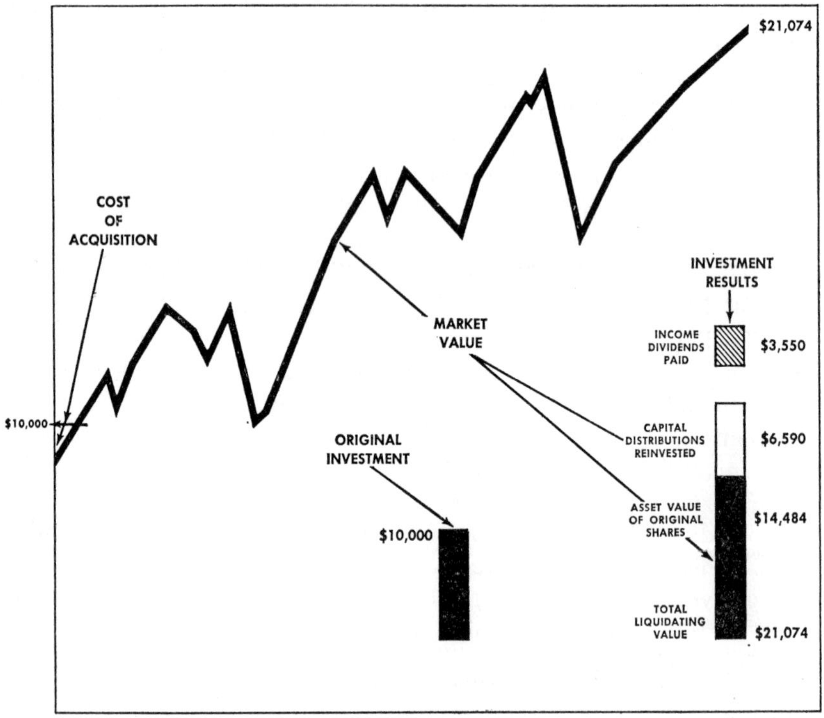

Fig. 14–7. Illustration of the Johnson Stock Fund Average. Annual record: income, capital gains, liquidating value. Assumed investment of $10,000 with realized capital gains taken in additional shares. (Reproduced with permission, from *Johnson's Investment Company Charts, 1965.* Buffalo, N. Y.: Hugh Johnson & Co.)

are provided showing the comparable data for the Dow-Jones Industrial Average, several of the Standard & Poor's stock indexes, the cost-of-living index, records of some of the leading industrial companies, and Johnson's own investment company averages. By placing the overlay on the particular investment company chart, the particular investment company's performance can be compared with that of the particular stock index or average diagrammed on the overlays. Figure 14–7 shows what is contained on the Johnson Stock Fund Average overlay issued in connection with diversified common stock funds (such as the fund shown in Fig. 14–6, on page 522). The charts are drawn to a logarithmic scale. The company charts and the chart of the averages make no provision for taxes on either ordinary income or on capital gains.

An inexpensive booklet dealing with both open- and closed-end investment companies is *Investment Trusts and Funds From the Investor's Point of View*. This is published, and revised frequently, by the American Institute for Economic Research, Great Barrington, Massachusetts. The performance record of a number of the leading funds is given and this is compared with the composite average. Recommendations classified into three groups are given: for investment, for speculative investment, and for speculation.

Leading financial magazines frequently contain information on investment companies. Every three months *Barron's* (*Barron's National Business and Financial Weekly*) runs its mutual fund record, showing the net asset value per share at the end of the last quarter and the dividends from ordinary income and capital gains for the preceding twelve months, and similar figures for the past ten years.

Each year, the August 15 issue of *Forbes* magazine contains a study of the shares of the leading investment companies. The article shows what would happen to an investment of $100 at net asset value for the most recent bull and bear markets. The dividend performance for the past twelve months and the selling charges on the shares of the various companies are also shown. Figure 14–8 shows one page of the *Forbes* study.

Interesting items and articles about mutual funds are contained in a monthly publication called *Fundscope*, which is published by Fundscope, Los Angeles, California. Included is a "Basic Buying Guide" showing, for the leading mutual funds, the past ten-year relative appreciation, the ten-year relative overall performance, the relative current yield, and the relative risk involved. Helpful information may be obtained also from *Vickers Guide to Investment Company Portfolios*, published annually, which is available from Vickers Associates, Inc., Huntington, N. Y.

1965 FUND RATINGS

Assets in Millions	Maximum Sales Charge %	Annual Expenses (Cents per $100)		CONSISTENCY OF PERFORMANCE: In UP Markets	CONSISTENCY OF PERFORMANCE: In DOWN Markets	MANAGEMENT RESULTS ($100 ended as): 1953-1965	MANAGEMENT RESULTS ($100 ended as): Latest 12 Months	Dividend Return %
			Standard & Poor's 500 Stock Average	—	—	**$360.26**	**$102.97**	**3.1%**
			Average of 10 stock funds in FORBES Index	C+	C+	**$383.94**	**$102.76**	**2.4%**
			CLOSED-END INVESTMENT COMPANIES*					
$ 42.2	—	$0.60	Abacus Fund, Inc. (started 6/57)	B+	B	—	$104.84	none
115.4	—	0.40	Adams Express	C	C+	$293.12	102.61	2.5%
51.7	—	0.51	American International	C	C+	300.16	101.00	2.5
21.9	—	0.72	Carriers & General Corporation	C+	B+	378.87	104.60	2.4
88.4	—	0.14	Consolidated Investment Trust	C+	C	366.20	103.82	2.7
48.1	—	0.41	Dominick Fund	C	C	257.04	102.26	1.9
73.8	—	0.79	General American Investors	C+	D+	306.89	101.59	1.3
93.8	—	0.38	General Public Service	C	A	325.44	103.22	2.4
84.6	—	0.53	International Holdings	D	B	248.23△	97.18	3.4
397.7	—	0.34	Lehman Corp.	B	C+	333.66	104.58	1.9
174.3	—	0.51	Madison Fund	C	C	299.21	100.52	2.4
55.0	—	0.65	National Aviation	B+	B	470.06	113.15	2.4
87.0	—	0.49	Niagara Share Corp.	C+	C+	374.22	103.01	1.9
46.3	—	0.32	Petroleum Corp. of America	C+	B	279.38	102.78	3.1
51.9	—	0.53	Standard Shares (started 3/56)	C	B+	—	99.99	2.0
538.9	—	0.20	Tri-Continental	C	B	268.56	96.81	2.7
143.0	—	0.53	The United Corporation	D	A	254.90	108.54	1.9
135.3	—	0.52	U.S. & Foreign Securities	C+	C+	297.87	100.80	2.5
			STOCK FUNDS (LOAD)					
$36.4	8.5%	$0.80	Aberdeen Fund	B	C	$392.36	$104.74	1.5%
2.1	8.5	0.80	Advisers Fund	D	A	242.76	106.79	2.2
1,134.1	7.5	0.36	Affiliated Fund	C+	A	303.66	101.53	3.1
1.6	1.0	2.36	Leon B. Allen Fund	C+	B	393.93	99.60	0.4
7.7	7.5	1.00	American Growth Fund (started 8/58)	—	B	—	100.68	1.4
285.1	8.5	0.64	American Mutual Fund	B	B	368.41	103.24	2.6
58.4	8.5	0.74	Associated Fund Trust	D	B	232.28	103.90	3.1
5.2	2.0	0.95	Associations Investment Fund (started 4/60)	—	—	—	103.46	1.6
40.3	8.25	0.95	Atomics, Physics & Science Fund (started 12/53)	D+	C	210.80△	108.85	1.9
9.3	8.5	1.02	Axe-Houghton Stock Fund	C+	B+	268.42	107.53	1.8
21.2	8.0	0.95	Axe Science Corp. (started 2/55)	C	C+	—	109.07	0.6
37.9	8.5	0.82	Blue Ridge Mutual Fund	D	C+	298.79	99.27	2.6
7.7	8.5	0.87	Bondstock Corp.	C	D+	265.24	101.78	2.2
338.0	7.5	0.20	Broad Street Investing Corp.	D	B+	308.87	102.06	3.1
2.2	8.5	0.81	The Brown Fund of Hawaii	D+	A	245.33	100.36	2.7
105.3	8.67	0.40	Bullock Fund	C	B+	335.05	101.35	2.7
117.1	8.75	0.99	Capital Life Insurance Shares and Growth Stock Fund (started 1/60)	—	—	—	83.07	0.2
121.1	8.5	0.35	Century Shares Trust	C+	C+	344.35	83.49	1.2

***All data based on net asset values.** *△Fund not operating for full period.*

WHAT THE RATINGS MEAN

We have selected eight distinct market movements over the past 12 years—four major up moves, four major down moves. For each period we have compared each stock fund's performance against that of the broadly based Standard & Poor's 500 stock average. The balanced funds have been compared against the FORBES balanced fund index. A high rating indicates a consistent ability to outperform the average; a low rating indicates a consistent inability to do as well as the average.

Fig. 14–8. First page from *Forbes* investment company report. (Reproduced with permission, from *Forbes*, August 15, 1965.)

SMALL BUSINESS INVESTMENT COMPANIES

A special type of investment company is the Small Business Investment Company (SBIC), formed under the Small Business Investment Company Act of 1959. Although these companies may receive their original capital from both government and private sources, they are formed in a manner somewhat similar to the closed-end investment companies, previously discussed. One important difference, however, should be noted. Instead of investing their capital in securities of large, established companies, these small business investment companies supply venture capital to small or new business concerns that would otherwise have difficulty in obtaining funds.

Many of the Small Business Investment Companies have sold their stock publicly, and several are listed on securities exchanges. They must register under the Investment Company Act of 1940, and they may elect to be taxed as a "regulated investment company."

Most of the small investment companies have had a rather rocky existence to date, and the prices of the stocks of those which have gone public have been subject to violent fluctuations. From the standpoint of safety, they cannot be compared to the typical closed- or open-end investment companies discussed in this chapter.

REAL ESTATE INVESTMENT TRUSTS

The investment company idea was applied to real estate a number of years ago, but after the Supreme Court ruled that they were subject to the ordinary business corporation income tax, nothing much was heard about them. In 1960, however, Congress enacted legislation which provided that if real estate investment companies meet practically the same requirements as the typical kind of investment company, they would be treated taxwise similar to a "regulated investment company." Since then, quite a number of real estate investment companies have been formed.

It should be emphasized that the assets behind this type of company are real estate, and not securities of large, established companies. These companies are also new. It should therefore be realized by the investor that as a class they are not as safe as the ordinary kind of investment company.

QUESTIONS

1. Explain the general nature of investment companies. What name or names, other than "investment company," are sometimes used for them? Do these all have exactly the same meaning? Explain.

2. What problems commonly encountered by the average investor in investing in ordinary corporation stock are overcome by buying shares of an investment company? What problems still remain?
3. Investment companies may be divided into three types: (a) face-amount certificate companies, (b) unit investment companies, and (c) management investment companies. Distinguish among these three. Which is the most popular? Why?
4. In what different ways may investment companies be classified? What types of investment company portfolios would you as an investor prefer? Why?
5. Management investment companies are of what two different types as regards the purchase and sale of their shares? Which types are referred to as mutual funds? Why are they so called?
6. Where a selling charge of 8½ per cent is specified as the selling charge for a mutual fund, is the charge this percentage of the net asset value per share or of the selling price? What would the percentage be if it were based on the other value? On which value do you think it should be based? Why?
7. Indicate the difference in the quotation for closed-end and open-end shares. How is the bid quotation for an open-end company share determined? The asked quotation?
8. Explain what is meant by a "letter of intention" in connection with the purchase of mutual shares.
9. Indicate the different types of accumulation plans which are used in the sale of mutual fund shares.
10. Can an investor make an arrangement with a mutual fund to have his dividends automatically reinvested in the shares? Is a selling charge made on the shares sold in this manner?
11. Compare the relative merits of buying a mutual fund with the accumulation plan and buying a closed-end company share under the Monthly Investment Plan.
12. What advantages may accrue to the investor from buying investment company shares under one of the accumulation plans or under the Monthly Investment Plan?
13. What types of systematic withdrawal plans are available to mutual fund buyers?
14. Compare the relative selling costs involved in buying mutual funds and listed closed-end company shares.
15. Indicate the various circumstances or procedures that would result in a reduction or elimination of the sales charge of an open-end investment company share.
16. Why do many closed-end company shares usually sell at a discount? Do you think that mutual funds should sell at similar discounts for the same reasons? Explain.
17. Explain what is meant by "leverage" in an investment company. In what types of investment companies is it found? Why?
18. List the relative advantages of buying open-end and closed-end investment company shares.

19. Indicate the main provisions of the Investment Company Act of 1940.
20. List the requirements of a "regulated investment company" as provided for by the Internal Revenue Service. What are the advantages of being a "regulated" company?
21. Why are the dividends of some domestic investment companies tax-free to the shareholders?
22. Why is it sometimes said that the buyer of investment company shares is buying a tax liability?
23. List the factors that should be considered in buying any investment company shares. How would you proceed to measure the success of the management of a particular investment company?
24. Indicate the specific sources of information that are available to the prospective buyer of investment company shares.
25. Explain the differences that exist between the shares of an open-end investment company and the shares of a small business investment company.

CASE PROBLEMS

1. Company A and Company B are both no-load mutual funds which pay out 100 per cent of their earnings and realized capital gains each year. At the beginning of the year, Company A's shares sold at $20, and Company B's shares sold at $10 a share. During the year Company A paid an ordinary income dividend of 40 cents and a capital gain dividend of 80 cents. Company B paid an ordinary dividend of 30 cents and a capital gain dividend of 30 cents. At the end of the year, Company A stock was selling for $21, and Company B stock was worth $11. Compare the performance of the two companies for the year. Which one would you rather own? Why?
2. Williams is considering buying the shares of a mutual fund under their cumulative savings plan. What features of this plan should he look up before making a decision? Bradshaw is buying the shares of a closed-end company through the Monthly Investment Plan. Compare the merits of these two types of plans.
3. Assume that you purchased some open-end regulated investment company shares for $10 per share. This price included the customary selling charge of 8½ per cent. Assume that the same day you purchased shares of a closed-end regulated investment company which had a net asset value per share exactly the same as the open-end company, but that you were able to buy the shares at a discount of 20 per cent below the net asset value, plus a commission of 2 per cent. How much per share did you pay for the closed-end shares? Assume that at the end of one year each company paid a dividend equivalent to 3 per cent of the net asset value per share at the beginning of the year. What was the yield to you on each investment? (Include selling charges in your purchase price.)
4. Assume that in Problem 3 above, the book value of the open-end company shares included an unrealized capital gain of 20 per cent. Further assume that immediately after you purchased the shares the company sold all the securities in which it had a capital gain, that it distributed the

capital gain to its shareholders, and that you had to pay a tax of 25 per cent on the capital gain dividend. What would be the new net asset value per share? How much did it really cost you to get the net assets of this amount?

5. Mac Dougall and Fern Flat were arguing about the relative merits of open-end and closed-end investment companies. Mac prefers the closed-end shares because he says they can be bought at a discount below net asset value and, furthermore, that the buying commissions are less. But Fern prefers the open-end shares because she says you can always sell the shares at their full book value. Comment on the arguments used by Mac and Fern. Which of the two types of shares would you prefer? Why?
6. Bill Hogan sought his broker's opinion on the idea of buying some shares of a closed-end investment company. The broker recommended a particular company and, among other things, indicated that the company had a high degree of leverage. Hogan said that he did not understand what was meant by "leverage," so the broker explained it to him, and concluded by saying that buying a high leverage company share was something like buying a stock on margin. That ended the interview and Hogan did not buy the shares because he thought that buying on margin was the same as gambling. Do you agree with the broker's comment relative to leverage and buying on margin? Explain. Do you agree with Hogan's idea that buying on margin is the same as gambling? Why or why not? How would you define "gambling"? Is speculation the same as gambling? Is speculation the same as investing? Explain.
7. Mr. and Mrs. X. Y. Greer, who are 70 and 66 respectively, are at the present time drawing a total of $130.50 from social security. Mr. Greer is getting and will continue to get for life a company pension of $75 a month. They have $2,000 (maturity value) in United States savings bonds, Series E, which will mature in approximately five years and on which the yield will be 3¾ per cent if held to maturity. The couple also has $4,000 in two savings and loan associations in the city on which they get a return of 4 per cent a year. Mr. Greer says that they have absolutely no hedge against inflation and that they should cash in their savings bonds and savings and loan accounts and invest the money in a large mutual fund which last year showed an income return of approximately 4 per cent on the offer price of the shares at the beginning of that year. Should they do as Mr. Greer says? Why or why not? Should they attempt to hedge against inflation? Why or why not?

SELECTED READINGS

Doane, C. Russell, and Hills, Edward J. *Investment Trusts and Funds From the Investor's Point of View.* Great Barrington, Mass.: American Institute for Economic Research, 1965.

Forbes Investment Company Report. Published annually in the August 15 issue of *Forbes* magazine. Reprints available from *Forbes,* New York, N. Y. 10011.

Investment Companies. New York: Arthur Wiesenberger & Co. Latest edition.

Investment Companies Fact Book. Latest edition. Single copies available free from Investment Company Institute, New York, N. Y. 10006.

Investment Company Shares: An Aid to Bankers and Trust Officers. Latest edition. Single copies available free from Investment Company Institute, New York, N. Y. 10006.

Jenkins, David. *How to Build Capital and Income in Mutual Funds.* Larchmont, N. Y.: American Research Council, 1961.
Johnson's Investment Company Charts. Latest edition. Hugh Johnson & Co., Buffalo, N. Y. 14203.
Management Investment Companies. (The Library of Money and Credit, Investment Company Institute.) Englewood Cliffs, N. J.: Prentice-Hall, Inc., 1962.
Mutual Fund Shares: An Aid to Attorneys. Single copies available free from Investment Company Institute, New York, N. Y. 10006.
Mutual Funds Charts & Statistics. New York: Arthur Wiesenberger & Co. Latest edition.
Smith, R. L. *The Grim Truth about Mutual Funds.* New York: G. P. Putnam's Sons, 1963.
Study of Mutual Funds, A. (Wharton School Study of Mutual Funds.) Washington, D. C.: Government Printing Office, 1962.
Vickers Guide to Investment Company Portfolios. Published annually by Vickers Associates, Inc., Huntington, N. Y.
Weisman, R. L. *Investments Made Easy.* New York: Harper & Row, 1962.

15

Obtaining Investment Information

Since investment company shares are a special type of investment, we discussed sources of information relating specifically to them in the last chapter. The present chapter will deal with investment information in general, which in most instances will apply also to investment companies.

Before buying or selling securities, the investor should carefully investigate his planned purchase or sale. When one buys a security, he buys an intangible claim against a company whose real value is contingent upon the future earning power of that company and its recognition by other investors in the market. Regardless of his experience and training, no one knows for certain the future earning power of any company nor does anyone know positively that any specific security is going to go up or down in market value. On the other hand, there is a great deal of information available about many potential investments which can help one judge the future earnings and market position. While no infallible formula for investing has been developed, the study and analysis of available information is a prerequisite to successful investing.

A substantial amount of information is available about past business conditions, present business situation, and future forecasts of business and industry in general. In addition, further literature is available on the past, present, and probable future of specific industries, and there is a wealth of information on certain specific companies. To this, add all the publications, articles, pamphlets, brochures, and books available on the general subject of investing and on specific investment techniques and market problems, and the investor has enough information to keep him busy for many years. One of the major advantages that the professional investor has over the non-professional is the additional available time that can be devoted to the study of security information. Although it is impossible for the average investor to read and study all the available information relative to any specific investment, analysis of sufficient information is still an important investment consideration for any individual. The individual should, therefore, select enough data from the wealth available to guide him in making a reasonable investment decision.

A knowledge of the sources of information can be very helpful in saving time for the individual investor. Certain firms collect data and put them into useful form to save time for the investor. Efforts have been made by many institutions to make the information more understandable to the average individual. A knowledge of the quickest and easiest ways to collect and use the necessary information for investment decisions can thus be very helpful. Anyone who does not want to take time to collect and use a reasonable amount of information should not be investing in securities.

The importance which the authors place upon the use of available investment information in making investment decisions is indicated by the fact that a full chapter in this book is devoted to this subject. Some of the more important types and sources of investment information are discussed below.

FINANCIAL INFORMATION SOURCES

Financial information may be classified in two ways—by type of information and by source. Classification by type of information would be as follows:

1. General business and economic data
2. Specific industry data
3. Specific company data
4. Specific security data
5. General investment data
6. Investment market data

Information in all of the above areas is important to security investment decisions. When one purchases a security, he buys a specific type of security in a specific company in a specific industry operating under given business and economic conditions. Furthermore, he purchases the security in the securities market, and it must fit into his total investment plan. None of these areas may be ignored in making an investment decision. The emphasis on types of information, however, may vary from one investment to another. For example, if the individual has decided that he is going to purchase common stock, little additional information need be obtained on the type of security other than to ascertain that it is a common stock. Even here, however, the investor may be interested in whether or not the stock carries the preemptive right, the kinds of voting features it might have, and what limitations might be imposed upon dividend payment. A classification of investment information by source would be as follows:

1. Published books
2. General and business periodicals
3. Investment and financial periodicals and newspapers
4. Financial information services
5. Financial institutions, including investment bankers and brokerage firms
6. Investment advisory firms
7. The issuer of the security—the company whose security you are buying

In using investment information it is important to recognize the source and to have in mind any biases which that particular source might have. For example, the company itself is unlikely to paint a dark picture of its own future. Brokerage firms are not very often inclined to suggest to investors that they refrain from buying or selling securities. On the other hand, most of the investment information obtained today from published sources or from established, recognized financial institutions and issuing companies is sufficiently reliable for purposes of making investment decisions. Federal and state legislation has been enacted to help insure reliability in investment data. The Securities Exchange Commission and the various state security commissions work diligently to see that the investor is supplied with reasonable and accurate information for purposes of selecting an investment. No amount of legislation, however, can insure that the individual investor will use the information which is made available to him. The person who does use the information is much less likely to be "taken" in his purchase of securities.

The following discussion of investment information and its sources combines the two classifications discussed above. Because of the importance of the issuing company as a source of information, the discussion of this source and the type of information presented by it is considered separately at the end of this chapter.

General Business and Economic Data

Newspapers, magazines, and special reports are the most important sources of general business and economic data. It is not difficult to keep abreast of general business conditions through general reading. While most local newspapers do not emphasize business and economic information, a few newspapers in the United States have excellent coverage in these areas. *The Wall Street Journal* is a newspaper specifically designed to meet the needs of the business and investing community. *The Wall Street Journal* is published five mornings a week in a number of different locations throughout the country and is available on the publication date in practically every large city in the nation. The *Commercial and Financial Chronicle* is another business and investment publication which supplies general business and economic information. The *New York Times* has an excellent business section daily and a comprehensive business and financial section in its Sunday edition. Other large city newspapers also devote considerable space to business and economic conditions.

Weekly and monthly periodicals are also important sources of information on general business and economic conditions. Some of the business publications include *Business Week, Journal of Commerce, Fortune, Nation's Business,* and *Burroughs Clearing House.* Some of the more general weekly and monthly publications also attempt to keep their readers abreast of current business developments. These would include such publications as *Time, U. S. News and World Report,* and *Newsweek.* Some magazines are devoted more specifically to the fields of finance and investment. These would include *Forbes, Magazine of Wall Street, Financial World,* and *Barron's National Business and Financial Weekly.* Certain government publications are particularly useful in understanding current business conditions and in forecasting the future. The *Federal Reserve Bulletin,* published monthly by the Board of Governors of the Federal Reserve System, includes a wealth of statistical data on the national economy. The *Survey of Current Business,* published by the United States Department of Commerce, also contains a great deal of statistical information on the nation's economic progress. The President's Council of Economic Advisors issues a monthly publication entitled *Economic Indicators* which is designed to help interested people interpret the trends in business and in the economy.

Many private organizations also publish data on present business conditions and future expectations. Most of the large financial institutions publish an annual economic forecast. For example, the Prudential Insurance Company of America makes available free of charge each December a publication entitled *Prudential's Economic Forecast* in which the company attempts to estimate the direction and level of business and economic activity during the coming calendar year. Bankers' Trust Company of New York annually issues *Investment Outlook* for the coming year. The National Securities & Research Corporation annually prepares a forecast for the coming calendar year. This is available through many brokerage and investment banking firms throughout the country. Unfortunately, the techniques for longer-term forecasting are not sufficiently developed to provide good reliability. As a result, few sources are available which specifically attempt to predict the movement of business and the economy beyond a one- or two-year period.

Specific Industry Data

Not all industries move in the same direction as the economy, nor do all industries have the same expected future growth rate as that of the economy in general. Thus in making any specific investment decision, it is important to study the present condition and future prospects of the particular industry in which the contemplated investment is located. Some industries, such as electric power, have varied little with the general business cycle. Other industries, such as railroads, have been relatively depressed in both good and bad times. Certain industries are expected to have a much greater future growth rate than the economy as a whole; others are considered mature and should level off or decline in the future.

A great deal of information on the present and future prospects of specific industries is available in published sources. Most public libraries carry a large number of trade association publications. These publications (commonly issued monthly or quarterly) devote several pages to a discussion of the past and present condition of the industry as well as estimates of its expected future progress. It would be difficult to find an industry for which a trade publication was not available. Many trade associations have substantial staffs devoting time to the study of future industry prospects. The results of the work of these staffs is generally published in the trade association publications. Such publications would include *Railway Age, Electrical World, Iron Age, Paper Trade Journal, Farm Implement News, Consumer Finance News, Hardware Age, Oil and Gas Journal, The American Artisan,* and many others. A list of trade associations by industry is available in *National Trade and Professional Associations* published by the United States Department of Commerce. The Department of Commerce also has available bibliographies of sources of information on specific industries entitled *Basic Information Sources.*

In addition to the industry itself as a source of information, many financial and reporting institutions collect and publish data on industry prospects. Most brokerage firms, from time to time, make studies of the prospects of specific industries and supply these studies free of charge to interested parties. Many commercial banks and trust companies do the same. Dun and Bradstreet, Inc. collects financial information on a large number of industries and periodically publishes this information. The newspapers and magazines mentioned under general business and economic data also publish information on specific industries.

An outstanding source of information on past trends and indexes for general business and for various industries is *Trade and Securities Statistics,* published by Standard & Poor's Corporation. These statistics are designed to aid the investor in studying the future prospects of investment in a specific industry. This publication uses the following classifications for its statistics:

- Banking and finance
- Production and labor
- Commodities
- Income and trade
- Building materials
- Transportation and public utilities
- Fuels
- Metals
- Autos, rubber and tires
- Textiles, chemicals, etc.
- Agricultural products

Merrill Lynch, Pierce, Fenner & Smith gives a description of industry prospects in its quarterly publication, *Security and Industry Survey.* Figure 15–1 gives a page from this booklet.

Specific Company and Security Data

Sources of data on the company and on the specific type of security are discussed together because most sources which provide information on the features of the specific security also provide information on the company being considered. The most important source of data of this type is the company itself. Much of the information from the company comes to the average investor indirectly through certain financial institutions and information intermediaries. These institutions and intermediaries may add data which were not provided by the specific company. In addition to information obtained directly from the specific company, institutions which deal in securities, financial services, and investment advisory services are important sources of information on specific securities and their issuing companies.

Institutions Which Deal in Securities. A large number of different types of financial institutions buy and sell or aid in the process of marketing corporate securities. These include brokerage firms, investment banking houses, odd-lot dealers, security dealers, stock exchanges, bond houses, and trust companies. Many of these institutions make available to the general public data about specific securities and companies. All of them gather information for the use of their own customers. The type of information available from these different kinds of institutions tends to be rather similar. As a result, they will be discussed together.

Figure 15–2 is a page from a monthly stock digest. A publication of this type giving information on all listed securities and some non-listed

AEROSPACE

Outlook appears favorable for selected companies

The recent market performance of selected aerospace shares has been excellent. Investors' renewed enthusiasm for the group reflects, we believe, a number of significant developments, including the escalation of the Vietnamese conflict; a surge of orders for commercial aircraft; and indications that defense expenditures may remain at a reasonably high level for the next several years instead of falling sharply as some prognosticators have suggested.

It is apparent that the completion of some defense programs and cancellations or cutbacks of others are responsible for the modest declines in certain segments of defense spending. For instance, the completion of some of the strategic retaliatory missile programs is reflected in the budget for fiscal 1966. Procurement of missiles is expected to drop from an estimated $2.5 billion in fiscal 1965 to an estimated $1.8 billion in fiscal 1966. Procurement of military aircraft, however, is estimated at some $6.37 billion for 1966, or slightly more than the $6.24 billion for fiscal 1965. This shift in spending is largely the result of increases for programs such as the F-4 fighter, the C-141 transport, the Navy and Air Force versions of the F-111 fighter bomber, and the Grumman A6A Intruder. In summary, total procurement of military hardware in fiscal 1966 should be virtually unchanged from the $13.275 billion estimated for fiscal 1965.

The budget for fiscal 1966 includes new funds for improved versions of the Minuteman missile and the SRAM, the Nike-X anti-missile missile, the C-5A transport plane, and the Manned Orbiting Laboratory, among other programs. Although funds available for research, test, development, and evaluation are expected to be modestly less than the $6.7 billion budgeted for fiscal 1965, they should remain at relatively good levels in coming years.

Offsetting this decline are the higher expenditures expected for space research. The National Aeronautics and Space Administration has requested $5.1 billion for fiscal 1966 compared with $4.9 billion estimated for the current fiscal year.

Excellent sales of commercial transport aircraft have been counterbalancing the plateau in military spending. Operations of the private-plane manufacturers should also remain favorable.

The industry's over-all volume should approximate $20 billion again in 1965; profit margins, however, should continue to improve as a result of a larger number of production contracts on which profit margins are generally higher, an increase in the number of incentive-type contracts for research projects, and further improvement in the commercial aircraft segment of the industry.

The outlook for earnings varies from company to company. Thus, we reaffirm our opinion that selectivity is of utmost importance for investments in the industry. We believe that Boeing, Grumman, United Aircraft, General Dynamics, Northrop, and TRW, Inc. appear to be well situated to record substantial gains in earnings this year.

AEROSPACE	Fiscal Year Ends	Earnings—$ a Share		Interim			Dividends—$ a Share			Price Range				Approximate	
							Consec.	Paid	Cur. or Indic.	1955-64		1965		Price	Yield
		1964	1963	Period	1965	1964	Yrs. Pd.	1964	Annual Rate	High	Low	High	Low	5-17-65	%
LIBERAL INCOME															
Bendix Corp.	Sept.	4.00[n]	4.09	6 mo. 3-31	1.68	1.61	27	2.40	2.40	89	42	52¼	44⅛	51	4.7
Lockheed Aircraft	Dec.	4.17[o]	4.03	3 mo. 3-27	1.01	0.98	18	1.60	2.00	44	9¾	50	36⅝	50	4.0
Martin-Marietta	Dec.	1.67	1.54[n]	3 mo. 3-31	0.19	0.24	4[s]	1.00	1.00	31¼[r]	17[r]	22¾	17⅞	21	4.8
*North Amer. Aviation	Sept.	5.86	4.91	6 mo. 3-31	2.61	2.45	18	2.40	2.80	72⅛	20⅛	55⅛	49¾	54	5.2
GOOD QUALITY: WIDER PRICE MOVEMENT															
*TRW, Inc.	Dec.	2.45[g]	1.98	3 mo. 3-31	0.64	0.52[g]	8[s]	0.90[2]	1.00	44⅞	18⅞	35⅞	28½	35	2.9
United Aircraft	Dec.	4.23	3.12	3 mo. 3-31	1.39	0.84	30	2.00	2.00	80⅜	32⅜	80⅜	60½	77	2.6
SPECULATIVE															
*Boeing Co.	Dec.	5.64	2.71[l]	3 mo. 3-31	1.76	0.98	24	2.00	2.00	65⅜	23	76¾	60⅜	75	2.7
General Dynamics	Dec.	3.77	3.28[n,2]	3 mo. 3-31	0.59	0.61	1	Nil	1.00	68⅝	20	45½	35	43	2.3
*Grumman Aircraft#	Dec.	4.74	3.40	3 mo. 3-31	1.53	1.03	32	1.50	1.50	55⅞	15¼	61¼	49	57	2.6
McDonnell Aircraft	June	3.26	2.37	9 mo. 3-31	2.90	2.31	17	0.53[q]	0.60	39⅝	3⅝	42⅜	31¼	42	1.4
*Northrop Corp.	July	1.66	2.16	9 mo. 4-25	1.50	1.15	15	1.00	1.00	34⅝	7⅞	26⅜	20	25	4.0

[2]—Restated on a fully taxable basis.

Fig. 15–1. A sample page from *Security and Industry Survey* (New York: Merrill Lynch, Pierce, Fenner & Smith Inc., Summer, 1965.) (Reproduced with permission of Merrill Lynch, Pierce, Fenner & Smith Inc.)

OVER-THE-COUNTER INDUSTRIAL and UTILITY STOCKS

No. Institutions Holding Stock ▼	Some Cash Div. Paid Ea.Yr. Since	Dividends Per Sh. Latest 12 Mos.	% Yield Indicated 12Mo. Divs	Recent Bid Price Per Sh.	OVER-THE-COUNTER INDUSTRIAL AND UTILITY STOCKS	EARNINGS PER COMMON SHARE @ — Earnings Trend ◇ TREND	12 Months End'g Latest Reported Quarter	12 Months End'g Next Preceding Quarter ◆	Fiscal Year Ending 65 = 1965 64 = 1964 63 = 1963
4	......	0	0	36½	ACME VISIBLE REC'DS ..	↗	Mr^{65} $1.63	Dc $1.49	Sp^{64} $1.40
0	1960	$0.80[5]	1.9	41¾	ALBERTSON'S INC.	↗	Mr^{65} 2.05[54]	Dc 2.00[38]	Mr^{64} 1.40[2]
4	......	0	0	10	ALICO LAND DEVELOP. .	↗	Au^{64} 0.30	Au 0.05	Au^{62} 0.14
0	1937	[1]0.80[5]	3.6	22	ALLIS (LOUIS)	↗	Mr^{65} 2.13	Dc 2.03	Dc^{63} 1.67
5	'59	0.40[5]	2.0	20¼	ALLYN & BACON	↘	Ap^{64} 0.73	Ap 1.07	Ap^{62} 0.95
3	'35	1.40[5]	4.4	32	AMERICAN AIR FILTER. .	↘	Ja^{65} 2.55	Oc 2.63	Oc^{63} 2.51
50	1870	1.40	2.2	64½	AMERICAN EXPRESS ..	↗	Dc^{64} 2.83	Dc 2.54	Dc^{62} 2.29
4	1965	0.15[15]	1.0	14⅞	AMERICAN FINANCIAL ..	↗	Mr^{65} 1.94[122]	Dc 1.90[122]	Dc^{63} 1.76[122]
1	'40	0.24[5]	3.3	7⅜	AMERICAN FURNITURE.	↗	Nv^{64} 0.55	Nv 0.35	Nv^{62} 0.53
27	1950	0.70[5]	1.8	38⅝	AMER. GREETINGS "A".	↗	Fb^{65} [40]2.20[54]	Nv 2.12[40]	Fb^{64} 1.90[40]
0	......	0	0	6	AMERICAN GYPSUM ...	..	Dc^{64} [38]0.39[141]	Je 0.42	Je^{63} 0.51[10]
0	'29	0.80[5]	2.5	31½	AMER. MAIZE-PRODS. ..	↗	Mr^{65} 2.24	Dc 2.05	Dc^{63} 1.40
2	'39	0.50	4.4	11⅜	AMER. PIPE & CONST.	↗	Fb^{65} 1.05[12]	Nv 1.00[12]	Nv^{63} 0.95[1]
9	'14	0.60	2.4	25¼	AMERICAN STERILIZER .	↗	Mr^{65} 1.01[12]	Dc 0.92[12]	Dc^{63} 1.36
3	'37	1.70[14]	1.7	103	ANGLO-CAN. TEL. "A" .[3]	↗	Mr^{65} 5.36[73]	Dc 5.26[73]	Dc^{63} 4.61[73]
50	1932	1.00[5]	2.2	46½	ANHEUSER-BUSCH	↗	Mr^{65} 2.19	Dc 2.00	Dc^{63} 1.59
1	'44	0.60	2.4	25⅛	ARDEN-MAYFAIR	↗	Mr^{65} 1.35	Dc 1.21	Dc^{63} 0.84[2]
4	'37	0.60	3.1	19⅝	ARKANSAS-MO. POWER.	↗	Mr^{65} 0.93	Dc 0.87	Dc^{63} 0.76
5	'39	[5]0.60[52]	3.2	18¾	ARK. WESTERN GAS ...	↗	Mr^{65} 1.00	Dc 0.99	Dc^{63} 0.72
7	......	0	0	9½	ARMSTRONG (A.J.)	↗	Mr^{65} 0.52	Dc 0.50	Dc^{63} 0.73
8	'29	3.00	4.9	61¼	ARROW-HART & HEGE. .	↗	Mr^{65} 4.78[93]	Dc 4.66[93]	Dc^{63} 3.99[93]
0	1965	0.10	0.7	14½	ART METAL, INC.	↗	Fb^{65} 1.70[159]	Nv 1.25[159]	My^{64} 1.16[159]
8	......	0	0	5⅛	ARVIDA CORP. "A"	↗	Ja^{65} 0.17[40]	Jl 0.04[40]	Jl^{63} d0.06[40]
6	'63	1.40[5]	2.9	48¾	ASSOCIATED TRANSP'T Ⓐ	↗	Mr^{65} 4.87	Dc 4.55	Dc^{63} 4.11
9	'39	0.76	3.2	23¾	ATLANTA GAS LIGHT ..	↘	Fb^{65} 1.10	Nv 1.35	Sp^{64} 1.28
5	'64	0.24[5]	1.1	21	AVERY PRODUCTS	↗	Fb^{65} 1.08	Nv 1.01	Nv^{63} 0.86
2	......	0	0	18⅜	AVIS, INC.	↗	Fb^{65} 1.51[33]	Nv 1.43[33]	Au^{64} 1.40[159]
8	......	6%Stk	[121]	18⅝	AZTEC OIL & GAS	↘	Mr^{65} 0.42[159]	Dc 0.52[159]	Dc^{63} 0.67[159]
4	......	0	0	4¾	BAIRD-ATOMIC	↗	Mr^{65} 0.14[14]	Sp d0.46[41]	Sp^{63} d0.38[41]
3	1925	1.00[5]	4.4	22½	BANGOR HYDRO-ELEC. .	↗	Mr^{65} 1.40	Dc 1.38	Dc^{63} 1.30
2	'39	1.00	5.7	17½	BANK BUILDING & EQ. ..	↘	Oc^{64} 1.46	Oc 1.49	Oc^{62} 1.27
2	'60	[3]0.70[5]	1.8	37⅞	BARD (C. R.)	↗	Mr^{65} 1.43	Dc 1.38	Dc^{63} 1.17
2	'57	0.60	6.3	9½	BAYLESS (A. J.) MKTS. .	↘	Mr^{65} 1.05	Dc 1.18	Dc^{63} 1.13[1]
22	1928	[1]1.00[5]	3.1	32¼	BAYSTATE CORP.	↗	Dc^{64} 2.25[140]	Sp 2.18[140]	Dc^{63} 2.06[140]
19	'44	1.40	5.0	27¾	BEAUTY COUNSELORS .	↘	Mr^{65} 1.42[11]	Dc 1.55[11]	Dc^{63} 1.70
3	'30	1.00[5]	3.0	33	BEMIS BRO. BAG	.	Mr^{65} 1.92[141]	Dc 1.95	Dc^{63} 1.84
23	'29	0.95	2.7	35	BENEFICIAL CORP.	↗	Dc^{64} 1.03[30]	Je 0.99[30]	Dc^{63} 0.97[30]
0	......	0	0	20⅝	BERKSHIRE HATHAWAY.	↗	Mr^{65} [154]1.99[159]	Dc 0.78[159]	Sp^{64} [10]0.15[159]
7	'64	0.30[5]	1.5	19½	BERYLLIUM CORP.	↗	Mr^{65} 0.85	Dc 0.76	Dc^{63} 1.03
4	1913	1.20[5]	4.4	27⅛	BIBB MFG.	↗	Au^{64} 1.85[12]	Au 1.31	Au^{62} 1.27
0	'24	1.25	3.9	32¼	BIRD & SON	↗	Dc^{64} 3.65	Je 2.62	Dc^{63} 1.40
11	'42	1.96	4.5	44	BLACK HILLS PWR. & LT.	↗	Ja^{65} 2.51	Oc 2.44	Oc^{63} 2.67[1]
2	......	0	0	11	BLACK, SIVALLS & BRY.	↘	Dc^{64} d3.99[41]	Je d0.92[41]	Dc^{63} d0.08[41]
3	'65	1.50	3.5	43	BOSTON HERALD-TRAV. .	↗	Dc^{64} 3.46	Dc 2.59	Dc^{62} 3.05
1	......	0	0	10⅝	BOURNS, INC.	↗	Mr^{65} 0.73	Dc 0.70	Dc^{63} 0.46
4	1947	0.23[19]	3.8	6	BOWATER PAPER ....[3]	↗	Dc^{64} 0.56	Je 0.51	Dc^{63} 0.43
0	'09	2.00[5]	4.3	46½	BRIDGEPORT GAS	↗	Dc^{64} 3.16	Sp 3.00	Dc^{63} 3.05
4	'26	1.00	3.2	31	BROCKWAY GLASS "A".	↘	Mr^{65} 2.28[12]	Dc 2.36[12]	Sp^{64} 2.50
7	'34	1.00[5]	3.0	33	BROWN & SHARPE	↗	Mr^{65} 2.64	Dc 2.47	Dc^{63} 2.70[1]
0	'34	0.96[5]	4.5	21½	BRUNSWIG DRUG	↗	Mr^{65} 1.72	Dc 1.66	Dc^{63} 1.37[2]
13	......	0	0	10⅝	BRUSH BERYLLIUM ...	↗	Mr^{65} d0.08[41]	Dc d0.11[41]	Dc^{63} 0.44
10	1953	0.95	3.4	28¾	BURNS INT. DETECTIVE .	↗	Dc^{64} 1.70[40]	Sp 1.53[40]	Dc^{63} 1.51[40]
11	'31	0.60	1.5	39½	CABOT CORP.	↗	Mr^{65} 3.70[20]	Dc 3.56[20]	Sp^{64} 3.37[20]
2	'54	0.84	1.9	43¾	CALIF. INTERSTATE TEL.	↗	Mr^{65} 1.48	Dc 1.24	Dc^{63} 1.10
6	'59	0.40	2.2	18½	CALIF. LIQUID GAS	↗	Dc^{64} 1.23	Je 1.11	Je^{63} 0.98
6	'43	1.00[5]	3.0	33¼	CAL.-PACIFIC UTIL.	↗	Mr^{65} 1.60	Dc 1.53	Dc^{63} 1.26
4	'31	1.30	4.3	30⅜	CALIF. WATER SERVICE.	↘	Mr^{65} 1.97	Dc 1.98	Dc^{63} 1.80
11	'48	3.40[5]	3.6	95½	CANNON MILLS "B" ...	↗	Dc^{64} 8.76[40]	Dc 4.24[40]	Dc^{62} 7.10[40]

Fig. 15–2. Section of a *Monthly Stock Digest* page (New York: Data Digests, Inc.).

securities is usually available from most of these financial institutions. In addition, most brokerage firms publish a monthly market survey or business letter commenting on current business conditions with specific information about certain industries and companies. Many of these same firms also have more comprehensive quarterly or semiannual publications giving additional information about specific companies and prospects. Most financial institutions with research departments publish reports on specific companies from time to time. These reports may range from less than one printed page to booklets of 50 or 60 pages.

Merrill Lynch, Pierce, Fenner & Smith, the largest brokerage firm in the United States, publishes a *Security and Industry Survey* (see Fig. 15–1) which covers 34 major industries and approximately 644 individual companies. This survey is published every three months and is available free of charge. Individual securities are listed according to investor appeal –investment type: growth; investment type: stability; liberal income; good quality: wider price movement; speculative.

Bache and Company, another large brokerage firm, regularly offers the following publications: *The Bache Selected List, Comparative Values, Listening Post,* and the *Bache Review.* E. F. Hutton and Company lists the following publications which provide information on specific companies to investors: *Market and Business Survey, Industry and Company Reports, Market Outlook and Select Securities, Morning Market Wire, Morning News Wire, Special Field Reports,* and *Investor's Aid.* Other brokerage and investment banking firms have similar lists of publications. *The Wall Street Journal* has a daily listing of the special industry and company reports available to the public which have been prepared by the various financial institutions.

Financial Services. The two large standard financial services—Moody's and Standard & Poor's—publish daily, weekly, monthly, and yearly summaries about industries and individual companies. These summaries describe the specific securities issued as well as the issuing companies. At least one of these services is almost always available through local financial institutions such as banks or brokerage firms. Most public and educational-institution libraries subscribe to one or more of these services. The basic service of these companies is providing financial information to the general public. By making information readily available through the nearest library or financial institution, these financial services save a great deal of time for the individual investor. In addition to the straight reporting of information, most of the financial services perform investment counseling and some analytical services for the investor.

Moody's Investors Service is best known for its annual manuals, which contain a summary of past financial statements and other important information about leading companies and their securities. Separate manuals are issued annually for companies in the following classifications: industrials, public utilities, transportation companies, financial institutions, and governments. The manuals are kept up to date by the issuance of biweekly supplements. Moody's also publishes a bond survey and a stock survey each week. Moody's Investors Service also has an investors' advisory service which offers subscribers a review of their portfolio and gives recommendations on buying and selling.

Standard & Poor's Corporation publishes information similar to that contained in Moody's Manuals. This is available in looseleaf form in what is called the *Standard Corporation Records.* Daily, weekly, and monthly supplements are issued which are inserted in the looseleaf binder, keeping the information current. Standard & Poor's *Trade and Securities Statistics* was mentioned above. The company also publishes standard listed and unlisted stock reports (Moody's has these also), which is a bulletin service on all the leading companies. On two sides of one page all of the important financial information about the company and its outlook is presented. An example of a stock report issued by Standard & Poor's will be found in Fig. 15–3. A new bulletin is issued on each company as often as substantial additional information is available. *The Outlook*, a weekly magazine published by Standard & Poor's Corporation, describes the outlook for investment opportunity and gives information on specific companies and industries. Standard & Poor's also publishes a *Security Owner's Stock Guide* which is a pocket-size handbook, issued monthly, two pages of which are illustrated in Fig. 15–4. This publication carries the stock ratings (described in Chapter 12). The company has a daily facts and forecast service and an investment advisory service. In addition, Standard & Poor's Corporation publishes a daily dividend record which carries a listing of all dividends declared and paid by leading companies.

The Value Line Investment Survey offers an investors' service which indicates the stock performance of the leading companies on a chart basis relative to other companies in the same industry and to securities generally. Value Line then indicates how it expects the stock to move in the coming year and in the coming five-year period. An example of the Value Line chart is given in Fig. 15–5. The information and rating for each stock is revised quarterly. In addition, Value Line publishes a special report on "special situations," which is a letter on market comments and advice. Value Line rates stocks according to quality, probable performance for the next twelve months, desirability of holding for three to five years, and yield. Each of these qualities is given one of five ratings ranging from I (top) to V (lowest). Index numbers are assigned to each of these ratings of 10, 8, 6, 4, and 2 (from highest to lowest). The investor can determine how a particular stock would suit him (according to Value Line ratings) by giving a weight of 4, 3, 2, and 1 to each of the rated qualities such as yield, etc., according to the relative importance to him of these four factors. A weighted average is then calculated for the particular stock. Fig. 15–5 shows a section providing for this kind of calculation. Each week Value Line publishes a *Weekly Summary of Advices and Index* which keeps up-to-date the ratings of the 1,123 stocks which Value Line follows.

Other more limited financial services include the Babson Statistical Organization, Investograph Service, the Investment Bulletin of the American Institute for Economic Research, the Bondex Service, the International Statistical Bureau Service, and the United Business and Investment Service Weekly Report.

While Dow, Jones & Co., Inc., is not normally classed as a standard financial service, its importance in the providing of financial information to the investor merits its special mention at this point. The major publications of Dow-Jones have already been mentioned. They include *The Wall Street Journal,* and *Barron's Financial Weekly.* This company also owns the Dow-Jones news tickers throughout the country which make minute-to-minute information available (referred to as the "broad tape") wherever a Dow-Jones ticker is located. As the owner of the ticker system and the publisher of the largest financial daily newspaper in the country, this company is the outstanding source of daily information in the fields of investment and finance.

Investment Advisory Services. Most of the financial services mentioned above offer what is called an investment advisory service. In addition, a number of other specific institutions make general information available and advise investors of purchases and sales of securities through daily, weekly, or monthly publications. An example of an organization of this type is David L. Babson and Co., Inc. This company publishes a weekly staff letter in which it describes important business and financial information along with data on specific industries and companies. In addition, Babson will make specific recommendations for individuals who subscribe to their service. Most investment advisory services offer personal investment counsel.

The investment counselor can personalize his service in that he makes specific recommendations for specific individuals in light of the investor's own personal circumstances and present portfolios. Investment counseling, therefore, does not include the publication of general data or general recommendations for purchase or sale. Each recommendation made by an investment counselor is made with the specific investor in mind. The investment counselor has the customer submit a list of the securities he owns and then, for a fee, makes current recommendations for the purchase and sale of securities. The annual fee charged for advice is usually a percentage, commonly ½ of 1 per cent, of the value of the fund being administered. The great disadvantage of this type of agency is that the average investor, due to the small size of his investment fund, cannot afford the services of the more reliable firms. Some of the reliable firms

GM[1] 978

General Motors

Stock—	Approx. Price	Dividend	Yield
COMMON	110	[2] $5.00	[2] 4.5%
$5 PREFERRED	115	5.00	4.3
$3.75 PREFERRED	89½	3.75	4.2

RECOMMENDATION: Considering GM's entrenched competitive position, strong finances, and favorable earnings prospects for 1965 and the longer term, its COMMON stock, a logical split candidate, deserves consideration for any well-rounded investment portfolio. The PREFERREDS are high-grade income issues.

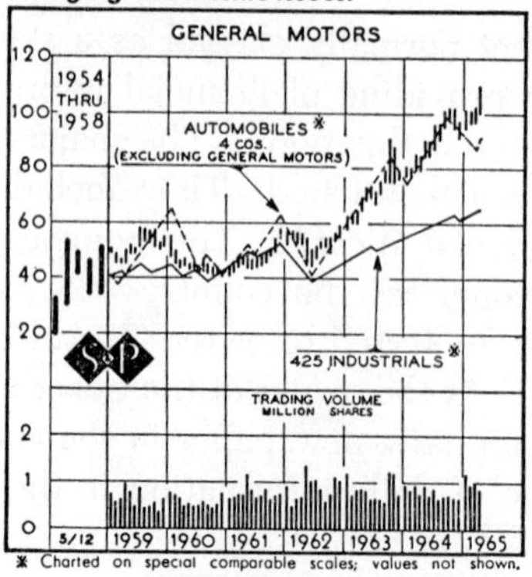

✱ Charted on special comparable scales; values not shown.

SALES (Million $)

Quarter:	1965	1964	1963	1962	1961
March......	5,558	4,786	4,147	3,665	2,724
June........		5,082	4,517	4,026	3,088
Sept........		3,291	3,017	2,760	1,968
Dec.		3,838	4,814	4,149	3,616

Sales for 1964 increased 3.0% from those of 1963 to a new peak on a 2.3% advance in world-wide factory shipments of vehicles. Output of cars and trucks in the U. S. declined 1.4% because of strikes of up to six weeks which began September 25. With results penalized by strike disruptions and higher wage rates, operating income was down 2.3%. Pretax profits decreased 2.1%. However, after a much lower effective tax rate of 47.2%, against 52.5%, net income was ahead 9% to a new high.

In the first quarter of 1965, sales rose 16%, year-to-year, on a 14% increase in factory shipments of vehicles. Higher labor and materials costs reduced the gain in pretax net to 14%. After taxes at 48.8%, against 50.8%, net income was up 19%.

COMMON SHARE EARNINGS ($)

Quarter:	1965	1964	1963	[3] 1962	1961
March.....	2.22	1.87	1.45	1.31	0.65
June........		2.11	1.62	1.41	0.88
Sept........		0.77	0.72	0.64	0.30
Dec.		1.30	1.77	1.74	1.28

PROSPECTS

Near Term—Sales for 1965 are expected to be well above the record $17 billion of 1964, aided by the strike-caused postponement of automobile registrations from late 1964 into the forepart of 1965 and the need to rebuild dealer inventories of new cars which were depleted during the strike. Industry-wide demand for passenger cars will advance further this year from the excellent level of 1964, and the important styling changes made on GM's 1965 models should bolster the company's share of the total domestic passenger car market. Foreign automotive volume should continue to grow, demand for trucks appears likely to rise, and deliveries of GM's non-automotive products are expected to increase.

Despite higher costs of pensions and materials, results will benefit from the greater volume, a more favorable product mix, and the lower corporate tax rate. Earnings for 1965 are estimated in the vicinity of $7.25 a share, up from the peak $6.05 of 1964. Dividends of $0.75 were declared for the first and second quarters of 1965, compared with $0.65 a year earlier, and a $0.75 special dividend is being paid in June, 1965, up from $0.50 a year earlier. Total payments for 1965 appear likely to exceed the $4.45 total disbursed in 1964.

Long Term—Allowing for interim fluctuations, an outstanding automotive trade position and diversification point to growth.

RECENT DEVELOPMENTS

On January 4, duPont made the last of three distributions of GM shares in compliance with the Supreme Court's ruling. The 23 million shares were issued on the basis of one-half of a share of GM common for each share of duPont common held.

DIVIDEND DATA

Payments in the past 12 months were:

Amt. of Divd $	Date Decl.	Ex-divd. Date	Stock of Record	Payment Date
0.65...	Aug. 3	Aug. 10	Aug. 13	Sep. 10'64
2.00Y.E.	Nov. 2	Nov. 6	Nov. 12	Dec. 10'64
0.75...	Feb. 1	Feb. 8	Feb. 11	Mar. 10'65
0.75...	May 3	May 10	May 13	Jun. 10'65
0.75spl.	May 3	May 10	May 13	Jun. 10'65

[1] Listed N.Y.S.E.; com. & $5 pfd. also listed Midwest, Phila.-Balt.-Wash. & Pacific Coast S.Es.; com. listed Detroit, Toronto & Montreal S.Es. & Paris Bourse, & traded Cincinnati, Pittsburgh & Boston S.Es. [2] Indicated rate, incl. $0.75 special payable June 10, 1965 and assuming continuance of $2.00 year-end dividend as paid in 1964. [3] Incl. $0.27 non-recurring income.

STANDARD LISTED STOCK REPORTS **STANDARD & POOR'S CORP.**

Published at Ephrata, Pa. Editorial & Executive Offices, 345 Hudson St., New York, N. Y. 10014
Vol. 32, No. 90 Wednesday, May 12, 1965 Sec. 10

Fig. 15–3. Sample pages from *Standard Listed Stock Reports* (New York: Standard & Poor's Corporation, 1965).

978 GENERAL MOTORS CORPORATION

[1]INCOME STATISTICS (Million $) AND PER SHARE ($) DATA

Year Ended Dec. 31	Net Sales	[3]% Op. Inc. of Sales	Amort. Depr. & Depl.	Equity Earns. Unconsol. Subs.	Net Bef. Taxes	[4]Net Inc.	Common Share ($) Data: [4]Earns.	*Cash Generated	Divs. Paid	Price Range	Price-Earns. Ratios HI LO
1965--	------	---	-----	---	------	-------	---	---	2.25	110¼-94⅝	-----
1964--	16,997	21.3	494.8	45.0	3,283.68	1,734.78	6.05	7.88	4.45	102⅝-77¼	17-13
1963--	16,495	22.4	475.2	47.5	3,353.9	1,591.82	5.56	7.37	4.00	91⅜-57⅞	16-10
1962--	14,640	21.7	444.6	50.6	2,934.5	1,459.08	5.10	6.72	3.00	59⅝-44½	12- 9
1961--	11,396	18.1	408.5	58.1	1,768.0	892.82	3.11	4.54	2.50	58 -40⅝	19-13
1960--	12,736	18.0	388.5	56.0	2,037.5	959.04	3.35	4.72	2.00	55⅞-40¼	17-12
1959--	11,233	18.6	413.7	51.2	1,792.2	873.10	3.06	4.52	2.00	58⅞-45	19-15
1958--	9,522	15.2	420.2	61.2	1,115.4	633.63	2.22	3.71	2.00	52 -33¾	23-15
1957--	10,990	17.8	414.9	51.3	1,648.7	843.59	2.99	4.47	2.00	47½-33⅛	16-11
1956--	10,796	18.4	347.2	57.2	1,741.4	847.40	3.02	4.26	.2.00	49¼-40¼	16-13
1955--	12,443	22.2	293.8	45.6	2,542.8	1,189.48	4.30	5.32	2.17	54 -29⅞	13- 7

[1] PERTINENT BALANCE SHEET STATISTICS (Million $)

Dec. 31	Gross Prop.	[2]Capital Expend.	Cash Items	Inventories	Receivables	Current Assets	Current Liabs.	Net Workg. Cap.	Cur. Ratio Assets to Liabs.	Long Term Debt	($) Book Val. Com. Sh.
[5]1965--	9,061	----	1,959.1	2,779.2	1,531.4	6,269.8	2,260.1	4,009.7	2.8-1	205.34	26.27
1964-- --	8,865	929.6	1,390.5	2,677.8	1,387.2	5,455.5	1,804.5	3,651.0	3.0-1	231.98	25.22
1963-----	7,967	647.2	1,890.7	2,221.2	1,250.6	5,362.6	1,635.2	3,727.4	3.3-1	260.46	23.53
1962-----	7,510	645.1	2,082.8	2,006.5	1,069.6	5,158.9	1,630.8	3,528.0	3.2-1	344.18	21.87
1961-----	7,005	503.2	1,696.1	1,800.1	987.3	4,483.5	1,424.9	3,058.6	3.1-1	365.32	19.69
1960-----	6,667	526.0	1,637.5	1,811.0	608.6	4,057.0	1,257.7	2,799.3	3.2-1	305.37	19.02
1959-----	6,186	319.9	1,261.8	1,799.8	643.2	3,704.8	1,138.7	2,566.2	3.3-1	308.30	17.55
1958-----	5,954	269.4	1,123.3	1,529.5	585.5	3,238.2	1,139.5	2,098.7	2.8-1	329.92	16.39
1957-----	5,765	472.9	733.4	1,730.8	553.4	3,017.6	1,156.2	1,861.4	2.6-1	342.20	16.04
1956-----	5,272	890.5	672.2	1,719.6	570.7	2,962.5	1,216.5	1,746.0	2.4-1	341.78	14.94
1955-----	4,354	608.1	1,201.5	1,601.7	580.4	3,392.6	1,334.3	2,058.3	2.5-1	300.00	13.92

[1]Consol.; incl. all subs. engaged in mfg. or wholesale marketing opers.; does not incl. G.M. Acceptance Corp. & Yellow Mfg. Acceptance or their subs. [2]Excl. additions for spec. tools. [3]Bef. depr., but aft. amort. of special tools & employee bonus. [4]Incl. non-recurring inc. of $0.27 a sh. in 1962. [5]As of Mar. 31.

*As computed by Standard & Poor's.

Fundamental Position

General Motors derives approximately 89% of total sales from automotive products, including cars, trucks, buses, parts and accessories. The Frigidaire and Delco appliance divisions, and the Allison, Diesel Electro-Motive, and Euclid divisions contribute most of the remainder. Defense work represented 2.5% of 1964 sales.

Chevrolet (including the Corvette, Chevelle, Corvair, and Chevy II), Buick (including the Special and Riviera), Cadillac, Oldsmobile (including the F-85), and Pontiac (including the Tempest) accounted for 49.1% of total new domestic registrations (including foreign-built cars) in 1964, compared with 51.0% in 1963 and 51.9% in 1962. Comparable figures for Chevrolet and GMC trucks are 42.8%, 41.3%, and 41.8%. There are about 16,000 U. S. and Canadian car and truck dealers. World-wide factory sales of cars and trucks in 1964 were 6,114,000 units, compared with 5,974,000 in 1963 and 5,239,000 in 1962. Domestic production in these years was 4,598,000, 4,662,000, and 4,223,000, respectively.

The company operates as a decentralized organization, with about 124 plants in 19 states, five plants in Canada, and assembly, manufacturing, and warehousing operations in 22 other countries. About 13% of consolidated net income in 1964 resulted from participation in markets outside of the U. S. and Canada, compared with 8% in 1963 and 7% in 1962. Investments in non-consolidated subsidiaries, including General Motors Acceptance Corp. and Yellow Mfg. Acceptance Corp., totaled $473 million at the 1964 year-end. The interest in Ethyl Corp. was sold in Nov., 1962.

Dividends, paid since 1915, averaged 69% of available earnings in the five years through 1964. Employees (world-wide): 738,000. Shareholders (common and preferred): 1,187,000.

Finances

Growth has been financed primarily from retained earnings, but this source has been supplemented since the end of World War II by $98 million of preferred stock sold in 1946, $300 million of debentures in 1953, and $325 million of common stock sold in 1955, plus borrowings by foreign subsidiaries. Finances are impressive, with a current ratio of at least three to one in recent years and with cash items substantial.

CAPITALIZATION

LONG TERM DEBT: $205,341,300 (divided $85,054,000 3¼% debs. due 1979 and $120,287,300 foreign subsidiary notes to 1977).

$5 CUM. PREFERRED STOCK: 1,835,644 shares (no par); redeemable at $120.

$3.75 CUM. PFD. STOCK: 1,000,000 shs. (no par); red. at $102 through Nov. 1, 1966, then less.

COMMON STOCK: 285,217,720 shares ($1.66-2/3 par).

Incorporated in Del. in 1916. **Office**—3044 W. Grand Blvd., Detroit 2. **Chairman & Chief Exec Officer**—F. G. Donner. **Pres**—J. F. Gordon. **Exec VPs**—L. C. Goad, J. E. Goodman, J. M. Roche, G. Russell. **Secy**—G. A. Brooks. **Treas**—O. A. Lundin. **Dirs**—H. C. Alexander, L. D. Brace, A. Bradley, L. D. Clay, E. N. Cole, F. G. Donner, L. W. Douglas, E. F. Fisher, L. C. Goad, J. E. Goodman, J. F. Gordon, O. E. Hunt, J. R. Killian, Jr., R. M. Kyes, J. W. McAfee, R. S. McLaughlin, R. K. Mellon, H. J. Morgens, C. S. Mott, J. L. Pratt, J. M. Roche, G. Russell, G. F. Towers, W. K. Whiteford. **Transfer Offices**—Company's office, 1775 Broadway, NYC; Wilmington Trust Co., Wilmington, Del.; Continental Illinois Natl. Bank & Trust Co., Chicago; National Bank of Detroit; Bank of America, N.T. & S.A.; San Francisco; National Trust Co., Toronto and Montreal; (Pfd.), National Bank of Detroit. **Registrars**—Chase Manhattan Bank, NYC; Bank of Delaware, Wilmington, Del.; Northern Trust Co., Chicago; Wells Fargo Bank, San Francisco; Royal Trust Co., Montreal and Toronto (Pfd.) Detroit Trust Co., Detroit.

Fig. 15–3. (Continued).

20 Ame-Ame

STANDARD & POOR'S CORPORATION

INDEX	Ticker Symbol	STOCKS NAME OF ISSUE (Call Price of Pfd. Stocks)	Market	Earns & Div Ranking	Par Val.	★ Inst. Hold Cos	Shs. (000)	STOCK CHARACTERISTICS Principal Business	PRICE RANGE 1936-63 High	Low	1964 High	Low	1965 High	Low	Mar Sales in 100s	March, 1965 O-C Monthend High	Low	Last	% Div. Yield
1	AMO	American Motors Corp.	[2]NYS	B	1⅔	5	7	Rambler cars; Kelvinator appl	a32¼	1	18⅜	13½	15⅛	13¼	6233	14⅝	13¼	13⅞	7.2
2		American Mutual Fund	UNL	NR	1	....	....	Diversified, mainly com stks	10.87	5 16	10.70	9.58	10.56	9.90	....	....	10.44B	11.41A	‡2.3
3		American National Insurance Co.	UNL	NR	1	27	1256	Life insurance	18¾	2⅛	24½	18⅜	20⅛	16⅝	....	....	16¾B	17¼A	1.7
4	ANG	American Natural Gas	NYS, Bo, De	A−	10	181	1780	Subsids serve Detroit & Milw	55¼	a2⅝	48⅛	39⅝	50¾	45⅝	407	50¼	48	48½	3.5
5	ANC	American News Co.	NYS	B+	No	3	41	Distr papers, books, food	49½	a4⅜	26½	18⅝	22⅝	18⅞	258	21⅞	20⅛	21¾	4.6
6	AOC	American Optical Co.	NYS, Bo	B+	1	36	145	Ophthalmic & optical products	a40¾	a7¼	40	a33½	44⅛	38	311	44⅛	41½	42⅞	‡2.9
7	API	American Petrofina. Cl A.	ASE	B−	1	1	5	Integrated oil company	18⅜	3¼	8¾	5½	7½	6	259	6½	6	6¼	2.4
8	APY	Amer. Photocopy Equip	NYS, Bo, De, PB	B	No	2	4	Photocopy machine & paper	46⅜	a1½	13	6½	9⅛	6¾	7529	9⅛	7⅛	7⅝	2.6
9		American Pipe & Construction	UNL	B+	5	2	103	Mfr reinforced concrete pipe	24½	a1⅜	12⅞	9½	11⅞	9⅝	....	....	10B	10⅜A	4.8
10	APO	Amer. Potash & Chemical	NYS, PB, PC	B+	No	42	491	Produces variety of chemicals	66¾	a7¾	40⅞	31	43	35	981	43	40	40½	3.0
11		Amer. Precision Industries	UNL	NR	55⁵/₉¢	....	....	Electronic coils; missile pts	15¼	3	4	2⅜	3⅜	2½	....	....	2⅞B	3½A	....
12	AST	Amer. Rad. & Standard Sanitary	[3]NYS	B	5	42	1042	Large producer of heating	29½	3¾	25	18	22¾	20¼	1853	22⅜	20⅝	20¾	4.8
13		7% cm Pfd (175)	NYS•	A	100	18	11	equip & sanitary ware	186	135	163	158	165	161¾	....	....	161¾B	163A	4.3
14	AXR	Amer. Realty & Petroleum	ASE	NR	10c	....	....	Develop real estate; oil, gas	7½	2	2⅞	1¾	3⅞	2⅛	137	3¾	3⅛	3¼	....
15		American Re-Insurance Co.	UNL	NR	5	29	339	Mainly surety & auto re-ins	a75½	a4⅜	72½	53¾	59	54	....	....	58½B	60A	†2.5
16	ARD	American Research & Development	NYS	NR	1	9	244	Non-diversified invest. co.	42¼	a3⅜	27⅜	18⅛	25½	21⅛	416	24⅛	22⅛	22¼	‡0.5
17		American Rubber & Plastics	UNL	NR	1	3	10	Sponge rubber; plastic foam	32⅜	15	23	12¼	15⅞	13	....	....	13½B	14A	5.7
18	ASQ	American Safety Equipment	ASE	NR	25¢	....	....	Supplier safety seat belts	9¾	a4⅜	12⅜	8	21¼	10⅛	911	21¼	17	20⅞	1.5
19		American Saint Gobain Corp.	UNL	B−	7¼	1	15	Important mfr sheet glass,	28	½	10¼	4¼	11	7½	....	....	10¾B	11⅛A	....
20		5% cm Pfd ([6]25¼; SF 25)	UNL	NR	25	2	8	full line flat glass products	19⅞	8¾	17¾	7⅞	17	13¼	....	....	15¾B	16¾A	....
21	AMK	American Seal-Kap Corp.	ASE	B	2	1	1	Mach & paper prod; electronics	24⅞	1¾	18¾	11¼	15½	11⅝	563	15½	13	13¼	‡1.9
22	AMZ	American Seating Co.	NYS, De	B+	10	9	30	Largest mfr public seating eqp	50½	a1¾	41⅞	34½	43	35⅝	250	43	41⅜	42	†4.3
23		American Service Co.	UNL	C	1	....	....	Drive-in food stores	18	⅛	8	3½	5¾	5¼	....	....	5¾B	6¾A	....
24	ABG	American Ship Building Co.	NYS	B	No	....	....	Shipconstruction, Great Lakes	26¼	a4½	14⅞	10¾	15⅜	13	144	15¼	13¾	14	2.5
25	AR	American Smelting & Refining	[4]NYS	B+	No	110	1173	Largest in field; mining oper	a44⅞	a5⅞	56½	a41¾	58½	48⅛	687	57⅝	53⅝	53⅞	†4.6
26	SNU	American Snuff Co.	NYS	A−	8⅓	5	11	Garrett, Honest, Peach, Dental	a31	a9⅝	25	22⅝	33	24⅛	184	33	29⅛	32¼	†3.9
27		6% non-cm Pfd (NC) vtg	NYS•	A	100	8	4	snuff; chewing tobacco	172	113	132½	125	129½	127½	4.9	129½	127½	128⅜	4.7
28	ASA	Amer-South African Investment	[5]NYS	NR	z	1	5	Closed-end invest co.; So Afr'a	39½	18	50¼	29⅜	54¾	41½	1010	54¾	47½	54½	1.8
29		American Sterilizer Co.	UNL	B+	3⅓	12	54	Sterilizers; surgical tables	47½	a13	23¾	15⅝	23⅝	18⅞	....	....	23½B	24A	2.5
30	ASR	American Sugar Co.	NYS, PB	B+	12½	11	396	Leading domestic cane sugar	30½	a1½	24⅞	17⅞	21⅞	19⅝	525	21	20	20¾	4.8
31		5.44% cm Pfd (13½) vtg	NYS, Bo	BB	12½	23	182	refiner	14⅛	13⅛	14	12⅞	14	13	130	13½	13	13	5.2
32	T	American Telephone & Telegraph	[3]NYS	A+	16⅔	1067	8581	'Bell' system, electronics	a70⅝	a16⅞	75	65⅜	70	66¼	9555	67⅝	66¼	66⅜	3.0
33	TH	American Thread, 5% cm Pfd (NC)	*ASE*	B	5	3	9	Cotton thread & yarns	8½	2½	5	4⅝	5	4⅝	57	5	4⅝	4¾	5.3
34	AT	American Tobacco Co.	[1]NYS, MW	B+	6¼	168	2590	Pall Mall, Lucky Strike, Dual	a55¾	a8⅝	37⅜	26⅜	38⅜	32¼	4220	38⅜	35⅛	35⅝	4.5
35		6% cm Pfd(NC) vtg	NYS•	A	100	119	79	filter Tareyton cigarettes	174	111⅜	138	122½	145	136½	65.1	144	141	141¼	4.2
36		American Vitrified Products	UNL	NR	1	....	....	Sewer pipe, bricks & flues	33½	⅛	17	11	11½	10½	....	....	11B	....	....
37	AWK	American Water Works Co.	NYS, PB	B+	2½	9	566	Operating subsidiaries form	a15⅜	a3⅜	a15¾	a13½	21¼	16¾	172	20¾	17⅝	18⅜	3.0
38		5% cm Pfd (25¼ from 1-1-67)	NYS•	BBB	25	9	36	largest group of privately	28½	23	27	24⅝	27½	26	11.5	27½	27	27	4.6
39		5% cm Pref ([6]25½)	NYS	BB	25	15	158	owned waterworks systems	26	22½	25⅞	24⅛	31	24½	20	25¾	25	25⅛	5.0
40	ZA	American Zinc, Lead & Smelt.	NYS, PB	B	1	2	5	A leading zinc custom smelter	24¼	a2¼	35⅜	21⅜	32	27¾	153	31¼	27¾	30¼	4.6

Uniform Footnote Explanations—See Page 1. Other: ‡Net invest income only. [1]Bo, Ci, De, PB, PC. [2]Bo, Ci, De, MW, PB, PC. [3]Bo, Ci, De, MW, PB, PC, Pi. [4]Bo, PB, PC. [5]Excl trades subj to int equalization tax. [6]To 12-31-65; then $25¼. [7]As computed by Standard & Poor s. r—Excl spec cr, a$0.48, 60. s—‡$0.19, '65; ‡$0.55, 64. t—On aver shrs. u—‡$0.03, '65; ‡$0.49, '64. v—Excl spec cr $0.54, '62; $0.12, '64; spec chg $1.57, '63. w—Fiscal Dec '61 and previous. x—9 mos, excl $0.51 spec cr; prior fiscal Dec. y—Max issuable. z—2 Rands. aa—Fiscal Oct. bb—'62 & pr yrs Dec. cc—Incl $0.22 spec cr.

Fig. 15–4. Sample pages from *Standard & Poor's Stock Guide* (New York: Standard & Poor's Corporation).

COMMON AND PREFERRED STOCKS

INDEX	Same Divs. Ea. Yr. Since	DIVIDENDS — Latest Payment — Per. $	Date	Ex. Div.	$ So Far 1965	Total Ind Rate	$ Paid 1964	FINANCIAL POSITION — Mil-$ — Cash & Equiv.	Curr. Assets	Curr. Liabs.	Balance Sheet Date	CAPITALIZATION — Long Term Debt Mil-$	Shs. 000 Pfd.	Com.	Yrs. End ▼	ANNUAL EARNINGS — $ Per Share $ — 1960	1961	1962	1963	1964	INTERIM EARNINGS OR REMARKS — Period	$ Per Share $ — 1963	1964	INDEX
1	1959	Q0.25	3-19-65	2-23	0.25	1.00	1.00	45.1	233	138	9-30-64	....	....	19065	Sep[11]	2.68	1.31	1.85	2.01	1.38	3 Mo Dec	0.58	0.50	1
2	1950	0.06	4-28-65	4-1	s‡0.13		s‡0.26	Net Asset Val $10.29			10-31-64	....	....	26241	Oct	#8.00	#9.83	#7.78	#9.56	#10.29				2
3	1923	Q0.07½	12-15-65	11-22	0.30	0.30	0.28	Equity per shr $9.77			[7]12-31-63	....	....	33000	Dec	X0.27	X0.33	X0.33	X0.61					3
4	1904	Q0.42½	5-1-65	4-12	0.85	1.70	1.60	31.0	126	133	12-31-64	493	....	14714	Dec[15]	a1.97	2.08	2.16	2.32	2.50				4
5	1864	Q0.25	3-20-65	3-5	0.25	1.00	1.00	7.59	29.2	16.9	1-3-64	7.00	....	1498	Dec[14]	n1.71	n1.29	0.75	0.83	P1.32				5
6	1939	Q0.31¼	4-1-65	3-10	0.58	‡1.25	‡1.02½	4.16	65.0	14.7	1-1-65	20.9	....	1856	Dec[24]	a1.74	a1.70	a1.90	a1.98	2.55				6
7	1958	0.15	6-9-64	5-26	....	0.15	0.15	5.91	44.1	33.8	12-31-64	27.6	....	+7041	Dec	+0.18	+0.15	+0.15	+0.64	+0.22				7
8	1957	Q0.05	4-1-65	3-9	0.10	0.20	0.33⅓	2.22	16.1	5.33	11-30-64	....	....	7964	Nov[17]	a0.57	0.66	0.58	0.36	0.33	3 Mo Feb△	0.09	0.08	8
9	1939	Q0.12½	2-15-65	*1-25	0.12½	0.50	0.50	3.45	28.7	7.63	11-30-64	11.4	....	2109	Nov[18]	a1.39	1.34	0.86	0.95	1.00				9
10	1936	Q0.30	3-15-65	2-24	0.30	1.20	1.20	4.18	24.6	5.68	12-31-63	15.7	44	2290	Dec	2.18	2.01	1.74	n1.99	P2.61				10
11	......	....	....	....	....	Nil	....	0.51	2.17	1.05	12-31-64	0.53	....	672	Dec	0.24	0.19	d0.07	d0.27	cc0.05				11
12	1936	0.25	3-24-65	2-15	0.25	1.00	1.00	42.9	234	79.2	12-31-64	13.3	43	10034	Dec	1.11	1.19	1.13	n1.64	2.03				12
13	1929	Q1.75	3-1-65	2-15	1.75		7.00						43		Dec	300.7	317.6	297.7	380.1	479.8				13
14	......		None paid		....	Nil	....	Equity per shr $3.92			4-30-64	4.64	....	2568	Apr	....	....	1.01	0.99	0.24	9 Mo Jan△	0.08	0.25	14
15	1922	Q0.35	3-15-65	3-2	0.35	1.50	†1.50	Equity per sh $56.39			[7]12-31-64	....	....	1584	Dec[19]	X2.93	X2.85	X2.37	X3.22	X3.58				15
16	1959	‡0.11	4-2-65	3-16	u‡0.11		u‡0.13	Net Asset Val $25.28			12-31-64	....	....	1535	Dec[11]	#25.33	#24.14	#20.01	#22.65	#25.28				16
17	1960	Q0.20	3-5-65	*2-19	0.20	0.80	0.95	2.50	3.94	0.90	2-29-64	....	....	498	Feb	1.64	1.91	2.20	1.72		9 Mo Nov	1.47	0.95	17
18	1964	a0.08	4-30-65	4-9	a0.13	0.32	0.15	0.35	2.18	1.21	12-31-63	....	....	600	Dec[23]	d0.14	a0.40	0.32	0.44	P1.28	Vote Apr 14, 2-for-1 split			18
19	......	0.15	9-3-57	*8-15	....	Nil	....	4.47	17.6	3.63	12-31-64	44.8	159	1163	Dec	d0.68	d0.83	d0.89	d3.99	d0.15				19
20	......	0.31¼	3-1-61	*2-17	....	Nil	....	Arrears $5.00¼ on 3-1-65					159		Dec	d3.75	d4.84	d4.26	d26.82	1.32				20
21	1934	0.25	12-31-64	12-9	....	0.25	‡0.25	3.33	17.6	4.82	12-31-63	6.43	....	989	Dec	0.80	0.63	1.01	k0.81		9 Mo Sep	0.62	k0.71	21
22	1936	Q0.40	3-5-65	2-8	0.40	1.80	†1.80	1.52	27.0	9.30	12-31-64	1.40	....	666	Dec	2.77	2.47	2.53	2.49	2.80				22
23	......	1.00	1-5-50	....	....	Nil	....	0.66	1.27	0.59	9-27-64	0.97	5	94	Sep	d2.18	d2.16	xd1.89	kd0.56	kd0.15				23
24	1963	0.35	9-30-64	8-26	....	0.35	0.35	1.13	10.1	6.80	6-30-64	0.02	....	584	Jun[16]	n2.36	0.96	vd0.97	v0.58	v0.70	6 Mo Dec	d0.06	0.62	24
25	1936	Q0.50	2-26-65	2-2	0.50	2.50a	†2.10	94.6	264	78.3	12-31-64	40.9	....	11124	Dec[13]	ar1.86	a1.64	a2.22	a2.41	k3.77				25
26	1903	†0.50	4-1-65	3-1	†0.75	1.25	†1.15	2.37	25.0	5.52	12-31-64	0.24	28	1383	Dec[21]	a1.53	a1.69	1.77	1.70	2.01				26
27	1901	Q1.50	4-1-65	3-1	3.00		6.00						28		Dec	77.59	86.19	91.53	88.38	104.0				27
28	1959	‡S0.50	11-30-64	11-2	....	1.00	‡1.00	Net Asset Val $53.69			2-28-65	....	....	1200	Nov	#33.45	w#34.53	#41.42	#44.16	#47.65				28
29	1914	Q0.15	3-15-65	2-16	0.15	0.60	0.60	1.25	22.7	4.73	12-31-63	4.42	....	1288	Dec[11]	1.18	0.99	n1.05	1.36	k0.92				29
30	1941	Q0.25	4-2-65	3-10	0.50	1.00	‡1.07½	7.76	95.1	39.6	12-31-64	87.6	1797	3639	Dec[22]	a1.85	a1.84	a2.17	2.26	1.76				30
31	1963	Q0.17	4-2-65	3-10	0.34		0.68						1797		Dec	....	....	....	5.61	4.25				31
32	1881	Q0.50	4-1-65	2-24	1.00	2.00	a1.95	1972	3340	2724	12-31-64	8725	....	522393	Dec[12]	t2.77	t2.76	t2.90	t3.03	t3.24				32
33	1899	S0.12½	1-1-65	12-8	0.12½		0.25	3.16	24.5	4.20	12-28-63	4.95	978	1796	Dec	0.68	1.28	k1.59	1.87					33
34	1905	Q0.40	3-1-65	2-2	0.40	1.60	1.60	16.1	723	114	12-31-64	69.1	528	25999	Dec[20]	n2.28	2.40	2.53	2.51	2.69	Propose merge Consolidated			34
35	1904	Q1.50	4-1-65	3-5	3.00		6.00						528		Dec	118.5	124.2	131.0	130.3	138.7	Foods Corp.			35
36	1947	0.10	1-17-64	*1-3	....	Nil	0.10	0.36	8.17	1.84	12-31-63	2.93	....	317	Dec	2.40	aa0.82	k2.47	0.12		6 Mo Jun	....	d0.35	36
37	1948	Q0.14	2-15-65	1-27	0.14	0.56	a0.52½	14.8	28.0	17.0	12-31-64	244	p1823	6579	Dec[25]	k0.76	a0.74	a0.94	a1.11	k1.29				37
38	1962	Q0.31¼	3-1-65	2-9	0.31¼		1.25						71		Dec	....	....	10.00	11.07	12.38	Propose acquisition of			38
39	1962	Q0.31¼	3-1-65	2-9	0.31¼		1.25						365		Dec	....	....	18.20	21.27	24.38	Southern Gas & Water			39
40	1947	Q0.35	3-19-65	2-23	0.35	1.40	1.20	2.66	18.9	6.49	6-30-64	1.62	....	1368	Jun	2.12	0.45	bb0.87	1.01	1.86	6 Mo Dec	0.82	1.17	40

▼Stock Splits & Divs: [11]3-for-1, '60. [12]2-for-1, '64. [13]100%, '64. [14]2-for-1, '60. [15]5-for-2, '61. [16]5-for-1, '60. [17]3-for-1, '61. [18]40%, '60; 2-for-1, '61. [19]10%, '61. [20]2-for-1, '60, '62. [21]3-for-1, '62. [22]2-for-1, '63. [23]200%, '62. [24]100%, '64. [25]2-for-1, '65.

Fig. 15–4. (Continued).

119 GENERAL MOTORS NYSE-GM

Recent Price 108	Estimated Yield (9) 4.2-4.4%	Next div'd meeting 5/3 goes ex about 5/10

8.5 X Cash Earnings (5 yr. Avg. Centered)
Growth 1953-57 to 1960-64, Actual (7) 5.6%
Growth 1960-64 to 1967-71, V.L. Est. 7.5%

HOW SUITABLE FOR YOU?	YOUR Weights (4, 3, 2 or 1—use each weight only once)	
Quality (B+)	8×	=
12 mos. (III)	6×	=
3-5 years (V)	2×	=
Yield (4.4%)	8×	=
Sum (100 perfect, 60 average) =		

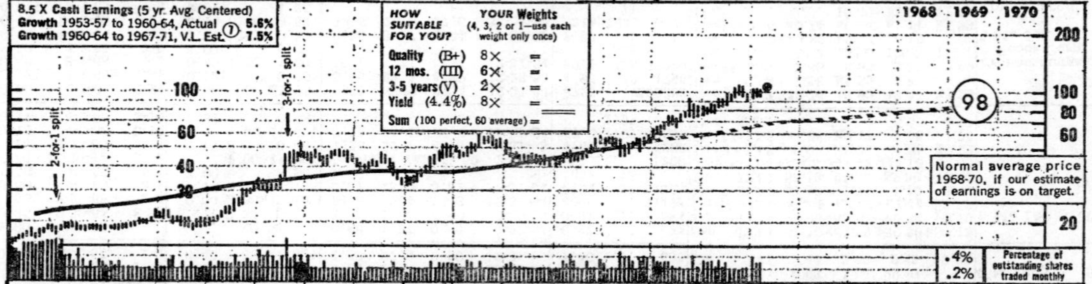

1950	1951	1952	1953	1954	1955	1956	1957	1958	1959	1960	1961	1962	1963	1964	1965	1966	1967		1968-70
7531	7466	7549	10028	9824	12443	10796	10990	9522	11233	12736	11396	14640	16495	16997	*18800*			Sales ($ mill.)	*20500*
25.3%	21.3%	20.7%	17.4%	18.4%	22.2%	18.4%	17.8%	15.2%	18.6%	18.0%	18.1%	21.7%	22.4%	21.3%	*22%*			Profit Margin (1)	*22%*
1506	1457	1191	1236	1351	2058	1746	1861	2099	2566	2799	3059	3528	3727	3651				Working Cap'l ($ mill.)	
284	284	284	284	584	584	584	626	613	592	589	649	628	544	516				Bonds & Pfd. ($ mill.)	
802	942	1263	1536	2161	2353	2968	3118	2963	2838	3010	3029	3207	3336	3900				Net Plant ($ mill.)	
45.7%	42.2%	41.5%	45.6%	52.2%	50.2%	52.8%	46.1%	51.1%	45.7%	47.7%	49.4%	53.9%	53.4%	51.1%	*53%*			Market Share (2)	*52%*
34.6%	19.5%	20.3%	20.1%	22.1%	26.2%	17.6%	16.2%	12.0%	15.4%	15.7%	14.0%	19.9%	21.6%	22.2%				%Earned Total Cap'l	*Italicized numbers are*
38.6%	21.3%	22.1%	21.7%	25.5%	29.4%	19.4%	17.9%	13.0%	16.8%	17.1%	15.3%	21.5%	23.1%	23.6%				%Earned Common Eq'ty	
8.11	8.82	9.45	10.28	11.83	14.49	15.48	16.62	16.96	18.15	19.61	20.28	22.40	24.01	25.58				Book Value per sh.	*estimates*
19.6%	11.7%	13.5%	15.4%	18.9%	21.8%	14.6%	14.9%	10.1%	13.9%	13.9%	10.1%	15.1%	13.4%	13.0%				Capital Growth Ratio (3)	
28.67	28.47	28.85	38.22	37.43	45.07	38.92	39.42	33.94	39.88	45.04	40.19	51.56	57.95	59.60				Sales per sh.	
3.59	2.36	2.61	2.91	3.91	5.33	4.26	4.47	3.71	4.52	4.72	4.54	6.39 (11)	7.22	7.77	*8.75*			Cash Earn'gs per sh.	*10.00*
.67	.99	1.31	1.91	2.88	2.20	3.21	1.70	.96	1.14	1.86	1.77	2.27	2.27	3.26				Capital Spending per sh.	
3.13	1.88	2.09	2.23	3.02	4.26	3.01	2.98	2.21	3.05	3.35	3.10	4.82 (11)	5.55	6.04	*6.75*			Reported Earn'gs sh.	*7.50*
2.00	1.33	1.33	1.33	1.67	2.17	2.00	2.00	2.00	2.00	2.00	2.50	3.00	4.00	4.45	*4.50–4.75*			Div'ds Declared sh.	*5.25*
56%	58%	52%	47%	43%	41%	47%	45%	54%	45%	43%	55%	45%	56%	57%	*52–55%*			Div'd Payout Ratio (8)	*53%*
4.6	8.9	9.1	9.1	8.4	9.1	15.1	13.6	18.7	16.8	13.2	15.4	11.1	13.0	15.0				Av'ge Annual P/E Ratio	*13.0*
13.8%	8.0%	7.0%	6.5%	6.5%	5.6%	4.4%	4.9%	4.8%	3.9%	4.5%	5.2%	5.6%	5.6%	4.9%				Av'ge Annual Div'd Yield	*5.4%*

Price to Earnings Ratio		Dividend Yield		Estimated 12 months to 9/30/65		to 3/31/66	Quality	12 Mos. Perform'ce	Desirability as 3-5 Yr. Holding		
'50-64 Median 13.0	Current (5) 17.0	'50-64 Median 5.6%	Current (9) 4.2-4.4%	Cash Earnings $8.25	Reported Earnings $6.35	Div'd Declarations $4.50-4.75	B+	III (Average)	V (Lowest) (6)	Characteristic Growth Index 55; Characteristic Stability Index .60	(Range 100 to 5)

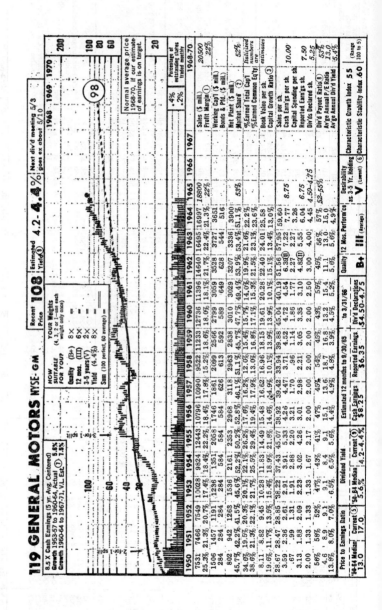

CAPITAL STRUCTURE as of 12/31/64

Debt $232.0 mill. **Interest** $11.4 mill. (Includes $141.5 mill. debt of foreign subsidiaries)

Pfd Stock $283.6 mill. **Div'd** $12.9 mill. 1,000,000 shares $3.75 cum. (no par) 1,835,644 shares $5.00 cum. (no par)
Common Stock 285,184,950 shares ⑩

Calendar	QUARTERLY SALES ($ Millions) Mar. 31	June 30	Sept. 30	Dec. 31	Full Year
1961	2724	3088	1968	3616	11396
1962	3665	4026	2760	4189	14640
1963	4147	4517	3017	4814	16495
1964	4786	5082	3291	3838	16997
1965					*18800*
1966					
1967					

Calendar	QUARTERLY EARNINGS (per sh.) Mar. 31	June 30	Sept. 30	Dec. 31	Full Year
1961	.65	.88	.30	1.27	3.10
1962	1.26	1.40	.64	1.55	4.82⑪
1963	1.44	1.62	.72	1.77	5.55
1964	1.87	2.10	.77	1.30	6.04
1965					*6.75*
1966					
1967					

Calendar	QUARTERLY DIVIDENDS PAID ④ Mar. 31	June 30	Sept. 30	Dec. 31	Full Year
1961	.50	.50	.50	1.00	2.50
1962	.50	.50	.50	1.50	3.00
1963	.50	1.00	.50	2.00	4.00
1964	.65	1.15	.65	2.00	4.45
1965	.75				
1966					
1967					

Appraisal: General Motors is riding the crest of its industry's prosperity wave, and relative to other blue-chip stocks in today's lofty market, it is perhaps still reasonably priced. But note that the current price/earnings ratio is higher than any that has prevailed for this issue during the past 15 years (save for 1958, a year of depressed earnings). And this company's 1965 earnings, on the contrary, are not depressed, but cyclically inflated and probably unsustainable. Accordingly, the risks in holding this stock now appear to be greater than the figures would suggest; not only are the issue's current capitalization rates generous by past standards, but profits will likely come down in 1966. Thus, as we estimate further into the future, this stock (which even now is classified no better than the average equity for year-ahead performance) can be expected to decline in rank. Investors not locked into their holdings of this stock by tax considerations can probably find better opportunities for capital growth over the next few years elsewhere in the market. . . Fund holdings of this equity reached a new all-time high at the end of 1964, largely reflecting the final distribution of GM shares to DuPont stockholders. But more individual Funds were sellers than buyers during the fourth quarter. Option exercises and bonus awards to officer-directors have materially exceeded their sales of company stock in recent months.

Analysis: General Motors' 1965 share of U.S automobile and truck production is being artificially inflated by the strike losses of 1964, which could not be fully made up before the end of last year. Thus, GM in 1965 is benefiting not only from the boom in auto demand, but from a concentration of its production in a compressed time span. Nevertheless, the high performance in prospect, and the likelihood of a stock split and/or further dividend boost, may continue to provide strong propulsion for this stock in the months ahead.

What does GM have left in its arsenal for a bad year? Product-wise, it could offer a Mustang-type vehicle, now that Ford has built this market up to respectable proportions; hitherto, GM has been content to ride with its highly successful BOP-ettes, the heroes of the compact car counter-revolution. Due for beefing up (or abandonment) is the Chevrolet second line: Chevelle, Chevy II, and Corvair. When the Chevelle threatened to dispossess Rambler from the auto scene altogether, GM toned down its promotion of this make. But where GM really leaves its rivals at the post is in its financial strength - it boasts a hoard of cash that has permitted a billion dollar a year capital spending program and a pay-out of 70% of reported earnings, with over $1 billion of idle cash left at the 1964 year-end for "incidentals". E.P.S.

BUSINESS: General Motors is the world's largest automobile manufacturer; 1964 output 51% of U.S. total. Makes Chevrolet-Corvair, Pontiac-Tempest, Buick-Special, Oldsmobile-F-85, and Cadillac cars; Chevrolet and GMC trucks; Frigidaire and Delco appliances; GM Diesel locomotives and engines; Allison aircraft engines; and Euclid earth-moving equipment. Plants in 22 foreign countries make Vauxhall cars and Bedford trucks, Opel cars and trucks, and Holden cars and trucks. Defense business 3% of 1964 sales; foreign, about 16%. Since 1947-49, sales have increased 259% (GNP, 149%). Labor costs, 30% of 1964 sales; materials costs, 45%. Has 660,977 employees, about 1,187,000 stockholders. Chrmn.: F.G.Donner. Pres.: J.F.Gordon. Inc.: Del. Add.: 2044 W. Grand Blvd., Detroit, Mich. 48202.

①-Before Interest, Depreciation, Income Tax. ②-Co. % of U.S. passenger car production. ③-Cash Earn. retained as % of Book Value. ④-Dividend payment dates: Mar. 10, June 10, Sept. 10, Dec. 10. ⑤-Current price, related to 12 mos. earn'gs (6 mos. past, est'd 6 mos. future). ⑥-Desirability=Appreciation Potential+Risk Allowance. ⑦-Compounded Annual. ⑧-% Cash Earns. paid out in pfd. and common div'ds. ⑨-Current price, related to est'd div'ds next 12 mos. ⑩-Excl. 1,823,267 treasury shares. ⑪-Excl. extraordinary income from Ethyl Corp., equal to 27¢ a share.

Value Line Survey

APRIL 23, 1965

Fig. 15–5. A sample page from *Value Line Investment Survey* (New York: Arnold Bernhard & Co., Inc.).

either will not accept an account of less than $100,000 or, if they do accept it, a minimum annual charge of $500 or $1,000 will be made. Obviously, this service is too expensive for the small investor. If an investment counselor is used, his selection should be made with very great care. The Investment Advisory Act of 1940 requires that all investment counselors register with the Securities and Exchange Commission and make information on their qualifications available to their customers.

Other Sources. In addition to the above-named sources, data relating to specific securities and companies are available from the company itself and from various industry sources. Many trade association publications present financial data on members of the industry. Newspapers and periodicals (discussed under general business and economic data) present, from time to time, articles and financial data on specific securities and companies. The wide variety of sources of information indicates that enough data are available on many securities to enable the prudent investor to make a suitable decision. It would also follow that since sufficient data are available on many securities, it would be unwise for the average investor to buy a security on which he could not obtain sufficient information to analyze his investment properly.

General Investment Market Data

The bibliography at the end of this chapter lists a number of textbooks on the general subject of investing. Almost all of the publications mentioned above have some information on the general field of investing and many of them carry specific market data. The various financial institutions in the securities market provide valuable information. For example, the New York Stock Exchange has available, among others, the following publications: *Understanding the New York Stock Exchange, The Exchange, Fact Book, The Language of Investing, Investment Facts, How to Get Help When You Invest, How to Invest on a Budget, Investment Clubs,* and *Understanding Financial Statements.* Additional information may be obtained from the American Stock Exchange, the Association of Stock Exchange Firms, the odd-lot companies, the Investment Bankers Association of America, and the National Association of Security Dealers, Inc.

Specific market price and sales data of securities are included in the information offered by the financial services. Daily newspapers, in varying degrees, report market prices. *The Wall Street Journal* and the various New York City newspapers carry the most complete listings. The *New York Times* and the *New York Herald Tribune* have both published pamphlets on this subject.

INFORMATION FROM THE COMPANY

The company which issues the security is the basic source of almost all financial data relating to the security and the company itself. Part of this information is supplied by the company because it is legally required to do so, but there was a large amount of information coming directly from companies long before there were legal requirements for its publication. Most publicly held corporations find it advantageous to make public certain information about themselves in order to maintain good stockholder and bondholder relations. Also, those companies which intend to sell new issues of securities have found it almost a necessity to provide financial information to prospective purchasers of these securities.

It is commonplace today for most large companies to make public a balance sheet and an income statement. Much of the data which the company makes public are picked up by newspapers, magazines, and financial services and disseminated to present and potential security holders. Public announcements by officials of the company are generally reported in financial publications. The information contained in prospectuses and registrations is collected by the financial services and made available by them. Quarterly, semiannual, and annual report information is carried in many financial publications and services. However, some of this information comes directly from the company to the present or potential security holder. Annual reports are made available by the company to its stockholders. Prospectuses must be made available by the company or by its agent to all prospective purchasers of a new issue of securities.

Prospectus

The Federal Securities Act of 1933, sometimes called the "truth in securities act," requires that companies selling new issues of securities must register with the Securities and Exchange Commission. Moreover, the seller must make available to the public a condensation, called a prospectus, of the registration statement. This prospectus must contain all the information the Securities and Exchange Commission feels is essential for the average investor to make a reasonable decision regarding purchase of the proposed security. While certain issues of new securities are exempt from the legislation (private sales, sales under $300,000, intrastate sales, and United States government, municipal, bank, railroad, savings and loan, short-term, non-profit corporation, and life insurance securities), a sufficient number of new issues of securities are covered by this legislation to allow the investor a wide selection of registered securities from which to make his choice. It is generally recommended that investors refrain from buying new issues of non-government securities not covered by this legislation.

A prospectus is a very complete document containing a wealth of company information. Included are balance sheets and income statements for several years preceding the sale. Certifications of independent auditors are given, as are important notes to the financial statements describing the accounting processes used in making up the statements. The normal prospectus would include a complete description of the company's property, its management, management compensation plans, depreciation policies, and capital expenditure plans. The typical prospectus will run twenty-five to forty pages in length. Whenever this document is available, it should be carefully studied before purchasing the security. The issuing company or investment banker is not allowed to distribute the prospectus until the Securities and Exchange Commission determines that the information included therein is sufficient for an average investor to make a reasonable decision. While waiting for the SEC to allow the sale of the security, many issuers publish a "red herring" prospectus. The investor should recognize that the red herring prospectus is not final, and in situations in which he has made investment decisions on the basis of the red herring prospectus, he should obtain the real prospectus before acting upon his decision.

The major limitation of the prospectus as a source of information to potential security buyers is that it is available only on new issues of securities. Most small investors do not buy new security issues—they buy securities from other investors in the secondary market through stock exchanges or security dealers. Many companies whose stock is actively traded have not had a new issue of securities in the last twenty-five years. The prospectus is, of course, only current at the time of the new issue.

Company Financial Reports

Since the prospectus covers only new issues, periodic additional information is necessary for the investor in making buying and selling decisions in the secondary market. Many companies have for years made quarterly, semiannual, or annual reports available to the general public. These reports primarily carry financial data for the preceding period for the company. The Securities Exchange Act of 1934 requires that all companies whose securities are listed on an organized exchange, or sold over-the-counter if the company has assets of at least $1 million and at least 500 shareholders, file annual reports regarding earnings and financial position with the Securities and Exchange Commission. These reports are designed to make information available to the investing public between new issues of securities.

The information required annually by the SEC is similar to but less extensive than that required for a registration statement for a new issue. As it would be very expensive for the company to provide this information in written form to all prospective purchasers, the law requires that the annual registration statement be given to the Securities and Exchange Commission only. Any interested party may see this statement by visiting the Securities and Exchange Commission offices in New York or Washington. In addition, for a fee, the Securities and Exchange Commission will photostat any portion of any registration statement which any individual requests. As it is rather expensive to go to New York or Washington to look up information in the offices of the Securities and Exchange Commission, and since it is also expensive to photostat any substantial portion of the registration statement, the information in these statements is made available to the general public through the financial services which collect the information from the Securities and Exchange Commission offices and publish it in their periodic manuals or reports. Companies whose securities are listed on organized exchanges must also furnish the exchanges with all pertinent information relating to their security issues.

Today, many companies make available substantial annual reports carrying a complete description of the company's activities during the past period and some estimates of future activity on the part of the company. In addition, these annual reports include financial statements, such as balance sheets and income statements. Most companies provide these annual reports to all registered stockholders and make them available to others upon request. It would generally be advisable for the prospective investor to study the annual statement of the company whose security he is considering purchasing. The information made available by most companies on a quarterly basis is much less expansive than that included in annual reports. However, many companies do make very important information available quarterly—particularly data on earnings.

The Balance Sheet

One of the two most common financial statements made available to investors by corporations is the balance sheet. Figure 15–6 is an example of a corporate balance sheet. The balance sheet presents a statement of financial position as of a specific date—normally the end of the company's fiscal year. The balance sheet includes the assets of the corporation (the things of value owned by the corporation), and the liabilities (amounts which the corporation legally owes to others), and the stockholders' equity in the company at the specific date of the balance sheet.

Those items listed under current assets on the balance sheet include cash and other assets that can be turned into cash in the normal course of

THE XYZ COMPANY
Balance Sheet
As of December 31, 1965

Assets		
Current assets		
Cash		$ 9,000,000
Marketable securities		1,000,000
Accounts receivable, *net*		16,500,000
Inventory		36,000,000
Total current assets		$ 62,500,000
Investments		$ 10,500,000
Fixed assets		
Plant and equipment	$85,000,000	
Less depreciation allowances	31,500,000	
Net plant and equipment	$53,500,000	
Land	10,500,000	
Total fixed assets		$ 64,000,000
Total assets		$137,000,000
Liabilities and Stockholders' Equity		
Current liabilities		
Accounts payable		$ 26,000,000
Bank notes payable		5,000,000
Accrued liabilities		3,500,000
Accrued taxes		10,500,000
Total current liabilities		$ 45,000,000
Long-term liabilities		
6% Debentures		$ 10,000,000
Stockholders' equity		
Preferred stock	$ 5,000,000	
Common stock	45,000,000	
Retained earnings	32,000,000	
Total stockholders' equity		$ 82,000,000
Total liabilities and stockholders' equity		$137,000,000

Fig. 15–6. A balance sheet.

business operation, in a short period of time—usually one year. Cash is the most liquid of all the assets of the corporation and is therefore listed first. Many companies, from time to time, own readily marketable securities such as United States government bonds which may be sold in the government bond market when the corporation needs money. Accounts receivable include the total amount of money owed to the company by its regular business debtors. Because some people fail to pay their bills, the company sets up a reserve for doubtful accounts, which it subtracts from the money owed. Inventory includes the raw materials, goods in process, and finished goods which a corporation has on hand. Investments are securities in other companies held for income or control. The fixed assets are those assets which are not expected to be sold during the coming fiscal period and which are more or less permanent in the business. Primary items in fixed assets include land, buildings, production equipment, office equipment, and delivery equipment. As these items decline in value over a period of time, an amount is subtracted from their value each year (except in the case of land) to take into account the factor of depreciation.

Liabilities are those obligations which the company is legally committed to pay at some time in the future. Like the current assets, current liabilities are those claims against the company which must be paid within a one-year period of time. The normal items in current liabilities are trade accounts payable and various accruals which arise through the operation of the business. The fixed liabilities include the bonds which the company has outstanding and any other claims which must legally be paid in the future but which are not due within the immediate one-year period.

The total of the net worth or equity section of the balance sheet is the total value of the stockholders' ownership in the company as of the date of the balance sheet. If there is only one class of stock outstanding, the stockholder may divide the total value in the equity section by the number of shares outstanding in order to determine his book value (net asset value) per share—the amount of assets behind each share of stock as shown on the books of the company. If two classes of stock are outstanding, the senior stock would have to be subtracted from the total equity before determining book value of the common stock. Preferred and common stock accounts carry the par or stated value of the securities outstanding. Surplus accounts (retained earnings and capital surplus) represent the stockholders' equity over and above par or stated value of the stock. The earned surplus account tends to represent the portion of the net gains from ordinary operation of the company which have been retained in the business.

The balance sheet, therefore, is a statement of financial position as of a specific point in time. It may be used to show the relative position of the various claimants against the company. It gives an indication of the liquidity or solvency of the company. The current assets may be compared to the current liabilities in order to get some indication of the company's ability to meet its current obligations. Proportion of bonds, preferred stock, common stock, and current liabilities can be determined in order to have a better understanding of the risk which the various claimants against the company are taking. Generally speaking, the more equity relative to debt, the safer the company.

The Income Statement

The income statement is a statement of income and expense for a given period of time, usually one year or one quarter. This statement is also commonly called the statement of operations, the profit and loss statement, or the income and expense statement. Figure 15-7 is an example of an income statement.

THE XYZ COMPANY
Statement of Income
Year ended December 31, 1965

Sales		$120,500,000
Cost of goods sold		85,000,000
Gross profit		$ 35,500,000
Less:		
Selling expenses	$6,500,000	
General expenses	3,500,000	
Administrative expenses	3,500,000	13,500,000
Operating profit		$ 22,000,000
Less interest expense		1,000,000
Earnings before income taxes		$ 21,000,000
Provision for income taxes		10,073,500
Net income for period		$ 10,926,500
Dividend on preferred stock		500,000
Balance of net income available for common		$ 10,426,500
Common stock dividends		5,000,000
Reinvested earnings		$ 5,426,500

Fig. 15-7. An income statement.

The first item on the income statement is sales, receipts, or gross income. This figure represents the dollar volume of business of the corporation during the period covered by the statement. The sales figure is normally followed by a cost-of-goods-sold figure. In a manufacturing operation, this would include the cost of manufacturing. In a merchandising company, the cost of goods sold would be the price which the company paid for the goods which it in turn resold in the channels of distribution. Subtracting cost of goods sold from sales gives gross profit—the amount which the corporation has available to pay its operating expenses (other than manufacturing) and to return a profit. Selling expense, administrative expense, and general expense would be subtracted from the gross profit to give net profit from operations. Other income and other expense items are then added or subtracted as the case may be. These are generally transactions arising from financial operations rather than from the primary production or distribution operation of the firm. The most common items in other income would be rents, royalties, dividends, interest, and purchase discounts earned. Other expenses would include interest paid and sales discounts. Adjusting for other income and other expense leaves net income before provision for federal income taxes.

Federal income taxes are then subtracted to give the net income figure. Federal income taxes are, of course, an expense of the business, but they are based on the net income before taxes. The net income or net profit figure left after subtraction of federal income tax is the net gain which the company has experienced during the period covered by the statement. This amount is available for payment of dividends to stockholders or for reinvestment in the company. Subtracting dividends from net income leaves the balance which is reinvested in the company and which is carried in the retained earnings on the balance sheet.

The income statement gives the investor a great deal of information about the operations of the company. It enables him to determine profit margin and operating ratios. The investor can compare the income statement for the company he is considering with those statements of other similar companies, in order to obtain a measure of efficiency. He may also compare income statements from one year to another for the same company in order to obtain an indication of trend. The income statement allows the bondholder to determine his interest coverage and the stockholder to determine his earnings per share. The importance of using past financial data of the company in selecting investments cannot be overemphasized. Figure 15–8 shows some of the financial statement ratios of a hypothetical situation which may be studied in reaching a conclusion on the purchase of a specific security. Incidentally, the liquidity ratio is the ratio of cash and equivalent (marketable securities) to total current liabilities. It is also expressed as a percentage figure and results from dividing cash and equivalent by the total current liabilities. The current ratio is current assets to current liabilities.

MARKET INFORMATION

The importance of the proper timing of security purchases for investors as well as speculators was discussed in Chapter 13. Proper timing means buying when market prices are "reasonable." In order to make good timing decisions, information on market prices and price trends is necessary. Some of the general sources of investment and market information were discussed above. Market prices are generally available in a wide variety of newspapers and other publications. Most of these publications also carry some information on market price trends. The interpretation of market price data and techniques for measuring trends

		1964	1963
1	Pre-tax Profit Margin	19.5%	18.5%
2	Current Ratio	2.24	2.38
3	Liquidity Ratio	41.7%	44.1%
4	Capitalization Ratios:		
	Long Term Debt	24.4%	20.8%
	Preferred Stock	5.7	6.3
	Common Stock and Surplus	69.9	72.9
		100.0%	100.0%
5	Sales to Fixed Assets	1.1	1.2
6	Sales to Inventories	4.3	4.5
7	Net Income to Net Worth	12.3%	12.5%

Fig. 15–8. Ratios to consider in investing. (Reproduced with permission, from *Understanding Financial Statements.* New York: The New York Stock Exchange, 1965.)

are discussed below along with the price-earnings ratio—an indicator of earnings relative to market price of a security.

Security Price Information

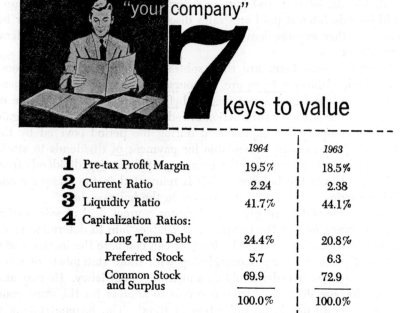

Many daily newspapers carry the price quotations for New York Stock Exchange stocks for the preceding day. Some newspapers also carry quotations from other exchanges and from the over-the-counter market. *The Wall Street Journal* has the most complete daily listings of security prices. Figure 15–9 is a portion of the New York Stock Exchange stock

A

— 1965 — High	Low	Stocks Div.	Sales in 100s	Open	High	Low	Close	Net Chg.
45	41½	Abacus 1.52f	1	41⅞	41⅞	41⅞	41⅞	+ ⅛
50	42½	Abbott Lab 1	47	45⅝	46⅛	45¼	46⅛	+ ½
23⅝	16¾	ABC Con .70	13	19⅞	20¼	19⅞	20	+ ⅜
93	72¾	ACF Ind 3a	24	79	79	77	78½	−1
73½	63⅞	Acme Mkt 2b	2	66⅝	66⅝	66⅝	66⅝	− ⅜
28¾	26¼	AdamE 2.05g	11	27⅝	27⅞	27⅝	27⅞	+ ¼
18¼	12½	Ad Millis .40a	2	14½	14½	14½	14½	
55⅞	41⅛	Address 1.40	33	44⅛	44⅞	43⅞	44½	+ ¾
33⅛	15⅝	Admiral	125	28⅛	29⅜	27¾	28⅞	+ ⅞
33¼	25⅜	Aeroquip .70	5	26¼	26¼	26⅛	26⅛	
63⅞	51⅛	Air Prod .20b	9	57	57	56⅛	56⅛	−1⅝
66⅛	53¾	Air Red 2.50	74	59	59½	59	59	+ ⅜
3⅛	2⅜	AJ Industries	15	2½	2⅝	2½	2½	
39⅜	34½	Ala Gas 1.70	6	35¼	35¼	35⅛	35⅛	− ⅛
25¾	19½	AlbertoCu .28	11	21	21	20¾	20⅞	− ⅛
12	8¾	Alleg Cp .20e	7	9½	9½	9⅜	9⅜	− ⅛
40⅜	27½	Alleg 6pf .60	1	31¼	31¼	31¼	31¼	− ½
47⅛	39¾	Allegh Lud 2	19	43⅜	44¼	43¼	43¼	+ ⅛
31	26½	Alleg Pw 1.06	11	28¼	28¼	27¾	28	
116	111½	Alleg & W 6	z10	112½	112½	112½	112½	+ ½
31¾	27¾	AllenIn 1.40a	1	28½	28½	28½	28½	− ¼
58¼	47	Allied C 1.90b	94	48	48⅜	47½	47⅝	
20⅞	14⅞	AlliedKid .85	3	17½	17½	17½	17½	
45¼	39	Allied Mills 2	4	41¼	41½	41¼	41½	+ ½
30¾	10⅛	Allied Pd .40	16	25¼	25½	25¼	25⅜	− ⅛
89¼	68⅝	Allied Strs 3	18	79¼	80¼	79¼	80¼	+ ½
17	13	AlliedSup .60	15	14⅛	14⅛	13⅞	13⅞	− ¼
26⅛	18½	AllisChal .50	29	20½	20½	20⅛	20⅜	
94½	93½	AllisCh pf4.20	2	93¼	93¼	93¼	93¼	− ¼
104	94	AllisCh pf4.08	1	95½	95½	95½	95½	+ ½
15⅛	11⅛	AlphaPC .50	30	11⅞	11⅞	11⅜	11⅜	− ¼
13¼	9¼	Alside Inc	5	9⅝	9⅝	9½	9½	− ¼
32⅛	25½	Alum Ltd .80	104	26¼	26¼	25¾	26¼	− ¼
79⅝	60½	Alcoa 1.40	59	72½	73⅛	72¼	72½	− ¼
24¾	21	AmalSug .80a	4	21⅜	21⅜	21⅜	21⅜	− ¼
27⅞	23	Amerace 1b	3	24½	24½	24½	24½	− ⅛
87½	70⅛	Amerada 2.40	x33	71¾	72⅜	71¾	71⅞	− ⅛
30¾	30½	AAirFiltr 1.40	2	30⅝	30¾	30⅝	30¾	+ ¼
59¼	44⅛	AmAirlin 1.25	37	53⅜	54¼	53⅛	54	+1
27½	20½	Am Baker 1	19	23⅝	23⅝	23¼	23⅜	− ⅛
74½	72	AmBkN pf 3	z30	74	74	74	74	
22½	15½	A Bosch .50e	28	19	19⅛	19	19⅛	− ⅛
69	56⅝	Am Brk 2.80	6	60⅜	61¼	60⅜	61¼	+ ⅞
65	48	AmBdcst 1.40	24	57¼	57½	56¾	56¾	−1
48⅝	42⅛	Am Can 2	94	48⅛	48¼	47½	47½	− ⅞
13⅜	10⅝	Am Cem .60	14	11⅛	11⅛	11	11	
36⅝	29½	AmChain 1.40	7	32⅛	32⅞	32⅛	32⅞	+ ⅞
52	38	AmCom 1.60b	21	40⅞	41	40¾	41	+ ⅜
22⅜	16	A Consum 1a	1	17	17	17	17	− ¼
19⅝	16½	AmCrySug 1	9	17¾	17¾	17¼	17¼	− ⅜
82⅛	67⅝	Am Cyan 2	30	75¾	75⅞	74¾	75	− ½
34½	29¼	Am Dist 1.20	1	31	31	31	31	+ ¼
47⅝	40⅞	AmElPw 1.24	41	44⅛	44⅜	43⅞	44⅜	+ ⅛
46¼	33	Amer Enka 1	35	40¾	40⅞	40½	40⅞	+ ¼
34⅜	23⅝	AmExp Isbrn	9	26⅝	26⅝	26½	26½	+ ¼
20	16½	Am FPow 1	1	17⅞	17⅞	17⅞	17⅞	
29¼	23	AmHoist 1.20	8	24⅝	24⅝	24	24	− ¾
74⅞	64⅞	AHome 1.80a	18	70⅞	70⅞	70⅛	70⅛	− ⅜
31¼	22⅞	Am Hosp .35	59	26¾	27⅜	26¾	27⅜	+ ⅜
16¾	15⅛	Am Intl 1.20g	3	16	16	16	16	+ ⅛
24⅜	22	AmInvCo 1.10	6	22¼	22¼	22⅛	22¼	
20⅜	16⅛	Am MFd .90	62	17½	17½	17⅛	17⅛	− ⅜
89½	88¼	AMF pf 3.90	z10	89¼	89¼	89¼	89¼	+1
54¼	40⅜	AMet Cl 1.60	22	45½	46⅛	45½	46⅛	+ ½
134½	111⅜	AMet pf 4.25	3	117¼	117¼	117¼	117¼	− ¼
26	19⅛	A MetPd 1.20	9	25	25¼	25	25¼	+ ¼
52	40½	A Meter 1.60	4	46¼	46¾	46¼	46½	+ ½
15⅛	10⅞	Am Motors 1	77	12	12⅛	12	12	

Fig. 15–9. Daily stock quotations. (Reproduced with permission, from *The Wall Street Journal*, July 13. 1965.)

quotations from *The Wall Street Journal.* These are typical of those from most other sources.

Properly reading the security price listings requires a knowledge of the type of information presented. The quotations from Fig. 15–9 for American Cyanamid Common stock "Am Cyan" are described here. The figure in the first column (82⅛) is the highest price per share at which this stock was traded on the New York Stock Exchange since the beginning of the year 1965. The figure in the second column (67⅝) is the lowest price per share at which this stock was traded since January 1, 1965. The figure given immediately after the name of the company (2) is the current dividend rate in dollars. Thus, American Cyanamid has a current dividend rate of $2.00 per year. The figure given is an annual rate, regardless of when dividends are paid, unless footnoted otherwise by a small-case letter. Explanations of the footnotes are given at the end of the listings. Unlike the yearly high and low quotations, the dividend is for a twelve-month period rather than for the year to date.

The column "sales in 100s" gives the number of shares traded during the day. The volume in American Cyanamid was 3,000 shares. Only round-lot transactions are included in the total. For most securities, the round lot is 100 shares. Several hundred stocks, such as American Bank Note preferred ("AmBkN pf"), are traded in lots of ten and actual number of shares traded is quoted (prefixed "z" in front of sales). Thirty shares of American Bank Note preferred were traded.

The next four columns—open, high, low, and close—describe the trading for the day. The first transaction made in American Cyanamid was at 75¾ per share. The last transaction of the day was at 75. During the day, the highest price paid for any American Cyanamid was 75⅞ and the lowest price paid during the day was 74¾. Most heavily traded stocks fluctuate both up and down during the period of one day.

The final column in the listing—labeled "net change"—describes the change in the closing price from the closing price the preceding day. Since American Cyanamid is minus ½, it is apparent that the closing price the preceding day was 75½ (75 + ½). Looking at American Distilling Company ("Am Dist"), only 100 shares were traded during the day. Thus, open, high, low, and close are all the same—31. Nonetheless, net change shows +¼, indicating that the stock closed the day before at 30¾.

If a stock is not traded in during the day, it is quoted elsewhere in the paper. Since there would be no figures for sales, only bid and asked figures are given. These quotations are obtained from the specialist in the stock at the close of trading for the day. The bid price is the highest price at which anyone will buy the stock. The asked price is the lowest price at which anyone was willing to sell. The asked price is always higher than the bid, for as soon as they become equal, a sale takes place. Since the market in over-the-counter securities is much less organized, sale prices of securities are not available. Instead, the financial papers obtain bid and asked prices on these securities from leading security dealers.

The price quotation "75⅞" means \$75.87½ per share. Any accrued or anticipated dividend is reflected in the quoted price. On the New York Stock Exchange, stocks are quoted in dollars and eighths of dollars rather than in dollars and cents. This is true in most other organized exchanges and in the over-the-counter market. The smallest possible variation in price in a New York Stock Exchange listed stock (except for very low-priced stocks) is \$.12½—this is a fairly substantial variation percentagewise on a low-priced security. On high-priced securities, the variation is relatively minor. It would be expected that high-priced securities would have higher dollar fluctuations than low-priced securities.

Price-Earnings Ratio

For practical purposes the value of a stock is expressed by its market price. The appraisal put upon the stock by buyers and sellers fixes the market price. This appraisal is determined from a complex set of factors which would include the following: the industry; position of the company in the industry; property owned and debts owed by the company; type of stock and number of shares outstanding; past, present, and prospective future earnings; dividends; taxes; and management. No definite weights can be given these different factors in the determination of a proper value for stock. Sometimes the market price of a particular stock appears to have little or no relation to these factors. Just why a particular stock should sell for \$75 instead of for \$70 or \$80, for example, usually cannot be explained.

The determination of the value of a high-grade bond is relatively easy, compared with the determination of the value of a common stock. If it is known, for example, what the face rate of interest is on a United States Government bond, and the call and maturity dates, the value of the bond can be determined with a high degree of accuracy. The valuation of preferred stock is much more difficult, but, after giving proper consideration to the estimated degree of risk involved, the amount of the fixed dividend is of great importance in arriving at a valuation.

The problem of valuation is most difficult when it comes to common stock. Not only is the risk greater, but it is much more difficult—in fact, practically impossible—to measure the degree of risk involved in the purchase of a particular common stock. Then, too, most common stocks have no fixed rate of dividends. But even if custom has more or less established some dividend rate on the common, this does not give us all the information available because the undistributed earnings are considered to belong to the common stockholders even though they are not then or later distributed to them in the form of dividends.

The amount paid out in dividends usually varies, however, according to the size of the earnings. Unless the earnings are relatively small, corporations commonly pay out from 40 to 70 per cent of their earnings in the form of dividends. The stockholder can usually conclude that the amount he will receive in future dividends depends upon the amount of the future earnings. After giving due consideration to the estimated degree of risk involved, the market price of common stocks is determined more from the estimated future earnings than from any other single factor.

With the emphasis thus put on prospective future earnings, anything which will shed some light on the probable future earnings would be of great value in the determination of a fair price for the common stock. The amount and trend of past and present earnings is probably more indicative of the expected future earnings than any other factor. Thus, some relationship should exist between the past earnings and the existing market price of the stock.

It should be noted that earnings per share on the common stock is what is left after bond interest, income taxes, and preferred dividends. In speaking of earnings here, it has not been indicated whether we have in mind current earnings or average past earnings. The more recent earnings, of course, are more indicative of the probable future earnings than the earnings of some years past. The profits of the most recent year may be used in the price-earnings ratio if they have been more or less normal, and if the trend of the earnings has been up. The financial services, which frequently give price-earnings ratios for particular stocks, usually use the current earnings. If the profits of the last or current year are not representative, an average of the past five, seven, or ten years should be used. If the past five years have been a prolonged period of prosperity or depression, the larger number of years should be used.

If the current earnings are used, it might be expected that the price-earnings ratio would be higher during a prosperous year than one in which there was a depression, since people usually expect existing trends to continue. But the earnings of many corporations sink so low during a period of depression that their stock might be selling for 100 times earnings, for example, when the market price is only $1 per share. The inadvisability of using the current earnings at such a time is apparent.

The price of common stocks at any particular time is determined largely by the prospective future earnings of the company. It would therefore be more logical to compare the present price of a stock with the expected future earnings than with the past or present earnings. Unfortunately, no one can predict the future earnings, over a period of years, with any fine degree of accuracy. But the past earnings over a period of, say, seven years, the trend of the earnings, the current earnings, and the future outlook for business in general and for the particular industry and company, are all important tangible factors which can be used to make an intelligent guess as to the probable future earnings. Graham [1] states that a common stock with neutral prospects for the future should sell for about 12 times the estimated average annual earnings. And he says that, except for unusual cases, the multiplier should not be greater than 20, nor less than 8.

If 12 times earnings is taken as a yardstick, it would seem to follow that stocks selling at a lower ratio would be a bargain, while those selling at a higher ratio would be overpriced. Such a conclusion should not be drawn. If a particular stock is selling for more than 12 times earnings, it may be indicative of the fact that this stock has a better than average prospect for the future. If the ratio gets too high, the stock may be overpriced. It should be kept in mind that these ratios apply to investment rather than speculation. Relatively new companies which offer excellent growth possibilities may appear attractive to the speculator even when their stocks are selling at a relatively high price-earnings ratio. In fact, stocks may offer good speculative possibilities when no profits at all are being earned by the company.

The same reasoning, in reverse, can be applied to a stock selling at less than 12 times earnings. A lower ratio than this may indicate that the future prospects of the company are so unfavorable that people do not want to buy the stock. Thus, despite the low price-earnings ratio, the stock might not be low priced in relation to future prospects. In a period of depression, however, people may become so pessimistic that they are afraid to buy stocks and this causes the price to fall so low that a very low price-earnings ratio results. Then the low ratio may indicate a favorable purchase price. Naturally, it is not easy to determine which interpretation should be put on a low price-earnings ratio.

The normal price-earnings ratio would also vary among different types of industries. As public utilities are generally considered safer than industrials, it can be expected that the price-earnings ratio for these stocks over a long period of time will be higher than for industrial stocks. Within the same industry, the stocks of the older and larger companies usually sell on a higher price-earnings basis than the smaller or newer companies. The stock of companies which have relatively stable earnings and pay regular dividends of a more or less fixed amount sell at a rela-

[1] Benjamin Graham, *The Intelligent Investor*, 3d rev. ed. (New York: Harper & Row, 1965), p. 193.

tively high price. Growth stocks sell at very high price-earnings ratios in times of prosperity. Companies in a relatively new industry which offer good opportunity for the future would appear more attractive than those which are in a field which is on the decline.

During the mid-1960's the stocks comprising the Dow-Jones Industrial Average sold in the neighborhood of 18 to 19 times earnings. The price-earnings ratio of the 500 Standard & Poor's Composite Index for a long number of years is shown on page 428.

Stock Price Averages

During the course of a day on the New York Stock Exchange some stocks will advance in price, some will go down, others will not change. By looking over the financial page of the newspaper and seeing the various plus signs for the advances over the preceding day's close, and the minus signs for the declines, it would be difficult for a reader to determine whether the market in general advanced or declined for the particular day, and the extent of the change. To determine this accurately it would be necessary to add the closing prices of all the stocks traded on the Exchange for the preceding day, and then do the same for the particular day, and compare the results. This could then be reduced to a per-share basis by dividing the day's totals by the number of different issues traded in for the day. All this would be a quite laborious task.

In order to facilitate the work, and give the investor or speculator information as to the trend of the market, several stock price averages are computed and published daily. The most popular of these are the Dow-Jones averages. These averages are printed daily in *The Wall Street Journal,* which is published by Dow, Jones & Co., Inc., and in many other newspapers and financial magazines throughout the country. The Dow-Jones industrial average is computed by taking the hourly and closing prices of thirty common stocks of leading and representative industrial companies, adding these together, and dividing, at the present time, by 2.245. The latter figure, rather than 30, is used in order to make the present-day average comparable to that of the past. During the course of time many of the companies included in the list have had stock dividends and stock split-ups. The effect of these is to reduce the price of the stock independently of the general trend of the market. For example, if a company included in the Dow-Jones list, whose stock was selling for $50, paid a 100 per cent stock dividend, or split its stock by giving the stockholders two new shares in exchange for each old share, the tendency would be to reduce the market price of the stock from $50 to $25 a share. If the Dow-Jones industrial average were always computed by adding the prices of the stocks and dividing by 30, the average would be distorted and show a lower figure than would be warranted from the actual trend of the market. The divisor is changed from time to time to give effect to stock dividends and stock splits that occur in the stocks which are used in the average. By dividing at the present time by 2.245, the same effect is produced as if the companies had not had these types of changes in the capital structure and the sum of the closing prices had been divided by 30. It is thus evident that if all the stocks included in the average would advance one point during the day, the average, at the present time, would go up slightly more than 13 points.

In addition to the industrial average, Dow, Jones & Co., Inc., also publishes a railroad average, a public utility average, and a composite average of industrials, rails, and public utilities. These are computed in a slightly different manner from the industrial average. The same company also publishes averages for different types of bonds. Figure 15–10 shows the Dow-Jones Industrial, Railroad, and Utility averages for the years 1915–1964.

The *New York Times* publishes a daily average of 25 industrial stocks, an average of 25 railroad stocks, and a composite average of the 50 stocks. The high, low, and closing prices are given. In order to give immediate effect to stock splits and stock dividends, the price of the stock of these companies is multiplied by such a number that will make the price comparable to the old price. As soon as possible, however, another comparable stock is substituted. A bond average is also carried by the same paper.

Believing that the above averages contained too few stocks, the *New York Herald Tribune* many years ago began publishing an average based on 70 industrial stocks, and an average of 30 railroad stocks. This average is computed for the high, low, and closing prices of the stocks. This paper also publishes a composite average of the 100 stocks contained in the other two averages, as well as a bond average.

Several criticisms of the above averages may be made. Some think that the number of stocks used is not sufficient to be representative of the market as a whole. The averages do not give effect to the total amount of stock which the various corporations included in the averages have outstanding. Also, the averages show absolute increases. If the averages were at 10, and over a period of time advanced to 20, this would of course show as a 10-point increase, or an increase of 100 per cent. But if the averages were at 100, and advanced only 10 per cent, this would result in a 10-point increase in the averages, to 110. This last increase of 10 points should not be given the same weight as the similar increase when the averages were only 10.

The Standard & Poor's Corporation publishes a stock price *index* which tries to overcome the shortcomings of the stock price *averages*

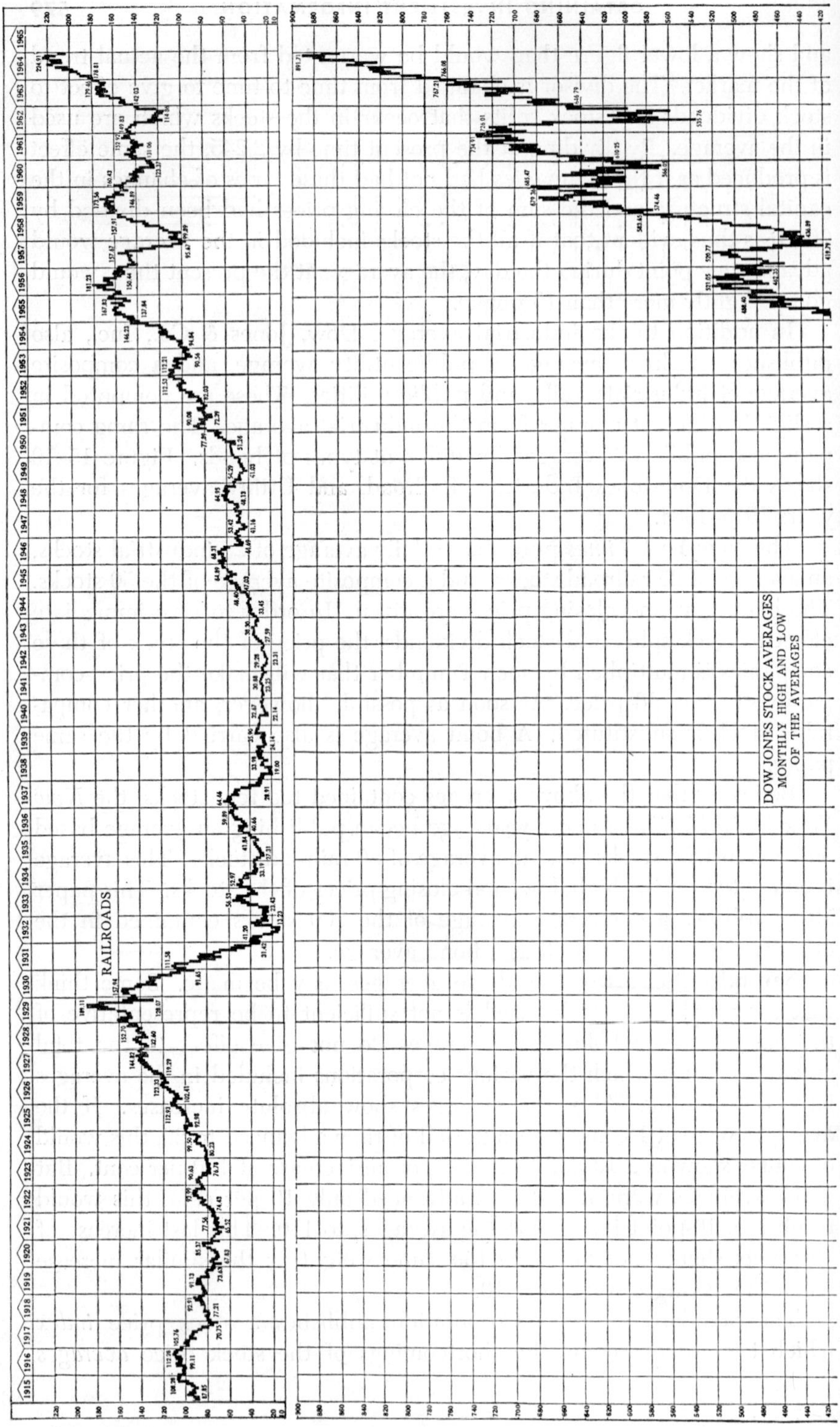
DOW JONES STOCK AVERAGES
MONTHLY HIGH AND LOW
OF THE AVERAGES
RAILROADS

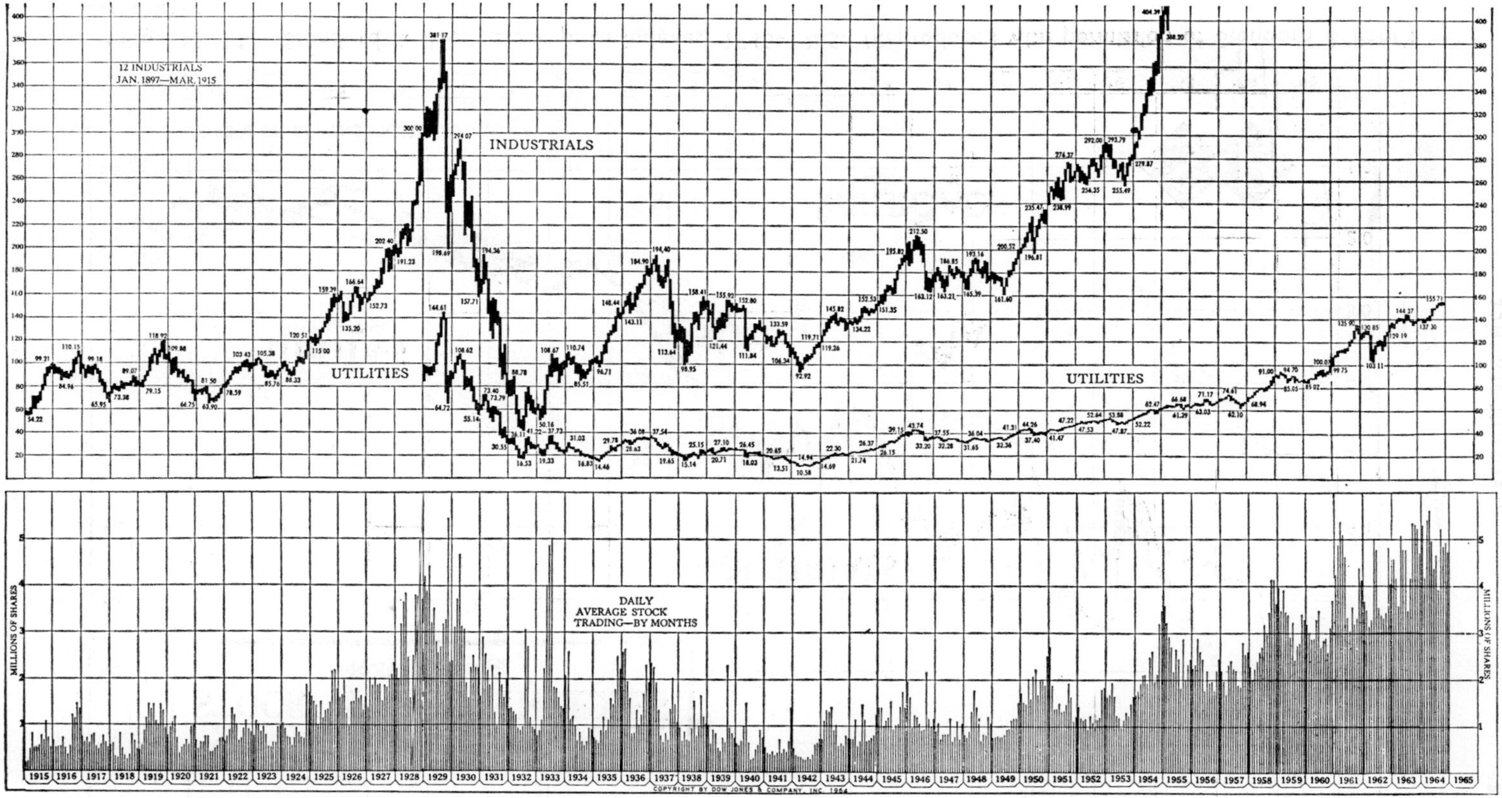

Fig. 15–10. Dow-Jones stock averages, 1915–1964. (Reproduced with permission of Dow, Jones & Company, Inc.)

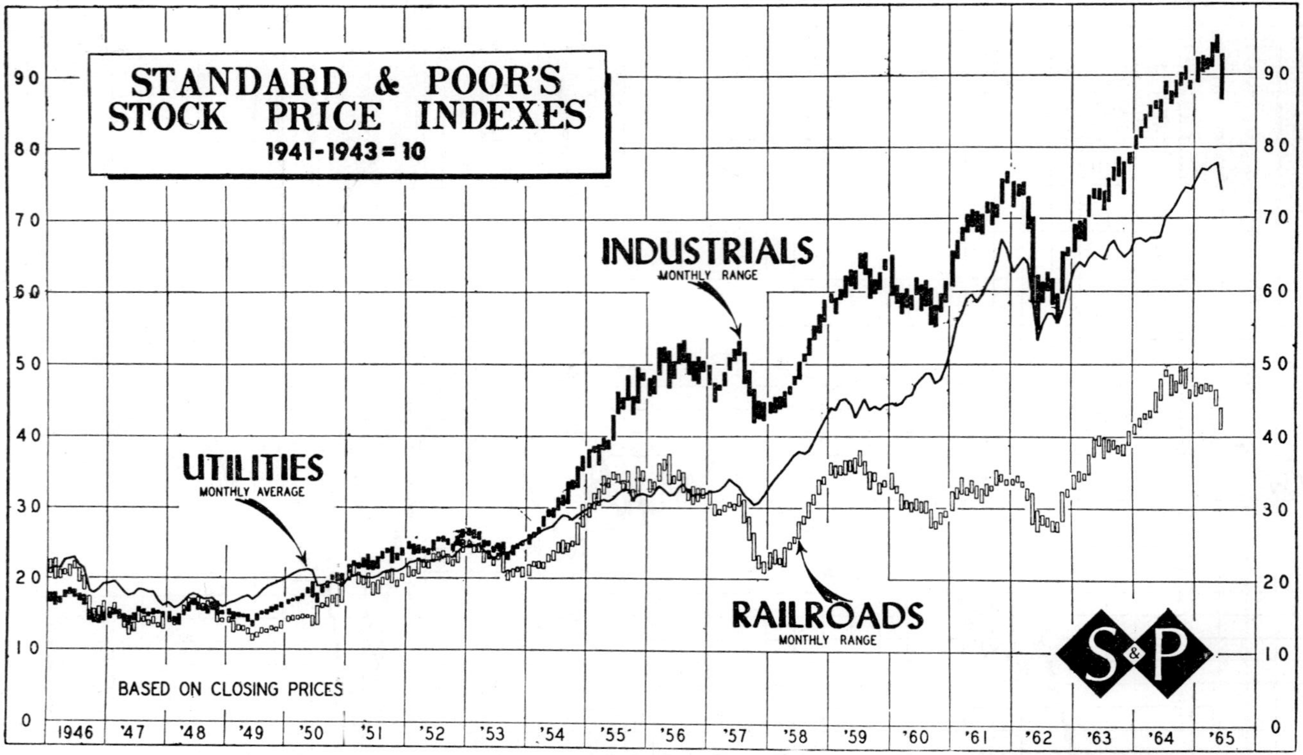

Fig. 15–11. Standard & Poor's stock price indexes, 1946–1965. (Reproduced with permission of Standard & Poor's Corporation.)

mentioned above. Their list of stocks includes 425 industrials representing the various types of companies, 50 utilities, and 25 railroads. An index of the composite 500 stocks is also compiled. The index takes the hourly and closing prices, and this is multiplied by the total number of shares which the particular corporation has outstanding. This total market value of each company's stock is expressed as a percentage of the average total market value of the stock for 1941–1943. This period is taken as the base, and the index for that period is 10. Due consideration is given to changes in the capital structure. Preferred stock and bond indexes are also published by Standard & Poor's Corporation. Figure 15–11 shows the Standard & Poor's industrial, railroad, and utilities indexes for the years 1946–1965.

Stock averages or indexes are published also by the Associated Press, Moody's Investors Service, and the Securities and Exchange Commission.

QUESTIONS

1. What procedures do you think could be used to get the average investor to secure more information than he does about securities which he is contemplating purchasing?
2. Name six different types of information which are important to the potential security buyer.
3. Why are general business and economic data of interest to the potential security investor?
4. What sources of data are available on specific companies and the securities they issue?
5. What types of information would be more useful to the speculator than to the investor? Why?
6. How much information should the average investor obtain before making a security purchase decision?
7. How reliable is the information which is obtained from the company issuing the security? What problem does the investor face in the reliability of other data?
8. Describe the services offered by Moody's and Standard & Poor's.
9. What are sources of trade and industry statistics?
10. Describe the information available in a Standard Listed Stock Report.
11. Describe the services offered by Value Line.
12. Differentiate investment advisory services from investment counselors.
13. What is the most important primary source of financial data for a given company?
14. When is a prospectus under the Securities Act of 1933 useful to the investor?
15. Why is the Securities Act of 1933 sometimes called the "truth in securities act"? How does the investor obtain the information required by the Act?

16. Of what use are the corporation's financial statements to the average investor? Differentiate the balance sheet from the income statement. Which of these statements is more useful? Why?
17. Discuss ratio analysis from the point of view of the average investor.
18. Explain specifically each figure given for Alcoa in Fig. 15–9.
19. Why is the price-earnings ratio considered important to investors?
20. Of what use are stock price averages or indexes? What problems are inherent in the reliability of these indexes?

CASE PROBLEMS

1. David Jenkins has been working on his first job, since his graduation from college almost a year ago. He finds he is earning more than his immediate spending requirements and desires to invest the remainder periodically in common stocks. However, David has had no experience in security investing and knows almost nothing about selecting securities. Since he is not knowledgeable in the field, would you recommend that he consider other investments instead of common stocks? If he is determined to invest in common stocks, how should he go about preparing himself to be an investor? To whom could he go for advice? What kinds of information should he attempt to obtain?
2. Robert Brussel's grandfather died recently and Robert is due to inherit $10,000 to $15,000. Robert has a well paying job and a sufficient insurance and savings program, and has decided to invest his inheritance in something that would offer a hedge against inflation. Since the money is not large enough in amount to allow a significant investment in real estate, he has concluded that he should invest in common stocks. However, Robert has had no experience in common stock investing and his knowledge is very limited. He has talked to a representative of a local brokerage firm who suggested that his firm would make recommendations to Robert concerning potential purchases with the money. He has also learned of a local investment advisor who makes the buy-and-sell decisions for his customers. Evaluate these two alternatives. What other alternatives are available to Robert? If Robert decides to use an investment advisor, how should he make the selection? How should he choose from among the available brokerage firms if he decides to utilize the services of such a firm?
3. James Pilsner's father died recently and James is due to inherit between $40,000 and $60,000. He has a steady job with good income. He also has an adequate insurance program. A friend has suggested that James put the money into common stocks. As James knows nothing about common stock investing, the friend suggested he contact Mr. Robert Barrister, an investment counselor, and let Mr. Barrister handle his investment program. Is this a wise move? Will it cost James anything to use Mr. Barrister's services? If so, on what basis should Mr. Barrister be paid? Should James talk to other investment counselors also? How can he find out something about Mr. Barrister?
4. In June, 1965, Dick Johnson obtained the Standard & Poor's Corporation card on General Motors Corporation given in Fig. 15–3. Dick is an

average small investor. What use should he make of the information on this card? Should he buy this stock? Why or why not?

5. The price-earnings ratio for the XYZ Chemical Company for the past eight years has been 12, 15, 18, 19, 22, 28, 33, 38, and is currently 41. What does this information indicate to you? What could account for this rapid rise in the price-earnings ratio? Is this sufficient information for you to make an investment decision on this stock?
6. Look at Fig. 15–10 and determine the relative trend of the stock market from 1915 to 1965, 1922 to 1929, 1930 to 1932, 1934 to 1945, 1949 to 1965. Have all three averages moved together during these periods? Which period includes the most substantial rise in the market? What trend would you project for 1965 on?
7. The Value Line Investment Survey gives a particular stock a rating of I for probable performance for the next twelve months, and II for desirability of holding for three to five years. The stock is yielding 1 per cent (which would give it a rating of V) and its quality rating of A would put it in the top rating of I for this category. Using the Value Line method of measuring the suitability of the stock, would this particular stock be a better investment for Mr. Jones or Mr. Smith if they sought the following features in the order indicated?

Jones	*Smith*
Quality	Yield
Prospects—12 months	Quality
Yield	Prospects—12 months
Prospects—3–5 years	Prospects—3–5 years

SELECTED READINGS

Barnes, Leo. *Your Investments.* Larchmont, N. Y.: American Research Council. Latest edition.

Bogen, Jules I. (ed.) *Financial Handbook,* Fourth Edition. New York: The Ronald Press Co., 1964. Sections 7 and 8.

Clendenin, John C. *Introduction to Investments,* Fourth Edition. New York: McGraw-Hill Book Co., 1964.

Engel, Louis. *How to Buy Stocks.* New York: Bantam Books. Paperbound. Single copies may be obtained free from any office of Merrill Lynch, Pierce, Fenner & Smith, Inc.

Foulke, Roy A. *Practical Financial Statement Analysis,* Fifth Edition. New York: McGraw-Hill Book Co., 1961.

Graham, Benjamin. *The Intelligent Investor,* Third Revised Edition. New York: Harper & Row, 1965.

———, Dodd, David, and Cottle, Sidney. *Security Analysis: Principles and Techniques,* Fourth Edition. New York: McGraw-Hill Book Co., 1962.

Hazard, John W., and Chrystie, Milton. *The Investment Business.* New York: Harper & Row, 1964.

How to Invest. New York: Merrill Lynch, Pierce, Fenner & Smith, Inc. Latest edition. Available from any of the firm's offices.

How to Read a Financial Report. Merrill Lynch, Pierce, Fenner & Smith, Inc. A free copy may be obtained from any of the firm's offices.

List of Free Materials Available to Professors. Princeton, N. J.: Dow, Jones & Co., Inc. Latest edition.

Monthly Stock Digest. New York: Data Digests, Inc. Available free from stock brokerage offices.

Moody's Manuals. New York: Moody's Investors Service. Separate manuals are published annually for companies in the following classifications: industrials, public utilities, transportation companies, financial institutions, and governments. These are available in stock brokerage offices and libraries.

Moody's Stock Survey. New York: Moody's Investors Service. Published weekly. Available in stock brokerage offices and libraries.

Outlook, The. New York: Standard & Poor's Corporation. Published weekly. Available in stock brokerage offices and libraries.

Security and Industry Survey: A Guide for Investors. New York: Merrill Lynch, Pierce, Fenner & Smith, Inc. Published quarterly. Available free from any of the firm's offices.

Stabler, C. Norman. *How to Read the Financial News.* New York: Harper & Row, 1965.

Standard & Poor's Standard Corporation Records. New York: Standard & Poor's Corporation. Available in stock brokerage offices and libraries.

Standard & Poor's Stock Guide. New York: Standard & Poor's Corporation. Published monthly. Available in stock brokerage offices and libraries.

Understanding Financial Statements. New York: New York Stock Exchange, 1965. Available from member firms of the New York Stock Exchange.

Value Line Investment Survey. New York: Arnold Bernhard & Co., Inc. Available in libraries and some stock brokerage offices.

See also Selected Readings at the end of Chapter 13 (page 504) for publications of the New York Stock Exchange.

16

Income Taxes

Many years ago, Benjamin Franklin said, "In this world nothing is certain but death and taxes." Practically every consumer is a taxpayer and most of us pay a great many different kinds of taxes.

Taxes are levied by the three forms of government—the federal government, the states, and the local governments. All three of these agencies have been collecting more and more in taxes as time goes on. For many people the federal income tax is the one that hits the hardest. The federal debt increased tremendously before and during World War II, and this resulted in a sharp increase in the income tax rates. With the huge debt hanging over our heads, it is probable that relatively high tax rates will continue into the indefinite future.

It would require many pages to list the various taxes which are levied by the federal government, the states, and their political subdivisions. Such an undertaking is not the purpose of this chapter. Here we will discuss the federal income tax.

History

The federal government enacted a type of income tax in 1861 to aid in the financing of the Civil War. This tax law was repealed in 1872. The present income tax law (not the present rates) was authorized in 1913 by the Sixteenth Amendment to the Constitution.

Prior to 1943, people filed their income tax forms on March 15 of each year and either paid their taxes then or paid one quarter of them and paid the balance in three quarterly installments. The taxes were always computed on the income of the previous year. Many people spent all or most of their money about as soon as they received it and were therefore unable to pay the taxes that were owed on the previous year's income. If they had filed a correct income tax report, but did not have the money to pay the taxes, nothing could be done about it. The tax liability, however, remained.

Realizing this and other shortcomings in the method being used, the government changed the laws in 1943 and put people on a pay-as-you-go basis in paying their taxes. Employers are compelled to withhold from the pay of their employees an amount that approximates the amount of taxes owed by the workers. Discrepancies between the amount withheld and the amount actually owed are settled on April 15 of the following year. Certain taxpayers are required to file estimates of their income and the amount to be withheld, and if that withheld is less than the total tax, then one quarter of the difference must be paid every three months.

Generally speaking, it is the people who work in factories, shops, stores, mills, mines, and for the federal, state, or local governments, etc., whose taxes are withheld from their pay. Professional people, the self-employed, domestic servants, etc., are required to pay their taxes directly to the Internal Revenue Service.

As may have been inferred from the above, this change put tax collection on a current basis. The taxes being collected by the withholding method or by annual or quarterly payments are the taxes due on the income received for that particular year. In recent years the tax laws and rates have been changed frequently.

The material which follows gives effect to the 1964 tax laws and the tax rates which became effective in 1965.

Getting Information About Income Tax

Income taxes have become a major expense. It is to the advantage of every individual to use every legal means available to reduce the tax as much as possible. The tax laws prescribe certain deductions which can be taken, and the tax rates are set with this in mind. If a person does not list all the deductions which are allowed, he will be paying more in taxes than is expected of him.

The tax laws are quite complicated, and the average person knows little about them. Most people could save something if they consulted a competent person when filling out their tax forms. There are some free and some relatively inexpensive sources of income tax information. In the offices of the Director of Internal Revenue in the various cities, there are competent governmental employees who will, without any charge, give information and suggestions on filling out the form.

Two inexpensive booklets, *J. K. Lasser's Your Income Tax*[1] and *Your Federal Income Tax*,[2] which are published annually, are informative and easy to understand. Many people would find in these booklets methods of saving in taxes which would more than offset their cost. This is particularly true of those people who own property or businesses, or of those who buy and sell property, both real and personal, or those who have extraordinary expenses or income.

For those whose incomes are very large, it is usually advisable to consult a competent public accountant or attorney. This, of course, would cost more than the published sources of advice, but the tax savings which may be effected may well justify the expense.

Who Must File a Tax Return?

Every citizen or resident of the United States—whether an adult or minor—who had a "gross income" (generally speaking, that means total income) of $600 or more in a taxable year must file a federal income tax return. People 65 and over, however, are not required to file a return unless their gross income is $1,200 or more for the year. It should be noted that age (aside from those 65 and over) and marital status make no difference so far as the filing requirement is concerned. Due to deductions and exemptions a person may not owe any taxes, but he nevertheless must file the return if his gross income is as stated above.

In some instances a person should file a tax return even if his gross income is less than $600 for the year. Employees have income taxes withheld from their pay by their employers. If they work part time, for example, and earn less than $600 for the year, they should file a return in order to get a refund of the taxes that have been deducted from their pay.

The income tax return must be filed with the office of the District Director of Internal Revenue for the district in which the taxpayer lives, not later than April 15 of the following year. It may be filed, however, any time after the close of the year up to April 15.

DIFFERENT TAX FORMS

There are two different tax forms on which income tax returns may be made. In some instances a person has the option of selecting which one he wants to use; in other cases he has no choice. Where it is optional, the taxpayer may save himself something in taxes by using one form rather than another. These forms are Form 1040A and Form 1040.

[1] Simon and Schuster, Inc., New York.
[2] Superintendent of Documents, Government Printing Office, Washington, D. C.

Form 1040A

Form 1040A may be used by anyone whose total income is less than $10,000 for the year and consists only of (a) wages or salaries from which taxes have been withheld and reported on withholding statements (Form W-2), and (b) not more than $200 total of dividends, interest, and other wages from which there has been no withholding of taxes.

Form 1040A is simply a card (see Fig. 16–1) on which the taxpayer fills in the required information. If the reported income is less than $5,000, the taxpayer can let the government figure the amount of taxes due. He will be billed for any taxes due (after giving effect to the taxes that have been withheld from his pay), or if he has overpaid, the government will send him a check for the amount of the refund. If the reported income is $5,000 or more, the taxpayer must compute the amount of the taxes in

Form 1040A U.S. INDIVIDUAL INCOME TAX RETURN (LESS THAN $10,000 TOTAL INCOME) 1964

Please print →
1. Name (If a joint return of husband and wife, use first names and middle initials of both)
Home address (Number and street or rural route)
City, town or post office, State and Postal ZIP code
2. Your social security number (Husband's if joint return)
3. Wife's number, if joint return
4. Check one:
☐ Single;
☐ Married filing joint return (even if only one had income);
☐ Married filing separately—If your husband or wife is also filing a return give his or her first name and social security number.

Enter the name and address used on your return for 1963. (If the same as above, write "Same.") If none filed, give reason.

If item 7 is $10,000 or more, or if interest, dividends and nonwithheld wages are over $200, use Form 1040.

NOTE.—Married taxpayers: If you are changing from filing separate returns to a joint return or from a joint return to separate returns, enter names and addresses from the 1963 joint or separate returns.

If your income was $5,000 or more, you must compute your tax. However, if your income was less than $5,000, you may have the Internal Revenue Service compute your tax by omitting items 8, 10, and 11. *If you compute your own tax, pay balance (item 10) in full with return to your District Director.*

5. Enter total wages, salaries, tips, etc. Enclose Forms W-2, Copy B. If not shown on enclosed Forms W-2 attach explanation. Yours → Wife's →
6. Interest and dividends Yours → Wife's →
7. Total income (add items 5 and 6)
8. Enter tax from Tax Table or from tax computation schedule →
9. Total Federal income tax withheld (from Forms W-2) →
10. If item 8 is larger than item 9, enter **balance due** →
11. If item 9 is larger than item 8, enter **refund** →
Apply refund to: ☐ U.S. Savings Bonds, with excess refunded; or ☐ Refund only.

U.S. TREASURY DEPARTMENT • INTERNAL REVENUE SERVICE (OVER) LIST YOUR EXEMPTIONS AND SIGN ON OTHER SIDE. 8

12. EXEMPTIONS FOR YOURSELF—AND WIFE (only if all her income is included in this return, or she had no income)
Check boxes which apply
(a) Regular $600 exemption ☐ Yourself ☐ Wife
(b) Additional $600 exemption if 65 or over at end of 1964 ☐ Yourself ☐ Wife
(c) Additional $600 exemption if blind at end of 1964 ☐ Yourself ☐ Wife
Enter number of boxes checked →
13. NUMBER OF YOUR DEPENDENT CHILDREN WHO LIVED WITH YOU →
14. DEPENDENTS OTHER THAN THOSE CLAIMED IN ITEM 13.

(a) NAME ▶ Enter figure 1 in the last column to right for each name listed (If more space is needed, attach schedule)	(b) Relationship	(c) Months lived in your home. If born or died during year also write "B" or "D"	(d) Did dependent have income of $600 or more?	(e) Amount YOU furnished for dependent's support. If 100% write "ALL"	(f) Amount furnished by OTHERS including dependent. See instruction 14	
				$	$	→
						→
						→

15. Total exemptions from items 12, 13, and 14 above →

If you had an expense allowance or charged expenses to your employer, see instructions for "Reimbursed Expenses" and check here ☐ if appropriate.

SIGN HERE → Under penalties of perjury, I declare that to the best of my knowledge and belief this is a true, correct, and complete return.

If joint return, BOTH HUSBAND AND WIFE MUST SIGN even if only one had income. Date B

Fig. 16–1. Form 1040A, U. S. individual income tax return, front *(top)* and reverse *(bottom)*.

a manner similar to that on Form 1040, which will be explained later. A standard deduction is taken (explained later). Tax rates are supplied on an instruction sheet. If any tax is due, payment should be made at time of filing the form. A refund will later be made if taxes have been overpaid.

Form 1040A is the simplest form and the easiest to use. It therefore would probably be preferred by those who earned less than $600 for the year and want to file a return in order to secure a refund. If a person's actual deductions do not exceed the standard deduction, he would probably also prefer to use this form. Those with actual deductions (explained later in the chapter) in excess of the standard deduction may prefer to use Form 1040. If a person had an income of $10,000 or over he could not use Form 1040A. Also, this form cannot be used if a person's income includes more than $200 total of dividends, interest, and wages from which there have been no taxes withheld.

Form 1040 with Use of Tax Table

Form 1040 can be used in two different ways. The form, with use of the tax tables, may be used only by those whose total income is less than $5,000. Tax tables supplied by the government in the "Instruction Booklet" (see Table 16–1) are used to ascertain the amount of taxes. These tables give effect to standard deductions. Separate tax tables are made out for single persons (not head of household), heads of household, married persons filing jointly, and married persons filing separate returns.

Form 1040 with Computation of Taxes

Anyone can "compute" his taxes with Form 1040. It *must* be done by anyone whose income is $10,000 or over. It must be used if the taxpayer itemizes his deductions. When this filing is used, the taxpayer computes his own taxes by applying the appropriate tax rates found in the proper schedule of the "Instruction Booklet" (see Tables 16–2 and 16–3). Although "deductions" may be itemized, a standard deduction may be taken. Whenever a taxpayer's actual deductions exceed the standard deduction, it is advisable to list them.

DECLARATION OF ESTIMATED TAX

For some persons, the taxes withheld from their wages or salaries are sufficient to cover their total taxes due on their annual incomes. Any slight difference is accounted for when they file their annual returns on April 15 of the following year. For other people, however, the taxes with-

Table 16–1.

TAX TABLE A—FOR MARRIED PERSONS FILING JOINT RETURNS★

This table is designed to allow for the standard deduction

Read down the income columns below until you find the line covering the total income (line 1, page 2, Form 1040–ES). Then read across to the appropriate column headed by the number corresponding to the number of your exemptions, this is your tax.

If your total income is—		And the number of exemptions is—		If your total income is—		And the number of exemptions is—				
At least	But less than	2	3 If 4 or more there is no tax	At least	But less than	2	3	4	5	6 If 7 or more there is no tax
		Your tax is—				Your tax is—				
$0	$1, 600	$0	$0	$2, 800	$2, 825	$172	$72	$0	$0	$0
1, 600	1, 625	2	0	2, 825	2, 850	176	75	0	0	0
1, 625	1, 650	5	0	2, 850	2, 875	179	79	0	0	0
1, 650	1, 675	9	0	2, 875	2, 900	183	82	0	0	0
1, 675	1, 700	12	0	2, 900	2, 925	187	86	0	0	0
1, 700	1, 725	16	0	2, 925	2, 950	191	89	0	0	0
1, 725	1, 750	19	0	2, 950	2, 975	194	93	0	0	0
1, 750	1, 775	23	0	2, 975	3, 000	198	96	0	0	0
1, 775	1, 800	26	0	3, 000	3, 050	204	102	4	0	0
1, 800	1, 825	30	0	3, 050	3, 100	211	109	11	0	0
1, 825	1, 850	33	0	3, 100	3, 150	219	116	18	0	0
1, 850	1, 875	37	0	3, 150	3, 200	226	123	25	0	0
1, 875	1, 900	40	0	3, 200	3, 250	234	130	32	0	0
1, 900	1, 925	44	0	3, 250	3, 300	241	137	39	0	0
1, 925	1, 950	47	0	3, 300	3, 350	249	144	46	0	0
1, 950	1, 975	51	0	3, 350	3, 400	256	151	53	0	0
1, 975	2, 000	54	0	3, 400	3, 450	264	159	60	0	0
2, 000	2, 025	58	0	3, 450	3, 500	271	166	67	0	0
2, 025	2, 050	61	0	3, 500	3, 550	279	174	74	0	0
2, 050	2, 075	65	0	3, 550	3, 600	286	181	81	0	0
2, 075	2, 100	68	0	3, 600	3, 650	294	189	88	0	0
2, 100	2, 125	72	0	3, 650	3, 700	302	196	95	0	0
2, 125	2, 150	75	0	3, 700	3, 750	310	204	102	4	0
2, 150	2, 175	79	0	3, 750	3, 800	318	211	109	11	0
2, 175	2, 200	82	0	3, 800	3, 850	326	219	116	18	0
2, 200	2, 225	86	0	3, 850	3, 900	334	226	123	25	0
2, 225	2, 250	89	0	3, 900	3, 950	342	234	130	32	0
2, 250	2, 275	93	0	3, 950	4, 000	350	241	137	39	0
2, 275	2, 300	96	0	4, 000	4, 050	358	249	144	46	0
2, 300	2, 325	100	2	4, 050	4, 100	365	256	151	53	0
2, 325	2, 350	103	5	4, 100	4, 150	372	264	159	60	0
2, 350	2, 375	107	9	4, 150	4, 200	379	271	166	67	0
2, 375	2, 400	110	12	4, 200	4, 250	386	279	174	74	0
2, 400	2, 425	114	16	4, 250	4, 300	394	286	181	81	0
2, 425	2, 450	117	19	4, 300	4, 350	401	294	189	88	0
2, 450	2, 475	121	23	4, 350	4, 400	408	302	196	95	0
2, 475	2, 500	124	26	4, 400	4, 450	415	310	204	102	4
2, 500	2, 525	128	30	4, 450	4, 500	422	318	211	109	11
2, 525	2, 550	131	33	4, 500	4, 550	430	326	219	116	18
2, 550	2, 575	135	37	4, 550	4, 600	437	334	226	123	25
2, 575	2, 600	138	40	4, 600	4, 650	444	342	234	130	32
2, 600	2, 625	142	44	4, 650	4, 700	451	350	241	137	39
2, 625	2, 650	146	47	4, 700	4, 750	459	358	249	144	46
2, 650	2, 675	149	51	4, 750	4, 800	467	366	256	151	53
2, 675	2, 700	153	54	4, 800	4, 850	474	374	264	159	60
2, 700	2, 725	157	58	4, 850	4, 900	482	382	271	166	67
2, 725	2, 750	161	61	4, 900	4, 950	490	390	279	174	74
2, 750	2, 775	164	65	4, 950	5, 000	497	398	286	181	81
2, 775	2, 800	168	68							

★ This table may also be used by certain widows or widowers who qualify for special tax rates.

held or paid during the year fall far short of what they actually owe. For those whose incomes are derived from sources other than wages and salaries, such as business earnings, professional services, or investments, there is no withholding for taxes. The law provides that certain taxpayers must, by April 15, when they file their final return for the previous year, report (on Form 1040–ES) an estimate of what they expect their income taxes for the current year will be, the amount they expect to be withheld from their income for the year, and the excess of estimated taxes over estimated withholding. Payments of this excess are due in quarterly installments on April 15 (when the income tax form is filed), June 15, September 15, and January 15. Taxpayers are required to file a

Table 16–2.

Schedule I. (A) Single Taxpayers Who Do Not Qualify for Rates in Schedules II and III, and (B) Married Taxpayers Filing Separate Returns

If the amount on line 5, Tax Computation Schedule, page 2, Form 1040–ES, is: / *Enter on line 6, Tax Computation Schedule:*

Not over $500............ 14% of the amount on line 5.

Over—	*But not over—*		*of excess over—*
$500	— $1,000....	$70, plus 15%	— $500
$1,000	— $1,500....	$145, plus 16%	— $1,000
$1,500	— $2,000....	$225, plus 17%	— $1,500
$2,000	— $4,000....	$310, plus 19%	— $2,000
$4,000	— $6,000....	$690, plus 22%	— $4,000
$6,000	— $8,000....	$1,130, plus 25%	— $6,000
$8,000	— $10,000...	$1,630, plus 28%	— $8,000
$10,000	— $12,000...	$2,190, plus 32%	— $10,000
$12,000	— $14,000...	$2,830, plus 36%	— $12,000
$14,000	— $16,000...	$3,550, plus 39%	— $14,000
$16,000	— $18,000...	$4,330, plus 42%	— $16,000
$18,000	— $20,000...	$5,170, plus 45%	— $18,000
$20,000	— $22,000...	$6,070, plus 48%	— $20,000
$22,000	— $26,000...	$7,030, plus 50%	— $22,000
$26,000	— $32,000...	$9,030, plus 53%	— $26,000
$32,000	— $38,000...	$12,210, plus 55%	— $32,000
$38,000	— $44,000...	$15,510, plus 58%	— $38,000
$44,000	— $50,000...	$18,990, plus 60%	— $44,000
$50,000	— $60,000...	$22,590, plus 62%	— $50,000
$60,000	— $70,000...	$28,790, plus 64%	— $60,000
$70,000	— $80,000...	$35,190, plus 66%	— $70,000
$80,000	— $90,000...	$41,790, plus 68%	— $80,000
$90,000	— $100,000..	$48,590, plus 69%	— $90,000
$100,000	....	$55,490, plus 70%	— $100,000

Table 16–3.

Schedule II. (A) Married Taxpayers Filing Joint Returns, and (B) Widows and Widowers Who Qualify for Special Tax Rates

If the amount on line 5, Tax Computation Schedule, page 2, Form 1040–ES, is: / *Enter on line 6, Tax Computation Schedule:*

Not over $1,000......... 14% of the amount on line 5.

Over—	*But not over—*		*of excess over—*
$1,000	— $2,000....	$140, plus 15%	— $1,000
$2,000	— $3,000....	$290, plus 16%	— $2,000
$3,000	— $4,000....	$450, plus 17%	— $3,000
$4,000	— $8,000....	$620, plus 19%	— $4,000
$8,000	— $12,000...	$1,380, plus 22%	— $8,000
$12,000	— $16,000...	$2,260, plus 25%	— $12,000
$16,000	— $20,000...	$3,260, plus 28%	— $16,000
$20,000	— $24,000...	$4,380, plus 32%	— $20,000
$24,000	— $28,000...	$5,660, plus 36%	— $24,000
$28,000	— $32,000...	$7,100, plus 39%	— $28,000
$32,000	— $36,000...	$8,660, plus 42%	— $32,000
$36,000	— $40,000...	$10,340, plus 45%	— $36,000
$40,000	— $44,000...	$12,140, plus 48%	— $40,000
$44,000	— $52,000...	$14,060, plus 50%	— $44,000
$52,000	— $64,000...	$18,060, plus 53%	— $52,000
$64,000	— $76,000...	$24,420, plus 55%	— $64,000
$76,000	— $88,000...	$31,020, plus 58%	— $76,000
$88,000	— $100,000..	$37,980, plus 60%	— $88,000
$100,000	— $120,000..	$45,180, plus 62%	— $100,000
$120,000	— $140,000..	$57,580, plus 64%	— $120,000
$140,000	— $160,000..	$70,380, plus 66%	— $140,000
$160,000	— $180,000..	$83,580, plus 68%	— $160,000
$180,000	— $200,000..	$97,180, plus 69%	— $180,000
$200,000	....	$110,980, plus 70%	— $200,000

declared estimate (unless they expect to owe less than $40 in taxes) and pay their current taxes at the time just indicated if:

1. Expected income *not* subject to withholding taxes is more than $200; or
2. Expected income *not* subject to withholding taxes is $200 or less, and

Taxpayer is	And gross income from all sources exceeds
Single	$ 5,000
Married (but not entitled to file a joint return)	5,000
Married (entitled to file a joint return)	10,000
Surviving spouse (spouse died within past two years)	10,000
Head of household	10,000

Naturally it is impossible in many cases to determine accurately in advance what the total tax bill for the year will be. But the government will not penalize the taxpayer unless his estimated tax is less than 70 per cent of what the actual figure turns out to be. If he underestimates by more than 30 per cent, the government will charge interest at the annual rate of 6 per cent on the difference between 70 per cent (66⅔ per cent for farmers) of the amount which should have been paid and the amount that was actually paid. As the year goes on, however, and he sees that he has greatly underestimated the amount of taxes due, the taxpayer may change the estimated tax from quarter to quarter.

JOINT RETURNS

Eight of the states have community property laws which provide that half of the husband's income belongs to the wife, and vice versa. Married people in these states had been enjoying a tax saving as compared to those who live in other states because, due to the progressive tax rates, the combined income tax on the husband's share and the wife's share of the income would be less in most instances than that which would have to be paid by the husband if he reported all the income in his own name.

In 1948, the federal income tax laws were changed to give people in the other states the same tax saving. To secure this saving it is necessary that the husband and wife file a joint return, in which the income of both is reported on the same form. When the joint filing first went into effect the combined taxable income of the husband and wife was "split" in half and the tax rate applied to the half, and then the result was multiplied by two. Since the tax rates are higher as the amount of the taxable income increases, the joint filing results in lower taxes because the taxes on the two halves would be at lower rates than if the tax were computed on the whole amount. At the present time it is not necessary to "split" the income when filing a joint return. The joint filing tax rate schedule made up by the government gives effect to this "split" income feature. The schedule for those filing separate returns indicates that the rate on the first $500 of taxable income is 14 per cent, and the rate on the next $500 is 15 per cent. Thus, a single person would pay a tax of $145 on a taxable income of $1,000. But the joint filing table indicates a tax rate of only 14 per cent on the first $1,000 of taxable income. So, a tax of only $140 would be paid under joint filing by a person with an income of $1,000. The difference in taxes between separate and joint filing, however, shows up more as the size of the income mounts. For example, a single person would pay a tax of $55,490 on a taxable income of $100,000, but a person filing jointly would pay a tax of only $45,180 on the same amount of income. This is a saving of $10,310 with the joint filing.

Joint Filing Details

The only two people who can file a joint return are husband and wife. If they are married any time during the year they may file a joint return for that year. If one of the spouses dies during the year the surviving spouse can file a joint return for that year. If husband and wife are divorced or legally separated on or before December 31, they cannot file a joint return for that year.

In a joint return all the income, exemptions, and deductions of both the husband and wife are included on the same tax form. A joint return may be filed even if the wife had no income for the year. Both husband and wife must sign the joint return, and the wife is responsible along with the husband for what is reported or not reported in the return.

If the taxpayer is married, files a return on Form 1040A, and does not compute his own tax, the government will compute the tax under both the separate and joint filing bases and charge him with the lesser of the two. If he computes his own tax on Form 1040A or Form 1040, he must decide whether to use the figures for the separate or joint filing. In practically all instances where the combined taxable income of the husband and wife is in excess of $500 it would be advisable to use the joint filing.

Widows and Widowers

Under certain conditions a taxpayer whose husband (or wife) has died during either of her two preceding taxable years may compute her tax by including only her income, exemptions, and deductions, but otherwise computing the tax as if a joint return had been filed. However, the exemption for the decedent may be claimed only for the year of death.

The conditions are that the taxpayer (a) must not have remarried, (b) must maintain as her home a household which is the principal place of abode of her child or stepchild for whom she is entitled to a deduction for an exemption, and (c) must have been entitled to file a joint return with her husband (or wife) for the year of death.

UNMARRIED HEAD OF HOUSEHOLD

An unmarried person or one separated from his spouse or divorced may be maintaining a home for himself and others and thus have about as much expense as a married person. But he cannot use the joint filing. Some years ago the laws were amended to tax the head of the household at rates that are about halfway between those paid under the separate and the joint filings.

To file as head of a household, the taxpayer must have furnished over half the cost of maintaining his home as a household and occupied it as a principal residence for himself along with (a) any related person for whom he is entitled to a deduction for an exemption or (b) his unmarried child, grandchild, or stepchild, even though such child is not a dependent or (3) his married child, grandchild, or stepchild for whom he is entitled to a deduction for an exemption. If his father or mother or both qualify as dependents, he may file as head of a household even though he maintains them in a different home. But if he maintains them in a nursing home, that is not considered to be the maintenance of a household.

The cost of maintaining a house includes such items as rent, property insurance, property taxes, mortgage interest, repairs, utilities, and cost of food. It does not include cost of clothing, education, medical treatment, vacations, life insurance, and transportation.

WHAT INCOME IS TAXABLE?

Generally speaking, all income received or earned during the year must be reported for tax purposes except the types of income which are specifically exempt by law. The income listed is the "gross income"—provision is made in the tax form for certain expenses, deductions, and exemptions. The following includes most of the different types of income that must be reported:

Wages, salaries, commissions, bonuses, fees, tips, and gratuities
Military pay
Profits from a business (unincorporated) or profession
Share of partnership profits
Interest from savings accounts and bonds and notes (except state and municipal bonds)
Dividends on stock
Rents and royalties
Profits from sale of real estate and securities
Industrial and civil service pensions (not social security)
Annuities
Contest prizes
Gambling winnings
Share of estate or trust income

The following types of income are exempt and therefore are not to be reported in the income tax return:

Interest from state and municipal bonds
Scholarships and fellowships
Gifts and inheritances
Workmen's compensation and damages for sickness and injury
Proceeds from health and accident insurance policies
Casualty insurance proceeds
Disability and death benefits
Social security benefits
Life insurance proceeds paid in a lump sum
Unemployment compensation
Railroad Retirement Act benefits
Government benefits to veterans and their families
Dividends on veterans' government life insurance

The total amount of wages or salaries earned is reported although the taxes may have been paid on them through withholding on the part of the employer. Later in the tax form credit is given for withheld taxes.

Gross wages or salary are reported even though the employer may have made deductions from salary for social security, insurance, savings bonds, pension fund, stock purchase plans, community fund, etc. Where an employee receives as part of his wages or salary such things as board and room, merchandise, or other things of value, he is supposed to report these items as income at their "fair market value."

Adjusted Gross Income

All of the includible items listed above go to make up total "gross income." The next step in determining taxes is to subtract from the gross income certain expenses or losses to arrive at the "adjusted gross income." Provision is made in several places in the tax form for the listing and subtracting of these items. Included in these expenses and losses that may be subtracted are the following:

Expenses of unincorporated business or profession
Expenses of rental property owned
Transportation expenses paid in connection with work
Travel expenses including board and room paid away from home (at least overnight) in connection with work
Losses incurred in sale of securities, real estate, and other types of property
Sick pay (if included in gross income, and subject to the limitations stated below)

A short explanation relating to the last item in the above list is necessary. Some employers have a wage continuation plan under which employees will be paid a specified amount per week while they are off the job because of illness or injury. In some instances the employee contributes part of the cost of the plan while in others the employer foots the entire bill. If the employee pays part of the cost, then he may deduct the amount of his pay during this period which is attributable to his share of the cost of the program. If the employer finances the plan, then the deduction of sick pay is subject to the following limitations (these apply to the first thirty calendar days the employee is absent from work due to illness or injury). If sick pay is more than 75 per cent of the employee's normal salary or wage, he cannot exclude any of his sick pay. If his sick pay is 75 per cent or less of his normal pay, then he may exclude his sick pay up to a maximum of $75 a week. But he cannot exclude the pay for the first seven calendar days of absence unless he is hospitalized at least one day during that absence. After he has been absent from work due to illness or injury for thirty days, he may exclude his sick pay up to a maximum of $100 a week. A space is provided on Form 1040 for the subtraction of allowable sick pay. Also, Form 2440 should be filed with the tax return, giving the details relating to the illness.

For most wage earners and those on salaries, the adjusted gross income would be the same as the total gross income. These would usually be different if a person is in business or if he has investments in real estate or securities.

The "adjusted gross income" is an important figure for several reasons. When a taxpayer has total income of less than $5,000 and files Form 1040A, or when he files Form 1040 and uses the tax table, the tax that is paid is the amount indicated opposite the particular adjusted gross income bracket in the tax table. When "deductions" are not itemized, the adjusted gross income may govern the amount of the standard deduction. When Form 1040A is filed and total income is $5,000 or more, or when Form 1040 (with tax computation) is filed, the "adjusted gross income" is the figure from which deductions and exemptions are subtracted in order to arrive at the taxable income.

AVERAGING YOUR INCOME

Professional people, artists, authors, professional athletes, and, in some instances, businessmen, will sometimes within one year have a much larger income than in previous or subsequent years. Due to the progressive tax rates, the percentage of the income that must be paid in income taxes for that particular year may be unusually high. Such persons may benefit considerably by taking advantage of the provision in the tax laws that permits averaging of the income. Since the typical taxpayer would not be interested in this procedure, we will here state only a few of the essentials relating to it.

Averaging of income is available to a person only to the extent that his income for the particular year is in excess of 133⅓ per cent of the average for the past four years. Furthermore, to be "averaged," the excess over the 133⅓ must be more than $3,000. The computation of the tax is complicated, but in general the following is done. Compute the tax on one fifth of the amount (the fifth is considered the top income) that can be "averaged" (the amount in excess of the 133⅓) and multiply this figure by 5. Add the amount of the tax thus computed on "averaged" income to the tax computed in the usual way on the income not subject to averaging.

Averaging of income cannot be applied to long-term capital gains, to *net income* received on property recently acquired as a gift or inheritance, or to gambling gains.

In general, averaging can be used by individuals (not corporations, estates, or trusts), including partners, shareholders, and beneficiaries.

TAX TREATMENT OF SELECTED SOURCES OF INCOME

Dividends

Generally speaking, all dividends paid in cash on corporate stock which represent a distribution of the net income or surplus of a company must be reported and are taxed as regular income. Dividends which are paid in property other than cash must also be reported as ordinary income at the market value of the property. If a stockholder has the option of taking a dividend in either cash or stock of the company, he must report the dividend as ordinary income even though he elects to receive the stock. If a dividend is paid in stock to the preferred stock in lieu of a cash dividend for the current or the preceding year it also is taxed as ordinary income. All other dividends paid in stock of the paying company do not have to be reported for taxation. But a dividend paid in stock (nontaxable) results in an adjustment in the "cost" of the stock for purposes of computing the capital gains tax upon the sale of the stock. Assume, for example, that a person paid $100 for a share of stock. Later a 100 per cent stock dividend is paid. This dividend is not taxable. This reduces the "cost" per share to $50. If a share of this stock is later sold for $70, a capital gains tax must be paid on the gain of $20 per share.

At least part of the dividend paid by many investment companies comes from a gain made by the company on the sale of some of its securities holdings. This is considered a *capital gain.* When the investment company shareholder receives such a dividend he reports it as a long-term capital gain. This will be discussed later in connection with capital gains.

When a shareholder receives part of his principal investment back from the company in the form of a dividend, it is not reported as income. Such dividends are often paid by "wasting asset" companies, such as mining companies. The amount of these dividends, however, is deducted from the cost of the share in order to arrive at an "adjusted" cost for the purpose of computing capital gains (or losses) upon sale of the shares.

"Dividends" paid at the end of the year to policyholders in mutual insurance companies or to veterans holding government life insurance are actually a return of part of the premium paid, and therefore are not reported as income for tax purposes.

Dividends paid by credit unions, mutual savings banks, and savings and loan associations are not reported as "dividends"; rather, they are reported as "interest."

It is commonly said that shareholders are doubly taxed. By this is meant that a corporation must pay the regular corporate income tax, and then on that part of the income which is paid out in dividends the shareholder must pay the personal income tax. (We will now be referring to dividends that are taxable as ordinary income.) The corporate shareholder receives a little relief from this double taxation through the *dividend exclusion.* The taxpayer may exclude from his taxable dividends received from domestic corporations the first $100 thereof. On a joint return the first $200 of dividends may be excluded if the securities giving rise to the dividends were jointly held by the husband and wife. If the husband and wife individually held the securities they may each exclude $100, provided each had that amount of dividend return. But if the husband's securities returned $120 and the wife's $25, only $125 may be excluded—$100 for the husband and $25 for the wife.

Corporations must report to the government all dividends and interest paid to taxpayers when the amount is in excess of $10 a year.

Interest

Practically all interest income received by a taxpayer must be reported for tax purposes. Thus interest which is received on all savings accounts or credited to savings accounts, and which may be withdrawn must be reported regardless of whether the interest is entered in the passbook. Dividends received on accounts in credit unions, mutual savings banks, and savings and loan associations must also be reported, the same as interest.

Interest received or accrued on all bonds directly issued by the United States Government are fully taxable. If income is reported on a cash basis (rather than the accrual basis) the taxpayer may elect to report the interest on Series E bonds in one of two ways. He may report the increase in the redemption value each year as income, or he may wait until he redeems the bond and then report the interest for the entire period he has held the bond as income for that particular year. The latter method is the easier way of doing it. Furthermore, the taxpayer may be retired at the time he cashes in the bonds and therefore he may be in a lower top-income bracket due to smaller total income. A college student, on the other hand, who has a relatively small income or none at all, would probably be ahead by reporting the income currently.

If the taxpayer is now deferring the reporting of income on Series E bonds until redemption and wants to switch over to reporting the increase in redemption value each year as income, he may do so without the necessity of obtaining permission from the government. In the year in which he makes the switch, however, he must report all the interest accrued on all Series E bonds, and this method must be continued in the future on the bonds then owned and any subsequently acquired, unless permission is obtained to change to the other method.

Although dividends paid by life insurance companies on participating policies are merely a return of part of the premium paid, and therefore not taxable, if the dividends are left with the company the interest earned on such dividends should be reported annually.

Rents and Royalties

Royalties received by authors and composers as compensation for their work must be reported. Rents ordinarily represent the income received by landlords for the use of their real estate. The total gross rental income is reported, but from this is deducted all expenses connected with the maintenance and repairs of the property. If an improvement is made to the property, such as the addition of another room, this cannot be charged off against the rent. Rather, it is considered to be a capital outlay and the cost of the improvement is added to the cost value of the property.

When property is rented, depreciation may be charged as an expense by the landlord even though there is no outlay of cash at the time for this item. Only the cost value of the house, and not the lot, can be depreciated. The remaining useful life of the house is determined and the cost value of the house is charged off over this period of time. Usually the straight-line method is used, which means the same amount of depreciation is charged each year. Other more complicated methods may be used if the property was acquired after January 1, 1954.

Assume that a person bought a piece of new rental property for $20,000. Possibly the lot alone was worth $4,000. That leaves $16,000 for the value of the house. If this is a new frame house its usable life may be determined to be forty years. Using the straight-line method, $400 depreciation could be charged off against the rent annually. The average useful life of various types of property is contained in a government booklet referred to as *Bulletin F*, which may be obtained from the Government Printing Office. These data may also be obtained from the tax services.

Capital Gains, Pensions, and Annuities

Due to the special nature of income from capital gains, pensions, and annuities, these sources of income will be discussed after we have completed a description of deductions and exemptions.

Other Income

Any other source of income such as from estates and trusts, alimony, prizes, etc., must also be reported.

DEDUCTIONS

Deductions are the amount that may be subtracted from income to cover such items as contributions to charity, interest expenses, taxes, medical and dental expenses, and casualty losses to the extent permitted.

If the taxpayer reports on Form 1040 and uses the tax table, or has total income of less than $5,000 and uses Form 1040A, the tax tables used in computing his tax automatically allow a "standard deduction." If his income is $5,000 or more and he reports on Form 1040A, he is allowed a "standard deduction."

If he reports on Form 1040, he may either list his actual deductions or take a standard deduction. If actual deductions exceed the amount of the standard deduction, he should list or itemize the deductions since this will result in lower taxes. But if the standard deduction allows more than was actually expended for the "deduction items," then the standard deduction should be taken. If adjusted gross income is less than $5,000, the tax table must be used to take the standard deduction.

The Standard Deduction

A taxpayer may take a standard deduction of an amount equivalent to 10 per cent of his adjusted gross income, up to a maximum of $1,000 ($500 for a married person filing a separate return). Beginning in 1964, a taxpayer may use a "minimum standard deduction" in lieu of the 10 per cent standard deduction (which he would elect to do if it gave him a larger deduction). The minimum standard deduction is $300 ($200 for a married person filing a separate return) plus $100 for each exemption (exemptions are explained later in the chapter) over one. This minimum standard deduction is also subject to the "maximum" of $1,000 ($500 for a married person filing a separate return).

Example: Williams is married, has two dependent children, and earns $5,000 (adjusted gross income) a year. The 10-per-cent rule would give him a deduction of $500. But the minimum standard deduction would amount to $600 ($300 plus 3 times $100). He would thus elect the latter.

The tax table (such as the one shown in Table 16–1) gives effect to deductions being computed by the method which gives the larger amount, and thus the lower tax.

It should again be noted that if a person's actual deductions are more than the standard deduction, he should list his deductions on Form 1040, and thus get the benefit of a lower tax.

We will now discuss the various "deduction" items. (These "deductions" should be distinguished from the items that may be subtracted from the total gross income to arrive at the adjusted gross income. This was discussed above.)

Contributions

Generally speaking, a taxpayer may deduct the amount of his contributions to religious, charitable, educational, scientific, or literary organizations, and organizations for the prevention of cruelty to children and animals, unless the organization is operated for personal profit or conducts propaganda or otherwise attempts to influence legislation. Gifts made to fraternal organizations may also be deducted if they are to be used for one or more of the purposes just enumerated. For the gift to be deductible, the organization must be organized or created in the United States or its possessions, or under the laws of the United States. Gifts made to individuals may not be deducted regardless of how worthy the purpose may be. The following illustrate the types of gifts that may and may not be deducted.

Deductible: Gifts to
Churches and temples
Salvation Army
Red Cross and united funds
Non-profit schools and hospitals
Veterans' organizations
Boy Scouts, Girl Scouts, and similar organizations
Non-profit organizations primarily engaged in conducting research or education for the alleviation and cure of such diseases as tuberculosis, cancer, multiple sclerosis, muscular dystrophy, cerebral palsy, poliomyelitis, diabetes, and diseases of the heart, etc.

Non-deductible: Gifts to
Relatives, friends, and other individuals
Political organizations or candidates
Social clubs
Labor unions
Chambers of commerce
Propaganda organizations

In general, deductions for contributions may not exceed 20 per cent of adjusted gross income. However, this limitation may be increased to 30 per cent if the extra 10 per cent consists of contributions to churches, a convention or association of churches, tax-exempt educational institutions, tax-exempt hospitals, certain medical research organizations, and in general, publicly supported charitable organizations such as Red Cross, American Cancer Society, or Community Chests. Of course the total of 30 per cent could be given to these organizations alone. Gifts of the "30 per cent type" which cannot be deducted in the particular year because they exceed 30 per cent of adjusted gross income may be carried over for a five-year period. Allowable gifts made in property other than cash may be deducted (within the limitations) at their fair value at the time of making the gift.

Interest

In general, interest paid on debts may be listed as a deduction. This would of course include interest on the following types of obligations:

Loans from banks, consumer finance companies, and credit unions
Home loans and other real estate loans
Indebtedness for installment purchase of goods
Loans on life insurance policies (with some exceptions)

The largest interest payment made by most people is that on their home mortgage. Most home mortgages are paid off on the installment plan, on a monthly basis. The total monthly payment includes payment on the principal and, in some instances, payment for taxes and insurance. These items, however, may not be listed as a deduction under the caption of "interest" (real estate taxes may be deducted under "taxes"). Only that part of the payment which represents interest may be deducted. If mortgage interest is being paid on property which is rented out, the interest on the mortgage should be deducted from the rent rather than listed as a deduction, since the taxpayer may save in taxes by taking the standard deduction rather than itemizing the deductions. In this way he gets his deduction and still saves taxes on the rent income. If interest is paid on a home mortgage on a double house, half of which is rented, then one half the interest should be deducted from the rental income.

In connection with installment purchases, if the amount of the interest is specifically stated, then that is the amount that would be deducted. But in many instances it is not clear as to the amount of the interest payment since there may be other carrying charges in addition to interest. When this is the case the law permits a deduction as interest of an amount equivalent to 6 per cent of the average monthly balance under the contract. The average monthly balance is computed by adding up the unpaid balance at the beginning of each month and dividing by 12. (The figure 12 is used regardless of the number of months paid.)

The typical taxpayer will not be confronted with the situations in which interest cannot be listed as a deduction. Following are a few examples of non-deductible interest:

Interest paid to buy tax-exempt securities
Interest paid on a loan to purchase a single premium life insurance pol-

icy, or one where substantially all the premiums are paid within four years
Interest paid on the debt of another person for which the taxpayer had no liability
Interest added to the principal of a life insurance policy loan
Interest paid on a gambling debt

Taxes

It is rather difficult to generalize on what taxes may be listed as a deduction and what ones may not, but the following statement is fairly accurate: State and local taxes may be deducted but federal taxes may not be deducted. The following lists may be helpful.

Deductible state and local taxes:
Gasoline (state only)
Income (state and city only)
Personal property
Real estate
Sales

Non-deductible state and local taxes:
Admission fees
Alcoholic beverages
Auto and drivers' license
Boat license
Cigarettes and tobacco
Dog license
Hunting and fishing licenses
Water

Non-deductible federal taxes:
Excise taxes on such things as telephone, cigarettes, and tobacco
Tax on automobiles
Income tax
Estate and gift taxes
Social security taxes
Medicare taxes

Medical and Dental Expenses

Medical and dental expenses and cost of medicines and drugs for a taxpayer, his spouse, and any dependent who received over half his support from him may be listed as a deduction, subject to the limitations which follow. Any reimbursement for the expenses, such as through insurance, reduces to that extent the amount that may be deducted. The procedure for computing the part of the total medical and dental expenses which may be deductible is as follows. List in the appropriate place on

Form 1040 the cost of medicines and drugs in excess of 1 per cent of adjusted gross income. Then add to this other medical and dental expenses. The amount which can be deducted is only that part of the total expenses which is in excess of 3 per cent of adjusted gross income. Assume, for example, that a taxpayer has an adjusted gross income of $7,000, that his medicine and drug expenses for the year amount to $80, and that his other medical and dental expenses are $300. The total that he may deduct for all these expenses is $100. The computation for this is shown below in the schedule which is taken from Form 1040 ("line 9, page 1" refers to the adjusted gross income).

PART IV.—ITEMIZED DEDUCTIONS—Use only if you do not use tax table or standard deduction.

Medical and dental expense.—Attach itemized list. Do not enter any expense compensated by insurance or otherwise. NOTE: If you or your wife are 65 or over, or if either has a dependent parent 65 or over, see page 8 of instructions for possible larger deduction.

1. Enter excess, if any, of medicine and drugs over 1% of line 9, page 1	10	00
2. Other medical, dental expenses (include hospital insurance premiums)	300	00
3. Total (add lines 1 and 2)	310	00
4. Enter 3% of line 9, page 1 (see note above) .	210	00
5. Subtract line 4 from line 3; see page 8 of instructions for maximum limitation	100	00

If either the taxpayer or his wife is 65 or over, however, he may list the total medicine and drug expenses (not just the amount that exceeds 1 per cent of adjusted gross income). Also, he may (subject to the limitations stated below) deduct the total medical and dental expenses (not just the part that exceeds 3 per cent of adjusted gross income). What has just been stated relative to deductible medicine and drug expenses and medical and dental expenses applies to those expenses of dependent parents (of either the taxpayer or his wife) 65 or over even if the taxpayer is under 65.

Generally speaking, the maximum that may be deducted for medicines, drugs, and other medical and dental expenses is $5,000 multiplied by the number of exemptions (explained later) claimed on the tax form (other than for age and blindness). This, however, is subject to the following limits on the total medical and dental deductions:

$10,000 on a separate return
$20,000 on a joint return, or a return filed as a surviving spouse or as a head of household
$20,000 if either the taxpayer or his wife is 65 *and* disabled; $40,000 on a joint return if both taxpayer and wife are 65 or over and disabled (but no more than $20,000 for each spouse's expenses)

With respect to the types of medicines and drugs that may be deducted as expenses, about the only limitation is that they be legal medicines and drugs. Whether a prescription is required to purchase them makes no difference. Such things as toothpaste, toilet articles, or cosmetics, however, may not be deducted.

Under medical expenses, amounts paid for the prevention, cure, correction, or treatment of a physical or mental defect or illness are deductible. This includes payments not only to doctors of medicine, but also to chiropodists, chiropractors, oculists, opticians, optometrists, osteopaths, podiatrists, practical nurses (for actual medical services), psychiatrists, and registered nurses. Payments for various types of medical and laboratory examinations and tests, including blood tests and X ray, both in and out of a hospital, can be deducted. Various types of hospital services, including board and room, anesthetist, oxygen, use of operating room, and vaccines, can be deducted. Equipment and supplies needed because of illness, injury, or physical defects can be deducted. These include payments for ambulance, artificial teeth and eyes, back supports, braces, crutches, elastic hosiery, eyeglasses, hearing aids, invalid chair, iron lung, orthopedic shoes, sacroiliac belt, splints, and trusses. Costs of medical treatments including payments for blood transfusion, diathermy, electric shock treatments, insulin treatments, nursing, prenatal and postnatal treatments, psychotherapy, radium, whirlpool baths, and X ray can be deducted.

Traveling expenses may be deducted as medical expenses under certain circumstances, as follows:

- To visit a specialist in another city
- A trip prescribed to relieve a specific ailment, such as to Arizona or Florida for the relief of arthritis
- Travel to and from a doctor's office

The following types of travel expenses may not be deducted:

- Travel for the general improvement of health
- Travel to a particular place for medical treatment if the treatment can be obtained locally
- Living expenses, including board and room, while on a trip for medical treatment, even if the travel expenses are deductible
- Travel to a place for "spiritual aid" rather than medical help

Practically all types of dental expenses including X rays and cleaning of teeth are deductible to the extent indicated above.

Premiums paid for hospitalization and surgery insurance, such as Blue Cross and Blue Shield, or for medical insurance are deductible. On health and accident insurance (including auto), only that part of the premium which covers the medical or hospital expenses can be deducted. The part of the premium that compensates for loss of earnings while incapacitated cannot be deducted. The taxpayer's insurance company can tell him what part of his premium is deductible. That portion of a medical bill for which the taxpayer is reimbursed through insurance cannot be deducted.

The following are not considered to be medical expenses and therefore their costs cannot be deducted: funeral, burial, cremation, cemetery lot, monument, or mausoleum.

Other Deductions

The tax form specifically provides for deductions for contributions, interest, taxes, and medical and dental expenses. The final section for listing deductions is simply called "other deductions."

Casualties and Theft. Casualty and theft losses of individuals (nonbusiness) can be deducted only to the extent the loss from *each* casualty or theft exceeds $100. To the extent that a loss is covered by insurance, it cannot be deducted.[3] Deductible casualty losses must result from some sudden and destructive force such as would result from action of natural physical forces or other sudden or unexpected cause. The following lists should prove helpful in deciding what types of losses are deductible:

Deductible losses:

Property such as a home, clothing, or automobile destroyed or damaged by fire

Loss or damage of property by heavy rains, flood, lightning, storm, hurricane, tornado, cyclone, landslides, earthquake, drought, freezing, explosion, termites (when damage is sudden), or airplane crash

Damage to an automobile resulting from icy roads, or from a collision when it is not due to owner's willful negligence

Theft of cash, jewelry, automobile, clothing, furniture or other personal property

Non-deductible losses:

Personal injury to oneself or another person

Accidental loss of cash or other personal property

Property lost in transit or in storage

Damage by rust or gradual erosion, or from termites over a long period of time

Animals or plants damaged or destroyed by disease

Expenses for Care of Children. A deduction is allowed in certain instances for payments made for care of children. A taxpayer may deduct (not to exceed a $600 total) for expenses paid by a woman or widower

[3] For people carrying "$100 deductible" automobile collision insurance it is thus apparent that on collision damages of $100 or less no insurance can be collected, and the amount cannot be listed as a deduction.

(including men who are divorced or legally separated under a decree and who have not remarried) for the care of one dependent ($900 for two or more dependents), if such care is to enable the taxpayer to be gainfully employed or actively seek gainful employment. For this purpose the term "dependent" does not ordinarily include the husband (wife) of the taxpayer and is limited to the following persons for whom the taxpayer is entitled to a deduction for an exemption: a person under 13 years of age, or a person who is physically or mentally incapable of caring for himself. If the payment for child care, however, is made to a person for whom the taxpayer claimed an exemption then the deduction is not allowed.

Unless her husband is incapacitated, the deduction is allowed to a working wife only if she files a joint return with her husband; the deduction is reduced by the amount (if any) by which their combined adjusted income exceeds $6,000.

Example: A qualifying working wife who has a joint adjusted gross income (including husband's income) of $6,400 pays $1,200 a year for the care of two qualifying children. The $900 deduction is reduced by $400 (the amount of the income in excess of $6,000), which leaves an actual deduction of only $500.

If a husband files a joint return, he can list a "child-care" deduction for a wife who has been incapacitated for at least ninety consecutive days (or until her prior death). This deduction would also be reduced by an amount by which their joint income exceeded $6,000. If the wife is institutionalized for at least ninety consecutive days (or until her prior death) the deduction would not be reduced even if the income exceeded $6,000.

Education Expenses. Expenses for education may be deducted if the education was undertaken primarily for the purpose of: maintaining or improving skills required in employment or other trade or business, or meeting the requirements of an employer, or the requirements of applicable law or regulations, imposed as a condition of the retention of salary, status, or employment.

Expenses incurred for the purpose of obtaining a new position, a substantial advancement in position, or for personal purposes are not deductible. The expenses incurred in preparing for a trade or business or specialty are personal expenses and are not deductible.

Employee Business Expenses. If a taxpayer works for wages or a salary, he may deduct ordinary and necessary business expenses connected with his work.

Deductible business expenses:

Safety equipment
Dues to union or professional societies

Entertaining customers
Tools, supplies and special uniforms
Fees to employment agencies

Non-deductible business expenses:
Travel to and from work
Entertaining friends
Bribes and illegal payments

Expenses To Produce Income. Expenses connected with earning income through securities or real estate are deductible to the extent that they are necessary for the conservation and management of the property or to the collection of the investment income. Thus the various expenses incurred with renting of real estate are deductible. The same is true of amounts paid for investment advisory services, such as Standard & Poor's, Moody's, or The Value Line Investment Survey. The cost of a safe-deposit box is deductible if the box is used for the safekeeping of securities. (But it is non-deductible if rented for the storage of jewelry or valuable papers other than securities.)

The expenses of acquiring and maintaining an automobile for purely personal pleasure cannot be deducted by the taxpayer. (It was pointed out above, however, that amounts paid for state gasoline taxes, and interest on money borrowed to purchase a car may be deducted.) If a person uses his automobile for business purposes, then all the costs, including depreciation, may be deducted. If an automobile is used partly for pleasure but partly for business purposes, all the costs incident to the business use may be deducted. For example, if it is used 25 per cent of the time for business, then 25 per cent of the costs may be deducted. Taxpayers who use their automobile in connection with renting real estate may deduct the proportion of the costs that can be attributable to this use.

Alimony Payments. Payments of alimony or separate maintenance made under a court decree may be deducted. The wife or ex-wife must report these amounts as income in her tax return. The following, however, may not be deducted: voluntary payments to the wife not under a court order, lump-sum settlement to the wife, or maintenance payments for the support of minor children.

EXEMPTIONS

The next step in determining the amount of income taxes after subtracting the amount of deductions is to subtract the amount allowed for *exemptions*. For each exemption claimed, the taxpayer is permitted to subtract $600 from his income.

Taxpayer as an Exemption

Every taxpayer is permitted to count himself as an exemption. If the taxpayer is 65 or older he gets another exemption for himself, thus making a total of two exemptions. If he is blind he is entitled to one additional exemption. Thus if he is 65 or older and also blind he can claim three exemptions.

Spouse as an Exemption

A taxpayer is allowed one exemption for his wife (husband) if he (she) files a joint return. If he files a separate return he may claim her as an exemption only if she had no income for the year and did not receive more than half her support from another taxpayer. If the wife can be claimed as an exemption, then additional exemptions may be claimed for her if she is 65 or older or if she is blind. Thus a husband and wife both 65 or older who file a joint return can claim four exemptions (six if both are blind) or a total of $2,400 ($3,600 if both are blind) in exemptions.

Children as Exemptions

The taxpayer is entitled to one exemption for each child (including a stepchild, or legally adopted child), if during the taxable year, the child:

1. Received less than $600 gross income (unless the child was under 19 or was a student, in which case the limitation does not apply), and
2. Received more than half of his or her support from the taxpayer (or from husband or wife if a joint return is filed), and
3. Did not file a joint return with her husband (or his wife), and
4. Was either a citizen or resident of the United States or a resident of Canada, Mexico, the Republic of Panama, or the Canal Zone; or was an alien child adopted by and living with a United States citizen abroad.

In regard to what constitutes *support,* this is defined to include food, shelter, clothing, medical and dental care, education, and the like. Generally, the amount of an item of support will be the amount of expense incurred by the one furnishing such item. If the item of support furnished by an individual is in the form of property or lodging, it will be necessary to measure the amount of such item of support in terms of its fair market value. In computing the amount of support, include amounts contributed by the dependent for his own support and also amounts ordinarily excludable from gross income. In figuring whether more than half of his support is provided for a student, disregard amounts received by him as scholarships.

As noted above, a child may be claimed as an exemption even if he or she makes $600 or more a year, provided he (she) is a student. A student is defined in the law as an individual who, during each of five calendar months during the year, is a full-time student at an educational institution, or is pursuing a full-time course of institutional on-farm training under the supervision of an accredited agent of an educational institution or of a state, or a political subdivision of a state.

Other Exemptions

In addition to his wife and children, the taxpayer is entitled to one exemption for each other dependent who meets all the following requirements for the year:

1. Received less than $600 gross income, and
2. Received more than half of his or her support from the taxpayer (or from husband or wife if a joint return is filed) (see definition of support), and
3. Did not file a joint return with her husband (or his wife), and
4. Was either a citizen or resident of the United States or a resident of Canada, Mexico, the Republic of Panama or the Canal Zone, and
5. Either (a) for the entire taxable year had the taxpayer's home as his principal place of abode and was a member of the household; or (b) was related to the taxpayer (or to husband or wife if a joint return is filed) in one of the following ways:

Mother	Stepbrother	Son-in-law
Father	Stepsister	Daughter-in-law
Grandmother	Stepmother	*The following if*
Grandfather	Stepfather	*related by blood:*
Brother	Mother-in-law	Uncle
Sister	Father-in-law	Aunt
Grandson	Brother-in-law	Nephew
Granddaughter	Sister-in-law	Niece

COMPUTING TAX

The procedures for determining taxes when filing Form 1040A and Form 1040 with use of tax tables were described above. If the tax tables are not used, the amount due in taxes is computed on Form 1040. The completion of the section of Form 1040 shown here can be illustrated with the following example. Assume that a married couple with one dependent minor child has a total gross income of $11,000 for the year, and that they file a joint return and take the standard deduction of $1,000. We will further assume that they have nothing to subtract from their gross income to arrive at their adjusted gross income (which is the typical case). After subtracting the deduction of $1,000 and the exemptions totaling $1,800, there is a *taxable income* of $8,200. Table 16–3, which is taken from the instruction booklet furnished by the government, shows that the tax on this amount of income is $1,424. If a single person with only himself as an exemption had an adjusted gross income of $11,000 and he took the standard deduction of $1,000, his *taxable income* would be $9,400. Table 16–2 shows that his tax would be $2,022. Those reporting as head of a household would use another schedule of tax rates (not shown here) which are lower than for separate returns but higher than for joint returns.

● Attach Copy B of Form W-2 Here ●

	INCOME—If joint return, include all income of both husband and wife	
	5. Wages, salaries, tips, etc. If not shown on attached Forms W–2 attach explanation	$ 11,000 00
	6. Other income (from line 9, Part II, page 2)	
	7. Total (add lines 5 and 6)	11,000 00
	8. Adjustments (from line 5, Part III, page 2)	
	9. Total income (subtract line 8 from line 7)	11,000 00
	FIGURE TAX BY USING EITHER 10 OR 11	
TAX COMPUTATION	10. Tax Table—If you do not itemize deductions and line 9 is less than $5,000, find your tax from tables in instructions. Do not use lines 11 a, b, c, or d. Enter tax on line 12.	
	11. Tax Rate Schedule—	
	a. If you itemize deductions, enter total from Part IV, page 2 If you do not itemize deductions, and line 9 is $5,000 or more enter the larger of: (1) 10 percent of line 9 or; (2) $200 ($100 if married and filing separate return) plus $100 for each exemption claimed on line 4, above. The deduction computed under (1) or (2) is limited to $1,000 ($500 if married and filing separate return).	1,000 00
	b. Subtract line 11a from line 9	10,000 00
	c. Multiply total number of exemptions on line 4, above, by $600	1,800 00
	d. Subtract line 11c from line 11b. (Figure your tax on this amount by using tax rate schedule on page 10 of instructions. Enter tax on line 12.)	8,200 00
	TAX—CREDITS—PAYMENTS	
	12. Tax (from either Tax Table, line 10, or Tax Rate Schedule, line 11)	1,424 00

CAPITAL GAINS AND LOSSES

Capital gains and losses are those which arise through the sale of capital assets. We will concern ourselves with the sale of assets which are not used in a business. Capital assets are of two different types: non-income-producing assets, and income-producing assets. Examples of non-income-producing assets are a home and an automobile. If a home or an automobile is sold for more than was paid for them (unlikely in the case of the automobile), the profit made should be reported as a capital gain. (More will be said later about the sale of a home.) But if a loss is sustained upon their sale, the loss cannot be deducted.

Examples of income-producing assets are stocks, bonds, and rental property (assuming the taxpayer is not in the real estate business). Profits made on the sale of such assets are reported as capital gains and any losses experienced upon their sale are reported as capital losses.

Reporting Capital Gains and Losses

To simplify the discussion, we will confine ourselves to income-producing capital assets. Capital gains and losses are of two types: short-term and long-term. A short-term capital gain or loss is one experienced on capital assets that are held for only six months or less. If the asset is held for more than six months before it is sold, the gain or loss is considered long-term. In general it is said that 100 per cent of any short-term capital gain or loss is reported, but that only 50 per cent of a long-term capital gain or loss is reported. But this is not an accurate statement. The following is the procedure for reporting capital gains and losses.

The short-term gains and losses for the year are balanced against each other to obtain the net short-term capital gain or loss. Then the long-term capital gains and losses (both at 100 per cent) are merged to obtain the net long-term capital gain or loss. The net long-term gain or loss is then added to (or subtracted from) the net short-term gain or loss to determine the net capital gain or loss. If the net long-term gain is more than the net short-term loss, only 50 per cent of the difference must be reported. But if the net short-term gain is more than the net long-term loss, 100 per cent of the difference must be reported. If, however, a net loss results, regardless of whether it is a net short-term or net long-term loss, all of the loss up to a maximum of $1,000 for the year can be deducted from ordinary income. If the net loss is more than $1,000, the excess can be carried forward and can be deducted from any future net capital gains. In addition, $1,000 of the loss can be deducted annually from ordinary income in future years. If there is both a net long-term gain and a net short-term gain, 50 per cent of the net long-term gain and 100 per cent of the net short-term gain are reported. The following examples, listed in the same order as described above, illustrate the amount to be reported as capital gains or losses under the circumstances indicated.

	Long-Term		Short-Term			
	Gain	Loss	Gain	Loss	Pay Tax On	Carry-Over to Later Years
(1)	$2,000	$1,000	$ 250	$ 500	$ 375	
(2)	250	500	2,000	1,000	750	
(3)	250	500	1,000	2,000		250 (loss)
(4)	500	250	2,000	1,000	1,125	

In (3) above, $1,000 of the loss could be charged off in the current year against other income. In determining capital gains and losses, brokers' commissions are added to the cost of the asset and the commissions are subtracted from the selling price of the asset.

Capital gains and losses are reported on separate Schedule D of Form 1040. Although the computations above may appear complex, by entering the capital gains and losses in the proper place in the Schedule the procedure prescribed in the tax form will result in an easy computation of the proper amount of gains or losses. The amount of the gains or losses is then carried to Form 1040 proper and it is added to or subtracted from other income.

If a taxpayer has a taxable income (after deductions and exemptions) of more than $26,000 on a separate return or more than $52,000 on a joint return he would be interested in using the "alternative" method of reporting his net long-term capital gains. Incomes in excess of the amounts just indicated are taxed at rates in excess of 50 per cent. Thus by reporting 50 per cent of a net long-term gain and being taxed at a rate in excess of 50 per cent the result would be that the taxpayer would be paying a tax in excess of 25 per cent of the net long-term gain. The "alternative" method of handling a net long-term capital gain (the excess of the long-term gain over the net short-term loss, or the entire gain if there is a net long-term capital gain only) results in the taxpayer's paying a tax of only 25 per cent on the entire net long-term capital gain. It is because of this alternative method that it is said that the maximum tax on a long-term capital gain is 25 per cent. Schedule D provides a place for the use of the alternative method.

Because of the distinction made between short- and long-term capital gains and losses, a person should watch the timing of his sales. If a particular stock is held for five months and sold at a profit, the entire amount of such profit is taxed, but if the sale is postponed for another month, only 50 per cent of the profit will be taxed.

Many people attempt to make their profits through an appreciation in the value of the stock rather than from the dividend return because of the difference in taxes. The total amount of the dividends, less the exclusion, is taxable, but only 50 per cent of the gain made from the sale of a stock which is held for more than six months is reported (with a maximum tax of 25 per cent of the gain). For persons in the higher brackets the difference is appreciable.

PROFIT ON SALE OF A HOME

If a person sells his home for more than he paid for it, the profit (less selling costs), except under circumstances stated below, is to be reported as a capital gain. If it is sold for less than the purchase price, however, the loss cannot be deducted. The factor of depreciation is ignored in either case. If the house was rented at the time of sale, any gain is reported as a capital gain, but the full amount of any loss is reported, and depreciation must be taken into account from the time the house was rented until it was sold, before computing the gain or loss. In determining the gain or loss on sale of property which has been inherited, the tax valuation at the time of the death of the person from whom it is inherited is taken as the cost price. Some people feel that it is desirable to have a low appraisal put on inherited property in order to reduce the inheritance taxes. But if it is contemplated that the property will be sold, it would be desirable to have a relatively high valuation. Any amount realized above the appraised value of inherited property must be reported as a capital gain on the income tax blank, and the income tax rates are much higher for most people than the inheritance tax.

If a homeowner sells his home at a profit, but buys a new home for as much or more than he received for his old one, the profit made on the old home will not have to be reported as income if the new home is purchased and occupied within a year before the sale or within a year after the sale. If he is building the home rather than buying an existing one, he must occupy it within a year before the sale or within eighteen months after the sale. If the new home is subsequently sold for enough to realize some of the profit not reported when the old home was sold, then it must be reported upon the sale of the new home, unless the profit is put into still another home. The following example illustrates the rule.

Let us assume that a person paid $8,000 for a home and after some years sells it for $15,000. If he purchases a new home for $15,000 within the time limitation stated before, none of the $7,000 profit will have to be reported. If, however, the new home is later sold for $18,000 and the proceeds are not invested in another home, a capital gain of $10,000 must be reported. It should be noted that the rule we have been discussing applies only to a house used as a home, and not to rental property.

In determining the amount of profit made on the sale of a home, broker's commissions and expenses incurred in putting the property in shape to sell, such as painting and papering, for example, may be deducted from the selling price in order to arrive at an "adjusted" selling price. Furthermore, the expenses must have been incurred within ninety days prior to the sale and paid for within thirty days after the sale. The costs of permanent improvements, such as a furnace, for example, cannot be deducted as a "fix-up" expense.

Break for Senior Citizens

If a person 65 or over sells his home at a profit he may not have to pay any tax on the gain even if he does not reinvest the profit in a new home. To get this relief he must have used the property as his principal residence for at least five of the eight years immediately before the sale. If the adjusted selling price (selling price less fix-up expenses incurred within ninety days prior to the sale and paid for within thirty days after the sale), is $20,000 or less, any profit does not have to be reported. If the adjusted selling price is more than $20,000 the profit (if any) is tax-free in the ratio that $20,000 is to the adjusted selling price.

Example: Mr. Henry made a gain of $9,000 when he sold his home for $30,000. $6,000 of the gain $\left(\frac{\$20{,}000}{\$30{,}000} \times \$9{,}000\right)$, is tax-free. If he bought a new home a year before or a year after the sale (the rule discussed in the above section), and paid at least $24,000 (adjusted selling price of $30,000 less tax-free gain of $6,000) for it, no tax would be paid on any of the gain.

If the home is jointly owned by husband and wife and they file a joint return, only one of them needs to be 65 or older to qualify for this favored tax position. If only part of the property is used as a residence, the tax relief applies to only that portion of the gain which is derived from the residence itself. The rule applies also to co-op apartments and condominiums.

To secure the tax relief just discussed the taxpayer must "elect" to have the profit so treated in a manner fixed by the Internal Revenue Regulations. Such election, however, is available only once during his lifetime. But if he thinks he may want to use the election again, he may revoke the election, provided he does so within three years from the year of sale of the house.

MOVING EXPENSES

According to the law, if a new employee is reimbursed for moving expenses, he is supposed to report this as taxable income. But he can deduct the amount of his moving expenses from his gross income. An old employee (as contrasted to a new employee) is not required to list his reimbursed moving expenses as income, and he is permitted to deduct the amount of his unreimbursed moving expenses. Since these deductions are from the gross income, the taxpayer benefits even if he takes the "standard deduction."

Moving expenses may be deducted only if the change in job location would have required at least twenty miles of additional commuting if the employee had not changed his residence.

In order to deduct unreimbursed expenses (but not reimbursed expenses), the taxpayer must be employed full-time in the general vicinity of the new job location for thirty-nine weeks during the twelve months following the move.

"Moving expenses" is interpreted to mean only the expenses of moving household goods and personal effects, and the expenses of the employee and his family for traveling (including meals and room) from the old home to the new one.

INCOME FROM ANNUITIES AND PENSIONS

The tax status of income from annuities and pensions is difficult to understand because some types are tax exempt, some are fully taxable, and some are partly taxable. Payments received from social security or from veterans' pensions are not subject to taxation. If an employee contributes nothing toward the purchase of an annuity or pension and his employer paid for the entire amount, then all the payments received from this annuity or pension are fully taxable. This is referred to as a noncontributory annuity or pension. The tax status of other types of annuities and pensions becomes complex.

If the employer contributes part of the cost and the employee contributes part, and if the amount contributed by the employee will be completely recovered by him within three years from the date the first payment is received, then the payments received by the employee are not taxable until he has recovered his contribution in full. But the entire amount received is fully taxable after the full cost to the employee has been received. If, on the other hand, the employee will not recover his entire cost within three years from the date of the first payment received by him, then the tax status is the same as for other types of annuities which will now be explained.

Most annuities and pensions are not of the types just described. Usually the employee will not recover his entire contribution within three years. Also, commonly, the employee and the employer both contribute toward the purchase of the annuity or pension. Or, the employer pays the cost but the amount paid by him must be reported as taxable income by the employee. The income received from such annuities and pensions is partly tax exempt and partly taxable. This is due to the fact that part of the payments received are a return of the investment or the cost, and of course this part is not taxable. But the part of the payment received that represents interest or a return on the investment is taxable.

The first step in determining the taxes that must be paid on the amounts received is to establish the amount of the total investment, or in other words, the net cost of the contract. This is the sum of all the premiums paid (less any dividends received). It includes the amount paid by the employee and the amount paid by the employer which had to be included in the taxable income of the employee at the time of the payment of the premium.

The next step is to determine the amount of the expected return over the years from the annuity or pension. If the employee or his beneficiary is to receive the payments for a fixed period of years—such as ten years—after the annuity payments begin, then the expected return is found by multiplying the annual payments to be received by the number of years it is to be paid, in this case ten years. If the annuity payments are to be received for life, then the annual payments to be received are multiplied by the number of years of life expectancy after the annuity payments begin—this can be ascertained from tables provided by the Internal Revenue Service.

Having determined the total investment and the total expected return, the next step is to figure out what percentage of the annual payments to be received represents a return of the investment. This can be found by dividing the amount of the investment in the contract by the total expected return. This percentage remains the same over the life of the contract regardless of whether the person receiving the payments lives a shorter or a longer period of time than was originally calculated. By multiplying the amount of the annual payments received by the percentage indicated, the amount of the annual payments received which represent a return of the investment—and are therefore non-taxable—can be found. Subtracting this amount from the total amount received will give the amount of the annual payments which will be taxed.

The above is illustrated by the following example. A person has a total investment of $9,600 in an annuity contract, and is receiving a total of $1,200 a year in annuity payments. According to the government tables, he will live ten years from the time the annuity payments begin. Thus his total expected return would be $12,000.

$$\frac{\text{Investment}}{\text{Expected return}} \times \text{Annual payment received} = \text{Amount non-taxable}$$

$$\frac{\$9{,}600}{\$12{,}000} \times \$1{,}200 = \$960 \text{ non-taxable income}$$

$$\$1{,}200 - \$960 = \$240 \text{ taxable income}$$

Thus each year $240 would be reported as taxable income.

RETIREMENT INCOME CREDIT

The retirement income credit is quite complicated and if the taxpayer cannot qualify for it there is no reason for him to try to understand the confusing details of the law relating to it. So at the outset it will be stated that this credit cannot be claimed under the following three conditions.

1. If pensions or annuities of $1,524 or more were received from social security or railroad retirement ($2,286 if husband and wife are both 65, or over, and file jointly)
2. If under 62 years of age and "earned income" is $2,424 or more
3. If 62 or over but under 72, and "earned income" is $2,974 or more ($3,736 if husband and wife both 65 or over, and file jointly)

The above stated incomes, of course, refer to those received for the taxable year. "Earned income" means income received from wages, salaries, or fees for personal services as distinguished from income from such things as pensions, annuities, interest, dividends, etc.

Prior Earnings Requirement

In order to qualify for the retirement income credit, one of the requirements is that the taxpayer must have had more than $600 of "earned income" in each year for any ten calendar years before the current year (that is the year in which he wants to claim the retirement income credit). These ten years need not be the last ten years nor do they have to be consecutive years. Where husband and wife, both 65, or over, file jointly, each will meet this earnings test if either does.

Retirement Income Requirement

Since the credit we are here discussing is a "retirement income credit" it follows that the taxpayer must have "retirement income" before he can claim the credit. According to the law, age is a factor in determining what may be included in retirement income. If under 65, retirement income includes only a pension or annuity received from a public retirement system, such as is provided for public school teachers, policemen, and firemen. But only the portion of an annual pension on which income taxes must be paid is included in the retirement income for the purpose of computing the credit. If 65 or over, retirement income consists of various types of annuities and pensions (the taxable portion of them), interest (taxable), dividends (after the exclusion), and rents (gross).

Amount of Retirement Income Included

The next step in the process of figuring the credit is to determine how much of the retirement income, if any, will be allowed for this purpose. The law states that the maximum annual allowable retirement income for any individual is the lesser of the following two amounts:

1. The taxpayer's retirement income
2. $1,524 ($2,286 if husband and wife are both 65, or over, and file a joint return), less any amounts received from social security (and

railroad retirement and certain veterans' pensions), and, unless the taxpayer is 72, or older, "earned income" of the following amounts:

(a) All over $900 if taxpayer is under 62

(b) Half of earned income between $1,200 and $1,700, and all over $1,700 if taxpayer is 62, or over, but under 72

Having arrived at the amount of the retirement income, the law says the "credit" that may be taken is 15 per cent of the allowable retirement income. The amount of this credit is deducted from the amount figured as income *taxes* (before applying the credit). Since the maximum amount of allowable (for this purpose) retirement income for anyone would be $1,524 ($2,286), and since the retirement income credit is 15 per cent of this amount, it is obvious that the maximum credit (that could be subtracted from the tax bill) in any case would be $228.60 ($342.90).

An example will be of help in understanding the above. Assume that a person is 66 (wife is under 65) and has had the ten years of more than $600 of earned income. Income (pertinent to computing the credit) for the year was as follows:

Earned income from various jobs	$1,300
Interest income (taxable)	600
Dividends (after $100 exclusion)	600
Rent income (gross)	900
Annuity from private company (total of $1,200 a year, of which $960 is non-taxable)	240
Social security retirement benefits	1,340

After giving effect to expenses which may be deducted from the rent income, exemptions, and deductions, we will assume that the income tax for the year for this person is computed to be $144. The retirement income credit would be computed as follows:

Retirement income (for purpose of computing credit)		
Interest		$ 600
Dividends		600
Rent		900
Annuity		240
Total retirement income		$2,340
Maximum allowable retirement income		$1,524
Less		
Half of earned income over $1,200	$ 50	
Social security	1,340	1,390
Allowable for computing the credit		$ 134

Taking 15 per cent of $134.00, we get $20.10, which is the retirement income credit. Subtracting $20.10 from the computed tax bill of $144.00, we arrive at $123.90, which is the amount that must be paid in taxes for the year.

If the taxpayer is married and his wife has retirement income and qualifies for the retirement credit according to the provisions stated above, she too may take it. This may be done on either separate returns or on the joint return. If both husband and wife are 65, or over, however, they should compute the retirement credit by the alternative methods and use the one which results in the least amount in taxes. By following the procedure indicated in the tax form a person may compute his retirement income credit without too much difficulty.

TAXATION OF BUSINESS OR PROFESSIONAL INCOME

Many people have taxation problems connected with a business which they own or partly own. If the business is incorporated, the various corporate expenses are deducted from the gross income to arrive at the taxable income. The regular corporate tax rates are then applied to this taxable income. But we are interested here in the personal tax and not in corporate taxation. When the corporation pays out dividends to its shareholders, the latter must report them for personal taxation. The taxation of dividends has already been explained.

If a person is an owner or part owner of an unincorporated business, such as a sole proprietorship or a partnership, or is in a profession, he must report his business or professional income, or his share of it, on his personal income tax form. This is done on a separate schedule and is carried forward to Form 1040. Farmers who report on a cash basis list their farming income and expenses on a separate schedule.

The total gross business income is listed and from this is subtracted the business expenses. The latter includes all the ordinary and necessary expenses of running the business, such as cost of merchandise sold, salaries and wages, rent, interest, repairs, supplies, depreciation, and taxes. Depreciation may be charged as an expense on owned property such as buildings, machines, equipment, and fixtures. If some property is used partly for business and partly for personal purposes, such as an automobile, depreciation and operating expenses may be charged off against the business income only to the extent that it is used in the business. If one automobile is used entirely for business purposes and another one entirely for pleasure, the entire costs of the former may be charged off against the business income, but none of the expenses of the other car may be so charged.

If a business or profession suffers a loss for the year, this loss may be deducted from other income, for tax purposes. If such losses exceed other income, the balance may be carried backward to offset income for the three previous years. If there still remains a loss balance this may be carried over and subtracted from income during the next five years. If the loss carry-back entitles the taxpayer to a refund of taxes, he can get the refund by filing Form 1045.

Self-employed and professional people who net at least $400 a year must report their self-employed income for social security purposes on part of Schedule C. The social security taxes are paid along with the income tax.

CASH OR ACCRUAL REPORTING

Income and expenses may be reported on the accrual basis or the cash basis. Under the accrual basis all income items are reported in the year in which they are earned even though the income has not yet been received, and all expenses are deducted in the year in which they are incurred even though they are not paid for that year. Under the cash basis, income is reported in the year in which it is actually or constructively received, and allowable expenses which are actually paid for during the year are deducted. Income is considered to be "constructively" received when it is made available, for example, as a credit to a savings account. Thus, income in the form of credits to a bank or savings and loan association for interest or dividends, uncashed salary or dividend checks, and matured bond coupons are treated as constructively received and these must be reported. Over a period of years the taxes paid out under the accrual and the cash basis would be about the same, although they may differ for individual years. Most people use the cash basis because they believe this is the only way they may report or because they find this is the easiest way of doing it.

GOVERNMENT CHECK OF YOUR RETURN

The Internal Revenue Service does not have the staff to check carefully all the tax forms that are filed. In general, the forms of those in the lower tax brackets are checked in the office only for errors in arithmetic. Sample checking is employed for the bulk of the tax returns. As the size of the income increases, the chance of a complete checking or audit increases. When deductions are itemized there is a greater probability of checking than when the standard deduction is taken. Self-employed and professional people are more apt to have their returns checked or audited than those who receive wages or salaries.

If the Internal Revenue Service calls a taxpayer and indicates that he has underpaid his taxes, the burden is more or less on him to prove otherwise. If, after discussing it with the Internal Revenue Service, he still believes he is right but cannot convince them of it, he has a right to appeal the matter to the tax court or to the federal courts. This, of course, takes time and money, so it would be inadvisable to appeal unless the disputed sum is an appreciable amount of money.

In general, the government has a three-year period dating from the time of filing to examine a return and collect additional taxes. This three-year period is not applicable, however, under the following three circumstances:

1. When no return at all is filed, there is indefinite liability for the tax.
2. If a proven fraudulent return is filed, there is indefinite liability for the taxes due.
3. If more than 25 per cent of total gross income is not listed on the return, the government has a period of five years to collect the tax or to start court proceedings to collect the tax due.

Various penalties are provided for different kinds of failure to conform to the law. Penalties may be inflicted for failure to file a return, or for failure to pay taxes within the prescribed time. A taxpayer must pay 6 per cent interest on taxes not paid when they are due, unless he can convince the government that the delay in paying was not caused by willful negligence. A taxpayer also has to pay a penalty if he underestimates his tax by more than 30 per cent (33⅓ per cent in the case of farmers). But if he reported not less than his previous year's income and used the current tax rates and exemptions, or if he reported the same tax as in the previous year, the penalty is not applicable. Both fines and jail sentences are provided for the filing of fraudulent returns.

TAX-SAVING IDEAS

It is not immoral or unpatriotic for an individual to use all legal means available to keep his taxes at the lowest possible figure. Those with large incomes can afford to hire accountants and lawyers who are experts in the field of taxation to advise them on legal methods and procedures for minimizing their taxes. It is unfortunate that the millions of people with smaller incomes cannot avail themselves of the services of an expert. Taxes now consume an appreciable part of practically every working man's wages or salary and this will probably continue to be true in the indefinite future. A taxpayer can personally use only the part of his income that is left after taxes. To effect a tax saving means the same as an increase in income. In fact, percentagewise, it nets him more because any increase in income will result in part of that added income going out in the form of additional taxes. A tax saving of $1.00 is a net saving of $1.00, but an increase of $1.00 in income will leave only 86 cents, 50 cents, or even 30 cents, depending upon the income tax bracket. The tax rates are relatively high because the government figures that people will use all legitimate deductions available in order to keep their taxable income at the lowest possible figure. If the taxpayer does not do this, he will be paying more in taxes than the government expects of him.

Married couples will practically always save in taxes by filing a joint return rather than separate returns. It will be recalled that a husband may file a joint return even if his wife has no income. The next point to watch is deductions. It is a good idea to always list the amounts of "deductions" on scrap paper and compute taxes after subtracting the actual deductions from adjusted gross income. Then figure the taxes using the standard deduction. Naturally, a taxpayer would use the standard deduction only if it resulted in lesser taxes than listing the deductions. If he uses Form 1040 with tax table he is forced to use the standard deduction, but if he computes his tax on Form 1040, he may list his deductions. If his adjusted gross income is $5,000 or more, he may use a standard deduction even though he uses Form 1040. When deductions are listed make sure to list all the items that may be included. Many taxpayers annually overpay their taxes simply because they do not list all their deductions.

Some taxpayers who are on a cash basis pay all the bills for deductible expenses in a particular year and list the deductions when completing the form. Then the next year they postpone paying all bills that they can, such as doctor bills, and then take the standard deduction for that year if it amounts to more than could be obtained from listing the deductions. Then the year following they pay all their current and past bills and list the deductions again.

In some instances it is possible to arrange with an employer to defer paying some wages or salaries in a year in which other income is relatively large, and then pay them the following year when other income may be lower. This could be done only when reporting on a cash basis. Some corporate executives have a deferred compensation plan with their company, whereby part of their salaries is deferred until after they retire; and then they receive a fixed amount per month for a specified number of years. If this deferred part of the salary had been paid to them while they were working, it may have been taxed at the rate of, for example, 70 per cent. The same amount received after retirement would be taxed at rates much less than this.

"Fringe" benefits of one kind or another may result in tremendous tax savings. For example, take the matter of insurance. If an executive is in the 70 per cent tax bracket he must earn $3.33⅓ in salary in order to have $1 left (after taxes) to use for insurance premiums. But it would cost the company only $1 to pay this premium. If the company can deduct this for its tax purposes, the net cost to the company would be only 52 cents (assuming a 48 per cent tax). Thus having the company carry insurance on its executives would be as helpful to the executives as raising their salaries an amount equivalent to 3⅓ times the amount of the insurance premiums. Consider the amount that an executive must earn before taxes in order to have enough left after taxes to purchase a summer resort cottage at which to spend his vacations. If the company, on the other hand, purchased the cottage and let its executives use the property without charge, this may be more profitable to the executives than a handsome salary raise.

People in high tax brackets who invest in securities for the interest or dividend return find that they have little of the income left after taxes. Many of these individuals would find it more profitable to purchase tax-exempt bonds. Another procedure is to purchase stocks which appear to have great growth potentialities even if the current yield is low. Profits made from the sale of these stocks (after they have been held for more than six months) are in effect taxed at only half the rate that dividends are taxed. And the maximum tax on such long-term capital gains is 25 per cent, while on dividends the maximum tax may be 70 per cent.

If an individual knows the real estate market, has the time available for property management, and is willing to spend the necessary amount of time in connection therewith, the purchase of rental property, particularly older properties, may prove to be a good investment taxwise. Depreciation (as well as all other expenses incident to the property) may be charged off against the rent before reporting the net rent for tax purposes. But depreciation is not an out-of-pocket current expense. Thus an appreciable amount of the rent may be received tax-free so far as current operations are concerned. Older properties may bring in about as much rent as comparable new houses, but the cost of the older houses may be written off in depreciation much faster than in the case of new houses. In other words, a larger percentage of the rent is currently tax-free.

People who are in business can charge off much more against their incomes than can those who are on salary. The operating expenses, including travel and entertainment expense (to the extent permitted) may be charged against the income.

The transfer of income-producing property to children's names can effect a material saving in taxes. Assume that a parent is sending his son $2,000 a year for college expenses. If the father is in the 50 per cent tax bracket he would need the imposing sum of $100,000 invested at 4 per cent in order to have the $2,000 left after taxes. Assume that the father transfers $50,000 of the income-producing property to the son's name. If the mother joins with the father in making the gift to the son, this sum could be given away without paying any gift taxes on it. The son may be married and have a child, in which case he would not have to pay any income taxes on the earnings of $2,000. In the meantime the father still has $50,000 of the investment left, which will yield him $1,000 after taxes, as compared to nothing under the former setup. Furthermore, upon the death of the father the estate tax would be paid on only the $50,000 investment rather than on $100,000.

QUESTIONS

1. How many jurisdictions may tax an individual? To which of these does he usually pay the most taxes?
2. Do you think it is fair for the federal government to force us by means of the income tax to pay such a large portion of our income for many foreign aid purposes which we may believe to be unjustified? Explain.
3. Indicate what individuals are legally required to file federal income tax returns. Who must file the declaration of estimated tax?
4. Where would you advise someone to go to secure free reliable advice regarding his income taxes? What inexpensive sources of information are available to a person who is capable of reading and understanding ordinary material?
5. Indicate what is meant by the joint income tax return. Who can use it? When is it advisable for them to do so?
6. What are the requirements for a person filing as head of a household? What are the advantages of doing so?
7. Under what circumstances would you advise a person to file Form 1040A? Form 1040?
8. Distinguish between the tax table and the tax schedule which are contained in the instruction booklet supplied by the federal government.
9. Indicate the circumstances under which you would recommend that a person use the tax table, when filing with Form 1040, to determine his taxes.
10. When should a person ignore the tax table and compute his taxes?
11. Indicate the circumstances under which sick pay may be deducted from the gross income. Indicate the amount allowable.
12. (a) What is meant by "income averaging" under the tax laws?
    (b) Indicate in general how income averaging is accomplished.
13. (a) What is meant by the double taxation of dividends?
    (b) What is the amount of the dividend exclusion?
14. Indicate how interest on Series E bonds may be reported for income tax purposes. Which way would you follow? Why?
15. What items are included in deductions which a person may list on his tax form or for which he may take a standard deduction?
16. Indicate the circumstances under which it would be advisable and inadvisable to take the standard deduction.
17. If a person is paying mortgage interest on a house that is rented, should he list the interest as a deduction or should he subtract it from the rent received? Why?
18. In general, what types of taxes may be listed as deductions and what types may not be so listed?
19. Explain the amount of drug and medical and dental expenses which people of the different ages may list as deductions.

20. Explain the number of exemptions which may be taken by taxpayers of different ages. How much may be subtracted from income for each exemption? How is a child going to school treated differently for exemption purposes than one who is not attending school?
21. (a) What is meant by a capital gain or loss?
    (b) Distinguish between a short-term capital gain and a long-term capital gain. How is each reported?
22. How are profits and losses incurred on the sale of a home treated for tax purposes? Does the age of the taxpayer make any difference? Explain.
23. Indicate how reimbursed and unreimbursed moving expenses are handled taxwise both for new and old employees.
24. (a) What types of pensions or annuities are tax-free?
    (b) When the receipts from a pension or annuity are partly tax exempt, explain how you would determine how much you would report for tax purposes.
25. Indicate ways that people of moderate incomes may save on income taxes. What additional ways may be used by those with large incomes?
26. Can a person ever reach the point when the receipt of any additional income would increase his taxes to the extent that he would have less left after taxes than he had before? Explain.

CASE PROBLEMS

1. Mr. Will Henry in 1965 signed up under the Medicare program for insurance which became effective July 1, 1966. In the autumn of 1966 he incurred doctors' bills of $280, and was compelled to go into a hospital for one week. The cost of the latter was $140. His Medical Insurance reimbursed him $184, and the Hospital Insurance paid $100 of the hospital bill. If Mr. Henry listed his "medical and dental" expenses on Form 1040, ascertain how much of these expenses he can list.
2. Indicate in which of the following situations a declaration of estimated tax must be filed:
   (a) Mr. and Mrs. Bill Henry, whose annual income is $8,000, file a joint return. This income includes interest of $90.
   (b) The same situation exists as in part (a), except that the interest income is $350 instead of $90.
   (c) Mr. and Mrs. Edwin Brown, whose total income is $12,000 a year, all of which was subject to withholding, file a joint return.
3. George and Ruth Smith are both employed. Smith had taxable income of $4,800, and his wife had taxable income of $3,200. Mrs. Smith's mother lives with them and is entirely dependent upon them. They have no children. Their deductions for the year amount to $500. Should they file a joint return or separate returns? Why? What would be the savings in filing a joint return? What would their total tax be? Should they use the standard deduction? Which one? What is the advantage of the standard deduction in this case?
4. Robert Brown is married and has three children. Two children are in high school and live at home. The third child is 22 and away at college. Brown gives this child $700 per year toward his annual expense budget of $1,350. The other $650 is earned in part-time jobs. Brown's annual income is all

from salary and amounts to $4,800. His deductions total $750. Which form should he file? Why? How many exemptions does he have? Figure his income tax both by using the tax table and by listing his deductions. What tax does the child away at college have to pay?

5. Joseph Adams has kept track of his expenses all year. He has paid the following items from his income of $5,600: food $1,000, mortgage principal payments $600, mortgage interest payments $300, clothing $600, utility bills $300, excise tax on telephone $3, church contributions $100, country club dues $100, property taxes $100, life insurance $200, property insurance $50, auto expense $400, state gasoline tax $30, license fee $15, auto depreciation $300, state sales tax $25, federal cigarette and liquor tax $25, household supplies $50, Blue Cross $30, doctor bills $80, drugs $30, withholding tax $1,000. What deductions is Adams allowed to take on his income tax? If he were a traveling salesman, would the allowable deductions be different?

6. On January 30, Pete Jackson purchased 100 shares of ABC Corporation for $5,430, including all expenses. In February, he purchased DEF Corporation common for $5,400. In April, he sold some bonds he had held for 6 years at a net profit of $65. In May, he bought GHI common for $3,210. In August, he sold the ABC stock for $4,900 net after expenses of sale. In September, he purchased JKL preferred for $9,800, and sold the GHI common for $4,000. In December, he sold the JKL preferred for $9,600. What is his net gain or loss figure for determination of the capital gains tax? What is a capital gain? What is the advantage of a long-term capital gain over a short-term capital gain? Would you prefer long- or short-term capital losses? If Jackson had no dependents and no other income for the year, what would his tax be? If he had no dependents and $100,000 in other income for the year, what would his tax be? (He files a single tax return.)

7. Mr. Allen Holden, who is 67 (wife is under 62), has earned more than $600 annually for a period in excess of ten years. He asks you to determine if he can claim a retirement income credit, and if so, the amount of each credit. From his records you obtain the following data:

Earned from odd jobs	$1,300
Interest income (taxable)	75
Dividends (after $100 exclusion)	250
Rent income (gross)	900
Annuity from private company ($1,000 of this is non-taxable)	1,200
Social security retirement benefits	1,200

SELECTED READINGS

Bardes, *et al.* (eds.) *Montgomery's Federal Taxes: 39th Edition.* New York: The Ronald Press Co., 1964.

Dickerson, William E., and Stone, Leo D. *Federal Income Tax Fundamentals,* Second Edition. San Francisco: Wadsworth Publishing Co., 1966.

Explanation of the Revenue Act of 1964. Englewood Cliffs, N. J.: Prentice-Hall, Inc., 1964.

Farmer's Tax Guide. (Publication No. 225.) Washington, D. C.: U. S. Treasury Department, Internal Revenue Service.

Federal Tax Course. Englewood Cliffs, N. J.: Prentice-Hall, Inc. Latest edition.

Federal Taxes. Englewood Cliffs, N. J.: Prentice-Hall, Inc. Latest edition.
How to Prepare Your Personal Income Tax Return. Englewood Cliffs, N. J.: Prentice-Hall, Inc. Latest edition.
Instructions for Preparing Your Federal Income Tax Return, Form 1040. Washington, D. C.: U. S. Treasury Department, Internal Revenue Service. Latest edition.
Investor's Tax Guide. New York: Merrill Lynch, Pierce, Fenner & Smith, Inc. Latest edition.
J. K. Lasser's Your Income Tax. New York: Simon and Schuster, Inc. Latest edition.
Olson, R. L., and Gradishar, R. L. *Saving Income Taxes by Short-Term Trusts.* Englewood Cliffs, N. J.: Prentice-Hall, Inc., 1956.
Standard Federal Tax Reporter. New York: Commerce Clearing House, Inc. Latest edition.
Tax Guide for Small Business. Washington, D. C.: U. S. Treasury Department, Internal Revenue Service (Publication No. 334). Latest edition.
Tax Ideas. Englewood Cliffs, N. J.: Prentice-Hall, Inc. Latest edition.
Teaching Federal Income Taxes. Washington, D. C.: U. S. Treasury Department, Internal Revenue Service (Publication No. 19).
Your Federal Income Tax. Washington, D. C.: U. S. Treasury Department, Internal Revenue Service (Publication No. 17). Latest edition.

17

Social Security and Medicare

Young people may be acquainted with social security and Medicare only because of the substantial deductions which are withheld from their check to pay for these governmental programs. But to elderly individuals or their survivors, and to the sick, they take on a different meaning.

In 1965, a person who met the requirements could retire and receive \$135.90 a month for life. This will eventually be raised to \$168.00. Or, if he were disabled, he could draw these amounts every month for life. The retired worker and his wife could draw a total of \$203.90 a month for life in 1965, and this total will be raised later to \$252.00. In order to earn an equivalent amount (\$252) at 4 per cent interest, it would be necessary to have savings of \$75,600. If the dependent family is large enough, a retired worker may receive benefits as high as \$309.20 a month, and this will increase to \$368.00 in the future. To get \$368 a month from a 4 per cent savings account would take the imposing sum of \$110,400. A worker's widow and children may also draw up to a maximum of \$309.20 a month.

Then there is the financial crisis brought about from illness or an operation. Take the case of Tom and Mary Hill, both 65 or older. One of them had to go into a hospital for an operation. The surgeon charged \$275. After a stay in the hospital which cost \$300, it was necessary to go to a nursing home for twenty-three days, and the bill there was \$250. Of the hospital bill of \$300, the Hills would have to stand the first \$40, but Medicare would take care of the remaining \$260. Medicare also picks up the tab for the first twenty days in the nursing home, but the Hills would have to pay at the rate of \$5 a day thereafter; the nursing home would then cost them only \$15. Doctors' and surgeons' fees are not covered under the basic Medicare program, so the Hills would have to pay the surgeon $275. Of the total expenses of $825, Medicare would take care of $495, and the Hills would stand the balance of $330.

But the Hills could have reduced their bill further if they had taken out a voluntary insurance program under Medicare. If they pay $3 each per month (this is in addition to the amount that must be deducted from any wages received) Medicare will pay 80 per cent of their doctor's or surgeon's bills after the first $50. So, if they carried this supplemental insurance, Medicare would have paid the surgeon $180 and the Hills would have stood $95 of the bill. Under this setup, Medicare would have taken care of $675 of the total expense of $825, and the Hills would be burdened with only $150. The details relating to Medicare will be explained later in the chapter. Although Medicare is a part of the social security system, we will first discuss the original social security program as amended, and then take up the new Medicare provisions.

Programs Administered

The Social Security Act passed by Congress in 1935, and its later amendments, is designed to keep individuals and families from destitution, to keep families together, and to give children the opportunity to grow up in their own homes. The 1965 amendments added health benefits to the aged through the Medicare provisions. There are really ten different programs provided for in the Act:

1. Social Insurance
   (a) Old-age, survivors', and disability insurance
   (b) Health insurance for the aged (Medicare)
   (c) Unemployment insurance
2. Public Assistance to the Needy
   (a) Old-age assistance
   (b) Aid to needy blind
   (c) Aid to dependent children
   (d) Aid to totally disabled
3. Health and Welfare Services
   (a) Child-welfare services
   (b) Services for crippled children
   (c) Maternal and child-health services

Although the Social Security Act is a federal law, the federal government operates only the first two programs listed above—old-age, survivors', and disability insurance, and Medicare insurance. The other eight are operated by the various states with the federal government cooperating and contributing funds. The nature and administration of these eight programs vary widely in operation and administration among the states. No attempt will therefore be made here to explain any features of these programs. What is said below will apply only to that part of the Social Security Act which pertains to *old-age, survivors', and disability insurance* (OASDI) and *health insurance for the aged.* These are the parts of the program which interest the average worker in the United States. Few workers know anything about this insurance except that deductions are made from their wages for social security. Approximately 76 million people in the United States are making payments into the social security fund. Effective July 1, 1966, approximately 19 million people came under the Medicare provisions. A person's principal interest in the social security program, other than how much he contributes, is what benefits he will receive and when. This is based on a number of different factors which are discussed below. The material in this chapter gives effect to the amendments made in the law in 1965.

Covered Employment

All people whose work comes under *covered employment* are subject to the social security taxes and are entitled to the benefits from the system. Generally speaking, such people may be classified into two groups—employees and the self-employed.

Employees. All the wage earners and salaried executives of business concerns (whether or not they are incorporated) come under social security. Farm employees (not owners) are covered if they receive $150 or more cash wages from one employer during a calendar year, or if they work for an employer on twenty or more days in a year for cash wages figured on a time basis, such as an hourly, daily, or weekly rate. Domestic or household workers, such as maids, housekeepers, cooks, nursemaids, or gardeners are covered by social security if they receive from an employer cash wages of $50 or more in a calendar quarter for work performed in or about the employer's private home. In general, employees of the federal government who do not have their own public retirement system may come under social security. Employees of states and local governments may come under the system if the state enters into an agreement with the federal government for coverage, and provided at least a majority of the eligible employees vote in favor of the plan. Employees of religious, charitable, educational, scientific, and other non-profit organizations may be covered if the organization makes an agreement for coverage with the government. Social security will not be forced on members of the Old Order Amish and others who have religious scruples against insurance if they applied for exemption by April 15, 1966. Members of the armed forces are covered by social security, and those who have served after January 1, 1957, have had the taxes deducted from their pay the same as civilian employees. Those who were in the service prior to that time can get wage credits for service. This is explained later in the chapter.

The following are among the types of employees who are not covered by social security, regardless of the amount of their earnings or their desire for coverage:

- Railroad worker (he is covered by the Railroad Retirement System)
- Child under 21 employed by his parents
- Person employed by his wife or husband
- Person employed by his son or daughter if the employment is in the child's household
- College student employed as a domestic by a local fraternity, sorority, or club
- College student employed by his college or university
- Student nurse
- Person doing casual work outside his trade and for which he receives less than $50 a calendar quarter
- Newsboy under 18

Self-Employed. Generally speaking, all self-employed persons now are covered by social security if they have net earnings of $400 or more during a calendar year. Thus all persons who are proprietors or partners of businesses or professions must pay the social security taxes and are subject to the benefits. Clergymen may elect to be covered by the system if they make application within the prescribed period of time. Farmers are considered to be self-employed and thus come under the system. (Effective 1966, some changes were made in the method of reporting farmers' income.) For purposes of the law, a farmer is defined as anyone who operates, cultivates, or manages a farm for profit. Persons who are appointed or elected to a public office, such as a judge, mayor, or sheriff, are not considered to be self-employed. Persons such as waiters, earning tips (of $20 or more a month), are supposed to report these to their employers who will count them into paycheck deductions for both income tax and social security. (Employers, however, are not required to "match" this.)

Requirements for Insured Status

A person must have earned at least a minimum specified amount in a given number of calendar quarters before he or his family will be entitled to any social security benefits (some exceptions for Medicare benefits). A calendar quarter is any three-month period beginning January 1, April 1, July 1, and October 1. An employee is given credit for each quarter in which he earns $50 or more. If he earns $6,600 or more in a year he will be given credit for four quarters even if he earned less than $50 in any of the quarters. A self-employed person is given credit for four quarters for each year that he makes net earnings of $400 or more. This $400 could be earned in one quarter and he would still get credit for the four quarters. If he earned less than $400 in any year he will get no credit for that year.

OLD-AGE, SURVIVORS', AND DISABILITY INSURANCE

The Medicare provisions which were added to the legislation in 1965 will be discussed later in the chapter. We will first discuss the social security benefits which take one of three forms: (1) retirement benefits, (2) survivors' benefits in event of the insured's death, and (3) disability benefits. The nature of these will be explained later in the chapter. In order for benefits to be received, it is necessary that the worker be *fully insured, currently insured,* or both.

Fully Insured Worker

Due to the fact that the Social Security Act has been amended a number of times to, among other things, permit new people who were near the retirement age to enter the system, the requirements for a fully insured worker have had to be changed several times. Effective 1966, the

Table 17–1. Number of Quarters of Coverage Needed To Be Fully Insured

Year Of Birth	Quarters Needed		Year Of Birth	Quarters Needed	
	Men	Women		Men	Women
1889 or earlier	3	3	1910	24	21
1890	4	3	1911	25	22
1891	5	3	1912	26	23
1892	6	3	1913	27	24
1893	7	4	1914	28	25
1894	8	5	1915	29	26
1895	9	6	1916	30	27
1896	10	7	1917	31	28
1897	11	8	1918	32	29
1898	12	9	1919	33	30
1899	13	10	1920	34	31
1900	14	11	1921	35	32
1901	15	12	1922	36	33
1902	16	13	1923	37	34
1903	17	14	1924	38	35
1904	18	15	1925	39	36
1905	19	16	1926	40	37
1906	20	17	1927	40	38
1907	21	18	1928	40	39
1908	22	19	1929 or later	40	40
1909	23	20			

number of "quarters of coverage" needed to be *fully insured* (and a worker must be fully insured before he can draw retirement benefits) are shown in Table 17–1.

The required quarters of coverage stated in the table need not be consecutive. Once they have been acquired the worker remains fully insured for life. It is noted that for those born in 1929 or later, 40 quarters of coverage are needed. This, of course, amounts to ten years.

A fully insured worker is also entitled to disability benefits, and upon his death qualified relatives are entitled to survivors' benefits. These will be explained later.

Currently Insured Worker

A worker is currently insured when he has at least six quarters of coverage during the preceding three years. Another way of stating this is that he must have at least six quarters of coverage during the thirteen-quarter period ending with the quarter in which his death occurs.

If he is only currently insured, his family is entitled to survivors' benefits upon his death, but he will not be entitled to retirement benefits or disability benefits.

CALCULATING AVERAGE WAGES

People naturally are interested in the nature and amount of their social security benefits. Within limits, the benefits an insured person gets are based on his average earnings.

If a person has not yet reached retirement age, it will of course be impossible to figure out the exact amount that he will get upon retirement, or what his survivors will get, because it is not definitely known how much his earnings will be in the future. If he figures on the basis of present earnings and those earnings are increased in the future, benefits will be higher than figured. If earnings decline, the reverse, of course, would be true. To determine benefits, the amount of earnings must be estimated.

Number of Years That Must Be Counted

The law specifies the number of years that must be counted in determining average monthly earnings. This depends upon whether the person is a man or a woman, and also upon the date of his birth. This is shown in Table 17–2. It is noted that the minimum number of years is five (for a man born in 1896 or earlier, or a woman born in 1899 or earlier), and the maximum is 38 (for a man born in 1929 or later).

Table 17–2. Number of Years That Must Be Counted in Figuring Average Earnings

Year of Birth	Number of Years	
	Men	Women
1896 or earlier	5	5
1897	6	5
1898	7	5
1899	8	5
1900	9	6
1901	10	7
1902	11	8
1903	12	9
1904	13	10
1905	14	11
1906	15	12
1907	16	13
1908	17	14
1909	18	15
1910	19	16
1911	20	17
1912	21	18
1913	22	19
1917	26	23
1921	30	27
1925	34	31
1926	35	32
1927	36	33
1928	37	34
1929 or later	38	35

Average Earnings

In arriving at average earnings a person may take into consideration every year beginning with 1937, when social security began, or the years beginning with 1951. Since wages and salaries have been advancing over the years, it is probable that his annual earnings have been higher from 1951 on than they were before 1951. Furthermore, he can count as his earnings only the amount from which social security taxes were actually deducted. The following shows the maximum earnings from which the taxes were deducted for the years stated:

$3,000 a year from 1937–1950
$3,600 a year from 1951–1954
$4,200 a year from 1955–1958
$4,800 a year from 1959–1965
$6,600 a year from 1966 and thereafter

Table 17–3. Examples of Monthly Cash Benefit Payments *

Average Yearly Earnings After 1950	$800 or Less	$1,800	$3,000	$3,600	$4,200	$4,800	$5,400	$6,600
Retirement at 65 / Disability benefits	$ 44.00	$ 78.20	$101.70	$112.40	$124.20	$135.90	$146.00	$168.00
Retirement at 64	41.10	73.00	95.00	105.00	116.00	126.90	136.30	156.80
Retirement at 63	38.20	67.80	88.20	97.50	107.70	117.80	126.60	145.60
Retirement at 62	35.20	62.60	81.40	90.00	99.40	108.80	116.80	134.40
Wife's benefit at 65 or with child in her care	22.00	39.10	50.90	56.20	62.10	68.00	73.00	84.00
Wife's benefit at 64	20.20	35.90	46.70	51.60	57.00	62.40	67.00	77.00
Wife's benefit at 63	18.40	32.60	42.50	46.90	51.80	56.70	60.90	70.00
Wife's benefit at 62	16.50	29.40	38.20	42.20	46.60	51.00	54.80	63.00
One child of retired or disabled worker	22.00	39.10	50.90	56.20	62.10	68.00	73.00	84.00
Widow age 62 or over	44.00	64.60	83.90	92.80	102.50	112.20	120.50	138.60
Widow at 60, no child	38.20	56.00	72.80	80.50	88.90	97.30	104.50	120.20
Widow under 62 and 1 child	66.00	117.40	152.60	168.60	186.40	204.00	219.00	252.00
Widow under 62 and 2 children	66.00	120.00	202.40	240.00	279.60	306.00	328.00	368.00
One surviving child	44.00	58.70	76.30	84.30	93.20	102.00	109.50	126.00
Two surviving children	66.00	117.40	152.60	168.60	186.40	204.00	219.00	252.00
Maximum family payment	66.00	120.00	202.40	240.00	280.80	309.20	328.00	368.00
Lump-sum death payment	132.00	234.60	255.00	255.00	255.00	255.00	255.00	255.00

* Generally, in figuring average yearly earnings after 1950, five years of low earnings or no earnings can be excluded. The maximum earnings creditable for social security are $3,600 for 1951–1954; $4,200 for 1955–1958; $4,800 for 1959–1965; and $6,600 starting in 1966. Because of this, the benefits shown in the last two columns on the right will not generally be payable for some years to come. When a person is entitled to more than one benefit, the amount actually payable is limited to the largest of the benefits.

We will therefore proceed on the assumption that the average earnings from 1951 on were higher.

Select the years of highest annual earnings for the exact number of years shown in Table 17–2.[1] For example, a man who was born in 1906 must take fifteen years into consideration in computing his average earnings. So he would pick out the fifteen years (beginning with 1951) of highest earnings, add these figures, and divide the sum by 15. The amount of his social security benefits would be based on the amount of these average earnings, as will be shown later.

Referring to Table 17–1, it is seen that a person born in 1906 needs only twenty quarters (five years) of coverage to be eligible for retirement. Suppose that a person had exactly twenty quarters of coverage and met the age requirement for retirement benefits. How can he average his earnings over a fifteen-year period (this is a requirement for him), when he has worked in covered employment only five years? The answer is that he will have to record "zero earnings" for ten of these years, add the five years of earnings, and still divide by fifteen. That, of course, will bring down the average considerably, and thus give him relatively small benefits. Of course, it is highly probable that a man born in 1906 would have at least fifteen years of coverage (unless he is an M.D. and first became covered by social security in 1965).

If a person keeps on working after he is 62 or even 65, he can take those years of earnings into consideration in calculating his average earnings.

RETIREMENT BENEFITS

Prior to the Medicare amendments in 1965, the retirement benefits were the ones in which people were most interested. The amount of the retirement benefits are of importance also in computing disability benefits and survivors' benefits, which will be discussed later.

The Primary Insurance Benefit

The amount of the retirement benefit at age 65 is officially referred to as the *primary insurance benefit* (also called *primary insurance amount* or *basic benefit*). These amounts are fixed by the legislation, and vary according to the amount of the "average wage," discussed above. These amounts are shown in Table 17–3.

[1] The number of years stated in Table 17–2 is calculated in the following manner. In figuring the average earnings the law provides that a man may drop out five years of lowest earnings (a woman born after 1898 can drop out eight years). The table therefore shows the number of years after 1950 until the person reaches 65, less the five or eight years' dropout.

Any man or woman reaching the age of 62, and having the minimum quarters of coverage specified in Table 17–1, is eligible to retire and start receiving the benefits. Application for retirement benefits would, of course, have to be made to the social security office. A person who retires at ages 62, 63, or 64, however, will receive lower benefits than if he had waited until 65 to retire (assuming calculation on same average wage). The 62-year-old retiree would get only 80 per cent as much as if he had waited until 65 for retirement. If he had waited until 63 for retirement he would draw 86⅔ per cent, and retirement at 64 would bring it up to 93⅓ per cent of the age 65 retirement figure. These amounts are shown in Table 17–3 for specified average earnings.

For example, a retiree whose average annual earnings were $4,800 would be entitled to retirement benefits of the following amounts if retirement began at the ages stated:

Retirement at Age	Monthly Benefits Received
65	$135.90
64	126.90
63	117.80
62	108.80

After the early retiree reaches 65, his retirement allowance is not increased—it stays the same as when he retired. Although early retirement cuts down the amount of the monthly benefit, it should be realized that the benefits will be paid over a longer period of time. The increased monthly benefits that go with age 65 retirement will result in more money to the retiree only if he lives long enough. How long? If the 62-year-old believes that he will die within fifteen years, he would receive more social security money by retiring immediately. If he should live for more than fifteen years, he would have been further ahead by waiting until 65 to retire. (Of course, many other factors may decide the retirement year.)

Limits

The minimum monthly retirement benefit (at age 65) at the present time is $44. This applies to a worker with average annual earnings of $804 (usually rounded off to $800 in tables) or less. If a person today can report average annual earnings of $4,800 (which was the top income from which social security taxes were withheld prior to 1966), his monthly benefit would be $135.90 (retirement at age 65). By the year 2000, some workers (women) will be able to show average annual earnings of $6,600 and can qualify for the top monthly benefit of $168 (the year 2003 for men). The amounts stated here refer to the retirement benefits for a retired worker; later we will state the maximum family benefit.

Working After Retirement

The retirement benefits continue for life. But if the retired person goes back to work, his retirement benefits will either be reduced or eliminated entirely, depending upon how much he earns. This will be discussed later. But a person 72 or older can earn any amount without his retirement benefits being reduced.

Retirement Benefits for Retired Worker's Wife

A wife 62 or older of a retired worker is also entitled to some retirement benefits. If the wife's benefits begin at age 65, she can draw an amount equivalent to half of what the husband would be entitled to based on his retirement at age 65. For example, Table 17–3 shows that a worker who retired at age 65 with average earnings of $4,200 would be entitled to a monthly benefit of $124.20. His 65-year-old wife could draw an amount equal to half of this, or $62.10. It will be noted from the table that the wife would be entitled to this amount (if her benefits started at age 65) even though the husband retired at an earlier age.

If the wife elected to start receiving the benefits at age 62, however, she would get only 75 per cent of the amount that she would have received starting at age 65. Using the above example, she would receive $46.60 instead of $62.10. If she elects to have her benefits start at age 63, or 64, it can be seen from the table that the amount of the benefits would increase.

If the wife is under 62 but is caring for an unmarried child (or children) under 18 (or one incapable of self-support due to a disability incurred before age 18), she can claim the same amount as the 65-year-old wife stated above. This also is shown in Table 17–3. When the child becomes 18, marries, or leaves the care of the mother, this benefit ceases. Of course, when the wife becomes 62 she can apply for the wife's ordinary benefit.

Benefits for Retiree's Children

Children of a worker who is drawing retirement benefits are entitled to benefits, provided they are dependent, unmarried children under 18. Each child is entitled (subject to the maximum family benefits) to an amount equivalent to one half of the retired parent's primary insurance amount (based on retirement at age 65) (see Table 17–3). These benefits cease when the child becomes 18, or is married, or is no longer dependent. Children who were permanently disabled before 18 and continue to be disabled after 18 continue to receive the benefits.

If a child is in school, however, he can continue to draw the benefits until he is 22 (effective first in 1965).

Family Limits to Benefits

Despite what has been said above, however, there is a ceiling on what one family can draw in retirement benefits. This amount is dependent on the worker's average earnings, and at the present time ranges from $66 to $309.20 a month. The maximum family benefits will rise in some cases in 1967 to $368 a month. The figures in Table 17–3 show the maximum family benefits. When the total family benefits exceed the maximum permitted, the primary insurance amount of the retired parent is not reduced, but the other family benefits are reduced proportionally to conform to the maximum.

Special Provision for Those 72 Years of Age

An amendment added in 1965 permits a retired worker who reaches 72 before 1969 to draw a flat $35 monthly benefit regardless of his average earnings if he worked a specified number of months—in some cases as few as nine—under social security at any time since January 1, 1937. And his wife can collect $17.50 a month if she reaches 72 before 1969. This new provision was designed to benefit those 72 and over who have not worked long enough under social security to meet the ordinary requirements for benefits.

Retirement Benefits to Husbands of Retired Wives

If a working wife is both fully and currently insured when she is entitled to retirement benefits, her husband (65 or over) can claim a benefit equal to one half the wife's basic benefit provided he is at least 50 per cent dependent upon his wife for a living. (Benefits can begin at age 62 at reduced rates.) If he was married to the wife for less than one year before filing for the benefit, he will not get it unless he is the father of his wife's son or daughter. A husband cannot claim the benefit if he on his own record is entitled to social security benefits equal to or greater than the benefit based on the wife's record.

Retirement Benefits for Divorced Women

A divorced woman (not currently married) 62 and older can receive retirement benefits based on her former husband's account, provided she was married to him at least twenty years before the divorce and provided he had been contributing (or obligated by the court to contribute) to her support when he became entitled to social security benefits. A woman who is divorced while she is receiving benefits based on her husband's earnings may continue to receive benefits if she and her husband had been married at least twenty years. These provisions for divorced women became effective in 1965.

A divorced woman meeting the above requirements may also qualify for disability benefits under her ex-husband's account. A discussion of disability benefits follows.

DISABILITY BENEFITS

If a worker is so severely disabled that he is unable to work, he may be eligible to receive social security disability benefits even though he has not reached the age of 65. When a person who is receiving disability benefits reaches 65, the disability benefits will be converted to retirement benefits.

In order to be entitled to disability benefits a worker must have worked under social security at least five of the ten years immediately preceding the beginning date of the disability.

Degree of Disability Required

In order to qualify for disability benefits the worker must be so physically or mentally disabled that he cannot "engage in any substantial gainful activity." Even though he is so disabled that he cannot engage in his regular work, so long as he can still do some other substantial gainful activity, he cannot qualify for disability benefits. Furthermore, to be entitled to the benefits, the disability:

1. Must have lasted for at least twelve consecutive months, or
2. Is expected to last for at least twelve months, or
3. Is expected to result in death.

Worker's Disability Benefit

If a worker qualifies for disability benefits, he or she will be entitled at age 65 to exactly the same benefit as the retirement benefit discussed above. This is shown in Table 17–3 for selected average monthly earnings. The latter is figured the same as if the worker reached 65 at the time he became disabled. If and when the disabled worker reaches the age of 65 his disability benefits will be changed automatically to retirement (old-age) benefits. If a disabled worker should recover before 65, his disability benefits would be stopped, subject to what is mentioned below.

After an application for disability benefits has been approved, the benefits may begin with the seventh full month of disability and the first benefit check will be received the following month.

Benefits for Dependents of Disabled Workers

If a worker is receiving disability benefits the dependent members of his family are entitled to the same amount in benefits as if the worker were receiving retirement benefits. As discussed above, these benefits are equivalent to 50 per cent of the amount that is paid to the disabled worker. The benefits are paid to the disabled worker's:

1. Dependent children under 18, or over 18 if disabled and the disability began prior to age 18
2. Dependent children under 22 who are in school
3. Wife, regardless of age, who has the care of children eligible for dependents' benefits
4. Wife when she reaches age 65, if no children eligible for benefits (wife age 62 can collect benefits at the reduced rate)

As with retirement benefits, the total that may be received by a disabled worker's family is limited to the amount set forth in Table 17–3.

Working After Disability

Beneficiaries who go to work despite severe handicaps can continue to be paid their benefits for twelve months—whether they go to work under a vocational rehabilitation plan or on their own.

Not until after the first nine months (not necessarily nine consecutive months) of this twelve-month period must a decision be made as to whether the work done by the beneficiary in those nine months shows that he has regained his ability to work. If he is found able to engage in substantial work, and therefore is no longer disabled within the meaning of the law, he will still be paid his benefits for three months longer.

Beneficiaries who recover from their disabilities before they have worked in each of nine months, as well as beneficiaries who recover before they have tested their ability to work, will have their benefits paid to them for three months after they recover. Disability beneficiaries who regain their ability to work but become disabled again within five years after their benefits have been stopped, and whose disability is expected to last at least one year or to result in death, do not have to wait another seven months after the beginning of their second period of disability before their benefits can start again.

SURVIVORS' BENEFITS

When an insured worker dies, his widow, children, or parents may be entitled to *survivors' benefits* (sometimes called *death benefits*). For some of these benefits to be collected the deceased worker had to be fully insured; for others, either fully insured or currently insured; and for others, both fully and currently insured. This will be mentioned as we take up each of the different kinds of benefits. These benefits, along with the other benefits, are summarized in Table 17–4 on page 648.

Widow's Survivors' Benefits

Widows of *fully insured* workers are entitled to survivors' benefits when they reach the age of 62 (actually 60, as explained below). The amount of the benefit is equivalent to 82½ per cent of the husband's primary insurance amount (retirement benefit starting at age 65). It should be pointed out that it is not necessary that the husband be retired and receiving the basic benefit at the time of his death for his widow to be entitled to the survivors' benefit. It is only necessary for the husband to have been fully insured at the time of his death. The fact that the widow has the benefits start at age 62 instead of 65 does not reduce the amount of the benefit. Since 1965, a qualified widow can start getting benefits at age 60, but the amount is reduced to 71½ per cent of the husband's primary insurance amount. If the benefits begin at age 61 the percentage goes up to 77 per cent.

The widow's survivor benefits continue for life unless she remarries or becomes entitled to a larger amount in benefits based on her own social security record. Since 1965, if a widow qualified for benefits remarries after reaching age 60, she will be eligible for whichever benefit is larger: either one half of the former husband's retirement benefit, or a wife's benefit based on the earnings of her present husband.

If a widow of any age of *either* a fully insured or a currently insured worker is left with a dependent, unmarried child under 18 (or any age if disabled and was so before the age of 18) she is entitled to a survivor benefit equivalent to 75 per cent of her husband's primary insurance amount. This benefit is the same regardless of whether there is one child or a number of dependent children. The benefit continues only so long as there is a child in her care under 18 (unless any disability continues). The amount of a widow's benefits for specified average earnings are shown in Table 17–3.

In addition to the survivor benefits just discussed, a widow of either a fully insured or a currently insured husband is entitled to a lump-sum death benefit equivalent to three times her husband's basic benefit, but the total amount of this lump-sum benefit cannot exceed $255. The lump-sum death benefits for specified average earnings are shown in Table 17–3.

Dependent Child's Survivors' Benefits

Unmarried, dependent children under 18 years of age (under 22 if in school) of either a fully insured or a currently insured parent are entitled to survivor benefits upon the death of the insured parent. If the child was disabled before reaching the age of 18 and the disability continues after age 18, the benefits are still collectible. Each surviving child gets an amount equivalent to 75 per cent of the primary insurance amount of the deceased insured parent. This is also subject to the maximum family benefit. Children's survivor benefits for specified average earnings are shown in Table 17–3.

Widower's Benefits

If a wife who is *both* fully and currently insured dies, her widower is entitled to survivors' benefits at age 62 if the wife had contributed at least 50 per cent toward his support. The amount of the benefit is 82½ per cent of the wife's primary insurance amount. The husband would not be entitled to these benefits if he was entitled to that much or more on his own social security record. The benefits also stop if he remarries. If the husband earns $1,500 or more a year in covered employment, his benefits would be either reduced or eliminated, as will be explained later.

If the deceased wife was *either* fully or currently insured her widower will be entitled to the lump-sum benefit equivalent to three times the wife's basic benefit, but this amount cannot exceed $255. The husband does not have to be dependent or age 62 in order to collect this lump-sum settlement.

Survivors' Benefits for Divorced Women

A divorced woman who meets the above requirements (of a widow) can receive survivors' benefits based on her former husband's account, provided she was married to him at least twenty years before the divorce and provided he had been contributing (or obligated by the court to contribute) to her support when he died. This is another of the 1965 amendments to the law.

A divorced woman (under 60) is entitled to death benefits also if she was dependent on her husband pursuant to an agreement or court order and has in her care his child who is also entitled to benefits.

Dependent Parent's Benefits

A dependent parent of a fully insured worker is entitled to survivors' benefits at age 62. The insured child must have contributed at least 50 per cent toward the support of the parent. Furthermore, to be entitled to this benefit the parent must not marry after the death of the insured child. The amount of one parent's benefit is 82½ per cent of the deceased child's primary benefit. If both parents are living and dependent, each can collect 75 per cent (subject to the maximum family benefit).

No Others Entitled to Benefits

No person other than those mentioned above are entitled to survivors' benefits, with one exception. If there is no widow or widower to claim the lump-sum death benefit, arrangements can be made for the lump-sum death benefit to be paid to a funeral home for any part of the expenses that have not been paid. When the funeral home has been paid in full, the lump-sum death benefit may be paid as reimbursement to those who paid the burial expenses. This is subject, however, to the maximum of $255. This benefit is allowable if the deceased was either fully or currently insured.

SUMMARY OF BENEFITS

In order not to complicate unduly the discussion on benefits, not all the details have been given. For those interested it is suggested that they contact their social security office to ascertain their particular benefits. From the limited amount of material stated above, the reader may not have an overall picture of the nature of the different types of social security benefits, to whom they are payable, and the amounts of the benefits. It is for this reason that the summary in Table 17–4 is given. It should be noted that for simplicity's sake the summary does not contain all the data or limitations that are included in the above discussion.

PAYMENT FOR SOCIAL SECURITY

People have no choice as to whether to come under social security. If they work in covered employment, which includes practically every type of work except certain governmental jobs and railroad employment, or are self-employed in business or are in the professions, they are compelled to pay social security taxes and are subject to the benefits of the system.

If an individual is employed by someone else, his employer is compelled to deduct social security taxes from his wages or salary, and is compelled to pay into the system for the employee's benefit the same amount that is deducted from his wages. A self-employed person must take the initiative and pay social security taxes along with his federal income tax. This is reported in Schedule C of Form 1040.

Table 17–4.

Monthly Benefits Paid	Percentage of Primary Benefit Paid	If You Are
Retirement (old age) Benefits		
You, a retired worker, age 65	100 (reduced rates at ages 62–64)	Fully insured
Your wife, age 65 or over	50 (reduced rates at ages 62–64)	Fully insured
Dependent child (under 18, under 22 if in school, or disabled)	50	Fully insured
Wife (regardless of age), if caring for minor or disabled child	50	Fully insured
Dependent husband age 65 or over	50 (reduced rates at ages 62–64)	Both fully and currently insured
Disability Benefits		
You, before age 65, if totally disabled	100	Fully insured (and have five years of coverage in past ten years)
Dependent child (under 18, under 22 if in school, or disabled)	50	Fully insured
Wife (regardless of age), if caring for minor or disabled child	50	Fully insured
Wife at age 65	50 (reduced rates at ages 62–64)	Fully insured
Survivors' Benefits		
Widow, age 62 or over	82½ (reduced rates at ages 60–61)	Fully insured
Widow (regardless of age), if caring for minor or disabled child	75	Either fully or currently insured
Dependent child (under 18, under 22 if in school, or disabled)	75	Either fully or currently insured
Dependent widower, age 62 or over	82½	Both fully and currently insured
Dependent parent, age 62 or over	82½ (for one parent; 75 for each of two parents)	Fully insured
Lump-sum benefit to widow or widower, or person paying burial expenses	Three times basic benefit (not over $255)	Either fully or currently insured

The Tax Rates

The social security tax rates have been raised a number of times since the system began. The tax rates are applied to covered earnings up to a maximum of $6,600 a year ($550 a month). Rates were raised in 1966 and also, for the first time, deductions were made for the hospital insurance coverage of the Medicare program for the aged. These tax deductions do not cover the charge for the voluntary supplemental medical insurance part of Medicare. If this insurance is taken out, the premiums for it are either paid directly by the individual, or they are taken out of the social security benefits being received by the individual. Medicare is discussed in the last part of the chapter.

Table 17–5 shows the percentage which is deducted from employees' covered earnings to pay for the old-age (retirement), survivors', and disability insurance and the new hospital insurance. The employer must pay social security taxes of exactly the same amount for each employee.

Table 17–5. Contribution Rate Schedules (percentage of covered earnings)

Years	For OASDI Benefits	For Hospital Insurance	Total
Employees and employers (each)			
1966	3.85	.35	4.20
1967–1968	3.90	.50	4.40
1969–1972	4.40	.50	4.90
1973–1975	4.85	.55	5.40
1976–1979	4.85	.60	5.45
1980–1986	4.85	.70	5.55
1987 and after	4.85	.80	5.65
Self-employed people			
1966	5.80	.35	6.15
1967–1968	5.90	.50	6.40
1969–1972	6.60	.50	7.10
1973–1975	7.00	.55	7.55
1976–1979	7.00	.60	7.60
1980–1986	7.00	.70	7.70
1987 and after	7.00	.80	7.80

It will be noted that the tax percentage is scheduled to advance until 1988. Table 17–5 shows also the social security taxes which must be paid by self-employed persons on their earnings up to $6,600 a year. It is noted that the hospital insurance taxes are the same as for employees, but the taxes paid by the self-employed for the other social security benefits are higher.

Table 17–6 shows the monthly social security taxes on monthly earnings of $550 (earnings of $6,600 a year), which is the maximum on which social security taxes are paid, both for employees and self-employed persons (employers must match the amount paid by employees).

People who are both employed and self-employed will of course have deductions taken from their pay where they are employed. If their employed earnings are $6,600 or more per year, they will not have to pay any taxes on their self-employed earnings. But if their wages are less than

Table 17–6. Social Security Taxes on Monthly Earnings of $550

Years	Employee	Self-employed
1966	$277.20	$405.90
1967–1968	290.40	422.40
1969–1972	323.40	468.60
1973–1975	356.40	498.30
1976–1979	359.70	501.60
1980–1986	366.30	508.20
1987 and after	372.90	514.80

this amount they must pay the taxes on that part of their self-employed income necessary to bring the total earnings for the year up to $6,600.

Those who work for more than one employer will have the social security taxes deducted on earnings up to $6,600 a year from their pay by each employer. It may, therefore, result that the taxes will have been deducted on annual wages in excess of $6,600. If this is the case, the worker should claim taxes withheld on that portion of his wages in excess of $6,600 as a credit on his income taxes for that year. Those working for more than one employer should keep a record of their employers and the amount of their wages in order to be able to supply the data necessary for the refund or claim. If they do not take the initiative in this regard they will lose the amount of the excessive taxes.

WHEN TO TAKE ACTION

Social security benefits are never paid automatically to the persons who are entitled to the benefits. An application for benefits must be filed with the social security office before any benefits can be collected from any of the types of insurance. A person is never sure whether he is entitled to benefits until he consults with the social security office. If application for monthly benefits is not filed on time a person may lose all of the benefits up to that time with the exception of the last six months. To collect on the lump-sum death benefit the claim must be filed within two years after the death of the insured person. The safest thing to do is to consult with the nearest social security office when any of the following occur.

When Retirement Age Is Reached. When a person reaches the age of 62 it is advisable to contact the social security office to ascertain whether he is eligible for benefits. Although he may not be eligible for retirement benefits at that time, he can find out what is needed to qualify.

When the Age of 72 Is Reached. An individual may not be eligible for retirement benefits or complete benefits at 62 because he is earning more than $1,500 (investment income not included) a year. After he reaches 72, however, he can get the retirement benefits regardless of the amount of his earnings in employment. If earnings from employment have kept him from receiving the benefits, there is no reason why he should not file for the benefits upon reaching 72.

When Disabled Before 65. A person under 65 who has become severely disabled should contact his social security office to ascertain if he is eligible for disability benefits.

When Someone in a Family Dies. If a member of a family dies, his survivors should consult with the social security office to ascertain whether the deceased was insured in order that the designated family members may be able to collect any survivors' benefits that may be due. The age for a widow's survivors' benefits was lowered in 1965 from age 62 to 60 (at reduced amount).

Dependent Child Under 22 in School. Prior to 1965, retirement, disability, and survivors' benefits based on a parent's earnings, and paid to dependent children ceased when the child reached 18 (unless disabled). Now (since 1965) such benefits continue until age 22 if the child is in school. Any families having such children for whom the benefits stopped when they reached 18 should immediately contact their social security office and have the benefits resumed.

Divorced Women. The 1965 amendments permit divorced women who were married to their former husbands for twenty years or more to receive benefits based on their former husband's earnings in the manner discussed above.

Persons 72 and Over. Persons 72 and over who have not been receiving social security benefits because they (or their husband) did not work long enough under social security may, since the 1965 amendments, be entitled to some benefits. They should immediately contact their social security office to ascertain whether they are eligible for any benefits.

Periodic Check. An employer must furnish an employee with receipts showing the amount of his wages and the amount that has been deducted for social security. This must be done at least once a year and when the employment is terminated. It may be advisable for the employee to check with the proper social security office soon after he goes on the social security rolls to make sure that he is getting proper credit for the taxes he is paying. Perhaps shortly after the first year of covered employment would be an ideal time. Checks can be made thereafter at intervals of a number of years. If several employers are making deductions from the employee's wages and he is not sure whether such deductions have been taken from annual earnings in excess of $6,600, it would be advisable to get the information directly from the Social Security Administration, P. O.

REQUEST FOR STATEMENT OF EARNINGS

ACCOUNT NUMBER			
DATE OF BIRTH	MONTH	DAY	YEAR

Please send me a statement of the amount of earnings recorded in my social security account.

NAME { MISS / MRS. / MR. ______________________

STREET & NUMBER ______________________

CITY, STATE AND ZIP CODE ______________________

} *Print Name and Address In Ink Or Use Typewriter*

SIGN YOUR NAME AS YOU USUALLY WRITE IT ______________________

Sign your own name only. Under the law, information in your social security record is confidential and anyone who signs someone else's name can be prosecuted.
If your name has been changed from that shown on your social security account number card, please copy your name below exactly as it appears on that card.

Fig. 17–1. Request for statement of earnings card.

Box 57, Baltimore, Maryland 21203. A postcard may be obtained from the nearest social security office to be used for mailing for this information (see Fig. 17–1). To request the "quarters of coverage" recorded, "QC" should be written on the card.

WHEN THE BENEFITS STOP

The occurrence of certain events will terminate the social security benefits that are being paid to an individual and to his family, based on their status. If these events happen, they are compelled by law to report them to the social security office. Penalties are imposed for failure to give this notice.

Working After Retirement

If a person under 72 who is drawing retirement benefits makes in wages or self-employment, or both combined, over $1,500 a year he will not be entitled to his social security benefits, or at least not entitled to the full benefits. In counting his wages, the amount earned even in non-covered employment is counted. Income earned from interest, dividends, rentals, pensions, annuities and other investments, veterans' benefits, gifts, inheritances, and capital gains, however, are not included. In other words a person may make $50,000 a year from investments, but so long as he does not earn over $1,500 a year from wages or salary and self-employment his social security benefits will not be affected.

Since 1965, persons 65 and older can treat royalties as investment income (for benefit purposes), rather than earned income, provided the copyright or patent giving rise to the income was obtained before the person was 65.

A beneficiary who earns more than $1,500 in a year will have $1 taken off his total year's benefit for each $2 earned from $1,500 up to $2,700, and for annual earnings above $2,700, $1 of benefits will be subtracted for each $1 earned. Applying these rules, a person under 72 could earn from $2,556 to $5,811 a year (depending on the size of the monthly bene-

Table 17–7. How Earnings Affect Social Security (effective 1966)

This table shows how much you can collect in social security benefits even if you continue working. First, look at the column on the left for the amount closest to the monthly benefit which you are getting or which your family is drawing on your social security account. Then look under the figure closest to your estimated earnings for the year to get a rough idea of how much social security you may still draw.

Monthly Benefit	Benefits for Year If Earnings Total				
	$0–$1,500	$2,100	$2,700	$3,300	$3,900
$ 44	$ 528	$ 228	$ 0	$ 0	$ 0
50	600	300	0	0	0
60	720	420	120	0	0
70	840	540	240	0	0
80	960	660	360	0	0
90	1,080	780	480	0	0
100	1,200	900	600	0	0
110	1,320	1,020	720	120	0
120	1,440	1,140	840	240	0
130	1,560	1,260	960	360	0
140	1,680	1,380	1,080	480	0
150	1,800	1,500	1,200	600	0
160	1,920	1,620	1,320	720	120
170	2,040	1,740	1,440	840	240
180	2,160	1,860	1,560	960	360
190	2,280	1,980	1,680	1,080	480
200	2,400	2,100	1,800	1,200	600
210	2,520	2,220	1,920	1,320	720
220	2,640	2,340	2,040	1,440	840
230	2,760	2,460	2,160	1,560	960
240	2,880	2,580	2,280	1,680	1,080
250	3,000	2,700	2,400	1,800	1,200
260	3,120	2,820	2,520	1,920	1,320
270	3,240	2,940	2,640	2,040	1,440
300	3,600	3,300	3,000	2,400	1,800

Note: Regardless of how much you make, you may still draw your regular check for any month in which your earnings don't exceed $125 or, if you are self-employed, for any month in which you don't perform "substantial services."

fit) before losing all his social security family benefits. Table 17–7 shows the amount of the annual benefits that will be received by persons (under 72) receiving specified monthly family benefits if they earn the amounts stated.

What has just been said, however, must be qualified by another rule. A person will not lose the social security retirement check for any month in which he neither received wages of more than $125 nor rendered substantial services in self-employment. For example, assume that a person received wages of $600 a month for each of the twelve months of a year (total of $7,200 for the year). According to the above-stated rule he would lose social security checks for each of the twelve months. But assume that he earned $7,200 during the year and that during four of the months he made only $125 (or less). He will be entitled to benefits for these four months, and will lose checks for only eight months instead of twelve months.

It is possible for a person actually to receive more than $125 in a particular month in wages or salary and still not lose his social security check for that month. Some companies will enter into a deferred salary contract with some of their employees or officers. The contract will provide that as part of the payment for services rendered, the officer or executive will receive after retirement a salary of a specified amount per month for a given number of years. If the retired employee does not "render any service" (or at least not over $125 of service) that month for his salary, even though it is in excess of $125, he will not lose his social security benefits for that month. Another arrangement would be to pay the executive an amount, such as $8,000, for a special one-to-four-weeks' (in the same month) consulting job. He would then draw benefit checks from social security for the remaining eleven months. But if the company's executive spent several days out of each month at the consulting office and received $8,000 a year, he would lose his social security checks for all twelve of the months.

If a self-employed retired person makes over $1,500 a year from his business he will not lose social security checks for any month in which he does not perform "substantial services" in the business. This is difficult to define since there is no monetary amount which decides the issue. Generally, devoting more than forty-five hours to the business during one month would be considered to be performing "substantial services." The following example, however, is clear-cut. Assume that a person who is drawing retirement benefits operates a hot dog stand for a three-month period in the summer, and that he clears $2,500 for the three summer months. He could still draw social security checks for the other nine months of the year (assuming he did not operate some other business or earn wages).

If a retired person loses social security checks because of his earning more than the amount permitted, any of his dependents who are drawing benefits based on his status also lose their benefit checks for the same months that the insured lost his. If a dependent who is drawing benefit checks earns more than the prescribed amount, he will lose his benefits in the same manner as has been described for the insured person. But the loss of benefits on the part of the dependent because of his own earnings will not affect the status of the insured person. In other words, the latter's benefit checks would be paid (assuming his own earnings do not exceed the maximum permitted). A widow's earnings will not count against her children's benefits—and her children's earnings do not count against her benefit.

A retired person who is earning in excess of $1,500 a year can notify the social security office of such excess earnings and his benefit checks will be reduced or withheld during that year. If he does not do this, he must report such excess earnings on a special form when he files his income tax form not later than April 15 of the following year. Benefit checks would then be withheld that year for the excess earnings of the previous year.

It should be noted that the above discussion is related to an insured person who is under 72. If a person is 72 or over he may earn any amount from any source and he will not lose his social security benefits.

Other Reasons for Termination of Benefits

If a person who is receiving any kind of social security benefits dies, his or her benefits are, of course, terminated. The last benefit check would be for the month immediately preceding death.

When a person receiving retirement benefits dies, the retirement benefits being received by any member of his family based on his insured status would also be terminated. But any qualified family members would then be entitled to survivors' benefits.

If a person who is receiving monthly benefits as a dependent or as a survivor gets married, his or her benefits stop, except for qualified widows who remarry after reaching age 60.

Benefits being received by a wife or dependent husband are stopped if they become divorced, except for divorced women who were married to their former husbands for twenty or more years.

Benefits being received by a child not in school stop when the child becomes 18, unless he is disabled and such disability continues.

If a wife under 62 or widow under 60 is receiving benefits because of the care of a minor child, her benefits will stop when the child becomes 18 (unless disabled).

Benefits being paid to children in school will stop when the child becomes 22, or quits school (if over 18).

When a person is receiving benefits and any of the above events occur, he must take the initiative and notify the social security office of this event.

THOSE WITH MILITARY SERVICE

Individuals who were in the military services during or after World War II may benefit from social security even though they were not in covered employment before entering the service.

Service Before 1957

Anyone in military service during World War II (September 16, 1940, through July 24, 1947) or the post-World War II period of July 25, 1947, through December 31, 1956, who was discharged under conditions other than dishonorable after at least 90 days' service (latter not required if discharge was for service-connected disability), can qualify for special treatment under the social security laws. Although social security taxes were not deducted from servicemen's pay during these periods, a veteran can get a social security wage credit of $160 a month for the time he was in service. This time also counts, of course, in determining his period of coverage and his insured status. The $160 a month wage credit is not actually listed on the veteran's social security record. At the time he or his family claims benefits it will be necessary to prove the military service and honorable discharge.

Service After January 1, 1957

Since January 1, 1957, those in the military services have been covered by social security in the same manner as a person in covered employment in civilian life. The social security taxes are deducted from the base pay of the serviceman, and the time in service is of course counted as covered employment. From what has just been said it should be apparent that a flat wage credit of $160 a month has not been granted since December 31, 1956.

THE SOCIAL SECURITY CARD

At the time when a person first becomes covered by social security he is given a social security card. If this is not received the individual should immediately request it. This card contains his name and his social security number. This number remains the same throughout his life. Since many different people may have the same name, the number is important in identifying the proper person. It is advisable always to show a new employer the card in order that he may report the taxes applicable with the exact information appearing on the card. If a person's name changes from that on the original card, a new card bearing his (her) new name should be obtained from the nearest social security office. If the card is lost, a request should be made for a new one.

WHAT IS DONE WITH THE MONEY

The social security taxes that are collected by the Internal Revenue Service are deposited in the Federal Old-Age and Survivors Insurance Fund, and the Federal Disability Insurance Trust Fund. The funds are used for overhead administration expenses of the agency and to pay benefits to insured members and their qualified dependent family members. The part remaining is invested in United States Government securities. People should not worry over the safety of the fund or the ability of the agency to make future social security benefit payments.

Many people who were temporarily employed in covered work and had deductions made for social security, and who are no longer employed, are wondering what happened to the deductions that were made from their wages. Most of these people are in the dark as to what rights or benefits, if any, they have under social security.

The answer to this question is easy. If the person cannot meet the requirements of either a currently or fully insured worker, as defined above, then he has no rights under social security, as the law is at the present time. The amounts which were deducted from his wages go into the funds set up by the government. The deductions made, however, remain to the worker's credit and may be supplemented by future deductions. Eventually he may become fully insured.

CRITIQUE

The social security system has been both praised and condemned. There can be no doubt, however, that to many people social security benefits are a godsend. Criticisms of the system are directed more at some of the details of its organization and operation, or at its inadequacies and inequities, rather than at the system itself.

Most people and families in the United States do not save enough to provide an adequate income in the event of disability or retirement. Many people who are 65 or over have incomes of less than $1,000 a year. The problem has become worse in recent years with the mounting cost of living resulting from the inflation that has taken place. Income is earned, and savings and investments are made, at one level of prices; but upon retirement, the prices that must be paid for the essentials of life have increased. This makes it difficult even with the added social security benefits, but it would be still worse if there were no social security.

At the present time, a man who has had average earnings in covered employment of $350 a month can retire at age 65 and, if he has a wife age 65, collect a total of $186.30 a month for life. In the future a person may retire and get the following monthly benefits (assuming he has a wife 65 or over):

Average Monthly Earnings	Monthly Benefits
$400	$203.90
450	219.00
550	252.00

These amounts may not be adequate for normal living, but they are certainly better than nothing. Or, they may serve as an adequate addition to other retirement income such as pensions, interest and dividends, annuities, etc. Looking at it in another way, a person would have to have the imposing sum of $55,890 invested at 4 per cent to yield $186.30 a month. But with social security he gets this monthly income (his wife's benefit included) from his average earnings of the past of $350 a month. If a man and wife receive $186.30 a month in social security benefits they will in ten years' time have collected a total of $22,356. If the husband then dies, the wife will continue to get monthly survivors' benefit checks in the amount of $102.50 for the rest of her life.

If a man is totally disabled he can collect the following amounts (assuming his wife and children do not qualify for benefits):

Average Monthly Earnings	Monthly Benefits
$350	$124.20
400	135.90
450	146.00
550	168.00

Another important feature of social security benefits is that they are not subject to income taxes.

Social security taxes and the benefits received have been increased a number of times in the past. If inflation continues it is probable that they will be further increased.

One of the criticisms frequently heard is that a retired person cannot make a decent wage thereafter or his social security benefits will be reduced or eliminated entirely. This applies to the ages of 62 to 72, and was discussed above. It is argued that if a person pays his social security taxes he should be entitled to the benefits regardless of how much he earns. Perhaps in the future the present age of 72, at which a person may earn any amount and not lose social security benefits will be lowered (it was 75 originally).

Another criticism many make is that a person who is so fortunate as to earn a large amount from investments will not lose any of his social security benefits regardless of how much he may earn from the return on the investments. But the less fortunate individual who has no income from investments and who, therefore, needs to work in order to live, cannot earn over $125 a month without losing some or all of his social security benefits.

Naturally many people complain about the amount of the social security taxes which must be paid. When the social security system went into effect in 1937, $3,000 was the top annual wage that was subjected to the tax, and the amount of the annual tax on this amount was only $30. Both the top wage figure and the rate of taxation have steadily advanced over the years. In 1966, the top annual wage was advanced from $4,800 to $6,600, and the rates also took another step up. Furthermore, taxes for the hospital insurance part of the Medicare program were added in 1966. The annual social security tax that had to be paid on annual wages of $6,600 in 1966 was $277.20. On self-employed earnings of the same amount the tax was $405.90. These amounts are scheduled to advance over the years until 1987, when the wage earner will have to pay annual social security taxes of $372.90, and the self-employed, $514.80—based on annual earnings of $6,600. For many people, the social security taxes are more than their federal income tax.

MEDICARE

In Chapter 8, health and medical insurance were discussed, that is, either individual or group policies taken out in private companies. The balance of the present chapter dealing with Medicare is related to the material in Chapter 8, but since the Medicare provisions were first adopted in 1965 as part of the total social security system operated by the government, it was thought advisable by the authors to discuss Medicare in the present chapter on social security. It is advisable for people 65 and over to reappraise their personal insurance program in the light of their insurance coverage under the Medicare program.

In the past, many elderly people in the United States have had a difficult time trying to make ends meet. In 1965, of 34.6 million people in the United States classed as "poor," 5.2 million, or 15 per cent, were 65 or older. Although the elderly account for one in ten of our population, they represent one in seven of our poor. The average income of the country's elderly couples is only $2,900—as compared to $5,800 for the under-65 couple. The social security benefits described in the first part of the chapter have helped tremendously in alleviating their situation. But when illness strikes, or prolonged hospitalization is necessary, a financial catastrophe occurs, even for those who have been able to get along under ordinary circumstances. About the only kind of insurance that many of them have carried has been Blue Cross or Blue Shield, both of which have limited application. Most of the ordinary medical or hospitalization insurance which some of them carried ran only to age 60 or 65. In recent years insurance has in some instances been made available to those 65 or older, but the premiums have been extremely high and the benefits limited. The majority of the aged cannot afford to carry private insurance which would give them adequate protection.

Attempts in the past to have Congress enact a national program of health and hospitalization insurance were unsuccessful until 1965, when the Medicare amendments to the Social Security Act were finally adopted.

At the outset approximately 19 million Americans 65 and over were almost automatically covered by the Medicare insurance. But to help defray the added cost of the new program the 76 million younger Americans who are paying social security taxes had their taxes increased effective January 1, 1966, and further increases are scheduled for successive periods up until 1987.

Persons Covered by Medicare

Generally speaking, all men and women in the United States age 65 or older are eligible for Medicare benefits.[2] At the time Medicare went into effect, this was true regardless of whether the person had ever paid any social security taxes. Another way of stating this is that any person who was born before 1903 is eligible for Medicare benefits even if he is not covered by social security. But those born in 1903 need at least six quarters of social security coverage to be eligible. The coverage needed for persons of various ages is shown in Table 17–8.

How to Enroll for Medicare Benefits

People who are already eligible for Medicare and are receiving monthly social security, civil service, or railroad retirement benefits will automatically get a form from the government to sign up for Medicare. Those 65 or over who are not receiving any of these benefits should go to their

[2] Federal workers and their dependents who are enrolled in the health plan established for them by the Federal Employees Health Benefits Act of 1959 are not covered by Medicare. The following are also excluded: (1) aliens who have not been admitted to the United States for permanent residence; (2) other aliens who have not lived in the United States continuously for the five years just before filing a Medicare claim; (3) members of subversive organizations; and (4) persons convicted of such high crimes as sabotage, espionage, and sedition. But if a federal employee or an alien who because of previous employment is entitled to social security or railroad retirement benefits, then he would be eligible for Medicare.

Table 17–8. Quarters of Social Security Coverage Needed To Qualify for Medicare Benefits

Year of Birth	Quarters Needed	
	Men	Women
1902 or earlier	0	0
1903	6	6
1904	9	9
1905	12	12
1906	15	15
1907	18	18
1908	21	19
1909 or later	Same as for social security retirement benefits	

social security office and file an application to establish eligibility for Medicare. The supplemental insurance may be bought during a seven-month period starting with the third month before their 65th birthday. A card similar to a Blue Cross card will be given to the person. This card will also show whether the individual has bought the supplemental insurance, which will be explained later. If a person is eligible to receive the Medicare hospitalization insurance, he can still get the benefits when he enters a hospital even if he has not received his card. But registration and the payment of the premiums are necessary to get the supplemental medical benefits which are discussed below.

The Medicare Program

The term *Medicare* is not used in the new health insurance amendments which were made to the social security legislation in 1965. This is merely a popular term which is used to apply to the particular legislation which is officially titled *Health Insurance for the Aged.* This legislation provides for two distinct types of insurance: (1) *Hospital Insurance* (provided for in Part A of the legislation and sometimes called "Plan A"), and (2) *Medical Insurance* (provided for in Part B of the legislation, and therefore sometimes referred to as "Plan B").

As the title would indicate, the Hospital Insurance covers hospital and post-hospital bills. It is sometimes referred to as the basic insurance plan. It is the one that was automatically applicable to all persons 65 or over. The cost of this plan is being met by the increased payroll deductions for social security taxes. But, as was stated earlier, people who were born prior to 1903 are eligible for the benefits even though they have paid no social security taxes. Younger workers started paying for the cost of this insurance for the elderly, as well as for themselves, on January 1, 1966.

The Medical Insurance is also officially referred to as the *Supplementary Medical Insurance Program*, and it is sometimes referred to as the voluntary insurance plan, or the voluntary supplementary insurance plan. This insurance covers doctors' bills and other medical and health expenses (as distinguished from hospital bills). Anyone eligible for the Hospital Insurance can also buy the Medical Insurance. In addition, the latter is available to federal employees who cannot qualify for Hospital Insurance. To get the benefits of the Medical Insurance a person must subscribe to the plan and pay his insurance premiums. People who are drawing social security benefits can arrange to have their premiums deducted from their benefits.

Hospital Insurance Benefits

The benefits of the Hospital Insurance which apply to practically all persons 65 and older can be classified into three different types, those covering (1) hospital bills, (2) nursing home expenses, and (3) home health services.

Hospital Bills. The need for insurance to cover hospital bills is apparent when it is realized that the American Hospital Association reported that in 1964 the average bill for each day in a general hospital in the United States was $40.40. This was the eighteenth year in a row that hospital bills had increased. In 1964, the bill for the average stay in a hospital was $307.00. Older people are more likely to need hospitalization than the average person and, furthermore, their average stay in the hospital is longer than the average.

Perhaps this part of Medicare could have been more aptly called "Hospicare." These benefits became effective July 1, 1966. If a person 65 or over enters an approved hospital, he must stand the first $40 of his hospital bill. The insurance pays for the remaining part of the bill for a period of 60 days, and all but $10 a day of the bill for the next 30 days (assuming the doctor certified hospital need). Thus, the insurance provides substantial hospital benefits for up to 90 days for each "spell of illness." If the patient stays in the hospital longer than 19 days, however, the doctor must recertify the need at intervals specified by the government. A "spell of illness" begins the day a patient is admitted to a hospital or nursing home, and ends once the patient has been outside for 60 straight days.

The coverage applies not only to general hospitals, but also to psychiatric and tuberculosis hospitals, provided a doctor certifies that the hospital treatment can be "reasonably expected to improve" the patient's condition. But if a patient is already in a mental or TB hospital when Medicare becomes available to him, the time he has spent there will be counted against the 90-day limit for a "spell of illness." Furthermore, Medicare benefits to a person in a mental hospital will cease after payments have been made (during his lifetime) for 120 days of care. If the patient goes into a Christian Science sanitarium, the insurance covers up to 120 days of care. The patient stands the first $40, plus $10 for each day after the first 60 days, and $5 for each day after the first 90 days. The government (insurance) stands the balance.

The hospital expenses covered are for board and room in a semiprivate room (two to four beds), unless the doctor orders a private room, in which event the latter is covered. In addition to the "board and room" expenses, the insurance covers the following additional hospital services:

Regular nursing services (but not a private nurse)
Services of residents and interns
Blood transfusions after the first three pints
All prescribed drugs and biologicals
Service of technicians in X ray, pathology, and anesthetics (but not doctors)

Hospital expenses for non-overnight patients who go into a hospital for diagnostic tests are also partly covered for a 20-day period. The patient pays the first $20 and one fifth of the balance of the bill and the insurance stands the rest.

Nursing Home Expenses. The coverage discussed here applies to what the law calls an "extended-care facility," and becomes effective January 1, 1967. This must be more than an ordinary nursing or rest home which offers only custodial care. To qualify, the home must generally be licensed or approved by the particular state, and must have a written agreement governing patient transfers with at least one hospital that has signed up for the Medicare program. The patient must be under a physician's supervision, and a doctor must always be available for emergency care. At least one registered nurse must be employed full-time.

To qualify for "extended-care facility" (under the Hospital Insurance) benefits, the patient must have spent at least three days in a hospital and entered the nursing home within 14 days after leaving the hospital. If the patient re-enters the nursing home within 14 days after leaving, he is covered even though he did not go back to the hospital again. The nursing home benefits apply only when a doctor has certified the need for skilled nursing care.

Nursing home benefits apply up to 100 days for each "spell of illness." The government pays for the first 20 days, and all but $5 a day for each additional day up to 80 more days.

Like hospital coverage, nursing home benefits apply to bed and board in a semiprivate room. Additional services are as follows.

Nursing care (but not a private nurse)
Services of interns and residents attached to qualified hospitals
Physical, occupational, and speech therapy
Services of medical social workers
Drugs and appliances

Home Health Services. Basic home health services (under hospital insurance) coverage applies only after the patient has been hospitalized for at least three days, and within 14 days after he returns home from the hospital or nursing home and the doctor certifies the specialized services needed. The home health services must be supplied by approved public or private home health agencies (other than those primarily for mental patients) and supervised by a doctor or registered nurse. Medicare benefits for those services became effective July 1, 1966. Included in the covered services are the following:

Part-time or intermittent nursing care provided by or under supervision of a registered nurse (but not a private nurse)
Physical, occupational, and speech therapy
Services of medical social workers
Medical supplies such as dressings and splints
Use of wheelchairs and crutches

The coverage applies to the first 100 "visits" after the patient returns from the hospital or nursing home, but the benefits end one year after the patient's discharge from the hospital or nursing home. If the patient is rehospitalized after being home at least 60 days, however, it will be regarded as a new "spell of illness," and he will again be eligible for 100 more visits upon returning home. Each type of service rendered is considered a "visit." Thus, if a nurse and a therapist both call on the patient at the same time, it will be counted as two visits.

If the patient is directed to go to a hospital or rehabilitation center for such treatment as hydrotherapy, this will also be covered. But he cannot stay overnight, and he must pay for his own transportation.

Medical Insurance

This part of the insurance program does not come automatically to persons 65 and older. To get this insurance, it is necessary for the person to sign up for it, and pay his premiums. The plan became effective on July 1, 1966, for persons who qualified. The insurance becomes effective three months after signing up.

People 65 or older who get or will be getting social security benefit checks will automatically receive their Medicare cards from the government. They can then sign up for the Medical Insurance if they wish.

Others can sign up for the insurance during a seven-month period starting with the third month before their 65th birthday. People who failed to sign up during this time may still sign up for the insurance during the last three months of any odd-numbered year starting with 1967. The amount of the premium, however, increases 10 per cent for each year delayed. The insurance may be dropped at the end of any calendar year. If premiums are not paid after a 90-day grace period, the government will drop the individual's insurance. Dropped insurance may be reinstated during any general enrollment period which begins within three years after the insurance was dropped. Higher premiums, however, are charged. But if the insurance is dropped a second time, it cannot be reinstated.

Premiums. The cost to the insured of this supplementary insurance is $3 a month. If husband and wife both want to be covered they each must sign up for the insurance and each pay the $3 monthly premiums. Those receiving social security, civil service, or railroad retirement benefit checks can have the premiums deducted from their checks. Others must pay the premiums to the social security office.

The government matches each $3 premium with its own contribution of $3, which is paid into the insurance fund. Thus, the government really pays half the cost of this insurance. Because of this, and the nature of the benefits received, it can generally be said that no person eligible for this insurance can afford *not* to sign up for it.

States and counties may pay the premiums in order to have their welfare claimants covered by the insurance.

Medical Expenses Covered. The supplementary insurance will pay 80 per cent of doctors' bills (assuming the doctors have agreed to participate in Medicare) after the first $50 for each calendar year. In other words, the patient must stand the first $50 of his annual doctor bills, and 20 per cent of the amount which is in excess of $50. The government pays the balance. It makes no difference whether the doctor treats him in his office, clinic, hospital, nursing home, or in his own home—he is covered. The doctor may be a general practitioner, or a specialist in pathology, radiology, physical therapy, anesthesia, etc. Doctor bills for mental illness treatments outside a hospital, however, are covered only up to 50 per cent, with a maximum benefit of $250 in any one year. Routine physical exams and vaccine shots are not covered. Dental bills are covered only in the event of jaw or other facial bone surgery required by accident or disease. Charges made by chiropractors and podiatrists are not covered. Drug bills are *not* covered under the Medical Insurance.

In addition to the regular charges made for a doctor's services, the following services are included under medical bills coverage.

Diagnostic tests, including X ray and laboratory tests performed in an approved laboratory
Radiation therapy
Surgical dressings, splints, and casts
Rental of iron lungs, oxygen tents, hospital beds, and wheelchairs
Artificial limbs, artificial eyes, and braces (but not orthopedic shoes, false teeth, hearing aids, or eyeglasses)
Ambulance service to nearest hospital when needed

Home Health Services. The supplemental insurance also provides coverage for the same "home health services" as were listed under the hospital insurance above, and under the same circumstances, with the following exception: prior hospitalization is not necessary under the medical coverage. Also, 100 "visits" per year under the Medical Insurance are in addition to the 100 provided in the Hospital Insurance. These home health service expenses are included under the medical costs and therefore the coverage is subject to the $50 annual exclusion and then 80 per cent of the balance of the expenses are covered.

Reasonable Customary Charges

Schedules of "reasonable, customary" medical charges are worked out for the particular community by the agency representing Medicare, with the cooperation of the medical profession. If a doctor charges a particular patient more than is provided for in the schedule, the insurance will cover only 80 per cent (after the first $50) of the "reasonable, customary" charge. The same is true regarding the hospital coverage under the basic plan. Naturally, if a patient wants better care, or more services, he will have to pay for this out of his own pocket.

Free Health Benefits to Needy and Near-Needy

One part of the social security program which will not be discussed is that which applies to the needy and near-needy. All the states have some kind of health benefits for recipients of "old-age assistance." And most of the states have put into effect the so-called Kerr–Mills programs to care for the "medically indigent." These are people 65 or older who are not poor enough to get regular welfare checks, but who cannot afford to pay their medical bills. The federal government through social security and the assistance of states will provide for free health services for such persons. The 1965 amendments to the law extended free health services to some needy persons under 65, such as children and their parents, the blind, and those totally and permanently disabled.

Use of Medicare Funds

The financing of the Medicare program is kept separate from the rest of the social security program. In the case of the Hospital Insurance, the amount contributed by employees, which is matched with an equal amount by the employer, and the amount contributed by the self-employed (these amounts are shown in Tables 17–4 and 17–5) are set aside in the Hospital Insurance Trust Fund, from which the program's administrative costs and benefits will be paid.

The $3 a month (per person) premium for the Supplemental Medical Insurance is matched with an equal amount from the general revenues of the federal government, and these amounts are turned over to the Supplementary Medical Insurance Fund, and the administrative costs and benefits arising from the medical insurance program will be paid from the Fund. Surpluses left in both trust funds will be invested in United States Government securities.

QUESTIONS

1. Do you believe that the social security system represents a big step toward socialism in the United States? Explain.
2. Are all employed and all self-employed persons in the United States covered by social security? Explain.
3. How much a year must be earned by each of the following to come under social security:
   (a) Self-employed
   (b) Factory worker
   (c) Domestic servant
4. Indicate the requirements for a *currently* insured worker.
5. Explain specifically how the "average monthly wage" is computed.
6. The following apply to retirement benefits:
   (a) How old must a worker be to qualify?
   (b) To whom are the benefits paid?
   (c) Is a currently insured worker entitled to the benefits?
7. (a) Explain what is meant by the "primary insurance amount."
   (b) What determines the amount of this benefit?
8. (a) How long must a person live in order that his retirement benefits beginning at age 65 would give him more money for life than if the benefits began at age 62?
   (b) Does the wife of a retired worker get less if her benefits begin at age 62 rather than at age 65? Explain.
9. What percentage of her husband's primary insurance amount is a wife (age 65) of a retired worker entitled to?
10. (a) Are children of a retired worker entitled to benefits?
    (b) What percentage of a father's basic benefits are eligible children entitled to?

11. Under what circumstances are husbands of retired wives eligible for benefits based on the wife's retirement benefits? What percentage of the latter are they entitled to?
12. Indicate the conditions that are necessary in order that a worker will be entitled to disability benefits.
13. If a worker is eligible for disability benefits, what percentage of the basic benefit is he entitled to?
14. What relatives of a worker drawing disability benefits are also entitled to benefits? How much can they get?
15. When is a widow (age 62) entitled to monthly survivors' benefits? How much does she get?
16. When is a widower (age 62) entitled to monthly survivors' benefits? How much can he get?
17. Indicate the circumstances under which a child of a deceased worker would be entitled to monthly survivors' benefits. How much are such children entitled to?
18. How much can a person drawing retirement benefits earn in wages and still be entitled to his full social security benefits?
19. If you are covered by social security, does this relieve you of the need for retirement planning? Explain.
20. What are the principal criticisms or shortcomings of the social security system (OASDI) at the present time?
21. At what age do the Medicare provisions of social security become effective? Must a person have worked in covered employment under social security before the Medicare provisions apply to him? Explain.
22. Do the social security taxes which are deducted from an employee's pay cover the hospital and medical insurance, or must a person pay an extra insurance premium for them? Explain.
23. Indicate specifically what is covered under the Hospital Insurance of Medicare.
24. Indicate specifically what is covered under the Supplemental Medical Insurance of Medicare.
25. Are the qualifications for home health services any different under the Hospital Insurance than they are under the Medical Insurance? Explain.
26. Define what is meant by a "spell of illness" under the Medicare provisions.

CASE PROBLEMS

1. Harold Washburn, who was born in 1901, having reached the age of 65 in late 1966, decided to retire at the end of the year. He had worked in covered employment continuously since 1950, and received the following amount in annual wages for the years stated:

Years	Annual Wages
1951–1953	$4,300
1954–1958	5,200
1959–1963	6,200
1964–1965	7,200
1966	6,000

(a) Is he entitled to retirement benefits? Why?
(b) How many years of earnings would he count to get his average earnings?
(c) Specifically which years of earnings would he use, and what would be the amount of his "average annual earnings"?

2. Mike Rooney, who is 65, is retiring this year. He is fully insured and his "average annual earnings" come to $4,200. Rooney's wife is 55 years old, and they have two unmarried dependent school children ages 16 and 18.
(a) What amount would they receive in family retirement benefits? Explain.
(b) Specifically, what is the amount of the benefits that would go to each member of the family?
(c) What event or events would alter the amount of the family benefits? (Assume neither the husband or wife takes a job.) Indicate how the event would affect the family's benefits.

3. John Wilson, age 57, is unable to work any longer because he is suffering from incurable cancer. He has worked in covered employment for the past fifteen years, during which time his "average annual earnings" were $3,600. Wilson has a wife age 55, and a 16-year-old unmarried dependent daughter.
(a) Is John Wilson entitled to disability benefits? If so, how much?
(b) Are any other members of his family also entitled to benefits? Explain.
(c) Under what circumstances will the family benefits be altered?

4. Frank Clark, who was fully insured under social security, was killed in an automobile accident. He left a widow age 54, and a 16-year-old unmarried dependent son. Mr. Clark's average annual earnings were computed to be $5,400.
(a) Who would be entitled to death benefits? How much?
(b) What events would change the amount of the family's benefits?
(c) If Mrs. Clark decided to have her widow's benefits (other than because of child care) begin at 60 instead of 62, what monthly benefits would she get?
(d) If Mrs. Clark had her benefits begin at 62 instead of at 65, would they be any less?
(e) If Mr. Clark had not been fully insured but had worked under social security continuously for the past five years before his death (assume same average earnings), would the answers to any of the above questions have been different? Explain.

5. Dr. Will Hopewell, who was born in 1899, retired from the general practice of medicine in 1964. He suffered a heart attack in December, 1966, which required hospitalization in The University Hospital for 70 days. His hospital bill was $1,950, which included $25 a day for a semiprivate room, and the usual hospital charges (which would be covered under Hospital Insurance). During the last ten days the only charge was for the room. Private nurses cost $280.00. Dr. Hopewell's private physician refused to bill him, but on the insistence of Dr. Hopewell, he billed him for a nominal amount of $75. Dr. Hopewell had opposed the Medicare legislation both publicly and in his local medical association meetings, because, he said, he was opposed to socialized medicine, and he had at the time of his attack not signed up for any part of the Medicare program.
(a) Could Dr. Hopewell claim any benefits under Medicare? Explain.

(b) If he could sign up for hospital insurance in the hospital and receive benefits, how much would he be entitled to?
(c) Considering his opposition to Medicare, do you believe he should accept any of the benefits?
(d) Could he sign up for Medical Insurance? If so, could he collect for this particular illness? Explain.

6. Howard Blackson suffered a stroke and was hospitalized for three weeks, after which time his doctor recommended a nursing home where he stayed for four weeks. Mr. Blackson was 67 at the time of the stroke. His hospital bill was $460, and the nursing home cost $280 (board and room). Mr. Blackson did not carry Medical Insurance. Could he collect anything under Medicare? If so, how much?
7. During the past year, Mr. Cook's doctors' bills amounted to $480, and his prescription–drug bill was $175. He carried the government Medical Insurance. How much could he collect from the government? Explain. If Mr. Cook listed his deductions when he filed his federal income tax return, could he list as medical expense that amount which he paid the government for hospital insurance (if he was employed) and medical insurance? Should the amount collected under these programs be deducted when he lists his medical expenses?

SELECTED READINGS

Department of Health, Education, and Welfare, Social Security Administration, Washington, D. C. Copies may be obtained from local Social Security offices, or the Government Printing Office, Washington, D. C. 20402.

Benefits for Students, 1965.
Benefits for Widows at Age 60, 1965.
Changes in Social Security Benefits, 1965.
Essentials of Social Security in the United States. Latest edition.
Health Insurance for the Aged, 1965.
Social Security Amendments, 1965.
Social Security Benefits, 1965.
Social Security Bulletin (Vol. 28, No. 9), September, 1965.
Social Security for Physicians, 1965.
Tips As Wages Under Social Security, 1965.
Your Social Security. Latest edition.

Matteson, William J. *What Will Social Security Mean to You?* Great Barrington, Mass.: American Institute for Economic Research. Latest edition.

Myers, Robert J. *Social Insurance and Allied Government Programs.* Homewood, Ill.: Richard D. Irwin, Inc., 1965.

Segal, Martin E. *Medicare and Social Security: 99 Questions and Answers on the New Social Security Program.* New York, N. Y.: Associated Press Newsfeatures, 1965.

Troan, John. *What You've Got Coming from Medicare and Social Security.* Cleveland, Ohio: Special Services Division, Newspaper Enterprise Association Inc., 1965.

Turnbull, John G., Williams, C. Arthur, Jr., and Cheit, Earl F. *Economic and Social Security—Public and Private Measures Against Economic Insecurity,* Second Edition. New York: The Ronald Press Co., 1962.

18

Retirement Planning and Annuities

In the past, most people gave little thought to retirement. Perhaps it was just as well, since in many instances they could not afford to retire, or they died before they reached the age at which they expected to retire. But things are different today. Due to the progress made in the improvement of medical technology and the development of many new wonder drugs, the life span of the average person in the United States is increasing. And in our affluent society more people are building up larger estates during their working years, pension plans among American business firms are increasing, unions are pressing for still lower retirement ages, and social security benefits are increasing in amounts and are payable to younger persons. All of this means that more people will be financially able to retire at earlier ages, and they will live a longer number of years in retirement than was formerly the case.

RETIREMENT PLANNING

In planning for retirement, a person should strive for two basic objectives: to be happy during retirement and to have enough money, property, or income to make it possible to be happy. Unfortunately, during their early life most people are so busy working to make enough money to make ends meet that they give little thought to the problem of retirement. If an older person wants to continue to enjoy things to the utmost, he would probably continue to work for life, because it has been found that in most instances a person is happiest when he is gainfully employed.

Most people, however, do not have this choice—they become incapable of working because of health, or their employer must retire them because of company policy on age. Since retirement is, therefore, an experience to be expected by most adults, how can a person best prepare himself for retirement?

Too many people make the mistake of waiting until a few months or years before they reach retirement age to begin to think about the problem. That is too late. Perhaps everyone should start to do some thinking about retirement as soon as he becomes gainfully employed.

Non-financial Factors

This is a book dealing with personal finance, and our primary concern in this chapter is discussing methods of providing proper finances for retirement. But it would probably be a mistake if we did not recognize the fact that non-financial factors are probably more important than money matters in planning for retirement.

The cultivation of an interest in learning should be an objective of every person. Some are able to do this without many years of schooling, but most persons acquire this interest, or develop it, only by formalized courses in schools. The goal of practically all high school graduates should be to go to college, and students in the latter institutions should attempt to graduate. The interests developed from education make life more interesting, both before and after retirement. Furthermore, the educated person usually has more money upon retirement than those who lack an education.

A family can be a source of trouble and worry to people in their old age, but at least it gives them something to think about. To most retired people, however, a family which has been properly reared can be the source of their principal enjoyment. The person who waits until retirement to think about the desirability of raising a family is naturally too late.

From observation it is rather apparent that the happiest people both before and after retirement are those who have the most friends. It is generally true that people who have not developed friends before retirement do not do so after retirement. It therefore appears that one requisite for happiness after retirement is abundant friendship and the ability to make new friends. Learning how to get along with people and developing a personality that is pleasing to other people are requisites to the making of friends. Taking a genuine interest in other people and in their accomplishments helps considerably in this respect.

When most young people think about retirement they think about doing *nothing*. Very few people can enjoy doing nothing. Happiness comes from doing *something*. Hobbies are commonly recommended for retired persons. But a person who forces a hobby upon himself after retirement merely to occupy himself usually does not enjoy the pastime and will quickly discard it. The development of a real interest in hobbies or other things throughout life will prove to be more lasting. An interest and active participation in charitable and civic affairs is often worthwhile and enjoyable to a retired person. The active person usually enjoys leisure time and the things he can then do, because he has so little of it. When one has nothing but leisure time, it ceases to be enjoyable.

Some retired people find that they can be happy only when they are employed on a regular job. If that is the case then an effort should be made to secure new employment of some kind even though the pay is not high. For many businessmen a continuing financial interest in the business may prove to be interesting. For those retired persons who are fortunate financially, an active and continuing interest in investments can be quite stimulating. Some who have stockholdings, or who acquire them after retirement, find that following the stock market can be an interesting and, in some cases, quite profitable hobby; or perhaps it becomes more than a mere hobby. Good judgment, care, and prudence, however, should be observed because the typical retired person cannot afford to deal in the stock market.

Having mentioned the above general factors relating to retirement, we will now turn to the financial ones.

Place of Life Insurance

Life insurance was discussed earlier in the book, where it was pointed out that the primary purpose of life insurance is to give protection to the insured's family in event of the death of the insured. Life insurance should not be thought of as a means of providing for retirement. Naturally one of the first things a married man should think of is the protection of his family in the event of his early death. Due to the limited earnings and small property holdings of the young married man, and the years of dependency of his young wife and small children, the purchase of life insurance is about the only way he can provide any degree of protection for his family in the event of his early death. To the extent that savings must be used to purchase life insurance, the young married man does not have the cash to start providing for his own possible retirement needs.

If a person has an endowment life insurance policy, or an ordinary life insurance policy which can be converted into installment payments upon retirement, and the need for the protection is over, such insurance could, of course, be used for retirement purposes. But the wisdom of buying these types of policies is questionable. Endowment or retirement provisions cost money. If the insurance protection is needed, the same amount of insurance could be purchased with less money, and the excess could be put into a more profitable form of retirement benefit. If more life protection is needed, a larger amount of other insurance could be carried for the same cost. As is true of any type of fixed dollar investment, life insurance benefits provide no hedge against inflation.

In some instances the only way a person can save any money is to obligate himself to some type of more or less forced savings, such as an endowment policy. If such a policy is not taken out, the money may be squandered. So in the end some people may benefit through the use of an endowment policy for retirement purposes. But there are other forms of more or less forced savings that might be more desirable for retirement purposes.

A relatively large percentage of the people who are employed are covered by some form of group life insurance at their place of employment. Such insurance would be terminated when the person retires from his job. But in most cases such insurance may be converted into an individual policy upon retirement by the payment of a higher premium. If the life protection is still needed at the time of retirement, consideration should be given to the conversion of the insurance.

Health and Accident Insurance

A large portion of the working population in this country is covered by Blue Cross and an increasing number is insured in the Blue Shield Plan. These were discussed earlier in the book (pages 279–283). When these are taken out at the place of employment they are group plans and the employee's protection would terminate upon his retirement. But upon retirement the worker may have the coverage continued under an individual contract for the payment of a slightly higher premium. Once a person has Blue Cross or Blue Shield it can be continued for life, regardless of the age of the insured. Since an older person is more prone to have illnesses and require hospitalization, and since the income of a retired person is usually less than formerly, it is recommended that retired persons continue their Blue Cross and Blue Shield or other medical insurance plans upon retirement, at least until they become fully covered by Medicare.

In the past, individual health and accident insurance could be taken out only by persons under age 60 or 65. And for those who had such insurance, the policies would terminate at age 60 or 65. At the present time, however, some companies will continue the insurance for life. Furthermore, a number of companies are now selling health and accident insurance to new customers who are 65 or older.

The enactment of the Medicare program, described in the preceding chapter, has been a tremendous help to persons 65 and over, and it is recommended that these people purchase the voluntary medical insurance which is available under the plan.

Emergency Fund

Families need an emergency fund to fall back on in the event of accident, sickness, temporary loss of a job, or temporary loss of some form of income. This is needed before retirement and the need for it continues through retirement. The amount needed for such a fund varies according to many factors. Certainly a month's income should be a minimum for such a fund. Funds equivalent to six months' income would be a better goal. The emergency fund should be invested in order to secure some income, but the type of investment should be one that provides maximum liquidity. Savings accounts in commercial banks, savings banks, and savings and loan associations are recommended.

Home Ownership

One thing that a retired person can be sure of is that he must have a place in which to live. Rent becomes a relatively heavier burden to the retired person whose income has been reduced from that which he enjoyed when he was employed. The retired person who owns his home but is still making mortgage payments on it likewise finds it more difficult to make the loan payments after retirement. In fact, some people overextend themselves so much, late in life, in the purchase of a home that they are unable to continue to make the loan payments after retirement and, as a consequence, are forced to sell their homes. It should be the goal of every man or woman to have his home paid for in full before retirement. The reduced retirement income is thus, in part, compensated for by the absence of home loan payments.

Home ownership is important to the retired person for still another reason. If a retired person has any income it usually consists of social security payments, interest on savings accounts, and possibly interest or principal on United States savings bonds, and payments from a company pension. All of these are fixed-dollar investments. Before World War II many families planned their affairs so that they could retire comfortably on a monthly income of $150, $200, or $250, for life. But inflation has reduced the purchasing power of the dollar to such an extent that these people are no longer able to live comfortably on their planned income. Unfortunately, the retired person can do little or nothing about it. The typical retired person or family has no hedge against inflation. Many experts are predicting continued inflation for the indefinite future.

The ownership of a home constitutes one of the best inflation hedges for the typical family. A well-constructed house bought at not too high a price, in a good neighborhood, will probably increase in value if we have inflation. Furthermore, there is probably less risk involved in buying a home than any other type of investment which offers a hedge against inflation. It is sometimes argued that home ownership is not a good inflation hedge since the owner may not wish to sell the house even if its value increases, and, therefore, he has no more dollars with which to purchase the higher-priced goods. But it should be realized that if the family does not own a home, the rent they would be forced to pay would probably go up with inflation. Or, the price that would have to be paid to purchase a home in the future would be greater under inflation. Therefore, home ownership is an inflation hedge even if the home is not sold in the future. A further fact should be noted. Many couples feel the need for a smaller home upon retirement. This may result from the children's leaving home or the desire of the housewife to cut down on the amount of space to be kept clean. So a smaller house may be purchased. Although the effects of inflation will be felt in the purchase of the new home, the larger amount obtained from the sale of the larger house will usually more than compensate. So, in this case, home ownership would prove to be an inflation hedge. The authors appreciate the fact that home ownership costs money, but after the mortgage has been paid off, it is cheaper than renting.

A final point on home ownership. Perhaps the greatest enjoyment that can come to retired persons is peace of mind. The ownership of a home free and clear will help tremendously in this respect.

United States Savings Bonds

At the start of World War II many people began buying Series E United States savings bonds. Many are still buying them regularly at their place of employment. Although the patriotic motive may have been dominant at the start, the investment idea or the retirement objective is uppermost in the minds of the buyers today. For those who own these bonds or are buying them today, they naturally fit into their retirement program.

The Series E bonds have several attractive features when purchased for retirement purposes. They can be purchased through the payroll deduction plan in many places of employment. This is a relatively painless way of saving money. Furthermore, it is a regular and systematic way of saving—a very important point. The interest is not paid currently, so it cannot be spent by the investor; and the interest does not have to be reported for income-tax purposes until the redemption of the bonds.

Since a person's income is usually less after retirement, the reporting of the Series E bond interest then, when the bonds are redeemed, will result in its being taxed at a lower rate than if reported currently as earned. Furthermore, the maturity may be extended into the future. From the standpoint of safety of principal and certainty of income, there is no better investment than United States Government bonds.

If a person does not already own Series E bonds, he might consider several shortcomings of the bonds as a source of retirement income. One is that the rate of return is not high. Another is that the bonds must be held for some years before the rate of return is even comparable with that which may be received from similar investments. Although retirement may be the objective in buying the bonds, it is never known when they may have to be cashed in for emergency purposes. For a person who needs current income the Series H savings bonds (discussed in Chapter 6) are recommended. If a person holding Series E bonds wants or needs current income from his investment, he can convert them into Series H bonds, and he will not have to pay income taxes on the accumulated interest on the Series E bonds until he redeems the Series H bonds. Perhaps one of the principal disadvantages of the Series E and H bonds, which can of course be applied to many types of investments, is that they provide no hedge against inflation.

Stocks

Since the principal types of income for a retired person are fixed-dollar investments, the person who can afford it should consider some stock investments in his program as a hedge against inflation. If a person does not have sufficient funds to secure proper diversification in investing in stocks, he may consider the purchase of shares of a large and successful investment company. Those who can invest a fixed sum of money at regular intervals should think about using the Monthly Investment Plan to purchase one of the successful closed-end companies listed on the New York Stock Exchange, or using the accumulation plan for buying shares in one of the successful mutual funds.

It is admitted that there is a risk involved in purchasing stocks, but it is the belief of many in recent years that stock should have a definite place in the retirement program for those who are competent to determine and minimize the risk and can afford the inherent risks.

Mutual Fund Systematic Withdrawal Plan

More and more retirees are finding the systematic withdrawal plan of mutual funds quite attractive in providing funds. On ordinary investments a person cannot expect to earn more than 4½ per cent with any degree of safety. At this rate, it takes a considerable amount of principal to earn a fair amount of return. With the mutual fund systematic withdrawal plan, the investor may arrange to receive annually 6 per cent or even 10 per cent of his original principal. Since the earnings on his original principal investment would be insufficient to provide this amount, some of the shares represented by his investment would be liquidated to provide the balance. This, of course, would represent a return to him of part of his principal annually, and thus less of the principal would be available for future earnings. Judging from past experience, however, over a period of years, the value of the remaining shares should increase in value (as well as decrease in value in some years) to offset, or partly offset, the sale of some of the shares. If too high a percentage is withdrawn, however, the retiree may find himself still living but with all of his income and principal from the investment gone. For this reason, a person should be fairly conservative in arranging the plan, and he should make other provision for a certain income (or already have it provided through social security, annuities, company pension plans, or other investments).

Most mutual funds have a systematic withdrawal plan, and most of them provide for a minimum initial investment of at least $10,000. If a person invests this amount at any one time he runs the risk of buying the shares when prices are relatively high, and thus obtaining relatively few shares. In anticipation of use of a systematic withdrawal plan, a person should give some thought to the use of the accumulation plan over a relatively long period of time to build up the principal through dollar-averaging. Accumulation and withdrawal plans of mutual funds are discussed in Chapter 14.

Company Pensions

More and more companies are providing pensions for their retired employees. In the past, pensions were often given only to retired executives, but today many forms of pensions are provided for the rank and file of employees. For many persons, the social security payments and the company pension are about the only sources of retirement income. In most instances either of these or the two combined are not sufficient in amount to provide a living for a retired worker and his family.

A worker cannot depend too much on his company's pension plan because he is never sure that he will be employed by the particular company at the time he reaches retirement age. Some companies fail and go out of business. Pensions are another form of fixed-dollar income and thus provide no hedge against inflation. Most employees will find that it will be necessary for them to supplement their company pensions and social security with additional sources of income if they expect to live comfortably after retirement.

In some instances the employer will contribute to a pension fund a certain percentage of the profits earned by the company. Some companies invest a relatively large percentage of the pension fund in their own stock, or the stock of other companies, and the exact amount paid in pensions to retired employees depends upon the earnings of the fund.

Other Company Plans

In the case of executives or some key employees, some companies will work out a plan of deferred compensation to provide retirement income. Not only does such a contract provide for retirement income, but by deferring the earned income until after retirement, when other income may be less, income taxes are saved.

An increasing number of companies are providing savings programs for their employees. A typical program permits the employee to put up a designated percentage of his monthly salary, which amount is usually invested in Series E United States savings bonds. The employer then contributes the same amount as the employee, or half the amount invested by the employee. The employer's contribution is usually invested in the company's common stock. At the end of a specified number of years, such as five years, the employee gets back his contribution plus that of the employer, and the compounded tax-free return on the investments. As indicated above, this is a type of savings program rather than a retirement program, but a person could continue it until retirement with the intention of using the proceeds as part of his retirement benefits. In 1956 General Motors started a savings plan which terminates at the time of the employee's retirement. A company savings plan of this type is highly recommended. It is a regular, systematic, payroll deduction plan—which is the best type of savings plan. Furthermore, the employer contributes an appreciable part of the savings without cost to the employee. In addition, there is a tax saving to the employee while the savings are being accumulated.

Real Estate

Some persons are able to live comfortably in retirement on the income from rental properties. In the past, investment in real estate has generally proved profitable, particularly because of the increase in property values which has taken place in the United States over a period of years.

For the person who does not now own rental property, considerable thought should be given the question before undertaking the acquisition of real estate. Prices are historically high, but of course they may go still higher in the future. It takes a considerable amount of money to purchase one piece of real estate, and a person should hesitate to tie up a relatively large amount of money in one particular property. A person should know real estate and the real estate market before investing in this kind of property. An added problem is that of worry, time, and attention. New tenants must be found for those moving out. Repairs and maintenance must be made constantly, and if a person cannot take care of most of the routine types of repairs, he will find it quite costly to hire the work done.

Generally speaking, business property investment is riskier than residential property. The purchase of farm land may prove unwise unless the purchaser is an experienced farmer or knows the farm market quite well. Investment in double houses, duplexes, or apartment houses may prove more profitable for rental purposes than single dwellings.

One advantage of rental real estate investment is the fact that depreciation, which is a non-cash expense, may be charged off against the rent for income-tax purposes. The inflation hedge is of course another advantage.

TAX SAVINGS RETIREMENT PLAN FOR THE SELF-EMPLOYED

It has become common for corporations to set up retirement plans for their officers and employees. In some instances the company makes the entire contribution toward the program, while in others the employee and the company both contribute to the fund. The employee benefits taxwise since he does not have to pay an income tax at the time of payment to the fund on the amount contributed by the company. Formerly, if the self-employed person, or one who practiced a profession, wanted to set up his own retirement program, however, he had to pay income tax on all the money earned which he used for his retirement program. This situation was altered in 1962 when Congress approved the Self-Employed Individuals Tax Retirement Act (better known as the Smathers–Keogh Act, or simply the Keogh Act).

The Keogh Act applies to professional people such as doctors, dentists, lawyers, accountants, architects, artists, and writers, and to self-employed people such as sole proprietors, partners in businesses, and farmers.

The Tax Savings

Under the Keogh Act a qualified person may make annual contributions to his own (approved) retirement fund of amounts up to 10 per cent of his earned income, but not more than $2,500 annually. Half of the amount contributed—up to a maximum of $1,250 a year—is deductible from taxable income. We are here referring, of course, to the federal income tax. (In New York State, the same amount is deductible in computing the state income tax.) It is thus apparent that the higher the income tax bracket, the larger would be the tax savings.

Income earned on the entire fund, and any capital appreciation of the fund, are also not taxable at the time.

At the time the retirement benefits are taken, the untaxed part of the initial contributions, the accrued income, and capital appreciation, if any, would be taxable. But it is probable that at this time the person's income would be smaller, and thus his top tax rates would be lower. Furthermore, since no tax was paid as the fund was being built up, the entire amount was invested for the period. Thus earnings accrue on amounts that would otherwise have been paid in taxes. The exact amount of taxes paid would depend upon whether the retired person elected to receive the benefits in a lump sum or in installments.

Time Limits

Practically speaking, the retirement benefits cannot begin until a person is at least 59½ years old (if they begin before that time a penalty must be paid). The law provides that the retirement benefits must begin by the time he reaches 70½.

Where the Funds Can Be Invested

To qualify under the Keogh Act, the retirement funds must be invested under an "approved" plan with a proper agency such as a bank, trust company, insurance company, mutual fund, or profession or trade association. Most of the leading mutual funds, a number of banks, and several professional associations have already set up approved plans. Investment in a special issue of United States Retirement Plan Bonds also is permitted.

Provision for Employer

If a self-employed person qualifies under the Act but has full-time employees working for him, he must make contributions for the latter and bring them under the plan in order that he himself can be covered.

ANNUITIES

In the preceding chapter we discussed social security benefits, which are the principal source of retirement income for many people. Thus far in this chapter we have discussed a number of possible sources of retirement income. There remains one important type of retirement income—annuities.

Nature of an Annuity

An annuity is a type of contract in which an insurance company agrees to pay to a person a fixed amount of money at stated intervals during his life. Life insurance gives protection to dependents in the event of the death of the insured, but an annuity gives protection to the annuitant (the person to whom the payments are made). The amount of money necessary to buy a fixed income may be paid in a lump sum to the insurance company, or it may be paid in fixed installments over a period of years. In the first case the annuitant can have the insurance company start the annual or monthly payments to him immediately, or he can wait until he reaches a certain age. When the premiums are paid over a period of years, the payments to the annuitant would begin at some future date.

Reasons for Buying an Annuity

There are good reasons for buying an annuity. In fact, looking at it from the selfish viewpoint of the individual himself, an annuity may be preferred over life insurance. The two types of policies, however, are different and one is not intended as a substitute for the other. Life insurance gives protection after death, the annuity gives protection before death.

It appears to be human nature for an individual to seek security. Most of us work for at least two reasons: to make enough money to live on and to provide for our old age, and to provide something for our dependents in the event of our death. The latter is accomplished, at least in part, through life insurance. We depend upon our wages or salary to provide us with a living during our active lives, but providing for old age is a problem. People try to save something out of their incomes in order to have some money, real estate, or securities which they hope will yield them enough to live on in later years. But they are never sure that the income will be sufficient.

The annuity offers a solution to the problem. With the proper amount of annuities in a safe company, a person does not need to worry about the future. But with the prospect for inflation in the future it is difficult to determine in advance just what is the proper amount. The annuity offers about the only safe way of using both principal and interest and, at the same time, not reducing the future income. Another advantage of the annuity as a means of saving is the fact that the premium notices come to the individual and are looked upon as a bill which has to be paid. If he did not have the annuity, it is probable that he would not set aside the same amount of money in some other form of savings. This more or less forced saving is the only kind of saving many people are able to accomplish.

It is well known to insurance companies that people who have annuities live longer than other individuals. Part of this is undoubtedly due to the fact that only relatively healthy people feel that an annuity is an economical investment. But some of the explanation lies in the fact that an annuity takes a lot of worry off the shoulders of a person, and thus tends to prolong his life.

TYPES OF ANNUITIES

Immediate Annuity

Annuities are classified into two groups according to the time when the annuity payments begin: immediate annuities and deferred annuities. As the title indicates, an immediate annuity is one on which the annuity payments begin immediately after the contract is purchased. A lump sum must necessarily be paid for this type. This is sometimes called the "single premium" annuity, but it should be noted that not all single premium contracts are immediate annuities. The proceeds of an immediate annuity are paid out only in the manner provided for in the policy at the time the contract is sold.

The amount of money needed to purchase an immediate annuity would necessarily be relatively large, the exact amount depending, of course, on the age of the individual. A man 60 years old, for example, could purchase an immediate annuity of $100 a month for life for the sum of $16,057. To get the same immediate monthly income a man of 40 must pay $23,968.

A person who is comparatively young would probably not purchase an immediate annuity for several reasons. First, he may not have the money necessary to buy a life income of any appreciable amount. And secondly, if he did have the money, he probably would not want the contract at that time, as he would be capable of keeping himself by working, unless he was in poor health. Immediate annuities are therefore ordinarily purchased by older people who have accumulated some money.

It was pointed out at the beginning of the chapter that the annuity is probably the safest way for a person to assure himself of an income for life. Furthermore, since both the principal and interest are being received, the return to the annuitant is higher than on any other form of safe investment. It was stated above that a person aged 40 could obtain an immediate life annuity of $100 a month by the payment of a single premium of $23,968. Otherwise, to obtain the same monthly income, assuming a return of 4 per cent on his investments, it would be necessary for him to have an estate amounting to $30,000.

The immediate annuity works in just the opposite way from life insurance. In the case of life insurance, the person pays premiums in installments over a period of years and the company eventually pays the face value of the policy to the beneficiary (in some instances, to the insured) in a lump sum or, in some instances, in installments. With an immediate annuity, the annuitant pays the insurance company a lump sum for the annuity, and the company makes installment payments directly to him for the remainder of his life.

Deferred Annuity

In the case of the deferred annuity, payments by the insurance company to the annuitant do not begin until some future time, which is stated in the contract. A single premium may be paid, as is the case with the immediate annuity, or the premiums may be paid in installments which continue until the time designated for the annuity payments to begin. All annual premium annuities are necessarily deferred annuities, just as all immediate annuities must be single premium annuities.

The annual premium type of deferred annuity is more common than the single premium form of deferred annuity. Most individuals who purchase a deferred annuity do not have sufficient money at the time to buy the single premium type. This can be better appreciated when we realize that anyone purchasing a deferred annuity would, in all probability, be relatively young as compared with the purchaser of an immediate annuity. The annual premium method of payment is thus more practical and convenient, just as the installment method of paying for life insurance is better suited to the individual's ability to pay than the single premium form.

In the immediate annuity, the money necessary to buy it must be saved and invested in something until the contract is purchased. In investing his own money the individual runs all the risk which has been mentioned before. When the annual premium or installment type of annuity is bought, the insurance company does the investing, thus relieving the individual of this risk, care, and worry. The advantages of the annuity as a means of saving money, discussed above, apply particularly to the annual premium type.

As originally issued, a deferred annuity had no cash surrender value or death benefit during the "deferred" period. Assume that a person age 30 started paying annual premiums of $300 on an annuity that was to start paying him a fixed amount for life beginning at age 65. If the person for some reason discontinued paying the premiums at age 60, for example, he would get nothing back from the policy. Or, if he died at age 60 nothing would be paid to his estate or to his beneficiaries, despite the fact that a total of $9,000 had been paid in to the insurance company. Compensating for this is the fact that if the annuitant lived until age 65 and started receiving the annuity payments, the latter would be larger in amount than if a cash surrender value had been provided. Policies of this kind, however, usually have a non-forfeiture provision to the effect that if the premiums are discontinued after the policy has been in force for a designated period, the installments already paid will be used to purchase a paid-up annuity of a smaller amount. Because of the absence of a cash surrender value or death benefit, few policies of this kind are sold today. Most deferred installment annuities are purchased under some form of retirement annuity which provides for cash surrender values. This type of annuity will be discussed later in the chapter.

TYPES OF PAYMENTS

The purchaser of an annuity may select one of a number of different plans for receiving the annuity payments. The following plans are those most commonly used:

1. Straight life annuity
2. Refund annuity
3. Life annuity with guaranteed number of payments
4. Retirement annuity
5. Joint and survivorship annuity
6. Variable annuity

Payments under these various types may be made to the annuitant annually, semiannually, quarterly, or monthly. The more frequent the payments, the greater is the cost to the annuitant. Although annual payments would be the most economical, this may be inconvenient to the annuitant. The types of annuity payments outlined above will now be discussed briefly.

Straight Life Annuity

The straight life annuity, or "life annuity," was the first type of annuity. Starting at a specified age, payments are made to the annuitant for life, but the contract is terminated upon the death of the annuitant, and no further payments are made to anyone, regardless of how much or how little of the purchase price has been paid out by the insurance company.

Because of the nature of the straight life annuity, the annual payments to the annuitant are larger than for any of the other types of annuities with the same cost. Since there is no residual estate in the contract after the death of the annuitant, the straight life annuity would appeal only to individuals who either have no dependents, or have provided for them in some other manner. It can be purchased either as an immediate or a deferred annuity.

Refund Annuity

This is similar to the straight life annuity in that payments are made by the insurance company to the annuitant for life. But if the annuitant dies before the company has paid him the total cost (value at time annuity payments begin) of the annuity, the balance will be paid to a designated beneficiary. For example, if the annuity cost $10,000, and at the time of the death of the annuitant the insurance company had paid $7,000, the balance of $3,000 would be paid to the beneficiary. This balance can be paid to the beneficiary either in installments or in a lump sum. When paid in installments, some companies call it an *installment refund annuity;* when paid in a lump sum, it is called a *cash refund annuity*. If the company had, at the time of the death of the annuitant, paid out more than the cost of the policy—for example, if it had paid the annuitant a total of $12,000—then the beneficiary would not receive anything.

The annuity payments under this type are smaller than for the straight life annuity. If a man aged 60 bought a $10,000 contract of each of these two types of immediate annuities in a leading company, he would receive an annual income for life of $775 under the straight life annuity, but only $706 under the installment refund annuity contract. Despite this lower annual return, the refund annuity would be preferred by persons who have dependents, and those who feel that they, or rather their estates, would be cheated with the life annuity by an early death. The refund annuity can be purchased in either the immediate or deferred form.

Life Annuity with Guaranteed Number of Payments

This is similar to the refund annuity. Payments are made by the insurance company to the annuitant for life, but if the annuitant dies before the end of a stipulated period, such as ten years, for example, the payments will be made to a designated beneficiary for the remaining part of the stated period. Thus if the annuitant dies at the end of six years, the beneficiary would receive the annuity payments for the remaining four years. If the annuitant dies after the ten-year period has ended, nothing will be paid to the beneficiary. If a man aged 60 paid $10,000 for an immediate life annuity with ten years certain, he would receive an annual income of $737.

This type of contract is similar to, but should not be confused with, the refund annuity. In the case of the refund annuity, as explained above, if the annuitant dies before an amount equivalent to the cost of the contract has been paid to the annuitant, the beneficiary will receive the balance. Both types may be purchased either as immediate or deferred annuities.

Retirement Annuity

The term "retirement annuity" is used by some to apply to any form of annuity which is designed to provide income upon retirement. Practically all types of annuities would thus qualify as retirement annuities. The term is usually used in the trade, however, to apply to some form of the deferred installment annuity. Formerly it could be purchased with a single premium, but now most companies write it only on the annual premium basis. Being an annual premium annuity, it is of course a type of deferred annuity, and is the most liberal and flexible of the various types of annuities. As the title indicates, it is admirably suited for the building up of a retirement income. It may be preferred to life insurance by a young person who has no dependents. It is a good investment for current savings, and can be changed into various forms of life insurance.

Unit Plan. The retirement annuity may not have a fixed face value. The amount of the contract is expressed in "units," and an annual premium of $100 will usually buy one unit. Or the premium may be quoted in terms of the amount necessary to purchase an annuity of $10 a month.

Participating. In recent years an increasing number of retirement annuities have been of the participating form. That is, if the earnings of the company warrant it, dividends are paid to the annuitant. These dividends may be taken in cash, they may be applied toward the next premium, or they may be left with the company to accumulate with interest at a stipulated rate.

Cash Value. After payment of the early premiums, the contract has a cash surrender value. This amount, of course, increases as premiums are paid and compound interest is added to the account. The cash value increases much faster than in the case of a life insurance policy because no part of the premium goes for protection. The contract may also have loan privileges.

Death Benefit. If the annuitant dies before the annuity payments to him have begun, a death benefit will be paid to the designated beneficiary. It is usually provided that this death benefit will be the cash value, or the total amount of the premiums which have been paid, whichever is greater.

Annuity Payments. The contract will state the age at which the annuity payments will begin, but if the annuitant subsequently wants to change this to an older age or a younger age, he may do so, provided the change is made before the maturity age has been reached. It is usually provided that the maturity age must be between 50 and 70. Any change in the maturity age would, of course, alter the amount of the annuity payments.

The type of annuity payments is stated in the contract, but it is usually provided that the annuitant can change this to another form, provided he does so before the annuity payments have started. Such a change would also affect the amount of the annual annuity payments. One of the following types of annuity payments is usually provided in the retirement contracts:

1. Deferred life annuity
2. Deferred refund annuity
3. Deferred life annuity with guaranteed number of payments
4. Deferred joint life and survivorship annuity

Exchange for Life Insurance. The retirement annuity may provide that it can be exchanged (at any time before its maturity) for a type of life insurance which the company sold at the time the annuity was issued. The amount of life insurance obtainable is that amount which the annuity premium would have bought at the time the contract was issued. Although no medical examination is required to take out a retirement annuity or any other form of pure annuity, such examination is required if the annuitant wants to exchange his annuity for life insurance.

Joint and Survivorship Annuity

In this type of annuity there are two or more annuitants who, upon reaching a specified age, jointly receive the annuity payments during their lives, and upon the death of any of the parties, payments of the same amount are made jointly to the remaining annuitants as long as they live. Usually there are only two annuitants. Provision may be made for the surviving annuitant to receive only one half or two thirds of the amount that the two annuitants were receiving jointly, instead of the total amount. This would increase the amount that would be received while the two annuitants are living.

This type of annuity may fit the needs of an elderly man and wife who either have no dependents or have provided for them in some other manner. The premiums for such an annuity are based on both the husband's and wife's ages, but more weight is usually put on the wife's age, for reasons which will be explained later. If a man has no dependents other than his wife, this type of contract may be preferred to life insurance and would be more economical. For an annuity, however, the yield is not very high. A higher yield can be obtained, or the same yield at a lower cost, by a variation in the contract to provide a separate life annuity for the husband and the wife, and a joint and survivorship annuity on both their lives. Thus, instead of taking out a joint and survivorship annuity for an income of $300 a month, they may each take out a life annuity for $100, and a joint and survivorship annuity on both their lives for $100 a month. This would give them a return of $300 a month during their lives, and upon the death of one of them the survivor would have an income of $200 a month. It is probable that the amount necessary to keep one of them would be less than that needed for both of them. This type of annuity may be purchased in either the immediate or deferred form.

COST OF ANNUITIES

The cost of annuities varies according to the age and sex of the person and the type of annuity purchased. Contrary to life insurance, the premiums paid for immediate annuities are less, the older a person is at the time the policy is issued. But for deferred annuities, particularly the installment type, the younger the person, the lower the premiums. Life insurance premiums are figured on age at the nearest birthday, but annuity premiums are based upon quarterly fractions of a year. Rates for life insurance are lower if purchased just before the age change, which would be six months after the last birthday, but it would be more economical to buy an immediate annuity right after the age had changed.

Annuity rates for women are higher than for men because they live longer than men. For immediate annuities, some insurance companies use the same rate table for women as for men, but charge women the same premiums they would charge men five years younger. This is the reason why the rates charged for a joint and survivorship annuity purchased by a man and wife are usually based more on the wife's age than on the age of the husband. Furthermore, the wife is generally younger than the husband.

Table 18–1 shows the premiums charged by one of the leading stock companies for a single premium immediate life annuity of $100 a month. Rates are given for both males and females for straight life annuities (no refund), ten years certain, and refund life annuities. Since immediate life annuities are usually purchased only by elderly persons, we have given the rates for only selected ages from 60 to 80.

Table 18–2 shows the premiums charged (if paid annually, semi-annually, quarterly, and monthly) for males at selected ages for a life income, with ten years certain, of $100 a month, beginning at age 65. The lower part of the table shows the amount of the monthly income

Table 18–1. Single Premium Rates for Immediate Life Annuities of $100 a Month, at Selected Ages *

Age at Issue	No Refund		10 Years Certain		Refund	
	Male	Female	Male	Female	Male	Female
60	$16,057	$18,019	$16,783	$18,401	$17,556	$19,009
62	15,174	17,094	16,025	17,564	16,789	18,206
65	13,825	15,660	14,915	16,306	15,623	16,975
70	11,545	13,187	13,210	14,289	13,660	14,878
75	9,422	10,817	11,896	12,624	11,182	12,877
80	7,453	8,549	10,969	11,363	10,055	10,916

* The company (a large stock company) whose premiums are shown here adds a small "Income Factor" to the amount of the premiums quoted. The amount added varies according to the frequency of the annuity payments. In addition, if the purchaser of the annuity resides in a state which taxes the insurance company on the amount of annuity premiums collected, the amount of the tax is added to the quoted premiums. The tax is typically 1 or 2 per cent.

Table 18–2. Annual Premiums—Male—per $100 Monthly Life Income, Ten Years Certain, at 65; Monthly Life Income, Ten Years Certain; Cash Refund at Ages 60, 62, 65, and 70 Obtainable from Premiums of Same Amount *

Premiums Paid	Age 30 Premiums	Age 35 Premiums	Age 40 Premiums	Age 45 Premiums	Age 50 Premiums
Annually	$289	$362	$465	$623	$907
Semiannually	147	184	236	316	460
Quarterly	74	92	119	159	231
Monthly	25	31	40	53	77
Starting at Age	**Monthly Life Income—Ten Years Certain**				
60	$ 70	$ 68	$ 65	$ 61	$ 54
62	81	80	78	75	71
65	100	100	100	100	100
70	140	143	147	153	163
Starting at Age	**Monthly Life Income—Cash Refund**				
60	$ 62	$ 60	$ 58	$ 54	$ 48
62	71	70	69	66	62
65	88	88	88	88	88
70	123	125	129	134	142

* Figures are rounded to nearest dollar. They are the rates quoted by a large stock company. The company adds a small "Income Factor" to the above quoted rates. Also, in states having a premium tax the rates will be slightly higher.

Table 18–3. Annual Premiums—Female—per $100 Monthly Life Income, Ten Years Certain, at 65; Monthly Life Income, Ten Years Certain; Cash Refund at Ages 60, 62, 65, and 70 Obtainable from Premiums of Same Amount *

Premiums Paid	Age 30 Premiums	Age 35 Premiums	Age 40 Premiums	Age 45 Premiums	Age 50 Premiums
Annually	$323	$405	$521	$692	$1,018
Semiannually	164	206	265	351	517
Quarterly	82	103	133	176	260
Monthly	28	34	44	59	87
Starting at Age	**Monthly Life Income—Ten Years Certain**				
60	$ 70	$ 68	$ 66	$ 62	$ 54
62	81	80	78	76	71
65	100	100	100	100	100
70	140	143	147	152	162
Starting at Age	**Monthly Life Income—Cash Refund**				
60	$ 64	$ 62	$ 59	$ 56	$ 49
62	73	72	70	68	64
65	89	89	89	89	89
70	123	125	129	134	142

* Figures are rounded to nearest dollar. They are the rates quoted by a large stock company. The company adds a small "Income Factor" to the above quoted rates. Also, in states having a premium tax the rates will be slightly higher.

that premiums of the same amount would purchase under a ten-years-certain life annuity and a cash refund life annuity with the income starting at ages 60, 62, 65, and 70.

Table 18–3 shows the same information as Table 18–2 but applies to females. Table 18–4 shows the cash surrender values at given years for the $100-a-month life income annuity quoted in Table 18–2 (male). The cash surrender values for annuities bought by women (shown in Table 18–3) would, of course, be higher since the amount of the annual premium is greater.

ADDITIONAL CONSIDERATIONS

Contract Provisions

In discussing life insurance it was pointed out that some policies are participating, while others are non-participating. In the annuity field immediate annuities are ordinarily non-participating. An increasing number of participating deferred annuities have been issued in recent years, and the trend is definitely toward the participating type of contract.

Table 18–4. Cash Surrender Values on Annual Premiums Paid on Life Annuity Income of $100 Per Month, Ten Years Certain, at 65—Male *

Premiums Paid	Age 30 Premiums	Age 35 Premiums	Age 40 Premiums	Age 45 Premiums	Age 50 Premiums
Annually	$289	$362	$465	$623	$907
Semiannually	147	184	236	316	460
Quarterly	74	92	119	159	231
Monthly	25	31	40	53	77
At End of Year			Cash Value		
1	$ 150	$ 190	$ 250	$ 350	$ 530
5	1,340	1,710	2,240	3,070	4,480
10	3,050	3,880	5,080	6,940	10,110
15	5,030	6,400	8,380	11,430	16,640
20	7,330	9,330	12,210	16,640	22,480
At Age			Cash Value		
60	$13,070	$12,710	$12,210	$11,430	$10,110
62	14,440	14,210	13,900	13,420	12,610
65	16,640	16,640	16,640	16,640	16,640

* Cash surrender values are for the same company whose rates are quoted in Table 18–2.

Medical examination is not required when purchasing an annuity, unless the policy has some life insurance feature. Proof of age, however, is required. While the purchase of life insurance may prove to be a good investment for an unhealthy person, or at least for his beneficiary, such a person should hesitate to buy a life annuity. The healthy individual whose ancestors lived a long time may find the annuity to be a good investment. Despite the prospect of a relatively early death, the person in poor health may, nevertheless, find the annuity to be extremely valuable if he is unable to work in later years.

Buying Annuities with Insurance Proceeds

Upon maturity, holders of endowment life insurance policies frequently buy annuities with the proceeds. Beneficiaries of various types of life insurance policies often elect to have the proceeds paid to them in the form of an annuity, or installments. Such a plan is highly recommended because it insures that the beneficiary will have some income for a certain number of years, or for life. Too frequently, when the proceeds of life insurance are paid in a lump sum, they are dissipated within a relatively short time after they are received. Life insurance trusts provide another way of insuring regular income payments to the beneficiary.

Combination Life Insurance and Annuity

Another form of combination life insurance and annuity has been increasing in popularity in recent years. This policy provides life insurance for the purchaser up to a specified age, such as 60, 65, or 70, and thereafter he will receive an annuity for life. The annuity is usually guaranteed for a stated period, such as 100 or 120 months. If the policyholder dies before the end of this time, the annuity payments will be made for the remaining part of the period to a designated beneficiary. Before the annuity payments begin, the policy has a loan and cash surrender value. Since this is a life insurance policy, it would naturally have a death benefit. The amount of such benefit would, of course, be much greater than the loan or cash surrender value during the early years of the policy. At the time that the annuity payments are to begin, the insured may elect to receive the cash value of the policy instead of the annuity payments.

This type of contract gives insurance protection and at the same time provides savings for the insured. The cost is, therefore, relatively high in comparison to the amount of life insurance obtained. A medical examination is of course necessary for this type of policy. Contrary to a pure annuity contract, waiver of premium can be obtained for a slight additional cost, and it is recommended.

Tax Status

The federal income tax laws give effect to the fact that part of the annuity payments received by a person constitutes a return of his principal and should, therefore, not be taxed. On a life annuity, to determine the amount of the annuity payments that are taxed, the cost of the annuity is divided by the number of years (from the time the annuity payments begin) the person is expected to live (as determined by tables approved by the government), and this figure is subtracted from the amount of the annual annuity payments. The computation can best be understood by the following example.

Assume that a person paid $15,000 (either in a lump sum or in installments) for an annuity which will pay him $1,200 a year for life after he reaches the age of 65. If the tables show that the life expectancy of this person at age 65 is 15 years, then we divide $15,000 by 15, which gives $1,000, the amount per year which represents the return of the principal. Subtracting this $1,000 from the annuity receipts of $1,200 gives $200, which is the amount that should be reported annually as income for tax purposes. If the person lives longer than 15 years, he still continues to report only the $200 as taxable income from the policy.

If the annuity payments run for a fixed number of years, and not for life, the taxable income is found by subtracting from the annual receipts the cost of the annuity divided by the number of years payments are to be made. If we assume that payments are to be made for a fifteen-year period, then the procedure to ascertain the taxable income would be the same as in the above example. If the contract is a refund life annuity, or a life annuity with a fixed number of years certain, the taxable income is found by subtracting from the annual receipts the cost of the annuity—reduced by the undiscounted value of the refund feature (as determined from tables approved by the government)—divided by the number of years the annuitant is expected to live. Any benefits received by a beneficiary of such an annuity after the death of the annuitant are not considered taxable income.

The taxable income from a joint and survivor life annuity is computed in the same way as for a single life annuity, except that the joint life expectancy of both annuitants (as determined by government-approved tables) is used instead of the life expectancy of the one person. The taxable income would thus be determined by subtracting from the annual annuity receipts the cost of the annuity divided by the joint life expectancy of the two annuitants. After the death of one of the annuitants, the survivor would report the same amount of taxable income from the annuity as the two annuitants formerly reported.

Choosing the Company

The same degree of care should be used in selecting the company in which to buy an annuity as in choosing the one in which to purchase life insurance. Generally speaking, the large companies are safer because they have a greater diversification of risks.

The rates for different kinds of annuities naturally vary, and the rates for the same kind of an annuity differ among the various companies. The prospective purchaser should attempt to measure the degree of risk involved and other factors, in addition to the relative costs, before selecting the particular company. Some companies offer lower rates on some types of annuities, but other companies may have lower rates on other types.

THE VARIABLE ANNUITY

We have already seen that one of the shortcomings of an annuity is that it provides no hedge against inflation. A person may purchase annuities which at the time he believes will be sufficient in amount, after giving effect to his other retirement income, to provide him with a comfortable living upon retirement. But, due to the increase in prices which may take place over a period of years, he may find that the income is inadequate. The variable annuity offers a method of compensating at least in part for the effects of inflation.

Nature of the Variable Annuity

As in any other form of annuity, the purchaser pays a single premium of a fixed amount or makes installment payments of a fixed amount over a stated period of time. The premiums are used to purchase "units" of the annuity fund. (These units should not be confused with the "units" of the retirement annuity previously discussed.) The value of a unit is determined at any one time by dividing the total market value of the annuity fund by the number of units outstanding. The insurance company will invest the amount received from the premiums (after deducting operating expense, etc.) primarily in common stocks.

Fluctuations in the value of the common stock portfolio held by the fund will result in changes in the value of a unit. If stock prices go down, the value of a unit will decrease; if stock prices go up, the value of a unit will increase. Furthermore, earnings on the portfolio will add to the value of a unit.

At a given age, such as 60 or 65, the annuitant will discontinue the premium payments (assuming they are the installment type) and the insurance company will start making the annuity payments to the annuitant. The amount of the annual annuity payments, however, will probably vary from year to year for the following reason. At the time the annuity payments begin the company will determine the exact number of units which have been credited to the annuitant. The company's tables will show how many units per month this total will buy for life, or how many monthly units may be bought for life with a guarantee, for example, for ten years. But the exact number of dollars received in any particular month or year will depend upon the value of a unit at that time.

The theory is, of course, that if prices in general go up, the value of the stock portfolio and its earnings will likewise increase. Thus the amount paid out per unit to the annuitant would be greater. This larger amount is needed in order to pay the higher living costs. It is true, of course, that should stock prices and earnings decline, the value of a unit would likewise decline in value, and thus the amount that would be paid to the annuitant would be less per unit. But if stock prices have declined, it is probable that the cost of living would also have declined and therefore the annuitant would not need so many dollars.

Some companies offer a package deal to the annuitant. Half of the premiums paid by him go to purchase an ordinary fixed annuity of the type described previously in the chapter. The other half of the premium dollar goes to purchase a variable annuity. These two annuities are embodied in the same contract. This type of annuity contract thus provides a hedge against both inflation and deflation. If a person, however, has adequate fixed-dollar retirement income from other sources such as interest, social security, or pensions, he may feel protected against deflation. Protection against inflation may be his objective in purchasing the variable annuity.

Slow Development

Until recent years, only a few of the states permitted insurance companies to sell variable annuities, and in these states only a few companies have offered them. In 1959, however, the Prudential Life Insurance Company, after a campaign of a number of years, was successful in getting the State of New Jersey to enact legislation permitting life insurance companies formed in that state to sell variable annuities. (To date, however, Prudential has concentrated on group variable annuities.) In the same year, the United States Supreme Court ruled that companies selling such annuities would come under the jurisdiction of the Securities and Exchange Commission in a manner similar to investment companies. Although some important differences exist, it should be apparent to the reader that some similarity exists between companies offering variable annuities and investment companies (mutual funds) which offer shares (particularly under some accumulation plans) to investors which may be withdrawn under some systematic plan.

A number of life insurance companies, particularly Metropolitan Life Insurance Company, have opposed the enactment of legislation that would permit the sale of variable annuities. This opposition in part grows out of the fact that life insurance companies have always paid off their contracts in fixed-dollar amounts. Many people in the securities business have likewise opposed the sale of variable annuities, since it was thought that their sale would be in competition with the sale of securities, particularly those of investment companies.

The pioneer insurance companies in the variable annuity field were The Variable Annuity Life Insurance Company of Washington, D. C., the Equity Annuity Life Insurance Company, also of Washington, D. C., and the Participating Life Insurance Company, which is located in Little Rock, Arkansas. In most instances these companies in the past have been confined in their business operations to their particular state.

In recent years a number of private companies have offered their employees a type of group variable annuities. Included in the list are American Airlines, Boeing Airplane Company, Bristol-Myers Company, Delta Airlines, Jersey Central Power and Light, Long Island Lighting Company, and Pan American Airlines.

In 1965, the legislatures of New York and Connecticut passed bills which enable life insurance companies domiciled in these states to sell group variable annuities. This brings to 29 the number of states now permitting (in most instances group only) variable annuities.

College Retirement Equities Fund

In 1918 the Carnegie Foundation for the Advancement of Teaching and the Carnegie Corporation of New York established the Teachers' Insurance and Annuity Association of America (TIAA) to provide contributory annuity benefits to teachers and other educators. The organization offered on a group basis the regular fixed annuity from the interest income from the bonds and mortgages in which the funds were invested. With the rising prices which have taken place, the purchasing power of the fixed dollar incomes of retirees has been materially reduced.

In order to provide its members with a hedge against the decline in the purchasing power of the dollar, TIAA, in 1952, organized and put into operation the College Retirement Equities Fund (CREF). The funds of CREF are invested in common stocks which, in the past, have provided a good hedge against inflation. Members of TIAA may elect to have ¼, ⅓, or ½ of their contributions to the annuity plan (including the employer's contribution) invested in CREF, the variable annuity company, and the balance invested in TIAA. Upon retirement, members get from TIAA a life annuity of a fixed amount of money, and if they have contributed to CREF, they will receive an amount of money which will vary from year to year according to the current value of their ownership in CREF.

Premiums paid by teachers to CREF go to purchase a certain number of "accumulation units," the exact number of which depends upon the current value of the accumulation unit. The value of a unit is calculated each month by dividing the current market value of all the common stocks in CREF's accumulation fund by the total number of accumulation units outstanding. If stock prices rise, the number of units which can be purchased with a premium of a given amount will decline, but, of course, the value of the accumulation units already credited to the member will increase in value. Figure 18–1 shows that the value of an accumulation unit increased from $10.00 in 1952 (when the company was started) to $33.96 at the beginning of 1965.

When a member retires, his CREF retirement income is expressed, not as a fixed number of dollars, but as a fixed number of annuity units payable each month for life. The dollar value of the annuity unit varies from year to year according to the market value and dividend income of the company's common stock investments. The table below the chart in

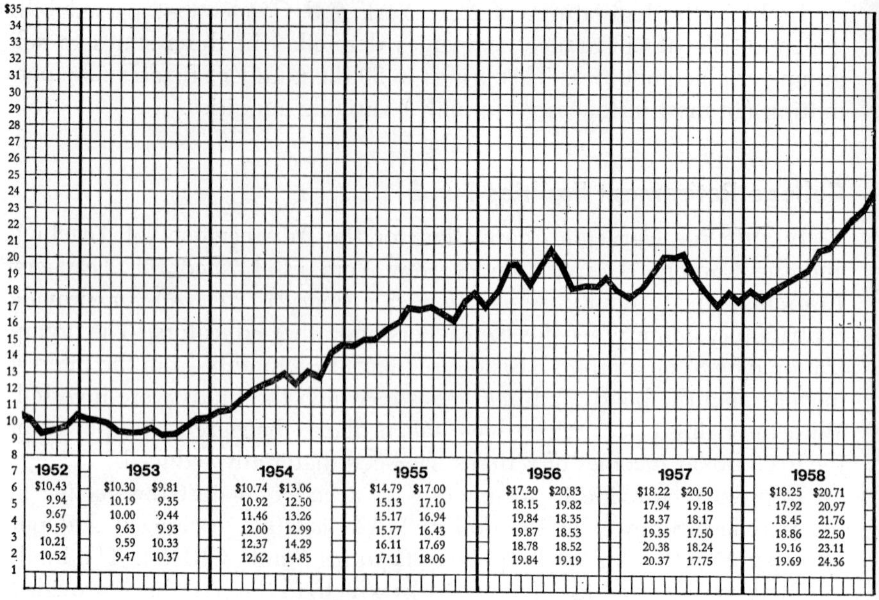

CREF Annuity Unit

Annuity Year May through April	Annuity Unit Value
Initial Value	$10.00
1953–1954	9.46
1954–1955	10.74
1955–1956	14.11
1956–1957	18.51
1957–1958	16.88
1958–1959	16.71

Fig. 18–1. Monthly value of the CREF accumulation

Fig. 18–1 shows that the value of an annuity unit has increased from $10.00 in 1952, to $26.48 in 1965.[1]

At the beginning of 1965 there were 1,330 schools and colleges that had group retirement plans in TIAA–CREF. Approximately 85 per cent of new TIAA policyholders concurrently go into CREF, and 9 out of 10 of these place the maximum of half of their premiums in CREF. The amounts shown in Fig. 18–1 illustrate the fact that to date CREF has been highly successful. It is appreciated, however, that the short period

[1] The annuity unit is revalued each year on March 31, and this sets the amount of CREF annuity income for the subsequent May through April.

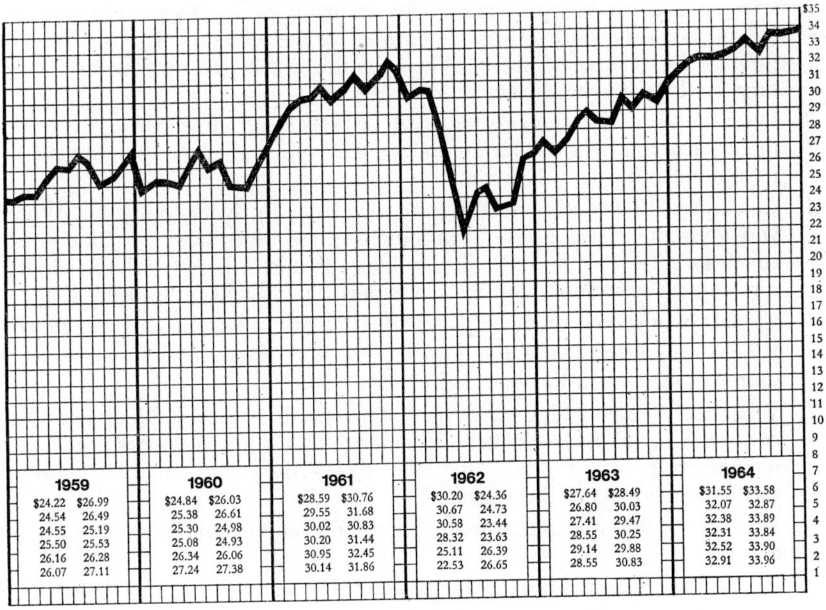

Values Since 1952

Annuity Year May through April	Annuity Unit Value
1959–1960	$22.03
1960–1961	22.18
1961–1962	26.25
1962–1963	26.13
1963–1964	22.68
1964–1965	26.48

unit, 1952–1965. (TIAA–CREF 1965 Annual Report.)

of time lapsing since 1952 may not be representative, but judging from the experience of similar investment programs covering a very long period of time, it appears that CREF, and other comparable variable annuity programs, will offer the retiree a good inflation hedge.

QUESTIONS

1. It is sometimes said that happiness is the goal of life. If this is true, should a person attempt to continue to work for life, or should he retire at a relatively early age? Explain.

2. Assume that a person is required by company policy to retire at age 65. When should he start to prepare himself for the adjustment? How may he prepare for the adjustment? When should he start to provide the necessary funds to live on during retirement?
3. Does life insurance prepare for death or does it aid in preparing for retirement? Do you believe that an endowment policy is a good investment for retirement purposes? Explain.
4. Can an aged person buy health insurance from a private company? Would you advise it? Can a person continue his group Blue Cross and Blue Shield coverage after he has retired? Explain. Should a person who is eligible for Medicare continue his Blue Cross and Blue Shield insurance? Explain.
5. Explain why home ownership is usually highly advisable for the retired.
6. Would you recommend the purchase or acquisition of real estate as a source of retirement income? Why?
7. What are the strong and weak points of retired persons' holding or buying corporate stocks for retirement income? What types of stocks would you recommend? Why? Why may the shares of a good mutual fund be recommended to a retired person?
8. Explain the different retirement or pension programs of American business companies.
9. Explain the reasons for and the principal provisions of the Keogh Act.
10. (a) What is an annuity?
    (b) How does an annuity differ from a life insurance policy?
    (c) Against what risk does an annuity offer protection?
11. Do you agree with the statement that the older people get, the more they worry about having enough to live on for the rest of their lives? Why is this true? When do people ordinarily start to worry about the future?
12. Comment on the status of annuities in a period of inflation.
13. Explain why investment in an annuity may be a safer and better way to provide for old age than investment in United States Government bonds.
14. Comment on the following statement: "A person can ordinarily save more through an annuity than an ordinary savings account because it represents forced savings."
15. People who have annuity policies live longer than those who do not have them. Why is this true? If you purchased an annuity policy, do you think you would live longer?
16. Because of the advances in medical science the life span is gradually increasing. How does this affect the holders of annuities?
17. Distinguish between immediate and deferred annuities. Is the immediate annuity necessarily a single premium policy? Are all single premium annuities immediate annuities?
18. "The immediate annuity works just the opposite way from life insurance." Indicate what is meant by this statement.
19. Indicate the distinguishing features of each of the following types of annuity policies:
    (a) Straight life annuity
    (b) Refund annuity
    (c) Life annuity with guaranteed number of payments

(d) Retirement annuity
(e) Joint and survivorship annuity
(f) Variable annuity

20. Does the cost of an immediate annuity increase or decrease as a person advances in age? Why is this? Is the same true for life insurance?
21. Why are annuity rates different for women than for men?
22. Why may the cost of a joint and survivorship annuity for husband and wife appear to be rather high as far as the husband is concerned?
23. Does a deferred annuity policy have any death benefit? Explain.
24. Is a medical examination necessary to buy an annuity? Would healthy or unhealthy people profit more from an annuity policy?
25. From what type of insurance are the proceeds often used to purchase an annuity?
26. Indicate how the annuity payments are treated under the federal income tax law. Do annuities have a tax advantage?
27. To what extent are company pension plans and social security a substitute for annuity policies?
28. Explain the nature of a variable annuity.

CASE PROBLEMS

1. Mr. and Mrs. Gary Holmes, ages 68 and 65 respectively, have the following monthly retirement income:

Social security (combined)	$186.30
Company pension	100.00
Mutual fund dividends	50.00
Interest on bank savings account	50.00
Total	$386.30

The mutual fund dividends are from shares with a present market value of $20,000, and the interest is from a $20,000 commercial bank savings account. They also have $20,000 (present redemption value) in Series E United States savings bonds, which cost them $13,000 (current taxes not being paid on the interest accumulation). Mr. Holmes will become the beneficiary of a substantial amount of money in ten years from the dissolution of a trust fund, but in the meantime he is finding that it is extremely difficult to make ends meet on a $386.30 monthly income. What recommendations would you make to remedy the situation?

2. Will Willis has been a successful manager of a large chain grocery store for many years. He is now 60 and expects to retire at 65. Mr. Willis believes that he will be financially adequately prepared for retirement with the company pension, social security retirement benefits, Medicare, annuities, and a sizable investment in common stocks. The mortgage on his house is paid off and he owes no debts—in fact he has often said that he will have nothing to worry about after retirement. Mrs. Willis, who is now 58, is not looking forward to her husband's retirement. Outside her household duties, her main interests have been playing bridge and going to an occasional movie. Mr. Willis has not been interested in either of these—his principal interest has been his job. During the week he says he is too tired to play

bridge or go out, but he enjoys watching western movies and wrestling on TV. On Saturday night after work he likes to go to the corner bar and drink beer for the evening, and on Sunday he likes to "loaf." Mrs. Willis is afraid that neither of them will be happy after her husband's retirement. Do you think Mrs. Willis is correct in her thinking? Mr. Willis, however, is eagerly looking forward to retirement. Do you believe that he will enjoy it? Why or why not? What would you recommend that Mr. Willis start doing now in order to better enjoy retirement?

3. Mr. and Mrs. J. F. Goodman, aged 69 and 65 respectively, are eagerly looking forward to Mr. Goodman's retirement from his factory job next year. They have been living quite frugally over the years in order to have an adequate income upon retirement. Their home is fully paid for and they owe no debts. It is expected that their retirement income from all sources will be approximately $320 per month. The Goodmans have lived in the same house for the past 31 years. They have stayed home most of Mr. Goodman's vacations in order to save money. Mr. Goodman has always been interested in reading about traveling. They have subscribed to *The National Geographic Magazine* and *Holiday* for some years. When Mr. Goodman is retired next year it is his intention to sell their home, buy a mobile home, and spend the rest of their days traveling over the United States, Canada, and Mexico seeing all the things they have read about for many years. It is expected that the home at present inflated prices would bring approximately $20,000, and they think the mobile home will cost about $5,000. They plan to invest the balance of $15,000 in a local savings and loan association at 4 per cent. This would boost their monthly income from $320 to $370. Mrs. Goodman is not too sold on the idea of selling their home and living in a "trailer" while traveling all over the country. Do you think they should sell the home? Do you think they would be happy living in a mobile home and traveling? Do you think they could afford to do this? What retirement plan would you suggest to the Goodmans?

4. Following are nine things which people have indicated they would like to do upon retirement. We will assume that the income would be barely adequate to do each of them.

   (a) Do nothing
   (b) Live the same life with the same job and income as before retirement
   (c) Travel
   (d) Retire and live in Arizona, Florida, or California
   (e) Play golf
   (f) Fish
   (g) Teach in a college or university
   (h) Take a trip around the world
   (i) Do the things you have always wanted to do

   List the above in the order of their importance or interest to you. Ask your father to do the same. Then ask a retired (third) person to do it. What differences do you observe in the opinions? Why is this the case? In view of the opinions of the others, do you believe you will change your opinion as you get older?

5. Ralph Swift is 26 years old, married, and has two children. His company has offered him the opportunity to purchase a retirement annuity through a payroll deduction plan. It would require a $12 per month deduction from

salary. Swift is eligible for social security when he reaches retirement 40 years from now. If he goes into the plan, the company will contribute $6 per month to be added to his $12. The company is offering this plan since it has no retirement or pension program of its own. Should Swift purchase the annuity? Would this annuity cover his insurance needs? Would it cover his retirement needs? What kind of protection does this annuity offer Swift's family?

6. Walter Jones is 65 years old and ready to retire. He has no family or dependents. During his working years, he has saved $60,000 and now wants to buy an annuity to pay him an income for the rest of his life. The insurance agent has suggested a straight life annuity, but Jones doesn't like the idea of "losing" his entire estate in event of an early death. He is thinking in terms of a refund or guaranteed number of payments annuity. Which annuity do you think would be best for him? What are the advantages of the straight life annuity for Jones? What are the advantages of the refund annuity for him? Why should Jones buy an annuity when he has $60,000 in savings? Would the type of annuity he should buy be different if he were married and his wife living? Explain.

7. Jerry Hudson finished college four years ago. One year later, he married Ruth and they now have two children. He is earning $650 per month with substantial opportunity for advancement over the years in his present employment. They have made a down payment on a home and are paying on a $12,000 mortgage. Hudson's job is covered by social security and in addition he has a $5,000 group term insurance policy. He is still carrying his $10,000 term National Service Life Insurance. They have several hundred dollars in a savings account besides their normal $100 balance in a checking account. They feel they should start planning for the future. Is it too early for them to start providing for his retirement in 40 years? Are his life insurance needs fully covered? Set up an insurance, retirement, and savings program for Jerry and Ruth Hudson.

SELECTED READINGS

Barnes, Leo. *Your Investments.* (Section on "How to Select Investment Companies and Operate Personal Retirement Plans.") Larchmont, N. Y.: American Research Council, Inc. Published annually.

Dusenbury, George, and Dusenbury, Jane. *How to Retire to Florida,* Fourth Edition. New York: Harper & Row, 1959.

Greenough, William C. "Is The Variable Annuity Making The Grade in College?" *Pension & Welfare News,* November, 1964.

J. K. Lasser Tax Institute, *J. K. Lasser's Estate and Gift Tax Planning That Builds Family Fortunes.* Larchmont, N. Y.: American Research Council, Inc., 1962.

J. K. Lasser Tax Institute, and Shulsky, Sam. *Investment for Retirement,* Revised Edition. Larchmont, N. Y.: Business Reports, Inc., 1965.

Magee, John H., and Bickelhaupt, David L. *General Insurance,* Seventh Edition. Homewood, Ill.: Richard D. Irwin, Inc., 1964. Chapter 25.

Masteller, Kenneth C. *How to Avoid Financial Tangles.* Great Barrington, Mass.: American Institute for Economic Research, 1965.

Matteson, William J., and Harwood, E. C. *Life Insurance and Annuities From the Buyer's Point of View.* Great Barrington, Mass.: American Institute for Economic Research. Latest edition.

Moore, Elon H. *The Nature of Retirement.* New York: The Macmillan Co., 1959.

Spinney, William R. *Estate Planning,* Tenth Edition. Chicago: Commerce Clearing House, 1963.

Teachers Insurance and Annuity Association—College Retirement Equities Fund, Annual Report, 1964.

Turnbull, John G., Williams, C. Arthur, Jr., and Cheit, Earl F. *Economic and Social Security—Public and Private Measures,* Second Edition. New York: The Ronald Press Co., 1962.

Wormser, René A. *Personal Estate Planning in a Changing World.* New York: Simon and Schuster, Inc. Latest edition.

Wright, Clarence. *Successful Retirement: Plan It Now.* Washington, D. C.: Kiplinger Washington Editors, Inc., 1964.

19

Estate Planning, Wills, Trusts, and Taxes

As is true of many financial matters, too many people start thinking about estate planning too late in life. The first serious thought that many individuals give to estate planning comes when they are about to retire, or in many instances when they start to realize that they will not be on this earth forever. Usually little can be done at this late date to *build up* an estate.

Too many people think of an estate as something that will come into being only *after they are dead.* To them estate planning means making arrangements for the disposition of this estate to the appropriate heirs. But this is only the final part of the planning. An estate is a person's property while he is living as well as after he is dead. And it is usually only by careful estate planning during his entire adult life that he will have a sizable estate to leave to his family. Complete estate planning really involves three objectives:

1. The acquisition and use of property during working years to provide an adequate balance between current enjoyment, security, and provision for the future.
2. Adequate property and income to maximize enjoyment and security during retirement.
3. Property adequate for the needs of a family after an individual's death, and planning proper methods of passing on this property to various members of the family both before and after his death with the least possible expenses and taxes.

Building an Estate

It is the hope of the authors that what has been said heretofore in this book will aid a person in the building of an estate. The following will be repeated as a summary:

1. Acquire the necessary education and experience to earn a respectable salary or profit.
2. Carry adequate life insurance to protect one's family in the event of an early death.
3. Maintain a budget.
4. Attempt to establish a proper balance between current spending and savings.
5. Buy or acquire a home.
6. Follow a rather conservative investment program, with proper diversification, and provide a hedge against both inflation and deflation.

In the previous chapter planning for retirement was discussed. All of this is, of course, part of estate planning. A conservative approach to retirement planning would anticipate a long life. If death occurs at an average age, the estate that is left to the heirs would properly be larger than contemplated.

Transferring an Estate

Many people dislike giving away any of their property during their lifetime, even to their spouses or children. In fact some dislike thinking about their property going to somebody else even after their death. There are three inescapable events everyone should recognize: (1) you are going to die, (2) "you can't take it with you," and (3) someone else is going to get your property. A sensible person makes suitable plans to transfer his estate.

In many instances provision has already been made for the transferral of certain property upon death without the need for provisions in a will. Some of these have already been mentioned—the payment to the beneficiary of the face value of life insurance, the right of the person named on a United States savings bond to ownership of the bond upon death of the registered owner, the right of co-owners of real estate and savings accounts, etc. Additional procedures discussed in this chapter are the passing on of property by means of a will or according to the laws of descent and distribution, the making of gifts, and the creation of trusts. We will discuss also the taxation aspects of the various methods of distributing an estate.

It is particularly important that a person have competent advice in regard to the distribution of his estate. This can be obtained from a lawyer experienced in handling estates, officers of trust companies and trust departments of commercial banks, and investment counselors. Many life insurance and mutual fund salesmen are competent to give advice on these matters, but the client should be on guard against overzealous salesmen trying to make commissions.

WILLS

Regardless of the size of your estate, there is one thing you can do immediately to help the situation—make a will. Practically everybody intends to make a will before they die, but court records show that only about half of us really do it. Why don't more people do it? Let's face it, we don't like to talk about death—particularly our own. For those who are superstitiously inclined it should be pointed out that there has never been one bit of evidence to show that making a will has hastened death. In fact, it could be argued that the peace of mind resulting from the making of a will may even tend to prolong life. For most people, just plain inertia is probably the reason a will is not made. It seems peculiar that so many people will spend a lifetime in working and saving in order to build up an estate and then they will not take the relatively few minutes required to draw up a will. It is the privilege of every person to see to it that particular relatives or friends get what is intended for them. But if a person dies without a will, the estate will go to those persons designated by the statutes of the particular state, regardless of the intentions of the deceased. If an individual wants his estate divided in some manner other than that specified by the law, he should make a will specifying just how he wants it distributed.

A person should not put off making a will. Putting it off usually results in no will at all. The time to make a will is *right now.* An individual can make out his own will, but it is advisable to get the assistance of a lawyer. A form for a will is found later in the chapter, but, since the laws of each state specify the requirements for a valid will, a person should consult an attorney in his own state.

DISTRIBUTION OF PROPERTY IN THE ABSENCE OF A WILL

State Statutes

It is of some interest to an individual to know what the statutes of descent and distribution of his particular state specify in regard to the distribution of property upon death, when there is no will. If the statutes prescribe the exact distribution desired by the individual, there is less

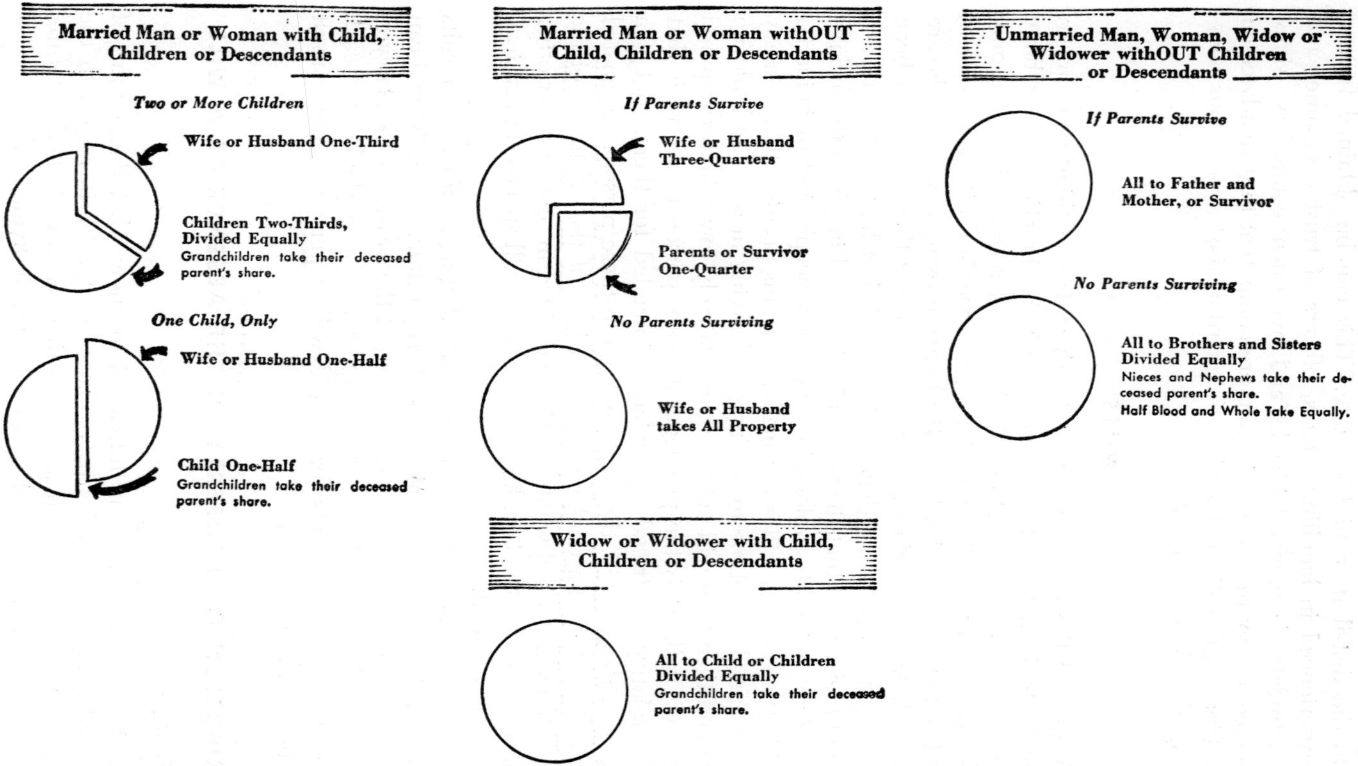

Fig. 19–1. Distribution of property upon death of owner, under Ohio law, in the absence of a will. (Reproduced with permission of D. D. Staples, Financial Advertising, Richmond, Va.)

need to make a will. Since these statutes differ among the states, it is impossible to set forth the laws of the various states here, but the following distribution is followed in a number of states.[1]

Distribution of Property upon Death of Unmarried Man or Woman, or Widow or Widower

1. *When no children or their descendants.* Property is distributed one half to the father, and one half to the mother, and if one of the parents is dead the survivor gets it all.

2. *When no children or parents.* Property is equally divided among the brothers and sisters. If one of them is dead, his or her share is equally divided among his or her children.

3. *When no children, parents, brothers or sisters, or their descendants.* Property is equally divided among next of kin. In Ohio one half goes to the paternal grandparents or survivor, and one half to maternal grandparents or survivor.

4. *When no relatives.* Property goes to the state in which the deceased resided. In Ohio, if there are stepchildren or their descendants, it goes to them.

Distribution of Property upon Death of Married Man or Woman

1. *When no children or their descendants.* A fixed amount, such as $5,000 or $7,500, plus half of any balance left after deducting this fixed amount goes to the spouse, and the remainder goes to the parents of the deceased. In case the parents are dead, some state laws provide that the spouse gets it all. The estate is divided between the spouse and the parents of the deceased, for example, in California, Michigan, New York, and Pennsylvania. But in Colorado, Florida, Kansas, Minnesota, and some other states the entire estate goes to the surviving spouse. In some states, such as Illinois and Indiana, it is divided among the surviving spouse and the parents and brothers and sisters of the deceased. In Ohio three quarters goes to the spouse and one quarter to the parents or surviving parent; if there are no parents then the spouse gets it all.

2. *When children or their descendants.* One third or one half goes to the surviving spouse, and the other two thirds or one half is divided equally between the children. If one of the children is deceased, his or her share is equally distributed among his or her children. In Ohio, if there is only one child or its descendants, the spouse gets one half and the child or its descendants gets the other half; if there is more than one child or its descendants surviving, only one third goes to the spouse and the other two thirds is divided equally among the children.

[1] This distribution is followed in Ohio, unless otherwise indicated.

The amount stated above for the surviving wife or husband is in addition to the life estate in certain real estate which may be given to her or him by the homestead statutes of the particular state. Where dower or curtesy exists (see page 358), the surviving spouse is usually given an option of taking the property under this right, or of taking the share which the statutes on descent prescribe. This is true regardless of whether there are children.

Distribution of Property upon Death of Widow or Widower with Children or Their Descendants. The property is divided equally among the children. If one of the children is dead, his or her children have a right to an equal part of their parent's share. In some states the statutes governing the distribution of real property (real estate) are different from those relating to personal property. In Ohio no distinction is made.

Ancestral Property

The laws on descent in some of the states make a distinction between property purchased by an individual and property which he acquired from an ancestor by gift, devise, or descent. If a person dies, and no children or their descendants are living at the time of his death, property which the deceased inherited from his father, for example, would, according to such laws, go to certain designated blood relatives of the father. The purpose of such laws is to keep ancestral property in the line of blood whence it came. The statutes of Ohio provide that there shall be no difference made between ancestral and non-ancestral property.

NEED FOR A WILL

Choice of the Beneficiaries

We have just seen what happens to the estate when a person dies intestate (without a will). Some of the injustices that can arise from the distribution of the property in the manner prescribed by the law may already be apparent, but we will enumerate a few of them.

Adams married a wealthy girl. During his lifetime he has accumulated a considerable amount of property. He also carries a large amount of life insurance for the protection of his wife and child. Mr. Adams' parents, in contrast to those of his wife, are quite poor and depend upon him for most of their support. This has caused some friction with his wife. Mr. Adams dies without a will. The law says that all the property will go to his wife and child. And possibly Mrs. Adams may give or will part of this property to her parents—who do not need any money. In the meantime Mr. Adams' parents, who are desperately in need of money, get nothing. Furthermore, they have no legal claim to any of the son's estate.

If Mr. Adams had made a will he could have left his parents any amount of his estate after giving effect to the part which his wife would be entitled to by the law of descent and distribution or by dower.

Now consider an entirely different situation. Mr. and Mrs. Smith have no children. Mr. Smith has never taken out any life insurance because he has always said that he did not "believe" in life insurance. They have accumulated an estate with an estimated value of $45,000. Mrs. Smith is entirely dependent upon her husband for a living. Mr. Smith's parents are quite wealthy. Since he kept "putting it off," Mr. Smith died without having made a will. According to the law of their state, Mrs. Smith gets $5,000 and half of the remaining $40,000, or $20,000. This amount is wholly inadequate for her. Mr. Smith's parents, who do not need the money, get $20,000 (taxes and expenses ignored). By means of a will Mr. Smith could have left the entire estate of $45,000 (expenses ignored) to his wife—which is probably what he intended to do. It is realized that $45,000 may be insufficient for Mrs. Smith, but she would certainly be better off than with only $25,000.

The Browns, who have a son aged 6, have accumulated very little property. Mr. Brown dies without a will. According to the law of the state in which they reside, Mrs. Brown gets only half the estate; the other half goes to the son. The latter being a minor, it becomes necessary for the court to appoint a guardian for the son. Although the mother would probably be appointed guardian, she can use the son's share only for his necessary expenses. When he becomes of age, he will get the residue of the share. In the meantime Mrs. Brown must struggle along on the half of the estate which she inherited. It was probably the intention of Mr. Brown that his wife would get his entire estate and use it as was necessary, but he failed to so provide in a will.

Mr. Henry died at the age of 64 without a will, and left an estate valued at $58,000. At the time of his death his wife was 61. Mrs. Henry has no income or property other than that which her husband left her. She is probably too old to secure employment, particularly since her only experience has been keeping house, and she is probably too old to remarry. The Henrys have one son, aged 37, who has done quite well financially and who has an annual salary of $14,500. The law of descent and distribution in their state decrees that Mrs. Henry will get only half the estate, or $29,000, and the other $29,000 goes to the son. Mrs. Henry really needs the entire estate and the son probably could get along just as well without any part of it. Had Mr. Henry made a will he could have left the entire estate of $58,000 to his wife—which is probably what he intended to do.

A final example. Mr. Williams' only source of income has been from his retail business. Most of the business income other than that which has been needed for living expenses has been plowed back into the business. Mrs. Williams also helps out in the business. Mr. Williams dies without a will and leaves his wife and two minor children. The court appoints Mrs. Williams guardian for the children, but it also appoints an administrator to oversee Mrs. Williams' disposition of the estate. It is the duty of the administrator to liquidate the estate as quickly as possible and settle the estate, and the court will see to it that this is done. A quick sale of the entire business or a piecemeal sale of the assets will bring only a fraction of the "going concern" value of the business, but the law must be carried out. Had Mr. Williams made a will and left the business to his wife as a going concern, she could have continued to run the business and enjoyed the income for the support of herself and the two children.

Avoidance of Legal Complications

If a person dies without a will, the court will appoint an administrator to handle the estate. If it is the husband who dies intestate, the court will often appoint his wife the administrator. The latter will have to provide and post a bond equal in amount to the estate. In some instances the family lawyer, brother of the husband, or the trust department of a bank may have been more competent to administer the estate, and had the husband made a will he could have designated such a person the executor of the estate. Furthermore, no bond is required of the executor if it is so provided in the will.

When no will is made, complications arise in connection with minor children who legally have a share in the estate. A guardian must be appointed for the children. Although the surviving spouse may be appointed guardian, a bond will be required by the court. A guardian must function in accordance with the laws and directives of the court, and an annual accounting must be filed with the court. If the deceased had, by means of a will, left all the estate to the surviving spouse, there would be no occasion to have a guardian appointed.

The absence of a will results in more expense and consumes more time in other ways. When some noted or wealthy individual dies without a will there may be hundreds or even thousands of people claiming kinship to the deceased. The legal proceedings and hearings may take years, with the result that the real heirs must wait a long time before they get anything from the estate.

A lawyer can include many devices in a will that will save the estate an appreciable amount in estate taxes. This applies particularly to the creation of trusts in the will, to become effective upon death of the creator. Trust plans and estate taxes are given separate discussion later in the chapter.

HOMESTEAD LAW AND OTHER RESTRICTIONS

Almost all states have some kind of *homestead law.* Such a law is designed to give protection to a man's wife against creditors and to prevent the gift of his property to someone else. In some states it is necessary for a person to file a homestead exemption with the proper authorities. If a homestead has not been selected before the death of the head of the house, the probate court is usually empowered to do this for the benefit of the wife and children. It usually covers the particular house in which the parties live, but there are limits, ranging up to $8,000, on the value of the property which may be exempt from debts, etc. The homestead law may absolutely give the property to the wife, or it may let her have it only for a limited period of time, or for life.

Our interest in the homestead law here is to point out that the right given by this law cannot be absolutely defeated by a will, except in the states of Mississippi and South Carolina.

A number of states have had laws giving the wife a *dower* right to her husband's property. This type of law gives the wife a one-third life interest in the real property owned by her husband, to take effect upon the death of the husband. In some states a similar law, called either *dower* or *curtesy,* gives the husband a similar interest in his wife's real property. Curtesy has been rather generally abolished, however, and many states have done away with the dower right of the wife. Where this has been done, new statutes have generally been enacted which give the wife or husband a portion of the estate of the other. It is usually provided that the property will be inherited in fee, rather than merely obtaining of a life interest. Such statutes usually cover not only real but personal property as well.

It is not possible to cut off the dower or statutory right of a wife by means of a will. Should property be granted to a wife in a will in lieu of the dower right, the wife may usually elect whichever one of the two she wants. If the wife is granted a gift in the will without reference to dower, it is sometimes assumed that it is in addition to the dower interest. In some instances it is necessary for a wife to choose between a homestead right and a dower estate. A husband may, by a will, leave his wife all his property, but he cannot, by means of a will, cut her off from everything he owns.

The other restrictions on the granting of property in a will relate to the creation of a trust. At common law a trust is limited in duration to named lives in being at the time of the creation of the trust plus 21 years and 9 months. The statutes of some states have codified the common law rule, while those in other states have changed it. The statutes of some states, however, permit the granting of perpetual trusts for charitable purposes.

In speaking above of homestead laws, dower, curtesy, and trusts, it should be kept in mind that these are governed by the statutes of the various states, and the individual should refer to the statutes of his particular state, or consult a competent attorney, in order to ascertain the nature of the law in that state.

DRAWING UP A WILL

The statutes of the particular state must be consulted in order to ascertain who is capable of making a valid will. All states prescribe the minimum age. Some, such as Massachusetts, fix the age at 21; others, like California, specify 18. New York fixes the age at 21 for real property and 18 for personal property. In some states the minimum age for males is 21, while for females it is 18.

The other requirement set forth by the statutes of the various states is that the person be of sound mind. He need not possess a perfect mind, such as a person who is in vigorous health will ordinarily have, to meet this requirement. It is sufficient if a person understands that he is making a will, has a knowledge, without prompting, of the extent of his property, and realizes his relationship to other parties who may or ought to be the objects of his bounty.

Terminology

A will is a legal document, and legal terminology is usually used throughout. The meaning of some of the words used in, or in connection with, a will follows:

Administrator. The person or institution appointed by the court to administer the estate of a person who dies leaving no will.

Beneficiary. A person named in a will to receive property.

Bequeath. The legal word used to apply to the giving of personal property.

Codicil. This is a supplement later added to the will, making some change in the original provisions. The requirements for this are the same as for the will itself.

Decedent. A deceased person.

Devise. The giving of real estate. The person to whom it is given is called a *devisee.*

Executor. The person or institution named in the will to pay the debts and distribute the property according to the provisions of the will. When it is a woman, the word *executrix* is used.

Holographic will. This is a will in the handwriting of the person making it. Such a will usually carries more weight than one which is typed. Several of the states do not require that this kind of will must be witnessed.

Intestate. This is used to refer to the situation when a person dies without having made a will.

Legatee. A person who is given personal property under a will.

Nuncupative will. This is an oral will which is made by a person during his last illness, or by a soldier or sailor in battle. It must be reduced to writing within a specified time by one or more of the witnesses and offered for probate within a specified time.

Personal property. Property other than real estate.

Probate. The name of the court which has jurisdiction over wills. The word is also used to apply to the procedure of the court in taking proof of the validity of the will.

Real property. Real estate.

Surrogate. Same as probate.

Testate. A person leaving a will is said to have died testate.

Testator. The person making the will. When it is a woman the word *testatrix* is used.

Formalities To Be Observed

In addition to making out the body of the will in proper form, certain formalities must be observed in order that the will be valid. These are as follows.

Signature of the Testator. The will must be signed by the person making it out, that is, the testator. It should be signed in ink, immediately after the last sentence in the body of the will, and in the presence of the required number of witnesses. It should be signed before the witnesses sign their names. The testator's signature should be exactly as his name appears in the body of the will, and his signature or initials should also be placed on the other pages.

Witnesses. The statutes of the various states usually require that there be at least two (in some states, three) witnesses. These witnesses should be adults, but younger than the testator. They should be persons of good standing and be well known to the testator. A witness should not be the spouse of the maker of the will, a beneficiary under the will, or a spouse of a beneficiary. If a beneficiary under the will signs as witness, he may lose what has been left to him in the will.

The witnesses should watch the testator sign, and they should watch each other sign, and the will should state that they all signed in the presence of each other. The addresses of the witnesses should be placed under their signatures. Both the testator and the witnesses should either sign or initial the other pages included in the will.

The witnesses need not read the will, but the testator should tell them that it is his last will and testament. The *attestation clause* which follows the signature of the testator should be read to the witnesses, so that they will know what they are signing.

No Alterations. After a will has been signed, no alterations of any character should be made in it. If this is done it may void the will. If it is later desired to make some change in the will, it should be done through a codicil, and all the requirements for the will itself should be observed in connection with this codicil.

Other Details. All the pages in a will should be numbered consecutively at the top. Where a standard form for a will is used, the inappropriate words should be deleted. The space for the date should not be filled in until the will is to be signed and witnessed.

Care Needed

A will is a legal document. It is more important to use the proper words and phrases in their correct positions in a will than in many other legal papers. The statutes of the various states have set forth the requirements for a will, and even a slight departure from the prescribed method may make it invalid. The maker of a will will not be on this earth when the time comes to interpret the provisions contained therein, so he should see to it that the will distributes the property in the way he desires, and that the phraseology used accomplishes this objective, and is in conformity with the requirements of the law.

Because of what has just been said, it is highly advisable that a good attorney be hired to draw the will. Sample forms of wills can be obtained which can be completed by filling in the blank spaces, but unless the simplest type of will is to be drawn this form should not be used. Even where it can be used, the maker may err in not having the proper number of witnesses, or by not signing in their presence, or in not having them sign in the presence of each other. The feeling of assurance that one's family will get the estate as he wants it distributed will justify the expenditure of a few dollars for the services of a competent attorney.

Although wills are often rather lengthy documents, this need not be the case when the estate is to be distributed to only one or two persons. The following, which in the body contained only 23 words, is the will of the late President Coolidge.[2]

[2] Preceding the body proper of the will was this statement: "*Will of Calvin Coolidge of Northampton, Hampshire County, Massachusetts.*" Following the signature of the late president was the following: "*Signed by us on the date above in the presence of the testator and of each other as witnesses to same and signature thereof.*

(Signed) *Everett Sanders*
Edward T. Clark
Erwin C. Geisser."

It will be noted that the will said, "*Drawn . . . this twentieth day December . . .*" The word "of" was apparently unintentionally omitted between the words "day" and "December." This will was written on a piece of folding White House stationery in the handwriting of the late president. The last word on the first page was "day," and the first word on the next page was "December." The turning of the page probably resulted in the omission of the word "of."

Not unmindful of my son John, I give all my estate, both real and personal to my wife, Grace Coolidge, in fee simple.

Drawn at Washington, District of Columbia, this twentieth day December, A.D., nineteen hundred and twenty-six.

(Signed) Calvin Coolidge

The late Chief Justice White of the United States Supreme Court left the following will.

Washington, D. C., June 26, 1915

This is my last will. I give, bequeath and devise to my wife, Leita M. White, in complete and perfect ownership all my rights and property of every kind and nature, whether real, personal or mixed, wherever situated, appointing her executrix of my estate without bond and giving her Seisin thereof.

Edward D. White

Signed, sealed, published and declared by the said Edward Douglass White as and for his last Will and Testament, in the presence of us who, in his presence, and at his request, and in the presence of each other, have subscribed our names as witnesses.

Richard H. Nugent,
1231 T St., N. W.
Bertram F. Shipman,
1745 Oregon Avenue.

Sample Form of a Will

The examples given above are rather short, but contain all the essentials of a will. The form shown in Fig. 19–2 could be completed by an individual to serve as his will until such time as he may have an attorney draw up a more complete and suitable one.[3]

[3] The following is the unusual and interesting will left by Charles Lounsbury, a distinguished newspaper man in Chicago in the 1870's. He died penniless in the 1880's.

I, CHARLES LOUNSBURY, being of sound and disposing mind and memory . . . do now make and publish this my last will and testament. . . . First, I give to good fathers and mothers, but in trust for their children, nevertheless, all good little words of praise and all quaint pet names, and I charge said parents to use them justly but generously as the needs of their children shall require.

Item: I leave to children exclusively, but only for the life of their childhood, all and every, the dandelions of the fields and the daisies thereof, with the right to play among them freely, according to the custom of children, warning them at the same time against the thistles. And I devise to children the yellow shores of creeks and the golden sands beneath the waters thereof, with the dragonflies that skim the surface of said waters, and the odors of the willows that dip into said waters, and the white clouds that float high over the giant trees.

And I leave to children the long, long days to be merry in, in a thousand ways, and the Night and the Moon and the train of the Milky Way to wonder at, but subject, nevertheless, to the rights hereinafter given to lovers; and I give to each child the right to choose a star that shall be his, and I direct that the child's father shall tell him the name of it, in order that the child shall always remember the name of that star after he has learned and forgotten astronomy.

Item: I devise to boys jointly all the useful idle fields and commons where ball may be played, and all snow-clad hills where one may coast, and all streams and

Selecting the Executor

The executor named in the will can be either an individual or a trust company. If the estate is small and is being left to an adult, such as a wife, who is capable of taking care of the simple details in connection with the administration of the property, it would simplify matters and save expense by appointing this beneficiary the executor (or executrix) of the will. Since some states provide that a bond must be furnished by the executor in the absence of any provision otherwise in the will, it is advisable to specify in the will that no bond is required.

If considerable property or a going business is left by the testator, it may be advisable to appoint a trusted business associate or the family lawyer the executor. Of course we occasionally read where such a person absconds with some of the money in the estate. It is advisable to get the consent of the individual before naming him the executor. Provision should also be made in the will for the appointment of another executor in the event that the one named refuses to serve, or if he dies. In event that none is named, or the individual specified does not accept, the probate court will appoint an administrator for the estate. If the estate is large, it may be advisable to appoint both the beneficiary and a lawyer the executors in the will.

An increasing number of people in recent years have made a trust company the executor. Due to its permanency of life, the trust company will probably be in existence to carry out the terms of the will. It is experienced in this kind of work and is equipped to safeguard the assets

---

ponds where one may skate, to have and to hold the same for the period of their boyhood. And all meadows, with the clover blooms and butterflies thereof; and all woods, with their appurtenances of squirrels and whirring birds and echoes and strange noises; and all distant places which may be visited, together with the adventures there found, I do give to said boys to be theirs. And I give to said boys each his own place at the fireside at night, with all pictures that may be seen in the burning wood or coal, to enjoy without let or hindrance and without any incumbrance of cares.

Item: To lovers I devise their imaginary world, with whatever they may need, as the stars of the sky, the red, red roses by the wall, the snow of the hawthorn, the sweet strains of music, or aught else they may desire to figure to each other the lastingness and beauty of their love.

Item: To young men jointly, being joined in a brave, mad crowd, I devise and bequeath all boisterous, inspiring sports of rivalry. I give to them the disdain of weakness and undaunted confidence in their own strength. Though they are rude and rough, I leave to them alone the power of making lasting friendships and of possessing companions; and to them exclusively I give all merry songs and brave choruses to sing, with smooth voices to troll them forth.

Item: And to those who are no longer children or youths or lovers I leave Memory, and I leave to them the volumes of the poems of Burns and Shakespeare, and of other poets, if there are others, to the end that they may live the old days over again freely and fully, without tithe or diminution; and to those who are no longer children or youths or lovers I leave, too, the knowledge of what a rare, rare world it is.

LAST WILL AND TESTAMENT

OF

____

I, ______________________________, a resident of ______________ (city) ______________ (county) State of ______________, being of full age, of sound mind and memory and not under restraint of duress, do make, publish and declare this my LAST WILL AND TESTAMENT, hereby revoking any and all wills and codicils by me heretofore made.

ITEM I. I direct that my just debts, including the expenses of my last illness and funeral, be paid as soon as may be practicable after my death.

Item II. I give and bequeath to my son, ______________________, the sum of Ten Dollars ($10.00).

ITEM III. I give and bequeath to my daughter, ____________________, the sum of Ten Dollars ($10.00).

ITEM IV. All the rest and residue of my estate, whether real, personal, or mixed, wheresoever situated, I give, devise and bequeath to my wife (husband) ______________________________, For her (his) own use and benefit forever.

ITEM V. I nominate and appoint my wife (husband) to be executrix (executor) of this, my LAST WILL AND TESTAMENT, and I direct that no bond be required of her (him) as such executrix (executor).

IN WITNESS HEREOF, I have hereunto set my hand to this, my LAST WILL AND TESTAMENT, at ____________ (city) ____________ (state) this ____________ day of ______________ A. D. __________

(Signed) ______________________________

This instrument was on the date hereof by the above named ______________________ signed, published and declared to be his (her) LAST WILL AND TESTAMENT in our presence, who, at his (her) request and in his (her) presence and in the presence of each other, we believing him (her) to be of sound and disposing mind and memory, have hereunto subscribed our names as witnesses the day and year above written.

(Signed) ______________________ *residing at* ______________________

(Signed) ______________________ *residing at* ______________________

(Signed) ______________________ *residing at* ______________________

Fig. 19–2. A will.

of the estate. One of the disadvantages of having a trust company act as executor is that it probably will not take the personal interest in looking after the administration of the estate that a friend would take. The other chief disadvantage is the cost.

When an independent executor or administrator is appointed, such as a lawyer or a trust company, a fee is customarily charged. The statutes of the particular state will prescribe the maximum fees. Those for the State of New York are shown in Table 19–1.

Table 19–1. Executor's Fees in New York State

Schedule of Fees	Portion of Estate
4% on first	$ 10,000
2½% on the next	290,000
2% on balance in excess of	300,000

Amount of Fees on Designated Estates

Size of Estate	Amount of Fees
$ 10,000	$ 400
25,000	775
50,000	1,400
100,000	2,650
250,000	6,400
500,000	11,650
1,000,000	21,650
5,000,000	101,650
10,000,000	201,650

An administrator who is appointed by the court to administer the estate in the absence of a will is rather narrowly limited by the law in the action he can take. An executor, on the other hand, can be given greater freedom of action. The testator should be careful, however, not to limit the executor too much by the provisions of the will. Unforeseen events may arise after the death of the testator which can be met by the executor for the best good of the beneficiary if he is not held down too closely by the will. If the executor can be trusted—and only a trusted person or institution should be appointed—he should specifically be given the power to use his own discretion in regard to the holding or selling of the property of the estate. Unless this power is specifically given him in the will, he will be personally responsible to the beneficiaries for any losses resulting from not selling the properties within a reasonable time after the death of the testator. This may result in sale of the property in an unfavorable market.

General Contents of a Will

The purpose of a will is to insure that the testator's property will be left to the person or persons he wished to receive the property. The following is a summary of what may well be included in a will:

1. Statement calling for prompt payment of all debts and funeral expenses
2. Nature of the funeral and burial services desired
3. Distribution of real and personal property to family and relatives
4. Distribution of property, if any, to servants and friends
5. Grants to charitable, religious, or educational institutions
6. Disposition to be made of personal effects
7. Appointment of executor
8. Appointment of guardian for minor children
9. Creation of trusts for wife or children, or others
10. Any special provisions desired

Some Suggestions in Drawing a Will

The following suggestions should be observed by an individual in having his will drawn up.

Distribute Property in Way Desired. It is the right of every individual to dispose of his property the way he desires. To most of us this means that we will take care of our immediate family first.

Try To Avoid Trouble. In many instances family quarrels result from the disposition of the property, particularly when there is an uneven distribution to relatives of the same kinship.

Consider Other Property. In distributing property by a will, due consideration should be given to any property owned by some members of the family, and the amounts and beneficiaries of life insurance policies.

Do Not Make the Will Too Rigid. At the time a will is drawn, it is impossible to foresee future events. If several pieces of property are being left to several children, it is usually better to give them an equal interest in all the properties, or the proceeds from the sale of the properties, than to give each separate properties. This is due to the fact that some real estate may go up in value while other properties may depreciate in value, and what was intended as an equal division may not turn out to be so. This may result in strife among the children. Of course, trouble may arise as a result of leaving one piece of property to several children who do not get along well.

Gifts of Fixed Amounts. Individuals sometimes will friends a fixed amount, such as $5,000. By the time the estate is settled it may have shrunk to the point that the payment of this amount to the friend may work a hardship on the family of the deceased. For this reason it may be advisable to state that the friend shall receive some fractional part of the estate, such as one twentieth, for example, with a provision that it shall not exceed $5,000.

Consider Stock Dividends and Splits. A person making out a will may own a definite number of shares of stock of a particular corporation, such as, for example, 100 shares of General Motors, and he may specify in his will that 100 shares of General Motors go to his son John. Subsequently, General Motors may split its stock 2 for 1, with the result that at the time of the death of the testator, there are 200 shares in his estate. Do the 200 shares go to the son? Or, is the latter entitled to only 100 shares, with the balance going to whoever is entitled to the residual estate? Provision should be made in the will for such a situation. A periodic review of the will would call attention to the need for clarification on such points.

Use Complete Names. The complete names of all persons mentioned in the will should be used, together with their proper addresses. The given name and middle initial of a married woman should be used rather than that of her husband.

Distribution of Property to Wife Only. As stated above, a wife is the only person who by law is entitled to property who cannot be entirely cut off by a will. So if a wife is not left her legal share of one third, or whatever it is in the particular state, she can still claim that amount.

In most instances, however, a man would want to leave all or the bulk of his estate to his wife. It will be recalled, however, that according to the laws of many states, if provision is not otherwise made in the will, in the absence of children, a wife is entitled to only part of the estate and the rest goes to the parents of the deceased or their survivors. As the parents would probably be more self-sufficient than the wife, in most instances the will should provide that the entire estate is to be given to the wife.

Distribution When There Are Children. When wife and children survive, the statutes of many of the states provide that, in the absence of a will specifying otherwise, the wife shall receive only one third of the estate and the other two thirds shall go to the children. If the children are minors, this will necessitate the appointment of a guardian. Although the mother may be appointed the guardian, she is permitted to spend their share only for their bare essentials. This may result in the wife's not getting enough to live on. It would thus probably be better in a situation of this kind to leave the entire estate to the wife.

If the children are old enough to be self-supporting by the time the father dies, it would undoubtedly be better in most instances to will the wife the entire estate. But if this is not done in the will, the children will be entitled to two thirds of the estate regardless of whether they need the money.

Provision in the Event of Simultaneous Death. If the husband wills his entire estate to his wife and he dies first, she will be entitled to the estate. Upon her death, in the absence of a will, the property will be divided among her family and relatives in the manner specified by the laws of descent and distribution in the particular state. If there are no children, that means that the property will go to her relatives rather than to the relatives of the husband.

With the widespread use of the automobile and airplane, there are an increasing number of accidents in which the husband and wife both die as a result of the same accident. If it can be proved that the husband died first, the wife would be entitled to the property given her by the will. But if both of them die at the same time, or if it cannot be proved which one died first, the will would be of no effect. Because of this possibility, it is advisable for the will to specify what disposition is to be made of the estate in event of the death of both the husband and wife in the same accident.

Some of the states have enacted statutes covering situations of the kind just discussed. In Ohio, for example, the statutes provide that when there is no evidence of the order in which death of two or more persons occurred, no one of such persons shall be presumed to have died first and the estate of each shall pass and descend as though he had survived the others. The statutes of this state further provide that when the surviving spouse or other heir at law, legatee, or devisee dies within thirty days after the death of the decedent, the estate of such first decedent shall pass and descend as though he had survived such surviving spouse, or other heir at law, legatee, or devisee. The Ohio statutes provide, however, that these sections of the statutes shall not apply in the case of wills wherein provision has been made for a distribution of property different from that set forth in the statutes.

Status of Children. It was stated above that if a person who has children dies without a will, the statutes of the various states provide that a fractional part of the estate, usually one third, will go to the spouse, and the remaining part, usually two thirds, will go to the children. It has also been mentioned that a man cannot by a will cut off his wife from the part that she is entitled to by law. But it is possible by a will to cut children off from any part of the estate. To will all the property to the wife, however, will not necessarily eliminate the children unless they are specifically mentioned in the will. This is sometimes done by leaving them a small amount, such as $1 or $10. Children born subsequent to the time the will is drawn up may also be entitled to part of the estate unless provision otherwise has been made in the will.

Need for Revision of a Will

It is not enough that a person make out a will. As time goes on he should review the contents of the will in the light of later events. After a will has been drawn, some of the parties mentioned therein may die before the testator. Or other children may be born or adopted. The testator may move to another state, or he may become legally separated from his wife or divorced or remarried. Some or all of these events may make it highly desirable that the will be changed.

Other Points on Validity of Wills

It is a general rule that a will must be probated in the state in which the testator was domiciled at the time of his death. This may require more than merely owning a residence in the state. Some people maintain residences in several states and they may die in any one (or some other) of the states. The domicile state would be the one in which the deceased maintained his *legal residence*—the one where he voted, paid his taxes, etc. (A wife's domicile would be that of her husband unless she has established another one for the purpose of getting a divorce, or unless she is legally separated from her husband.)

Death taxes, such as inheritance and estate taxes, are payable in the state of domicile. In some instances, however, several states have exacted the taxes since each claimed domicile.

A rather generally accepted rule of law is that the validity of a will which bequeaths personal property depends upon the law of the state where the testator had his domicile at the time of his death, but if the will devises real property (real estate) its validity depends upon the state in which the real property is located. At the present time, however, most states will recognize valid wills made in another state.

If after making out a will a person moves (his domicile) to another state, it is a good idea to have a competent lawyer in the new state check to determine whether the will is valid in that jurisdiction, or whether a new will is advisable. For example, only two witnesses may have been sufficient in the state in which the will was drawn, but the new state (where the will would be probated) may require three in order to be valid. A new will may be advisable also in order to have witnesses who will be more accessible when the will is to be probated. A number of states also require that the executor be a resident of the particular state.

Some states require a non-resident executor to post a substantial bond, or to appoint a resident agent.

Changing the Will

Any attempts to change some of the provisions in a will may result in the entire will being declared invalid, unless the statutes are closely observed. Changes in or additions to a will can be made by means of a codicil which is attached to the will. The same legal formalities required in the drawing up of the will must be observed when making a codicil. Perhaps a better method of making changes is to destroy the original will and make up an entirely new one to take its place.

Revocation of a Will

A will may be revoked in several ways. If a person makes out a new will bearing a later date which indicates an intention to revoke the previous will, or one which is inconsistent with the provisions of the other will, or one which disposes of the entire estate, this will constitutes a revocation of the previous will. The will or part of it can also be changed through the use of a codicil.

If the will is torn, burned, canceled, or destroyed by the testator or by some other person in the presence of and by direction of the testator, it will be deemed to be revoked. If after the death of the testator the will is found among his possessions in a mutilated condition, it will be deemed revoked unless there is proof of a contrary intention on the part of the testator. If a codicil is drawn up in such a way that it can stand alone, it will be effective even though the will is destroyed or cannot be found.

Care of the Will

People are often careless even in respect to important papers. Since the entire estate will be distributed by the will and the future welfare of the family or relatives of the testator may be dependent upon it, extreme care should be taken to keep the will in a safe place. But the will should not be kept in the safe-deposit box of the person making it out even if the spouse has access to the box. When a person dies, his safe-deposit box is sealed until it can be opened in the presence of a representative of the particular state's taxation department. This may be sometime after the person is buried. If the testator's spouse has a box in his or her name alone the will could be kept there. Otherwise the will should be kept in a safe place in the home or office and the spouse should know its whereabouts. Unsigned carbon copies of the will may also be left with the family lawyer and the executor of the estate.

THE LETTER OF LAST INSTRUCTIONS

It is advisable that a person prepare and keep in a place which is known to his spouse a letter of last instructions which will be quite useful in settling his estate. This is a better place than the will for any burial instructions. Many wives know little or nothing about the business or financial affairs of their husbands. Included in the letter should be the names and addresses of the particular individual's lawyer, accountant, executor, broker or investment banker, and possibly his insurance advisor. Forms may be secured from a trust company or trust department of a bank in which the detail of an individual's personal and financial affairs may be filled in. The exact location of the following should be stated:

1. The will
2. Safe-deposit boxes and the keys thereto
3. Bank accounts
4. Savings and loan accounts
5. Accounts in other types of savings institutions such as credit unions, postal savings, company savings systems, etc.
6. Cash other than that in savings accounts and safe-deposit box
7. Life insurance policies
8. Social security number and card
9. United States Government bonds
10. Stocks and bonds
11. Certificate of automobile ownership
12. Birth certificate and marriage certificate
13. Deeds, abstracts, insurance policies, and mortgages pertaining to any real estate owned
14. Copies of the income tax returns for the past several years
15. Canceled checks and receipted bills

If a person does not have a birth certificate, he should state the place and the date of his birth. A better procedure would be to go to the proper state office and have a birth certificate made out and put it in the safe-deposit box. Most life insurance companies require the beneficiary of a life insurance policy to establish proof of the date of birth of the insured. That is one reason why the birth certificate is important. If the insured wants to save time and trouble for his widow, he can establish proof of date of birth with the insurance company by sending in to the company a copy of his birth certificate. In the absence of a birth certificate some companies will accept proof by means of a baptismal certificate.

Figure 19–3 illustrates a good checklist which can be used in connection with putting estate plans in proper order.

Figure 19–4 shows where important records should be kept. Incidentally, a copy of the Letter of Last Instructions should be kept in the home file. As added insurance, a copy should also be kept in the safe-deposit box.

TRUST PLANS

A trust is a contract whereby the maker of the trust, called the *trustor*, places his property under the control of a *trustee* for the benefit of a certain party, or parties, called the *beneficiaries*, or *cestuis que trustent.* The trustee may be an individual or an institution such as a trust company. In selecting a trustee, at least the same degree of care should be exercised as in the case of an executor, but, due to the need for prudence and experience in investing the trust funds, it is recommended that a competent trust company rather than an individual be selected.

The beneficiaries who receive the income from the trust funds during their lives are called the *life tenants,* or *income beneficiaries,* and the person or persons designated to receive the principal at the termination of the trust are called the *remaindermen.*

Three types of trusts will be briefly described here: the living trust, the testamentary trust, and the life insurance trust.

Living Trust

The living trust is one which goes into effect during the life of the trustor. In this kind of trust the trustor may also be the beneficiary. Such a trust may be created by a person who is making a large salary, such as a movie actor or actress, who realizes that fortune may not be so kind in the future, and who wants to lay away part of his estate to provide for future contingencies. Or, this kind of trust may be set up by an individual who is too busy with other matters to give sufficient attention to the matter of investing his money. People who travel extensively or who live in foreign countries may find this kind of arrangement convenient. Then, too, it may be used by individuals (who may be included among those mentioned above) who realize their own incompetence when it comes to selecting investments.

The living trust may be set up to accomplish various purposes. The trustor may provide in the agreement that he is to receive the income from the trust for life and upon his death the principal of the trust shall go to his wife. Or, it may be provided that upon his death the wife will receive a life income and upon her death the principal shall go to the children. Or, it may be provided that someone else, such as an incompetent child, shall receive a life income from the trust starting immediately after the creation of the trust, and that upon the death of the child the

Your check lists

Are your affairs in order?
Use these to find out.

1. Are your records in order?

	yes	no	needs more work
will	☐	☐	☐
insurance policies	☐	☐	☐
real estate deeds	☐	☐	☐
stock certificates	☐	☐	☐
bonds	☐	☐	☐
notes receivable	☐	☐	☐
bank books	☐	☐	☐
safe-deposit key	☐	☐	☐
income tax returns for prior years	☐	☐	☐
marriage certificate	☐	☐	☐
divorce papers	☐	☐	☐
family birth certificates	☐	☐	☐
list of close relatives with addresses and dates of birth	☐	☐	☐
veteran's discharge paper or certificate	☐	☐	☐
social security card or record of number	☐	☐	☐
list of your assets	☐	☐	☐
burial instructions	☐	☐	☐
general instructions to wife, including list of advisers	☐	☐	☐

2. What is the value of your estate?

assets:

savings ______
securities ______
real estate ______
life insurance face value ______
other assets ______

total assets ______

estimated liabilities:

debts ______
burial expense ______
estate and inheritance taxes ______
income taxes due ______
administration expense ______

total liabilities ______
net estate ______

3. What would your wife's income be?

source	monthly income
life insurance	______
social security	______
veteran's pension	______
income from securities (Figure 3½% annual return on amounts to be invested. Omit value of home if wife is to occupy it.)	______
income from trust funds	______
any income wife might have of her own such as salary, if she would be working, help from relatives, etc.	______
total	______

What would your wife's minimum expenses be?

food ______
shelter ______
clothing, medical, miscellaneous ______
education ______

total ______

4. List of advisers (1st, 2nd, 3rd choice)

lawyer 1.______ 2.______ 3.______

bank officer or businessman 1.______ 2.______ 3.______

investment adviser 1.______ 2.______ 3.______

insurance adviser 1.______ 2.______ 3.______

5. Planning

	yes	no
Have you made an over-all plan for your estate?	☐	☐
Have you a will?	☐	☐
Has your wife a will?	☐	☐
Are your beneficiary arrangements up to date in insurance policies and pension plans?	☐	☐
Have you made provision for children's guardian?	☐	☐
Have you left burial instructions?	☐	☐
Have you minimized taxes and administration costs?	☐	☐
Have you gone over these matters recently with a lawyer?	☐	☐

Fig. 19–3. Checklist for management of personal financial affairs. [Reprinted by permission from *Changing Times,* the Kiplinger Magazine (November, 1961 issue). Copyright 1961 by The Kiplinger Washington Editors, Inc., 1729 H. Street, N. W., Washington, D. C. 20006.]

Family record guide

document	importance	where to keep
AUTO TITLES	Issued in 40 states and District of Columbia as evidence of ownership. Essential for transfer to new owner when car is sold.	safe-deposit box
AUTO BILL OF SALE	Submitted to state on new car to obtain title or to register. May be required as evidence of car ownership should you move from a nontitle to a title state.	safe-deposit box
NOTES & DEBTS	Promissory notes, instalment sales contracts, etc., serve as evidence of what you owe or what people owe you. Checks and receipts of payments are important for interest deductions on tax returns and to indicate fulfillment of contract terms.	Notes, contracts in safe-deposit box; others in home file
REAL ESTATE OWNERSHIP	Usually deed fulfills its legal function when recorded with proper county office, but worthwhile retaining for description of property.	home file
	In some areas, real estate transfers involve summation of legal actions affecting property. Difficult to prepare in many instances and expensive.	safe-deposit box
INSURANCE POLICIES	Easily replaced by insurance company if lost.	Policies in home file; keep list of policy numbers, amounts, companies in safe-deposit box.
MARRIAGE, BIRTH RECORDS	May take time and small fee to replace by writing to county or state bureau of vital statistics. If original birth record lost from state or county files, must use substitutes such as U.S. Bureau of Census record ($3 fee), baptismal certificate, or affidavit from doctor or hospital.	safe-deposit box
MILITARY DISCHARGE	Can't be replaced, but services will issue "certificate in lieu of discharge" at no cost.	safe-deposit box
SCHOOL RECORDS	Transcripts of courses and grades available from schools at modest fee.	home file
SOCIAL SECURITY CARD	Social Security Administration provides replacements at no cost and will furnish temporary certificates when employer insists employe have card before starting work.	home file
STOCKS, BONDS	Company securities and bonds difficult and expensive to replace.	Safe-deposit box or with your broker. Keep list in home file.
	Savings bonds are replaced by government at no cost, but it normally takes six months to get the new ones.	Safe-deposit box, but can be held in home file if you put in safe-deposit box a list of bonds with year of issue, name & address of owner, serial number & letter.
TAX RECORDS	Federal government can question tax return within three years of filing, and six years if you omit from gross income an amount exceeding 25% of the total. Keep checks, receipts, supporting evidence, copy of tax withholding statement for at least three years. Keep copies of returns.	home file
	Home improvement records should be handled differently. Tax on profit made on sale of a house is calculated on difference between price received and cost plus sums spent to improve property. Thus, these sums act to reduce taxable profit. Retain receipts, bills of sale, checks, etc., evidencing money spent for three years after you've reported sale of the house in your tax return.	safe-deposit box
WILLS	Vital. Make several copies.	Original with lawyer or corporate executor; copy in safe-deposit box. If executor is individual, give him copy, put another copy in home file and store original in safe-deposit box, but check law on access to box after your death.

Fig. 19–4. Key documents in management of personal financial affairs. [Reprinted by permission from *Changing Times,* the Kiplinger Magazine (August 1963 issue). Copyright 1963 by The Kiplinger Washington Editors, Inc., 1729 H. Street, N. W., Washington, D. C. 20006.]

income or principal shall be distributed in the manner provided in the trust agreement.

We have already seen that spouses and heirs have certain rights with respect to property of a deceased person by virtue of the law of descent and distribution. But property left to another by means of a living trust is not subject to such laws and therefore this type of property distribution cannot be contested. Wills are a matter of public record and the contents of those made by prominent or wealthy deceased persons will be carefully scrutinized by newspaper reporters. But the property already transferred by means of a living trust will not come to the attention of the public.

Revocable Living Trust

The living trust may by its terms be made *revocable* or *irrevocable*. In the usual case the trustor would make it *revocable*. The typical person dislikes parting with his property forever (except when death forces it—and he may still dislike the thought). Whatever may have been the reason or reasons at the time that prompted a person to create an irrevocable trust, unforeseen events may occur which will cause him to regret his action. Subsequent losses of property or a reduced income, illnesses, etc., may make it advisable for him to be able to revoke the trust and use the income or principal or part of the income or property to cover living expenses. In some instances the unwise use of the income on the part of the life tenant may make revocation desirable. Or perhaps other relatives have a better need for the income or principal.

Estate and gift taxes will be discussed later in the chapter, but the taxability of trusts will be briefly mentioned as we describe trust agreements. At the time a revocable trust is created, no gift taxes are paid on the principal amount because no actual gift has been made since the trust is revocable. Any income earned on the trust principal is taxable to the trustor the same as if the trust had not been created. This is true even if the income is paid to someone else. In the latter case the income would be considered a series of gifts after they had been finally made. Thus the trustor must pay the gift tax on the income given to the other party, provided of course that the amount of the income gifts exceeded the gift tax exclusions and exemptions. The principal of the revocable trust is part of the trustor's estate and upon his death it would be subject to the estate taxes. A second or third set of estate taxes would not have to be paid when successive income beneficiaries die, as will be discussed when we consider testamentary trusts.

Irrevocable Living Trust

The other kind of living trust is the *irrevocable* trust. The occasions in which this type of trust would be recommended are rare. One may be where a person has already lost one or two fortunes by his unwise handling of his property or business affairs. Or, he may recognize his own weaknesses with respect to spendthrift tendencies, addiction to drink, periodical unsoundness of mind, or approaching senility, and accordingly may create a trust that he cannot change in order to protect himself or his dependents, or both. In most instances when the irrevocable trust is used, however, it is done for tax-saving purposes. The taxes that may be saved are the estate taxes upon the death of the trustor and the income taxes that would otherwise have been paid by the trustor. To effect these savings, extreme care must be used in drawing up the trust agreement. It is desirable to consult an attorney for additional information.

Testamentary Trust

A testamentary trust is set up in a will and does not become effective until after the death of the maker. The trustee may be a different party from the executor of the will, but in most instances the same party, or trust company, is appointed to both offices. Unlike the irrevocable living trust, the testamentary trust becomes part of the estate. But one of the important advantages of the testamentary trust is that the person creating it does not part with any of his property until his death—when he would have to part with it anyway.

A man may be doing his wife a favor if he leaves his property in trust for her rather than willing her the property directly. Most women, particularly those who are married, are inexperienced in handling investment and business matters. An estate which may be adequate to maintain a widow for life may be quickly dissipated soon after the death of the husband because of the financial incompetency of the wife. Trust companies sometimes make mistakes in handling investments, but they do not make the financial mistakes that many women make.

Testamentary trusts are quite often set up to give the widow the income from the estate during her life, and upon the death of the wife the principal would be paid to the children. Or the property may be held in trust for the children until they reach a specified age, such as 21. Provision may be made in the contract for the trustee to draw on the principal if the income from the trust investments is inadequate.

If a parent wants to leave property to a minor child, all of the cost and trouble referred to previously may be avoided by establishing a testamentary trust in his will for the child. No guardian would then be appointed, and the trustee would have much greater freedom of action than a guardian. Furthermore, the parent can include flexible provisions in the trust to facilitate the administration of the trust estate. The trustee must of course be paid, but this is offset by the saving of the guardian's fee.

Trusts, particularly testamentary trusts, have long been used by wealthy people as a means of lessening the federal estate tax. Without the trust, here is what would happen. Brown dies and leaves his property outright to his wife. The estate tax (after the marital deduction, which will be explained later) would be paid upon Brown's death. When the wife dies she leaves what is left of the estate to her children. The estate is then again hit with the estate tax. When the children die they each leave their estates to their children (Brown's grandchildren). Once again the federal estate tax must be paid. Thus in passing the property down from Brown through his wife and children to his grandchildren three separate sets of estate taxes have been paid. Uncle Sam, rather than the grandchildren, may have obtained the bulk of Brown's estate.

In order to pay less federal estate taxes and thus preserve a larger part of the estate, the following practice has become common. Brown in his will creates a testamentary trust leaving his wife a life estate in all the property—she is to get the income from the trust for life. (The procedure would be altered somewhat as will be explained in connection with taxes.) The federal estate tax would have to be paid on the estate at this time. The trust provides that upon the wife's death, the children shall get the income for life and, upon their death, the grandchildren shall get the principal of the trust; or they will get the income from the trust until they are 21, at which time the principal will be paid to them. Under this arrangement no federal estate taxes will have to be paid on the trust estate upon the death of the wife or upon the death of the children, because due to the terms of the trust the federal law considers that there has been only one transfer of the property from Brown through his wife and children to his grandchildren and therefore only one federal estate tax is applicable. This may result in a tremendous saving in taxes and the successive generations can enjoy a larger estate.

The procedure of setting up trust funds and the arrangements for lessening the estate taxes are quite complicated, and it is suggested that persons interested in the matter consult their attorney or competent officers of trust companies or trust departments of commercial banks for advice and guidance. It may be found advisable to have the trust company or bank act as trustee.

Life Insurance Trusts

This is the type of trust created when a person makes a trust company or a bank, as trustee, the beneficiary of a life insurance policy or policies. The proceeds are invested and installment payments are made to the wife or children of the insured. The life insurance trust is really a form of testamentary trust. The income and principal can be paid out in the same manner as mentioned above in connection with the testamentary trust. An increasing number of people are leaving their life insurance in trust instead of having the proceeds paid directly to the wife or children. This may insure that the wife will currently receive an adequate amount.

When the proceeds of life insurance are paid directly to the beneficiaries in a lump sum, it is known that in many instances this money is unwisely invested or dissipated.

Because the face value of the policy is paid upon the death of the insured, it is obvious that the payment of one or a few premiums will, in event of the death of the insured, build up a trust fund many times the size of the premiums paid. Where the amount of the insurance carried is relatively small, it is not advisable to set up the life insurance trust. The income from the investment of the proceeds of a $5,000 or even a $10,000 policy, for example, would be inadequate to maintain a person. In such instances the proceeds should be paid directly to the beneficiary. Of course, if a number of such policies are held, all of them may be made payable to the trust company and thus provide a sufficient income.

It was pointed out in Chapter 7 that the insured can provide in the insurance contract that upon his death the proceeds will be paid to the beneficiary in regular installments, or that the proceeds shall be held by the insurance company and a regular rate of interest paid to the beneficiary. Either of these arrangements may accomplish the same objective as in the creation of a life insurance trust. One advantage of this is that it is cheaper. The insurance company does not make any charge for handling the proceeds in this fashion, whereas the trust company naturally receives compensation. Leaving the proceeds of the policy to a trust company, however, is more flexible, because the trust company, if so provided, can use its discretion in deciding whether any of the principal should be used to augment the income being earned.

Where the proceeds of life insurance are left with the insurance company, the funds are not segregated from the other assets of the company, but when the insurance trust is set up the trust company must keep the investments separated. The types of securities which may be purchased with trust funds, however, are more limited than those which can be bought by life insurance companies.

Powers of Appointment

One criticism of trust plans is that they are too inflexible and that subsequent events may make the distribution of property provided for in the trust an unfortunate one. It has already been pointed out that the person drawing up a will may include a provision therein giving the trustee power to draw upon the principal of the trust if the income being paid to an income beneficiary is insufficient.

Another point to consider is the inclusion of a provision giving the income beneficiary the right to alter the terms of the trust for the distribution of the trust property upon his death. Let us take the following typical example. Smith by means of a testamentary trust leaves his son a life income from the trust property and provides that upon the son's death the property shall be distributed to the son's living children in equal shares. Soon after Smith's death his son dies and the latter's children get the property. The son's wife does not have any means of support. Or, before the son's death it may become apparent to him that some of his children would have a much greater need for the trust property than others. Or, perhaps the family of a deceased child is destitute. But unless the trust agreement provides otherwise, the son's hands are tied. If Smith wishes to do so he may include in the trust plan provided in his will a provision giving his son the "power of appointment" to specify in his own will how the trust property shall be distributed upon his death. Of course Smith may want to make the decision himself and not entrust such power to his son. The inclusion of a power of appointment may change the tax status of a trust and therefore this point should be talked over with a lawyer before any action is taken.

Limitation on Life of Trusts

The law early recognized that if property could be held in trusts forever, in a matter of time practically all, if not all, of the property in the world would be so held. It is thus considered contrary to public policy to have the "dead hand" control the disposition of property for an unreasonable length of time. The common law rule, which still prevails in most of the states (in some by codification of the common law), is that a trust cannot extend beyond the lifetime of any number of named persons in existence at the time the trust becomes effective ("lives in being") plus 21 years and 9 months. The "named persons" need not be beneficiaries of the trust but they usually are income beneficiaries. As long as the "named" persons are living (plus 21 years and 9 months thereafter), unborn people, such as grandchildren, could be beneficiaries under the trust agreement. After the maximum period has expired the trust is terminated and the property is distributed in the manner prescribed in the agreement.

In some states the statutes specify a different maximum duration for a trust than that set forth by the common law. In New York, for example, a trust may not extend beyond the lives of two named persons who were living at the time the trust was created.

In the case of a testamentary trust and a revocable living trust, the "named persons" must be in existence at the time of the death of the person creating the trust. In the case of the irrevocable living trust they must be in existence at the time the trust agreement is drawn up.

Duties of Trustee

The trustee appointed under any of the different forms of trusts mentioned above may be an individual or an institution. In some instances both are appointed as co-trustees. Comparatively few individuals are equipped to handle this work in a satisfactory manner. Trust company executives are usually competent, are well acquainted with the laws, and have had experience in investing. They also have the facilities and the necessary clerical personnel to take care of the work.

It is the duty of the trustee to protect the principal of the fund, and to keep it constantly invested in such manner as to provide a maximum income consistent with the safety of the principal. If the trustor states in the agreement the kind of securities which may be purchased, then this must be followed by the trustee. In the event that no specific instructions have been given in the trust agreement, the trustee must observe the statutes of the particular state.

Where there are no statutes relating to trust investments, the common law must be observed. This varies somewhat among the states, but usually the decisions state that a trustee should act in good faith and with the degree of care and prudence that prudent men ordinarily use in investing their own money, giving due regard to income and safety of principal. Whether trust investments are governed by statutes or the common law in a particular state, it is apparent that the trustee must be conservative in his investment policies, and thus a relatively low rate of return is earned. In an effort to secure a hedge against inflation, more and more trusts set up in recent years give the trustee power to purchase some common stocks. Some of the states have amended their laws in recent years to permit trustees to invest trust funds to a limited extent in selected common stocks.

Although trustees are responsible for the funds entrusted to them, they are not personally liable for losses that occur unless such losses result from their own fraud or carelessness. If any loss occurs from the purchase of ineligible securities, they naturally can be held liable.

Trustees, whether individual or corporate, are entitled to compensation for their work. The statutes of the various states provide the method and amount of this compensation. This is based on the principal amount invested and the annual income. The amount varies among the states. The rates are usually based on a sliding scale, being smaller as the amount increases.

Trust officers of banks and trust companies are more experienced in trust affairs than is the average person.

Rights of Beneficiaries

The life tenants are entitled to the income earned on the trust fund after the expenses have been deducted. The income is paid at regular intervals and is accompanied by a detailed statement showing receipts and expenditures. The beneficiary has a right to see to it that the trustee discharges his duties in accordance with the terms of the trust agreement and the statutes of the state. It is his right to insist that all funds in the trust be fully invested, but he cannot, of course, tell the trustee what securities to purchase.

Rights of Remaindermen

The remaindermen are entitled to the principal of the trust fund upon the expiration of the trust agreement. It may be to their advantage to accept the securities in which the funds are invested rather than have the trustee liquidate them and return the cash.

Although the trustee is required to turn over the trust property to the remaindermen upon the termination of the trust, it should be realized that the value of this property may be more or less than it was when the trust was created. It is the right of the remaindermen to see to it that the trustee does not give the life tenants any part of the fund itself. Extraordinary dividends which encroach upon the capital of the trust fund, such as those often paid in the form of stock, should be returned to the trust fund for the benefit of the remaindermen rather than be paid to the life tenants.

STATE INHERITANCE AND ESTATE TAXES

All states except Nevada have an inheritance or estate tax. Estates of residents of Nevada which are subject to the federal estate tax, however, would be subject to as high a death tax as those in other states. This will be explained later when we consider the federal estate tax. Some of the states have both an inheritance tax and an estate tax. For all practical purposes an estate tax is a tax against the estate, while an inheritance tax is a tax on the beneficiaries to whom the estate is distributed.

Nature of Inheritance Tax

Since the inheritance tax is a state tax, it would be expected that the exact nature of the law would vary widely among the states. Expenses of closing the estate and debts of the decedent are deductible to arrive at the net estate. Usually the amount of the exemptions and the tax rates vary according to the degree of relationship between the heir and the deceased. In most instances the tax rates increase as the amount of property inherited increases. The law may provide that the exemption for a widow, or a minor child, or a husband, or all of these, is $750, $5,000, $15,000, $20,000, etc., depending upon the particular state. The amount of the exemption for the next class such as for an adult child, mother, or father is less in most states. The next class, which includes brothers and sisters, would have a still smaller exemption. The tax rates on the first two classes may begin at 1 per cent on the first $25,000 (after exemption) and be graduated up to 5 or 10 per cent on amounts in excess of $100,000 or $200,000. The rates on the other classes in most instances start at higher rates, such as 2 to 5 per cent, and may go up to 10 or 20 per cent on amounts in excess of a specified amount. In the case of estate taxes, ordinarily there is a single uniform exemption. As is true of the inheritance taxes, the rates of the estate taxes are usually graduated.

In addition to the inheritance tax, many of the states have an estate tax which is designed to make up the difference, if any, between the inheritance tax and the maximum credit allowed for state taxes under the federal estate tax. This will be explained when we discuss the federal estate tax later in the chapter. In most of the states the inheritance and estate taxes are not excessive, particularly on relatively small estates. It should be noted too that property received by way of inheritance is not subject to the income taxes. Income earned on such property thereafter of course would be treated the same as any other income.

Property Subject to Inheritance Taxes

Generally speaking, all property, both real and personal, in excess of the exemptions, is subject to inheritance taxes. Real property and tangible personal property are subject to taxes in the state where located. Intangible personal property, such as securities, is ordinarily taxed by the state of domicile of the deceased. The tax status of several types of property will now be mentioned because of the misunderstanding relating to them.

United States Government Bonds. Bonds issued by the United States Government are fully taxable under the inheritance and estate taxes. Thus, all Series E and Series H savings bonds and all Treasury bonds are subject to death taxes. In most states the tax authorities have to depend upon the honesty of people to report government bonds, since the state has no record of them. If the bonds are kept in a safe-deposit box, they will be listed by the state authorities when the box is opened in their presence.

Many people own Series E United States savings bonds. A person may have his wife's or child's name recorded on the bond as co-owner or beneficiary. There may be a difference in taxation where the survivor is a beneficiary instead of a co-owner. Upon the death of the registered owner, the beneficiary would be subject to the inheritance tax on the total amount of the bonds. They would be listed at their redemption value at that time rather than at the cost or maturity value. If a person is named on the bond as a co-owner instead of as a beneficiary, he would ordinarily pay the inheritance tax on only half of the value of the bonds. If it is obvious that the deceased co-owner contributed all the money to buy the bond, then the surviving co-owner would be subject to tax on the entire amount. On small estates the taxation authorities ordinarily do not go into this question. Under the federal estate tax, the surviving co-owner ordinarily must pay the tax on the entire amount, unless he can prove that he contributed some of the purchase price.

State and Municipal Bonds. These are fully taxable under the inheritance or estate tax laws, the same as any other property. A state may, however, exempt its own bonds from taxation within the state, if it desires.

Postal Savings. There is nothing in the federal law which would exempt postal savings from inheritance or estate taxes. Unless the particular state specifically exempts such accounts, they would be subject to full taxation.

Life Insurance. In most states the beneficiary of a life insurance policy does not pay any inheritance tax upon the death of the insured. In some states, however, he is taxed, but there is usually an exemption. Some of the states exempt the insurance from taxation when it is paid to the wife or dependent of the insured, but tax it when the proceeds are payable to someone else.

Joint Ownership Property. Where property such as savings accounts and real estate is held in the name of the husband and wife as joint owners with right of survivorship, some states will upon the death of a spouse tax only half of the property; others will apply the tax to the total valuation of the property unless the survivor can prove that he or she contributed on the investment.

Gifts Made in Anticipation of Death

If a person on his deathbed gives away part or all of his property, this property is fully subject to the inheritance tax, upon the death of the transferor. Generally speaking, property which is transferred in anticipation of death is subject to inheritance and estate taxes. In some jurisdictions, if property is transferred within two or three years prior to death, there is a rebuttal presumption that it was done in anticipation of death.

FEDERAL ESTATE TAX

In addition to the inheritance and estate taxes levied by the states, the federal government levies an estate tax. In a technical sense the federal tax is not imposed on the right to receive property, such as are the inheritance taxes, nor is it on the estate itself. The federal estate tax is a tax on the right to transfer the estate, but for all practical purposes we can consider it to be a tax on the estate.

The federal tax is applied to the net estate of a person at the time of his death. Included in the estate is any property which was transferred in anticipation of death. The executor or administrator may at his option value the property at the time of death or as of a date one year after his death. The taxing authorities or the courts, of course, may have the final word on some valuations. The estate tax must be paid within fifteen months after the death of the person.

All estates are subject to a flat exemption of $60,000, regardless of who may inherit the property. Since the net estates of most people are less than this amount, it follows that most estates are not subject to the federal estate tax. But with the inflation that has taken place in recent years, particularly in real estate values, and the higher incomes received by most individuals, more and more estates are becoming subject to the tax. In addition to the exemption mentioned, spouses are entitled to a marital deduction which will be explained later. The estate tax rate is graduated. It begins at 3 per cent on the first $5,000 (after deducting the exemption of $60,000), and higher rates are applied to the higher amounts. The top rate of 77 per cent is applied to that part of the net estate which is in excess of $10,000,000. The rates and taxes for specified estates are shown in Table 19–2.

Gross Estate

All property, real and personal, tangible and intangible, is included in the gross estate. That means house and contents, cash, bank and savings accounts, stocks and bonds, accounts receivable, library, tools, automobile, etc. Specific mention will now be made of certain property because of the doubt that may exist as to whether such property is included in the taxable estate.

Life Insurance. Although the proceeds of life insurance policies are not ordinarily taxed under the state inheritance taxes, they may be taxed under the federal estate tax. The proceeds will be taxed if the life in-

Table 19–2. Federal Estate Tax, Before and After Marital Deduction

Col. (A) Net Taxable Estate Before $60,000 Exemptions	Col. (B) Tax on Col. (A) Without Marital Deduction	Col. (C) Tax Rate on Amt. in Excess of Col. (A) *	Col. (D) Tax on Col. (A) with Maximum Marital Deduction
$ 60,000	$ 0	3%	$ 0
65,000	150	7%	0
70,000	500	11%	0
80,000	1,600	14%	0
90,000	3,000	18%	0
100,000	4,800	22%	0
110,000	7,000	25%	0
120,000	9,500	28%	0
130,000	12,300	28%	150
150,000	17,900	28%	1,050
160,000	20,700	30%	1,600
200,000	32,700	30%	4,800
250,000	47,700	30%	10,900
300,000	62,700	30%	17,900
310,000	65,700	32%	19,300
560,000	145,700	35%	56,700
810,000	233,200	37%	96,100
1,060,000	325,700	39%	136,100
1,310,000	423,200	42%	178,950
1,560,000	528,200	45%	222,700
2,060,000	753,200	49%	314,600
2,560,000	998,200	53%	411,500
3,060,000	1,263,200	56%	515,600
3,560,000	1,543,200	59%	627,200
4,060,000	1,838,200	63%	739,700
5,060,000	2,468,200	67%	983,500
6,060,000	3,138,200	70%	1,247,300
7,060,000	3,838,200	73%	1,526,400
8,060,000	4,568,200	76%	1,820,500
10,060,000	6,088,200	77%	2,449,300

* These percentages apply only in relation to column B, that is, when the marital deduction is *not* used.

surance was made payable to the estate, or if a particular person is named the beneficiary and the insured retained any "incidents of ownership" in the policy. The payment of premiums by the insured was formerly treated as an incident of ownership but this is no longer the case. In general, if the insured retains the right to make any change in the policy this is considered to be an incident of ownership. More specifically, the following rights would be so treated.

Right to change beneficiary
Right to surrender or cancel the policy
Right to sell, assign, or pledge the policy
Right to cash or loan value
Right to receive dividends
Right to disability benefits
Right to paid-up or extended insurance
Right to elect settlement options

Joint Ownership Property. Several types of property are commonly held jointly by two people. It is further provided that upon the death of either, title to the deceased's interest goes to the survivor. Although such property passes to the survivor without going through a will, it is nevertheless subject to the federal estate tax to the extent that the deceased contributed to the purchase price. In applying the federal estate tax it is assumed that the first joint owner to die contributed the entire purchase price or put up the entire amount of money in a joint account. If the survivor put up any of the money the burden is on him (or her) to prove it.

The types of property commonly held jointly by two people are real estate, particularly the home, bank accounts, and United States savings bonds. In the case of the latter what was said above applies when the bonds are registered in the joint names. If the bonds were registered in the name of the deceased owner or in his name with the survivor named as beneficiary, the surviving owner would always have to pay the estate tax on the entire amount.

In most instances jointly owned property of the kind mentioned above is held by a husband and a wife. The federal law, as will be more fully explained later, provides that a spouse can inherit half of her (or his) spouse's property free of any tax. So a wife (or husband) could upon death of the spouse get half of such jointly held property without paying any estate tax on it, even if it could not be proved that the survivor contributed anything toward the purchase price of the property. (If the marital deduction is taken on jointly held property, however, it reduces by that amount the marital deduction that may be taken on other property.)

Trusts. When we discussed trusts it was pointed out that the property in a revocable trust is taxed under the federal estate tax at the time of death of the trustor. Even in the case of an irrevocable living trust, if the trustor gets some benefit from the trust or if he can alter any of the terms of the trust, the trust property will be subject to the federal estate tax. Testamentary trusts set up in the will are, of course, subject to the estate tax.

Sometimes a parent will establish a bank account in trust for a child, with the parent reserving the right to make withdrawals from the account. The entire amount of such accounts is subject to the estate tax.

Gifts in Contemplation of Death. "Deathbed" gifts are also subject to the federal estate tax at the time of the death of the person making the gift. Any gifts made within three years of the death of the giver are assumed to have been made in contemplation of death, and are therefore taxable under the estate tax unless the executor of the estate can prove to the satisfaction of the taxing authorities that the gift was not made in contemplation of death. When the estate tax must be paid on such gifts, any gift taxes that had been paid on them will be credited against the estate tax.

Net Estate

Certain deductions and exemptions are subtracted from the total gross estate to arrive at the "net estate" which is the figure on which the taxes are computed. Last illness and funeral expense can of course be deducted. Debts owed by the deceased are deducted. Deductible also are all the expenses for the administration of the estate, including lawyers' fees and commissions paid to the executor or administrator of the estate. Bequests made to tax-exempt institutions and qualified charities are also deductible. Andrew Mellon left almost his entire estate of approximately $100 million to the A. W. Mellon Educational and Charitable Trust, which wiped out estate taxes of about $67 million. When Henry Ford died in 1947, out of his total ownership in the Ford Motor Company of approximately 1,900,000 shares of stock, he left 1,805,000 shares (tax-free) to the charitable Ford Foundation. This was all non-voting stock. The remaining 95,000 shares were voting stock and were left to his heirs.

To prevent the same property from being taxed twice under the federal estate tax within a relatively short period, the law affords some relief. This can best be explained by the following example. We will assume that B inherits property, which has been subject to the federal estate tax, from A. If B dies within two years from the time of A's death, the government will not tax the same property in B's estate. If B's death occurs within from two to four years afterward, a credit of 80 per cent of the tax will be allowed. If he dies within from four to six years later, the credit will be 60 per cent. If he dies within from six to eight years afterward, the credit will be reduced to 40 per cent, and if the death is from eight to ten years afterward, the credit will be only 20 per cent. If B's death occurs ten years or more after A's death, no credit will be allowed. In the case of property left by one spouse to another this credit applies only to the extent that it did not give the first estate a marital deduction.

The Marital Deduction

In the event of an estate being left by one spouse to another the most important deduction, particularly in the case of larger estates, is the marital deduction, which has been referred to several times above and will now be explained.

In 1948, when the split income provision for married couples filing a joint income tax return went into effect, a similar change was made in the federal estate tax law with respect to a wife (or husband) inheriting property from her husband (or wife). In other words, the federal law recognizes that a husband or wife is a half-owner in the property held by his or her spouse, and therefore if he leaves the spouse at least half of the property, this half will go to the spouse tax-free. Technically, the marital deduction applies to one half of the *adjusted gross estate,* which is the gross estate after all debts, expenses, and claims have been deducted but before any charitable bequests and before the $60,000 exemption have been taken out.

The importance of this marital deduction may be seen from the following examples. Assume that a husband leaves an adjusted gross estate of $100,000. Half of this, or $50,000, goes to the wife tax-free. After this marital deduction the size of the estate is reduced to $50,000. Since the flat exemption of $60,000 is then allowed, it is obvious that the wife would pay nothing in estate taxes. If the estate amounted to $500,000 the wife will get $250,000 tax-free. Subtracting the $60,000 exemption from the other half leaves only $190,000 which is taxable.

Due to the graduated rates, the marital deduction results in the estate tax being less than half as much as it would be otherwise. Referring to the examples above, an adjusted gross estate of $100,000 would, without the marital deduction, be subject to a tax of $4,800; with the marital deduction there would be no tax at all. A $500,000 estate would be taxed $126,500. With a marital deduction for half of the estate the tax would be only $47,700. Thus the marital deduction resulted in a saving of $77,800, or expressed in percentage a saving of approximately 61½ per cent. Table 19–2 shows estate taxes without and with the marital deduction for estates of various sizes.

In order to secure the full marital deduction, the husband or wife must leave his or her spouse the property or at least half of it outright, or if left in trust, the spouse must receive the income from the property at least annually and have the unrestricted right and power to dispose of the trust property during her or his lifetime or upon death, by will or otherwise. If less than half the property is left to the spouse the marital deduction will apply to only that part which is so left. If more than half of the property is left to the spouse the marital deduction applies to only half of the total estate.

Tax-Saving Devices

When we discussed trusts it was indicated that if a husband left his entire property in trust for his wife for life only, and upon her death it would pass to the children, the federal estate tax would have to be paid upon the husband's death, but it would not be subject to the tax again when it went to the children upon the wife's death. But this arrangement would lose the benefit of the marital deduction since the wife did not have control of the property after the husband died. The following procedure is now followed in many instances. The husband leaves half of his estate outright to his wife. Or he leaves half of the estate to his wife in trust for her life, and gives her the power to determine its disposition upon her death. We will call this Trust A. Either arrangement will permit her to claim the marital deduction on this half. The other half of the estate is left in Trust B to the wife for life and upon her death it is to pass to the children. This (after the exemption) will of course be subject to the estate tax, but upon the wife's death, no tax is paid on it when it is transferred to the children. Trust A, however, would be subject to the estate tax when it was passed to the children or to whomever the wife decided should get it.

By taking advantage of the marital deduction as just described, only half of the estate is taxed at the time of the husband's death. Thus the saving in taxes will result in a larger estate on which the wife may enjoy earnings, and a larger estate can be passed on to the children. Although the tax must be paid upon the wife's death on the half of the estate represented by Trust A, the effect of taxing the two halves of the estate at different times results in less taxes than taxing the entire estate once because of the graduated rates.

Credit for State Taxes

Persons inheriting from estates which are subject to the federal estate tax will, with the exception of Nevada, have paid an inheritance or estate tax to the state. Any such amounts paid to the states are deductible from the estate tax due the federal government, up to an amount equal to 80 per cent of the federal tax as computed under the 1926 law. The rates and exemptions under the 1926 law are much different, however, from those prevailing at the present time. Then the exemption was $100,000 instead of $60,000, and the maximum rate was only 20 per cent instead of 77 per cent, which obtains at the present time.

The application of the credit for state death taxes results in lowering the federal estate tax by varying amounts not exceeding .8 of 1 per cent on a taxable estate (after exemption) of from $40,000 to $90,000 (no credit allowed on the first $40,000), to 16 per cent of the portion of the taxable estate in excess of $10,040,000. Table 19–3 shows the extent to

Table 19–3. Federal Estate Tax, Before and After Maximum Credit for State Taxes, Selected Estates (without marital deduction)

Net Taxable Estate Before $60,000 Exemption	Tax Before Credit for State Taxes	Tax After Credit for State Taxes
$ 60,000	$ 0	$ 0
100,000	4,800	4,800
150,000	17,900	17,500
200,000	32,700	31,500
300,000	62,700	59,100
500,000	126,500	116,500
700,000	194,700	176,700
1,060,000	325,700	289,140
2,060,000	753,200	649,280
10,100,000	6,119,000	5,036,200

which the federal estate tax (before marital deduction) will be reduced with the maximum allowance for state inheritance or estate taxes.

A Final Word

A material saving in estate taxes may be effected through the proper handling of the estate. This is a complicated matter which requires the attention of expert lawyers or trust officers of financial institutions.

When large estates are going to be subject to the federal estate tax it is advisable that sufficient liquid assets or life insurance be available to pay the taxes. Otherwise part of the estate may have to be liquidated at forced sale (and possibly at times when security prices or real estate prices may be relatively low) in order to get the cash with which to pay the taxes.

Figure 19–5 shows the average estate settlement costs for over 10,000 estates of varying sizes in all parts of the United States.

STATE GIFT TAXES

Gift taxes have been enacted by twelve of the states [4] and by the federal government. In order to escape inheritance and estate taxes, many

[4] California, Colorado, Louisiana, Minnesota, North Carolina, Oklahoma, Oregon, Rhode Island, Tennessee, Virginia, Washington, and Wisconsin.

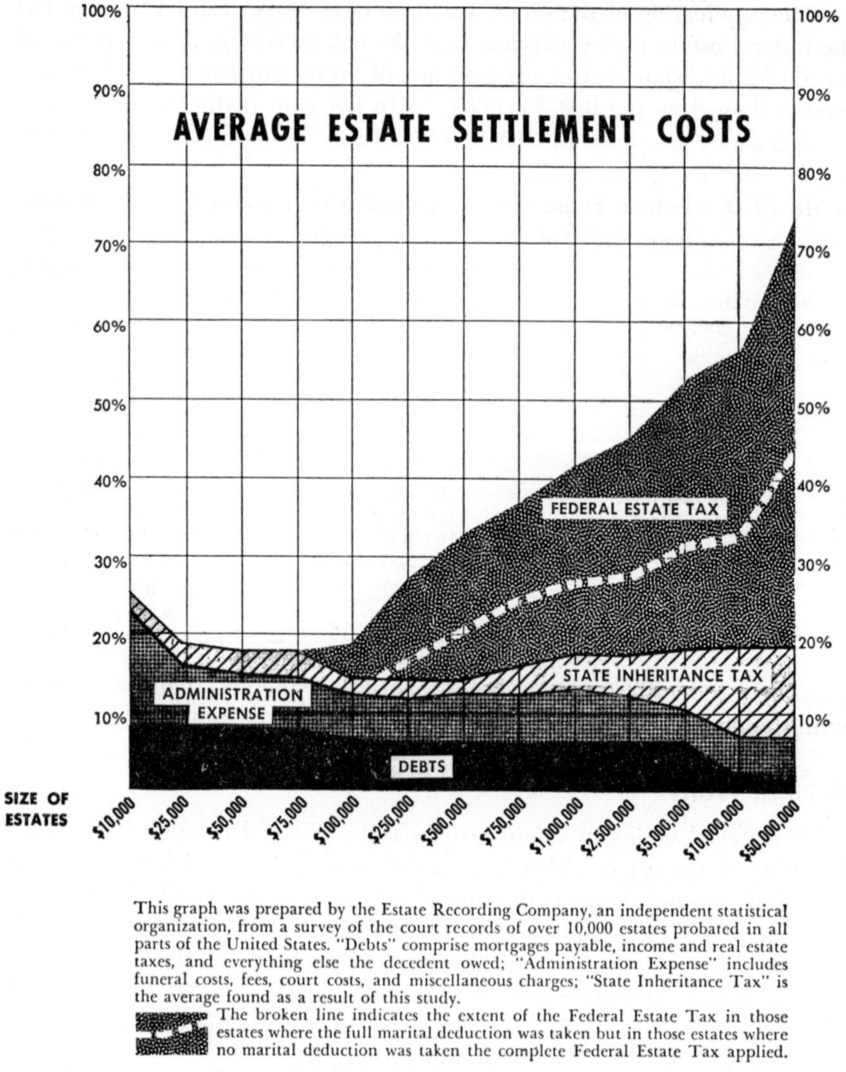

This graph was prepared by the Estate Recording Company, an independent statistical organization, from a survey of the court records of over 10,000 estates probated in all parts of the United States. "Debts" comprise mortgages payable, income and real estate taxes, and everything else the decedent owed; "Administration Expense" includes funeral costs, fees, court costs, and miscellaneous charges; "State Inheritance Tax" is the average found as a result of this study.

The broken line indicates the extent of the Federal Estate Tax in those estates where the full marital deduction was taken but in those estates where no marital deduction was taken the complete Federal Estate Tax applied.

Fig. 19–5. Average costs of settling an individual's estate. (Reproduced with permission of Estate Recording Co., Box 5356, San Diego, Calif. 92105.)

wealthy people have in the past given to their heirs a substantial part of their property before death. The gift taxes have been designed primarily to cover such situations. The state laws follow very closely their own inheritance or estate taxes. The state taxes are low compared to the federal gift tax. They cannot be deducted or used as a credit in figuring the federal gift tax. Also, the federal gift tax cannot be deducted in computing the state gift taxes. Space will not permit a discussion of the state laws, but a brief discussion will be given the federal law.

THE FEDERAL GIFT TAX

The federal gift tax works hand in hand with the federal estate tax, in that it taxes gifts that may have been made during a person's lifetime with the probable intent of lessening the amount of the estate tax upon his death. The tax is paid by the person making the gift (the donor). As is the case with inherited property, the person receiving the gift (the donee) does not have to pay income taxes on it.

Taxable Gifts

Direct and indirect transfers of all types of property, both real and personal, are subject to the gift tax. The gift must be made during the lifetime of the donor, but not all lifetime gifts come under the gift tax. If an individual purchases a house, automobile, bond or stock, or practically any other kind of property, and has it put in the name of himself and someone else as "joint tenants and right of survivorship," he is making a taxable gift equivalent to one half the market value of the property at the time. There is one important exception to this rule. If a husband (or wife) buys real estate and puts it in the name of himself and his spouse as joint owners no gift is deemed to have taken place unless the purchaser wants to treat it as an actual gift. If the couple later decide to split up the joint ownership of the real estate and the division of the property or the proceeds from its sale are derived disproportionately to the way it was originally paid for, a gift tax would be involved. If the property is held until one of them dies, there never would be a gift tax paid (although it may be subject, at least in part, to the estate tax).

If a person opens a joint bank account with someone else and he can withdraw funds from the account without the consent of the other party, he has made no gift until or unless the other party withdraws some of the funds for his or her own benefit. He would then be subject to the gift tax on the amount of money actually withdrawn. If a husband opens a joint account with his wife and she withdraws money to pay for some necessary clothes or household expenses, such amounts are not considered gifts because they were not solely for her benefit. If he buys United States savings bonds and puts them solely in the name of someone else, such as his son, it is considered a taxable gift in the amount of the cost of the bonds. If the bonds, however, are placed in the name of himself and the son as co-owners, it is not considered as a gift unless, while he is living, he permits the son to redeem the bonds and keep the proceeds.

People sometimes attempt to escape the gift tax by a more or less fictitious sale. If a person sells property worth $1,000 to his brother for $100, it will be considered that he made a gift of $900.

The creation of a living trust may or may not subject the property to the gift tax. If the trust is irrevocable and the trustor cannot make any changes in the terms of the trust, then it is subject to the gift tax. But if the trustor can make alterations even if he cannot revoke the trust, then it is not subject to the gift tax (of course the estate tax must be paid on it at the time of the trustor's death). A revocable trust is not subject to the gift tax (subject to estate tax).

Gifts made to tax-exempt institutions and qualified charitable and religious organizations and institutions are not subject to the gift tax.

As pointed out above, gifts made within three years from the time of death of a person subject the property given away to the estate tax unless it can be proved that the gift was not made in contemplation of death. If subject to the estate tax, any gift tax paid can be used as a credit.

If a minor gives away property or attempts to do so, such gifts would not be subject to the gift tax until after the minor becomes of age and does not disaffirm the gift.

Exclusions and Exemption

The first $3,000 in property given to any person or that amount given to each of any number of persons in any calendar year is excluded from the gifts which are subject to the tax. In addition to this annual exclusion, each person has a lifetime exemption of $30,000. This exemption may be taken in one year, or in any number of years, and it may be taken for gifts made to one person or to any number of persons. The $30,000 exemption applies to all gifts made since the law became effective June 6, 1932. To illustrate the application of the exclusions and exemption we will assume that Mrs. Smith, a widow, made gifts of $10,000 to each of her three children this year (relationship not necessary), and that she contemplates giving each of them $10,000 next year and the year following. (We will assume these are the first gifts she has ever made.) This year, Mrs. Smith would be entitled to an exclusion of $3,000 on each gift. That would take care of total exclusions of $9,000. That leaves $21,000 that could be applied on the $30,000 lifetime exemption. So she would pay no gift taxes this year. Next year Mrs. Smith again takes the annual exclusions of $3,000 on each of the three gifts—this totals $9,000. She would then apply the $9,000 remaining balance in her lifetime exemption against the gifts. Thus in the second year the exclusions and exemption would total $18,000, which therefore leaves a balance of $12,000 on which the gift tax must be paid. In the third year she could take only the three

$3,000 annual exclusions, which total $9,000. Thus in the third year Mrs. Smith must pay the gift tax on a total of $21,000.

The Marital Deduction

The joint ownership of income and property on the part of husband and wife which is recognized in the federal income and estate tax laws applies also with respect to the federal gift tax. In other words, if a husband makes a gift of $68,000 to his wife, since she is considered by the federal tax laws to have already owned half of this property, it is considered that a gift of only $34,000 has been made. The husband can then use his $3,000 annual exclusion against this $34,000. That leaves $31,000. If he has not yet used any of his $30,000 lifetime exemption, then this could be applied against this and that would leave only $1,000 that would be subject to the gift tax.

Joint Gifts by Husband and Wife

Since each person is entitled to the annual exclusion of $3,000 to each person to whom a gift is made, plus the $30,000 lifetime exemption, if the husband and wife jointly make gifts they would be entitled to annual exclusions of $6,000, and a lifetime exemption of $60,000. To accomplish this, both spouses must sign the gift tax return and indicate that they are jointly making the gift. If a joint gift is made any other gifts made by either spouse for that year must also be treated the same way. Since the exemptions are doubled it is obvious that a considerable savings in gift taxes may be made if the husband has the wife join in with him in making gifts.

The Gift Tax Rates

The federal gift tax rates begin at 2¼ per cent on the first $5,000 of taxable gifts in excess of the exclusions and exemptions and are graduated upward to the maximum rate of 57¾ per cent, which is applied to taxable gifts in excess of $10,000,000. The complete tax rates appear in Table 19–4. It should be noted that these rates are just three fourths as much as the federal estate tax rates.

The lowest rate of 2¼ per cent, however, cannot be applied to the first $5,000 of taxable gifts each year. A record must be kept of all taxable gifts made since 1932. The first $5,000 of gifts ever taxed bears the 2¼ per cent rate. If $5,000 in taxable gifts is made the next year, the rate applicable would be for the bracket $5,000 to $10,000, which is 5¼ per cent. If $5,000 in taxable gifts is also made the following year, it would be taxed at the rate of 8¼ per cent.

Table 19–4. Federal Gift Tax

Net Gifts (after exclusions and exemption)	Tax on Amount in Column 1	Rate of Tax on Excess over Amount in Column 1 (per cent)
—	—	2¼
$ 5,000	$ 112½	5¼
10,000	375	8¼
20,000	1,200	10½
30,000	2,250	13½
40,000	3,600	16½
50,000	5,250	18¾
60,000	7,125	21
100,000	15,525	22½
250,000	49,275	24
500,000	109,275	26¼
750,000	174,900	27¾
1,000,000	244,275	29¼
1,250,000	317,400	31½
1,500,000	396,150	33¾
2,000,000	564,900	36¾
2,500,000	748,650	39¾
3,000,000	947,400	42
3,500,000	1,157,400	44¼
4,000,000	1,378,650	47¼
5,000,000	1,851,150	50¼
6,000,000	2,353,650	52½
7,000,000	2,878,650	54¾
8,000,000	3,426,150	57
10,000,000	4,566,150	57¾

Tax Savings Through Gifts

A considerable saving in taxes for an estate may be effected by giving away property during the lifetime of the donor rather than leaving it in the estate subject to the estate taxes. And, as indicated above, despite the fact that the gift tax rates are only three fourths as high as the estate tax rates, the saving is greater than one fourth. Of course it is realized that gift taxes must be paid on any taxable gifts, whereas estate taxes come out of the estate.

From what has been said above, it is apparent that over a period of time a considerable amount of property may be given away, particularly if given to a number of different people, without paying any gift taxes—due to the gift tax exclusions and exemptions. Had this same property been left in the estate it may have been taxed at a relatively high estate tax rate. Another saving comes from the fact that a gift reduces the estate by the amount given, which means that the estate tax saved is that applicable to the top part of the estate. But if this was the first taxable gift made, the gift tax rates applicable would be the lowest rate. In other words, for an extremely large estate a taxable gift of the $5,000 would be taxed at 2¼ per cent, but had it been left in the estate until the donor died, it would have been taxed 77 per cent under the estate tax.

The tax savings through gifts can be illustrated with even a more modest estate. We will assume that Mr. Williams has a total estate of $300,000. If he were to die and leave at least half of his estate to his wife it can be seen from Table 19–2 that the estate tax would be $17,900 (after giving effect to the marital deduction). Let us assume that over the next ten years, Mr. and Mrs. Williams jointly gave their children half of the then existing estate, or gifts totaling $150,000. The joint total annual gift tax exclusions would be $6,000, or a total of $60,000 for the ten-year period. Adding to this the joint lifetime exemptions of $60,000 makes a total of $120,000 in exclusions and exemptions. Subtracting this from the total gifts of $150,000 leaves taxable gifts of only $30,000.

Referring to Table 19–4, it is seen that the gift tax on this amount would be only $2,250. If we assume that the size of Mr. Williams' estate remained the same except for the gifts given, then after ten years the estate would be reduced to $150,000. If Mr. Williams then died and left at least half of his property to his wife, the estate tax would be only $1,050. By giving away half of the estate the estate tax was reduced from $17,900 to $1,050. This resulted of course from the fact that the taxes were figured on an estate of half the size of the original one, and also because the top tax rates were only 11 per cent instead of 28 per cent. A total of $120,000 was given away under the exclusions and exemptions, and part of this came from the part of the estate that otherwise would have been taxed at the rate of 28 per cent. The $30,000 of taxable gifts were taxed at rates varying from only 2¼ to 10½ per cent. When the gifts were made the estate taxes were $1,050 and the gift taxes were $2,250, making a total tax bill of $3,300. If the gifts had not been made the estate tax would have been $17,900. Subtracting from the latter figure the $3,300 leaves $14,600, which is the overall tax saving resulting from the gifts. This represents a saving of approximately 81½ per cent.

QUESTIONS

1. What is meant by the "estate" of a person? Indicate what is involved in estate planning.
2. Specifically, why should most people make out a will?
3. Indicate the treatment that is accorded ancestral property owned by a decedent in some of the states.

4. In a state in which a homestead law exists, is it legally possible for a husband, by means of a will, to deprive his wife of the benefits of the law?
5. Assume that a spouse has been left property by provisions of a will. Can the spouse claim this property in addition to or in lieu of any right he or she may have had under any homestead law or curtesy or dower?
6. Can a husband, by means of a will, deprive his wife of a dower right?
7. Is it legally possible, by means of a will, for a husband to leave all his property to his wife when there are children?
8. Does the dower right exist in all the states? If not, what type of statute has replaced this right? How do such statutes differ from dower rights?
9. Indicate what legal restrictions there are, if any, on who may make a will.
10. Indicate what is meant by each of the following: administrator, beneficiary, bequeath, codicil, decedent, devise, holographic will, legatee, intestate, nuncupative will, probate, real property, testate, testator.
11. (a) How many witnesses are required for a will?
    (b) Who should sign first, the testator or the witnesses?
    (c) Is it necessary that the signature of the testator and the witnesses be made in the presence of each other?
    (d) Can anyone serve as a witness? Would it be advisable for a beneficiary under the will to act as a witness?
    (e) Is it necessary to read the will to the witnesses or to tell them what is contained therein?
12. Is it better to express the amount being left designated persons in a will in dollars or in fractional parts of the estate? Explain.
13. Where several properties of approximately equal value are being left to several children, is it advisable to will the properties to each one separately, or should they all be left an undivided equal interest in all the properties? Explain.
14. When there are children, should a husband will all his property to his wife? If this is not done, how much would she be entitled to?
15. Why may it be desirable for a husband to make provision in a will covering the disposition of his property in event he and his wife die as a result of the same accident?
16. If a man who has children wills all his property to his wife and does not specifically mention his children in the will, in event of his death can his widow claim all the property?
17. Indicate two ways in which changes in the provisions of a will may legally be made.
18. If a person moves to another state why may it be advisable for him to make out a new will?
19. (a) Indicate the nature of a trust.
    (b) Explain what is meant by each of the following: *cestuis que trustent*, trustee, trustor, life tenant, remainderman.
20. (a) What is meant by a living trust?
    (b) Indicate the circumstances under which this type of trust may be created.

(c) Indicate the circumstances under which no inheritance or estate taxes would have to be paid on the trust property at the time of the death of the trustor.

21. What are the relative advantages and disadvantages of the revocable and the irrevocable living trusts?
22. (a) Explain what is meant by a testamentary trust.
    (b) Under what circumstances would this type of trust be created?
    (c) Indicate how you think a testamentary trust should be drawn up when a man has a wife and children.
23. (a) Explain what is meant by a life insurance trust.
    (b) What advantage may accrue to the beneficiary from setting up this kind of trust?
    (c) What is the difference between leaving the proceeds of a life insurance policy with the insurance company to be paid out in the form of an annuity, and the creation of a life insurance trust?
24. Are the proceeds of a life insurance policy taxable under the state inheritance tax laws?
25. Explain the following relative to the federal estate tax:
    (a) General nature of the tax
    (b) The amount of the exemption
    (c) Tax status of proceeds of life insurance and jointly held property
    (d) Relief from tax from rapid successive deaths of beneficiaries
    (e) The marital deduction and its importance
    (f) Credit for state inheritance or estate taxes
    (g) Tax savings through creation of trusts for a married man with children
26. Explain the following relative to the federal gift tax:
    (a) General nature of the tax
    (b) What types of gifts are taxable and what types non-taxable
    (c) Exclusions and exemptions
    (d) The marital deduction
    (e) Exclusions and exemptions for joint gifts by husband and wife
    (f) Application of the tax rates
27. Explain how and why the making of gifts will save taxes for an estate.

CASE PROBLEMS

1. Max and Ruth Deveroux are in their early thirties and have two small children. Max is chief research engineer for a prosperous and growing electronics company. He is now earning $18,000 a year and expects to make more as time goes on. He has a modest amount of life insurance, a substantial equity in a home he is buying, and a small amount of stock in his company. By careful financial management they have, in view of their income, expenses, and payments on the home, a fairly good monthly savings. Both Max and Ruth are interested in using their savings to build up their estate in the best way possible. Ruth wants Max to use a considerable amount of the savings to pay premiums on additional life insurance (on his life). Max wants to pay off the home mortgage as quickly as possible, and then buy additional stock in the company. A mutual fund salesman is trying to interest them in putting most of their savings in his company under a systematic savings plan (front-end load). This fund also provides a sys-

tematic withdrawal plan for amounts of $10,000 and up. Max's father recommends Series E United States savings bonds. Indicate the advantages and disadvantages of the various courses of action stated. Do you have any recommendations? Explain.

2. Pete Hagan dies intestate leaving a sizable estate. Hagan is survived by his wife and their three children. One of the children is entirely dependent on him for support. His parents also survive him and are dependent on him for support. He had intended to make a will for some time and leave the entire estate to his wife, with the stipulation that she provide for his parents and for the dependent child. What difference does it make that Hagan dies intestate? In most states, how will his estate be divided? If his wife had died before he did, how would the estate be divided? If they had had no children, how would the estate be divided? What difference would it make if one child had died before Hagan and had left three children?

3. Fritz Keil has a very sizable estate. Under normal circumstances, he would will it all to his wife in the event that she outlived him, and then she in turn would will it to the children. However, because of large federal estate taxes under this method, Keil wants to work out some technique whereby the funds could be passed to the children but his wife have the use of the funds until her death. In this way, he feels that only one estate tax would be paid instead of two. Could he do this? How much of his estate need he put in trust for his wife? What is a living trust? Why should Keil consult an estate planner?

4. Jim Myers is the remainderman under a life trust set up for his mother under his father's will. The First Trust Company is trustee. Myers feels that the trustee is not earning enough on the principal of the fund as it is all invested in high-grade corporate bonds. Since Myers also believes that we are in a period of inflation, he wants the trustee to purchase some variable value investments as well as investing in higher yielding securities. He wants his mother to have more income as the inflation has cut her purchasing power considerably. The trustee refuses to switch investments. Why do you suppose the trustee will not switch investments along the lines requested by Myers? What can Myers do to change the portfolio of the trust? What could his mother do if she were also dissatisfied? When his mother dies, will he get the same amount as was originally put in the trust? Why or why not?

5. Ascertain from competent authority what disposition would be made in your state of property left without a will by a spouse, both when there are children and when there are no children. Is it legally possible for a married man by means of a will to leave all his property to his children? Explain.

6. Frank Peck left an estate of $600,000 (before the $60,000 exemption). Compute the amount of the federal estate tax (before credit for state taxes) due if the entire estate was left in trust to the wife for life and then upon her death the property was to pass to the children. Compute the amount of the federal estate tax if one third of the estate had been left to the wife outright and the other two thirds left to the children. Compute the tax if one half had been left outright to the wife and one half to the children. Would the tax be any different from that just calculated if two thirds of the property had been left outright to the wife and one third to the children?

7. Compute the amount of the federal gift tax under each of the following situations. You may assume that these are the first gifts made by the individuals unless otherwise indicated.
   (a) Ben Riley (a bachelor) gave his mother $40,000 this year.
   (b) Mr. and Mrs. Roy Sage jointly gave each of their two children $20,000 each year for a period of five years.
   (c) Carl Thomas bought a home for $50,000 in his own name and immediately thereafter transferred title to the home to the name of himself and his wife as "joint owners with right of survivorship." (Assume Mr. and Mrs. Thomas have not used any of their gift tax exclusions or exemptions.)
   (d) Howard Turner, who has used up his gift tax exclusions for this year and his lifetime exemption (but has never made a taxable gift) buys his son John a $10,000 (maturity value) Series E United States savings bond which is registered in the name of the son.
   (e) The bond in part (d) was registered in the names of the father and son as co-owners.

SELECTED READINGS

Casner, A. J. *Estate Planning.* Boston: Little, Brown & Co., 1963.

Federal Estate and Gift Taxes Explained. Chicago: Commerce Clearing House, 1965.

How Much Will It Cost to Settle Your Estate? Pamphlet. Free copy available from Manufacturers Hanover Trust, New York, N. Y. 10022.

Internal Revenue Service. *A Guide to Federal Estate and Gift Taxation.* Washington, D. C.: Government Printing Office, 1965.

Internal Revenue Service. *Regulations Relating to Estates, Trusts, Beneficiaries and Decedents.* (Publication No. 414.) Washington, D. C.: Government Printing Office.

J. K. Lasser Tax Institute, *Estate and Gift Tax Planning That Builds Family Fortunes.* Larchmont, N. Y.: American Research Council, 1962.

———. *53 New Plans for Saving Estate & Gift Taxes,* Revised Edition. Larchmont, N. Y.: American Research Council, 1965.

———. *10 Timely Plans for Saving Estate and Gift Taxes.* Larchmont, N. Y.: American Research Council, 1964.

———, and Wallace, Ralph. *How to Save Estate and Gift Taxes,* Revised Edition. Larchmont, N. Y.: American Research Council, 1965.

Masteller, Kenneth C. *How to Avoid Financial Tangles.* Great Barrington, Mass.: American Institute for Economic Research, 1965.

Practical Suggestions About Your Will. Pamphlet. Free copy available from Manufacturers Hanover Trust, New York, N. Y. 10022.

Spinney, William R. *Estate Planning,* Tenth Edition. Chicago: Commerce Clearing House, 1963.

Stephenson, Gilbert T. *Estates and Trusts,* Fourth Edition. New York: Appleton-Century-Crofts, 1965.

Your Estate. San Diego, Calif.: Estate Recording Co., 1965.

Wormser, René A. *Personal Estate Planning in a Changing World.* New York: Simon and Schuster, Inc. Latest edition.

20

Owning a Business

Do you want an exciting and demanding challenge for your vocation? Are you willing to work hard and take sizable financial risk for possible future self-satisfaction and financial gain? If so, you may consider owning your own business.

In spite of an increasing domination of American business by big concerns, small business is certainly not dead. Small businesses represent 95 per cent of all businesses in the country. In terms of numbers, small businesses are dominant in all fields. If measured by economic importance, small businesses are a less important factor in manufacturing; are still in the majority but are decreasing in importance in retailing; and almost completely dominate the fast growing service industry.

It is not easy to define *small business.* Most authorities in the field have developed different quantitative measures for different types of businesses. For example, the Small Business Administration (SBA) has the following definition of small businesses eligible for SBA loans:

Manufacturing–small if it has no more than 250 employees; large if it has more than 1,000 employees. Within these breaking points are specific size standards for specific industries.
Wholesale–annual sales of not more than $5 million.
Retail or service–annual sales or receipts of not more than $1 million.

Tables 20–1 and 20–2 illustrate the importance of small business in the United States. Less than one tenth of 1 per cent of all sole proprietorships had business receipts (sales) in excess of $1 million in 1962. Less than one per cent of all partnerships exceeded $1 million in business receipts. Approximately 2 per cent of all corporations had assets in excess of $1 million. It is readily apparent that the number of businesses classified as small is very great. While large businesses are relatively minor in

Table 20–1. Number of Corporate Returns, Total Compiled Receipts, Net Income, and Total Assets, by Size of Total Assets—All Industries, United States, 1962

Size of Total Assets	Number of Returns	Total Compiled Receipts (in thousands of dollars)	Net Income (less deficit) (in thousands of dollars)	Total Assets (in thousands of dollars)
Total	1,268,044	949,305,342	49,606,038	1,388,126,547
Under $100,000	740,884	64,107,294	509,237	25,132,145
$100,000 under $1,000,000	454,730	230,928,669	5,172,779	130,176,484
$1,000,000 under $25,000,000	67,208	227,853,718	9,052,306	271,953,380
$25,000,000 under $50,000,000	2,390	44,376,560	2,519,163	82,917,627
$50,000,000 under $100,000,000	1,289	46,679,856	2,917,269	89,558,972
$100,000,000 under $250,000,000	905	72,027,805	5,254,251	139,575,414
$250,000,000 or more	638	263,331,440	24,181,033	648,812,525

SOURCE: Internal Revenue Service, *Corporation Income Tax Returns, 1962.*

Table 20–2. Number of Sole Proprietorships and Partnerships, Business Receipts, Depreciation, and Net Profit, by Size of Business Receipts—United States, 1962

Size of Business Receipts	Number of Businesses	Business Receipts (in thousands of dollars)	Depreciation (in thousands of dollars)	Net profit less loss (in thousands of dollars)
Sole proprietorship				
Total	9,182,586	178,420,483	7,200,760	23,894,781
Under $5,000	4,266,312	8,358,779	932,763	1,764,119
$5,000 under $10,000	1,472,371	10,600,732	947,785	2,843,634
$10,000 under $25,000	1,679,769	26,774,948	1,917,680	6,095,192
$25,000 under $50,000	850,722	29,894,073	1,300,318	5,612,705
$50,000 under $100,000	472,221	32,599,539	945,223	4,229,531
$100,000 under $200,000	208,341	28,433,327	576,210	2,080,898
$200,000 under $500,000	81,190	23,790,545	359,390	1,021,746
$500,000 under $1,000,000	15,442	10,512,308	135,222	280,096
$1,000,000 under $5,000,000	4,610	6,817,032	53,543	120,246
$5,000,000 or more	61	639,200	2,356	7,454
Receipts not reported	131.547	—	30,270	160,840
Partnership				
Total	932,181	72,303,784	2,213,291	8,513,019
Under $5,000	198,416	386,389	84,878	38,366
$5,000 under $10,000	103,433	726,676	96,425	138,803
$10,000 under $25,000	169,878	2,763,115	247,555	660,591
$25,000 under $50,000	147,124	5,237,987	309,937	1,063,310
$50,000 under $100,000	130,454	9,227,147	363,188	1,672,976
$100,000 under $200,000	86,885	12,054,917	376,123	1,771,864
$200,000 under $500,000	50,781	15,150,519	363,788	1,620,637
$500,000 under $1,000,000	12,357	8,449,407	149,658	668,414
$1,000,000 under $5,000,000	6,639	12,137,129	153,382	715,076
$5,000,000 or more	593	6,170,498	59,295	355,624
Receipts not reported	25,621	—	9,062	115,910

SOURCE: Treasury Department, *Statistics of Income, 1962.*

number, they are much more important in economic activity. Nonetheless, almost one third of all receipts of corporations were accounted for by small businesses. Over 75 per cent of the business receipts of partnerships and over 90 per cent of the receipts of proprietorships were by small business. Ninety-eight per cent of all reporting units under the Social Security Act had 100 or less employees in 1962.

The data in Tables 20–1 and 20–2 are for 1962 only. It is important to note that the growth trend of small businesses has been upward. For example, there were one million sole proprietorships in 1939, but the number had increased to over nine million in 1962. Partnerships increased in number during this same time period by 300 per cent. Since most proprietorships and partnerships are small, this indicates the growing number of small businesses in the United States. In 1964, the nation as a whole averaged in excess of 16,000 *new* incorporations per month. In the early months of 1965, the average was running more than 1,000 better than 1964. A great majority of these new incorporations represent small business.

WHY OWN YOUR OWN BUSINESS?

There are probably as many combinations of reasons for owning your own business as there are privately owned businesses. Each individual makes a decision on this matter, based on his own background and circumstances. However, there are some relatively common advantages and disadvantages which should be considered before making a decision to own your own business.

Advantages of Ownership

A common reason given for owning a business is to receive greater income. On the other hand, one does not need to own his own business to increase his income; therefore, there are a great many non-economic considerations which have prompted many people to form their own businesses.

Perhaps first among the non-economic advantages of owning your own business is the ability to be your own boss. Some people do not like direction from above in an organization. Others feel stifled by people who have authority or control over them. It is generally assumed that you are your own boss when you own your own business. The authors would like to point out, however, that no one in business is entirely his own boss. While you may be the head of your concern, you still have to please your customers in order to continue in business. You must also pay attention to the desires of suppliers, employees, and creditors in order to keep your business operating satisfactorily. Therefore, while the area within which you may make your own decisions is perhaps broader if you own your own business, there are still restrictions imposed upon you by other people.

Pride of ownership is another intangible advantage of owning your own business. There is a great deal to be said for the self-satisfaction one obtains from founding and building a business from "scratch." Of course, people who work for others can also take pride in their business organizations and in records of growth and accomplishment. However, there is unquestionably an additional element of pride if you actually own the business, and the potential for self-satisfaction is probably greater.

People who are tremendously creative often find it more satisfactory to work for themselves than for others. Many organizations, particularly large ones, tend to put restrictions on activities of employees which limit their creativeness. A truly creative person may be able to accomplish more if he is self-employed.

For those who are unsuccessful in acquiring employment, starting a business may be the only thing left to do.

Disadvantages of Owning Your Own Business

Owning one's own business would certainly not appeal to a great many people. Being your own boss has many limitations. One of these limitations was stated—no business owner is totally his own boss in any set of circumstances. In addition, owning your own business tends to put a great deal more responsibility on the owner-manager than on the employee working for someone else. Because an owner-manager has a broader area for decision-making, he is more responsible for employees, customers, suppliers, and creditors than he would be in an organization that separates ownership and management.

The business owner-manager typically works extremely hard for his income. It is a rare circumstance when such a person restricts himself to a forty-hour workweek. Particularly in the early stages of development of the business, the owner-manager puts in many more hours than would a typical employee. In addition, much of his time away from the business is devoted to thinking about it and planning for it. Many owner-managers have time for no other enjoyments in life beyond the self-satisfaction they attain from owning their own business.

Growth in size leads to increased security. Therefore, the very small business offers less security to the owner-manager than he would attain if he were employed by someone else. In fact, the majority of the new businesses started as owner-manager businesses result in failure. If you start your own business and fail, you obviously accomplish none of the objectives that you had planned from business ownership. Even when successful, the financial pressures, particularly during the early stages of development, are very great for the typical owner-manager.

ARE YOU QUALIFIED?

Not everyone is qualified to own and manage his own business. The only theoretical requirement for ownership is sufficient capital to purchase or start the business. Therefore, anyone with capital is potentially an owner. However, in our free enterprise system, ownership of capital carries with it a responsibility for decision-making. The provider of all of the equity capital for a business has the right to make the important management decisions for that business. It is true that a 100 per cent owner of a business could hire a manager and turn all authority over to that manager. However, in this chapter, we are discussing primarily the owner-manager businesses in which the owner takes the major responsibility for management. To be a good business manager *and* a successful business owner requires certain attributes.

Personality

Certain types of personalities are more successful in business management than others. In addition, some businesses require one type of personality while other businesses require another. Any owner-manager of more than a one-man business must have a personality which enables him to get along with employees. It is difficult to envision a business in which the owner-manager does not need an unusual personality in order to deal successfully with some types of customers. A strong desire to be an owner-manager is encountered primarily in people who have the personality to perform this function, but this is not always the case. Drive and ambition are only part of the attributes required of a successful owner-manager—an even temperament is a necessary personality trait in many businesses in order to impart stability to the business.

Experience

Relatively few people become successful business managers without first acquiring experience in a related activity. It is said that experience is a dear teacher, and this is probably very true, but experience is also a relatively complete teacher compared to the alternatives of learning from textbooks and teachers. In many situations, it is only through personal experience that one learns to avoid pitfalls. If one can learn while working for others, he is less likely to experience difficulty once he becomes his own business manager.

Management Ability

Management ability is extremely difficult to define. However, this ability is necessary to operate a business successfully. The manager must be a decision maker. As such, he must have an ability to collect sufficient relevant and reliable data on which to base intelligent decisions. Further, he must be able to project the results of his decisions and to consider the effects of his actions on other people and on related and competitive enterprises.

Some authors have listed the primary management processes as planning, organizing, and controlling. A manager must be able to plan. He must be able to select from alternative courses of action those actions which will lead to the most desirable results. A manager must be able to organize; that is, he must be able to pull together the factors of production necessary to produce his product or service. He must be able to do this in the most economically efficient way. Finally, a manager must control. He must develop a process whereby he constantly checks on his organization to see that it is moving in the direction outlined. He must be "on top of things" enough to recognize undesirable trends in time to make corrections so that the planned results can be achieved even though circumstances change.

Financial Resources

We have listed financial resources last among the personal requirements for owning your own business, for two reasons. One is that many people claim that they would like to own their own businesses but cannot do so because they do not have financial backing. The authors do not necessarily agree with this point of view. A good manager with a good product or service idea stands a good chance of obtaining financial backing from others if he does not have available capital of his own.

The second reason is that a great many business activities require a relatively small amount of capital to start. Even where large amounts of capital are required, considerable financial backing may be obtained from others. But where outside financial help cannot be obtained, an adequate amount of personal capital is a necessity.

BUYING AN EXISTING BUSINESS

The business opportunity sections of leading metropolitan newspapers carry many notices of potential businesses for sale. Anyone with sufficient capital can buy an existing business from its present owners. If you desire to own your own business, the only alternative to buying an existing business is to create one yourself. Creating a new business requires development of the idea and assembling of all the factors of production necessary to produce the product or service, as well as acquisition of customers. In buying an existing business, a portion of this huge task has already been accomplished.

Advantages of Buying an Existing Business

The major advantage of buying an existing business versus starting an entirely new one is that the purchaser has a greater degree of certainty of results. The existing business has a past record which can be projected into the future. In addition, sufficient factors of production have been acquired by the existing business to operate at its present level. The new owner will only have to add new factors of production as he makes changes or expands. The existing business has a current customer list. The sales price of the product or service as well as its cost are known factors. The quality and acceptance of the product or service can be more readily determined for an existing business.

The past record of operation and the development of the organization and customer acceptance to the time of transfer is extremely important to the purchaser of an existing business. It is the major indication of results in the future.

Disadvantages of Buying an Existing Business

The major disadvantage of purchasing an existing business as opposed to starting a new one from the beginning is that the purchaser will normally either have to pay a price for the development that has already taken place or take over responsibility for a past development that has been relatively unsuccessful. The seller of a business often has a demonstrated earning power; the price at which he sells the business is based on this demonstrated earning power. Because the earning power is easier to estimate for the future in an existing business than in a new one, the multiple of expected earnings reflected in the selling price will be higher for an existing business when compared to the cost of developing an entirely new business to reach the same expected future earnings.

Many people start their own businesses because they cannot find for sale the kind of existing business they would like to own and manage. Highly successful businesses are not normally sold unless the present owners desire to change their way of life and do not wish to pass their business on to their children. There are many more unsuccessful businesses for sale than successful ones. The buyer of an unsuccessful business has to plan significant changes in past operations to justify the purchase of such a business.

What To Look For in Buying

There are many factors to be considered in purchasing an existing business. The most important is to estimate the future return from the business. The first step in estimating future earnings is to project past earnings. In so doing, the buyer must estimate his ability to maintain the past earnings. This depends upon the reliability of their measurement. An independent audit is extremely helpful, as is a check of stated earnings against tax returns. Even if the buyer is satisfied that the past earnings are realistically measured, he has the problem of determining whether he can maintain them.

The major problem of projecting past earnings into the future at the time of sale of a business relates to changing conditions which result from the sale. The past earnings may be due partially to a desirable lease on a location. If the new owner cannot continue the lease at the same price, his earnings will obviously be different in the future. The seller of the business may have been extremely important to its profitability. It is necessary for any buyer to make an estimate of loss to the business in its future earnings due to the departure of the prior owner. It may be that the present earnings have been due primarily to one or two large customers. A check should be made to be sure that these customers will continue with the business even though there is a change of ownership. The same check should be made relative to suppliers and key employees. The buyer has to make certain that the assets of the business are legally owned by the business and that there are no major undisclosed contingent liabilities. He must guard against past tax claims on the business and watch for regulatory changes and patents and copyright changes which can significantly influence future earnings. The buyer has to study changing market conditions insofar as they affect future earnings.

An important question for a buyer to ask is why the owner is selling. If he is selling because he has a better alternative for investing his money, the buyer may do well to consider this other alternative also. Many present owners sell because they anticipate changing conditions in the future which will reduce the profitability of their business. Buyers should be cautious of buying a business if they cannot determine a legitimate personal reason for the present owner to be selling.

Value of an Existing Business

From an economic point of view, a business is only worth what it can earn for the owner in the future. However, his earnings can come in two ways. One is through the normal operating earnings of performing services or producing products. The other is through sale of the assets of the business at a price in excess of purchase price. This latter case may be called a liquidation situation. If liquidation and sale of assets would normally produce more than the "going concern value" of a business, any buyer should expect that the seller would break up the business and liquidate it rather than sell it at a price less than he could get through liquidation. Because of this, it is unusual for a buyer of an existing business to expect to gain by merely buying the business and then liquidating the assets. Thus, his normal return comes through continued or changed operation of the business in the future. Its worth, then, is the present value of these expected future earnings.

The common approach is to estimate average future earnings per year and then multiply this by some factor to determine the present worth of the company. This factor or multiplier should vary with the type of business, the level of economic conditions, and the reliability of the estimate of future earnings. A common multiplier for a small business to be sold as a going concern would be no more than six or eight times expected average annual future earnings. A multiplier of six gives a 16⅔ per cent return on investment and a multiplier of eight gives a 12½ per cent return on investment. It should be stressed that the earnings figure to be multiplied is the expected future earnings. Furthermore, the future earnings are after depreciation and taxes as well as all other business expenses. The potential buyer should also subtract from these earnings a salary for the time he plans to devote to the company.

Finding an Existing Business

While there are a large number of businesses for sale at any particular time, it may be difficult to find one which exactly suits your specific needs. Classified ad sections of leading newspapers carry advertisements of businesses for sale. Some advertisements may be found also in certain business publications. Chambers of Commerce and local banks are often sources of information about businesses which are potentially for sale. An important way to find an existing business for sale is through a business broker. Charles Ford & Associates, one of the largest business brokerage firms, publishes the *Ford Business for Sale Directory* monthly. This directory and others like it are excellent sources of names of businesses for sale. The business broker commonly charges the seller rather than the buyer so there would be no cost to the buyer for contacting the broker. However, the broker is likely to encourage him to buy only a business which his firm has listed for sale. The broker typically charges a 1 per cent retainer to the seller for a listing and if a sale is consummated, the commission may run as high as 5 or 10 per cent. If buyer and seller manage to get together without the use of a business broker, this 5 or 10 per cent commission may be saved and potentially split between them.

Franchise Operations

A franchise is a way of starting a new business which you own yourself, but which is, in many ways, similar to buying an existing business. As holder of a franchise, you pay an initial fee and a percentage of either gross sales or cost of equipment and supplies furnished by the franchiser. The franchiser's participation may be limited to furnishing equipment and supplies, helping in the initial establishment of the organization, and allowing the use of his name. In other cases, the franchiser will continue to aid in supervision of the business, maintain quality checks on the operation, help train you and your employees, and provide you with advertising and merchandising help. Large, well-established franchisers will normally grant a franchise only to someone who, upon thorough investigation by the franchiser, appears to have the capability of operating a franchise in a successful manner. The parent company is as interested in the success of the operation as is the individual owner.

The major advantages of the franchise operation are that the parent company is able to hire experts to help in a variety of management and merchandising problems at much lower cost to the franchise holder than would be true if he attempted to obtain these experts himself. Because the parent company has a substantial reputation at stake in the franchise operation, it will put a fair amount of effort into assuring profitability for the franchise operation. An advantage of a franchise is the benefit to each individual franchise holder of national advertising by the parent company. Franchisers are often in a position to back financially a floundering franchise holder.

A major drawback to operating a franchise business is the problem of control. The franchise holder obviously gives up some of his control to the parent company. In addition, the parent company obviously receives part of the profit from the total operation. The rapidly growing number of franchise holders across the nation indicates that the disadvantages are often outweighed by the advantages of operating under franchise.

STARTING A NEW BUSINESS

Building a new business from scratch potentially offers the greatest opportunity for economic return and personal satisfaction. Unquestionably, however, it also involves the greatest probability of complete failure. If you are willing to take the risk of starting your own business, you can materially improve your chances of success by being as scientific as possible in selecting your product or service and in developing your business.

Many people are amazingly haphazard in the way they choose an enterprise in which they are going to invest their time and money. Starting a new business involves a great deal of management skill—much more than taking over an existing business or operating under franchise—and the decisions on what type of business to start and how to go about it should be made carefully and should be based on extensive study. Figure 20–1 is a checklist for going into business.

Selecting the Field

Clearly, one of the most important decisions in starting a new business is deciding what type of business to start. Some businesses are destined to be failures because they never should have been started in the first place. While many people have successfully relied entirely on chance in selecting a given business opportunity, others have been more careful in their selection. The major pitfall in most businesses is having sufficient customers for a product or service at the price at which it can be profitably produced. Some attempt should be made to determine the market potential for your product or service before you decide which type of business to enter. Market studies are available from market research or consulting organizations, or you may perform your own market study based on data available from local, state, and federal governments, as well as trade associations, business and financial publications, and published marketing studies.

Where to Locate

In many types of businesses, the choice of location is extremely important in its effect on the market potential for the product or service. In other businesses, the location is important in terms of cost of operation. Wages may be higher in one location than in another for a manufacturing operation. Transportation costs for incoming and outgoing goods may vary significantly based on the choice of location.

In studying location, you need to consider the overall community, a given section of a community, and a specific location. The local transportation pattern to and from the specific location and the amount of traffic may be important considerations. Obviously, the importance of the location varies considerably with the type of business. Certain technical factors must always be considered in selecting a specific location, such as zoning, and availability of utilities, land, and satisfactory existing buildings. A wise approach to selection of location would be to consider those factors which would affect the business income rather than those relative to the desirability of the location as a place for the owner-manager to live.

Prospective Enterprises

SMALL BUSINESS ADMINISTRATION • JOHN E. HORNE, Administrator

SMALL MARKETERS AIDS **No. 71**

Washington 25, D. C. **September 1961**

CHECKLIST FOR GOING INTO BUSINESS

By Staff Members of the Small Business Administration, Washington, D. C.

SUMMARY

People sometimes go into business for themselves without being fully aware of what is involved. Sometimes they're lucky and succeed. More often, they fail because they do not consider one or more of the ingredients needed for business success.

This checklist is designed to help you decide whether you are qualified or have considered the various phases of going into business for yourself. Careful thought now may help you to prevent mistakes and to avoid losing your savings and time later. Use this list as a starter. Consider each question as it applies to your situation. Check off each question only after you've made an effort to answer it honestly. Before you omit a question, satisfy yourself that it does not apply to your particular situation.

After each section, you will find a few references. If you have uncovered doubtful areas or weaknesses in your preparation, it is strongly recommended that you obtain these publications and study them. You will find it time well spent. Most of the references are available, free, on request from any SBA field office or the Small Business Administration, Washington 25, D. C. However, the notation "Supt. Docs." means that the item is for sale at the price indicated by the Superintendent of Documents, Washington 25, D. C. (not from SBA).

QUESTIONS TO CONSIDER

Are You the Type?

	Yes	No
1. Have you rated your personal traits such as leadership, organizing ability, perseverance, and physical energy?		
2. Have you had some friends rate you on them?		
3. Have you considered getting an associate whose strong points will compensate for your weak traits?		

REFERENCES: Starting and Managing a Small Business of Your Own (40¢ Supt. Docs.); SM 39, Balanced Skills; Measure of Effective Managers; SM 46, Essential Personal Qualities for Small Store Managers; SM 52, Are You Really Service-Minded?

What Are Your Chances for Success?

	Yes	No
4. Have you had any actual business experience?		
5. Do you have special technical skills, such as those needed by a plumber, electrician, mechanic, or radio repair man?		
6. Have you obtained some basic management experience working for someone else?		
7. Have you analyzed the recent trend of business conditions (good or bad)?		
8. Have you analyzed business conditions in the city and neighborhood where you want to locate?		
9. Have you analyzed conditions in the line of business you are planning?		
10. Have you determined what size business you plan to establish (dollar sales per year)?		
11. Have you built up a detailed set of figures on how much capital you will need to launch the business?		
12. Have you figured how much time you will need until the business income equals the expenses?		
13. Have you planned what net profit you believe you should make?		

Fig. 20–1. Checklist for going into business. (Reproduced through courtesy of the Small Business Administration, Washington, D. C.)

	Yes	No

14. **Will the net profit divided by the investment result in a rate of return which compares favorably with the rate you can obtain from other investment opportunities?** ____ ____
    REFERENCES: Appraise Your Competitive Position to Improve Company Planning, in _Management Aids Annual No. 2_ (55¢ Supt. Docs.); Appraising the Market for the Services You Offer, in _Marketers Aids Annual No. 2_ (40¢ Supt. Docs.); Practical Business Use of Government Statistics (20¢ Supt. Docs.)

How Much Capital Will You Need?

15. **Have you worked out what income from sales or services you can reasonably expect in the first 6 months? The first year? The second year?** ____ ____
16. **Do you know what net profit you can expect on these volumes?** ____ ____
17. **Have you made a conservative forecast of expenses including a regular salary for yourself?** ____ ____
18. **Have you compared this income with what you could make working for someone else?** ____ ____
19. **Are you willing to risk uncertain or irregular income for the next year? Two years?** ____ ____
20. **Have you counted up how much actual money you have to invest in your business?** ____ ____
21. **Do you have other assets which you could sell or on which you could borrow?** ____ ____
22. **Have you some other source from which you could borrow money?** ____ ____
23. **Have you talked to a banker?** ____ ____
24. **Is he favorably impressed with your plan?** ____ ____
25. **Do you have a financial reserve for unexpected needs?** ____ ____
26. **Does your total capital, from all sources, cover your best estimates of the capital you will need?** ____ ____
    REFERENCES: MA 105, Watch Your Cash; Term Loans in Small Business Financing, in _Marketers Aids Annual No. 2_ (40¢ Supt. Docs.); A Handbook of Small Business Finance (30¢ Supt. Docs.)

Should You Share Ownership With Others?

27. **Do you lack needed technical or management skills which can be most satisfactorily supplied by one or more partners?** ____ ____
28. **Do you need the financial assistance of one or more partners?** ____ ____
29. **Have you checked the features of each form or organization (individual proprietorship, partnership, corporation) to see which will best fit your situation?** ____ ____
    REFERENCES: MA 80, Choosing the Legal Structure for Your Firm; MA 111, Steps in Incorporating a Business; Equity Capital and Small Business (35¢ Supt. Docs.)

Where Should You Locate?

30. **Do you know how much space you will need?** ____ ____
31. **Do you know what type of building you will need?** ____ ____
32. **Do you know of any special features you require in lighting, heating, ventilating, air conditioning, or parking facilities?** ____ ____
33. **Have you listed the tools and equipment you need room for?** ____ ____
34. **If the proposed location does not meet nearly all your requirements, is there a sound reason why you should not wait and continue seeking a more ideal location?** ____ ____
35. **Have you checked the U. S. Census Bureau population figures?** ____ ____
    REFERENCES: MA 99, Plant Location Factors for Small Industry; Sizing Up Small Business Locations, in _Marketers Aids Annual No. 1_ (45¢ Supt. Docs.); SBB 16, Store Location.

Should You Buy A Going Business?

36. **Have you considered the advantages and disadvantages of buying a going business?** ____ ____
37. **Have you compared what it would take to equip and stock a new business with the price asked for the business you are considering?** ____ ____
38. **Have you learned why the present owner wants to sell?** ____ ____
39. **Have you checked the owner's claims about the business with reports from an independent accountant's analysis of the figures?** ____ ____
40. **Have you checked with the company's suppliers to obtain their ideas of the value of the business?** ____ ____
41. **Do the suppliers think well of the proposition?** ____ ____
42. **Is the stock of merchandise a questionable buy? (Would a large proportion of it have to be disposed of at a loss? Is any of it out of date, unsalable, or not usable?)** ____ ____

Fig. 20–1 (Continued)

	Yes	No
43. Are the physical facilities old or in poor condition and, hence, overvalued?		
44. Are you sure the accounts receivable are worth the asking price?		
45. Is the present company's good will fairly valued?		
46. Are you prepared to assume the liabilities, and are the creditors agreeable?		
47. Has your lawyer checked to see if the title is good and if there is any lien against the assets?		
48. Are there any back taxes to pay?		
49. Have the sales been temporarily increased by conditions which are not likely to continue?		

REFERENCES: Key Factors in Starting a New Plant, in _Management Aids Annual_ No. 5 (45¢ Supt. Docs.); SM 20, Buying a Small Going Concern.

Are You Qualified to Supervise Buying and Selling?

	Yes	No
50. Have you estimated your total stock requirements?		
51. Do you know in what quantities users buy your product or service?		
52. Do you know how often users buy your product or service?		
53. Have you made a sales analysis to determine major lines to be carried?		
54. Have you decided what characteristics you will require in your goods?		
55. Have you set up a model stock assortment to follow in your buying?		
56. Have you investigated whether it will be cheaper to buy large quantities infrequently or in small quantities frequently?		
57. Have you weighed price differentials for large orders against capital and space tied up?		
58. Have you decided what merchandise to buy direct from manufacturers?		
59. Will you make your account more valuable to your suppliers by concentrating your buying with a few of them?		
60. Have you worked out control plans to insure stocking the right quantities?		

REFERENCES: MA 120, Checking Your Marketing Channels; MA 123, Getting the Most From Your Purchasing Dollar; SM 28, Profitable Buying for Small Retailers; SM 56, Advertising for Profit and Prestige; SM 60, Sales Promotion Pointers for Small Retailers; SBB 37, Buying for Retail Stores.

How Will You Price Your Products and Services?

	Yes	No
61. Have you determined what prices you will have to charge to cover your costs and obtain profit?		
62. Do these prices compare favorably with prices of competitors?		

REFERENCES: How to Price a New Product, in _Management Aids Annual No. 3_ (45¢ Supt. Docs.); MA 100, Pricing Arithmetic for Small Business Managers; SM 21, Pricing and Profits in Small Stores.

What Selling Methods Will You Use?

	Yes	No
63. Have you studied the sales promotional methods used by competitors?		
64. Have you outlined your own sales promotion policy?		
65. Have you studied why customers buy your product (service, price, quality, distinctive styling, other)?		
66. Will you do outside selling?		
67. Will you advertise in the newspapers?		
68. Will you do direct mail advertising?		
69. Will you use posters and handbills?		
70. Will you use radio and television advertising?		

REFERENCES: SM 16, Improving Personal Selling in Small Business; SM 32, Methods of Improving Off-Season Sales; SM 56, Advertising for Profit and Prestige; SBB 20, Advertising-Retail Store.

How Will You Manage Personnel?

	Yes	No
71. Will you be able to hire satisfactory employees, locally, to supply skills you lack?		
72. Do you know what skills are necessary?		
73. Have you checked the prevailing wage scales?		
74. Have you a clear-cut idea of what you plan to pay?		
75. Have you considered hiring someone now employed by a competitor?		
76. Have you checked on the pros and cons of doing so?		
77. Have you planned your training procedures?		

REFERENCES: MA 102, Keeping Your Salesmen Enthusiastic; Sales Training for Small Wholesalers, in _Marketers Aids Annual No. 1_ (45¢ Supt. Docs.); SBB 23, Training Retail Sales People; Sales Training for the Smaller Manufacturer (20¢ Supt. Docs.)

Fig. 20–1 (Continued)

What Records Will You Keep?	Yes	No
78. Have you a suitable bookkeeping system ready to operate?		
79. Have you planned a merchandise control system?		
80. Have you obtained standard operating ratios for your type of business to use as guides?		
81. Have you provided for additional records as necessary?		
82. Have you a system to use in keeping a check on costs?		
83. Do you need any special forms?		
84. Have you made adequate provision for having your record keeping done?		

REFERENCES: MA 75, Protecting Your Records Against Disaster in Management Aids Annual No. 5 (45¢ Supt. Docs.); SM 36, Picking An Auditor For Your Firm; SBB 15, Record Keeping Systems--Small Store and Service Trade.

What Laws Will Affect You?

85. Have you investigated what, if any, licenses to do business are necessary? ____ ____
86. Have you checked the health regulations? ____ ____
87. Are your operations subject to interstate commerce regulations? ____ ____
88. Have you seen your lawyer for advice on how to meet your legal responsibilities? ____ ____

REFERENCES: MA 108, Selecting a Lawyer for Your Business; SM 42, FTC and Guides Against Deceptive Pricing; Small Business and the Federal Trade Commission, in Marketers Aids Annual 2 (40¢ Supt. Docs.)

What Other Problems Will You Face?

89. Have you worked out a system for handling your tax requirements? ____ ____
90. Have you arranged for adequate insurance coverage? ____ ____
91. Have you worked out a way of building a management team? ____ ____
92. Does your family (if any) agree that your proposed venture is sound? ____ ____
93. Do you have enough capital to carry accounts receivable? ____ ____
94. Will you sell for credit? ____ ____
95. Have you worked out a definite returned goods policy? ____ ____
96. Have you considered other management policies which must be established? ____ ____
97. Have you planned how you will organize and assign the work? ____ ____
98. Have you made a work plan for yourself? ____ ____

REFERENCES: MA 103, Organizing the Owner-Manager's Job; MA 113, "Tailor-Make" Your Executive Staff; Building Sound Credit Policies for Small Stores, in Marketers Aids Annual 1 (45¢ Supt. Docs.); SM 49, Improving Collections from Credit Sales; Business Insurance, in Management Aids Annual No. 1 (65¢ Supt. Docs.); How Good Records Aid Income Tax Reporting, in Management Aids Annual No. 3 (45¢ Supt. Docs.); Appeal Procedure for Income Tax Cases, in Management Aids Annual No. 4 (45¢ Supt. Docs.)

Will You Keep Up To Date?

99. Have you a plan for keeping up with new developments in your line of business? ____ ____
100. Have you a small group of qualified advisors from whom you can get help in solving new problems? ____ ____

REFERENCES: MA 117, Selecting Marketing Research Services; MA 125, Building Growth-Mindedness Into Your Business; SM 54, Store Modernization Check List

Fig. 20–1 (Continued)

Estimating Capital Requirements

An important part of promoting a new business is to estimate the amount of funds that will be necessary to start the business. Sometimes the amount of money that is put into the business is the full amount that a particular person or group of persons have or are able to obtain. Few businesses fail because of too much money. A common cause of failure is insufficient capital. The lack of cash may be merely a symptom of some other fault, but often the failure is due to too little capital being put into the business originally. Since most promoters are optimistic, it is common to overestimate income and underestimate expenses. In so doing, proper allowances are not made for the amount of money required. Keep in mind that it is easier to raise money before a company starts than after it has run into financial difficulty.

In determining the specific amount of money that will be needed, you must make an estimate of promotional and organizational expenses which will require outlays before the business is operating as a going concern. While these organizational expenses may be considered as assets to the business, they still require a cash expenditure and must be provided for in estimating total capital requirements. In addition, the promoter of a new business needs to determine the total amount of fixed assets required and their cost. Fixed assets include such things as buildings and equipment. Further, estimates must be made of the required amount of working capital (current assets). Working capital includes inventories and supplies, accounts receivable, and minimum cash requirements. A new business may make sales in the first month but have no inflow of money because all of the sales were on credit. A certain amount of accounts receivable will always be outstanding in a business which sells on credit, and these must be financed while waiting for the cash receipts on sales. A certain amount must always be tied up in inventory, and if sales are expanding, this amount will constantly increase.

In addition to the normal asset requirements and organizational expenses, the promoter of a new business must consider initial working capital. This is the amount that is necessary to provide for unusual outlays during the early months or years of the business and to overcome initial operating losses. Very few businesses start to make profits during the first day, week, month, or even year of operation. It takes time to build a clientele sufficient to utilize services at a profitable level. Losses during the early life of the business are really cash drains on the business and must be financed from the start. A great many businesses have failed because they have not provided for operating losses during the early life of the business.

Estimating capital requirements includes providing for all of the financing necessary for the business. As owner, you would usually have to count on providing at least 50 per cent of this yourself. In a typical small business, total requirements may range from $10,000 to $25,000. If you plan to obtain borrowed funds from others, you must project into your capital requirements the means to repay others as their loans come due.

Selecting Capital Sources

Once the estimate is made of the amount of funds needed by the business, possible sources of these funds must be studied to determine which should be used. The most common source of funds for expansion of existing businesses is retained earnings, but this is not available to new businesses. New businesses must rely entirely on other sources. The majority of funds in a small business generally comes from equity provided by the owner himself. In some cases, it is possible for a given owner to attract others into ownership in his business. This would require the establishment of a partnership or the sale of stock in a corporation. Commonly, in a new business, the only possible owners other than the promoter (owner-manager) are friends and relatives. Most outside investors are not willing to risk their capital in someone else's *new* business. This is particularly true if the new venture is small.

Thus, other than funds from the owner and his friends and relatives, most new businesses obtain their capital from various types of creditors. Because of the high risk in new businesses, it is uncommon for a new business to be able to sell bonds to the general public or to obtain much in long-term financing from financial institutions. Generally, the credit available to new businesses takes the form of trade credit from suppliers, with the added possibility of some short-term bank financing. Suppliers are often an excellent potential source of funds in that they benefit from the establishment of the new business through profit on sales as well as a return on any money they may invest in the new business. Most new businesses can count on some spontaneous sources of funds, including trade credit and tax and wage accruals. Trade credit enables the new business to acquire materials and supplies from a supplier and pay for them later—potentially after it has already sold them and collected from its customers.

Assembling the Factors of Production

In addition to acquiring capital, a new business must develop its sources of supply of goods and materials. Many sellers are eager to take on new customers, and sources of supply usually are not difficult to obtain. However, they may not always be readily available, particularly in times of war or strikes.

If the business requires employees other than the owner-manager, it must be assured of being able to hire these needed employees at reasonable rates. While unskilled and semiskilled labor is often available, there are many circumstances in which certain types of skilled labor and professional people are not available when a business desires them. In starting a new business it is just as important to be assured of having sufficient labor available as it is to have sufficient capital.

Of course, the number-one problem in most new businesses is securing sufficient customers to purchase the product or service of the business at a profitable price. There is greater uncertainty in obtaining customers than in securing capital, goods, or labor. Some businesses are started with advance purchase agreements from customers, but since this is relatively unusual, the greatest risk in most new businesses is that of not being able to attract sufficient customers to justify the continuance of the business.

THE SMALL BUSINESS ADMINISTRATION

The preservation and expansion of competition is basic not only to the economic well-being but to the security of the nation. Such security and well-being cannot be realized unless the actual potential capacity of small business is encouraged to develop. It is the declared policy of the Congress that the government should aid, counsel, assist, and protect insofar as it is possible the interest of small business concerns in order to preserve free competitive enterprise.[1]

This policy was implemented in 1953 by the establishment of the Small Business Administration (SBA). The SBA has three objectives: (1) to protect the welfare of small businesses through counsel and assistance; (2) to insure that a reasonable share of total federal government contracts for supplies and services is placed with small businesses; and (3) to make loans to small businesses. The administrator of the Small Business Administration is located in Washington, but the SBA has a number of regional and branch offices. The SBA has established both regional and local small business advisory groups to assist in developing and carrying out its programs.

Business Loans

In the SBA's business loan program, the agency's financial specialists counsel small business concerns on their financial problems and, if borrowing is necessary, help them to obtain funds from private lending sources. If a small business concern cannot obtain a loan from private financing agencies on reasonable terms, the SBA will consider making a loan to it, provided it meets necessary credit and other requirements. Loans are usually available to an existing small business rather than a completely new business. The agency prefers to make participation loans, that is, loans in which the agency shares with a local lending institution. Where participation loans are not possible, the SBA will make direct loans to the borrower. Figure 20–2 gives key features of the SBA's principal lending program.

The Small Business Administration supervises the Small Business Investment Act of 1958. Under this Act, Small Business Investment Companies (SBICs) are established with private capital and potential borrowing power from the federal government. These concerns are empowered to make loans to small businesses or to provide equity-type financing,

[1] Small Business Act of 1953, Public Law 163, Title II, 83rd Congress, First Session (1953), Section 202 (15 USC Section 631).

SMALL BUSINESS ADMINISTRATION

John E. Horne, Administrator

Washington 25, D. C.

Key Features of SBA's Principal Lending Programs

BUSINESS LOANS

	REGULAR BUSINESS	LIMITED LOAN PARTICIPATION PLAN	SIMPLIFIED BANK PARTICIPATION PLAN	SIMPLIFIED EARLY MATURITY PLAN
WHO IS ELIGIBLE?	Most businesses that are independently owned and operated and non-dominant in their fields; that cannot obtain private financing on reasonable terms and are not eligible for financing from other Government agencies, and that qualify as "small" under SBA's size standards, which generally are based on dollar volume of business or number of employees.	Any business that meets criteria stated under Regular Business Loan Plan. However, Limited Loan Participation Plan is of special interest to small retail, wholesale and service concerns.	Any business that meets criteria stated under Regular Business Loan Plan. However, this plan, under which the businessman deals entirely with his bank, is intended to assist the "stronger credits."	Same as under Simplified Bank Participation Plan. Major distinction between this plan and Simplified Bank Participation Plan is that bank provides at least 50% of loan and is repaid before SBA.
LOAN PURPOSES	Business construction, conversion or expansion; purchase of equipment, facilities, machinery, supplies or materials; and working capital.	Same as under Regular Business Loan Plan.	Same as under Regular Business Loan Plan.	Same as under Regular Business Loan Plan.
MAXIMUM AMOUNT	$350,000 to any one borrower. This is maximum SBA share of "participation loan" - - one made jointly by SBA and private lending institution - - and maximum SBA "direct loan" - - one made entirely by Agency.	Maximum SBA share of $25,000 or 75% of total loan, whichever is lesser; private lending institution's share must equal any outstanding loan to be repaid to it with part of participation loan or must be 25% of participation loan, whichever is larger.	$350,000 to any one borrower, as SBA share of participation loan or SBA direct loan.	Same as under Simplified Bank Participation Plan.
INTEREST RATE	Maximum of 5½% per annum on SBA share of "immediate participation loan" (where SBA and private lending institution each put up part of loan funds immediately) and on SBA direct loan. 1/ Where SBA "defers" providing its share of participation loan until asked by lending institution to do so, institution may set "reasonable and legal" rate on entire loan. However, if SBA later provides its share of "deferred participation loan," rate on SBA share then is maximum of 5½%. 1/	Maximum of 5½% per annum on SBA share of loan where Agency puts up its share immediately or where Agency has provided its share of deferred participation loan at request of participating institution. 1/ Participating institution may set "legal and reasonable" rate on its share of loan and on SBA share of deferred participation loan until SBA provides its share.	Same as under Limited Loan Participation Plan.	Same as under Limited Loan Participation Plan, but on immediate participation basis only.
MATURITY	Maximum of 10 years as a rule. However, working capital loans generally are limited to 5 years, while construction loans may have maximum of 10 years plus estimated time required to complete construction.	Maximum of 5 years.	Same as under Regular Business Loan Plan.	Same as under Regular Business Loan Plan.
TYPE OF COLLATERAL	Real estate or chattel mortgage; assignment of warehouse receipts for marketable merchandise; assignment of certain types of contracts, guarantees or personal endorsements; in some instances assignment of current receivables, and inventories stored in bonded or otherwise acceptable warehouse.	Real estate or chattel mortgage; assignment of accounts receivable or funds due on contracts; pledges of warehouse receipts; negative pledge agreements, and corporate guarantees or personal endorsements.	Same as under Regular Business Loan Plan.	Same as under Regular Business Loan Plan, except that collateral must be of a type not subject to rapid depreciation or obsolescence.

MARCH 1963

1/ 4% interest charged in areas classified by Federal Government as having substantial unemployment.

Fig. 20–2. Key features of SBA's principal lending programs. (Reproduced through courtesy of the Small Business Administration, Washington, D. C.)

primarily through purchase of convertible debentures. The SBICs were developed to provide the equity-type capital not available through the Small Business Administration. SBICs are given certain tax advantages and certain borrowing power from the federal government. An SBIC may make long-term loans to small firms, either entirely from its own funds or in participation with other lending institutions, on an immediate or a deferred basis.

Fair Share of Purchases and Sales

In the Small Business Act, Congress stated its intention that a fair proportion of total purchases and contracts for property and services for the federal government was to be placed in small business enterprises. The SBA works to carry out the provisions of this mandate by providing information to small businesses on available contracts, by setting aside certain purchases and sales for small business only, and by providing information on government buying and selling. The Small Business Administration will also offer assistance to small businesses in government subcontracting. Another SBA service to small businesses is helping them to obtain government contracts for research and development and to gain the benefits of research and development performed under government contract or at government expense.

Advisory Services and Management Assistance

Staff specialists of the SBA assist many types of businesses with management problems. Their services are available to established businessmen who have specific problems or who want information on various aspects of management, as well as to persons who are considering starting their own businesses. One feature of this counseling service is the system of business reference libraries which the SBA has established at a number of its regional offices. The SBA, in cooperation with certain educational institutions, sponsors courses in administrative management which are open to officers of small firms.

The SBA publishes several series of management and technical publications which are of value to established or prospective operators of small business concerns. A partial listing of SBA publications is given in the selected readings at the end of this chapter.

SELECTING THE FORM OF ORGANIZATION

The legal responsibilities and consequences attached to the various forms of business organization differ substantially. Since selection of the form of business organization is primarily a legal consideration, the legal (and tax) consequences of each form must be understood before selecting the proper form for your specific business. Such matters as the extent of personal liability, the sharing of profits, the transfer of interest, the length of business life, taxation, and government regulation depend upon whether a business operates as a sole proprietorship, a partnership, or a corporation.

Sole Proprietorship

The oldest, simplest, and most commonly used form of organization is the sole proprietorship; the business is owned, managed, and controlled by a single person. For legal purposes, there is really no distinction between the proprietor and the proprietorship.

The individual proprietorship is the most easily formed of the various forms of organization. If a person starts a business by himself and takes no steps to start another form of organization, the law will say that he has a sole proprietorship. No organizational papers need to be drawn nor are there any organizational taxes and fees to be paid. In the case of the sole proprietorship, the tax laws do not distinguish between the proprietor and his business. The business income is reported on the individual proprietor's personal income tax form. The tax must be paid when the profits are earned, regardless of whether they are withdrawn from the business.

One of the more important disadvantages of this form of organization from the viewpoint of the proprietor is that he has unlimited liability. If the assets of the business are insufficient to satisfy the firm's creditors, they may proceed against the individual's personal property. Thus, the proprietor subjects all of his personal property to the risks of his business.

The General Partnership

The general partnership may be defined as an association of two or more persons carrying on as co-owners a legal business for profit. This form of business is based on a contract between the co-owners. It is advisable that the contract be in writing and signed by the partners, but this is not a legal requirement. While for business purposes the partnership is looked upon as a firm or company, at law it is not generally treated as a legal entity.

In the absence of an agreement to the contrary, each partner has full authority to enter into ordinary business contracts for the firm. Such contracts bind the other partners just as if they had been made by the other partners themselves. Each partner is, in effect, an agent of the partnership. The liability of each partner is both joint and several. While partners are never liable for the personal debts contracted by their partners, they are liable for all business debts contracted by partners. This liability extends to the personal assets of each of the partners.

In many states, there is a partnership code which covers development of partnerships. Like the proprietorship, the partnership lasts only as long as the partners. Therefore, it has limited life. However, in a partnership, life may be even more limited because the partnership is automatically dissolved upon the death or withdrawal of *any one* of the partners. The partnership has an advantage over the proprietorship in ability to raise capital, in that more people are involved in ownership. However, it is often difficult to attract wealthy people to ownership in a partnership because of the unlimited liability which they must accept.

Partners are normally taxed as individuals on their share of the earnings of the partnership regardless of whether the profits are withdrawn from the business. However, it is now possible for a partnership with less than fifty partners to pay taxes as if it were a corporation.

The Corporation

A corporation is an artificial, or legalistic, person chartered by the state to perform the purposes stated in its charter. Since the corporation is a creature of the state, it must comply with all of the requirements laid down by its creator. Articles of incorporation must be drawn and bylaws must be adopted. These requirements necessitate services of experts, so incorporation can become an expensive procedure. Furthermore, an organizational tax must be paid, as well as an annual franchise fee to the state of incorporation. However, most larger business organizations have found that the corporate form has many advantages which justify the additional expenses of organizing the corporation.

A major advantage of the corporation is the fact that it is a legal entity. As such, it has a life separate and apart from the individuals who own it. Property is held in the corporate name and suit is brought by and against the corporation. The separate legal entity gives limited liability to owners. The original owner of corporate stock is liable only for the full par or stated value of the stock which he has purchased. Once this stock becomes fully paid to the corporation, the owner has no further liability. The legal entity concept has also led to permanent life for corporations. Death of a stockholder, or of all of the stockholders, does not have any legal effect on the life of the corporation. The legal entity concept has also led to transferability of shares. Corporate shareholders can sell their shares to anyone at any time without affecting the life of the organization. No consent to the transfer is necessary and other owners cannot normally prevent a given owner from selling his portion of the corporation.

Representative management is necessary to a corporation. In a general partnership, each partner has general agency powers to bind all of the other partners on all regular matters of business. This does not apply to owners in a corporation. According to the statutes, the stockholders do not have agency powers to contract for the company. They have the right to elect a board of directors to whom management is delegated. The directors in turn are given the right to appoint officers who carry out the policies adopted by the directors. The directors and officers, therefore, are the only ones with the right to manage the corporation.

Because of the problems of permanence, management, agency powers, and unlimited liability, the corporation is normally recommended for businesses in which more than one owner is involved. Present tax laws allow a corporation with less than ten owners to be taxed as a partnership. Until these laws were passed, corporations had an advantage for firms wishing to retain money in the business, and the partnership had an advantage for those wishing to withdraw all earnings. Since the corporation is a separate legal entity, it is taxed separately from the owners. While the basic tax rate on corporations is generally lower than personal taxes of some persons, if the earnings are, in turn, paid out to the owners, the owners must pay personal taxes (after exclusion of the first $100 in dividends) after the corporation has already paid the corporate tax. This double taxation is generally higher than would be true for the single taxation for proprietorships or partnerships. The federal income tax rate for corporations is 22 per cent on the first $25,000 of taxable income and 48 per cent of any excess over $25,000. Salaries, however, are deducted before computing the corporate tax.

In businesses with sole owners, costs and regulatory restrictions on corporations may make the proprietorship the more desirable form under given circumstances. The decision on form depends upon the type of business, its size, its requirements for permanence, and the personal financial position of the promoters and owners.

MANAGING A BUSINESS

This discussion is not intended to qualify any reader as a manager. Instead, we are merely providing an overview of management to indicate some of the problems of management and some techniques which may be helpful in solving them.

The management process consists of performance of various management functions. These functions are applied to various business resources in order to achieve the objectives of the organization. The management process is accomplished through utilization of certain managerial tools. It is in utilization of these tools that we rely upon "scientific" management. The results achieved depend upon how well the management functions are applied to the resources utilized.

The primary management functions are planning, organizing, motivating and directing, and controlling. Planning is forecasting future problems and events and selecting courses of action to handle the problems and events as foreseen. Organizing is getting ready to do what has been planned, or gathering together all of the resources required to accomplish the plan. Motivating is instilling in each subordinate the desire to do his assigned or directed tasks, and directing is training subordinates in a general way to do their jobs in the proper way and at particular times. Controlling is determining to what degree the plans have been achieved and taking appropriate action to keep future results in line with plans.

The business resources to which the management functions are applied are men, money, materials, machinery, methods, and markets. These are the factors with which management must deal. With the addition of time, this list comprises all of the ingredients that go into an enterprise.

All of the management process is related to the accomplishment of the organization's objectives or goals. These may be the goals of the firm or the goals of the owner or manager or employee of the firm. The firm's goals are organizational goals and the goals of the people in the firm are personal goals. There are both long-term and short-term goals in either case. It is extremely difficult for an owner-manager to separate organizational goals from personal goals. In most businesses, the organizational goals relate to growth of the business, return on investment or profitability, and product or service value. These various organizational goals may be in conflict in the short run, but must be properly balanced for long-run accomplishment. Most small businessmen claim profitability as their major business objective. Profitability is also a personal objective in that it represents return to the owner and could include both salary and return on investment.

The various managerial tools include policies and procedures. Policies are standard decisions created as stock answers for a type of problem that comes up repeatedly. A procedure is a standard way of doing something within the business. Where policies and procedures do not exist to handle any given activity or problem, a new management decision must be made. By having policies and procedures, management time is saved in the organization. Other managerial tools are the organizational structure, job descriptions, budgets, management reports, cost control, quality control, etc. These tools are discussed in most management textbooks and will not be given further treatment here.

SUCCESS OR FAILURE

While everyone starting a business does so with anticipation of success, it must be recognized from the outset that the chances of failure are relatively great. Some studies claim that as many as three out of every four new businesses fail or go out of existence within five years. The first five years are the hardest, and those which survive this time period have a high probability of continued existence and success. Table 20–3 gives failure trends from 1920 to 1964.

Table 20–3. Failure Trends—Selected Years, 1920–1964

Year	Number of Failures	Total Failure Liabilities	Failure Rate Per 10,000 Listed Concerns	Average Liability Per Failure
1920	8,881	$ 295,121,000	48	$33,230
1922	23,676	623,895,000	120	26,351
1926	21,773	409,233,000	101	18,795
1930	26,355	668,282,000	122	25,357
1932	31,822	928,313,000	154	29,172
1937	9,490	183,253,000	46	19,310
1944	1,222	31,660,000	7	25,908
1949	9,246	308,109,000	34	33,323
1955	10,969	449,380,000	42	40,968
1960	15,445	938,630,000	57	60,772
1961	17,075	1,090,123,000	64	63,843
1962	15,782	1,213,601,000	61	76,898
1963	14,374	1,352,593,000	56	94,100
1964	13,501	1,329,223,000	53	98,454

SOURCE: Dun & Bradstreet, Inc.

Failures occur for many reasons. The immediate reason for practically all failures is the inability to pay debts—the lack of cash or its equivalent. This is merely a superficial sign. The real reasons for failure are those underlying factors which resulted in the weak cash position.

Although we do not consider a company to have failed until it is unable to meet its debts, or is forced to undergo some compromise settlement with its creditors, or is reorganized, or closes its doors, the factors causing its failure will have been at work for many years. It is therefore often difficult to determine the real cause of the failure. Furthermore, there may be a number of different contributing factors.

A listing of external and internal causes of failure follows. Those causes which arise outside the business are considered external.

EXTERNAL CAUSES

Excessive competition
The general business cycle
Change in public demand
Governmental acts
Adverse acts of labor
Acts of God

INTERNAL CAUSES

Non-financial

Poor overall management
Unwise promotion
Unwise expansion
Inefficient purchasing
Inefficient production
Inefficient selling
Overextension of inventories

Financial

Poor management
Excessive fixed charges
Excessive funded debt
Excessive floating debt
Overextension of credit
Unwise dividend policy
Inadequate maintenance and depreciation

There can be no doubt that the most important single cause of failure of most business enterprises is incompetent and inefficient management. While management is listed above as an internal cause, it is really an influence on all of the other factors. During a given period, a number of companies will be operating under similar circumstances, but some will fail and others will survive.

QUESTIONS

1. Define *small business.*
2. Discuss the advantages and disadvantages of owning your own business.
3. What qualities do you consider necessary for an owner-manager of a small business?
4. How important is financial backing in establishing a small business?
5. How can you overcome lack of financial resources?
6. What are the advantages of buying an existing business relative to starting a completely new business?
7. Develop a checklist of things to look for in buying an existing business.
8. How can you place a value on an existing business?

9. If you are interested in buying an existing business, how can you determine which businesses are for sale?
10. Are "service" businesses increasing in relative importance? Why? Are they commonly operated as small businesses? Why?
11. What is a franchise operation? Why have they been growing in importance?
12. Discuss the problems of selecting a location for a completely new business.
13. How do you estimate capital requirements for a completely new business?
14. Describe the assistance program of the Small Business Administration.
15. Why did the Small Business Administration come into existence?
16. What is the Small Business Administration's advisory service?
17. Differentiate the following: (a) sole proprietorship, (b) general partnership, (c) corporation.
18. Should the owner-manager of a small business consider his salary as a business expense, or as part of the return from the business? Is his salary tax deductible? Explain.
19. What is "scientific management?" Why is this important to a business manager?
20. What are the major causes of failure of business organizations?

CASE PROBLEMS

1. Ralph Johnson is 21 years old. He quit college after his sophomore year because he said he was not "challenged." He has just completed his time in the service and is planning for his lifetime vocation. He inherited $10,000 from his grandfather a few years ago and is considering putting this into the purchase of a small business. Ralph is single and has no family responsibilities. His only prior work experience has been summer camp jobs before going into the service and work as an aircraft mechanic while in the service. Do you recommend that Ralph Johnson consider going into business? If so, what kind? What are some of the limitations Ralph faces as an owner-manager?
2. Paul Vincent is 34 years old, married, and has three children. All three children are now in school and Paul's wife Mary is considering getting a job. Paul has been employed as an assistant manager of a variety chain outlet but has not been very pleased with the rapidity of his promotions. Mary has an uncle who has suggested that Paul and Mary consider setting up some franchise retail operation where they can be their own boss and keep all the profits of their labor for themselves. The uncle would be willing to lend them some money to get them started. Since Mary is considering going to work anyway, she and Paul could open the business together. The uncle has suggested that they look into an ice cream store. A number of new ice cream stores have opened in their city in recent years under a specific franchise operation. They could get the franchise for a small area on the south side of the city. The stores sell expensive hand-packed ice cream in a variety of flavors. Evaluate the uncle's suggestion.
3. Sylvester Jones is the operator of a typical neighborhood gasoline station. He purchased the station five years ago on time from a major oil company. Syl-

vester has been having difficulty paying his normal living expenses and making his loan payments to the oil company. A friend of his has suggested that he talk to the Small Business Administration about a loan. Can a business this small consider SBA financing? What are the advantages and disadvantages of refinancing the purchase of the gas station with an SBA loan? What other possibilities should Sylvester consider?

4. Bob White and Chet Anders have worked for ten years for the Last State Bank of Anytown, U.S.A. Both men started work for the bank upon graduation from college. For several years they have been discussing the possibility of buying a small bank in a small community. They do not feel that the opportunities for significant promotions are very great at the Last State Bank in the next few years. Both boys come from upper middle-income families and can obtain financial aid from their families. How can they go about finding a bank to buy? What studies should they make of the bank they are considering purchasing? What other recommendations do you have for Bob and Chet?

5. Wilbur Best is a production worker in a middle-sized machine tool plant. Wilbur's income has been averaging $8,000 per year in recent years. He has difficulty paying on his house and two automobiles with this income. Wilbur is constantly complaining to his wife about his income level. He points out that Mr. Bastien, president of the company, owns a much larger house, belongs to the country club, owns a Chris Craft and travels a great deal. Mr. Bastien has been the manager of the company for some years and has built it from a small garage concern employing one other person to a company now employing 250 people. Wilbur thinks that Mr. Bastien makes much more money than his employees and that his contribution to the firm is no more important than that of the production worker such as Wilbur. Comment on Wilbur's point of view.

6. Frank Ford bought a small downtown restaurant four years ago from its retiring owner-manager. As Frank had no money, he borrowed enough to make the down payment from friends and agreed to make time payments to the former owner. While some of the payments have been made, Frank has gotten further and further behind in his payments to the owner and has been unable to pay off the money he borrowed for the down payment. In addition, he is as much as six months past due to some suppliers and was unable to meet his small payroll to his employees last week. As a result, the employees quit and some of the suppliers have attached his assets. Frank's attorney has advised him that there is no real possibility for saving the business and that he should go through bankruptcy. Frank has put the blame for his failure on competition from the larger, better financed downtown restaurants, and on his inability to buy from suppliers at the same price as his larger competitors. He particularly blames an outlet of the National Cafeteria Chain which is located near his establishment. What are the probable causes of Frank's failure? How important is competition as a factor in his failure?

7. Assume you suddenly inherited $50,000 on condition that within one year you use it to buy or establish a business. What type business would you select? Why would you select this type business? How would you prepare yourself to become the owner-manager of this business?

SELECTED READINGS

Bunn, Verne A. *Buying and Selling a Small Business.* Wichita, Kans.: University of Wichita, 1963.

Dun & Bradstreet, Inc., New York, N. Y. has the following publications:

- a) *Key Business Ratios*
- b) *Pitfalls in Managing a Small Business*
- c) *Profitable Management for Main Street*
- d) *How to Build Profits by Controlling Costs*
- e) *How to Control Accounts Receivable for Greater Profits*
- f) *Twelve Key Problems in Retailing and Suggested Solutions*
- g) *Growth in Importance of the Credit Function*
- h) *The Failure Record*

Fowler, F. Parker, and E. W. Sandberg. *The Relationship of Management Decision-Making to Small Business Growth.* Fort Collins, Colo.: Colorado State University, 1964.

Gibson, James L., and W. Warren Haynes. *Accounting in Small Business Decisions.* Lexington: University of Kentucky Press, 1963.

A Handbook of Small Business Finance. Washington, D. C.: Small Business Administration. Latest edition.

Internal Revenue Service. *Tax Guide for Small Business.* Washington, D. C.: Government Printing Office, 1966.

Lasser, J. K. *How to Run a Small Business,* Third Edition. New York: McGraw-Hill Book Co., 1963.

Preston, Lee E. *Managing the Independent Business.* Englewood Cliffs, N. J.: Prentice-Hall, Inc., 1962.

Starting and Managing a Small Business of Your Own, Revised Edition. Washington, D. C.: Small Business Administration, 1962.

Small Business Administration, Washington, D. C. 20416, also has the following publications along with many others:

Management Aids
#46 How to Analyze Your Own Business
#52 Loan Sources and the Federal Government
#80 Choosing the Legal Structure for Your Firm

Technical Aids
#61 Noise Reduction in the Small Shop
#62 Protective Packaging Problems
#89 Operations Research for Small Business

Small Marketers Aids
#79 Building Sales to Established Accounts
#89 Pricing Your Services for Profit
#112 Sales Potential and Market Shares

Small Business Bibliographies
#20 Advertising
#31 Retail Credit and Collections
#75 Inventory Control

Management Research Summaries
#131 Profitability and Size of Firm
#145 Factors in Small Business Success or Failure
#185 Problems in Small Business Management

Index